Macs
ALL-IN-ONE
FOR DUMMIES®
A Wiley Brand

4th Edition

by Joe Hutsko
and
Barbara Boyd

MAY 2014

Macs All-in-One For Dummies® 4th Edition

Published by
John Wiley & Sons, Inc.
111 River Street
Hoboken, NJ 07030-5774
www.wiley.com

Copyright © 2014 by John Wiley & Sons, Inc., Hoboken, New Jersey

Published simultaneously in Canada

For general information on our other products and services, please contact our Customer Care Department within the U.S. at 877-762-2974, outside the U.S. at 317-572-3993, or fax 317-572-4002. For technical support, please visit www.wiley.com/techsupport.

Wiley publishes in a variety of print and electronic formats and by print-on-demand. Some material included with standard print versions of this book may not be included in e-books or in print-on-demand. If this book refers to media such as a CD or DVD that is not included in the version you purchased, you may download this material at http://booksupport.wiley.com. For more information about Wiley products, visit www.wiley.com.

Library of Congress Control Number: 2013954222

ISBN 978-1-118-82210-4 (pbk); ISBN 978-1-118-82586-0 (ebk); ISBN 978-1-118-82593-8 (ebk)

Manufactured in the United States of America

10 9 8 7 6 5 4 3 2 1

Contents at a Glance

Table of Contents

Introduction

Whether you're a beginner, an intermediate user, or a seasoned computer expert, you can find something in *Macs All-in-One For Dummies,* 4th Edition. This book is divided into five minibooks so you can focus on the topics that interest you and skip over the ones that don't. We explored every menu and button of the Mac, its operating system, and Apple's iLife and iWork applications and wrote about most of them, focusing on the functions and features we think you'll use frequently or that will help you get the most out of your Mac and the applications.

About This Book

This book begins by focusing on the basics for all the aspects of using a Mac with the latest operating system, OS X 10.9 Mavericks. We start at the very beginning, from turning on your Mac, using the mouse and trackpad with multitouch gestures, and organizing your virtual desktop. We segue to creating your Apple ID and connecting your Mac to the Internet. In true *For Dummies* style, we show you step by step how to conduct all your online activities from setting up e-mail accounts to having video chats. We introduce you to more advanced but important tasks, such as protecting your Mac and your personal information; networking your Mac with other Macs, peripherals, and devices; and installing Windows on your Mac!

The fun begins when we explore Apple's iLife apps to manage tasks, such as editing and organizing your digital photos and videos, adding music to your Mac, and even creating and recording your own sounds. Along the way, we tell you how to share your finds and creations with people you know.

This book also shows you how to use and take advantage of Apple's iWork suite, which provides word processing, desktop publishing, a presentation app, and a spreadsheet app for calculating formulas and displaying your data as 3D charts. Whether you use a Mac for work, school, or just for fun, you'll find that with the right software apps, your Mac can meet all your computing needs.

If you're migrating to a Mac from a Windows desktop or notebook PC, this book can ease you into the Mac way of computing and show you how to install Windows on your Mac so you can still use your favorite Windows programs. By running Windows on a Mac, you can turn your Mac into two computers for the price of one.

If you're new to the Mac, you'll find that this book introduces you to all the main features of your Mac. If you're already a Mac user, you'll find information on topics you might not know much about. After reading this book, you'll have the foundation and confidence to delve deeper into your Mac's bundled apps as well as others you can find at the App Store.

To help you navigate this book efficiently, we use a few style conventions:

✦ Terms or words that we *truly* want to emphasize are *italicized* (and defined).

✦ Website addresses, or URLs, are shown in a special monofont typeface, `like this`. If you're reading this book as an e-book, URLs are active hyperlinks like this: `www.dummies.com`.

✦ Numbered steps that you need to follow and characters you need to type are set in **bold**.

✦ *Control-click* means to hold the Control key and click the mouse. If you're using a mouse that has a left and right button, you can right-click rather than Control-click. If you have one of Apple's trackpads, tap with two fingers. You find complete explanations of the multitouch gestures in Book I, Chapter 2.

✦ When we refer to the Apple menu — the menu that appears when you click the Apple icon in the very upper-left corner of your Mac's screen — we use this apple symbol: . When we talk about menu commands, we use a command arrow, like this: Choose ⇨Recent Items⇨Calendar. That just means to click the Apple menu; then, when it appears, slide your pointer down to Recent Items and drag slightly to the right to open a submenu from which we want you to click Calendar.

✦ We place figures where we think they help to explain the task at hand; however, we encourage you to follow along with your Mac so you have a full-color, full-size image to refer to.

Foolish Assumptions

In writing this book, we made a few assumptions about you, dear reader. To make sure that we're on the same page, we assume that

✦ You know something, but not necessarily a whole lot, about computers, and you want to find out the basics of using a Mac or doing more with your Mac than you are already.

✦ You have at least a general concept of this wild and crazy thing called the Internet — or more precisely, the phenomenon known as *the web* (or, more formally, the World Wide Web).

✦ You'll turn to the introductory chapters if you find yourself scratching your head at such terms as *double-click, drag and drop, scroll,* and *Control-click* — or any other terms that sound like things we assume that you know but you don't.

✦ You appreciate the speed at which technology-based products like the Mac (and the programs you can run on it) can change in as little as a few months, with newer, sleeker, faster models and app versions replacing previous versions.

✦ You can traverse the web to find updated information about the products described throughout this book.

✦ You know that keeping up with the topic of all things high-tech and Mac (even as a full-time job, as it is for us) still can't make a guy or gal the be-all and end-all Mac Genius of the World. You will, therefore, alert us to cool stuff you discover in your Mac odyssey so that we can consider including it in the next edition of this book.

✦ You're here to have fun, or at least try to have fun, as you dive into The Wonderful World of Mac.

Icons Used in This Book

To help emphasize certain information, this book displays different icons in the page margins.

The Tip icon marks tips (duh!) and points out useful nuggets of information that can help you get things done more efficiently or direct you to something helpful that you might not know. Sometimes Tips give you a second, or even third, way of doing the task that was pointed out in the step.

Remember icons mark the information that's been mentioned previously but is useful for the task at hand. This icon often points out useful information that isn't quite as important as a Tip but not as threatening as a Warning. If you ignore this information, you can't hurt your files or your Mac, but it may make the task at hand easier.

This icon highlights interesting information that isn't necessary to know but can help explain why certain things work the way they do on a Mac. Feel free to skip this information if you're in a hurry, but browse through this information when you have time. You might find out something interesting that can help you use your Mac.

Watch out! This icon highlights something that can go terribly wrong if you're not careful, such as wiping out your important files or messing up your Mac. Make sure that you read any Warning information before following any instructions.

Beyond the Book

Talk is cheap (so they say), but print is not, and we always have more information than we can squeeze into our page limits. The wonderful universe of the web comes to the rescue, so we put a bunch of cool stuff online to complement what you read here. Follow these links to find

✦ **Cheat Sheet**

www.dummies.com/cheatsheet/macsaio

Although the Mac uses menus for just about everything, the menu commands have key combination counterparts. We put together a table of the most common key commands that you can print and keep near your Mac. You also find a cheat sheet table that shows you how to type foreign letters and common symbols and one that summarizes the multi-touch gestures. To help you stay up to date with the latest Mac news, we provide a list of Mac websites with hot links, which you can simply click to go to the site.

✦ **Dummies.com online articles**

www.dummies.com/extras/macsaio

We posted four bonus articles — one each for minibooks II–V — to reinforce what you read about in each minibook. You can read suggestions for enhancing your online communications, advanced tips for working with Mac utilities, and specific examples of using Apple productivity apps in your daily Mac routine.

✦ **Updates**

www.dummies.com/extras/macsaio

When we write these books, the content is current, but sometimes products change the day after the book goes to press. So, we post updates online for you. If changes are important but minimal, you find an article online; if substantial changes happen, we post updates to the Downloads tab.

Where to Go from Here

In general, *For Dummies* books aren't meant to be read cover to cover. However, this book flows from task to task, chapter to chapter, in an order that would be logical if you're learning the Mac for the first time. In that case, feel free to start at Book I, Chapter 1 and go through the Book I chapters to familiarize yourself with how the Mac is organized and how you can make it do what you want it to do. Then mix it up, moving on to fun tasks, such as making FaceTime video calls (Book II, Chapter 3) or designing a flyer with Pages (Book V, Chapter 3), and then bounce back to a crucial task, such as backing up (Book III, Chapter 1).

If you're computer intuitive, you could start with Book I, Chapter 3 to get your Apple ID and Internet connection set up, and then move in the direction you want, whether it's learning about more advanced system functions in Book III or editing your digital home movies with iMovie.

If you're familiar with the Mac but want to brush up on the latest OS X — Mavericks — read about the Notification Center in Book I, Chapter 6; Maps in Book II, Chapter 4; iBooks in Book IV, Chapter 6, and the completely updated iWork apps in Book V, Chapters 3–6.

Book I
Getting Started with Mac Basics

Visit www.dummies.com for more great Dummies content online.

Contents at a Glance

Chapter 1: Starting to Use Your Mac

In This Chapter

✔ **Identifying your Mac model**

✔ **Powering on**

✔ **Conserving time and energy with Sleep mode**

✔ **Shutting down and restarting**

✔ **Getting to know your Mac**

Apple offers several different kinds of Macs, and understanding how your Mac is different from the others can help you navigate this book more quickly, gathering the information you need and skipping the rest. Before you can use your Mac, you have to start it up — which makes perfect sense — so we tell you how to do that. Now, get ready for the counterintuitive part. After you have your Mac up and running, you can just leave it on.

In this chapter, we cover current Mac models and how they're different and alike, show you how to start and restart your Mac (and give you an idea of what goes on behind the scenes), and then tell you how to put it to sleep and shut it down completely. Sprinkled throughout this chapter is technical information about the various Mac models and what goes on inside that makes your Mac tick, but we make our explanations as clear and simple as possible. At the end of the chapter, we introduce you to Mac processors and show you how to find out precisely which features your Mac has.

Examining Different Macintosh Models

Apple's Macintosh computer — Mac for short — enjoys the reputation of being the easiest computer to use in the world. Macs are so dependable, durable, and beautifully designed that they incite techno-lust in gadget geeks like us and ordinary Joes alike. For those doubly good reasons, you probably won't buy a new Mac to replace your old one because you *have* to, but because you *want* to.

The Macintosh has been around since 1984, and since that time, Apple has produced a wide variety of Mac models. Although you can still find and use older Macs (although many are not compatible with the latest and greatest OS or applications), chances are good that if you buy a newer Mac, it will fall into one of three categories:

✦ **Desktop:** Mac mini or Mac Pro, which require a separate display (monitor), keyboard, and mouse or trackpad.

✦ **All-in-one desktop:** iMac, which houses the display and computer in one unit and requires a keyboard and mouse or trackpad.

✦ **Notebook:** MacBook Air or MacBook Pro, which have built-in keyboards, trackpads that work like a mouse at the touch of your fingertip, and bright displays. A clamshell design lets you close and tote them in your backpack, messenger bag, or briefcase.

All the newest Mac models have USB and Thunderbolt ports to connect peripheral hardware, such as external drives and displays. They are also engineered for Wi-Fi and Bluetooth connections, which are used for data transfer and peripheral connectivity. Because most data transfer and storage happens online or with flash drives, optical disc (CD and DVD) drives have become almost obsolete and have been removed from all but one of the Mac models sold today, although optional external DVD drives are available if you still use CDs, DVDs, or software apps on discs. You can also connect to another (ahem) older computer on a network and access its optical disc drive.

The Thunderbolt port, standard on all newer Macs, is a data-transfer protocol used to connect peripheral devices, such as displays or hard drives. Thunderbolt transfers data faster than either USB or FireWire protocols.

Mac mini, Mac Pro, and iMac models use an external wireless or wired (usually USB) keyboard and a mouse or trackpad (sold separately from the mini and Pro). Apple's Magic Trackpad lets you use the multitouch gestures — such as swipe, pinch, and flick — to control the cursor and windows on whichever Mac desktop model you choose. If you use a trackpad, you don't need a mouse, but you can use both if you prefer.

By understanding the particular type of Mac that you have and its capabilities, you'll have a better idea of what your Mac can do. We highlight those capabilities in the sections that follow. No matter what the capabilities of your Mac are, chances are good that it will work reliably for as long as you own it.

The Mac mini and Mac Pro

The biggest advantages desktop Macs (the Mac mini and the Mac Pro) offer are that you can choose the type of display to use and place it anywhere you want on your desk — as long as you have a cable that can reach. The Mac mini, however, is small enough to hide under your desk, or situate in a corner of your desktop.

The Mac mini is a lower-priced version designed for people who want an inexpensive Mac for ordinary uses, such as word processing and writing, sending e-mail, browsing the web, and playing video games. At the same time, it packs a fast Intel Core i5 or i7 processor, between 500 gigabytes (GB) and 1 terabyte (TB) of storage, and an assortment of the latest ports and slots for audio, video, and USB connections — nothing to sneeze at. Alternatively, it can function as a terrific, cost-effective server for home or small business networks.

The Mac Pro was completely remodeled and released in December 2013. This higher-priced professional version Mac boasts ports to connect multiple monitors and lots of expandability for up to 64GB of memory and up to 1TB of flash storage, as well as greater graphics and processing capabilities with the latest Intel Xeon processor and dual graphics processors.

The iMac

The all-in-one design of the iMac is an evolutionary result of the original — 1984-era — Mac design. The iMac combines the computer with a built-in LED-backlit display, speakers, and FaceTime camera. You can configure up to 3TB of storage or choose flash storage instead of a hard drive, depending on your need for speed or space. On iMac models, you can connect external speakers and a second external display.

The advantage of the iMac's all-in-one design is that you have everything you need in a single unit. The disadvantage is that if one part of your iMac fails (such as the display or speaker), you can't easily replace the failed part, although our experience has been that Apple responds quickly and professionally to problems with their products.

The MacBook Air and MacBook Pro

MacBook Air and MacBook Pro are the notebook members of the Mac family. All the MacBook models run on rechargeable battery packs or external power. If you need to take your Mac everywhere you go, you can choose from the ultralight MacBook Air or one of the MacBook Pro models.

Although both MacBook Air and MacBook Pro models have full-size keyboards, neither includes the extra numeric keypad found on most external keyboards (but not on Apple's standard wireless keyboard) or on larger Windows notebooks. Also, instead of a mouse, MacBooks use a built-in trackpad, which responds to all the multitouch gestures you can use to control the cursor and windows on your Mac.

If you find the keyboard or trackpad of your notebook Mac too clumsy to use, you can always plug an external keyboard and mouse into your notebook.

The MacBook Air comes with an 11-inch or 13-inch LED-backlit screen, and the MacBook Pro models come in two screen sizes: 13-inch or 15-inch. The 13-inch LED-backlit MacBook Pro model comes with an internal optical disc (DVD) drive and an Ethernet port. The 13-inch and 15-inch LED-backlit Retina models don't have an internal optical drive or an Ethernet port although they do have an HDMI port.

Apple's Retina display uses an LCD (liquid crystal display) with a pixel density of about 220 pixels per inch (PPI). At this density, the human eye doesn't distinguish the individual pixels at a normal distance. Different screen sizes have different PPIs. For example, the iPhone 4 and later models have 326 PPI. Except for the LED MacBook Pro model (the one that still has a DVD drive), all MacBook Pros have the Retina display, as do some iPad, iPod, and iPhone models. The MacBook Air and other desktop models sport an LED-backlit screen.

Starting Your Mac

Here's the simple way to start your Mac — the way you'll probably use 99 percent of the time: Press the Power button.

Depending on the type of Mac you have, the Power button might be in back (Mac mini and iMacs), front (Mac Pro), or above the keyboard (on notebook models MacBook Air and MacBook Pro). Some Apple displays have a Power button that commands the computer it's connected to.

A few seconds after you press the Power button, your Mac chimes to let you know that it's starting. (Techie types say *booting up*, a term derived from the phrase "to lift yourself up by the bootstraps.")

The moment electricity courses through, your Mac's electronic brain immediately looks for instructions embedded inside a special read-only memory (or ROM) chip. While your computer is reading these instructions (also known as *firmware*), it displays the Apple logo on the screen to let you know that the computer is working and hasn't forgotten about you.

The firmware instructions tell the computer to make sure that all of its components are working; most often, they are. However, if some part of your computer (say, a memory chip) is defective, your computer will stop at this point.

Unless you know something about repairing the physical parts of a Mac, this is the time to haul your Mac to the nearest Apple Store or authorized repair shop, or to call Apple Support to arrange shipping your bummed-out Mac directly to Apple for repair (800-275-2273 in the United States).

Sometimes a Mac might refuse to start correctly because of software problems. To fix software problems, check out Book III, Chapter 6, which explains how to perform basic troubleshooting on a Mac.

After your computer determines that all components are working, the last set of instructions on the chip tells the computer, "Now that you know all your parts are working, load an operating system."

When you unpack your Mac and turn it on for the very first time, it asks you to type your name and make up a password to create an account for using your Mac. You use this name and password in the following situations:

✦ When you wake or restart your Mac, if you activate those types of privacy settings (see Book III, Chapter 2).

✦ When you install new apps or update the system software.

✦ When you change some settings in System Preferences.

✦ When you switch from one user to another, if you set up your Mac to work with multiple users (see Book III, Chapter 2).

This username and password is different than your Apple ID, which you use for iCloud and making iTunes, App, and iBooks Store purchases. You can learn about creating an Apple ID in Book I, Chapter 3.

To guide you through the process of setting up a Mac for the first time, a special application called Setup Assistant runs, which asks for your time zone, the date, and whether you want to transfer files and applications from another Mac to your newer one.

Normally, you need to run through this initial procedure only once, but you also have to perform it if you reinstall your operating system, which we refer to as *OS* throughout this book. We explain reinstalling the OS in Book III, Chapter 6. The most important part of this initial procedure is remembering the password you choose because you'll need it to log in to your account, change some of the settings in System Preferences, or install new software.

An *operating system* is the program that controls your computer and is almost always stored on your computer's built-in hard drive (rather than on an external drive). On the Mac, the operating system is named Mac OS X (pronounced as *Mac O S ten*) and is followed by a version number, such as 10.9.

Apple code-names each version of OS X. The current version is OS X Mavericks, version 10.9, which is the first of a new nomenclature that uses the name of surfing destinations in California. Before Mavericks, each operating system was named after a big cat, such as Mountain Lion, Snow Leopard, and Jaguar.

After the operating system loads and you log in, you can start using your computer to run other applications to do things: design a poster or send an e-mail, browse the web, calculate your yearly budget, or play a game — you know, all the cool things you bought your Mac for in the first place.

Turning Your Mac Off

You can choose one of three different ways — Sleep, Shut Down, or Restart — to turn your Mac off (or let it rest a bit). In this section, we explain when and why you would want to use each option and, of course, how.

Putting a Mac in Sleep mode

If you're taking a short break from working on your Mac, you don't have to always turn it off and back on again when you want to use it. To do the "green" thing by conserving energy, put your Mac into Sleep mode instead of leaving it running while you're away. When you put your Mac to sleep, it shuts down almost every power-draining component of your Mac and draws only a teensy trickle of power. The great part, though, is that you can instantly wake it up with a touch of the keyboard, click of the mouse, or opening the lid if you use a MacBook Pro or MacBook Air. Presto change-o! Your Mac immediately returns to the same state you left it in, without making you wait to power on as if it were completely shut down.

To put your Mac to sleep, you can go manual or automatic.

+ **Manual:** If someone walks into your office and you want to hide that secret project you're working on, you might want to put your Mac to sleep manually.

+ **Automatic:** So you don't have to remember to put your Mac to sleep when you stop using it (to take a phone call or go out to lunch) you can adjust your Mac's settings so that it automatically falls asleep after a certain amount of time.

If your Mac is doing a task, such as sending an e-mail or downloading a file, let it finish the task before putting it to sleep.

To put your Mac to sleep manually, choose one of the following actions:

+ **Choose Sleep.** The menu is in the upper left of the screen.

+ **Press the Power button or press Control+Eject.** (If you're having trouble finding your way around the keyboard, see Book I, Chapter 2.) Then, when a dialog appears, as shown in Figure 1-1, click the Sleep button (or press the S key on your Mac's keyboard).

Figure 1-1:
Put your
computer in
Sleep mode.

Are you sure you want to shut down your
computer now?

☐ Reopen windows when logging back in

[Restart]   [Sleep]   [Cancel]   [**Shut Down**]

✦ **Press ⌘+Option+Eject.** If you have a MacBook Air or Retina MacBook Pro,
   your Mac doesn't have an Eject key because it doesn't have a disc drive.

✦ **If you have a MacBook, just close its lid.** When a MacBook is sleeping,
   you can safely move it without worrying about jarring the built-in hard
   drive that spins most of the time your MacBook is "awake" and in use.

To put your Mac to sleep automatically, you set the amount of time your Mac
sits idle before it goes to sleep. Which Sleep mode options you see depend
on what type of Mac you're using.

✦ **Desktops:** On desktop Macs, you can adjust when your Mac puts the
   display to sleep and when it puts the computer to sleep.

✦ **Notebooks:** Your Mac knows whether it's using battery power or the
   power adapter, and you can adjust when the display and computer sleep
   in both instances.

Follow these steps to adjust how your computer sleeps automatically:

1. **Choose ⌘⇨System Preferences, and then click the Energy Saver icon.**

   The Energy Saver window appears, as shown in Figure 1-2. If you have
   an iMac, a Mac mini, or a Mac Pro, you won't see the Battery and Power
   Adapter tabs, which appear on MacBook models.

   If you're using a notebook, notice which tab (Battery or Power Adapter)
   you're on before you proceed with the next steps. When powered by
   the battery, you may want your Mac to go to sleep after a short time
   (say, 5 minutes) to make the battery charge last longer. Then when your
   Mac is connected to a power source, you could set it longer: say, after
   15 minutes.

2. **Drag the Computer Sleep timer to the amount of time you want your
   Mac to sit idle before it goes to sleep.**

   The exact time is shown above the timescale (on the right) as you move
   the slider.

   This setting puts the hard drive to sleep. You may want to set a longer
   time interval for Computer Sleep than for Display Sleep (the following
   step) because it takes your Mac slightly longer to wake from Computer
   Sleep than Display Sleep.

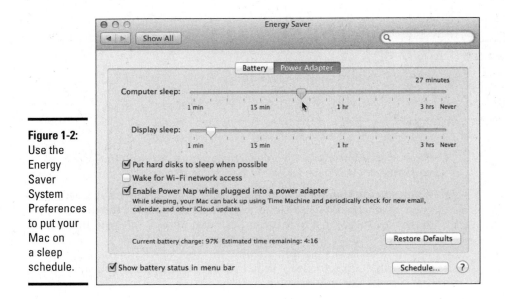

Figure 1-2:
Use the
Energy
Saver
System
Preferences
to put your
Mac on
a sleep
schedule.

3. Drag the Display Sleep timer to the amount of time you want your Mac to sit idle before the screen saver plays.

This setting puts the display to sleep. A *screen saver* is an image that appears when your Mac is inactive after the time interval you set here. It hides whatever you were working on from peering eyes when you're away from your Mac. You can find out how to choose a special image for your screen saver and set a password for it in Book I, Chapter 6.

If your computer is doing a task, such as downloading a sizeable file, set Computer Sleep to Never and set only Display Sleep with a time interval. This way, your Mac continues to do the task at hand even though the display is sleeping.

4. (For MacBook models) Select the Show Battery Status in Menu Bar check box (in the bottom-left corner).

This displays an icon at the top of your Mac's screen indicating how much charge is left on your battery.

5. (Optional) Select the check boxes next to the other options to set when your Mac goes to sleep or wakes.

For instance, if you access your Mac remotely, you want to select the Wake for Wi-Fi Network Access check box so your Mac will wake when you attempt to retrieve files and data from your Mac.

Select Enable Power Nap so your Mac continues to perform some functions while it's sleeping. When Power Nap is on, your Mac receives incoming e-mail, automatically updates any apps you share with other devices such as Contacts, Calendar, and Notes, and performs Time Machine backups.

MacBooks have two Power Nap settings: one for Battery and one for Power Adapter. By default Power Nap is on when your Mac is connected to a power source but off when running on the battery. To change either, click the Battery or Power Adapter tab and select, or deselect, the Power Nap checkbox. When you use Power Nap in Battery mode, the activities are limited to receiving e-mail and updating shared data.

To see if your Mac model supports Power Nap, visit `http://support.apple.com` and search *about power nap.*

6. **(Optional) Click the Schedule button and adjust those settings as desired.**

   A pane opens that lets you schedule the days and times you want your Mac to start or wake up and go to sleep. This is convenient if you don't want to accidently leave your Mac on when you leave your home or office or you do want to find it awake and waiting for you when you arrive.

7. **Save your setting by choosing System Preferences⇨Quit System Preferences or clicking the Close (red) button in the upper-left corner.**

To wake a sleeping desktop or all-in-one Mac or a MacBook with the lid open, click the mouse button or tap any key. To keep from accidentally typing any characters into a currently running application, press a noncharacter key, such as Shift or an arrow key. To wake your closed and sleeping MacBook, just open its lid.

Depending on which Mac model you own, you may notice a built-in combination power/sleep indicator light that softly pulses like a firefly when your Mac is in Sleep mode. On the MacBook Pro, the power/sleep indicator light is on the front edge below the right wrist rest. On the Mac mini, the indicator light is in the lower-right corner. No such light is anywhere on the iMac or the latest MacBook Air, which appear to be totally in the dark when they're asleep.

Shutting down your Mac

When you shut down your Mac, open applications are automatically closed, Internet and network connections are disconnected, and logged-in users are logged out. It may take a few minutes for your Mac to shut down. You know your Mac is shut down completely when the screen is black, the hard drive and fan are silent, and there are no blinking lights anywhere. Here are a few circumstances when you'd want to shut down your Mac:

✦ **Taking an extended break:** When you won't be using it for an extended length of time. Turning your Mac completely off can extend its useful life, waste less energy, and save you a few bucks on your yearly energy expense.

✦ **Traveling:** When you're traveling with your Mac and putting your MacBook Air, MacBook Pro, or Mac mini in your wheeled carry-on trolley. (Sleep mode is fine if you're carrying your Mac in a laptop bag or backpack.)

✦ **Repairing hardware:** If you want to open your Mac to install a new battery, additional memory, or a video graphics card.

✦ **Rebooting:** To resolve weird situations, such as unresponsive or slow-running applications, because your Mac runs a number of behind-the-scenes file system housekeeping chores every time you start it. (See the next section for instructions.)

Here are the ways to shut down your Mac:

✦ **Choose ⇨Shut Down.** A confirmation dialog appears (as shown in Figure 1-3) asking whether you're sure you want to shut down.

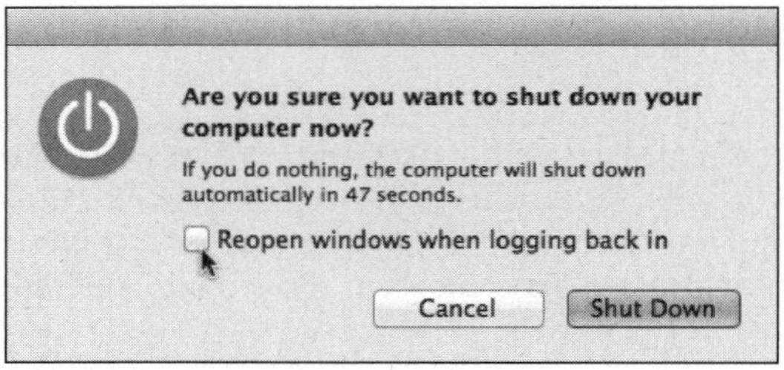

Figure 1-3: Use the menu to turn off your computer.

Are you sure you want to shut down your computer now?

If you do nothing, the computer will shut down automatically in 47 seconds.

☐ Reopen windows when logging back in

[Cancel]   [**Shut Down**]

Select the Reopen Windows When Logging Back In check box if you want everything you're working on to open when you turn your Mac on the next time.

Click the Shut Down button (or Cancel if you change your mind). If you don't click either option, your Mac will shut down automatically after 1 minute.

✦ **Press Control+Eject or press and hold the Power button.** When a dialog appears (refer to Figure 1-3), click the Shut Down button or press the Return key.

Make sure that your MacBook Air or MacBook Pro is completely shut down before closing the lid, or it may not shut down properly. Even more problematic, it may not start up properly when you next try to turn it on.

To shut down without seeing those bothersome dialogs, do this: Hold the Option key and then choose ⇨Shut Down. This bypasses the confirmation prompt asking whether you're sure that you want to shut down.

You have one more option for shutting down your Mac, but proceed with caution.

Press and hold ⌘+Control and then press the Power button to perform a *force shutdown,* which forces all running applications to shut down right away. However, this route should never be your first choice when shutting down. Use a force shutdown as your last resort only if your Mac — your *Mac,* not just a stubborn application —is unresponsive and appears to have frozen. If a single application is freezing or acting flaky, force-quit (close) that single application instead of shutting down your entire computer. (See Book III, Chapter 6 for information about how to force-quit a single application.) Performing a force shutdown can cause you to lose any changes you've made since the last time you saved them, so use force shutdown only as a last resort.

Restarting a Mac

Sometimes your Mac can act sluggish, or applications might fail to run. If that happens, you can shut down and immediately restart your Mac, which essentially clears your computer's memory and starts it fresh.

To restart your computer, you have three choices:

✦ **Press the Power button or press Control+Eject.** Then, when a dialog appears, click the Restart button (refer to Figure 1-1) or press the R key.

✦ **Choose ⌘⇨Restart.**

✦ **Press Control+⌘+Eject.**

When you restart your computer, your Mac closes all running applications; you will have the chance, though, to save any files you're working on. After you choose to save any files, those applications are closed, and then your Mac will shut down and boot up again.

Understanding Mac Processors

The *processor* acts as the brain of your Mac. A computer is only as powerful as the processor inside. Generally, the newer your computer, the newer its processor and the faster it will run.

The type of processor in your Mac can determine the applications (also known as *apps* or *software*) your Mac can run. Before you buy any software, make sure that it can run on your computer.

To identify the type of processor used in your Mac, click the Apple menu in the upper-left corner of the screen and choose About This Mac. An About This Mac window appears, listing your processor as Intel Core 2 Duo, Core i3, Core i5, Core i7, or Xeon.

If your Mac doesn't have one of the previously mentioned processors, you won't be able to run Mac OS X Mavericks, version 10.9. This means that Core Solo and Core Duo models can't run Mavericks. What's more, to use Mavericks, you also need at least 2GB RAM (random access memory).

The Intel family of processors includes (from slowest to fastest) the Core Solo, Core Duo, Core 2 Duo, dual-core i3, dual-core i5, quad-core i7, and quad- and six-core Xeon. Every processor runs at a specific speed, so for example a 2.0 gigahertz (GHz) Core 2 Duo processor is slower than a 2.4 GHz Core 2 Duo processor. If understanding processor types and gigahertz confuses you, just remember that the most expensive computer within a product line is usually the fastest.

Talk to your friendly, neighborhood Apple reseller when deciding which Mac model is best for you. The tasks you plan to do with your Mac determine the processor speed that will meet your needs. For example, if you plan to mostly write books, surf the Internet, and use productivity apps like Calendar and Contacts, a low-end processor is probably sufficient. If, instead, you're a video editor or game developer, you want the fastest processor you can afford.

In the About This Mac window, move the cursor over the More Info button and click to open the System Information utility and see an expanded window of information about your Mac, as shown in Figure 1-4.

Figure 1-4:
The About This Mac window identifies the processor used in your Mac.

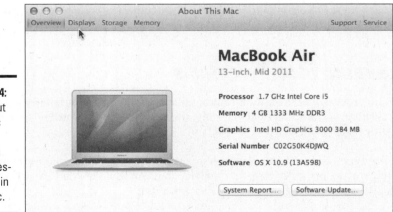

What Macs and PCs share

In Spring 2006, Macs started shipping with Intel processors, which are the same type of processors used in many Windows PCs. Intel processors are less expensive than earlier Macs' PowerPC processors and more powerful. Intel processors also give the Mac the capability to run the Microsoft Windows operating system (although dyed-in-the-wool Mac loyalists would wryly consider that a drawback — if not outright blasphemy!).

Click each tab at the top of the window to open panes that show more information about your Mac: Overview, Displays, Storage (shown in Figure 1-5), and Memory. Click Support (top right) for links to the Help Center and user manuals. Click Service (also top right) to access links to information about your Mac's warranty and AppleCare Protection.

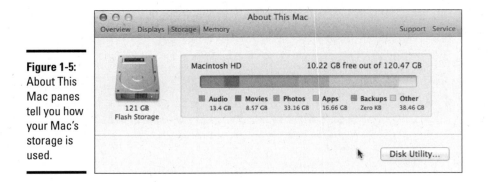

Figure 1-5: About This Mac panes tell you how your Mac's storage is used.

Exploring Your Mac's Inner Workings

By looking at your Mac, you can tell whether it's an all-in-one design (iMac), a notebook (MacBook Air or MacBook Pro), or a desktop unit that lacks a built-in screen (Mac mini or Mac Pro). However, looking at the outside of your Mac can't tell you the parts used on the inside or the details regarding what your Mac is capable of. You might need to look at the hardware information in the System Report window when you want to know about the health of your MacBook's battery or the type of graphics card in your Mac Pro. To identify the parts and capabilities of your Mac, follow these steps:

1. **Click the Apple menu (🍎) in the upper-left corner of the screen and then choose About This Mac.**

An About This Mac window appears.

2. **Click More Info, and then click System Report.**

3. **In the System Report window that opens, click the disclosure triangle to the left of the Hardware option in the category pane on the left (as shown in Figure 1-6) to view a list of hardware items.**

   If the list of hardware items (such as Bluetooth, Memory, and USB) already appears under the Hardware category, skip this step.

   Clicking a disclosure triangle toggles to open or close a list of options.

   You can also click the disclosure triangle next to Network or Software in the category pane on the left to see information about networks you're connected to or software installed on your Mac. (You can learn more about networking your Mac in Book III, Chapter 3; we tell you how to install software in Book I, Chapter 5; and we cover uninstalling software in Book I, Chapter 5.)

4. **Click a hardware item, such as Audio, Memory, or Disc Burning.**

   The right pane of the System Report window displays the capabilities of your chosen hardware, as shown in the figure.

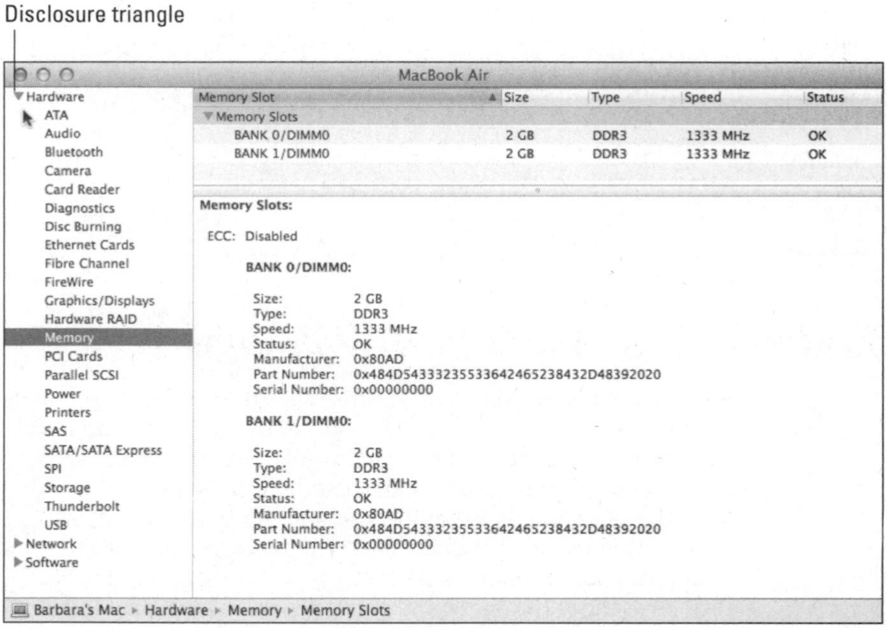

Disclosure triangle

Memory Slot	Size	Type	Speed	Status
▼ Memory Slots				
BANK 0/DIMM0	2 GB	DDR3	1333 MHz	OK
BANK 1/DIMM0	2 GB	DDR3	1333 MHz	OK

Hardware
- ATA
- Audio
- Bluetooth
- Camera
- Card Reader
- Diagnostics
- Disc Burning
- Ethernet Cards
- Fibre Channel
- FireWire
- Graphics/Displays
- Hardware RAID
- Memory
- PCI Cards
- Parallel SCSI
- Power
- Printers
- SAS
- SATA/SATA Express
- SPI
- Storage
- Thunderbolt
- USB
- Network
- Software

Memory Slots:

ECC: Disabled

   BANK 0/DIMM0:

     Size: 2 GB
     Type: DDR3
     Speed: 1333 MHz
     Status: OK
     Manufacturer: 0x80AD
     Part Number: 0x484D5433323553336424652384320482D48392020
     Serial Number: 0x00000000

   BANK 1/DIMM0:

     Size: 2 GB
     Type: DDR3
     Speed: 1333 MHz
     Status: OK
     Manufacturer: 0x80AD
     Part Number: 0x484D5433323553336424652384320482D48392020
     Serial Number: 0x00000000

MacBook Air

Barbara's Mac ▸ Hardware ▸ Memory ▸ Memory Slots

Figure 1-6: The System Report identifies the type and capabilities of the hardware in your Mac.

Don't worry if the information displayed in the System Report window doesn't make much sense to you right now. The main idea here is to figure out a quick way to find out about the capabilities of your Mac, which can be especially helpful if you have a problem in the future and a technician asks for information about your Mac.

If you really want to know, pick through the technical details to find the parts that you understand, and do some research for more info on the items you don't understand. I cover many of these items throughout the book, so use its table of contents and index to guide you. If you don't find it here, search the Internet to look up the details that you don't understand.

5. **When you finish scouting the contents of the System Report window, you can simply close it (click the red circle in the upper-left corner) to return to About This Mac.**

    To close both System Report and About This Mac, choose System Information⇨Quit System Information.

Chapter 2: Getting Acquainted with the Mac User Interface

In This Chapter

✓ Perusing menus and windows

✓ Using the mouse, trackpad, and keyboard

✓ Getting familiar with the parts of the Desktop

✓ Working with Dashboard widgets

✓ Getting help from your Mac

Theoretically, using a computer is simple. In practice, using a computer can cause people to suffer a wide range of emotions from elation to sheer frustration and despair.

The problem with using a computer stems mostly from two causes:

✦ Not knowing what the computer can do

✦ Not knowing how to tell the computer what you want it to do

In the early days of personal computers (PCs), this communication gap between users and computers arose mostly from ordinary people trying to use machines designed by engineers for other engineers. If you didn't understand how a computer engineer thinks (or doesn't think), computers seemed nearly impossible to understand.

Fortunately, Apple has mostly solved this problem with the Mac. Instead of designing a computer for other computer engineers, Apple designed a computer for ordinary people. And what do ordinary people want? Here's the short (but definitely important) list:

✦ Reliability

✦ Ease of use

From a technical point of view, what makes the Mac reliable is its operating system, OS X. An operating system is nothing more than an application that makes your computer actually work.

An operating system (OS) works in the background. When you use a computer, you don't really notice the operating system, but you do see its *user interface* (UI) — which functions like a clerk at the front desk of a hotel: Instead of talking directly to the housekeeper or the plumber (the operating system), you always talk to the front desk clerk, and the clerk talks to the housekeeper or plumber.

Apple designed a UI that everyone can understand. You control your Mac with multitouch gestures applied to the trackpad or mouse, making the UI even more intuitive and literally hands-on. In this chapter, we first explain what you see on the screen when you turn your Mac on, and then we explain how to use a mouse, trackpad, and keyboard to control your Mac. Then we introduce the Dock, Finder, and Dashboard, and tell you how to get help from your Mac if you need it.

Chances are if you work with a computer, you know how to click and drag and open menus, but we explain it step by step in the beginning in case this is your first time using a computer. After all, we were all newbies at one time or another. The layout and gestures you read about in this chapter apply to almost everything you'll ever do with your Mac.

Looking at Menus, Dialogs, and Windows

The Mac UI acts like a communication pathway between you and the OS, serving three purposes:

✦ To display all the options you can choose

✦ To display information

✦ To accept commands

This section tells you how menus and windows serve those three purposes.

One of the most crucial parts of the Mac user interface is an application called the *Finder,* which displays files stored on your Mac. You find out more about the Finder later in this chapter.

Exploring the menu bar

The menu bar runs across the top of your Mac's screen. The menu bar is always accessible and almost always visible (it's hidden when you use an app in full-screen view — be patient, we get to that soon) and provides a single location where you can find nearly every possible command you might need for your computer or the app you're using. The menu bar consists of three parts, the Apple menu, the app menus, and menulets. Figure 2-1 identifies the parts that appear on the left side of the menu bar.

Figure 2-1:
The left
side of the
menu bar.

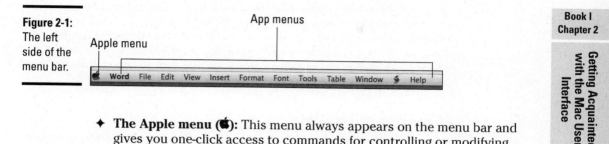

App menus

Apple menu

Word File Edit View Insert Format Font Tools Table Window Help

✦ **The Apple menu ():** This menu always appears on the menu bar and gives you one-click access to commands for controlling or modifying your Mac.

✦ **The App menus:** Here's where you find the name of the active app along with several menus that contain commands for controlling that particular app and its data. (If you don't run any additional apps, your Mac always runs the Finder, which you find out more about in this chapter.)

On the right side of the menu bar, you see the menulets, shown in Figure 2-2. Menulets are mini menus that open when you click the icons on the right end of the menu bar and give you quick access to specific System Preferences settings, such as Network, Time and Date, or Sound.

Menulets

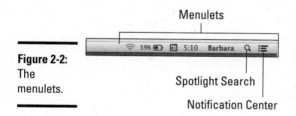

Figure 2-2:
The
menulets.

Spotlight Search

Notification Center

The icons on the right end of the menulets open menus that perform one or more system functions, such as providing fast access to Wi-Fi controls or battery status (MacBook models). The two icons to the right open Spotlight Search and the Notification Center.

If you don't want a menulet cluttering up the menu bar, you can typically remove it by holding down the ⌘ key, moving the pointer over the icon you want to remove, dragging (moving) the mouse pointer off the menu bar, and then releasing the mouse button.

Understanding menu commands

Each menu on the menu bar contains a group of related commands. The File menu contains commands for opening, saving, and printing files; the Edit menu contains commands for copying or deleting selected items; and the View menu gives you options for how and what you see on the screen. The number and names of different menus depend on the application.

To give a command to your Mac, drag your finger across the trackpad or move the mouse so the pointer points to the menu you want. Then tap the trackpad or click the mouse to call up a pull-down menu listing all the commands you can choose. Drag the pointer (with your finger on the trackpad or with the mouse) to highlight the command you want the computer to follow and click it (File⇨Save, for example).

Working with dialogs

When your Mac needs information from you or wants to present a choice you can make, it typically displays a *dialog* — essentially a box that offers a variety of choices. Some common dialogs appear when you choose the Print, Save, and Open commands.

Some dialogs (particularly Save and Print) often appear in a condensed version, but you can blow them up into an expanded version, as shown in Figure 2-3. For example, to switch between the expanded and the condensed version of the Save dialog, click its disclosure triangle, which looks like triangle to the right of the Save As field.

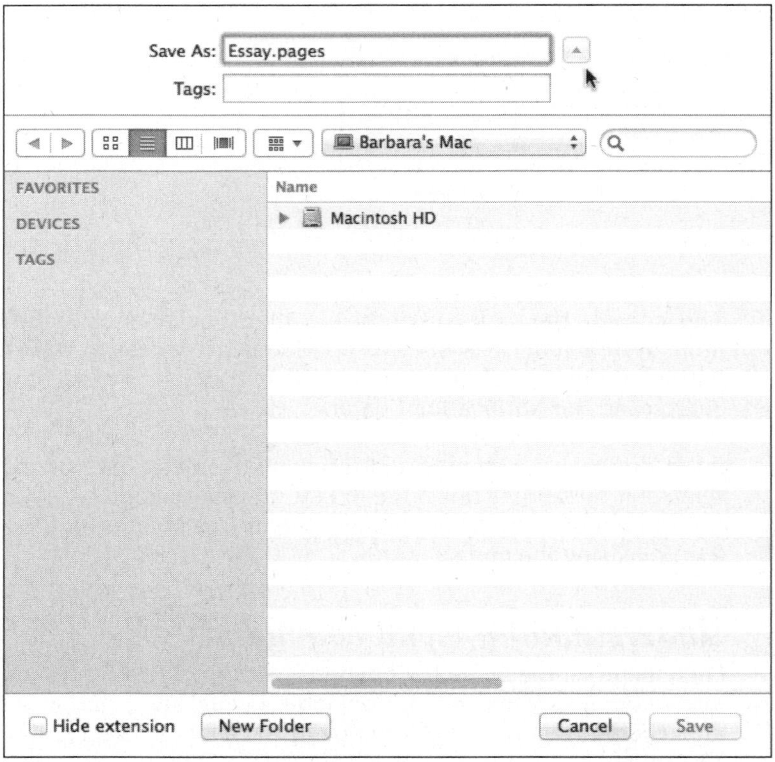

Figure 2-3:
When expanded, the Save dialog offers more options.

Whether expanded or condensed, every dialog displays buttons that either let you cancel the command or complete it. To cancel a command, you have three choices:

✦ Click the Cancel button.

✦ Press Esc.

✦ Press ⌘+. (period).

To complete a command, you also have two choices:

✦ Click the button that represents the command that you want to complete, such as Save or Print.

✦ Press Return or Enter to choose the default button, which appears in blue.

Managing windows

Every app needs to accept, manipulate, and/or display data, also referred to as *information.* A word processor lets you type and edit text, a spreadsheet app lets you type and calculate numbers, and a presentation app lets you display text and pictures. To help you work with different types of information (such as text, pictures, audio, and video files), every app displays information inside a rectangular area called a *window.* Figure 2-4 shows two app windows.

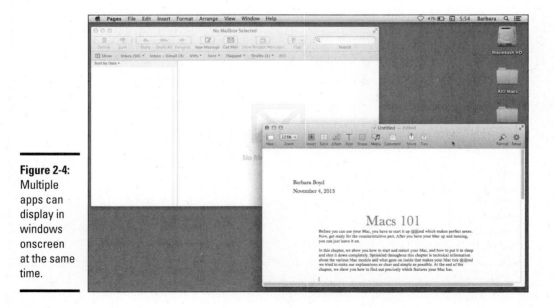

Figure 2-4:
Multiple apps can display in windows onscreen at the same time.

Dividing a screen into multiple windows offers several advantages:

✦ Two or more apps can display information on the screen simultaneously.

✦ A single app can open and display information stored in two or more files or display two or more views of the same file.

✦ You can copy (or move) data from one window to another. If each window belongs to a different app, this action transfers data from one app to another.

Of course, windows aren't perfect. When a window appears on the screen, it might be too big or too small, be hard to find because it's hidden behind another window, or display the beginning of a file when you want to see the middle or the end. To control the appearance of a window, most windows provide built-in controls, as shown in Figure 2-5. The following sections show you what you can do with these controls.

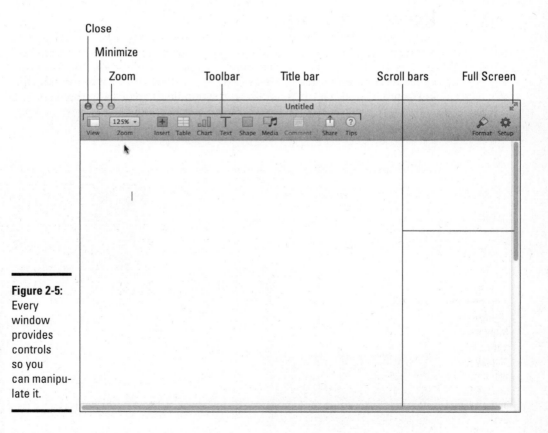

Figure 2-5:
Every window provides controls so you can manipu-late it.

Moving a window with the title bar

The title bar of every window serves two purposes:

✦ Identifies the filename that contains the information displayed in the window

✦ Provides a place to grab when you want to drag (move) the window to a new location on the screen, which we explain in the sections "Using the mouse" and "Operating the trackpad".

Resizing a window

Sometimes a window might be in the perfect location, but it's too small or too large for what you want to do at that moment. To change the size of a window, follow these steps:

1. **Move the pointer over any corner or edge of the window to reveal a resizing handle.**

   It looks like a dash with arrows on both ends if you can make the window larger or smaller; it has just one arrow if the window has reached its size limits and can only be made smaller (or larger).

2. **Hold down the mouse or trackpad button with one finger or your thumb and drag the mouse, or a second finger on the trackpad, to move the resizing widget.**

   • *If you have a two-button mouse,* hold down the left mouse button.

   • *If you have a trackpad,* you can also tap when the pointer becomes a resizing widget, and then with three fingers swipe in the direction you want the window to grow or shrink.

   The window grows or shrinks while you drag or swipe.

3. **Release the mouse or trackpad button (or tap in the window if you're swiping) when you're happy with the new size of the window.**

Closing a window

When you finish viewing or editing any information displayed in a window, you can close the window to keep it from cluttering the screen. To close a window, follow these steps:

1. **Move the pointer to the upper-left corner of the window and then click the Close button (the little red button) of the window you want to close.**

   If you haven't saved the information inside the window, such as a letter you're writing with a word-processing application, the application displays a confirmation dialog that asks whether you want to save it.

2. **In the dialog that appears, click one of the following choices:**

   - *Don't Save:* Closes the window and discards any changes you made to the information inside the window.

   - *Cancel:* Keeps the window open.

   - *Save:* Closes the window but saves the information in a file. If this is the first time you've saved this information, another dialog appears, giving you a chance to name the file and to store the saved information in a specific location on your hard drive.

Computers typically offer two or more ways to accomplish the same task, so you can choose the way you like best. As an alternative to clicking the Close button, you can click inside the window you want to close and then choose File➪Close or press ⌘+W.

Minimizing a window

Sometimes you might not want to close a window, but you still want to get it out of the way so it doesn't clutter your screen. In that case, you can minimize or hide a window, which tucks the window onto the Dock. We explain the features and functions of the Dock a bit later in this chapter.

To minimize a window, choose one of the following methods:

✦ Click the Minimize button — the yellow button in the upper left corner — of the window you want to tuck out of the way.

✦ Click the window you want to minimize and choose Window➪Minimize Window (or press ⌘+M).

✦ Double-click the window's title bar.

To open a minimized window, choose ➪Open Recent and then click the minimized app or document in the list, or click the minimized window on the Dock, as we explain in the section "The Dock."

Zooming a window

If a window is too small to display information, you can instantly make it bigger by using the Zoom button — the green button in the upper-left corner of most windows. (When you move the mouse over the Zoom button, a plus sign appears inside.) Clicking the Zoom button a second time shrinks the window to its prior size.

Zooming a window makes the window — not the contents — grow larger. Many apps have sliders or menus that increase, or decrease, the size of the contents: 100 percent is the actual size; a lower percentage (such as 75) shows more information at a smaller size; and a higher percentage (such as 200) shows less information but may be easier on your eyes.

Employing full-screen view

Most Apple apps and many third-party apps offer full-screen view. When available, a full-screen button (a line with an arrow on each end) appears in the upper-right corner of the title bar of the app window. When you click the full-screen button, the application fills the screen, and the menu bar is hidden from view. Hover the pointer at the very top of the screen to reveal the menu bar so you can point and click to use the menus. Move the pointer back to the window and the menu bar disappears again. Press the Esc key or Control+⌘+F to return to normal view or click the full-screen button again, which you find by hovering the pointer over the upper-right corner.

If you use several applications in full-screen view, swipe left or right with four fingers across the trackpad or Control+→ or Control+← to move from one application to another.

Scrolling through a window

No matter how large you make a window, it may still be too small to display all the information contained inside. If a window isn't large enough to display all the information inside it, the window lets you know by displaying vertical or horizontal scroll bars.

You can scroll what's displayed in a window two ways:

✦ **Mouse or trackpad scrolling:** See the next sections "Using the mouse" and "Operating the trackpad" to learn how to use both the mouse and trackpad. With either one, moving your fingers or the mouse up and down and left and right move the contents of the window up and down, left and right.

✦ **Scroll bars:** You can move the contents by

- *Dragging the scroll box:* Click and drag the gray oval scroll box in the scroll bar to move forward and backward in the window. This scrolls through a window faster than mouse or trackpad scrolling.

- *Clicking in the scroll bar:* Scrolls up/down or right/left in large increments or directly to the spot where you click.

  Although the scroll bar is the size of the window, it represents the length, or width, of the document; if you want to jump to page 25 of a 100-page document, click in the upper quarter of the vertical scroll bar; to go to page 90, click near the bottom of the scroll bar.

You can adjust the scroll bars' appearance — or eliminate them altogether — which we explain in Book I, Chapter 6.

Depending on your Mac model, your Mac's keyboard may have dedicated Page Up and Page Down keys, which you can press to scroll up and down. Not seeing Page Up and Page Down keys on your Mac or MacBook keyboard doesn't mean they aren't there. To use your Mac's invisible Page Up and Page Down keys, see the "Arrow and cursor control keys" section.

Mastering the Mouse, Trackpad, and Keyboard

To control your Mac, you use the mouse or trackpad and the keyboard. Using both the mouse or trackpad and the keyboard, you can choose commands, manipulate items on the screen, or create such data as text or pictures.

Using the mouse

A typical mouse looks like, and is about the size of, a bar of soap. The main purpose of the mouse is to move a pointer on the screen, which tells the computer, "See what I'm pointing at right now? That's what I want to select." To select an item on the screen, you move the mouse (which in turn makes the onscreen pointer move), put the pointer on that item, and then press and release (click) the mouse button, or press down the top, left side of the mouse if you have a mouse, such as Apple's Mighty Mouse or Magic Mouse, that doesn't have visible buttons.

The whole surface of the wireless Apple Magic Mouse uses touch-sensitive technology that detects your fingertip gestures just like the MacBook trackpads, whereas the Mighty Mouse (sometimes called simply "Apple Mouse") is touch-sensitive where your fingertips hit when you rest your palm on the mouse, but a scroll ball that doubles as a button on the top and squeezable side buttons. These are the basic mouse gestures to use with either mouse:

✦ **Clicking (single-clicking):** This is the most common activity with a mouse. With the Magic Mouse, move the mouse and tap anywhere on the surface. If you have an older mouse with buttons or an Apple Mighty Mouse, pressing the left mouse button, or the left side of the mouse, is *clicking*.

✦ **Double-clicking:** If you point at something and tap twice in rapid succession on the surface (that is, you *double-click* it), you can often select an item and open it at the same time. (If you're using an older mouse, click the left mouse button or the mouse's single button twice in rapid succession to double-click.)

✦ **Dragging:** Another common activity with the mouse is *dragging* — pointing at an item on the screen, holding down the left mouse button or the Magic Mouse's invisible single center button to select the item, moving the mouse, which drags the item in the direction you move the mouse, and then releasing the button. Clicking and dragging is often the way to open menus, too.

✦ **Control-clicking/right-clicking:** Holding down the Control key while you click, or clicking the right button on the mouse, commonly displays a menu of commands (a *contextual* or *shortcut menu*) at the point you clicked to do something with the item that the mouse is pointing at. For example, in some apps (such as Pages), right-clicking a misspelled word displays a list of properly spelled words to choose from. Or, in Word, access a list of synonyms by right-clicking a correctly spelled word and then dragging on the contextual menu to Synonyms, as shown in Figure 2-6.

On the Magic Mouse, hold down the Control key and tap to click. To simulate a right-click with a single-button mouse, hold down the Control key and click the mouse button. On a two-button mouse, click the right button (or the right side of a Mighty Mouse).

You can set up the Magic Mouse to function like an old-style two-button mouse by choosing the menu and choosing System Preferences. Click Mouse in the Hardware section and then select the Secondary Click check box. You can even choose left or right side, making it more natural if you're left-handed.

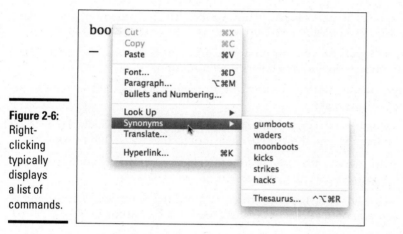

Figure 2-6:
Right-clicking typically displays a list of commands.

♦ **Scrolling:** The surface of the Magic Mouse has the sensitivity of a track-pad, so you can move a finger up or down to scroll up and down the onscreen image (say, a word-processing document or a web page). Hold down the Control key while you scroll with one finger to zoom in on items on the screen.

♦ **Swipe:** Swipe two fingers left and right on the Magic Mouse surface to move back and forth through web pages or to browse photos in iPhoto.

Likewise, you can use System Preferences to make the Mighty Mouse to function like a one-button mouse.

If you don't like the mouse that came with your Mac, you can always buy a replacement mouse or a *trackball*, which looks like a golf-ball embedded in a switchplate; you rotate the trackball with your fingers or palm to move the pointer instead of moving the entire mouse across your desktop or mouse-pad. Some mice are ergonomically molded to be a better fit for the shape of your hand, so find a mouse that you like and connect it via the USB port of your Mac. Or, get a wireless mouse that connects to your Mac using your Mac's Bluetooth wireless connection feature.

Operating the trackpad

All current MacBook models sport trackpads that can do more than most advanced multibutton mice. If you have a desktop model or find the track-pad on a MacBook model inconvenient, you can opt for the Magic Trackpad, which will give you all the multitouch gestures explained here.

Thanks to the trackpad's smart sensing abilities, *point-and-click* has a whole new meaning because you're often using your index (or pointer) finger to move the pointer and then tapping once on the trackpad to "click." A double-tap is the same as a double-click. Other gestures you can use with the trackpad are

✦ **Scroll:** Move what you see on the screen up and down or left to right is as easy as sliding or swiping two fingers up and down or across the trackpad. The items in the window follow the movement of your fingers, the window contents move up when you move your fingers up.

✦ **Rotate:** Move the window contents 360 degrees by placing two fingers on the trackpad and making a circular motion.

✦ **Swipe:** Swipe the tips of three or four fingers across the trackpad to per-form various tasks:

  • Swipe up with three or four fingers to open Mission Control (see Book I, Chapter 5), and then tap to close it or switch to a different window.

  • Swipe down with three or four fingers to open App Exposé (see Book I, Chapter 5), and then swipe up or down to close it.

  • Swipe left and right with three or four fingers to switch between full-screen applications or Spaces (see Book I, Chapter 5).

✦ **Pinch:** Place three fingers and your thumb slightly open on the track-pad, and then bring them together as if picking up a small item; doing so opens Launchpad (see Book I, Chapter 5). Tap to close it or double-tap to open a different app.

✦ **Unpinch:** Place three fingers and your thumb together on the track-pad and open them to move everything off the Desktop. Pinch to bring everything back.

✦ **Control-click:** Hold the Control key and tap the trackpad or tap with two fingers.

✦ **Click and drag:** Move the pointer to a menu, window title bar, file, folder, or just on the Desktop. Press and hold your thumb on the trackpad. Then, with another finger, drag down to open a menu, drag the title bar of an open window to move the window, or drag a closed file or folder to move the file or folder. On the Desktop, or if your windows are in Icon view (as explained in Book I, Chapter 4), drag around multiple objects, as if you were lassoing them, to select a group. Click and drag across text to select it in an app you can type in such as a word processing or e-mail app.

✦ **Two-finger tap:** Tap the trackpad once with two fingers to Control-click/right-click.

✦ **Two-finger double-tap:** Tap the trackpad twice with two fingers to zoom in on a web page.

✦ **Three-finger double-tap (in Apple apps):** Tap the trackpad twice with three fingers to look up a word in the built-in dictionary.

✦ **Three-finger drag:** Move the pointer to the title bar of a window and move it around on the desktop with three fingers.

Choose ⌘ ➪ System Preferences and then choose Mouse or Trackpad to specify how you want to use the mouse or trackpad and to see examples of how the multitouch gestures work, as shown in Figure 2-7.

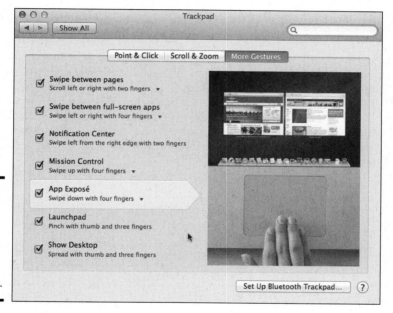

Figure 2-7:
See multitouch gestures in action in System Preferences.

Examining the parts of the keyboard

The primary use of the keyboard is to type information. However, you can also use the keyboard to select items and menu commands — sometimes more quickly than using the mouse. Figure 2-8 shows how the keyboard groups related keys. The next few sections cover each group of keys in detail.

Function and special feature keys

Depending on your particular keyboard, you might see 12 to 20 function and special feature keys running along the top of the keyboard. These keys are labeled F1 through F12/F19, along with an Esc key — short for Escape — and an Eject key that looks like a triangle on top of a horizontal line.

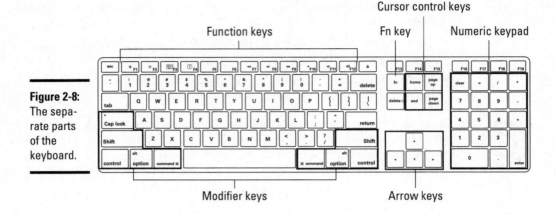

Figure 2-8:
The separate parts of the keyboard.

On Mac models made after April 2007, the function number appears in the lower right corner of the key and a larger icon represents the special feature task that happens when you press the key to do things, such as turn down the screen brightness (F1), play or pause music you're listening to in iTunes (F8), or open your Mac's Dashboard Widgets application to check the weather forecast (F4). Although the icons on each of these special feature keys are self-evident, check out Table 2-1 to find out what all your Mac's special features keys do when you press them.

Table 2-1	Mac Assigned Commands
Function Key	*What It Does*
F1	Decreases display brightness
F2	Increases display brightness
F3	Displays Mission Control
F4	Displays Launchpad (displays Dashboard on older Macs)
F5	Decreases keyboard backlight brightness
F6	Increases keyboard backlight brightness
F7	Video and audio rewind
F8	Video and audio play/pause
F9	Video and audio fast-forward
F10	Mutes sound
F11	Decreases sound volume
F12	Increases sound volume

You select the Mac's application-specific function keys by pressing and holding the Fn key and *then* pressing one of the function keys on the upper row of the keyboard. (You can see the Fn key to the left of the cursor control keys earlier in Figure 2-7.) In Microsoft Word, for instance, pressing Fn+F7 tells Word to run the spell checker; pressing Fn+F5 opens the Find and Replace dialog.

In other words, holding down the Fn key tells your Mac, "Ignore the special feature controls assigned to that function key listed in Table 2-1 and just behave like an old-fashioned function key."

To reverse the way the Mac's function keys work when you press them, choose ⌘⇨System Preferences and click the Keyboard icon. Click the Keyboard tab at the top of the window, and then select the check box next to Use All F1, F2, Etc. Keys as Standard Function Keys. When you activate this option, you *must* hold down the Fn key to perform the commands shown in Table 2-1, but you don't have to hold down the Fn key to use app-specific function keys.

Here are some additional tips for getting the most out of the function and special feature keys:

✦ **App Exposé:** Pressing Fn+F10 (or Ctrl+F3) shows you all windows that belong to the active app (this feature is called App Exposé). You can identify the active app by looking for its name on the left side of the menu bar. Pressing Fn+F11 or ⌘ +F3 shoves all windows out of the way so you can see the Desktop.

✦ **Dashboard:** Pressing Fn+F12 (F3 on older Mac keyboards) displays the Dashboard app and its widgets, which are simple mini-apps, such as a calculator, calendar, or a display of your local weather forecast. You find out more about Dashboard in the later section, "Exploring the Dashboard."

✦ **Shortcut commands:** As for the other keys — F1–F7 and (possibly) F13–F19 — holding the Fn key and pressing these fellows can carry out shortcut commands on a by-application basis.

✦ **Escape and Eject:** Turning to the two keys grouped near the function keys, here's what you need to know. The Esc key often works as a "You may be excused" command. For example, if a pull-down menu appears on the screen and you want it to go away, press the Esc key. The Eject key ejects a CD or DVD from your Mac. (If your MacBook Pro or Air came without a disk drive, there's no Eject key.)

Originally, function keys existed because some applications assigned commands to different function keys. Unfortunately, every application assigned different commands to identical function keys, which sometimes made function keys more confusing than helpful. You can assign your own commands to different function keys, but just remember that not every Mac will have the same commands assigned to the same function keys. (Not everyone thinks exactly like you, as amazing as that might seem.) To customize which function keys perform which commands, choose ❤️➪System Preferences➪Keyboard, and then click the Keyboard Shortcuts tab at the top of the window and adjust your Mac's keyboard shortcuts to your heart's content.

Typewriter keys

You use the typewriter (also known as the *alphanumeric*) keys to create *data* — the typing-a-letter-in-a-word-processor stuff or the entering-of-names-and-addresses-into-the-Contacts-app stuff. When you press a typewriter key, you're telling the Mac what character to type at the cursor position, which often appears as a blinking vertical line on the screen.

You can move the cursor by pointing to and clicking a new location with the mouse or by pressing the arrow keys as explained in the upcoming "Arrow and cursor control keys" section.

Just because you don't find a character labeled on your keyboard doesn't mean you can't type that character. Holding Shift, Option, and Shift+Option while pressing another key on the keyboard results in different symbols or letters, such as uppercase letters or the symbol for a trademark or square root.

To see all the key combinations, follow these steps:

1. **Choose ❤️➪System Preferences and then click Keyboard.**

2. **Click the Keyboard tab and then select the Show Keyboard & Character Viewers check box.**

3. **Close System Preferences.**

    A menulet for the Keyboard & Character Viewer appears in the menu bar at the top of your screen.

4. **Choose the Keyboard & Character Viewer icon and then Show Keyboard Viewer.**

    A graphic representation of the keyboard appears on your screen, as shown in Figure 2-9.

5. **Hold down the Shift, Option, or Shift+Option keys.**

    The keyboard changes to show the letter or symbol that will be typed when you hold down Shift, Option, or Shift+Option and type a letter or number.

    Refer to the Cheat Sheet at www.dummies.com/cheatsheet/macsaio for more information about typing special characters.

Figure 2-9:
Keyboard
Viewer.

In addition to keys that type letters and characters, you'll find keys that don't type anything but nevertheless play an important role.

✦ **Delete:** Appears to the right of the +/= key. The Delete key deletes any characters that appear to the left of the cursor. If you hold down Delete, your Mac deletes any characters to the left of the cursor until you lift your finger.

✦ **Tab:** This key indents text in a word processor and moves from cell to cell in a spreadsheet app, but it can also move from text box to text box in a form, like when you type a shipping address for an online bookstore or merchant.

✦ **Return:** Moves the cursor to the next line in a word processor, but can also choose a default button (which appears in blue) on the screen. For example, the Print button is the default button in the Print dialog, so pressing Return in the Print dialog sends your document to the printer.

The Return key is sometimes named Enter on third-party external keyboards you can buy to use with your Mac.

Modifier keys

Modifier keys are almost never used individually. Instead, modifier keys are usually held down while tapping another key. Included in the modifier keys category are the Function (Fn) keys mentioned in a few of the previous sections, along with the Shift, Control (Ctrl), Option, and ⌘ (Command) keys.

Here's an example of how modifier keys work. If you press the S key in a word-processing document, your Mac types the letter "s" on the screen. If you hold down a modifier key, such as the Command key (⌘), and then press the S key, the S key is modified to behave differently. In this case, holding down the ⌘ key followed by the S key (⌘+S) tells your word processing application to issue the Save command and save whatever you typed or changed since the last time you saved the document.

Most modifier keystrokes involve pressing two keys, such as ⌘+Q (the Quit command), but some modifier keystrokes can involve pressing three or four keys, such as Shift+⌘+3, which saves a snapshot of what you see on your screen as an image file, which is commonly referred to as a *screenshot*.

The main use for modifier keys is to help you choose commands quickly without fumbling with the mouse or trackpad to use menu commands. Every application includes dozens of such keystroke shortcuts, but Table 2-2 lists the common keystroke shortcuts that work the same in most apps.

Table 2-2	Common Keystroke Shortcuts
Command	*Keystroke Shortcut*
Copy	⌘+C
Cut	⌘+X
Paste	⌘+V
Open	⌘+O
New	⌘+N
Print	⌘+P
Quit	⌘+Q
Save	⌘+S
Select All	⌘+A
Undo	⌘+Z

The Caps Lock key, when active as indicated by the green light on the key, lets you type in all capital letters but doesn't effect the function of modifier keys combined with letters.

Most Mac apps display their keystroke shortcuts for commands directly on their pull-down menus, as shown in Figure 2-10.

Instead of describing the modifier keys to press by name (such as Shift), most keystroke shortcuts displayed on menus use cryptic graphics. Figure 2-11 displays the different symbols that represent shortcut commands.

Numeric keypad

The numeric keypad appears on the right side of the keyboard (if your keyboard has one!) and arranges the numbers 0–9 in rows and columns like a typical calculator keypad. It also features other keys that are useful for mathematical calculations. The main use for the numeric keys is to make typing numbers faster and easier than using the numeric keys on the top row of the typewriter keys.

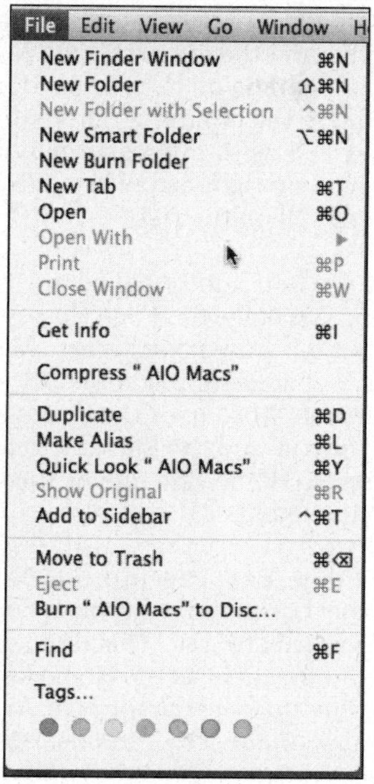

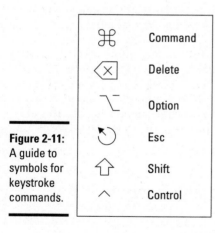

Figure 2-10: Most pull-down menus list shortcut keystrokes for commonly used commands.

Figure 2-11: A guide to symbols for keystroke commands.

⌘	Command
⌫	Delete
⌥	Option
↺	Esc
⇧	Shift
^	Control

Arrow and cursor control keys

The pointer becomes a cursor when you use the keyboard to enter data in any type of app or even when naming a file. The cursor often appears as a vertical blinking line and acts like a placeholder. Wherever the cursor appears, that's where your next character will appear if you press a keyboard key. You can move the cursor with the mouse or trackpad, or you can move it with the arrow keys.

The up arrow moves the cursor up, the down arrow moves the cursor down, the right arrow moves the cursor right, and the left arrow moves the cursor left. (Could it be any more logical?) Depending on the application you're using, pressing an arrow key might move the cursor in different ways. For example, pressing the right arrow key in a word processor moves the cursor right one character, but pressing that same right arrow key in a spreadsheet might move the cursor to the adjacent cell on the right.

On some Mac keyboards, you might see four additional cursor-control keys: Home, End, Page Up, and Page Down. Typically, the Page Up key scrolls up one screen, and the Page Down key scrolls down one screen. Many applications ignore the Home and End keys, but some applications let you move the cursor with them. For example, Microsoft Word uses the Home key to move the cursor to the beginning of a line or row and the End key to move the cursor to the end of a line or row, and ⌘+Home/End moves the cursor to the beginning or end, respectively, of a document.

 Just because you might not see the Home, End, Page Up, and Page Down keys on your Mac or MacBook keyboard doesn't mean those command keys aren't there. On the MacBook that I'm using to write this, holding down the Fn key and then pressing the left arrow key acts as the Home key, which moves the cursor to the start of the line that the cursor is in. Pressing Fn+→ jumps the cursor to the end of the current line, Fn+↑ scrolls the text up one page, and Fn+↓ scrolls the text down one page. Also, ⌘+Fn+←/→ moves the cursor to the beginning or end (respectively) of the document. Because seeing is believing, try it on your own Mac keyboard so you can see what I mean — even if you don't see keys bearing those actual labels.

To the left of the End key on a full keyboard, you might find a smaller Delete key. Like the bigger Delete key, this smaller Delete key also deletes characters one at a time. The difference is that the big Delete key erases characters to the *left* of the cursor, but the small Delete key, sometimes labelled Del, erases characters to the *right* of the cursor. If your keyboard lacks the Del key, holding the Function (Fn) key while pressing the delete key erases characters to the right.

Getting to Know the Parts of the Desktop

Consider your physical desk: You keep the things you use most frequently, like a calculator or day planner, out in the open so you can grab them easily. Likewise, if you start leaving documents about, sooner or later there are so many you can't see the surface, so you divvy up the documents and place related ones in folders, keeping only the most pertinent folders on your desk and putting the others in a filing cabinet to be pulled out when needed.

The theory behind the Mac Desktop — the screen you see most of the time — is the same. Windows open on the screen display the documents or files you're working on. Windows cover part of — or, when you use a full-screen app, all of — the Desktop. File and app icons are like those documents and tools you keep on your desk. Unfortunately, the more icons you store on the Desktop, the more cluttered it appears, making it harder to find anything — just like your physical desk. Organizing your app and files into folders makes things easier to find and your virtual desktop more orderly. In addition, you can place frequently used apps and files on the Dock, which is a quickly accessed area of the Desktop.

The Desktop generally shows an icon that represents your hard drive — think of it as your filing cabinet. If you have any additional storage devices attached to your Mac (such as an external hard drive, a CD or DVD, or a USB flash drive), you typically see icons for those storage devices on your Desktop, too. We describe the menu and menulets at the beginning of this chapter. Here we take a look at the other parts of the Desktop: the Dock and the Finder.

The cool thing about the virtual Mac Desktop is that you can have more than one, and we explain how to do that trick in Book I, Chapter 5.

The Dock

The *Dock* is a rectangular strip that contains app, file, and folder icons. It lies in wait just out of sight either at the bottom or on the left or right side of the Desktop. When you hover the pointer in the area where the Dock is hiding, it appears, displaying the app, file, and folder icons stored there. When you use your Mac for the first time, the Dock already has icons for many of the pre-installed apps, as well as the Downloads folder and a Trash icon. You click an icon to elicit an action, which is usually to open an app or file, although you can also remove the icon from the Dock or activate a setting so that app opens when you log in to your Mac. We tell you about working with apps in the Dock in Book I, Chapter 5; here we tell you how to change the Dock's appearance.

When you open an app that isn't on the Dock, a temporary icon appears there; when you quit that app, the icon is deleted from the Dock. You can add icons to the Dock for apps, folders, or files you use frequently. To help keep your icons organized, application icons appear on the left side of a divider and file icons on the right side, as shown in Figure 2-12.

Figure 2-12:
The Dock.

Applications   Files

By default, the Dock appears at the bottom of the screen, and the icons have a standard size. Like most things on your Mac, however, the Dock is flexible, and you can move it to the left or right of the screen and modify the size of the icons. If you move the Dock to the side of the screen, the application icons are above the divider, and the file icons are below.

The Dock grows longer each time you add more app and file icons to it. (You find out how to customize the icons on the Dock in Book I, Chapter 5.) If you have a lot of icons, depending on your screen size, you may not see them all at once. You can make the icons smaller so that you can see the whole length of the Dock at once, but the icons can then appear too small, making it hard to see which icon the mouse is pointing at. Fortunately, the name of the application beneath the pointer appears to tell you what application it is, and you can turn on magnification, which makes Dock icons zoom in size when you move the pointer over them (refer to Figure 2-12).

To make changes to the Dock's appearance, follow these steps:

1. **Choose** ⌘ ⇨ **Dock** ⇨ **Dock Preferences.**

   The Dock preferences pane appears, as shown in Figure 2-13.

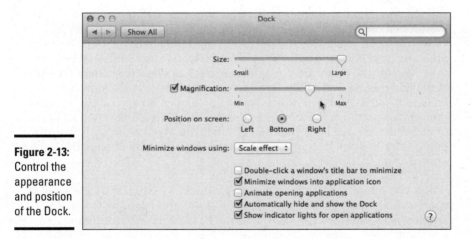

Figure 2-13: Control the appearance and position of the Dock.

2. **Drag the Size slider to adjust the size of all the icons on the Dock.**

3. **Select (or clear) the Magnification check box.**

4. **Drag the Magnification slider to adjust the magnification of the Dock.**

   Magnification makes the icons appear larger as you move the pointer over them, which is especially helpful if you have a small size Dock with a lot of items on it.

5. **Click your preferred location for the Dock: Left, Bottom, or Right.**

6. **Choose how you want apps and files to open when clicked in the Dock:**

   • *Genie Effect:* When you open or minimize a file or app, it exits and enters the Dock like a genie being pulled in and out of a magic lamp.

   • *Scale Effect:* Files or apps exit and enter the Dock in a simple, linear fashion.

7. **Select the check boxes next to the other display choices to turn them on or off.**

   We prefer to turn three of the five choices on, as shown in Figure 2-13. Minimizing windows keeps the Dock icons to a minimum; automatically hiding the Dock keeps it out of sight until you need it; and showing indicator lights lets you know which apps are open.

8. **Click the Close button of the Dock preferences window.**

For a fast way to turn Hiding or Magnification on or off, or to change the position of the Dock, choose Dock Turning Hiding Off (On)/Turn Magnification On (Off)/Position on Left/Bottom/Right.

When you click the Minimize window button — the yellow button in the upper-left corner — a minimized window icon on the Dock actually displays the contents of that window, and sometimes continues playing the content. If you squint hard enough (or have a large enough screen), you can see what each minimized window contains. Reopen minimized windows as you would any other file or app, hover the pointer over the window and then click; the window pops back up on the Desktop.

If you select Minimize Windows into Application Icon on the Dock Preferences (refer to Figure 2-13), any windows you minimize will be kept with the app icon. Click and hold the app icon, then drag to the name of the file that was in the window to open it.

The Finder

The Finder is an app that lets you find, copy, move, rename, delete, and open files and folders on your Mac. You can run apps directly from the Finder although the Dock makes finding and running apps you use frequently much more convenient.

The Finder runs all the time. To switch to the Finder, click the Finder icon on the Dock (the Picasso-like faces icon on the far left, or top, of the Dock) or just click an area of the Desktop outside any open windows. You know you're in the Finder because the app menu is Finder, as opposed to Pages, System Preferences, or some other app name.

Open a new Finder window by choosing File New Finder Window or choosing New Finder Window from the Finder's Dock menu. You can open as many

Finder windows as you want, although it's common just to have one Finder window open and several tabs within that window for the folders and devices you want quick access to.

Because the Finder helps you manage the files stored on your hard drive, a Finder window consists of two panes and multiple tabs, as shown in Figure 2-14.

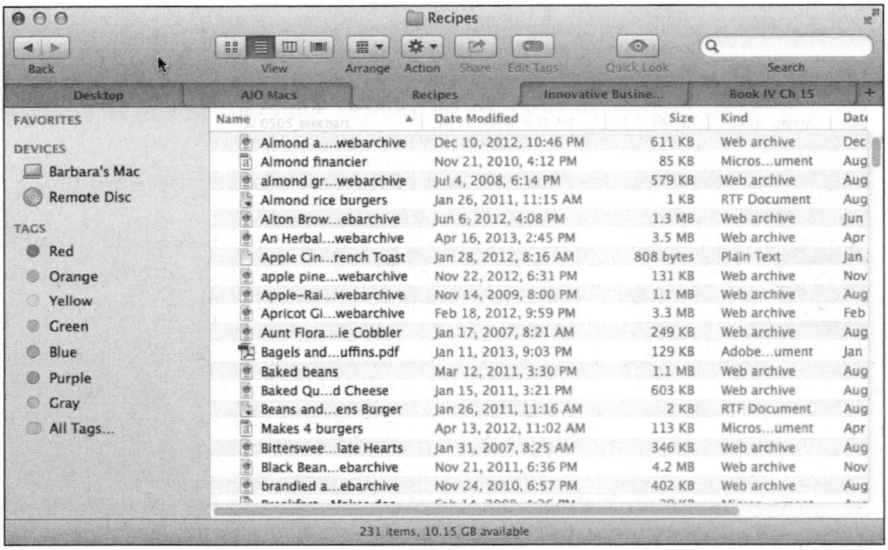

Figure 2-14:
The Finder displays panes and tabs to help you navigate to different parts of your hard drive.

The left pane — the *Sidebar* — displays up to four different categories:

✦ **Favorites:** Lists the Desktop, Home, Applications, and Documents folders, which are the default folders for storing files, as well as any others you select in Finder preferences so you can access them more quickly.

✦ **Shared:** Lists all shared storage devices (if any) connected on a local area network (LAN).

✦ **Devices:** Lists all the storage devices connected to your Mac, such as hard drives, flash drives, and CD/DVD drives.

✦ **Tags:** Lists tags you can apply to files; clicking a tag shows all the files tagged with that criteria.

The right pane displays the contents of an item selected in the Sidebar. For example, if you click the hard drive icon in the Sidebar, the right pane displays the contents of that hard drive. All apps and files displayed in a Finder window or tab appear as icons with text labels, regardless of which type of view you chose to view the Finder window.

You find out how to use the Finder and create tabs, tags, and folders in Book I, Chapter 4.

You can change what your Mac displays on the Desktop. To do so, click the Desktop to activate the Finder, and then choose Finder ➪ Preferences. In the Finder Preferences window, shown in Figure 2-15, check, uncheck, or change the different options to suit your style.

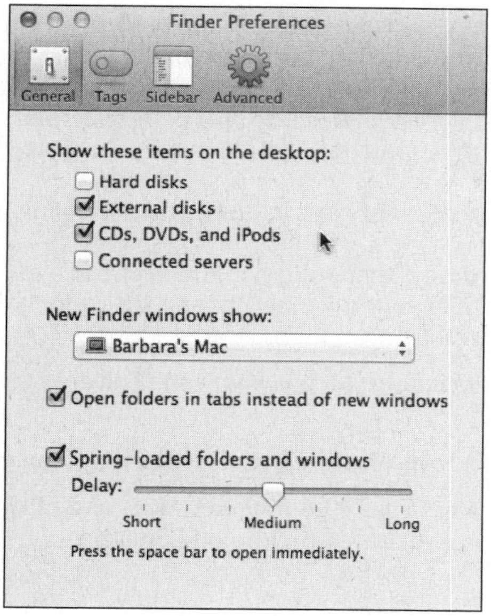

Figure 2-15:
Select what
you want
to see on
the Desktop
with Finder
Preferences.

Exploring the Dashboard

Many apps have so many features crammed into them that succeeding versions get more bloated and harder to use. If you want to perform a simple task, such as adding a few numbers together or printing an envelope, you probably don't need to load a full-blown spreadsheet or word-processing app. Instead, you're better off using a much simpler app specifically designed to solve a single task.

That's the idea behind Dashboard, which provides you with quick access to a collection of small, simple-task apps called *widgets*. Some typical widgets display a calendar, weather forecasts for your city, a calculator, stock market quotes, and movie times for your neighborhood movie theaters.

Widgets are designed to simplify your life, and Dashboard is the feature that helps you display, manage, and hide widgets. By using Dashboard, you can be more productive without having to master an entirely new application to do so. In this section, we tell you everything you need to know about using Dashboard widgets.

Viewing Dashboard widgets

The Dashboard can be a Desktop unto itself — remember that you can have more than one Desktop — or you can view widgets on top of whatever windows are open on your Desktop. As a Desktop space, it resides to the left of the first Desktop. (Discover how to add more Desktop Spaces in Book I, Chapter 5.) To choose where you want to view your widgets, choose ➡️System Preferences, and then click Mission Control or right-click (two-finger tap on the trackpad) the Dashboard icon on the Dock. Select the Show Dashboard as a Space check box to give Dashboard its very own Desktop space. Deselect the check box to make widgets appear on top of the open windows on your Desktop.

To view your widgets, open Dashboard in one of the following ways:

✦ **Press the Dashboard key.** Depending on the keyboard you use, Dashboard may have its very own key. It has a little clock on it and shares space with one of the function keys.

✦ **Press Fn+F12.** Do this if your keyboard doesn't (or does) have a dedicated Dashboard key.

✦ **Click the Dashboard icon on the Dock.** It looks like a speedometer.

✦ **Open Launchpad (press Fn+F4 on a newer Mac) and click the Dashboard icon.** You can find more info on Launchpad in Book I, Chapter 5.

✦ **Navigate to the Dashboard's Desktop space.** If your Dashboard has its own Space (as it does by default), you can do any of the above or swipe from left to right with four fingers on the trackpad, or hold the Control key and press the left arrow.

When you finish using a widget, you close it (and the Dashboard) the same way: by pressing the Dashboard key (if your keyboard has one), Fn+F12, or press Esc. If your widgets are on top of your windows, click anywhere on the Desktop. If you gave Dashboard its own Space, you can use the keys or click the arrow in the lower-right corner, swipe from right to left with four fingers on the trackpad, or press Control+→.

While most MacBook and recent Apple keyboards have a Function (Fn) key, other Mac keyboards don't always have the Fn key. If your Mac's keyboard doesn't have an Fn key, you can just press whatever function key we tell you to press and ignore our mention of the Fn key whenever you encounter it.

As soon as you open Dashboard, several widgets pop into view, as shown in Figure 2-16. The defaults that appear are the calendar, clock, calculator, and weather widgets.

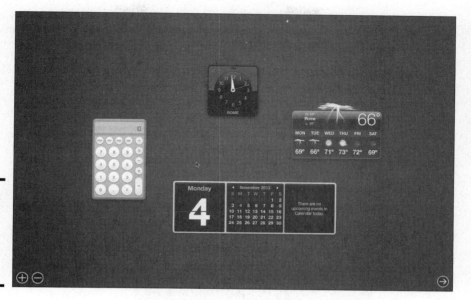

Figure 2-16:
Dashboard
displays
widgets on
their own
desktop.

The calendar widget lets you view dates for different months and years. The clock widget displays the time in a big clock, which can be easier to read than the tiny time display in the right end of the menu bar. The calculator widget acts like a typical four-function calculator, and the weather widget offers forecasts for a city of your choosing.

If you don't like the position of your widgets on the screen, you can always move them to a new location. To move a widget, click it and drag it to its new position. After you use a widget, you can hide Dashboard, and all its widgets are out of sight once more.

Many widgets, including the weather widget, rely on an Internet connection. If you aren't connected to the Internet when you display such a widget, the widget can't display the latest information.

Customizing a widget

Some widgets always appear the same way, such as the calculator widget. Other widgets let you customize them to change their appearance or the type of data they display. To customize a widget, follow these steps:

1. **Press the Dashboard key to open Dashboard and display all your widgets (or press Fn+F12).**

2. **Hover the mouse on the widget you want to customize and then click the Information (i) button.**

   The *i* button (the Information button) appears only for widgets you can customize, such as the weather widget.

3. **Select any check boxes the widget may provide to display additional information, type the new information you want the widget to display, and then click Done.**

In Figure 2-17, we clicked the Information button on the Weather widget. Type the city and state or zip code of a city whose weather forecast you want to keep track of, and then select the Include Lows in 6-Day Forecast check box if you want to see that information as well.

Figure 2-17:
Widget
options you
can modify.

Displaying and then clicking a widget changes or expands the information that appears. For instance, clicking the weather widget shows or hides the six-day forecast, and clicking the day/date display of the calendar widget toggles the month-at-a-glance and upcoming appointments displays. Click other widgets to discover whether they offer other additional displays.

Adding and removing widgets

When you open Dashboard, you see several widgets, even if you actually want to use just one widget. In case you don't want to see a particular widget, you can remove it from Dashboard. (Don't worry; you can always put it back on Dashboard again.) Conversely, you can also add more widgets to your Dashboard.

Removing a widget from Dashboard

When you remove a widget from Dashboard, you don't physically delete the widget. Instead, you just tuck the widget into storage where you can retrieve it later. To remove a widget from Dashboard, follow these steps:

1. **Press the Dashboard key or Fn+F12 to open Dashboard and display all your widgets.**

2. **Click the minus sign button that appears inside a circle in the bottom-left corner of the screen to display Close buttons (x's in circles) in the upper-left corner of every widget, as shown in Figure 2-18.**

If you hover the pointer on the widget you want to remove and hold down the Option key, a Close button appears in the upper-right corner of just that one widget (and you don't have to click the circled minus sign icon).

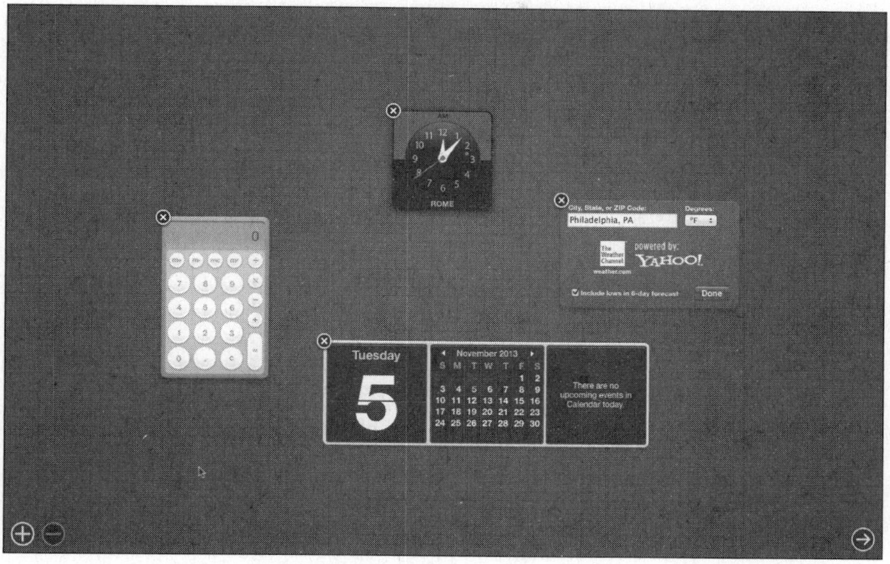

Figure 2-18: Click the Close button to remove a widget you no longer want to see.

3. **Click the Close button of the widget you want to remove to make it disappear from the screen.**

4. **Press the Dashboard key or Fn+F12 to close Dashboard.**

Clicking anywhere on the screen except on another widget is another way to close Dashboard.

Displaying more widgets in Dashboard

When you open Dashboard, you see only a handful of all the widgets in the Dashboard's library of widgets that come with every Mac. Table 2-3 lists all of Dashboard's available widgets that you can choose to display every time you open Dashboard, some of which are shown earlier in Figure 2-18. (*Note:* Apple may have changed the lineup since we wrote this, so keep in mind that your collection may vary.)

Table 2-3	Dashboard's Library of Widgets
Widget	*What It Does*
Contacts	Lets you search for names stored in the Contacts app.
Business	Displays a Yellow Pages directory for looking up business names and phone numbers.

(continued)

Table 2-3 *(continued)*

Widget	What It Does
Calculator	Displays a four-function calculator.
Dictionary	Displays a dictionary and thesaurus.
ESPN	Displays sports news and scores.
Flight Tracker	Tracks airline flights.
Calendar	Displays a calendar and any appointments stored within Calendar.
Movies	Displays which movies are playing at which times at a certain zip code.
Ski Report	Displays the temperature and snow depth at your favorite ski resort.
Stickies	Displays color-coded windows for jotting down notes.
Stocks	Displays stock quotes.
Tile Game	Displays a picture tile game in which you slide tiles to re-create a picture.
Translation	Translates words from one language to another, such as from Japanese to French.
Unit Converter	Converts measurement units, such as inches to centimeters.
Weather	Displays a weather forecast for your area.
Web Clip	Displays parts of a web page that you've clipped from Safari. (See Book II, Chapter 1 for more information about creating Web Clips.)
World Clock	Displays the current time.

To display a hidden Dashboard widget, follow these steps:

1. **Press the Dashboard key or Fn+F12 to open Dashboard, and then click the plus sign that appears inside a circle in the bottom-left corner of the screen to display a selection of widgets.**

2. **Click a widget that you want to display in Dashboard, such as ESPN or Stocks, to make it appear onscreen.**

3. **Move the cursor to the widget, click and drag the widget to wherever you want it to appear on your screen, and release the mouse button.**

4. **Press the Dashboard key or Fn+F12 to close Dashboard.**

   All your widgets disappear. The next time you open Dashboard, your newly added widgets appear onscreen.

You can have multiple instances of the same widget opened at the same time. For instance, to track the weather in two or more cities, you can just repeat Step 2 in the preceding steps for each additional instance of the weather widget you want to display.

Finding new widgets

Dashboard comes with a library of widgets, but people are always creating more, which you can browse and download by visiting Apple's website. To find the latest widgets, follow these steps:

1. **Press the Dashboard key or Fn+F12 to open Dashboard, and then click the plus sign that appears inside a circle in the bottom-left corner.**

2. **Click the More Widgets button.**

   The Widget Browser on Apple's download website opens.

3. **Scroll through the Widget Browser or click the Categories to display a list of the widgets.**

4. **Click a widget in the Widget Browser or one of the lists.**

   This displays details about the widget.

5. **Click the Download button if you decide to add the widget to your Mac's library of Dashboard widgets.**

   Your Mac downloads the chosen widget to the Downloads folder and displays a dialog confirming whether you want to install your newly downloaded widget in Dashboard.

   We found a lot of outdated widgets that OS X 10.9 Mavericks refused to open, but we can also assure you that valid widgets exist. A little patience and trial and error can help you find functioning widgets.

6. **Click the Install button to give your Mac permission to open Dashboard and install the new widget.**

7. **Click the widget and drag it to where you want it to appear on your screen.**

Disabling and deleting widgets from Dashboard

If you keep installing new widgets, eventually your list of available widgets can get crowded and overwhelming. To reduce the number of available widgets, you can disable or delete them.

Disabling a widget hides it from view but keeps it stored on your hard drive in case you change your mind and decide to display it after all. *Deleting* a widget physically removes it from your hard drive.

Disabling a widget

To disable a widget and temporarily remove it from view, follow these steps:

1. **Press the Dashboard key (or Fn+F12) to open Dashboard and then click the minus sign that appears in a circle in the bottom-left corner of the screen.**

   Widgets that are active on the Dashboard are displayed.

2. **Click the "x" in the upper-left corner to disable the widget and remove it from the Dashboard.**

3. **Press the Dashboard button (or Fn+F12) to close the Dashboard.**

To re-enable a widget you disabled, repeat the steps for adding widgets.

Deleting a widget

You can delete any widgets that you install (see the "Finding new widgets" section, earlier in this chapter, for more about downloading additional widgets) although you can't delete the widgets that came with your Mac. To delete a widget, follow these steps:

1. **Press the Dashboard key or Fn+F12 to open Dashboard and then click the plus sign that appears in a circle in the bottom-left corner of the screen to display installed widgets.**

2. **Click and hold any widget icon until they all begin to wiggle.**

3. **Click the "x" in the upper-left corner on the widget you want to delete.**

   A confirmation dialog appears, asking whether you really want to move the widget to the Trash.

4. **Click OK.**

5. **Repeat Steps 3 and 4 to delete other widgets or click anywhere to stop the wiggling.**

6. **Click the Escape key to return to the Dashboard.**

7. **Press the Dashboard key (or Fn+F12) to return to the Desktop.**

Getting Help

Theoretically, the Mac should be so easy and intuitive that you can teach yourself how to use your computer just by looking at the screen. Realistically, the Mac can still be confusing and complicated — there'd be no need for this book otherwise. We've done our best to give you steps and tips to handle any Mac task you come across, but we probably missed a few things. And sometimes it might just help to read the same task explained in a different way. So, any time you're confused when using your Mac and can't find the answers in this book, try looking for answers in the Help Center — you might find the answer you're looking for!

REMEMBER

You may have apps that we don't cover in this book, but look at the section "Reading Help topics" to find out how to access help for them, too.

Your Mac offers two types of help. First, it can point out specific menu commands to choose for accomplishing a specific task. For example, if you want to know how to save or print a file, Mac Help will point out the Save or Print command so you know which command to choose.

Second, the Help Center can provide brief explanations for how to accomplish a specific task. By skimming through the brief explanations, you can (hopefully) figure out how to do something useful.

Pointing out commands to use

To use the Help Center to point out commands you can use with the Finder or an application you're running, follow these steps:

1. **Click the Help menu at the right end of the menu bar for any application you're running.**

Or you can switch to the Finder by clicking the Finder icon on the Dock or clicking the Desktop outside any windows, and then click Help.

A Search text box appears.

2. **Begin typing a word or phrase.**

If, for instance, you want help with printing a document, type **print**. While you type, a list of possible topics appears.

Help topics for the application you're running appear first under the Menu Items category, followed by the Help Topics category, which lists topics for the Finder and any other applications stored on your Mac.

3. **Move your pointer over a Menu Items topic.**

A floating arrow points to the command on a menu to show you how to access your chosen topic for the application you are running, as shown in Figure 2-19.

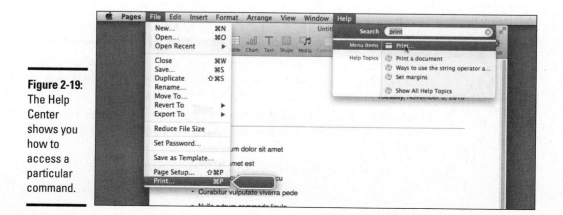

Figure 2-19:
The Help Center shows you how to access a particular command.

Reading Help topics

To read brief explanations of different topics, follow these steps:

1. **Click the Finder icon on the Dock.**

2. **Click the Help menu, and then choose Help Center.**

The Help Center window appears.

3. **Click a subject in the left column, and then click a topic in the right column.**

Alternatively, click the option Help for All Your Apps at the bottom of the left column to reveal the window shown in Figure 2-20.

Click the icon for the application you need help with to open a list of help topics for that application.

Figure 2-20: Access help for all your applications from the Help Center.

4. **Mac Help displays additional information about your chosen topic.**

Click the Bookmark icon at the upper right of the help window to bookmark that particular help explanation. Click the Book icon to the right of the bookmark icon to see explanations you bookmarked.

5. **Click the Back (or Forward) button to jump to a previously viewed topic or click the Home button to return to the original Mac Help window.**

6. **Click the Close button to close the Mac Help window.**

Chapter 3: Making Your First Connections

In This Chapter

✔ **Connecting to the Internet**

✔ **Creating your Apple identity**

✔ **Syncing and managing data with iCloud**

✔ **Adding e-mail and social network accounts**

For most people, an Internet connection is no longer an option but a necessity. You can use a computer all by itself, but to get the most out of your Mac, you need an Internet connection. An Internet connection gives you access to the World Wide Web, but equally important, it lets you use the Mail, FaceTime, Messages, and Maps apps; shop in the iTunes, App, and iBook Stores; sync Calendar, Contacts, Notes, and more across different devices; plus share photos and documents with iCloud and other Apple and third-party apps.

In this chapter, we explain how to connect your Mac to the Internet. Then we walk you through creating an Apple ID, which you use for iCloud, FaceTime, and shopping in the iTunes, Apps, and iBook Stores. After you have an Apple ID, we show you how to set up iCloud and explain the various iCloud options. At the end of this chapter, we explain how to add e-mail accounts from other providers, such as Microsoft Exchange and Google, as well as social networks like Facebook and LinkedIn. Many apps that came with your Mac access information from these accounts, so setting them up at the beginning makes your Mac experience easier down the road.

Setting Up an Internet Connection

From a technical point of view, to connect to the Internet, your Mac must connect to another computer, run by a company called an Internet Service Provider (ISP), through which your Mac actually connects to the Internet. The ISP may offer one or both of the following connections:

✦ Analog or dial-up, which is generally too slow to do more than send and receive text e-mail messages

✦ Broadband, which travels across digital service (DSL) phone lines, digital terrestrial television service, cellular data, or satellite connections

Most likely you already have a broadband Internet connection in your home either through your cable or phone service provider, but if you don't, ask around to find out what's available in your area. Some providers, including Xfinity (Comcast) and AT&T, let you connect to the Internet when you're away from home through Wi-Fi *hotspots,* which provide Internet access in public locations.

If you live in an area where Internet service is unavailable or limited to dial-up, check into using a cellular data modem or satellite Internet service.

Regardless of the type of broadband service, to connect your Mac to an ISP, you have two options:

✦ Ethernet (also called *high-speed broadband*): You connect your Mac physically to the modem with an Ethernet cable.

✦ Wireless (also called *Wi-Fi high-speed broadband*): Your Mac connects to the modem wirelessly.

Ethernet connection

A broadband Ethernet connection is the fastest way to connect to the Internet. Essentially, you connect a modem to the digital cable or DSL outlet, and then connect one end of an Ethernet cable to the modem and the other end to the Ethernet port of your Mac. (If you have a MacBook Air or a newer MacBook Pro, you need a USB-to-Ethernet adapter.) After you connect your Mac to the modem, you can usually start using the Internet right away.

To confirm your connection, choose ⌘↔System Preferences, click the Network icon, and look for "Ethernet Connected" in the list of services. For more information about setting up a network and sharing a single Internet connection with multiple computers, see Book III, Chapter 3.

You can usually rent a modem from your ISP or purchase one separately, although you want to be sure the one you purchase meets your ISPs specifications (check with your provider). Each modem comes with its own instructions, which you should refer to when setting up your Ethernet connection.

When you connect your Mac to a broadband modem by using your Mac's Ethernet port, your Mac can recognize the Internet connection right away through the Dynamic Host Configuration Protocol (DHCP): Your Mac automatically figures out the proper settings to connect to the Internet without making you type a bunch of cryptic numbers and fiddle with confusing technical standards.

Your Mac can also connect to your broadband modem wirelessly if the modem you buy (or rent from your ISP) has a built-in Wi-Fi router, which your Mac's built-in AirPort Wi-Fi feature can access. (See the next section for more on AirPort.)

Wireless (Wi-Fi) access

Wireless broadband access is popular because it allows you to connect to the Internet without stringing cables through your house to trip over. Every new and recent Mac comes with a built-in wireless capability called AirPort Wi-Fi.

You then connect to a wireless network, whether in your home or at another location if you're using a MacBook that you can take wherever you go. Public libraries and many coffee houses offer free wireless Internet access, as do many hotels and motels, which is handy when you're traveling. Your ISP may offer Wi-Fi *hotspots,* which let you access the Internet in public locations where they offer service. You can set up your own wireless network at home or work (see Book III, Chapter 3) by using a wireless router that lets several computers and other Wi-Fi-able gadgets (such as video game consoles, iPhones, iPads, and some printers) share a single Internet connection.

Choosing a wireless router

A *wireless router* connects to your modem — cable, DSL, cellular, or satellite — and broadcasts radio signals to connect your Mac wirelessly to the Internet. Most cable and DSL modems come with built-in Wi-Fi transmitters, giving you one device that does the job of two Wi-Fi devices.

If you choose to use a separate Wi-Fi router to connect to your modem, Apple sells three wireless router models:

✦ **AirPort Express:** Small and ideal for small homes, apartments, and dorm rooms.

✦ **AirPort Extreme:** Ideal for homes; four Ethernet ports to connect to Macs in the same room with an Ethernet cable; a built-in USB port lets you connect a printer or hard drive to share wirelessly with other people in your house or workplace.

✦ **Time Capsule:** Same features as AirPort Extreme but also includes a built-in hard drive for wirelessly backing up one or more Macs that connect to it.

Apple's Wi-Fi routers and the AirPort network admin tools make Internet management and setup easy.

Having said that, you can buy any brand of wireless router to connect to your modem and create a home Wi-Fi network. Here are the key considerations:

✦ **Speed:** The brand name of your wireless router is less important than the speed offered by the router, which is determined by the wireless standard the router uses. A *wireless standard* simply defines the wireless signal used to connect to the Internet.

✦ **Compatibility:** To connect to a wireless network, you need to make sure that your router and your Mac's built-in wireless use the same wireless standard. (See Table 3-1.) All new and recent Macs connect preferably to

Wi-Fi routers that use the 802.11ac standard but are compatible with all five types of the wireless network standards.

The 802.11n standard, which is the most common at the time of writing, offers good range and high speed. Most routers are compatible with multiple standards, and newer routers also include compatibility with the 802.11ac standard while offering *backward compatibility,* which means they work with older standards.

Table 3-1 lists the different wireless standards.

Table 3-1	Wireless Standards and Router Speeds	
Wireless Standard	*Speed*	*Indoor Range*
802.11a	Up to 54 Mbps	30 meters (98 feet)
802.11b	Up to 11 Mbps	35 meters (114 feet)
802.11g	Up to 54 Mbps	35 meters (114 feet)
802.11n	Up to 248 Mbps	70 meters (229 feet)
802.11ac	Up to 1.3 Gbps	90 meters (295 feet)

The upload/download speed of wireless standards is measured in megabits per second (Mbps) — or, with the super-fast 802.11ac, gigabits per second (Gbps), although this maximum speed is rarely achieved in normal use. The speed and range of a wireless Internet connection also degrade with distance and obstacles, such as walls or heavy furniture that stand between the Wi-Fi router and your Mac. The 802.11g standard also suffers interference from peripherals (such as wireless keyboards) that use the 2.4 GHz band. The 802.11ac standard uses 5 GHz signals, which make it almost impervious to interference and also uses a beaming (instead of broadcasting) technology, so it targets devices that are connected to it.

Connecting to a Wi-Fi network

Each router or modem will have its own set of instructions, which you should refer to when setting up your Wi-Fi network at home or in your office. In general, you connect the router to the modem that's connected to the DSL, digital terrestrial, or satellite outlet, turn the router on, and then access the router administration tools through a web browser (Safari on your Mac) to set up the network name and password.

You can connect your Mac to a wireless network (say, at a café or a Wi-Fi network in your home) by following these steps:

1. **Click the Wi-Fi icon in the right corner of the menu bar to open a pull-down menu displaying a list of any Wi-Fi networks within range of your Mac, and then select the network name you want to connect to, as shown in Figure 3-1.**

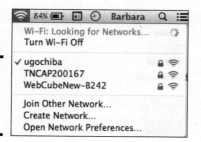

Figure 3-1:
See nearby
Wi-Fi
networks.

If you see WiFi: Off when you click the Wi-Fi icon on the menu bar, choose Turn WiFi On and then click the Wi-Fi menu icon again to display a list of any nearby wireless networks (refer to Figure 3-1).

If you don't see the Wi-Fi icon on the menu bar, choose ⌘⇨System Preferences, click the Network icon, and then select the Show Wi-Fi Status in Menu Bar check box.

A lock icon to the left of the network's signal strength indicates a *secured* (also known as *encrypted*) wireless network that is protected by a password. You must know what password to enter when prompted if you try to connect to a secured network.

2. **If a dialog appears indicating that the network you selected requires a password to connect to it (shown in Figure 3-2), type the password and then click Join.**

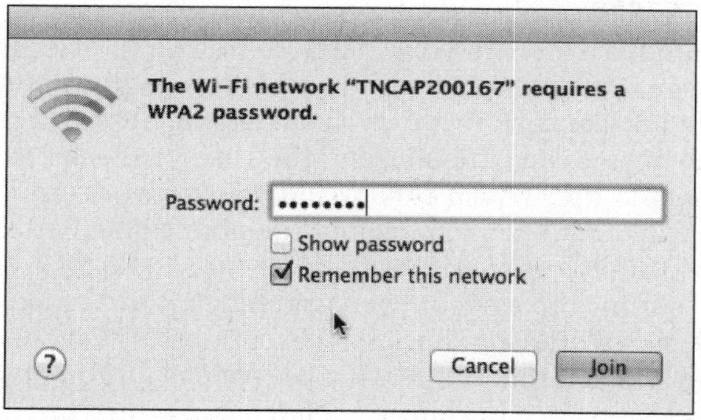

Figure 3-2:
A secure
Wi-Fi
network
requires a
password
to connect
to it.

> The Wi-Fi network "TNCAP200167" requires a WPA2 password.
>
> Password: ••••••••
>
> ☐ Show password
> ☑ Remember this network
>
> (?) Cancel Join

3. **(Optional) Select the following options on the password dialog prompt:**

   • *Show Password:* Displays actual characters you type instead of dots that hide your password. With long, mixed-character case-sensitive passwords, it can be helpful to see what you type — just make sure that no one is looking over your shoulder.

- *Remember This Network:* Remembers that you have connected to the selected network before and then connects to it automatically whenever you're within range of its signal. (If you chose to remember more than one wireless network in the same location, your Mac always connects to the one with the strongest signal first.)

The Wi-Fi icon on the menu bar shows black bars to indicate the strength of the Wi-Fi network signal your Mac is connected to. Like with mobile phone reception (and gold), more bars are better.

You're now free to choose any activity that requires an Internet connection, such as running Safari to browse the news on *The New York Times* website (www.nytimes.com) or launching Messages to partake in a video chat with a friend who's also connected to the Internet and signed in to Messages.

When you connect to a wireless network that doesn't require you to enter a password, your Mac essentially broadcasts any information you type (such as credit card numbers or passwords) through the airwaves. Although the likelihood of anyone actually monitoring what you're typing is small, tech-savvy engineers or hackers can "sniff" wireless signals to monitor or collect information flowing through the airwaves. Whenever you connect to a public Wi-Fi network, assume that a stranger is peeking at your data and type only such data that you're comfortable giving away to others. Connecting to a secured network that requires you to type a password to connect to it can lessen the likelihood that anyone is monitoring or collecting what you're typing.

Cellular data modem

If you're on the move a lot with your MacBook and go to places that don't have Wi-Fi service, a cellular data modem may be a good solution. These devices, which look like flash drives or small mobile phones, hold a SIM card just like the one in your smartphone, and they use your selected cellular carrier to connect to the cellular broadband data network. And, like your mobile phone, you don't have to plug into the phone line. With 3G, 4G, and LTE network availability, service is acceptable for simple tasks: reading and sending e-mail, surfing the web, or even watching a short video. Some cellular data modems are freestanding and can support Wi-Fi connections for three to five devices at a time. Others are *plug-and-play:* You plug the device into your Mac's USB port, enter the associated password (provided by the modem and cellular service provider), and *voilà!* You're online.

Establishing Your Apple Identity

When you first turn on your Mac (or install an upgrade to the operating system), a series of questions and prompts appear, including a prompt to sign in to your Apple ID account or create a new Apple ID.

The Apple ID identifies you and your devices in all things Apple that you do: registering new products, purchasing media and apps from the iTunes and App Stores, and signing in to your iCloud account.

iCloud is Apple's remote syncing and storage service. See the "Keeping Your Data in iCloud" section for more information on why you might want to use the app.

You might already have an Apple ID — in which case you can either skip this section or continue reading for information on adding an iCloud account to the mix. You can use the same Apple ID for everything, iCloud and iTunes included, or create separate Apple IDs for separate accounts. *Note:* If you've used Apple products long enough that you still have one of the old Apple IDs that isn't an e-mail address, you do have to set up a new account to use iCloud.

In the next sections, we explain two ways to create an Apple ID.

If you don't have an e-mail address or want to create an @icloud.com e-mail as your Apple ID and use it for all your Apple interactions, set up a new Apple ID from within iCloud in System Preferences (I tell you how to do that in the next section), not during the Mac setup. When you set up an Apple ID during the Mac setup, you must use an existing non-Apple domain e-mail address — because if you have an Apple domain e-mail address, that is your Apple ID and you use that to sign in.

Creating an Apple ID during Mac setup

When you first turn on your Mac, the onscreen dialog prompts you to sign in with your Apple ID or create a new one. Read through these steps to see what to expect:

1. **Click one of the following on the opening screen:**

- *Sign In with Apple ID:* Type in your existing Apple ID and password and then click Continue.

- *Create Apple ID:* The Apple ID website (https://appleid.apple.com) opens. Type the information requested in the fields on the form: Use an existing e-mail address as your Apple ID, choose three security questions and answers, and provide your date of birth and an optional rescue e-mail that's different than your Apple ID e-mail. Complete the form with your mailing address (so the products you order online can be shipped to you), select your preferred language from the pop-up menu, select the e-mail you want to receive from Apple, type the Captcha word, select the check box to concede your agreement to the Terms of Service, and finally, click the Create Apple ID button.

- *Use Separate ID for iCloud and iTunes:* The iCloud icon is highlighted in the center of the screen. Enter the Apple ID you use with iCloud or click Create Apple ID, which takes you to the Apple ID website as we explain in the previous bullet. Click Continue. The iTunes and App Stores icons are highlighted; type in the Apple ID you use with them or click Create Apple ID and repeat as above.

If you want to create an Apple ID with an @icloud.com suffix, click Don't Sign In and confirm your choice by clicking the Skip button in the dialog that appears. Go to the next section to create an Apple ID and e-mail address in iCloud.

2. **If you sign in with an existing Apple ID, you are prompted to do the following:**

   - Turn on Find My Mac, which we suggest you do.

   - Choose three security questions and answers.

   - Agree to the Terms of Service.

   The message in the window lets you know your Mac is being set up, and then the Desktop appears.

Creating an Apple ID in iCloud

We find creating and using an @icloud.com e-mail address as your Apple ID convenient because you need remember only one password for all your interactions with Apple, and we like to think there's added security for the information you sync across devices using iCloud when using an Apple domain rather than Google mail, Yahoo!, or one of the other e-mail service providers. (For more info on the benefits of iCloud, see the next section.)

If you use the iCloud e-mail only for exchanges with Apple, notifications about product updates or invoices don't get lost in the shuffle of myriad messages in a more active e-mail account.

Here we show you how to create an Apple ID with iCloud and then segue into managing your iCloud preferences in the next section.

1. **Choose **System Preferences or click the System Preferences icon on the Dock. Then click the iCloud button.**

   The iCloud preferences window opens.

2. **Click Create New Apple ID.**

3. **Choose your Location and Date of Birth, and then click Next.**

   The Create an Apple ID window opens, as shown in Figure 3-3.

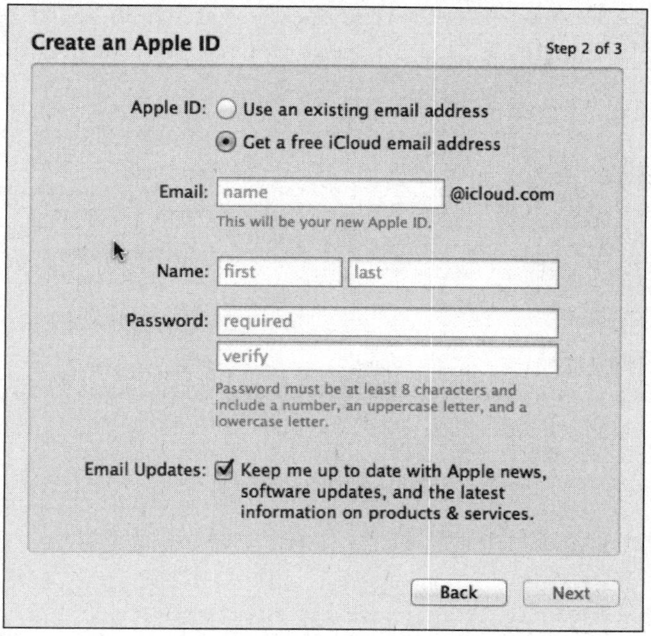

Figure 3-3:
Create
an icloud.
com e-mail
address to
use as your
Apple ID.

4. **Select the Get Free iCloud Email Address radio button.**

5. **Type in a name you want to use for your e-mail address and then complete the other fields: first name, last name, and password.**

   Your password must be at least eight characters and contain at least one number, one uppercase letter, and one lowercase letter.

6. **(Optional) Select the Email Updates check box for Apple news and update information.**

7. **Click Next.**

   If someone else already uses the name you chose, you're prompted to type an alternative. It may take a few tries to find an unused name.

8. **Select three security questions and answers from the pop-up menus that appear on the next window.**

9. **Type in a Rescue E-mail, which is different than the iCloud e-mail address you just created.**

   Apple uses this address to communicate with you in the event you completely forget your iCloud e-mail address and password.

10. **Click Next.**

11. **Select the check box to confirm that you read and agree to the Terms of Service, and then click Continue.**

12. **The iCloud activation screen opens, as shown in Figure 3-4.**

Leave both check boxes checked.

Figure 3-4:
Activate
iCloud
syncing and
Mac locating
features.

13. **Click Next.**

The iCloud Security Code window opens. This code is used to add security to *iCloud Keychain,* which is the iCloud feature that remembers your online usernames and passwords as well as credit card numbers.

14. **Type in a simple four-digit security code and click Next, or click Advanced to do one of the following, as shown in Figure 3-5, and then click Next:**

- *Use a Complex Security Code:* Prompts you to enter a longer, more complex code in place of the four-digit code.

- *Get a Random Security Code:* Tells iCloud to create a code for you.

- *Don't Create Security Code:* When you set up iCloud Keychain, you have to approve the set up from another device, like an iPhone or iPad, signed in to the same iCloud account.

15. **Select one of the Advanced options and then click Next, or click Back to use the simple four-digit security code, and then click Next.**

16. **Type your security code, short or long, to confirm it.**

Common four-digit codes, like 1-1-1-1, generate a warning that the code is too simple and easily guessed. You can choose to create a different code or just type your simple, easy code to confirm it.

17. **Type a mobile phone number that will be used to send approval codes to your mobile phone when you access iCloud Keychain from another device.**

This adds a second security to iCloud Keychain access.

18. **Click Next.**

iCloud opens, as shown in Figure 3-6.

A list of Apple apps that work with iCloud appears, and check marks indicate which are active. The data in checked apps will sync across all devices — computes, iPhones, iPads, iPod touches — that sign in to the same iCloud account.

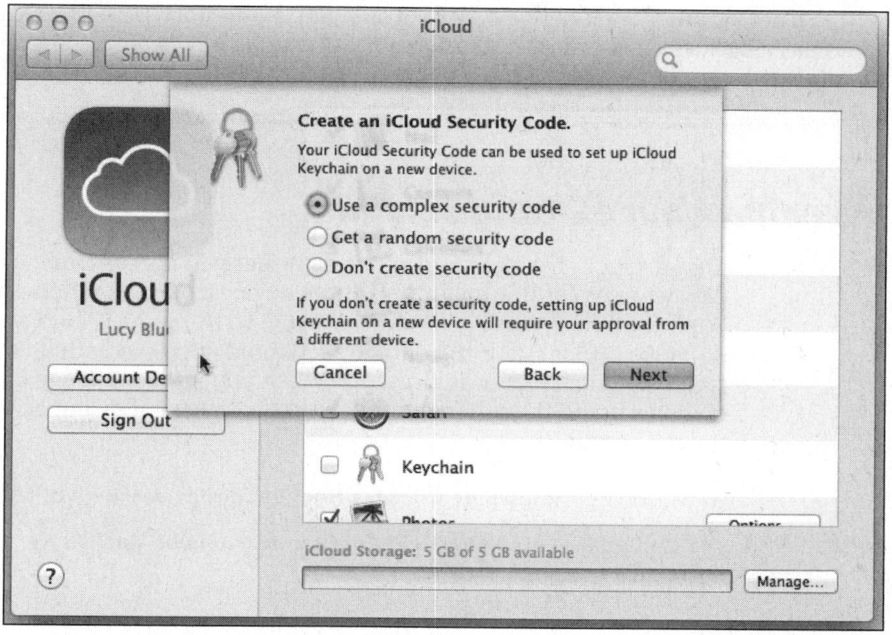

Figure 3-5:
Create a
security
code here.

Figure 3-6:
Sync apps
with iCloud
across
all your
devices.

Your legacy Apple ID

New Apple IDs take the form of an e-mail address. If you have an Apple ID that you created several years ago, it may be in the form of a name, such as barbaradepaula. If your Apple ID isn't an e-mail address, you can continue to use it for iTunes, App, and iBook Store purchases, though. Just know that you have to create a different Apple ID for iCloud because that service requires the e-mail address ID format.

Keeping Your Data in iCloud

iCloud remotely stores and syncs data that you access from various devices — your Mac and other Apple devices, such as iPhones, iPads, and iPods, and PCs running Windows. Sign in to the same iCloud account on different devices, and the data for activated apps *syncs;* that is, you find the same data on all your devices, and when you make a change on one device, it shows up on the others. iCloud works with the following Apple apps and the data within them:

+ Contacts (known as Address Book in earlier versions of Mac OS X)
+ Calendar (known as iCal in earlier versions of Mac OS X)
+ Reminders
+ Mail
+ Notes
+ Safari bookmarks, reading list, tabs, and viewing history
+ Photos from both iPhoto and Aperture
+ iTunes music and television shows
+ iWork apps (Pages, Numbers, and Keynote)
+ Preview
+ TextEdit
+ Keychain

iCloud also works with third-party iCloud-enabled apps, such as iA Writer.

Here are some situations where iCloud can make your life easier:

+ You want to back up your iTunes music and television show collections.
+ You use both a Mac and an iOS device, such as an iPhone, iPad, or iPod touch.

✦ You want to access Contacts, Calendar, and Mail from more than one computer — Mac or Windows — say, one for work and one at home.

✦ You keep a calendar that other people need to see and maybe even edit.

✦ You want to activate Find My Mac to keep tabs on your Mac's location and re-locate it should it be lost or stolen.

The initial setup on your Mac or the creation of an iCloud Apple ID as explained previously activates your iCloud account and places a copy of the data from Mail, Contacts, Calendar, Notes, Reminders, and Safari from your Mac to the cloud (that is, the Apple data storage equipment). Here, we show you how to work with the iCloud preferences, sync devices, and sign in to and use the iCloud website.

If you use a Windows PC in addition to your Mac, you can download the iCloud Control Panel 3.0 for Windows (Windows 7 or 8) at `http://support.apple.com/kb/DL1455`, which enables iCloud storage and syncing in Windows. You then access the iCloud apps through iCloud.com and Microsoft Outlook.

Selecting iCloud preferences

You can choose which apps you want to use with iCloud. For example, you may want to keep Contacts and Calendars synced across all your devices but prefer that Notes stay separate because you use Notes on your iPhone for shopping lists that you don't need on your Mac. Here's how to customize how you work with iCloud:

1. **Choose ⌘⇨System Preferences and then click the iCloud button.**

The iCloud preferences window opens (refer to Figure 3-6).

2. **If you haven't signed in to iCloud, click the Sign In button, enter your Apple ID and password, and click Sign In.**

The iCloud preferences window opens.

The check-marked apps sync across all the devices signed in to iCloud with the same Apple ID.

3. **Scroll down and click the Options button to find further options:**

• *Photos:* Lets you turn on My Photo Stream (automatically uploads and downloads photos from added to iCloud or your Mac to the other source) and Photo Sharing (creates online photo albums that you can share with other people and they can also add photos, videos, and comments). Learn more about both features in Book IV, Chapter 3.

• *Documents & Data:* Select the apps that store and share data in iCloud. See Figure 3-7.

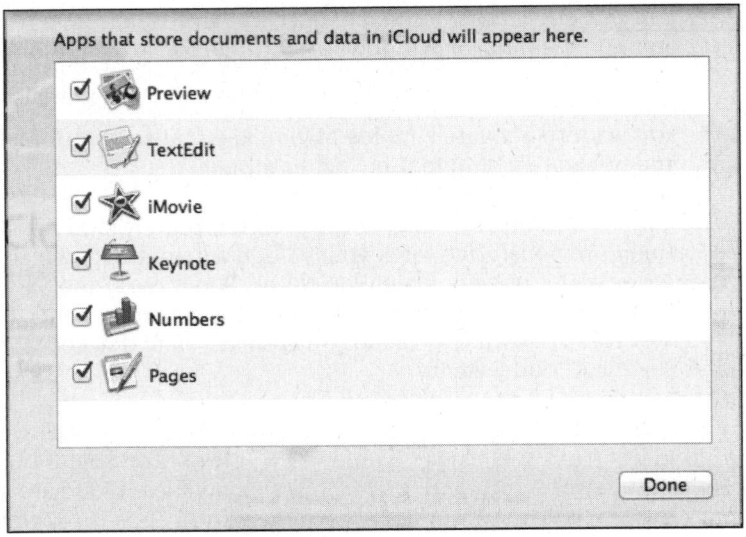

Apps that store documents and data in iCloud will appear here.

☑ Preview

☑ TextEdit

☑ iMovie

☑ Keynote

☑ Numbers

☑ Pages

Done

Figure 3-7:
Select the apps you want to use with iCloud.

Go to Book V to learn about using apps that work with iCloud.

4. **(Optional) Click the Manage button (refer to Figure 3-6) to see the data that occupies your allotted iCloud storage, as shown in Figure 3-8.**

Click each item in the list on the left to see the files for each. Backups (top of this list) keeps the backups of your iOS devices — *not your Mac.* iCloud keeps documents and data for iCloud-enabled apps but *does not back up your entire Mac.* See Book III, Chapter 1 to learn about backing up your Mac.

5. **(Optional) Click the Buy More Storage button.**

A free iCloud account gives you 5 gigabytes (GB) of storage — but songs purchased from the iTunes Store or up to 25,000 tracks in iTunes Match plus photos in PhotoStream don't count toward that amount. In PhotoStream, iCloud stores up to 1,000 photos from the last 30 days. You can purchase additional storage for a yearly fee if necessary, as shown in Figure 3-9.

Click the storage amount you want and then click Next. Follow the onscreen instructions to add your personal and payment information.

6. **Click Done.**

7. **Click the Close button in the upper left to quit System Preferences.**

Figure 3-8:
See the
documents
stored in
each app on
iCloud.

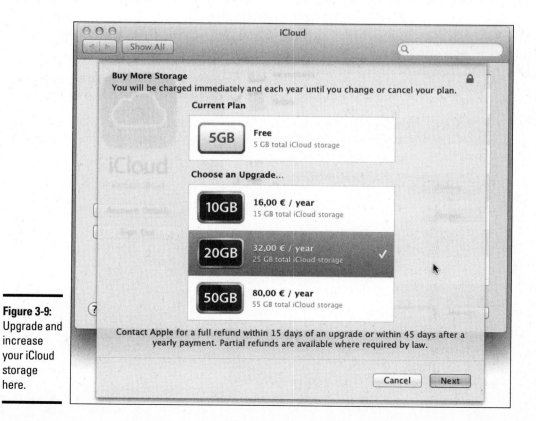

Figure 3-9:
Upgrade and
increase
your iCloud
storage
here.

Syncing with your other devices

The only reason this topic has a heading is so it stands out because it couldn't be simpler. To sync iCloud apps with your iOS devices, do the following:

1. **Tap Settings on the Home screen.**

2. **Tap iCloud.**

3. **Sign in to your iCloud account.**

4. **Tap the apps you want to use to the on position.**

 The data in each app is automatically synced between your Mac and your iOS device.

You must have an Internet connection to use iCloud.

Using the iCloud website

To manage your data on iCloud, you can go to the iCloud website. Follow these steps:

1. **Click the Safari icon on the Dock or from Launchpad. (See Book II, Chapter 1 to read about using Safari.)**

2. **Type** www.icloud.com **in the URL field in Safari.**

 The iCloud website opens with the sign in fields.

3. **Type in your Apple ID or the e-mail you used when you set up your iCloud account, and then type your password, as shown in Figure 3-10.**

4. **(Optional) Select the Keep Me Signed In check box if you want to stay connected to iCloud even when you go to other websites or quit Safari.**

Figure 3-10:
Signing in
to an iCloud
account.

5. **Press the Enter key or click the arrow button.**

   Your name appears in the upper-right corner, and icons that take you to your activated services appear in the window, as shown in Figure 3-11.

Figure 3-11: Click the icons to go to the data you want.

6. **Click any of the icons to go to the app you want.**

7. **From the app window, click the cloud button in the upper-left corner to return to the opening iCloud web page.**

8. **Click the arrow to the right of your name and choose Sign Out to close iCloud.com.**

What about iTunes?

You might have noticed that iTunes isn't mentioned in the iCloud preferences under System Preferences, nor is there an iTunes icon on the iCloud website. Nonetheless, all your iTunes purchases are automatically stored in iCloud, and you can set up iTunes to automatically download your purchases to all your devices, regardless of which device you use to make your purchase. Songs you didn't purchase through iTunes are not stored in iCloud. If you have a lot of songs that weren't purchased through iTunes, you may want to consider purchasing *iTunes Match* ($25/year), which downloads up to 25,000 songs you own that you didn't purchase from iTunes (but that exist in the iTunes Store) to your iTunes purchase history. You get the advantage of having iTunes quality songs included in the iCloud storage. See Book IV, Chapter 1 for more information about using iTunes.

Setting Up E-Mail and Social Network Accounts

Even if you've created an Apple ID and set up iCloud, you may use a different account for e-mail and associated services such as calendars and contacts, Additionally, you might want to link contacts and events from your social networks to Contacts and Calendar. You can sync the data between apps on your Mac (such as Mail, Calendar, and Contacts) and the online apps (such as Google or Twitter). Here we show you how to add accounts to your Mac and activate the services and data you want to share.

Adding accounts

Many e-mail accounts offer contact and calendar management, and even note-taking services, too. Your e-mail address and password identify and give you access to your account. The three types of e-mail accounts you can set up are

+ POP (Post Office Protocol)
+ IMAP (Internet Message Access Protocol)
+ Exchange

A POP e-mail account usually transfers (moves) e-mail from the POP server computer to your computer. An IMAP or Exchange e-mail account stores e-mail on its server, which allows access to e-mail from multiple devices. Most individuals have POP accounts, whereas many corporations have IMAP or Exchange accounts.

You can use dozens of e-mail applications, but the most popular one is the free Mail app that comes with your Mac. If you don't like Mail, you can download and install a free e-mail app, such as Thunderbird (www.mozilla.org/en-US/thunderbird) or Mailsmith (www.mailsmith.org).

You can access your e-mail from Mail (or a different e-mail app) on your Mac, from a web browser on your Mac, or on another computer, such as at your friend's house or in an Internet café. When you use a web browser, you go to the e-mail provider's website.

Gathering your account information

To make Mail work with your e-mail account or link Contacts and Calendar to a social network account like Facebook or Twitter, you need to gather the following information:

✦ **Your username (also called an *account name*):** Typically a descriptive name (such as nickyhutsko) or a collection of numbers and symbols (such as nickyhutsko09). Your username plus the name of your e-mail provider or ISP defines your complete e-mail address, such as nickyhutsko@gmail.com or lilypond@comcast.net.

✦ **Your password:** Any phrase that you choose to access your account. If someone sets up an e-mail account for you, he might have already assigned a password that you can always change later.

For Mail, you might also need the following two bits of information, so have them handy if you can:

✦ **Your e-mail account's incoming server name:** The mail server name of the computer that contains your e-mail message is usually a combination of POP or IMAP and your e-mail account company, such as pop.comcast.net or imap.gmail.com.

✦ **Your e-mail account's outgoing server name:** The name of the outgoing mail server that sends your messages to other people. The outgoing server name is usually a combination of SMTP (Simple Mail Transfer Protocol) and the name of the company that provides your e-mail account, such as smtp.gmail.com or smtp.comcast.net.

If you don't know your account name, password, incoming server name, or outgoing server name, ask the company that runs your e-mail account or search on the provider's website. If you're unable to find the information, chances are you might still be able to set up your e-mail account on your Mac, thanks to the Mail app's ability to detect the most popular e-mail account settings, such as those for Gmail or Yahoo!.

Configuring your account

After you collect the technical information needed to access your account, you need to add it to the Internet Accounts on your Mac by following these steps:

1. **Choose ⟹System Preferences or click the System Preferences icon on the Dock or from Launchpad.**

2. **Click the Internet Accounts button.**

The iCloud account you created is selected.

3. **Click the plus sign at the bottom of the window to reveal a list of other accounts you can add, as shown in Figure 3-12.**

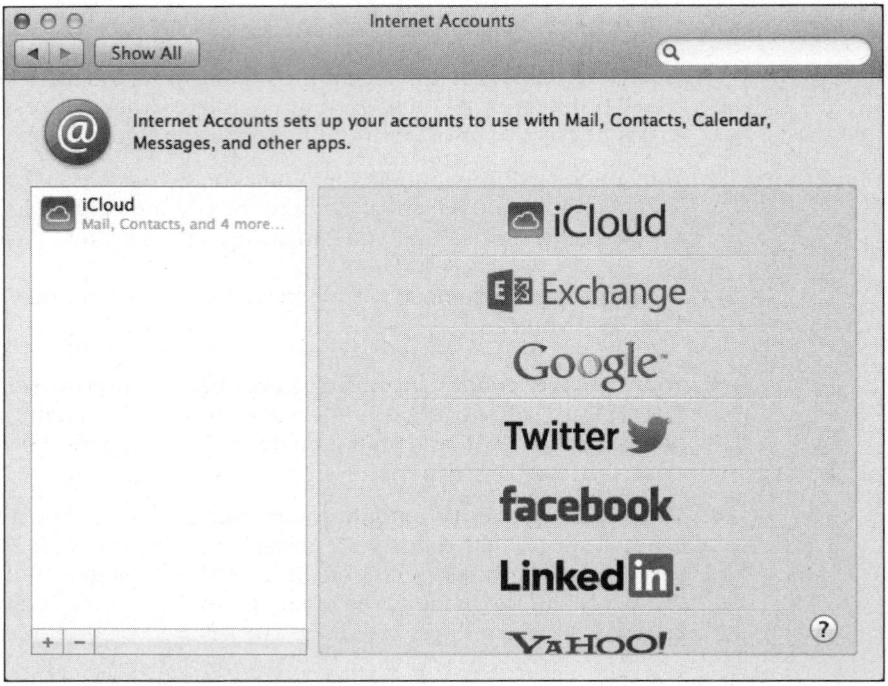

Figure 3-12:
Add
accounts
from those
listed.

4. **Click the name of the account you want to add, such as Google or Yahoo! or Twitter. Scroll down to see more options, including AOL, Vimeo, and Flickr, as well as an Add Other Account option.**

   An account information window opens, similar to Figure 3-13.

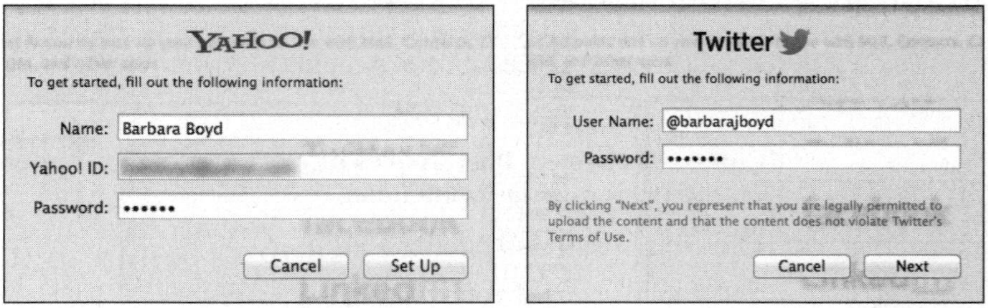

Figure 3-13:
Activate the
account.

5. **Type your name, e-mail address, and password, and then click Set Up.**

   Social networks, such as Twitter or LinkedIn have a Next button.

Exchange has a Continue button, and a second dialog prompts you for a Server address, which your network administrator can probably provide. Click Continue on the second dialog to verify the account.

Your account is verified and a list of services appears, such as contacts or calendar.

6. **Click the services you want to use.**

   For example, if you choose Contacts in Facebook, you will see them as a group in the Contacts app. Or choose Calendar in Google, and your events can be accessed from the Calendar app.

7. **(Optional) If you don't see the account you use listed, click Add Other Account.**

   A selection of account types appears, as shown in Figure 3-14.

Figure 3-14:
Set up other types of accounts in System Preferences.

8. **Click the account type and then click Create.**

   Type in the information requested, which varies for different account types. See specific chapters for more details: Mail — Book II, Chapter 2; Messages — Book II, Chapter 3; Calendar — Book V, Chapter 2; Contacts — Book V, Chapter 1.

   As you add accounts, they appear in the list on the left of the window (refer to Figure 3-14).

9. **(Optional) Edit or delete accounts:**

- *Edit:* Click an account to edit the services it provides, for example to add Notes to your Gmail account or deactivate Contacts from Facebook.

- *Delete:* Click an account and then click the minus sign to delete it from your Mac.

10. **Click the Close button to quit System Preferences.**

After you add an account, you access its contents in other apps, such as Mail, Contacts, Calendar, and Safari.

Chapter 4: Working with Files and Folders

In This Chapter

↳ **Using the Finder**

↳ **Organizing and viewing folders**

↳ **Tagging files and folders**

↳ **Searching with Spotlight**

↳ **Setting up Smart Folders**

↳ **Deleting files and folders**

*W*hen you need to organize stuff scattered around the house, one strategy would be to toss everything in the middle of the floor. However, it's probably easier to take a more organized approach by storing off-season clothes in one box, retired gadgets in another box (to be taken to the local recycling center), bills in one file folder, and new books you want to read — or your e-book reader — on your nightstand.

Computers work in a similar way. Although you *could* dump everything on the top level of your hard drive, it's more helpful to divide your hard drive in a way that can help you sort and arrange your stuff in an orderly, easy-to-get-to fashion. Instead of boxes or shelves, the Mac uses *folders* (which tech-types like Joe also refer to as *directories*). In a nutshell, a folder lets you store and organize related files.

This chapter is dense with information, but familiarizing yourself with the way your Mac organizes documents, applications, and files will make everything you do on your Mac a lot easier. We tell you several ways to do the same thing so you can choose the way that's easiest for you to do and remember. We begin by explaining the *Finder,* which is the tool you use to organize your files and folders. Next, we show you how to create and manage folders. We also tell you about *tags,* a feature added in OS X Mavericks, which helps you quickly identify and find folders and files. At the end of the chapter, we shine a light on your Mac's search tool, Spotlight Search. At the end of the chapter, we spell out the procedure for deleting files and folders.

Getting to Know the Finder

The *Finder* manages drives, devices, files, and folders on your Mac. To access the Finder, click the Finder icon (the smiley face icon on the far left or top) on the Dock. The Finder is divided into three parts, as shown in Figure 4-1:

✦ A *toolbar* that runs across the top of the window and contains buttons that you use to control and manage the files and folders in the Finder.

✦ A left pane showing the *Sidebar,* which is where you find a list of connected storage devices as well as commonly used folders.

✦ A right pane showing the contents of the selected drive or folder (or search results if one was performed). If you switch to List, Column, or Cover Flow view, which we explain in the section "Organizing and Viewing a Folder," the right pane also shows a hierarchy of files — and even other folders — stored inside folders.

The right pane may be further divided into *tabs*, which are essentially panes within the pane that display different folders open simultaneously, although only the one in view on top is active.

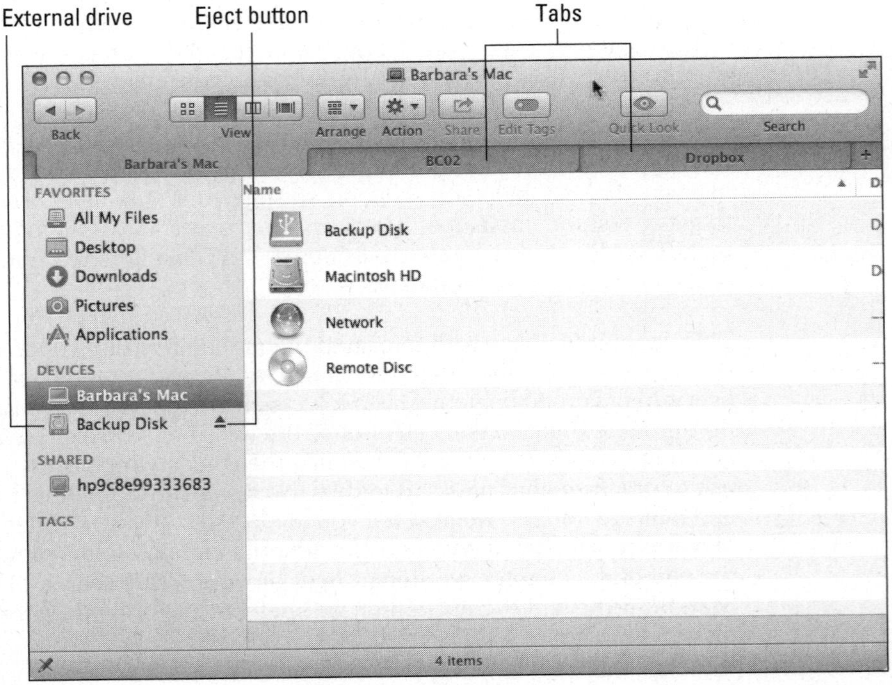

Figure 4-1:
The Finder displays the files, folders, and devices connected to your Mac.

You can choose to hide or show both the toolbar and Sidebar, or hide just the Sidebar from the Finder View menu. You can't hide the toolbar alone, nor do you have that option if you have active tabs.

Handling devices

The Devices category of the Sidebar lists your Mac (Barbara's Mac in Figure 4-1) and any devices, remote or cabled, connected to your Mac as well as any mounted disk images, which can appear when you download software updates or large files.

When you click your Mac in the Device category of the Sidebar, you see the internal hard disk drive (HDD) or solid state drive (SSD), which is named Macintosh HD by default. This is the drive that your Mac boots from. If your desktop Mac has a second hard drive installed, it appears in the Devices list.

The other devices listed here are those that you plug into your Mac, such as an external hard drive, a USB flash drive, or a digital camera. One external drive, Backup Disk, is connected in Figure 4-1. These removable devices can be connected and disconnected at any time.

To connect a removable device to your Mac, just plug it in with the appropriate FireWire, Thunderbolt, or USB cable. The icon for the device appears in the Devices list and on the Desktop.

You can eject a removable drive when you no longer need to access it or want to take it with you. Ejecting a removable hard drive or USB flash drive removes its icon from the Finder and Desktop and allows you to then safely disconnect it from your Mac.

If you physically try to disconnect a removable drive before you eject it, your Mac might mess up the data on that drive. Always eject removable drives before physically disconnecting them.

To remove a removable device from a Mac, do one of the following:

✦ Click the Finder icon on the Dock to open the Finder window, and then click the Eject button next to the connected drive you want to remove in the Finder window Sidebar.

✦ Click the device icon on the Desktop and choose File➪Eject.

✦ Click the device icon and press ⌘+E.

✦ Control-click the device icon and choose Eject from the shortcut menu that appears.

✦ Drag the device icon to Trash on the Dock (it turns into an Eject button); then let go of the mouse.

If the removable device is a CD/DVD, your Mac ejects it. If the removable device is plugged into a USB (Universal Serial Bus) port or a FireWire port on your Mac, you can then physically disconnect the device.

Understanding folders

All the data you create and save by using an application (such as a word-processing document or a photograph you copy from your digital camera to your Mac's hard drive) is stored as a *file*. Although you can store files on any storage device, the more files you store on a device, the harder it is to find the one file you want at any given time. Much like you would place related paper documents in a manila folder rather than stack them willy-nilly on your desk, folders on your Mac help you organize and manage electronic files on a storage device in a logical way. You can even store folders inside other folders.

Initially, every Mac hard drive contains the following folders:

✦ **Applications:** Contains all the apps installed on your Mac. When you open Launchpad, you also see all the apps that are stored in the Applications folder.

✦ **Library:** Contains data and settings files used by applications installed on your Mac, fonts, and plug-ins used by applications such as Internet web browsers.

✦ **System:** Contains files used by the OS X operating system. You shouldn't change this folder.

Never delete, rename, or move any files or folders stored in the Library or System folders, or else you might cause your Mac (or at least some apps on your Mac) to stop working. Files in the Library and System folders are used by your Mac to make your computer work. If you delete or rename files in either folder, your Mac might not operate the way it's supposed to — or (worse) grind to a halt.

✦ **Users:** Contains any files that you — and anyone else who uses your Mac — create and save, including documents, pictures, music, and movies.

Home folders are kept in the Users folder; each account on your Mac is assigned a Home folder when the account is set up. (See Book III, Chapter 2 for more information about creating accounts.) The Home folder has the same name as the account and shouldn't be renamed. The Home folder of the user who is logged in looks like a little house.

Each Home folder automatically contains the following folders when an account is set up. Notice that these folders have icons on them.

✦ **Desktop:** Contains any application and document icons that appear on your Mac's Desktop.

✦ **Documents***:* Contains any files you create and save by using different applications. (You'll probably want to organize this folder by creating multiple folders inside it to keep all your files organized in a logical, easy-to-manage way.)

✦ **Downloads:** Contains any files you download from the Internet. After being downloaded, you'll want to move them to an appropriate folder or, if you download apps, install them.

✦ **Library:** Contains folders and files used by any applications installed on your Mac. (***Note:*** There are three Library folders: one stored on the top level of your hard drive, another inside that Library folder, and one hidden inside your Home folder, which you can see by holding the Option key and choosing Go⇨Library.)

✦ **Movies:** Contains video files created by iMovie and certain other applications for playing or editing video, such as Final Cut Pro X or QuickTime Player.

✦ **Music:** Contains audio files, such as music tracks stored in iTunes; or created by GarageBand or another audio application; such as Audacity.

✦ **Pictures:** Contains digital photographs, such as those you import into iPhoto.

✦ **Public:** Provides a folder that you can use to share files with other user accounts on the same Mac, or with other users on a local area network (LAN).

✦ **Sites:** Provides a folder for storing any web pages you use on a website you manage.

Every drive (such as your hard drive) can contain multiple folders, and each folder can contain multiple folders. A collection of folders stored inside folders stored inside other folders is a *hierarchy*. It's important to know how to view and navigate through a folder hierarchy to find specific files, and we tell you how to do that in the "Navigating the Finder" section later in this chapter.

Setting Finder preferences

As you look at the figures in this book, you might say to yourself, "My Finder doesn't look like that." You probably have different Finder preferences than we do. You can choose the items you see in the Finder Sidebar and also how the Finder behaves in certain situations by setting the Finder preferences to your liking. Follow these steps, and remember you can always go back and change them later if you think of a better setup:

1. **Click the Finder icon on the Dock.**

   A Finder window opens.

2. **Choose Finder⇨Preferences.**

   The Finder Preferences window opens.

3. **Click the General button at the top, if it isn't selected.**

4. **Select the check boxes next to the items you want to see on your Desktop.**

   You can select any or all of the following: Hard Disks, External Disks, CDs, DVDs, and iPods, and/or Connected Servers.

5. **From the New Finder Windows Show pop-up menu, choose which window you want to open when you open the finder.**

6. **(Optional) Select the Open Folders in Tabs Instead of New Windows check box if you want this option in the Action menu, which you find in the Finder Toolbar.**

   You can have more than one folder open simultaneously. They can be opened in separate windows, which tend to clutter the Desktop, or in separate tabs within one Finder window. See the section "Working with tabs" to learn about tabs.

7. **Click the Sidebar button.**

   The Sidebar preferences pane opens, as shown in Figure 4-2.

8. **Select the check boxes next to the items you want to see in the Finder Sidebar.**

   When the Finder is open, you can show and hide the items in each category by clicking the Show/Hide button that appears when you hover to the right of the category title in the Sidebar.

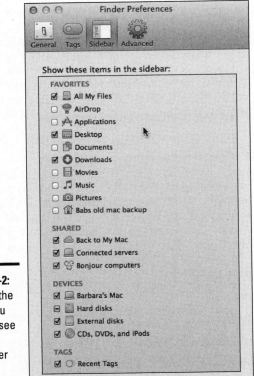

Figure 4-2:
Choose the items you want to see listed in the Finder Sidebar.

9. **Click the Advanced button to choose to activate one or more of the following options:**

   • *Show All Filename Extensions* displays the file extension on every filename on your Mac. File extensions are the two or more letters after a file name, such as `.doc` or `.xls`.

   • *Show Warning before Changing an Extension* opens a dialog if you save a file as a different type, such as saving a `.doc` file as `.txt`.

   • *Show Warning before Emptying the Trash* gives you time for second thoughts before you throw a document away.

   • *Empty Trash Securely* overwrites files when you empty the trash so a savvy hacker can't rebuild your documents. This is sort of like shredding your credit card bills before recycling the paper they're printed on.

   You can also set the search level for Spotlight search, which we discuss in the "Spotlight Preferences" section, later in this chapter.

10. **Click the red Close button in the upper-left corner to close the window.**

Navigating the Finder

To access files stored on your Mac, navigate the different folders and devices by using the Finder. First choose a connected drive or device, and then you can open and exit folders or jump between specific folders. We explain each method throughout these sections.

To open the Finder, click the Finder icon on the Dock or click the background of your Desktop and choose File➪New Finder Window. The Finder opens to the folder or device you specified in Finder preferences. The Finder opens when you double-click a folder, too, but it opens at the level of that specific folder, not at the highest point of the Finder hierarchy. See the section "Working with tabs" to learn about opening more than one Finder window or tab at a time.

Opening a folder

When you open the Finder and click a device, the Finder displays all the files and folders stored on that device. To open a folder (and move down the folder hierarchy), you have several choices:

✦ Double-click the folder.

✦ Click the folder and choose File➪Open.

✦ Click the folder and press ⌘+O.

✦ Click the folder and press ⌘+↓.

✦ Click the folder, and then click the Action button on the toolbar and choose Open in New Tab or Open in New Window (depending on whether you select the Open Folders in Tabs Instead of New Windows option from Finder➪Preferences➪General) or Open at the very bottom of the menu to open the folder in the existing tab or window.

✦ Control-click the folder and choose Open or Open in New Tab/Window from the shortcut menu that appears.

Each time you open a folder within a folder, you're essentially moving down the hierarchy of folders stored on that device.

Working with tabs

Tabs are a way of having several folders open in one pane at the same time so you don't have to close and open folders to switch between them or use the Back and Forward buttons. To open a folder in a new tab, click the folder, click the Action button, and choose Open in New Tab, as shown in Figure 4-3.

Hold down the Option key while clicking the Action button, and Open in New Tab becomes Open in New Window.

If you want to open a new tab as if it were a new Finder window, click the Add Tab button (the plus sign) on the far right end of the tabs. The Finder opens to the device or folder you specified from Finder➪Preferences➪General.You only see the Add Tab button when two or more tabs are open; if you don't see it, choose File➪New Tab or Open in New Tab from the Action menu.

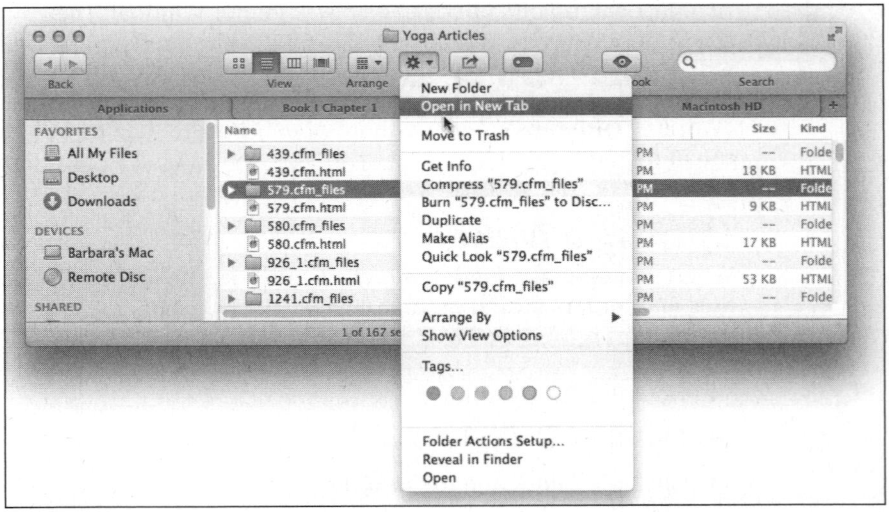

Figure 4-3:
Tabs help you navigate through folders on the Finder.

To close a tab, hover over the left end until you see the "x" and then click it.

When you hide, close, or minimize the Finder window and reopen it from the Dock, your tabs are still in place. If, instead, you click the Desktop and choose File⇨New Finder Window, you won't see your tabs, but you can still access them by clicking the Finder icon on the Dock.

Jumping to a specific folder

By moving up and down the folder hierarchy on a device, you can view the contents of every file stored on a device. However, you can also jump to a specific folder right away by choosing one of these options:

✦ Click the tab you opened for that folder.

✦ Choose a folder from the Go menu — for example, choose Go⇨Utilities — or press ⌘+Shift+U to open the Utilities folder. Other folders listed on the Go menu can also be accessed by pressing the appropriate shortcut keys, which appear next to the folder name on the menu.

✦ Click a folder displayed in the Sidebar.

✦ Use the Go⇨Recent Folders command to jump to a recently opened folder. (Using this command sequence displays a submenu of the last ten folders you visited.)

If you display the contents of a folder in List, Column, or Cover Flow views, you can view folder hierarchies directly in the Finder. (You find out more about using the List, Column, and Cover Flow views later in the "Organizing and Viewing Folders" section.)

Jumping back and forth

While you navigate from one folder to the next, you might suddenly want to return to a folder for a second look. To view a previously viewed folder, you can choose the Back command in one of three ways:

✦ Click the Back arrow.

✦ Choose Go⇨Back.

✦ Press ⌘+[.

After you use the Back command at least once, you can choose the Forward command, which reverses each Back command you chose. To choose the Forward command, pick one of the following ways:

✦ Click the Forward arrow.

✦ Choose Go⇨Forward.

✦ Press ⌘+].

Moving to a higher folder

After you open a folder, you might want to go back and view the contents of the folder that encloses the current folder. To view the enclosing folder (and move up the folder hierarchy), choose one of the following:

+ **Choose Go⇨Enclosing Folder.**

+ **Press ⌘+↑.**

  Each of these options changes the tab, if you're using tabs.

+ **Hold down the ⌘ key, click the name in the Finder window title bar to display the hierarchy of enclosing folders, and then click an enclosing folder.**

  Do the same on saved document titles in open app windows to see the folder heirarchy.

Following the folder path

Click the Finder icon on the Dock and then choose View⇨Show Path Bar. Displayed at the bottom of the Finder window is the series of folders that lead to the folder you're currently viewing. Double-click any of the folders in the series to switch to that folder's view. If you misplace or can't find a file, click in the Search field of the Finder window, and then type the name of the file or a word or phrase it contains. Click the file you seek from the list of matches that appears, and then use the Path Bar to see where it's hiding.

The Back command is not the same thing as the Enclosing Folder command. If you open an external drive and then switch to the Utilities folder on your hard drive, the Back command returns the Finder to the external drive, but the Go⇨Enclosing Folder command opens the Applications folder where Utilities resides.

Organizing and Viewing Folders

The Finder shows the contents stored on a device, such as a hard drive, which acts like a giant folder. To move, copy, or delete items within that folder or any of its subfolders, you first have to select the item(s), and we tell you how to do that. If your Mac's hard drive contains a large number of files and folders, trying to find a particular file or folder can be frustrating so we show you how to search for and tag files and folders. To organize a folder's contents, the Finder can display the contents of a folder in four views, which we discuss throughout this section. You can also preview files, and we tell you how to do that here as well.

To switch to a different view in the Finder, choose View and then choose As Icons, As Lists, As Columns, or As Cover Flow — or just click one of the view buttons on the toolbar shown in Figure 4-4.

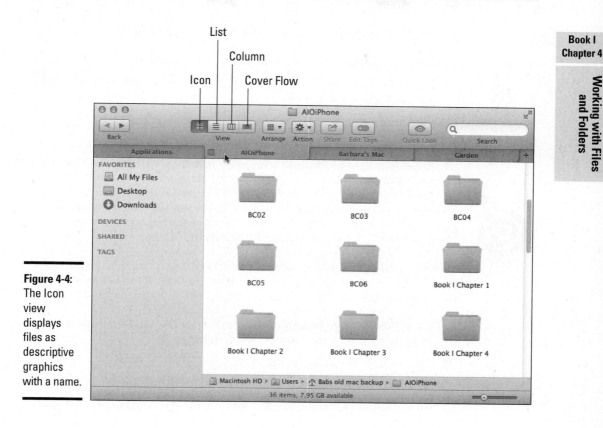

Figure 4-4:
The Icon view displays files as descriptive graphics with a name.

Selecting items in the Finder

No matter how you view the contents of a folder, selecting items remains the same. You always have to select an item before you can do anything with it, such as copy or delete it. You can select items three ways:

✦ Select a single item (file or folder) by clicking it.

✦ Select multiple items by holding down the ⌘ key and clicking each item.

✦ Selecting a range of contiguous items by clicking and dragging the mouse. Or, in List, Column, or Cover Flow view, click the first item, holding the Shift key, and then click the last item; all items in between the first and last are selected.

Using Icon view

Icon view displays all files and folders as icons (refer to Figure 4-4). To organize files in Icon view, you can manually drag icons where you want, or you can have your Mac automatically arrange icons based on certain criteria, such as name or date modified.

To arrange icons within Icon view manually, follow these steps:

1. **Move the pointer over an icon you want to move.**

   You can select two or more icons by holding down the ⌘ or Shift key and clicking multiple icons.

2. **Click and drag the mouse.**

   Your selected icon(s) moves when you move the mouse.

3. **Release the mouse button when you're happy with the new location of your icon(s).**

When you arrange icons manually, they might not align with one another. To fix this problem, make sure that no items are selected and then choose View⟿Clean Up Selection to straighten them up.

Manually arranging icons can be cumbersome if you have dozens of icons you want to arrange. As a faster alternative, you can arrange icons automatically in Icon view by following these steps:

1. **Click the Arrange button on the toolbar of the Finder window to open the pop-up menu, or choose View⟿Arrange By.**

2. **Choose one of the following options:**

   ✦ *Name:* Arranges icons alphabetically.

   All the following arrangements create sections to group like files and folders.

   ✦ *Kind:* Arranges items alphabetically by file extension, clustering together Microsoft Word files, JPG picture files, and music tracks, for instance.

   ✦ *Application:* Arranges items by application type.

   ✦ *Date Last Opened:* Puts files and folders you opened today in the Today section, those you opened yesterday in the Yesterday section, and so on for the Previous 7 Days, Previous 30 Days, and Earlier.

   ✦ *Date Added:* Same type of sorting as Date Last Opened but by when you added the file or folder. Added files may be ones that were copied or downloaded from another source as well as files or folders you created.

   ✦ *Date Modified:* Arranges the most recently modified items at the top of the window and divides the others in the time intervals as Date Last Opened.

   ✦ *Date Created:* Arranges the most recently created items at the top of the window and divides the others in the time intervals as with Date Last Opened.

✦ *Size:* Arranges the largest sized files and folders at the top of the window. Files are grouped by size divisions, such as 100MB to 10GB, 1MB to 100MB, and 10KB to 1MB.

✦ *Label:* Arranges icons alphabetically by color. Icons with no color appear near the top of the window, followed by icons colored blue, gray, green, orange, purple, red, and yellow.

If you don't see the buttons we describe in the toolbar, choose View➪Customize Toolbar. Click and drag the buttons you want to see from the bottom pane to the Finder toolbar. To delete those you don't want to see, simply click and drag them down to the bottom pane, and they disappear in a puff of virtual smoke.

Using List view

By default, List view displays each item by name, size, date it was last modified, and the kind of item it is, such as a folder or a PDF (Portable Document Format) file. The biggest advantages of List view are that it always displays more items in the same amount of space than the Icon view, it displays hierarchies of folders as indented items (shown in Figure 4-5), and you can select items from multiple folders at the same time.

You can change the width of the columns by hovering the cursor over the line between two headers until it becomes a vertical line crossed by a double-ended arrow. Click and drag left or right to make the columns wider or narrower. Rearrange the order of the columns by clicking and dragging

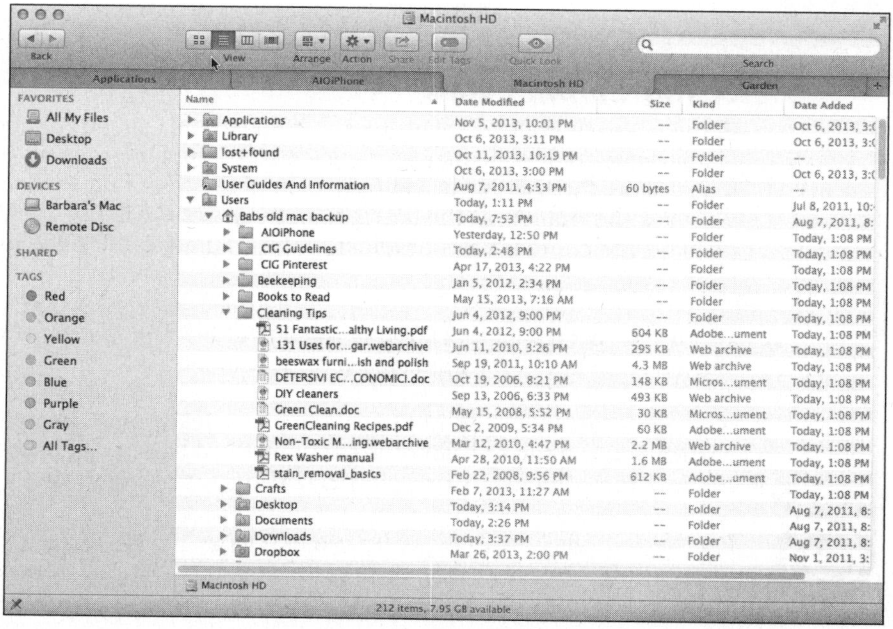

Figure 4-5:
List view displays items in rows and folders as hierarchies.

the header title. Only the Name column must remain as the first column. Additionally, if you click a column heading in List view (such as Name or Date Modified), the Finder sorts your items by that column in ascending or descending order.

When you view your Macintosh HD in List view, user folders are identified by a folder icon and a triangle symbol (which Apple officially refers to as a *disclosure triangle*) pointing to it. Clicking that triangle symbol expands that folder to display its contents — files, more folders, whatever. Clicking the triangle again collapses that folder to hide its contents. If you click a folder with a disclosure triangle, and then select Option+→, the top level folder and all folders contained within it open. Choose Option+← to collapse and close all the folders.

When you expand more than one folder, List view makes it easy to move files and folders from one folder to another. Select multiple folders or files at one time by holding down the ⌘ key and clicking each item you want to select. When you're done selecting folders and/or files, you can then click and hold on one of the selected items and drag them all to wherever you want to move them — to another folder in that view, to the Desktop, or to the Trash on the Dock. If you have another folder, device, or drive open in a separate tab, drag the items to the tab. Then when the tab is highlighted, release the mouse or trackpad button, and the items will be moved to that folder, device, or drive.

If you don't have many files or folders (or you just like everything sort of thrown together), the Finder has an All My Files option, which displays documents from your user account on your Mac, in the view you choose, sorted by the criteria selected from the Arrange pop-up menu.

Using Column view

Column view initially displays files and folders in a single column. As with List view, all folders display a triangle next to the folder name. (Okay, okay, in List view, the triangle is just to the left of the folder name, and Column view has the triangle at the far right, but you get the idea.) Clicking a folder displays the contents of that folder in the column to the right, as shown in Figure 4-6.

When you reach an application or document file, the rightmost column shows a preview of the application or document.

You can adjust the width of the columns by clicking and dragging the short, vertical lines at the bottom of the column divider. You can rearrange the order of the columns by dragging the headers, as in List view.

In any view, click the Arrange button to change the sorting criteria.

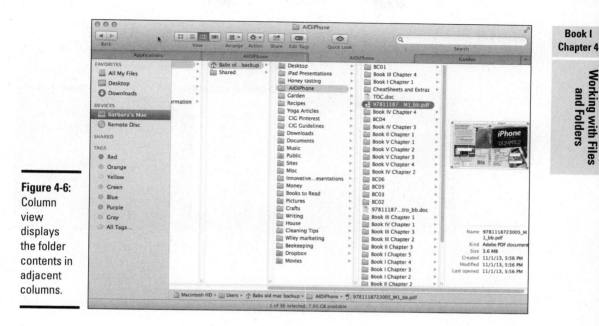

Figure 4-6:
Column
view
displays
the folder
contents in
adjacent
columns.

Using Cover Flow view

Cover Flow view combines List view with the graphic elements of Icon view, as shown in Figure 4-7. Cover Flow originated from jukeboxes that let you pick songs by viewing and flipping through album covers. In the Finder, Cover Flow lets you choose files or folders by flipping through enlarged icons of those files or folders, which can make finding a particular file or folder easier.

Click and drag the resizing button just below the Cover Flow scroll bar up and down to zoom in and out of the image pane. To scroll through items in Cover Flow view, you have a number of choices:

✦ Drag the scroll box in the Cover Flow scroll bar.

✦ Click in the scroll area to the left or right of the scroll box on the Cover Flow scroll bar.

✦ Click an icon on either side of the icon preview image that appears in the middle of the Cover Flow view.

✦ Press the up- and down-arrow keys to select a different file or folder in the list portion of the Cover Flow view. Each time you select a different file or folder, the Cover Flow icon for that file or folder appears.

If you don't see scroll bars, select ￼⇨System Preferences, and the click the General icon. Select the button next to Show Scroll Bars Always.

Resizing button

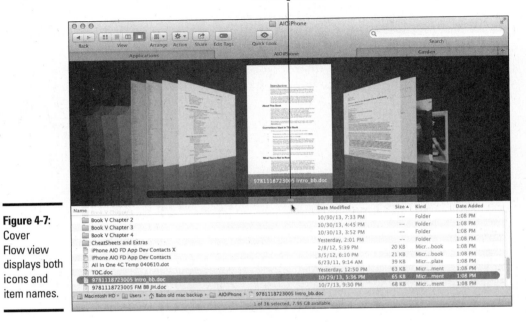

Figure 4-7:
Cover
Flow view
displays both
icons and
item names.

Changing your view options

In any view of the Finder or any folder — Icon, List, Column, or Cover
Flow — you can change the view options. You can also choose to make
one style view the default for every folder you open in a Finder window or
you can set different views for different folders. From any of the four views,
choose View➪Show View Options.

The View Options window opens, shown in Figure 4-8, displaying these
choices from left to right:

✦ **Icon view:** Scale the size of the icons and the grid spacing, adjust the
text size and position, and add color to the background.

✦ **List/Cover Flow view:** Set the same options. Choose small or large
icons, the text size, and the columns you want to see displayed.

✦ **Column view:** Choose the text size and whether you want to see icons
and the preview column.

In any of the View Options windows, you can choose how to arrange or sort
the folders and files.

✦ **Always Open in Icon/List/Column/Cover Flow View:** Select this option
if you want to see the selected folder in that view.

✦ **Browse in Icon/List/Column/Cover Flow View:** You want subfolders of this folder to open in the same view.

✦ **Use as Defaults:** You want the Finder and any folders to always open with this view.

Using Quick Look to view file contents

Quick Look enables you to see the contents of a file for many file types without having to run the application you would normally use to create, view, and save it. Just select a file icon and then click the Quick Look view button (or press the spacebar) to display an enlarged preview icon of the selected file, as shown in Figure 4-9. You have four options to close the Quick Look display:

✦ Click the Close button in the upper-left corner.

✦ Press the spacebar.

✦ Press the Escape key.

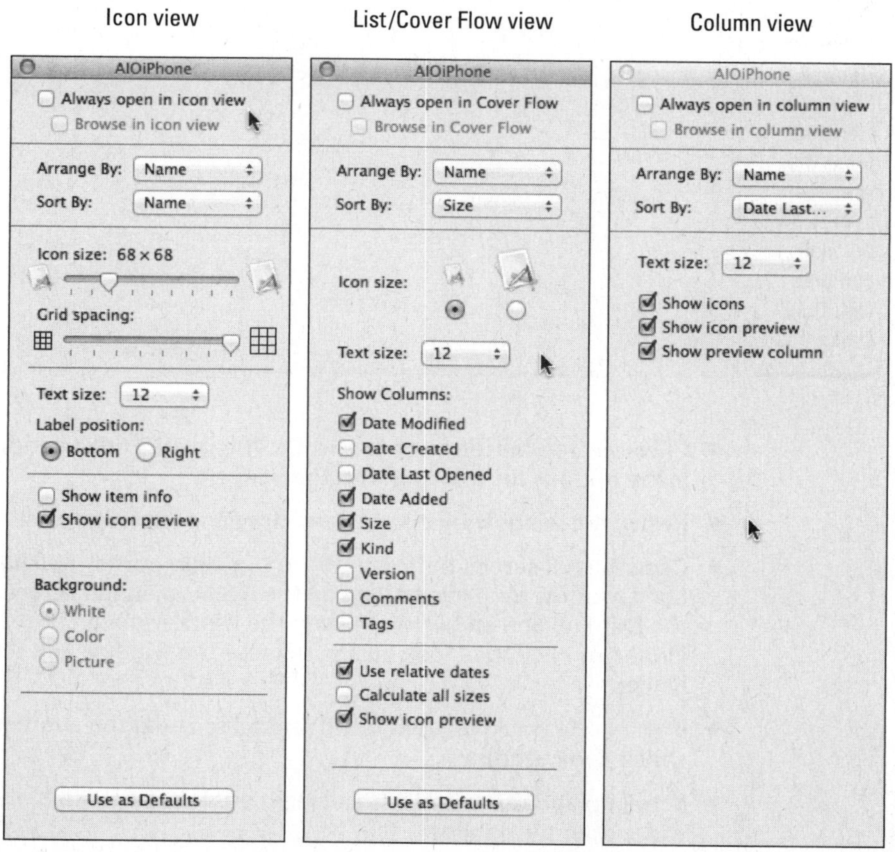

Icon view   List/Cover Flow view   Column view

Figure 4-8:
Use View
Options to
customize
how you
view the
Finder and
folders.

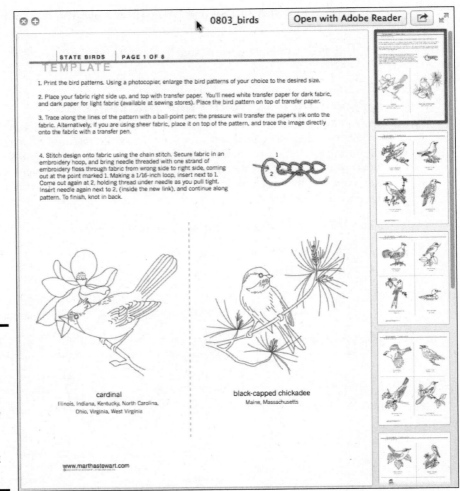

Figure 4-9: Click a file icon and press the spacebar to preview the file's contents with Quick Look.

✦ Click the app button to open the file. The Quick Look window offers many options for working with the image:

✦ Resize the window by clicking and dragging any edge or corner.

✦ Click the full-screen button in the upper-right corner to isolate the Quick Look window from everything on the Desktop. In full screen view, click the Exit Full Screen button to keep the window open but return to the Finder, or click the Close button to close the window and return to the Finder.

✦ If you use a trackpad, pinch and spread to zoom the contents of the Quick Look window.

✦ Scroll up and down and left and right on documents that are longer or wider than the window.

✦ Click the Share button to send the file to someone as an attachment to an e-mail in Mail, an instant message in Message, or to another computer on the same network with AirDrop. Some files can also be shared on Facebook, Twitter, or Flickr.

✦ (Available for some file types) Choose File⇨Print to immediately print the image.

The Quick Look view behaves differently, depending on the type of file you're peeking into:

✦ A recognizable audio file plays in its entirety, so you can hear its contents.

✦ A full-size picture file appears in a window, so you can see what the picture looks like.

✦ A recognizable movie file plays in its entirety, so you can see and hear its contents.

✦ PDF files and HTML files (web pages) appear in a scrollable window that lets you read their contents.

✦ A document file (created by other applications, such as spreadsheets and word processors) is scrollable if in a format that QuickLook recognizes, or displays the first screen of its contents along with a listing of its name, size, and date of last modification.

✦ A folder appears as an icon listing its name, size, and last modified date.

✦ An application icon is displayed along with a name, size, and last modified date.

If you don't have the app that a file was created in, chances are that you can view it as an image by using the Preview app. From Preview, you can search, copy, and print — but not edit — image and PDF documents. Click the Preview icon from Launchpad. Choose File⇨Open, and then click the file you want to view in the chooser, which looks and functions like the Finder.

You can also sign PDF documents, which we explain in the article "Signing on the Dotted Line in Preview" online at www.dummies.com/extras/macsaio.

Creating Folders

In addition to letting you navigate your way through different folders, the Finder also lets you create folders. The main purpose for creating a folder is to organize related files and folders together. You create a folder in the Finder or the Save As dialog. The next sections walk you through each method.

Creating a folder from the Finder menu

Although many Mac users consider the Documents folder as the repository for all folders and documents, we tend to create folders directly in the Home folder and keep the folders for active projects on the Desktop. Each folder relates to a project or category and often contains subfolders and files in the subfolders. For example, the folder for a book project could comprise folders for each chapter, which contain the word processing and image files for the respective chapter. You can create and organize your files and folders in a way that makes sense to you — and that's the beauty of the modern, flexible computer interface called Mac. To create a folder from the Finder menu, follow these steps:

1. **Click the Finder icon on the Dock.**

   The Finder appears.

2. **In the Sidebar of the Finder, click the location (for example, Macintosh HD) or device (such as an external USB flash drive) where you want to create a folder.**

3. **Navigate to and open the folder where you want to store your new folder, such as the Documents or Home folder or Desktop.**

4. **Choose File⇨New Folder (or press Shift+⌘+N).**

   An untitled folder icon appears with its name selected.

5. **Type a descriptive name for your folder and then press Return.**

   Your new folder is christened and ready for use.

Creating a folder from Save or Save As

The Finder isn't the only way to create a new folder. When you save a file for the first time or save an existing file under a new name, you can also create a new folder to store your file at the same time. You use the Save As command, which is the Duplicate command in apps that support Versions, such as Pages or Numbers. (To find out more about Mac's version control feature, see the nearby sidebar, "Saving multiple versions of documents.") To create a folder from the Save or Save As dialog, follow these steps:

1. **Create a new document in any application, such as Microsoft Word or Apple Pages.**

2. **Choose File⇨Save if this is the first time you're saving the document.**

   If you've already saved the document, choose Save As or Duplicate; choosing Save at this point only saves changes to the current document without opening a dialog.

   A Save As dialog appears, as shown in Figure 4-10.

3. **Click the arrow button to the right of the Save As field.**

   The Save As dialog expands to display your Mac's storage devices and common folders in a Finder-like presentation.

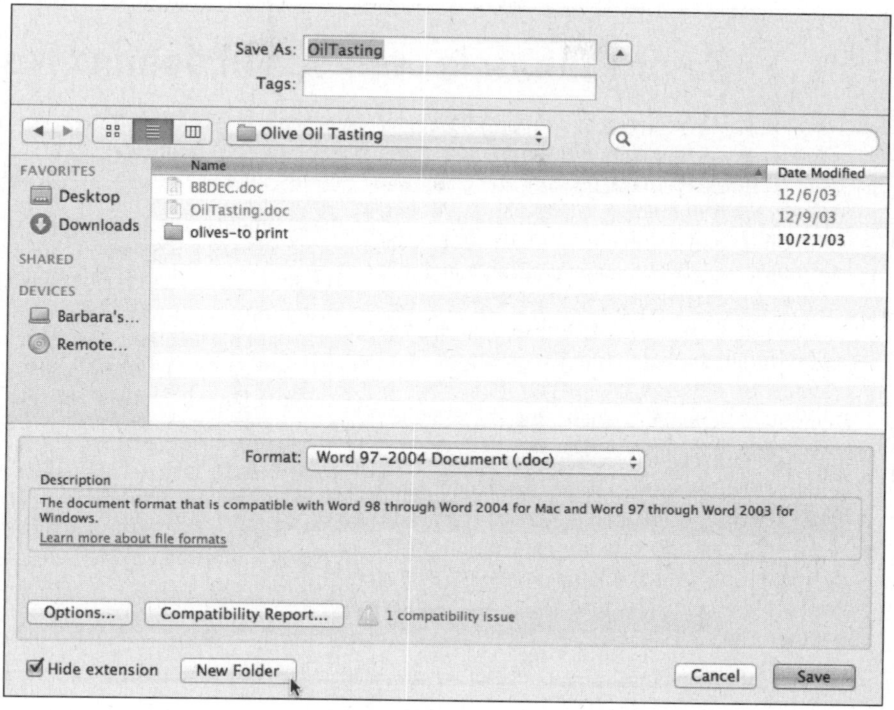

Save As: OilTasting

Tags:

◀ ▶ | 88 ≣ Ⅲ | 📁 Olive Oil Tasting ▾ | 🔍

FAVORITES
  🖥 Desktop
  ⊙ Downloads

SHARED

DEVICES
  🖥 Barbara's...
  ◎ Remote...

Name	Date Modified
📄 BBDEC.doc	12/6/03
📄 OilTasting.doc	12/9/03
📁 olives–to print	10/21/03

Format: Word 97–2004 Document (.doc) ▾

Description

The document format that is compatible with Word 98 through Word 2004 for Mac and Word 97 through Word 2003 for Windows.

Learn more about file formats

Options... | Compatibility Report... | ⚠ 1 compatibility issue

☑ Hide extension | New Folder | Cancel | Save

Figure 4-10:
Create a
new folder
while you're
saving a file.

4. **In the Sidebar of the dialog, click the device where you want to create a folder and open the folder where you want to create a new folder.**

5. **Click the New Folder button (or Shift+⌘+N).**

A New Folder dialog appears, as shown in Figure 4-11.

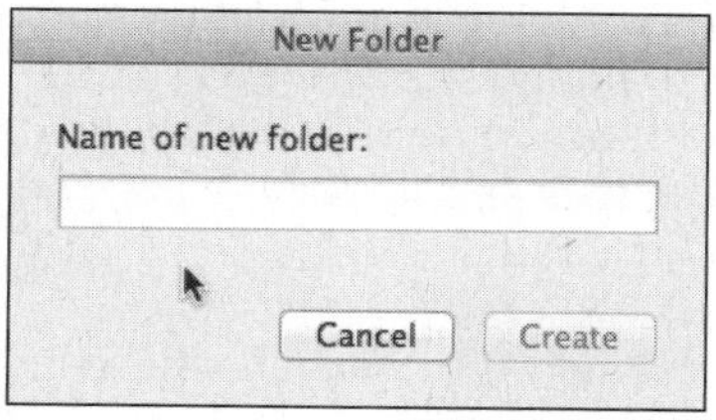

New Folder

Name of new folder:

▢

Cancel | Create

Figure 4-11:
Name your
folder.

---

6. **Type a name for your folder in the dialog's text box and then click Create.**

A new folder is created in the location you specified.

This name can't be identical to the name of any existing folder in that location.

7. **In the main window of the Save As dialog, type a name for your document in the Save As text box and click Save.**

Your new document is stored in your new folder.

REMEMBER

Saving multiple versions of documents

If you're using an app that supports Versions, such as Pages or Numbers, Versions keeps your current document, creates a snapshot of the changed document, and saves a version of the changed document once per hour. The new version doesn't have a different name but a timestamp that shows when each was saved. Instead of opening several files, you access the different versions from within the app and restore an older version if you don't like the changes you made to a more recent version.

To see the previous versions of a document, choose File⇨Revert To. The current document appears on the left and a stack of previous time-stamped versions appears on the right. Scroll through the stack to access a previous version, and click Restore when you find the version you want to use. Even when you close

the document, the interim versions remain so you can always retrieve a version from older (better) times.

The first time you save a document you create, you see the Save option in the File menu, just as you always do. After you save the document for the first time, you see the Save a Version option in the File menu. Versions automatically saves a copy of an open file you're working on once per hour. If you want to save a version in the interim, choose File⇨Save a Version.

If you want to save a copy of the document and create a new folder in which to place it, choose File⇨Duplicate, and then choose File⇨Save. Create a folder as explained previously and save the duplicated document in the newly created folder.

Playing Tag: Classify Files and Folders for Quick Access

You may have noticed the Tags button in the Finder preferences window. Added to OS X 10.9 Mavericks, *tags* provide a way to identify files, in addition to the name. Although every file should have a unique name (you can have duplicates if they're stored in different folders but we don't recommend this), you can apply the same tag to many files or folders and then search for or view files by tag. You can add tags to new files when you save them for the first time or add tags to existing files and folders — and then with a click, access everything attached to a single tag.

Initially, Mavericks offers seven colored tags. You can simply tag a file or folder by a color, but then you have to remember what each color means. Tags become more effective when you name the colors and add other named tags. You can also assign a color to the named tags, but your choices are limited to those seven predetermined colors.

Setting tag preferences

To give more meaningful names to the colored tags, click the Desktop outside a window and then choose Finder⇨Preferences⇨Tags. Click the color name of one of the tags to select it, and then type a new name. For example, Green could become Garden Ideas. Do two other tasks in the Tags preferences:

✦ **Display tags in the Sidebar.** Select the check box next to the tags you want to appear in the Finder Sidebar. When you click the tag in the Sidebar, all files with that tag will appear in the right pane of the Finder window.

✦ **Access tags from the Finder menu.** Drag tags from the list to the box at the bottom of the window to designate favorite tags that you want to see in the Finder's File menu.

✦ **Change tag colors.** Click the colored circle next to a tag name and choose a different color or no color from the list.

Tagging existing files and folders

If you have thousands of files on your Mac, you probably won't go through and tag them all, but you may want to tag those files that you access frequently or are related to a project. To tag an existing file or folder

1. **Click the Finder icon on the Dock to open a Finder window.**

2. **Click and scroll through the folders and files to find the one you want to tag.**

3. **Click the file or folder once to select it (double-clicking would open it).**

4. **Click the File menu and then do one of the following:**

   • *Click a color from the tags at the bottom of the menu.* The tag is added to your folder or file.

   • *Click Tags to see more tag options or create a new tag name.* The Tags window opens, as shown in Figure 4-12. Type a new tag name or click Show All (at the bottom of the Tags list) to see all the tags you use and click one from that selection. When you type a new tag name, it appears in the Tags list.

   Or, click the Edit Tags button in the Finder window toolbar and click the tag you want to add to the file or folder (click Show All if you don't see all your existing tags) or type a name to create a new tag.

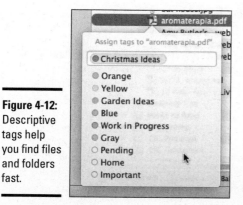

Figure 4-12: Descriptive tags help you find files and folders fast.

5. **Click or create other tags you wish to add to the file or folder.**

   You can add as many text tags as you want. You are limited to the seven preset colors, although you can use the same color for more than one tab. Go to Finder⇨Preferences⇨Tags and click the colored circle next to a tag to change a tag's color.

6. **(Optional) To delete tags from a file or folder, click the file or folder once, and then click the Edit Tags button in the Finder window toolbar. Click to place the pointer to the right of the tag you want to delete and then press the Delete key.**

Tagging new files

When you create a new file of any kind, you save it at some point with a name and location. The Save and Save As dialogs have Tag fields where you tag the new file with an existing tag or tags, or create a new tag that you can then use for other files as well. From the app, choose File⇨Save or Save As and then click the Tags field. The list of colored tags appears, and the Show All option is at the bottom. Click the tag you want to use from the list or type a new tag to add it to the Show All list.

Finding your tagged files

To find files with the same tag, click Finder on the Dock and then click the tag in the Sidebar (or click All Tags and then click the tag you want). All files and folders with that tag appear in the contents pane on the right side of the Finder window.

If you don't see Tags in the Sidebar, choose Finder⇨Preferences⇨Sidebar, and make sure the check box next to Tags is selected. Then, click the Tags button, and click the check box next to the Tags you want to see listed in the Sidebar — although clicking All Tags will open a list that shows all your tags, including those you choose not to see in the Sidebar.

Manipulating Files and Folders

After you create a file (by using an application such as a word processor) or a folder (by using the Finder or a Save As dialog from an application), you might need to change or edit the name of that file or folder to correct a misspelling or to change the name altogether. Additionally, you might need to move or copy that file or folder to a new location or delete it altogether.

To make sure that you're copying, moving, or changing the correct file, you may want to open it first. However, this can take time, and a faster way to view the contents of a file is to click that file in the Finder window and then click the Quick Look icon (or press the spacebar) to take a peek into the file's contents (refer to Figure 4-9).

Renaming files and folders

Keep these rules in mind when naming and renaming files and folders.

+ **Number of characters:** File and folder names can't be longer than 255 characters.

+ **Character restrictions:** You can't use certain characters when naming files or folders, such as the colon (:). Additionally, some applications might not let you use the period (.) or slash (/) characters in a filename.

+ **Duplicate folder names:** One folder can't have the same name as another folder in that same location. For example, you can't store two folders named Tax Info in one folder (such as the Documents folder). You can, however, store two folders with the same name in two different locations — and if you try to move one of them to the same place as the other, your Mac asks whether you want to merge the two folders into one folder with the same name or replace one with the other.

+ **Duplicate filenames:** You can store two identically named files in different folders. If you try to move a file into a folder that already contains a file with the same name, a confirmation dialog asks whether you want to replace the older file with the new one or keep the new one with a numeric suffix appended to the name.

+ **File extensions:** You can also store identically named files in the same location if (and only if) a different application created each file. That means you can have a word processor document named My Resume and a spreadsheet file also named My Resume stored in the same folder.

A file's complete name consists of two parts: a name and a file extension. The name is any arbitrary descriptive name you choose, but the file extension identifies the type of file. An application file actually consists of the .app file extension, a Microsoft Word file consists of the .doc or .docx file extension, a Pages file consists of the .pages file extension, and a Keynote file consists of the .key file extension.

Therefore, a My Resume file created by Microsoft Word is actually named My Resume.doc, and the identically named file created by Pages is actually named My Resume.pages.

To view a file's extension, click that file and choose File➪Get Info (or press ⌘+I). An Info window appears and displays the file extension in the Name & Extension text box, as shown in Figure 4-13. To view the file extensions for this file, deselect the Hide Extension check box. To view extensions for all files in the Finder, follow the instructions as explained in the earlier section, "Setting Finder preferences." You can also add tags to a file in its Info window.

Folders don't need file extensions because file extensions identify the contents of a file, and folders can hold a variety of different types of files.

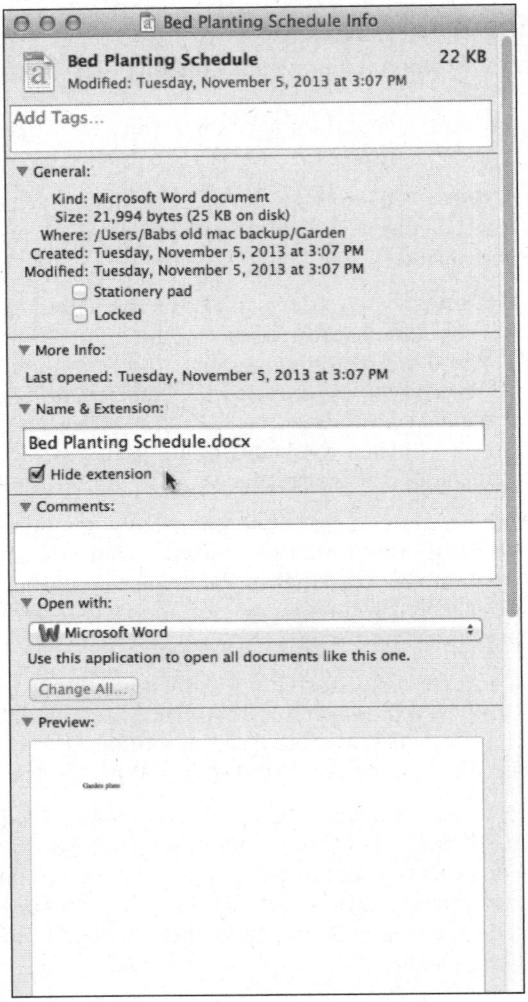

Figure 4-13:
Display file
extensions
or not.

For a fast way to rename a file or folder, follow these steps:

1. **Click a file or folder that you want to rename and then press Return.**

   The file or folder's name appears highlighted.

   When editing or typing a new name for a file, changing the file extension can confuse your Mac and prevent it from properly opening the file because it can no longer identify which application can open the file. Don't modify or remove the file extension.

2. **Type a new name (or use the left- and right-arrow keys and the Delete key to edit the existing name) and then press Return.**

   Your selected file or folder appears with its new name.

Copying a file or folder

At any time, you can copy a file or folder and place that duplicate copy in another location. When you copy a folder, you also copy any files and folders stored inside. To copy a file or folder, you can use either menus or the mouse.

Using menus to copy a file or folder

To copy a file or folder by using menus, follow these steps:

1. **Click the Finder icon on the Dock.**

   The Finder appears.

2. **Navigate to (and open) the folder that contains the files or folders you want to copy.**

   Use the Sidebar and the various other navigation techniques we outline earlier in this chapter to find what you want.

3. **Select one or more files or folders you want to copy and then choose Edit⇨Copy (or press ⌘+C).**

4. **Navigate to (and open) the folder where you want to store a copy of the file or folder.**

5. **Choose Edit⇨Paste (or press ⌘+V).**

   You have your own cloned file or folder right where you want it.

You can also create an alias of a file or folder, as we explain in Book I, Chapter 5. An *alias* — a shortcut — points to the actual file or folder, acting like a remote control for opening the file.

Using the mouse to copy a file or folder

Using the menus to copy a file or folder is simple, but some people find clicking and dragging items with the mouse to be more intuitive. You can drag between two separate devices (such as from a flash drive to a hard drive) or between different folders on the same device.

1. **Click the Finder icon on the Dock.**

   The Finder shows its face.

2. **Navigate to the folder where you want to store your copied files or folders.**

3. **Click the folder and choose File⇨New Tab.**

   A second tab opens for that folder.

4. **Click the first tab and navigate to the folder containing the file or folder you want to copy.**

5. **Using your mouse, click to select one or ⌘-click to select multiple files or folders.**

6. **Drag your selected file(s) and/or folder(s) to the second tab.**

If you want to drag a file or folder to a new location on the same device, hold down the Option key while dragging the mouse; otherwise, you just move the file or folder to the new location rather than placing a copy there.

A green plus sign appears near the pointer while you drag the mouse.

7. Release the mouse button when the second tab is highlighted.

Your selected files and folders appear as copies in the folder you selected.

Dragging a file or folder to a new location on the same device (such as from one folder to another on the same hard drive) always moves that file or folder (unless you hold down the Option key, which ensures that the original stays where it is and a copy is created in the new location). On the other hand, dragging a file or folder from one device to another (such as from a USB flash drive to a hard drive) always copies a file or folder — unless you use the ⌘ key, which creates a copy on the destination drive and deletes the original.

Moving a file or folder

Files and folders can be moved within the Finder following similar steps as for copying — just don't hold down the Option key.

However, thanks to your Mac's *spring-loaded folders* feature, you can also move files and folders without opening a second tab. Drag and hold the file or folder you want to move over the icon of the device or folder you want to copy to, and wait a moment or two until the folder springs open. (You can keep springing folders open this way until you reach the one you want.) Let go of the mouse button to move the file or folder. To adjust how long it takes for folders to spring open, click the Finder, choose Finder➪Preferences, and click the General tab. Then drag the slider at the bottom of the window to adjust how quickly (or slowly) folders spring open when you hover over them with a selected file or folder.

Drag the file or folder out of the Finder to the Desktop for a moment to spring back to your starting point, and then release the mouse or trackpad to leave things where they were.

Grouping files

You can select several files from different locations and move them into a folder by holding the ⌘ key and clicking each file, or by holding the Shift key while clicking the first and last file in a list to select all the files between the first and last file selected. Click and hold one of the selected files and begin to drag them toward the folder where you want to place them. They will be grouped together, and the number of files appears in a red circle on top of the group. Drag the group over the folder where you want to place them until the folder is highlighted, and then release them.

If you want to create a new folder for a group of files, select the files as we describe in the previous paragraph. From the Desktop, choose File➪New Folder with Selection. A new folder is created called New

Folder with Items, which you can rename as explained previously in the "Renaming files and folders" section.

Create a new folder, open that folder in a new tab, and then drag selected files and folders to the new tab. All the selected items are in the new folder.

Archiving Files and Folders

Files and folders take up space. If you have a bunch of files or folders that you don't use, yet want or need to save (such as old tax information), you can archive those files. *Archiving* grabs a file or folder (or a bunch of files or folders) and compresses them into a single file that takes up less space on your hard drive than the original file(s), unless you're archiving files that don't compress, such as JPEG, videos, and some audio.

After you archive a group of files, you can delete the original files. If necessary, you can later "unpack" the archive file to retrieve all its files.

You have two common ways to archive files and folders:

✦ **Creating ZIP files:** ZIP files represent the standard archiving file format used on Windows computers. (By the way, ZIP isn't an acronym. It just sounds speedy.)

✦ **Creating DMG files:** DMG files (DMG is shorthand for *disk image*) are meant for archiving files to be shared only with other Mac users. Generally, if you want to archive files that Windows and Mac users can use, store them in the ZIP file format. If you want to archive files just for other Mac users, you can use the ZIP or DMG file format. If you want to share the disk image with computers that use a different operating system, use the Disk Utility found on your Mac to create a Hybrid disk image, as explained in the section "Creating a DMG file."

The ZIP file format is faster and creates smaller archives than the DMG file format. However, the DMG file format offers more flexibility by allowing you to access individual files in the archive without having to unzip everything the way you must with a ZIP file. Most people use ZIP archives to store data. The most popular way to use DMG files is for storing and distributing software.

Creating a ZIP file

A ZIP file can contain just a single file or folder, or dozens of separate files or folders. To create a ZIP file, follow these steps:

1. **Click the Finder icon on the Dock.**

   The Finder comes to the fore.

2. **Navigate to (and open) the folder that contains the file or folder you want to archive.**

3. **Select one or more items you want to archive.**

4. **Choose File⇨Compress.**

   If, for instance, you select three items in Step 3, the Compress command displays `Compress 3 items`.

   An archive file named `Archive.zip` appears in the folder that contains the items you selected to compress. If you compress a named folder, the ZIP file has the same name as the folder with the `.zip` extension. You can see both in Figure 4-14. You can rename this file to give it a more descriptive name.

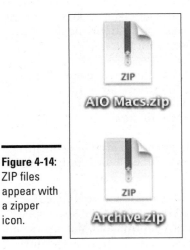

Figure 4-14: ZIP files appear with a zipper icon.

To open a ZIP file, just double-click it. Doing so creates a folder inside the same folder where the ZIP file is stored. Now you can double-click this newly created folder to view the contents that were stored in the ZIP file.

Creating a DMG file

Although ZIP files are handy for storing files, DMG files more often are used to compress and store large items, such as the contents of an entire folder, CD, or hard drive. To create a DMG file, follow these steps:

1. **Click the Finder icon on the Dock.**

   The Finder appears.

2. **Move or copy the files you want to store in the DMG file into a single folder.**

3. **Choose Go⇨Utilities and double-click the Disk Utility application icon.**

   The Disk Utility application loads and displays its window.

4. **Choose File⇨New⇨Disc Image from Folder.**

   The Select Folder to Image dialog appears.

5. **Using the Select Folder to Image dialog, navigate to and select the folder containing the files you chose in Step 2.**

6. **Click Image.**

   The New Image from Folder dialog appears, as shown in Figure 4-15.

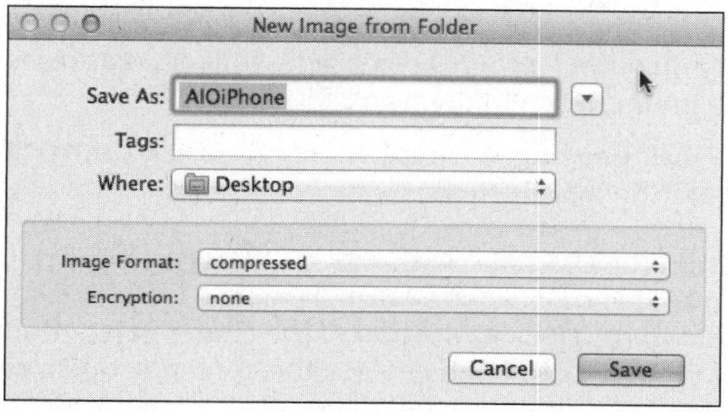

Figure 4-15: Name and define the location of your disk image file.

7. **In the Save As text box, enter a name for your disk image file.**

8. **(Optional) Add any tags that might help you find the file later.**

9. **(Optional) From the Where pop-up menu, choose a folder or device to store your disk image.**

   The disk image will be saved to the Desktop by default.

10. **Open the Image Format pop-up menu and choose one of the following:**

    • *Read-Only:* Saves files in the DMG file, but you can never add more files to this DMG file later.

    • *Compressed:* Same as the Read-Only option except that it squeezes the size of your DMG file to make it as small as possible.

    • *Read-Write:* Saves files in a DMG file with the option of adding more files to this DMG file later.

    • *DVD/CD Master:* Saves files for burning to an audio CD or a video DVD.

    • *Hybrid Image (HFS + ISO/UDF):* Saves files in a DMG file designed to be burned to a CD/DVD for use in computers that can recognize Hierarchical File Structure (HFS), ISO 9660 (International Organization for Standardization), or Universal Disk Format (UDF) for storing data on optical media. (Most modern computers can recognize HFS and UDF discs, but older computers might not.) Also saves files in a DMG file designed for transfer over the Internet.

11. **(Optional) From the Encryption pop-up menu, choose None, 128-bit AES, or 256-bit AES encryption.**

    If you choose encryption, you have to define a password that can open the DMG file.

    AES stands for *Advanced Encryption Standard,* the American government's latest standard for algorithms that scramble data. Choose one of these options if you want to prevent prying eyes from viewing your disk image file's contents (unless you share the password with those you trust).

12. **Click Save.**

    Disk Utility displays a progress message while it compresses and stores the files in your chosen folder as a DMG file.

13. **When the disk imaging is complete, choose Disk Utility⇨Quit Disk Utility to exit the application.**

Figure 4-16 shows the DMG file (with the .dmg extension). Double-clicking a DMG file unpacks it and displays a hard drive icon (also in Figure 4-16) on the Desktop and in the Devices section of the Finder. It functions like any other drive: Double-click to open and see the contents; open, copy, edit (read-write files), and print files contained within; use the Eject command to remove the drive. If you want to share the DMG file, you should share the file — not the drive.

Figure 4-16: Creating a disk image from a folder creates a DMG file.

Deleting files and folders

Like garages, basements, and attics, after a while your Mac probably has stuff that you can throw away, get rid of, or just plain delete. You can delete single files, single folders that contain multiple files, or multiple files and folders together with these steps:

1. **In a Finder window or on the desktop, select the single or multiple files or folders you want to delete in one of the following ways:**

   - Click the single file or folder.

   - Click and drag to select a group of contiguous files or folders in a window or on the desktop.

   - Shift-click the first and last of a group of contiguous files or folders.

   - ⌘-click multiple non-contiguous files or folders.

2. **Click File⇨Move to Trash and drag the selected files to the Trash icon on the Dock or press ⌘+Delete.**

   The files and folders are moved to the Trash file. From here, you can still retrieve your files and folders.

3. **When you're sure you want to eliminate the files and folders from your Mac's memory, click the Desktop, and do one of the following:**

   - Choose Finder⇨Empty Trash, and then confirm by clicking the Empty Trash button

   - Choose Finder⇨Secure Empty Trash, and then confirm by clicking the Secure Empty Trash button

While recovery utilities may be able to restore items deleted with the Empty Trash command, those deleted with the Secure Empty Trash button are irretrievable.

Searching Files

No matter how organized you try to be, there's a good chance you might forget where you stored a file. To find your wayward files quickly, you can use the Spotlight feature.

In Spotlight, just type a word or phrase to identify the name of the file you want or a word or phrase stored inside that file. Then Spotlight displays a list of files that matches what you typed. Say you want to find all the files related to your baseball collection. Type **baseball**, and Spotlight would find all files that contain *baseball* in the filename — or in the file itself, if it's one your Mac can peer into (such as a Word document or an Excel spreadsheet). If you type **image:baseball**, Spotlight will show you only the image files that have *baseball* in the name.

Using Spotlight

Spotlight searches for text that matches all or part of a filename and data stored inside of a file. *Hint:* When using Spotlight, search for distinct words. For example, searching for *A* will be relatively useless because so many files use *A* as part of the filename and in the content. However, searching for *ebola* will narrow your search to the files you most likely want.

Spotlight searches your entire computer. To restrict a search to a specific folder, be sure to check out the next section.

To use Spotlight, follow these steps:

1. **Click the Spotlight icon, which looks like a magnifying glass in the upper-right corner of the menu bar.**

   Alternatively, press ⌘+spacebar.

   If your application is open in full-screen mode, move the pointer up to the upper-right corner of your screen so the menulets appear, where you can click the Spotlight icon.

2. **Type a word or phrase.**

   While you type, Spotlight displays the files that match your text, dividing by file type. If you click one of the matching files, a quick view window opens, as shown in Figure 4-17.

3. **Click a file to open it or click Show All in Finder at the top of the list to see the entire list of matches in a Finder window.**

   Narrow your search by setting more limited criteria in the Show All in Finder window.

4. **Click the device you want to search.**

5. **Click the plus button next to Save on the right side to open two criteria fields, as shown in Figure 4-18.**

Figure 4-17: Click a matching file in the Spotlight list to see a preview.

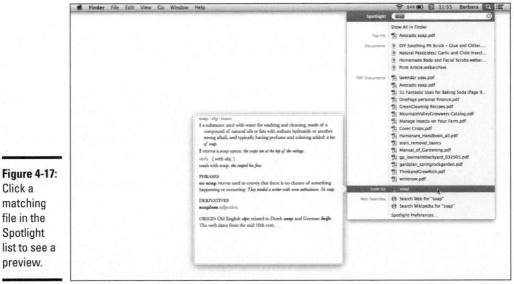

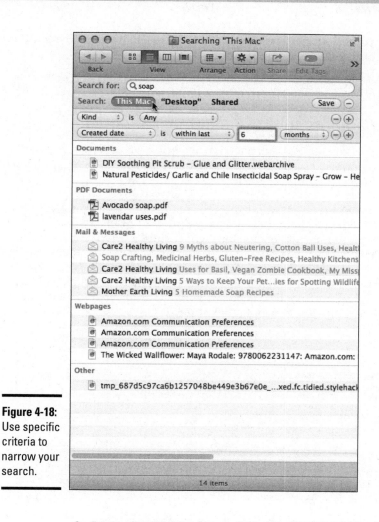

Figure 4-18:
Use specific criteria to narrow your search.

6. **In the first field, choose from Kind, Name, Contents, Visibility, and Creation and Modification Dates. Click Other to open a window that lets you choose more specific attributes to search by.**

7. **Enter information in the successive field (or fields) or pop-up menus to complete the search criteria, and then type the word or words in the file(s) you're seeking.**

   For example, if you choose Name in the first field, the second field enables you to select Matches, Contains, Begins With, and so on.

8. **Repeat Steps 4–6 to add another rule for the search criteria.**

9. **(Optional) Click Save to save this search criteria to use again in the future.**

   A button named after the search word appears next to the other searchable device names.

10. **When you find the file you're looking for, click the item to open it or drag and drop it to a new location.**

    You can even drop the files in an AirDrop box on a different Mac. Read about AirDrop in Book III, Chapter 4.

Spotlight Preferences

From Finder⇨Preferences⇨Advanced, you can specify whether you want Spotlight to perform searches by looking through your entire Mac or only in the active folder.

You can also set preferences for the types of results Spotlight gives you. Choose ⌘⇨System Preferences and click Spotlight or click Spotlight Preferences at the bottom of the Spotlight results window. Select the check boxes next to the types of files you want Spotlight to include when searching, as shown in Figure 4-19. Deselect check boxes next to types of files you want Spotlight to ignore. Then click and drag the names to put them in order of priority. For example, you may want documents listed before folders, and you may not want applications to be included in your search results.

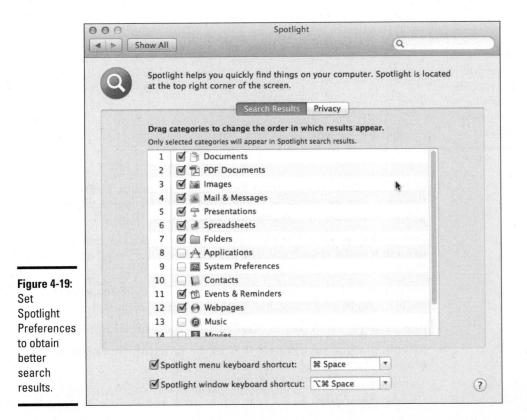

Figure 4-19:
Set
Spotlight
Preferences
to obtain
better
search
results.

Using Smart Folders

Spotlight can make finding files and folders fast and easy. However, if you find yourself searching for the same types of files repeatedly, you can create a *Smart Folder,* which essentially works behind the scenes with Spotlight to keep track of a bunch of files that share one or more common characteristics. For example, you can tell a Smart Folder to store info about only those files that contain *rose* in the filename or the file; and from now on, you can look in that Smart Folder to access all files and folders that match *rose* without having to type the words in the Spotlight text box.

Think of Smart Folders as a way to organize your files automatically. Rather than take the time to physically move and organize the files, you can have Smart Folders do the work for you.

A Smart Folder doesn't physically contain any files or folders. Instead, it contains only links to files or folders. This saves space by not duplicating files.

Creating a Smart Folder with Spotlight

To create a Smart Folder, follow these steps:

1. **Click the Finder icon on the Dock or click the Desktop to make the Finder active.**

2. **Choose File⇨New Smart Folder.**

3. **Click in the Spotlight text box and type a word or phrase.**

4. **Click the plus button next to Save on the right side to open two criteria fields. (Refer to Figure 4-18.)**

5. **In the first field, choose from Kind, Name, Contents, Visibility, and Creation and Modification Dates.**

    Click Other to open a window that lets you choose more specific attributes to search by.

6. **Enter information in the successive field (or fields) or pop-up menus to complete the search criteria, and then type the word or words in the file(s) you're seeking.**

7. **Repeat Steps 4–6 to add more criteria, which leads to more specific results.**

8. **Click the Save button that appears underneath the Spotlight text box.**

    A Save As dialog appears, as shown in Figure 4-20.

9. **Click in the Save As text box and type a descriptive name for your Smart Folder.**

10. **Choose a location to store your Smart Folder from the Where pop-up menu (or click the down arrow and navigate to the location where you want to save your Smart Folder).**

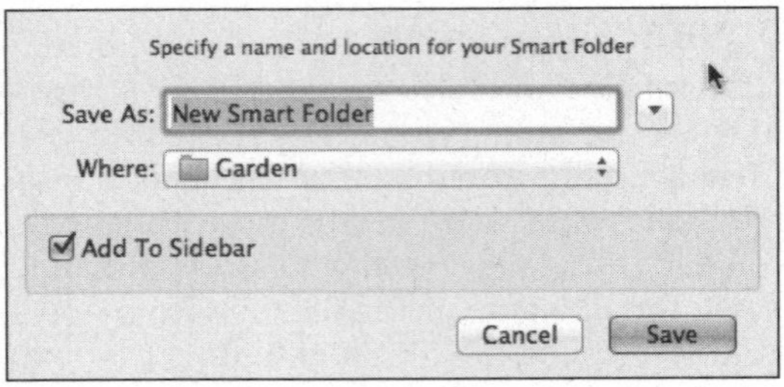

Figure 4-20:
Name
your Smart
Folder and
define
where to
store it.

Specify a name and location for your Smart Folder

Save As: New Smart Folder

Where: 📁 Garden

☑ Add To Sidebar

Cancel   Save

11. **(Optional) Select or deselect the Add to Sidebar check box.**

Select the check box if you want the Smart Folder to appear in the Sidebar in the Favorites section. Deselect the check box if you don't want to see your Smart Folder in the Sidebar.

12. **Click Save.**

Your Smart Folder appears in your chosen location. Instead of displaying an ordinary folder icon, Smart Folder icons always show a gear inside a folder.

After you create a Smart Folder, it automatically keeps your list of files and folders up to date at all times. If you create new files or folders that match the criteria used to define a Smart Folder, that new file or folder name will appear in the Smart Folder automatically. Delete a file, and the Smart Folder deletes its link to that file as well.

Deleting a File or Folder

To delete a file or folder, you first have to place that item in the Trash. But putting an item in the Trash doesn't immediately delete it. In fact, you can retrieve any number of files or folders you've "thrown away." Nothing is really gone — that is, permanently deleted — until you empty the Trash.

Deleting a folder deletes any files or folders stored inside. Therefore, if you delete a single folder, you might really be deleting 200 other folders containing files you might not have meant to get rid of, so always check the contents of a folder before you delete it, just to make sure it doesn't contain anything important.

To delete a file or folder, follow these steps:

1. **Click the Finder icon in the Dock, and then navigate to (and open) the folder that contains the file or folder you want to delete.**

2. **Select the file or folder (or files and folders) that you want to delete.**

3. **Choose one of the following:**

- Choose File⇨Move to Trash.

- Drag the selected items onto the Trash icon in the Dock.

- Press ⌘+Delete.

- Control-click a selected item and choose Move to Trash from the shortcut menu that appears.

Retrieving a file or folder from the Trash

When you move items to the Trash, you can retrieve them again as long as you haven't emptied the Trash since you threw them out. If the Trash icon in the Dock appears filled with a pile of crumbled up paper, you can still retrieve items from the Trash. If the Trash icon appears empty, there are no files or folders there that you can retrieve.

To retrieve a file or folder from the Trash, follow these steps:

1. **Click the Trash icon in the Dock.**

   A Finder window appears, showing all the files and folders you deleted since the last time you emptied the Trash.

2. **Select the item (or items) you want to retrieve, drag them onto a device or folder in which you want to store your retrieved items, and then release the mouse button.**

Emptying the Trash

Every deleted file or folder gets stored in the Trash, where it eats up space on your hard drive until you empty the Trash. When you're sure that you won't need items you trashed any more, you can empty the Trash to permanently delete the files and free up additional space on your hard drive.

To empty the Trash, do one of the following:

✦ Click the Finder icon in the Dock (or click the Desktop) and choose Finder⇨Empty Trash.

✦ Control-click the Trash icon in the Dock and choose Empty Trash from the shortcut menu that appears.

✦ Click the Finder icon (or the Desktop) and press ⌘+Shift+Delete.

A dialog appears, asking whether you're sure that you want to remove the items in the Trash permanently. Click OK (or Cancel).

Under Empty Trash, you see another option: Secure Empty Trash. Secure Empty Trash overwrites the deleted files with random data to foil any attempt to recover deleted files later with a special file recovery application. If you want to delete something sensitive that you don't want to risk falling into the wrong hands, choose the Secure Empty Trash option.

If you check Empty trash securely in Finder➪Preferences➪Advanced, you only have the Secure Empty Trash option.

Chapter 5: Managing Apps on the Dock, Launchpad, and Desktop

In This Chapter

🖊 **Running apps from the Dock and Launchpad**

🖊 **Switching between apps**

🖊 **Opening documents and files**

🖊 **Using aliases**

🖊 **Organizing the Dock**

🖊 **Working with Mission Control**

🖊 **Shopping at the App Store**

🖊 **Installing, updating, and uninstalling apps**

After you power-on your Mac and have OS X up and running, you have to use apps (*applications;* or software or programs) to actually do anything with your Mac, such as write a report with a word processor, edit a video, play a video game, browse the web, or read and write e-mail. The number of apps you can load and run simultaneously is limited only by the amount of hard-drive space and memory installed inside your Mac.

This chapter explains how to run, install, and uninstall apps for your Mac. Most of the time, you start or launch an app from the Dock (which we introduce to you in Book I, Chapter 2) or Launchpad, which we show you in this chapter. We explain how to use and organize both in this chapter. We also show you three other ways to open apps. Although your Mac comes with many great pre-installed apps, we give you pointers for finding new apps and take you window-shopping in the App Store (purchasing is optional).

Launching an App

Running an app is also referred to as *launching* an app or *starting up* an app.

To start an app, you can choose any of the six most common methods. Don't worry if some of the terms here are new to you; we show you how to do each throughout this chapter:

✦ Click an app or document icon on the Dock.

✦ Double-click an app or document icon in the Finder.

✦ Click an alias of the app or document in any of the locations just listed.

✦ Click Launchpad on the Dock (or open it with the F4 key on newer keyboard or Control+⌘+L on any keyboard) and click the app. The Launchpad icon looks like a rocket.

✦ Choose an app name from the Apple (🍎) menu's Recent Items.

✦ Find the app with the Spotlight search feature and then select it to run.

The *Dock* is the strip of animated icons that appears when you hover the pointer over the bottom of your Mac's screen (on the left or right side if you changed the Dock's position by choosing 🍎➪Dock➪Position).

Optionally, the Dock identifies running apps by displaying a glowing dash underneath the icon of each running app. The app menu — the menu to the right of the 🍎 menu that shows the name of an app, such as Word or iTunes — identifies the active app. You can run multiple apps and display multiple windows showing active files created with those apps, but only one window is active, and therefore only one app is active. The *active app* is the one that is front and center on your screen, ready to accept any data or commands you give. The window of the active app may be on top of any other app windows that are open, or it could be next to other windows if you have a large screen or are working with multiple displays.

When you attach a device, such as a digital camera or a mobile phone, an app such as iPhoto or iTunes may launch automatically, depending on the settings you choose. For those two specific examples, see Book IV, Chapters 3 and 1, respectively.

From the Dock

To run an app from the Dock, move the pointer over the app icon that you want to run and click. (What? Were you expecting something difficult?) The Dock contains icons that represent some (but not all) of the apps installed on your Mac. When you turn on your Mac for the first time, you see that the Dock already includes a variety of apps that Apple thinks you might want to use right away. However, you can always add or remove app icons to/from the Dock (that's next in this section).

You can use the Dock in several ways:

✦ **To gain one-click access to your favorite apps.**

✦ **To see which apps are running.** You see a small white illuminated dash under, or next to, the app icon (see Figure 5-1) if you turn on the Dock indicator lights in Dock Preferences. (We tell you how to adjust Dock Preferences in Book I, Chapter 2.)

Running applications

Figure 5-1:
The Dock
identifies
running
apps with
a glowing
dash.

✦ **To switch between different apps quickly.** Clicking a running app's
Dock icon makes it easy to switch among all the apps that are open
at the same time. So, if you want to switch to the iTunes app from the
Mail app, you just click the iTunes app icon. Doing so immediately displays the iTunes window(s) and displays the iTunes app name in the
Application menu on the menu bar at the top of the screen. (Clicking the
iTunes app icon brings iTunes to the forefront, but the Mail app doesn't
close or quit on you; it just moseys to the background, waiting for its
turn to step into the limelight again.)

✦ **To see which windows you have minimized.** *Minimized* windows are
tucked out of sight but are still open. By default, you see a miniature version of the minimized window on the right (or lower) end of the dock.
Simply click it to bring it back to full size.

You won't see minimized windows if the Minimize Windows into
Application Icon option is selected in Dock Preferences; click the app
icon to open the minimized windows of documents created in the app.
(We tell you how to adjust Dock Preferences in Book I, Chapter 2.)

✦ **To view a specific app window.**

✦ **To go to a specific window of a running app.**

✦ **To perform specific tasks of an app.**

✦ **To quit an app without switching to it.**

✦ **To show or hide all windows that belong to a specific app.**

You can add or remove app icons to or from the Dock so it contains only the
apps you use most often, and you can arrange the icons in the Dock to suit
yourself and make starting apps even easier. The following sections give you
all you need to know about the relationship between the Dock and its icons.

From Launchpad

If the app you want to open isn't stored on the Dock, you can go to
Launchpad, which shows all apps that are in the Applications folder. Click
the Launchpad icon (which looks like a rocket) on the Dock.

If you removed the Launchpad icon like we did, press the shortcut key (F4 on newer Apple keyboards or Control+⌘+L), to open Launchpad, as shown in Figure 5-2. If you use a trackpad, with three fingers and your thumb slightly open, place your finger`s and thumb on the trackpad and bring them together as if you were to pick up a small object. *Voilà!* Launchpad launches. (Sorry, but there's no default mouse equivalent although if you have a multibutton mouse, you can assign that function to one of the buttons.)

Figure 5-2:
Apps stored in the Applications folder on your Mac appear on Launchpad.

Launchpad shows all the apps that are in the Applications folder, using multiple screens depending on how many apps are installed on your Mac. That means all the apps that came with your Mac and all apps you install have an icon on Launchpad.

Each Launchpad screen can hold between 35 and 40 apps or folders, depending on your Mac's screen resolution. Each folder can hold up to 32 apps. You can have multiple Launchpad screens. To move from one Launchpad screen to another, hold the mouse button and move the mouse left or right, swipe left and right with two fingers on the trackpad, or use ⌘+→ or ⌘+←.

To open an app, just click the app icon on Launchpad, and the app opens.

To leave the Launchpad without opening an app, simply click anywhere on the background or press Esc.

You can do the following to manage the appearance of Launchpad:

✦ Click and drag an icon to move it on Launchpad; drag it to the very right or left edge to move the icon to another screen. You can move only one icon at a time.

✦ Click and drag one icon over another to create a folder that holds both icons, and then drag other icons into the folder. Click the folder once to open it, and then double-click the name to highlight the name and type in a new name. To remove an icon from a folder, just drag it onto Launchpad.

You can drag an icon from Launchpad to the Dock to add the icon to the Dock.

From the Apple menu's Recent Items

This one's a no-brainer: Choose ⌘➪Recent Items and then choose the app you want to run from the list of recently run apps. You can also choose a recently created or viewed document or other file to automatically launch the associated app and load the document or file.

From the Finder

Because an app's icon might not appear on the Dock, you have to be able to access icons another way. The Launchpad shows apps stored in the Applications folder, but the Finder can help you find any applications that are stored in another folder.

You can store an app icon in any folder on your hard drive, but you should store apps in the Applications folder. That way, if you need to find that app again, you just have to look on Launchpad or in the Applications folder instead of trying to remember where else you stored it.

To run an app from the Finder, follow these steps:

1. **Click the Finder icon on the Dock and then click the Applications folder in the Finder window's Sidebar to display the apps installed on your Mac.**

2. **Scroll through the Applications folder window until you see the app icon you want and then double-click the icon to run the app.**

   (You might have to double-click a folder that contains an app icon and then double-click the app icon.) Alternatively, you can single click the app icon and then choose File➪Open or press a keyboard shortcut, such as ⌘+O or ⌘+↓.

   Your chosen app appears, typically with a blank window, ready for you to do something application-y, such as typing text.

Typing the first letter of an app file or document you're looking for in any Finder window will instantly jump to and select the first icon that matches the letter you type. For instance, to locate Safari in the Applications folder quickly, press S to jump to and select Safari (or another app icon whose name starts with S that might come before Safari, if one is present).

If you're having trouble understanding how the Finder works, go to Book I, Chapter 2 to read a brief introductory overview and Book I, Chapter 4 to learn all the nitty-gritty Finder details.

With Spotlight

As an alternative to clicking an app's Dock or Launchpad icon, or locating an app or document by clicking through folders, you can use your Mac's handy Spotlight feature to quickly open apps or documents for you. We explain Spotlight in detail in Book I, Chapter 4. You can use Spotlight to run apps and open documents in two ways:

✦ **Via Finder:** Click the Finder icon on the Dock, click in the Search text box, type all or part of a document or app name (or the contents of a document you want to open), and then press Return. Double-click the document or app you want to open from the list of results.

✦ **From the menu bar:** Click the Spotlight icon in the far-right corner of your Mac's menu bar (or press ⌘+spacebar) and begin typing the first few letters of the app or file name (or contents of a file) you're looking for. Move the pointer to the app or document you want to open and click it.

Opening documents

A file on the Mac appears as a graphically descriptive icon with a name. Icons can represent applications and documents or a link, known as an *alias,* to either of those.

✦ *Application files* actually do something, such as play a game of chess; or send, receive, and organize your e-mail.

✦ *Document files* hold data created by applications, such as a report created in a word processing app, a budget created in a spreadsheet app, or a movie created in a video-editing app.

✦ *Application icons* are often distinct enough to help you identify the type of app they represent. For example, the iTunes app icon appears as a musical note against a blue circular background, the iPhoto icon appears as a camera over a photograph, and the Mail application icon (for sending and receiving e-mail) appears as a postage stamp.

✦ *Document icons* often appear as a dog-eared page showing a thumbnail image of the content and the suffix of the file type stamped on the bottom, such as *web, docx,* or *html,* as shown in Figure 5-3. Folders look like folders, and image files such as JPG or TIFF appear as thumbnails of the image.

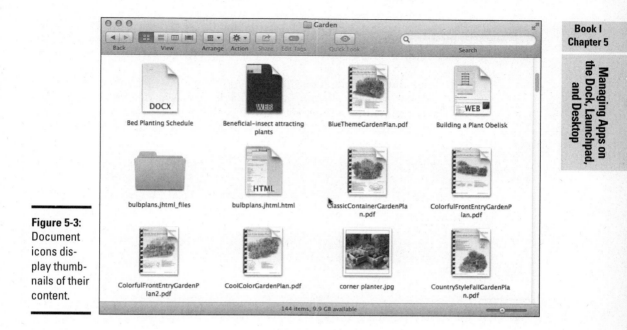

Figure 5-3:
Document icons display thumbnails of their content.

✦ *Alias icons* represent links to app icons or document icons. You find out more about alias icons in the "Creating Alias Icons" section, later in this chapter.

When you double-click an app icon in the Finder, you start (that is, *run* or *launch*) that particular app. If you want to use your newly opened app to work on an existing file, you then have to search for and open that file by using the app's File⇨Open command.

As an alternative to starting an app and then having to find and open the file you want to work with, the Mac gives you the option of double-clicking the document icon you want to open. This opens the app with your chosen document ready for action.

You have three ways to find and open a document stored in the Documents folder, which is stored in your Home folder but can be accessed from the Dock, the Finder sidebar, and the Desktop window as follows:

✦ Control-click the Documents icon on the Dock and then choose Open in Finder (or click and hold the Documents icon to see the folders and documents inside it, move the pointer to the one you want to open, and then let go of the mouse button).

✦ Click the Finder icon on the Dock and then click the Documents folder in the Sidebar to open the Documents window.

✦ Click the Desktop and press ⌘+Shift+D to open the Desktop window. Then click the Documents folder in the Sidebar.

If you store your document files in other folders, such as a folder that's specific to a project with all related files in that folder, you can find your document in three ways:

✦ Click the Finder icon on the Dock and then click All My Files from the Sidebar. You see all your documents on your Mac displayed — you won't see documents of other users. You can choose how to sort them — by Size, Name, Kind, Date Last Opened, and so on, as shown in Figure 5-4.

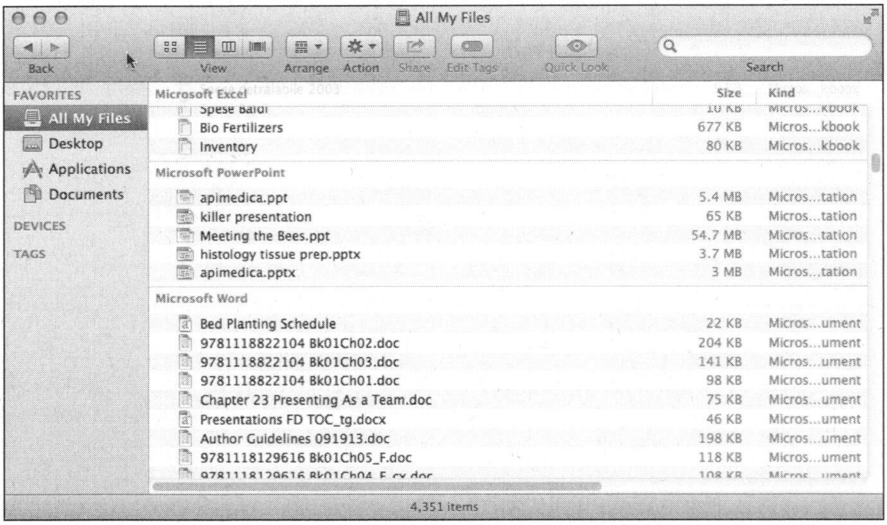

Figure 5-4:
See all the files on your Mac with the Finder All My Files feature.

✦ Click the Finder icon on the Dock and then click the location of the folder that contains your document, such as Desktop or the Home icon. Double-click the folder to see the documents within.

✦ Type the document name or a word or phrase it contains in the Spotlight Search field in the Finder window or menu bar.

Scroll through the documents wherever you find them — Documents folder, All My Files, Spotlight Search results, or another folder — and double-click your document file when you find it to open it.

Your Mac loads the application that created the document (if it's not already running) and displays your chosen document in a window. If your Mac can't find the application that created the document, it might load another application, or it might ask you to choose an existing application on your Mac that can open the document.

Sometimes if you double-click a document icon, an entirely different application loads and displays your file. This can occur if you save your file in a different file format. For example, if you save an iMovie project as a QuickTime file, double-clicking the QuickTime file opens the QuickTime Player rather than iMovie.

Switching among Applications

When you run multiple applications, multiple windows from different apps clutter your screen, much like covering a clean tabletop with piles of different papers. To help keep your screen organized, you can switch between different apps (say, a word processor and a web browser) as well as switch to different windows displayed by the same app (such as a word processor displaying a window containing a letter of resignation and a second window containing a résumé).

Your Mac offers quite a few different ways to switch among different apps, including using the Dock, using the Application Switcher, clicking a window of a different app, using Mission Control, or by hiding apps or entire Desktops, which we explain in the section "Organizing Multiple Desktops with Spaces," later in this chapter.

We discuss the first three ways of switching between running apps in the following list:

✦ **Using the Dock:** Refer to the section "From the Dock" earlier in this chapter to review this method.

✦ **Using the Application Switcher:** Press ⌘+Tab to open the Application Switcher, which displays icons of all active applications, even if the windows are closed or you hid the app with the *app menu⇨Hide app* command. Hold the ⌘ key to keep the Application Switcher open and then press the Tab key to move left to right from one running application to the next, as shown in Figure 5-5. When you release the ⌘ key, the chosen application moves to the front of your screen.

Pressing the Shift key while holding down ⌘ and pressing Tab will move the selection from right to left. You can also press ⌘+Tab and then let go of the Tab key and use the arrow keys to navigate left and right.

If an application has several files open in different windows, the Application Switcher just switches you to that application, but you still have to find the specific window to view.

Figure 5-5:
The
Application
Switcher
displays
icons of
running
applications.

✦ **Clicking different windows:** A fast but somewhat clumsier way to switch between applications is to rearrange your windows so you can see two or more windows at one time. To switch to another window, click anywhere inside that window.

✦ **Going to Mission Control:** To see all the open windows on your Desktop, as well as the Dashboard and other Desktops Spaces (which we get to in just a bit), press F3, swipe up on the trackpad with three or four fingers, or press Control+Shift+↑ to open Mission Control, as shown in Figure 5-6. Then click the window you want to work in.

To choose how many fingers you need to open Mission Control, click System Preferences on the Dock and select Trackpad from the list (you have this choice only if you use a trackpad). Click the More Gestures tab, and then choose Swipe Up with Three Fingers or Swipe Up with Four Fingers from the pop-up menu, which you see when you click the disclosure triangle.

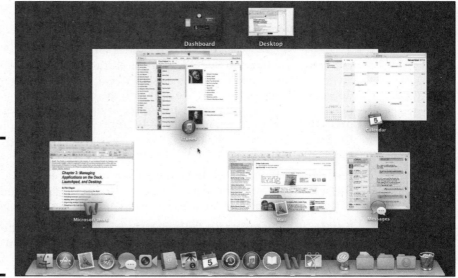

Figure 5-6: Mission Control shows everything that's open on your Desktop.

If you want to switch between two or more open windows from the same app, press ⌘+` (that's the accent grave character, which lives on the key to the left of numeral 1 on most keyboards). If you want to see all the windows from the same app, press fn+F10 or Control+Shift+↓ to open Exposé, as shown in Figure 5-7. Exposé shows you thumbnail versions of all the open windows from one running app. Then all you have to do is click the exact window you want to use.

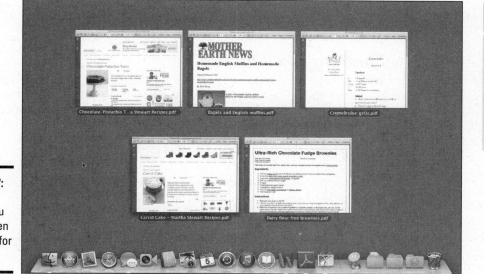

Figure 5-7:
Exposé
shows you
all the open
windows for
one app.

Quitting Apps

When you shut down an app, you also shut down all document windows that app may have open. However, if you simply close a document in an open app, the app keeps running.

If you leave apps running when you shut down your Mac or log out of your account, in the dialog that appears you can choose to automatically reopen the running apps when you start your Mac the next time, letting you pick up where you left off.

Closing a document

If you want to stop working with or viewing a specific document but want to keep the application running, you can close just that particular document. You have three different ways to close a document window:

✦ Choose File⇨Close.

✦ Press ⌘+W.

✦ Click the red Close button of the document window.

If you click the yellow button, the window is hidden on the Dock but isn't closed. Click the document or app icon on the Dock to quickly reopen it.

If you try to close a window before saving the file, a confirmation dialog appears, asking whether you want to save your file.

Shutting down an app

When you finish using an app, shut it down to free up your Mac's memory to run other apps. The more apps you have running at the same time on your Mac, the slower your Mac can become, so always shut down apps if you don't need them anymore.

To shut down an app, you have three choices:

✦ Click the application menu and choose Quit (such as iPhoto➪Quit iPhoto to shut down the iPhoto application).

✦ Press ⌘+Q.

✦ Control-click the app icon on the Dock and choose Quit from the contextual menu that appears.

If you try to shut down an application that displays a window containing a document that you haven't saved yet, a confirmation dialog appears asking whether you want to save your file.

Force-quitting an app

Despite the Mac's reputation for reliability, there's always a chance that an app will crash, freeze, or hang, which are less-than-technical-terms for an app screwing up and not reacting when you click the mouse or press a key. When an app no longer responds to any attempts to work or shut down, you might have to resort to a last-resort procedure known as a *force-quit*.

If you force-quit an app, you will lose any data you changed between the time of your last save and right before the app suddenly froze or crashed. For instance, say you're typing a sentence and then perform a force-quit press before pressing ⌘+S to save it — that sentence would be missing the next time you reopen that document.

As the name implies, force-quitting makes an app shut down whether it wants to or not. Here are the two easiest ways to force-quit an app:

✦ **Choose **⬀**Force Quit (or press **⌘**+Option+Esc).** The Force Quit Applications dialog appears, as shown in Figure 5-8. Frozen or crashed applications might appear in the Force Quit Applications dialog with the phrase Not Responding next to its name. Just click the application you want to force-quit and then click the Force Quit button. If you select Finder, the Force Quit button reads Relaunch.

Figure 5-8:
The Force
Quit dialog
shows you
all running
applications.

> ⊖ ○ ○   Force Quit Applications
>
> If an application doesn't respond for a while,
> select its name and click Relaunch.
>
> 📷 Grab
> 📬 Mail
> W Microsoft Word (not responding)
> 🧭 Safari
> 🖥 System Preferences
> 📑 Finder
>
> You can open this window by pressing   [Relaunch]
> Command-Option-Escape.

✦ **Control-click an app icon on the Dock and choose Force Quit from the shortcut menu that appears.** If the app hasn't really crashed or if your Mac thinks the app hasn't crashed, you won't see a Force Quit option in this pop-up menu. In that case, you may want to wait a minute or so to give your Mac time to correct the seemingly hung-up app. If you wait awhile, and the app still appears stuck but you don't see the Force Quit option, hold down the Option key, Control-click an app icon on the Dock, and then choose Force Quit.

Most apps present you with the original and a recovered version of the document you were working on before a force-quit. Look at both to determine which is the most recent or most correct version, and then proceed as follows, depending on which file is the better one:

✦ **Original file:** Save the file by choosing File⇨Save. Click the Close button (the red button in the upper-left corner) of the recovered file. When asked whether you want to save it, click Don't Save.

✦ **Recovered file:** Close the original file, and then click the window of the recovered file to make it active. Choose File⇨Save and give the recovered file the same name as the original file. Click Replace when asked in the confirmation dialog.

Creating Alias Icons

An *alias icon* acts like a link to another icon. Double-clicking an alias icon works identically to double-clicking the actual app or document icon. The biggest advantage of using alias icons is that you can move and place alias icons anywhere you want without physically moving (and perhaps losing) an app or document.

One way to use alias icons is to create alias icons to your app icons, store those alias icons in a folder, and then store that folder to the right of the divider on the Dock. This gives you easy access to lots of apps without cluttering the Dock.

You can do the following things with alias icons:

✦ **Create an alias icon.** Click the Finder icon on the Dock, scroll through your folders and files, and then click the one you want to select. Choose File⇨Make Alias. (You can also Control-click it and choose Make Alias, or press ⌘+L.) A copy of your chosen icon appears in the window. Notice that the new icon has an arrow in the bottom corner and *alias* is added to its name, as shown in Figure 5-9.

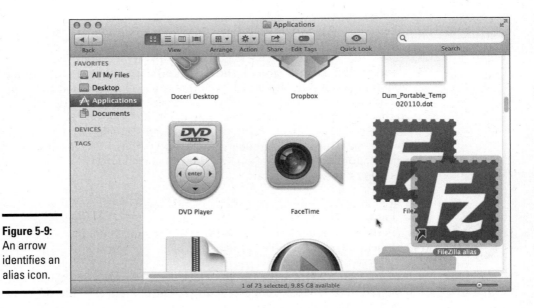

Figure 5-9:
An arrow identifies an alias icon.

✦ **Move an alias icon.** Because it's pointless to store the original icon and the alias icon in the same location, store the alias icon in a new location. To move an alias icon, click it to select it and then drag it to the Desktop, the Dock, or the folder you want to move it to.

✦ **Create and move an alias icon in one step.** Hold ⌘+Option when you click the icon you want to create an alias of and then drag it to the new position. The alias is created and positioned in the new location.

✦ **Delete an alias icon.** Simply Control-click it and choose Move to Trash, or move the pointer over the icon and press ⌘+Delete. Note that deleting an alias icon never deletes the original icon — meaning that if you delete an alias icon that represents an app, you never delete the actual application. The only way to delete an application or document is to delete the original application or document icon.

You can store alias icons on the Desktop for fast access or in specific folders to organize applications and documents without moving them to a new location. (Essentially, the Dock replaces the need to place alias icons on the Desktop, and Smart Folders duplicate the process of creating and storing alias icons in a folder. You can delve into Smart Folders in Book I, Chapter 4.)

Working with Dock Aliases

The Dock includes several apps already installed on your Mac, but if you install more apps, you might want to add their icons to the Dock as well. One way to add an app icon to the Dock is to click and drag the icon onto the Dock.

When you drag an app icon to the Dock, you aren't physically moving the app from the Applications folder onto the Dock; you're just creating a link, or *alias,* from the Dock to the actual app (which is still safely stashed in its folder). Here's how that's usually done:

1. **Click the Finder icon** (the Picasso-like faces icon) **on the Dock and then click the Applications folder in the Finder window's sidebar.**

   The Finder displays the contents of the Applications folder.

2. **Drag the app to the Dock.**

   To drag an app, move the pointer over the icon of the app you want to move, click and hold the mouse button or trackpad, drag the pointer where you want to place the icon on the Dock, and then release the mouse button.

   Make sure that you drag app icons on the Dock to the left of the divider, which appears as a gap near the Trash icon. To the left of the divider, you see app icons. To the right of the divider, you can store file or folder icons.

   Your chosen app icon now has its own place on the Dock.

Be careful not to drag the application icon to the Trash bin unless you really want to delete it from your hard drive.

You can also add an app icon to the Dock when the app is open. Remember that the Dock displays the icons of all running apps at all times, but when you exit an app, that app's icon — if it's not a Dock resident — will disappear from the Dock. To give a running app Dock residency, Control-click the running app's icon on the Dock — or click and hold down on the app icon — and choose Options⇨Keep in Dock from the shortcut menu, as shown in Figure 5-10. Now when you exit from this app, the app icon remains visible on the Dock.

Figure 5-10:
Dock icons
have short-
cut menus.

Adding file and folder aliases to the Dock

You can always find the files and folders you want by using the Finder. However, you might find that switching to the Finder constantly just to access the contents of a particular folder can be tedious. As a faster alternative, you can store aliases to files and folders directly on the Dock.

Accessing files from the Dock

If you have a file that you access regularly, consider placing an icon for that file directly on the Dock. That way, the file icon remains visible at all times (whenever the Dock is visible), giving you one-click access to your frequently used files.

To place a file icon on the Dock, follow these steps:

1. **Click the Finder icon on the Dock and navigate to the folder containing the file you use frequently.**

2. **Drag the file to the Dock into any space to the left of (or above) the Trash icon.**

   The icons on the Dock slide apart to make room for the icon. To open this file, just click its file icon, which looks like a thumbnail version of the original.

A file icon on the Dock is just an alias or link to your actual file. If you drag the file icon off the Dock to delete it from the Dock, your physical file remains untouched.

Creating Stacks on the Dock

Rather than clutter the Dock with multiple app or file icons, consider storing a folder on the Dock. A folder icon, when stored on the Dock, is a *Stack*. After you create a Stack on the Dock, you can view its contents by clicking the Stack.

To load the app or open the file, you can click the stack on the Dock and then click the app or file icon. The downsides include losing the shortcut menus for the items in the stack and not being able to open a document in an app other than the one in which it was created.

To store a Stack on the Dock, follow these steps:

1. **Click the Finder icon on the Dock to open a new Finder window, and then navigate to a folder you use frequently.**

2. **Drag the folder to the Dock into any space to the right of (or above) the divider.**

    The Dock icons slide apart to make room for your Stack to give your folder a place all its own.

Opening files stored in a Stack

After you place a Stack on the Dock, you can view its contents — and open a file in that Stack — by following these steps:

1. **Click a Stack folder on the Dock.**

    The files and folders in the stack appear in a window. If a file contained in the folder represented by the Stack is open, the icon shows a piece of paper emerging from the folder.

2. **Click the file you want to open in the grid or list.**

    Your chosen file opens.

    Or, click Open in Finder to see the folder in a Finder window.

Control-click (two-finger tap on a trackpad) a Stack icon to display a short-cut menu of options you can choose to customize the way a Stack folder appears on the Dock (as a Stack or Folder) and how its contents are displayed when you click it, as shown in Figure 5-11.

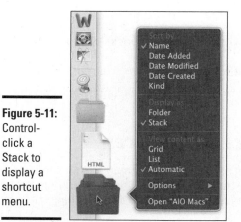

Figure 5-11:
Control-click a Stack to display a shortcut menu.

Rearranging icons on the Dock

After you place app, file, and folder icons on the Dock, you may want to rearrange their order. How you rearrange your Dock is up to you! To rearrange icons on the Dock, click the icon that you want to move, drag the mouse (or your finger on the trackpad) sideways (or up and down) to move the icon to its new position, and then release the mouse or trackpad button.

You notice that while you move an icon, its neighbors move to the side to show you where the icon will appear when you let go of the mouse button. Neat effect, right?

You can rearrange icons on the Dock how you want, but one icon you can't move or remove is the Finder icon, which won't budge no matter how hard you try to drag it from its Number One position on the Dock.

Removing icons from the Dock

Right from the get-go, you might see icons on the Dock for apps that you rarely use. Or, you might think having the Launchpad icon on the Dock is redundant because opening the Launchpad is a quick operation. Rather than let those icons take up precious Dock real estate, get rid of them and make room for the icons of apps and files you use frequently. It's like keeping salt and pepper on the counter and the mustard seed in the cupboard. You have two ways of removing an icon from the Dock:

✦ Click the icon that you want to remove from the Dock, drag it away from the Dock over to the edge of the screen, and then release the mouse button. Your unwanted application icon disappears in an animated puff of smoke.

✦ Control-click the app or file icon and choose Options⇨Remove from Dock from the shortcut menu. (This doesn't work for folders or stacks.)

Note: Removing an icon from the Dock doesn't remove or delete the actual file. To remove apps, see the "Uninstalling Applications" section, later in this chapter.

Here are two things you can't do with icons on the Dock:

✦ You can never remove the Finder and Trash icons from the Dock.

✦ You can't remove an app icon from the Dock if the app is still running.

Organizing Multiple Desktops with Spaces

Spaces multiplies your Mac's single display into as many as 16 separate virtual screens, or Desktops. The main purpose of Spaces is to help organize multiple applications running at the same time. Rather than cram multiple application windows on a single screen (Desktop), Spaces lets you store multiple applications in separate Desktops. One Desktop might contain only Internet applications, such as Safari and Mail, whereas a second Desktop might contain only Microsoft Word and the Mac's built-in Dictionary application. Each Desktop can have its own desktop picture and a customized Dock.

If one application has multiple windows open, you can store each application window on a separate Desktop. For example, if you have a word processor and open a personal letter and a business letter, you could store the personal letter's window on one Desktop and the business letter's window on a second Desktop.

You manage each Space individually, but you can see all of them and move windows from one Space to another in Mission Control.

Creating Desktops

Your Mac comes with one Desktop, also called a Desktop Space or Space, plus the Dashboard (see Book I, Chapter 2). You can see both by opening Mission Control, which is where you create additional Desktops. Apps in full-screen view, which you activate by clicking the full-screen button in the upper right corner, act as a Space, too. To create a Desktop, follow these steps:

1. **Open Mission Control by using one of these methods:**

    -   Press F3.

    -   Click the Mission Control icon on the Dock, which resides next to the Finder icon and looks like a miniature screen with three open windows.

    -   Press Control+Shift+↑.

    -   Swipe up on the trackpad with three or four fingers.

2. **Move the pointer to the upper-right corner until you see a plus sign.**

    If you have the Dock on the right, the plus sign will be in the upper-left corner.

3. **Click or tap the plus sign.**

    A new Desktop Space appears with the name Desktop 2. Subsequent desktops will be named Desktop 3, Desktop 4, and so on up to Desktop 16, as shown in Figure 5-12.

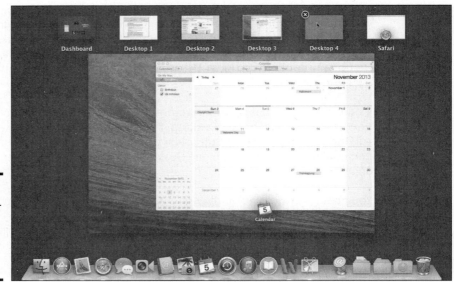

Figure 5-12:
Create additional desktops from Mission Control.

You can give each Desktop Space a personal desktop image and Dock. Open Mission Control and click the Desktop you want to work in. Then do the following:

✦ **Set the picture for that Desktop.** Go to ⌘➪System Preferences➪Desktop and Screensaver, as explained in Book I, Chapter 6.

✦ **Choose which icons you want on the Dock for that Desktop.** Click and hold an icon on the Dock and choose Options➪This Desktop (to use the icon only on this Desktop), All Desktops (to use the icon on every Desktop), or None (to not use this icon on the Dock in any Space).

Switching Desktops

Apps used in full-screen mode are treated as Desktop Spaces. When you create multiple Desktops and/or use applications in full-screen mode, you want to be able to move from one Space to another. To move from one Desktop Space to another, you can do the following:

✦ **Use the trackpad.** Swipe left or right with three or four fingers to move from one Desktop to another.

✦ **Use Mission Control.** Enter Mission Control and click the Desktop you want.

✦ **Switch between Desktops.** Hold the Control key and press the left- or right-arrow keys.

✦ **Switch to the first Desktop.** Press Control+1.

Moving app windows to different Desktops

When you run an app, it appears on the Desktop you're working in. For example, if you're on Desktop 1 and you run the Safari web browser, Safari appears on Desktop 1. Unless you choose the All Desktops option from the Safari icon on the Dock or turn off the related option in Mission Control preferences (see the next section), when you try to open Safari on another Desktop, you are sent back to Desktop 1. You can choose the All Desktops option, or you can move an app's window from one Desktop to another, so that the window appears where you want, by doing one of the following:

✦ **Move the window via Mission Control.** Go to Mission Control and click the Desktop that has the window you want to move. That Desktop is now active. Go to Mission Control again and drag the window from the active Desktop, which appears in the center of the screen, to the thumbnail (among those across the top of the screen) of the Desktop where you want to move the window.

✦ **Control-click and choose the Desktop from the menu.** Go to Mission Control and click the Desktop where you want the window to be. On the Dock, control-click the app that correlates to the app of the window you want to move, and then choose Options➪Assign to This Desktop. The window moves. For example, say you have a Word document window open on Desktop 3, and you want to move it to Desktop 6. Click Desktop 6 and then control-click the Word icon on the Dock. Choose Options➪Assign to This Desktop, as shown in Figure 5-13.

Figure 5-13: Use the Options for each app icon on the Dock to move windows from Desktop to Desktop.

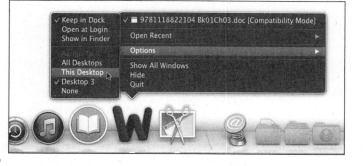

✦ **Drag the window to the desired Desktop.** From the Desktop, click the title bar of the window you want to move and drag to the far left or right edge of the screen until it shifts to the neighboring Desktop. Release the mouse or trackpad button or keep going until you reach the Desktop you want to move the window to.

Setting Mission Control preferences

Mission Control lets you choose some of the ways you view and interact with it. Choose ⌘⇨System Preferences and click the Mission Control icon, or Control-click System Preferences on the Dock and choose Mission Control (see Figure 5-14).

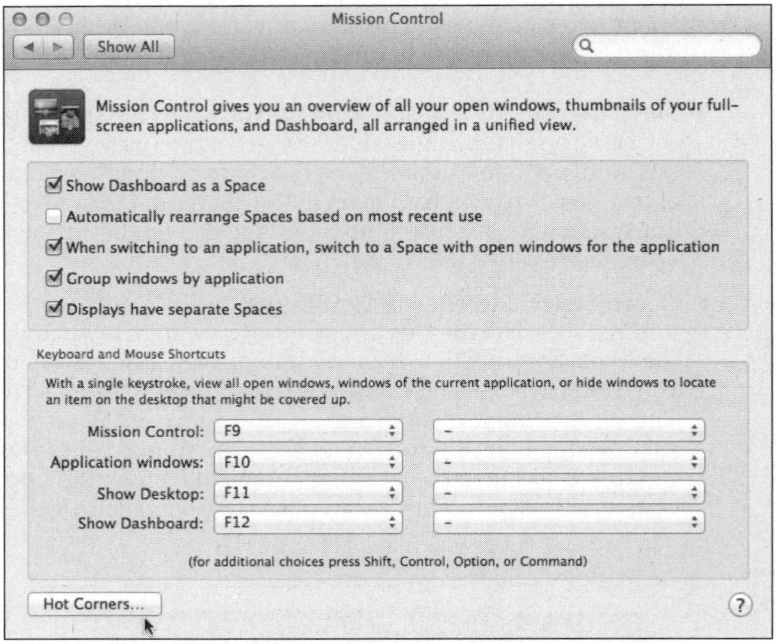

Figure 5-14:
Set Mission
Control
preferences.

Select the check boxes next to the features you want to activate:

✦ **Show Dashboard as a Space:** Shows Dashboard in Mission Control. When de-selected the Dashboard widgets appear on the desktop. Refer to Book I, Chapter 2 to learn more about Dashboard.

✦ **Automatically Rearrange Spaces Based on Most Recent Use:** Moves your Desktop Spaces around so the most frequently used are first. If you're a creature of habit and like to find things where you put them, leave this check box deselected.

✦ **When Switching to an Application, Switch to a Space with Open Windows for the Application:** When you open an app, your Desktop scrolls automatically to the Desktop that has a window open and uses that app. If this option is deselected, when you click an app on a Desktop, it opens on that Desktop even if the app is already open on another Desktop. And, just clicking the app icon on the Dock moves you from one window on a Desktop to another window of the same app on another Desktop.

✦ **Group Windows by Application:** When you have multiple windows of multiple apps open and go to Mission Control, the windows are grouped by app.

✦ **Displays Have Separate Spaces:** If you use multiple displays, this option lets you have different Spaces for each display.

In the Keyboard and Mouse Shortcuts section of the Mission Control preferences dialog, you can use the pop-up menus to set keyboard (left column) or mouse command (right column) shortcuts to access Mission Control, to see Application Windows, to Show Desktop, and to Show Dashboard.

Click the Hot Corners button to assign one of the screen's four corners to Mission Control. Open the pop-up menu next to the corner you want to assign to Mission Control, and choose it from the menu. When you move the pointer to that corner, Mission Control opens. You can also assign other tasks to the remaining three corners.

Acquiring New Apps

As we mention in Book I, Chapter 1, optical disc drives are practically obsolete, which means you put files on your computer with different means, sometimes in the form of a flash drive — or, more often than not, by downloading. The same goes for apps, with Apple in the lead by offering the OS X 10.9 Mavericks software only online as a free download from the App Store. In addition to the OS software, you also find a huge selection of apps in the App Store, but the App Store isn't the only game in town. Search the web to find other apps, which we break down into three types: commercial, shareware, and freeware/open source. The following list spells out how they differ:

✦ **Commercial:** These are the apps that you buy. You can still find some software applications in pretty boxes in an electronics superstore, but most companies sell the same commercial applications through the App Store or on their own websites — and if your Mac doesn't have an optical disc drive and you didn't buy an external one, that's the way you'll want to acquire software.

Many commercial applications downloaded from that company's website offer a trial version that you can download and use for a limited time, such as 30 days. After your trial period is over, the application will either stop working or run with many features turned off. If you pay for the software, the publisher will send you a registration key that converts the trial application into a fully functional version. To find trial versions of applications, just visit the websites of different software publishers.

✦ **Shareware:** Usually, *shareware* applications have limited functionality, are time-limited trial versions, or are fully functional applications written by individuals or small companies. The idea is for you to try out the application. If you like it, you're then supposed to pay for it.

✦ **Freeware:** *Freeware* applications, many of which you find in the App Store, are typically simple utilities or games although some commercial companies distribute freeware applications to promote their other products. Sometimes companies offer a freeware version of an application and then sell a more advanced version of that same application. As the name implies, freeware applications are available for you to copy and use at no cost. *Donationware* is a term for a freeware application whose creator welcomes donations to help the developer cover the cost of maintaining and developing new versions of the application.

A variation of freeware applications is *open source.* Like freeware applications, open source applications can be copied and used without paying for them. The main difference is that open source applications let you modify the application yourself if you know the specific application programming language that the application is written in.

Table 5-1 lists some popular open source applications and their commercial equivalents.

Table 5-1	Popular Open Source Applications	
Open Source Application	*Purpose*	*Commercial Equivalent*
NeoOffice www.neooffice.org	Office suite containing word processing, spreadsheet, presentation, drawing, and database applications	Microsoft Office or iWork
OpenOffice.org www.openoffice.org	Office suite containing word processing, spreadsheet, presentation, drawing, and database applications	Microsoft Office or iWork
AbiWord www.abisource.com	Word processor	Microsoft Word or Pages
Firefox www.mozilla.com	Web browser	Safari
Thunderbird www.mozilla.com	E-mail application	Mail
Tux Paint www.tuxpaint.org	Children's painting application	Broderbund Kid Pix
ClamXav www.clamxav.com	Antivirus scanner	Norton AntiVirus
Celtx www.celtx.com	Screenplay word processor (online only)	Final Draft

Besides being free, many open source applications offer additional features that their commercial rivals lack.

For example, the Safari web browser comes free with every Mac, but many websites are designed to work only when viewed through Internet Explorer or Firefox. If you use Safari, you might not be able to view some websites correctly, so you might want to switch to Firefox (or at least keep Firefox on your hard drive) in case you run across a website that Safari can't open.

To find an overwhelming number of shareware, freeware, and open source apps for your Mac, visit the following sites:

+ **Open Source Mac:** www.opensourcemac.org
+ **CNET Download.com:** http://download.cnet.com/mac/
+ **MacForge:** www.macforge.net
+ **Tucows:** www.tucows.com
+ **MacUpdate:** (www.macupdate.com)

The following sections tell you how to acquire and install apps from the App Store. If you'd like to know more about acquiring and installing apps from other sources, see the upcoming "Installing Applications" section.

Shopping in the App Store

If you have a new Mac or upgraded to OS X 10.9 Mavericks, the App Store app is on your Mac, and you find the App Store icon on the Dock.

If you've exhausted the freeware, shareware, and open source sources or prefer a more traditional online shopping experience, the App Store is a great place to look for new apps to add to your Mac. In this section and the next section, we give you a quick rundown of how the store is organized and how to purchase and download applications from the App Store.

Like the iTunes Store, the App Store is an online service, so you need to have an active Internet connection to browse, purchase, and/or download applications.

Although you can browse the App Store as much as you want, and download free apps, you need an Apple ID. You can use your iTunes Apple ID or an iCloud Apple ID, or set up a new Apple ID by choosing Store➪Create Account and following the onscreen instructions, which basically ask for an e-mail address and a password. You need a credit card or iTunes Store card to purchase apps.

When you first click the App Store from the Dock or Launchpad, a window opens similar to the one shown in Figure 5-15.

Figure 5-15:
The App
Store
window.

The opening window of the App Store is updated (at least) weekly. Across the top, you see rotating banner ads. Below the banner ads, the left three-quarters of the window contains more app ads, divided in three sections (you have to scroll down the window to see the sections you don't see in Figure 5-15):

✦ **Best New Apps:** These are a mix of the latest arrivals to the App Store and those that have generated user and shopper interest.

✦ **Best New Games:** These games are being downloaded a lot. This category could change occasionally to highlight another category, such as Best New Business Apps.

✦ **Previous Editors' Choices:** These apps are the ones that Apple staff liked the most in recent weeks.

The column running down the right side of the window is divided into sections, too:

✦ **Quick Links:** Tap any of these items to Sign In, go to your Account (if you have credit, it appears to the right of this button), redeem iTunes or Apple gift cards, and go to the Support page.

✦ **Categories:** Next down the list is a pop-up menu that lets you choose the category of apps you want to view. This helps narrow your choices when you're looking for a specific type of app. Choose from categories such as

Business, Games, Medical, Lifestyle, and Utilities. The Categories pop-up menu is followed by apps or groups of apps that Apple thinks will be useful to get you started, such as OS X Mavericks, Apple Apps, Editors' Choice, and Great Free Apps.

✦ **Top Paid/Top Free:** These two lists show the top ten most downloaded apps divided by paid apps and free apps. Click See All to view an expanded list of the top paid and free apps for the week.

✦ **Top Grossing:** These apps are the apps that made the most money, so you usually find higher-priced apps in this category unless there's a low-priced app that's sold thousands of copies or a free app that's sold in-app purchases. Again, click See All to view an expanded list.

You can change the view of the opening window by clicking the tabs across the top. Featured is the opening that we described at the beginning. The others are

✦ **Top Charts:** Shows an expanded view of Top Paid, Top Free, and Top Grossing.

✦ **Categories:** Displays a grid with an icon for each category and the names of three apps in that category. This can help you choose which category best suits your shopping needs.

✦ **Purchases:** When you sign in to your account, you can see all the apps you purchased using this Apple ID in your App Store history.

You can consult your past purchases by clicking the Purchases tab at the top of the window or by choosing Store⇨Purchases. You can also download purchases again to another Mac or if you accidentally delete it — when you buy something in the App Store, it's yours forever.

✦ **Updates:** Lets you know whether any apps you purchased in the App Store have updates available. If you do have updates, just click the Download Updates button, and the updates are downloaded immediately and applied to the apps on Launchpad. You also see a list of apps that were recently updated.

As you browse through top ten lists and ads, when you find an app that interests you, click the app name or icon to open the app information screen. You'll see the name and description for the current version of the app, and also these items, as shown in Figure 5-16:

✦ **Buy/Free button:** Click to download the application.

✦ **Pop-up menu:** Click the triangle next to the price/free button for a pop-up menu that has options to tell a friend about it or copy the link, which you can then paste somewhere else, such as an e-mail. You also have options to share on Twitter, on Facebook, or in Messages.

✦ **Links to developers' website and app-specific support website:** Click either to go to those websites.

✦ **Information box:** Check here for the category, release date and version number, the language used, an age-appropriate rating, and system requirements.

✦ **More By:** Lists other apps by the same developer.

✦ **Sample images:** In the center of the window, you see several sample images that you can click through to see what the app looks like and get an idea of how it works.

✦ **Reviews:** (Not shown in the figure.) Users can give a simple star rating, from zero to five, or write a review. Reviews help you decide if the item is worth downloading or purchasing.

Figure 5-16: The information screen helps you decide whether to download an app.

At the bottom, lists show items by the same software developers and other items purchased by people who bought that particular item.

Downloading apps from the App Store

When you find something you like, click the price or the Free button, and it's downloaded to the Applications folder and you find the icon on Launchpad on your Mac. Some apps have "in-app purchases," which you buy while using the app. Examples of in-app purchases are additional functions or features, chips for online poker games, or music for instrument apps.

You can switch over to Launchpad to see the app downloading or updating and pause or resume the download if you want. Some app downloads and updates are so quick that you won't have any reason to pause and resume. If, however, the power goes out or your Wi-Fi router dies in the middle of the download, when you're back up and running, clicking the app on Launchpad will resume the download at the point it was interrupted. Choose Store⇨Check for Unfinished Downloads to prompt completion.

Of course, when you buy, you have to pay from your Apple ID account. This happens two ways:

✦ **Credit Card:** Enter your credit card information into your Apple ID account. If you didn't enter credit card information when you created an Apple ID, you can do so by choosing Store⇨View My Account and clicking Edit to the right of Payment Information. A window opens where you can choose your preferred payment method, such as credit card or PayPal, and type in the necessary information: account number, expiration date, billing address, and so on.

✦ **Redeem:** You can redeem Apple or iTunes gift cards, gift certificates, or allowances. Click Redeem in the Quick Links section of the Featured, Top Charts, or Categories window. Type in the code from the card or certificate, or click Use Camera and follow the onscreen instructions to capture the code with your Mac's FaceTime camera (if it has one). The amount of the card or certificate is added to your account and appears to the left of the Apple ID account tab.

However you choose to pay for your app purchases, a prompt asks for your password to confirm your intent before making the final purchase.

If you ever have a problem with a purchase, choose Store⇨View My Account. Click Purchase History and then click the Report a Problem button next to the item that isn't working.

When your app cup runneth over

Because you have a physical limit on the amount of software and data you can install on your Mac, you have three choices when you're running out of room for your apps:

✔ **More hard drive space:** You can get another hard drive (an external drive or a larger internal drive) to store big byte-consuming files, such as videos or graphic-heavy documents, so you can keep installing more apps.

✔ **Cloud storage:** You can move things off your computer to a remote storage site such as iCloud, Dropbox, or SugarSync.

✔ **Purging:** You can delete some apps or files that you don't want or need, which makes room for more apps that you do want and need.

If you want to limit the types of downloads that others who use your Mac can make, you can set up separate user accounts and apply Parental Controls. If you apply Parental Controls to your account, those controls apply to you as well. See Book III, Chapter 2.

Installing Applications

Although purchasing, downloading, and installing apps from the App Store is one-stop shopping, if you purchase a packaged application from a store or download an app from a website, you have to install it yourself, and we tell you how to do that here.

The most common place to install software is inside the Applications folder, so you should specify that folder when installing software. You can store an app icon in any folder on your hard drive, but you should store apps in the Applications folder. That way, if you need to find that app again, you just have to look on Launchpad or in the Applications folder instead of trying to remember where else you stored it. Some apps store their app icon inside the Applications folder plain as day, but others hide their application icons within another folder.

An application icon actually represents a folder containing multiple files. Hiding these details from you and letting you treat a folder of files as a single application icon ensures that you can't accidentally delete or move a single crucial file that the entire application needs to work. For the technically curious, you can see the hidden files tucked inside an application by Control-clicking the application icon and choosing Show Package Contents from the shortcut menu. You're free to look around, but we strongly advise that you don't delete, move, modify, or rename any of the files you see because doing so might render the application inoperable.

Installing an app from the web

Although you can buy software in a box from your local computer store, it's becoming far more common to buy software directly from the web. Not only does this save the publisher the time and expense of packaging an application in a fancy box and shipping it to a store, but it also gives you the latest version of the software to use right away.

When you download an application off the Internet, the application usually arrives as a DMG (disc image) file. *Safari,* the OS X default web browser, stores all downloaded files in a special Downloads folder in your Home folder (unless you direct it to your Mac's Desktop or another folder of your choosing). A Downloads folder icon also appears right next to the Trash icon on the Dock. (If you're using a different browser, such as Firefox, you might need to define where it stores downloaded files.)

Distributing software as a DMG file is the most common way to compress files for sending via the Internet. A DMG file essentially copies the contents of an entire folder and smashes it into a single file. You can always identify a DMG file because its icon appears with a hard drive icon, and the name includes the three-letter .dmg extension.

After you have a DMG file on your Mac, you're set to install the software inside it. Just follow these steps:

1. **Control-click the Downloads folder on the Dock to see the contents, and then click the app's DMG file.**

   The DMG file displays a device icon on the Desktop and displays a Finder window that contains either an installer or the application icon and an alias for your Applications folder, as shown in Figure 5-17.

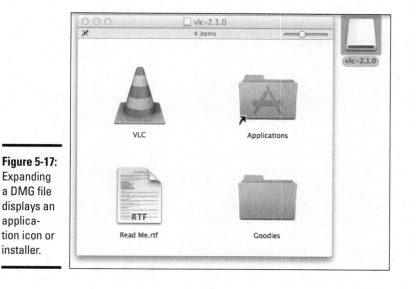

Figure 5-17:
Expanding a DMG file displays an application icon or installer.

2. **Drag the app icon to the Applications folder icon.**

   Doing so installs the application in your Applications folder.

   If a dialog appears, enter your Mac administrator account name and password; this is the user name you created for your Mac, not your Apple ID.

3. **Control-click the DMG device icon on the Desktop and choose Eject.**

When you open a DMG file, it creates a *device icon,* a space that acts like a separate storage device — specifically, a temporary disk from which you can copy files. After you install an application from the DMG file, you eject the DMG device icon just to clear it out of the way. (Leaving it on your Desktop won't hurt anything.)

After you install an application on your Mac, you can always find it again by looking in the folder where you stored it, which is usually the Applications folder. At this point, you might want to add the application icon to the Dock or place an alias icon on the Desktop (see the earlier section, "Working with Dock Aliases"). As long as it's in the Applications folder, you find it on Launchpad, too.

The first time you run a newly installed application, a dialog like that in Figure 5-18 might pop up, reminding you to be sure the application came from a secure source, informing you that the application was downloaded from the Internet, and/or you are running the application for the first time. To run the application, click Open. These dialogs pop up as a way of trying to protect you from malicious applications that might try to install and run themselves automatically. If you didn't try to run an application and see this dialog pop up, click Cancel.

Figure 5-18:
A dialog
alerts you
when you
first run an
app.

Installing an application from a CD/DVD

Software bought from a store will probably come on a CD/DVD, or there may be a code that you use to download the app from the developer's website. When you insert the CD/DVD into an optical disc drive connected to your Mac, you might see nothing but a single app icon, along with several other files labeled Read Me or Documentation.

Other times, you might insert a CD/DVD and see an icon labeled Install. When you see an Install icon, you need to run this installation application to install the app on your hard drive.

When installing software, your Mac usually asks for your admin name and password — the one you set up when you created your user account the first time you set up your Mac, which is different than the password you created if you created an Apple ID. (For more on user accounts, see Book III, Chapter 2.)

Requiring your password to install an app keeps unauthorized people (such as your kids) from installing apps that you might not want on your Mac, or applications you want to approve of before allowing another user to install on your Mac. (We write about Parental Controls and password protection in Book III, Chapter 2.)

Dragging an application icon off the CD/DVD

If you insert an app's installation CD/DVD into your computer and just see an app icon, you install the app by dragging the app icon into your Applications folder. To do this, follow these steps:

1. **Insert the software CD/DVD into your Mac (or an external drive if you have a new Mac sans optical disc drive).**

   A window appears, showing the contents of the CD/DVD.

2. **Click the Finder icon in the Dock and then choose File⇨New Finder Window (or press ⌘+N).**

   A second Finder window appears, ready to do your bidding.

3. **Move the CD/DVD window and the Finder so they appear side by side.**

4. **Click and drag the app icon displayed in the CD/DVD window to the Applications folder in the Finder Sidebar.**

   Doing so copies the app icon from the CD/DVD to the Applications folder.

Running an installer application

Instead of displaying an app icon, a CD/DVD might display an Install icon. The installer is simply a special app designed to copy an app from the CD/DVD and place it in your Applications folder, as well as copying other companion files to the appropriate folders on your Mac.

To install software by using an installer app on a CD/DVD, follow these steps:

1. **Insert the software CD/DVD into your Mac and look for an icon labeled Install in the window that appears showing the contents of the CD/DVD.**

   The Install icon typically looks like a cardboard box with its top opened up.

2. **Double-click this Install icon and click Continue on the dialog that appears asking whether you really want to continue installing.**

3. **Follow the onscreen instructions.**

   If you have multiple hard drives, the installation app might ask where to install the app. (Generally, you should choose your Mac's built-in hard drive unless you have a reason to store the app elsewhere.) Right before the app installs, you're asked for your password.

Updating Applications and System Software

Developers are constantly working to improve and enhance their applications or fix bugs that have been pointed out by disgruntled customers. Likewise, when Apple offers an operating system upgrade, developers must update their apps to make them compatible with the new OS. You want to keep your applications up to date to take advantage of these improvements.

You see a badge on the App Store icon on the Dock to let you know when any applications you downloaded from the App Store have been updated. Simply click the Update button on the App Store, and the updates will be downloaded.

You can set up your Mac to automatically check for updates to OS X and apps downloaded from the App Store by choosing ⌘➪System Preferences, and then choosing App Store. As shown in Figure 5-19, select the Automatically Check for Updates check box, which tells your Mac to check for updates without any further instructions from you. You can also leave the box deselected and check manually by choosing ⌘➪Software Update, but we suggest that you let your Mac worry about checking for updates for you. Select the other options that you want to activate:

+ **Download Newly Available Updates in the Background:** Updates will be downloaded but not installed until you manually do so.

+ **Install App Updates:** Updates will be automatically installed as soon as they are downloaded.

+ **Install System Data Files and Security Updates:** These types of software will be downloaded and installed automatically.

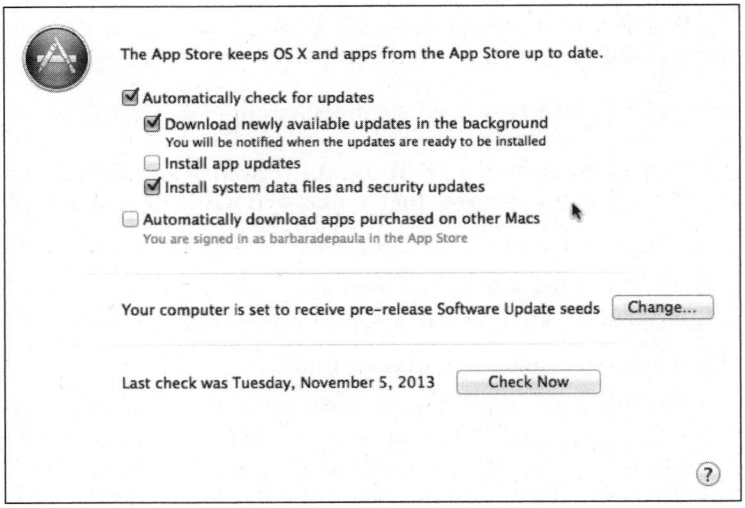

Figure 5-19:
Let
Software
Update
check auto-
matically
for system
software
updates.

The App Store keeps OS X and apps from the App Store up to date.

☑ Automatically check for updates
　☑ Download newly available updates in the background
　　　You will be notified when the updates are ready to be installed
　☐ Install app updates
　☑ Install system data files and security updates

☐ Automatically download apps purchased on other Macs
　　You are signed in as barbaradepaula in the App Store

Your computer is set to receive pre-release Software Update seeds ⟨ Change... ⟩

Last check was Tuesday, November 5, 2013 ⟨ Check Now ⟩

If you have more than one Mac, you may want to select the last check box so that when you download purchases on one Mac, they are automatically downloaded on other Macs that are signed in to the same Apple ID account in the App Store.

When new software is available, a message arrives, as shown in Figure 5-20.

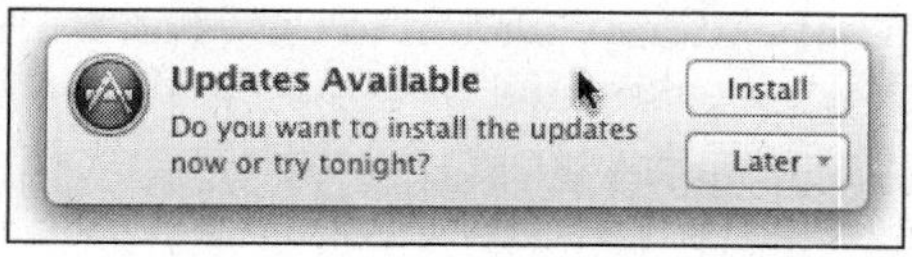

Figure 5-20:
Your Mac
tells you
when
updates are
available.

> **Updates Available**
> Do you want to install the updates
> now or try tonight?
>
> Install
>
> Later ▾

Apps you download or install from other sources may also have automatic software updates available. You usually find them either under the Help menu or in the Application menu. If you're having problems with a particular application, go to the developer's website to check for an update. If you're having a problem, others folks probably are, too, and an update can often be the remedy.

Uninstalling Applications

If you no longer use or need an app or if it's an old version that is no longer compatible with your OS X version, you can always remove it from your hard drive. By uninstalling an app, you can free up space on your hard drive.

Apps downloaded from the App Store remain available in your purchase records even if you remove them from your hard drive. You can download them again in the future, as long they are still available.

Don't uninstall an app from a non–App Store source unless you have the original disc or the website from which you downloaded it offers a lifetime download policy. Otherwise, you may have to purchase the app again.

Uninstalling an app can involve three parts, which we explain in detail:

✦ **Uninstalling the app**

✦ **Deleting app icons/alias icons**

✦ **Deleting app settings**

If an app you want to uninstall comes with an uninstaller application, double-click it to uninstall your app instead of dragging it to the Trash. However, the next few sections give you a more detailed look at what's involved when you uninstall an app by dragging it to the Trash.

Uninstalling an app

Uninstalling a Mac app is typically as simple as dragging and dropping its app icon into the Trash. If you've purchased an app in the App Store, you can remove it via Launchpad, and we explain how later in this section. Apps that are pre-installed on your Mac are extremely difficult to remove; we suggest that you don't try to remove them.

To uninstall an app, follow these steps:

1. **Make sure that the application you want to uninstall isn't running. If it is running, shut it down by choosing the Quit command (⌘+Q).**

2. **Click the Finder icon on the Dock.**

   The Finder appears.

3. **Click the Applications folder in the Finder Sidebar to display the apps installed on your Mac, and then click the app icon or folder that you want to uninstall.**

4. **Choose File⇨Move to Trash.**

   Alternatively, you can also drag the app icon or folder to the Trash icon on the Dock, or press ⌘+Delete to move the app icon or folder to the Trash.

   In some cases, you might be prompted for your password when you move an application file to the Trash. If so, type in your password and then click OK or press Return.

   The Trash icon displays an image showing the Trash filled with crumpled papers.

   Before emptying the Trash, make sure that you want to permanently delete any other apps or documents you might have dragged into the Trash. After you empty the Trash, any files contained therein are deleted from your hard drive forever.

5. **Choose Finder⇨Empty Trash.**

   Alternatively, you can Control-click the Trash icon and choose Empty Trash, or press ⌘+Shift+Delete to empty the Trash.

   Adiós, application!

From Launchpad, you can delete apps purchased in the App Store. Press the Option key, and all the icons begin to wiggle and jiggle. Those you can delete from the Launchpad have an "x" on the upper left of the icon. Click the "x." A confirmation dialog asks whether you really want to delete the app. Click Delete if you do; click Cancel if you don't.

Removing app alias icons from the Dock and Desktop

After you uninstall an app, it's also wise to remove all Dock or alias icons because those icons will no longer work. To remove an app icon from the Dock, click the app icon that you want to remove, drag the icon up and away from the Dock, and then release the mouse button. Your chosen app disappears in a puff of animated smoke.

If you created multiple alias icons of an app, click the Finder icon to open a new Finder window, click in the Spotlight text box, and then type the name of the app you uninstalled followed by the word *alias,* such as **PowerPoint alias** or **Stickies alias**. The Finder will display the location of the specified alias icons. Hold down the ⌘ key, click each alias icon you want to delete, and then press ⌘+Delete to move them to the Trash. *Au revoir!*

Deleting the alias is *not* the same as deleting the app because the alias is only a pointer to the app, not the app itself. Removing the alias is useful to eliminate clutter but won't eliminate the app.

Removing user setting files

Almost every app creates special user setting files that contain custom settings and preferences for the app, such as the default font used to type text when you use the app or your choice of toolbar icons displayed by the app. When you uninstall an app by dragging it to the Trash, the app's user setting files remain on your computer.

The more unnecessary files you have cluttering your hard drive, the slower your Mac might perform because it needs to keep track of these unused files even though it isn't using them anymore. To keep your Mac in optimum condition, you should delete the user setting files of apps you uninstall from your computer. You can do that manually or you can buy an app to do it for you automatically. We explain both ways.

Manually removing user setting files

Manually removing user setting files requires deleting individual files or entire folders from your Mac's hard drive. This process isn't difficult although it can be tedious.

If you feel squeamish about deleting files that you don't understand, don't delete them without an expert's help. If you delete the wrong files, you could mess up the way your Mac works.

Many apps store their user setting files in one or both of two folders: the Application Support folder and the Preferences folder. To find these two folders, click anywhere on the Desktop, then hold down the Option key, and choose Go⇨Library. Look inside the Application Support and Preferences folders and click any icons or folders bearing the name of the app you uninstalled; drag them to the Trash and choose File⇨Empty Trash (or press ⌘+Shift+Delete).

Automatically removing user setting files

Because manually deleting user setting and preference files might seem
scary and intimidating, you may prefer to remove these files automatically.
To do so, you have to buy and install a special uninstaller app. When you run
an uninstaller app, you tell it which app you want to uninstall. Then the uninstaller app identifies all the files used by that application.

Popular uninstaller apps include

✦ **AppZapper:** www.appzapper.com

✦ **Spring Cleaning:** http://my.smithmicro.com/

✦ **Uninstaller:** http://macmagna.free.fr

Chapter 6: Changing How Your Mac Looks, Sounds, and Feels

In This Chapter

✔ Changing the Desktop and screen saver

✔ Setting the date and time

✔ Adjusting alert sounds

✔ Making your Mac more accessible

✔ Talking to your Mac

✔ Listening to your Mac

The desktop user interface functions the same way regardless of the Mac model you have, but that doesn't mean they all have to look and feel the same. To personalize your Mac, you can change the way it looks and even how it behaves.

By customizing your Mac — and adjusting how it works to make things easier on your eyes, ears, or hands — you can stamp it with your personality and truly turn your Mac into a personal computer that feels like it's working with you and for you, rather than against you.

When you have a choice about how an application or function looks or responds, Preferences are where you go to specify your choices. There are two places to find preferences on your Mac:

✦ ⌘⇨System Preferences gathers all the preferences settings for your Mac operating system in one place. This is where you set up your Mac's appearance, connect to a network or printer, and establish the type of notifications you want to receive for incoming information such as an e-mail message or Facebook update. You read about keyboard, mouse, and trackpad preferences in Book I, Chapter 2.

✦ *Application menu*⇨Preferences lets you set application-specific preferences. In Book I, Chapter 4, you can read all about Finder preferences.

In this chapter, we discuss the System Preferences. We show you how to customize your Desktop image, set up screen savers, and adjust the screen resolution. We explain how to use Notification Center and how to set the date and time. At the end of the chapter, we introduce you to the *Universal Access functions,* which are the preferences you can choose to make working with your Mac easier if you have trouble with your vision, hearing, or movement.

If you share your Mac with other people and set up separate user accounts as explained in Book III, Chapter 2, some system preference settings, such as Network or Date & Time apply to all users, while others, such as Desktop, as well as app preferences, are specific to the user who sets them.

Changing the Desktop and Screen Saver

The Desktop fills the screen in the absence of any application windows, and the Screen Saver is the image that runs across the screen when your Mac sleeps. You set preferences for both from the same window, and we explain how to do that in the next few sections.

Choosing a Desktop image

Generally, the Desktop displays a decorative background image. Your Mac comes with a variety of images, but you can display any image, such as a photo captured with a digital camera or a favorite picture you downloaded from the Internet. To choose your Desktop image, follow these steps:

1. **Control-click anywhere on the Desktop and choose Change Desktop Background.**

   Or you can click the System Preferences icon on the Dock and choose Desktop & Screen Saver from the pop-up menu.

   The Desktop & Screen Saver preferences pane appears, as shown in Figure 6-1.

2. **Click one of the following to choose the Desktop image (click the disclosure triangle next to Apple if you don't see the first two choices):**

   - *Desktop Pictures* to browse images bundled with OS X.

   - *Solid Colors* to pick a solid background color.

   - *iPhoto* to choose a photo from your iPhoto library (learn all about iPhoto in Book IV, Chapter 3).

   - *Folders* for access to photos stored in your Pictures folder.

3. **Choose the image or color that you want to adorn your Desktop.**

   - *Set your favorite color (say, poppy red) as your Desktop.* Click Solid Colors, and then click the Custom Color button under the color chips. When the color picker opens, click to choose your preferred shade and then click the Close button.

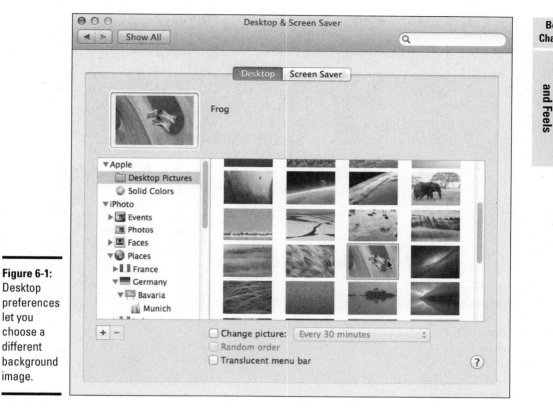

Figure 6-1:
Desktop
preferences
let you
choose a
different
background
image.

- *Use a personal photo.* Click the disclosure triangle next to iPhoto and then scroll through the choices. Click Photos to see all the photos you have stored in iPhoto or click successive disclosure triangles, such as Events or Places, to narrow your choices to specific albums in those sections.

- *Use something from your Pictures folder (inside Folders).* These are images downloaded from a website or from a digital camera. Images stored in separate folders inside the Pictures folder will not initially be visible; click the folder to see images inside.

- *Click the Add (+) button in the lower-left corner and use the dialog that appears to navigate to the folder that contains the image you want to use.*

4. **Click the image or color you want to use.**

5. **(Optional) If you choose an image from iPhoto or the Pictures folder, a pop-up menu appears above the images, as shown in Figure 6-2. Choose how you want the image to appear on the Desktop from the following options:**

- *Fill Screen:* Expands or contracts the image to fill the screen but might cut off edges, depending on the aspect ratio of the original image.

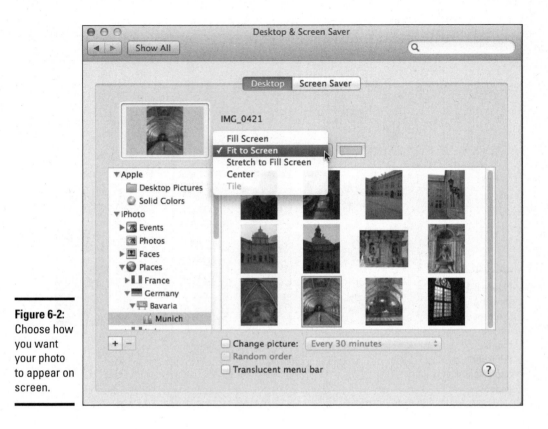

Figure 6-2:
Choose how
you want
your photo
to appear on
screen.

- *Fit to Screen:* Expands the image to fill most of the screen but might leave edges uncovered, depending on the aspect ratio of the original image. Click the menu to the right of this option to choose the color of the border that may surround the image.

- *Stretch to Fill Screen:* Stretches a picture to fill the entire screen, which might distort the image similar to the way a carnival mirror can.

- *Center:* Places the image in the middle of the screen at its original size, and might leave edges uncovered or crop out portions, depending on the image's dimensions. Click the menu to the right of this option to choose the color of the border that may surround the image.

- *Tile:* Duplicates the image in rows and columns to fill the screen. Some images are too large to tile and the option will be grayed (as in the figure). Resize your selected image in iPhoto or another photo manipulation app or choose a smaller image.

6. **(Optional) Select the check boxes next to the options at the bottom of the window to do the following:**

    • *Change Picture:* Click the pop-up menu to tell your Mac to change the Desktop background picture based on a time interval, when you log in to your Mac, or when you wake it from Sleep mode. Choices come from the category where you select the Desktop image, so if you choose an image from the Desktop Pictures folder, the selection is limited to those images. Choose a photo from an iPhoto Event, and the selection changes between photos in that album.

    • *Random Order:* Randomly changes the Desktop background image. Left unselected, the images change in the order they appear in the source.

    • *Translucent Menu Bar:* Gives your Mac's menu bar a translucent "see through" effect.

7. **Click the Close button in the upper-left corner of the window. (Or choose System Preferences⇨Quit or press ⌘+Q to close the System Preferences window.)**

Customizing the Screen Saver

A *screen saver* is an animated image that appears onscreen after a fixed period when your Mac doesn't detect any keyboard, trackpad, or mouse activity. When selecting a screen saver, you can choose an image to display and the amount of time to wait before the screen saver starts.

For an eco-friendlier alternative to using the screen saver, check out the Energy Saver setting described in the section about putting your Mac in Sleep mode in Book I, Chapter 1.

To choose a screen saver, follow these steps:

1. **Choose ⇨System Preferences from the Finder menu and click the Desktop & Screen Saver icon.**

    Or you can Control-click the System Preferences icon on the Dock and choose Desktop & Screen Saver from the pop-up menu.

    The Desktop & Screen Saver preferences pane appears.

2. **Click the Screen Saver tab to display the Screen Saver preferences pane, and then click one of the screen saver styles shown in the left column.**

    The preview pane shows you what your screen saver will look like. Scroll through the pane on the left side to see the different screen saver styles, which have slightly different options:

The first 14 styles all use photos and display a Source menu under the preview image. Open the pop-up Source menu and select from Recent iPhoto Events, Default Collections (which include some fabulous National Geographic photos), a folder, or photo library, as shown in Figure 6-3. Check Shuffle Slide Order (hidden under the pop-up menu in the figure) to randomly display the images in the chosen event, collection, or library.

- *Flurry, Arabesque, and Shell* display luminous, colorful, moving shapes.

- *Message* displays something you write, such as an inspirational phrase or reminder.

- *iTunes Artwork* displays a collage of album covers from your iTunes collection.

- *Word of the Day* shows a word selected from the dictionary you choose in the Screen Saver Options menu.

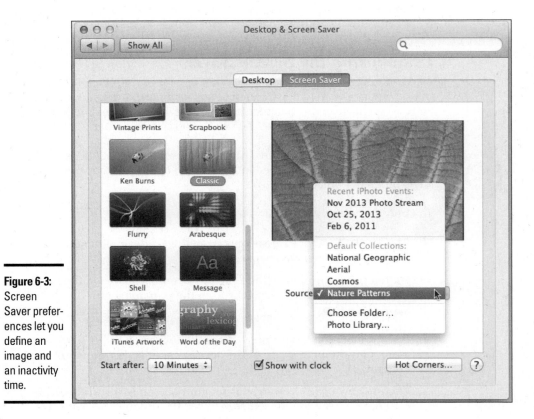

Figure 6-3:
Screen Saver preferences let you define an image and an inactivity time.

- *Random* picks a different screen saver image every time the screen saver starts. After your randomly chosen screen saver starts, that same animated image appears until you press a key to turn off the screen saver.

   You can download third-party screen savers from the App Store. When installed on your Mac, they appear after the Random choice.

3. **Open the Start After pop-up menu to specify an amount of time to wait before your screen saver starts.**

   Opting for a short amount of time can mean the screen saver starts while you're reading a web page or document, so you might have to experiment a bit to find the best time for you.

4. **(Optional) Select the Show with Clock check box to display the time with your screen saver.**

5. **(Optional) Enable Hot Corners.**

   a. *Click the Hot Corners button (refer to Figure 6-3).*

   b. *Open one (or each) of the four pop-up menus and choose a command that your Mac will carry out when you move your pointer to the specified corner, as shown in Figure 6-4.*

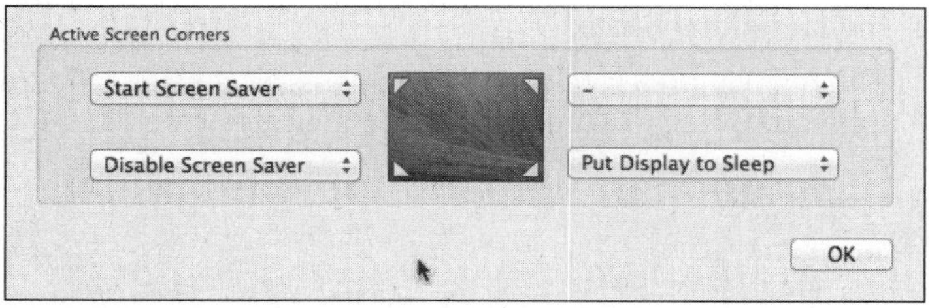

Figure 6-4:
Each pop-up menu defines a function for a hot corner.

Active Screen Corners

Start Screen Saver ⬍		– ⬍
Disable Screen Saver ⬍		Put Display to Sleep ⬍
		OK

Two common uses for a hot corner are to turn on the screen saver, or to put your Mac's display to sleep to save energy.

You can define multiple hot corners to do the same task, such as defining the two top corners to start the screen saver and the two bottom corners to put the display to sleep.

   c. *Click OK to close the Active Screen Corners dialog.*

6. **Click the Close button in the Desktop & Screen Saver preferences pane.**

You can customize the layout of the System Preferences window by choosing View➪Customize. Clear the check box next to the items you don't want to see. You still see all the preferences in the Show All menu and the System Preferences menu accessed from the Dock.

Changing the Display and Appearance

Because you'll be staring at your Mac's screen every time you use it, you might want to modify how the screen displays information. Some changes you can make include changing the Desktop size (resolution), or selecting another color scheme of your various menus, windows, and dialogs. The next sections show you how.

Changing the screen resolution

The display defines the screen resolution, measured in *pixels,* which are the dots that make up an image. The higher the display resolution, the more pixels you have and the sharper the image — but everything on your screen might appear smaller.

Selecting your Mac display's highest resolution generally puts your Mac's best face forward, so to speak, when it comes to making everything look sharp and correct on your screen.

To change the screen resolution, follow these steps:

1. **Choose System Preferences and click the Displays icon, or click the System Preferences icon on the Dock and choose Displays from the menu that opens.**

    The Display preferences window opens, as shown in Figure 6-5. Depending on your Mac model, the image may be different.

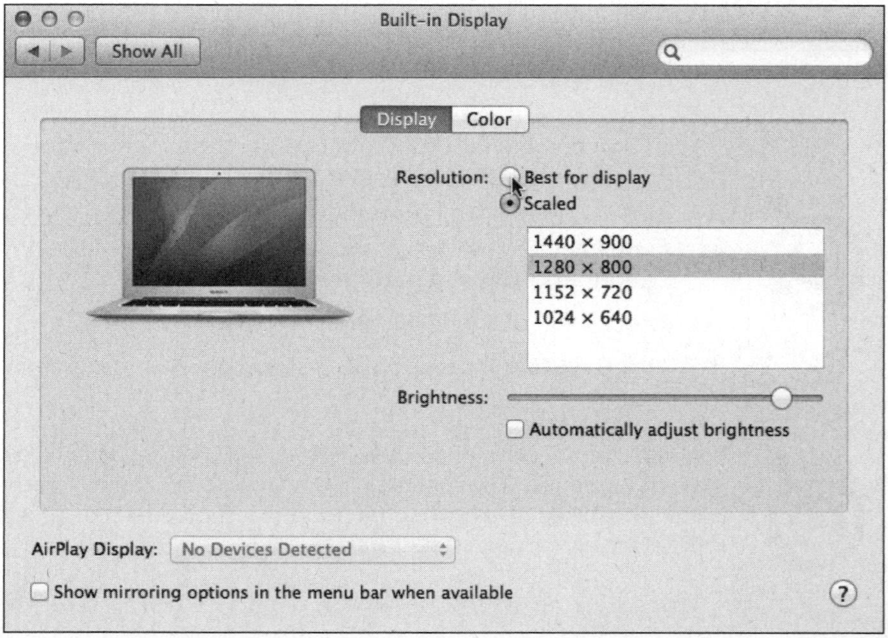

Figure 6-5:
Choose a different screen resolution.

2. **Click the Display tab (if it isn't already selected) and select one of the following:**

   - *Best for Display:* Sets the resolution to an optimal size.

   - *Scaled:* Choose a specific resolution to make objects appear larger on screen or to make them smaller so you see more objects on screen.

3. **Choose a resolution.**

   Your Mac immediately changes the resolution so you can see how it looks. If you don't like the resolution, try again until you find one that's easy on your eyes.

4. **Adjust brightness.**

   Move the brightness slider to adjust the luminosity of your screen or select the Automatically Adjust Brightness check box to have your Mac adjust the screen brightness based on the ambient light.

5. **(Optional) Adjust color.**

   Click the Color tab, click the Calibrate button, and then follow the steps that appear to tweak the way your Mac displays colors; click the Done button when you reach the final step to return to the Display preferences pane.

6. **Click the Close button in the System Preferences window when you're happy with the screen resolution.**

The AirPlay Display menu will be active when external monitors or displays are available on the same network. A Detect Displays button appears when you hold down the Option key. Do this and then click the display in the pop-up menu to connect your Mac to it. After you connect another display, hold down the Option key while clicking Scaled to adjust the resolution for that display.

Changing the color of the user interface

Another way to change the appearance of the screen is to modify the colors used in windows, menus, and dialogs. To change the color of these user interface items, follow these steps:

1. **Choose ⌘⇨System Preferences and click the General icon.**

   Or, Control-click the System Preferences icon on the Dock and choose General from the menu that opens.

   The General preferences pane appears, as shown in Figure 6-6.

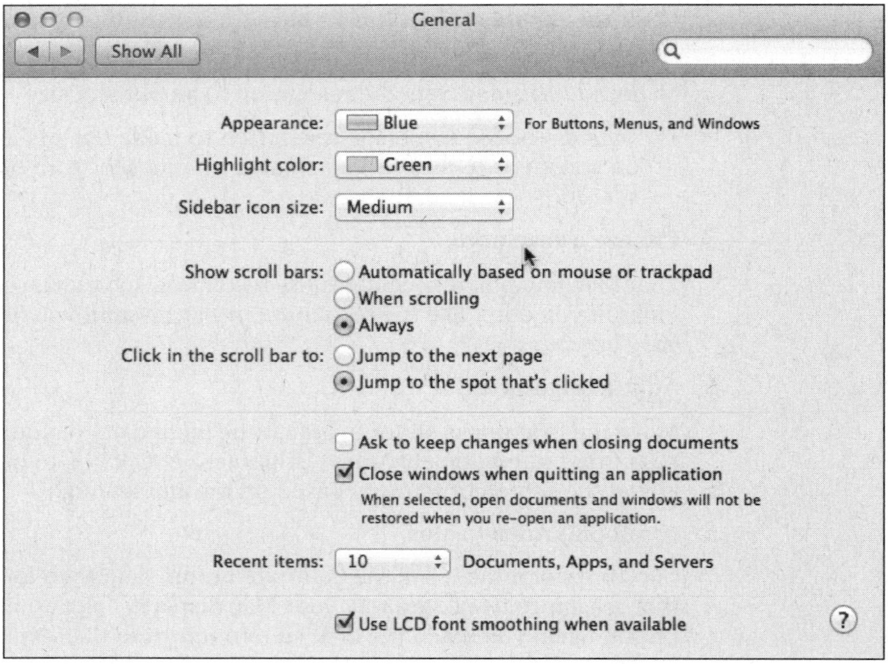

Figure 6-6:
Use
Appearance
preferences
to modify
colors.

2. **From the Appearance and Highlight Color pop-up menus, choose your color variations.**

   The Appearance pop-up menu defines the colors that normally show up on windows, buttons, and so on. The Highlight Color pop-up menu defines the color of items that you select.

3. **From the Sidebar Icon Size pop-up menu, choose the size of icons in the Sidebar of the Finder window.**

4. **Select the radio buttons and check boxes to adjust how the scroll bars work.**

   These changes will be seen only in applications that support these features. Choose from these three:

   • *Automatically Based on Mouse or Trackpad* reveals scroll bars only when the window is smaller than its contents. This gives you a visual clue that there's more than meets the eye.

   • *When Scrolling* uses a shadowy black oblong that appears only when you are hovering over the right edge of the window if you're scrolling up and down, or on the bottom of the window if you're scrolling left to right. The advantage is that scroll bars don't take up precious window real estate.

- *Always* puts right side and bottom scroll bars on your windows whether you need them or not.

  And then choose one of these:

- *Jump to the Next Page* moves your document up or down one page when you click above or below the scroller in the scroll bar.

- *Jump to the Spot That's Clicked* takes you to the position in your document more or less in relation to where you clicked the scroll bar. If you click near the bottom of the scroll bar, the window jumps toward the end of the document.

5. **(Recommended) Select the Close Windows When Quitting an Application check box to only open the app (and no windows) when you restart an app.**

   By default, when you quit an app, windows that are open in that app close. Then, when you restart the app, the windows that were open when you quit automatically reopen.

6. **From the Recent Items pop-up menu, choose how many items you want to appear in the Recent Items list under the menu.**

7. **Select the LCD Font Smoothing When Available check box to make fonts appear smoother.**

8. **Click the Close button to close the General preferences pane.**

To move quickly between one System Preferences pane and another, click and hold the Show All button to reveal a pop-up menu that lists all the preferences items in alphabetical order.

Changing the Date and Time

Keeping track of time might seem trivial, but knowing the right time is important. That way, your Mac can determine when you created or modified a particular file, and keep track of appointments you've made through applications, such as Calendar.

Of course, keeping track of time is useless if you don't set the right time to begin with. To set the proper date and time, follow these steps:

1. **Choose System Preferences and click the Date & Time icon.**

   Or, Control-click the System Preferences icon on the Dock and choose Date & Time from the menu that opens.

   The Date & Time preferences pane appears, as shown in Figure 6-7.

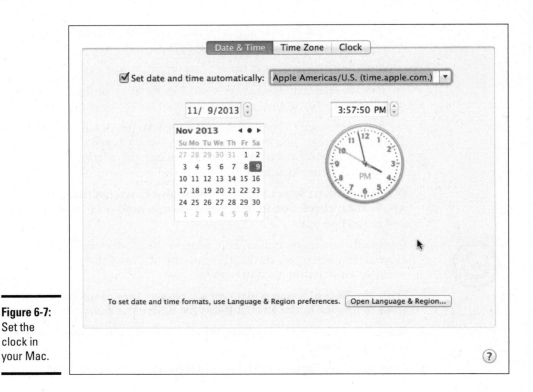

Figure 6-7:
Set the
clock in
your Mac.

2. **Select (or deselect) the Set Date & Time Automatically check box.**

   If you select this check box, open the drop-down list to choose a location.

   This feature works only if you're connected to the Internet. If you aren't connected to the Internet, click the calendar to pick a date and click the clock to set the time.

   You can use a different method to set the time. Instead of selecting the Set Date & Time Automatically check box, click the Time Zone tab at the top of the window and then click near your home city on the map.

   You can also click in the Closest City field and begin typing the name of the city nearest you in the same time zone, or click the drop-down list and select the city nearest you.

3. **(Optional) Click Set Time Zone Automatically Using Current Location if you want the clock to change automatically when you travel to a different time zone.**

   This feature works when you have an Internet connection and have turned on Location Services.

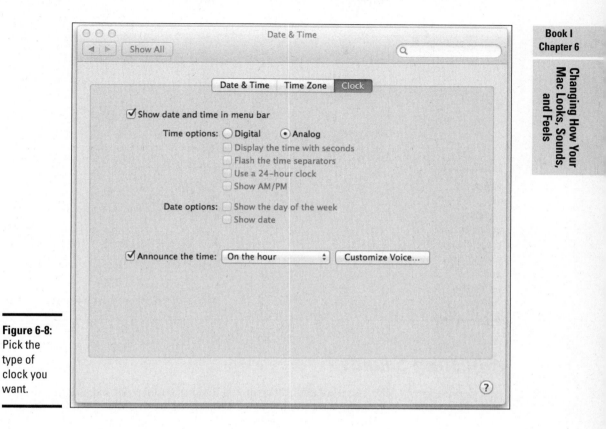

Figure 6-8:
Pick the
type of
clock you
want.

4. **Click the Clock tab and select (or deselect) the Show Date and Time in Menu Bar check box, as shown in Figure 6-8.**

   If selected, this displays the time on the right side of the menu bar. After you make your selection, you can select the other options to change the appearance of the clock, such as choosing between a digital or an analog clock, and choosing whether to show the day of the week (Digital option only).

5. **Select (or deselect) the Announce the Time check box if you want your Mac to recite the time by using a synthesized voice every hour, half-hour, or quarter hour.**

   The associated pop-up menu lets you specify when announcements are made; click the Customize Voice button to choose what kind of voice is used and how quickly and loudly it utters the time.

6. **Click the Close button to close the Date & Time preferences pane.**

   Click the Language & Region icon in System Preferences to change the time and date format based on your language and region. Use the pop-up menus as shown in Figure 6-9.

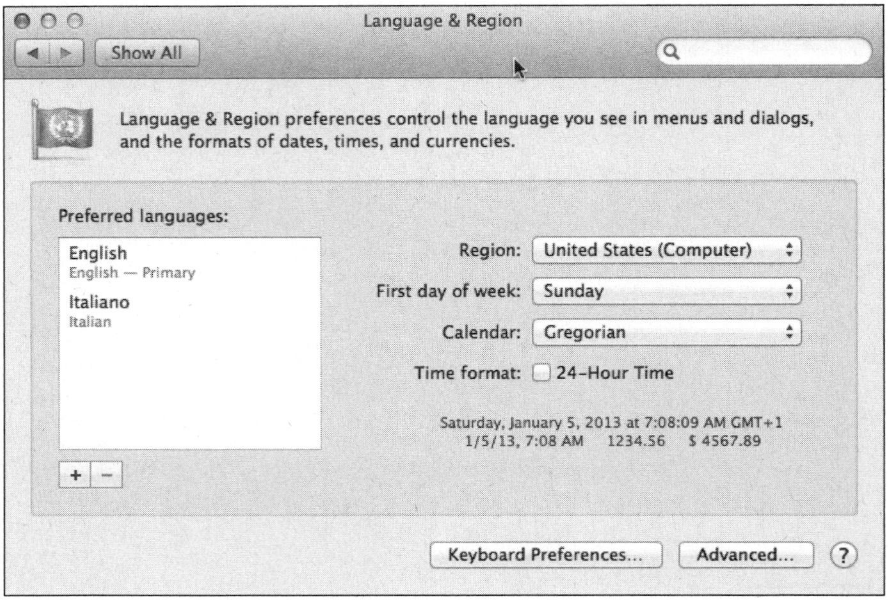

Figure 6-9:
The
Language
& Region
preferences
provide time
and date
formatting
options.

Adjusting Sounds

Every Mac can play sound through speakers (built-in or external) or head-phones, from making the simplest beeping noise to playing audio CDs like a stereo. Three primary ways to modify the sound on your Mac involve volume, balance, and input/output devices.

✦ **Volume:** Simply means how loud your Mac plays sound by default. Many applications, such as iTunes, also let you adjust the volume, so you can set the default system volume and then adjust the volume within each application, relative to the system volume, as well.

✦ **Balance:** Defines how sound plays through the right and left stereo speakers. By adjusting the balance, you can make sound louder coming from one speaker and weaker coming from the other.

✦ **Input/output:** Depending on your equipment, you might have multiple input and output devices — speakers and headphones as two distinct output devices, for example. By defining which input and output device to use, you can define which one to use by default.

To modify the way your Mac accepts and plays sound, follow these steps:

1. **Choose ⌘➪System Preferences and click the Sound icon.**

Or, Control-click the System Preferences icon on the Dock and choose Sound from the menu that opens.

The Sound preferences pane appears, as shown in Figure 6-10.

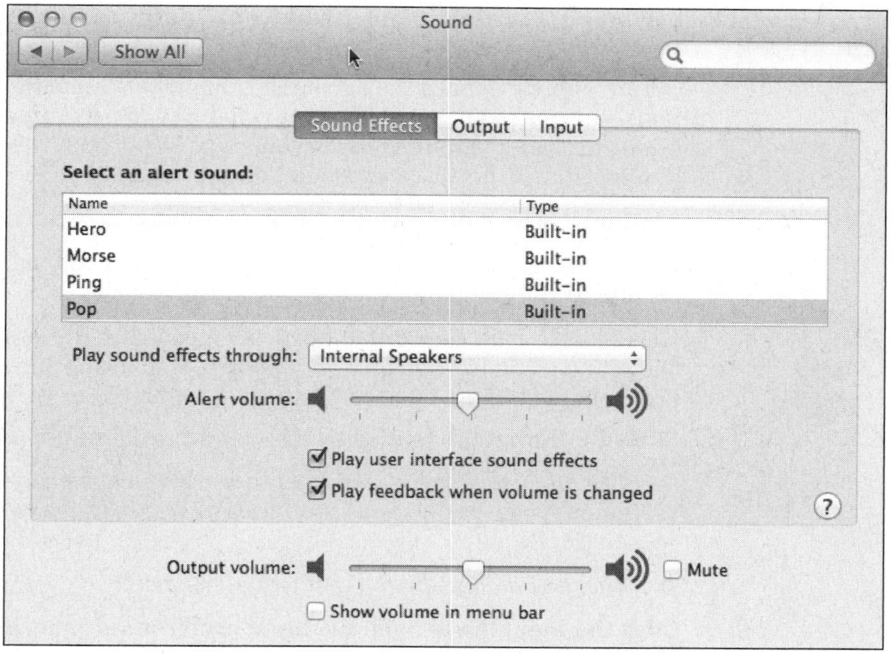

Figure 6-10:
Use Sound
Effects
preferences
to define
audible
alerts.

2. **Choose a sound effect.**

   Click the Sound Effects tab (if it isn't already selected) and scroll
   through the list to choose the sound your Mac will play when it needs
   your attention, such as when you're quitting an application without
   saving a document.

   In the last section of this chapter, "Setting up Dictation & Speech," we
   tell you how to hear a spoken warning when your Mac wants to alert you
   to something.

3. **(Optional) From the Play Sound Effects Through pop-up menu, choose
   whether your Mac plays sounds through its built-in Internal Speakers
   or through another set of speakers you might have connected to your
   Mac.**

4. **(Optional) Drag the Alert Volume slider to the desired location to set
   how loudly (or softly) your Mac will play the alert when it needs to get
   your attention.**

5. **(Optional) Select (or deselect) either of the following check boxes:**

   • *Play User Interface Sound Effects:* Lets you hear such sounds as the
     crinkling of paper when you empty the Trash or a whooshing sound
     if you remove an icon from the Dock.

   • *Play Feedback When Volume Is Changed:* Beeps to match the sound
     level while you increase or decrease the volume.

6. **(Optional) Drag the Output Volume slider or press the volume-up and volume-down keys on the keyboard.**

   Output volume defines the maximum volume that sound-playing applications can emit, so if you set Output volume at 75 percent and then play a song in iTunes with the iTunes volume at 50 percent, the song plays at 37.5 percent of the Mac's maximum output capacity.

7. **(Optional) Select (or deselect) the Show Volume in Menu Bar check box.**

   When selected, you can see and adjust your Mac's volume from the *menulet* in the menu bar.

   Menulets are mini menus that open when you click the icons on the right end of the menu bar and give you quick access to specific System Preferences settings, such as Network, Time and Date, or Sound.

8. **Click the Output tab to display the Output preferences pane.**

   • *Click the output device* you want to use if you have another output option connected to your Mac, such as headphones or external speakers.

   • *Drag the Balance slider* to adjust the balance.

9. **Click the Input tab to open the Input preferences pane, as shown in Figure 6-11.**

10. **Click the input device you want your Mac to use to receive sound.**

    For instance, you might choose a built-in microphone or the line in port as your input device.

    Your Mac may not have a Line In port — the MacBook Air does not.

    • *Drag the Input Volume slider* to adjust the default input volume.

    • *Select (or deselect) the Use Ambient Noise Reduction check box* to eliminate background noise.

      Select this option if you're recording with the built-in microphone or someone you're having a FaceTime or Messages voice or video chat with complains that they can't hear you clearly.

11. **Click the Close button to close the Sound preferences pane when you finish making adjustments.**

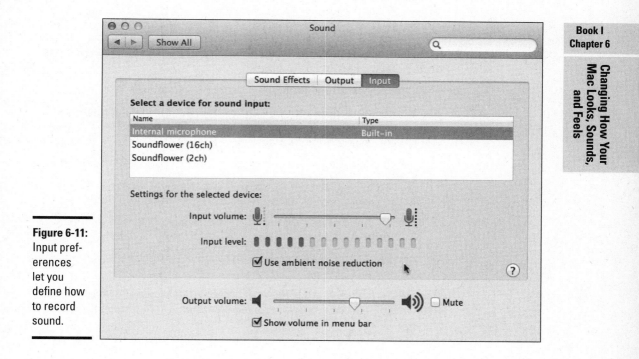

Figure 6-11:
Input pref-
erences
let you
define how
to record
sound.

Noticing Notifications

When your Mac wants to tell you or remind you of something, it alerts you. It used to be those alerts were few and far between, but today with bells ringing for birthdays, beeps telling you you've got mail, and banners flying across the screen with the latest tweet, your Mac can sound like a noisy traffic jam. From Notification Center, you can define how you want to be alerted by any app that might generate an alert. It's managed in System Preferences, and you view the Notification Center by clicking its button at the far right end of the status bar.

There are several types of notifications, which you can turn on or off for each app that notifies you of something:

✦ **Banners** are mini-windows that appear for a few seconds in the upper-right corner of your screen and then disappear automatically.

✦ **Alerts** are banners that remain onscreen until you click an action button, such as Reply or Later.

✦ **Badges** appear on the app icons on the Dock and Launchpad as white numbers in red circles, indicate the number of items that need attending, which can be messages to be read or apps to update.

✦ **Sounds** play to let you know an app or your Mac needs your attention.

✦ **Notification Center** holds items from various apps, such as a Facebook post by someone you follow or upcoming calendar events.

To personalize how you receive notifications, do the following:

1. **Choose ⬛️⇨System Preferences or click the System Preferences icon on the Dock or from Launchpad.**

2. **Click the Notifications icon.**

   The Notifications preferences window opens, as shown in Figure 6-12. Your preferences window may look slightly different based on the apps you have installed on your Mac.

   The list that runs down the left of the window is divided into different sections:

   • *Do Not Disturb* is its own section, and we explain it in Step 7.

   • *In Notification Center* lists all the apps that you choose to appear in the Notification Center.

   • *Not In Notification Center* lists apps you choose not to appear in the Notification Center.

   Words immediately under the app name indicate whether badges, banners, alerts, and/or sounds are used to notify you of information from the app.

Figure 6-12:
Manage how your Mac alerts you.

3. **In the list that runs down the left of the Notifications preferences window, click an app and choose how you want to be notified when that app has information for you.**

   Figure 6-12 shows the notification options for Calendar.

   - *Click the Calendar alert style you prefer.* Choose None, Banners, or Alerts.

   - *Select the check boxes for the type of notifications you want.* If you select Show in Notification Center, use the pop-up menu to choose how many recent notifications you want to see.

     If you deselect Show in Notification Center, the app will be moved to the Not in Notification Center section of the list on the left of the preferences window.

4. **Click the next app in the list and set your preferences.**

   Some apps have additional choices:

   - *Twitter:* Click the Notifications button of the Twitter alert preferences to choose to show notifications for Direct Messages and specify from whom you want to see mentions and replies.

   - *Mail and Messages:* Choose if and when you want to see a message preview.

5. **Open the Sort Notification Center pop-up menu and choose to sort**

   - *By Time,* which displays items in Notification Center in the chronological order in which they arrived

   - *Manually,* in which case you click and drag the apps in the preferences list into the order you wish them to appear in the Notification Center

6. **(Optional) Click Share Buttons and then select the Show Share Buttons in Notification Center check box.**

   This will let you write and send Messages and post to Facebook, Twitter, and Facebook directly from the Notification Center.

7. **(Optional) Click Do Not Disturb, as shown in Figure 6-13, to schedule an interruption-free work or rest time.**

   When Do Not Disturb is on, you don't hear any alert sounds and notification banners remain hidden. Choose the features you want to use:

   - *Turn on Do Not Disturb:* Select this check box and then use the arrows to set the From and To times to schedule a daily fixed time of silence. Deselect the checkbox to deactivate scheduled Do Not Disturb time.

   - *When Mirroring to TVs and Projectors:* Selecting this check box prevents interruptions such as a banner that might come across the projection screen during your multi-million dollar deal presentation.

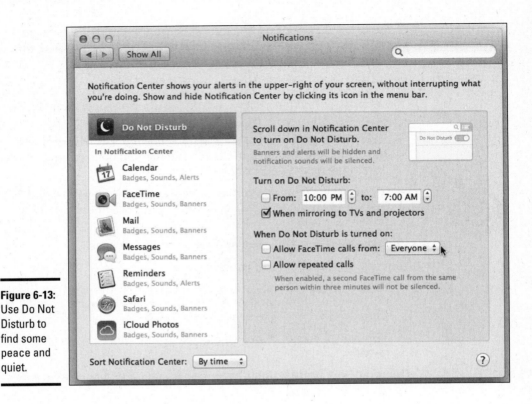

Figure 6-13:
Use Do Not
Disturb to
find some
peace and
quiet.

- *When Do Not Disturb Is Turned On:* Select the check boxes for the types of FaceTime calls you want to allow when Do Not Disturb is turned on. Choose Everyone or Favorites if you want to allow some or all FaceTime calls. Click Allow Repeated Calls if you want insistent callers to get through.

8. **Click the Close button to exit System Preferences.**

To see how your settings affect the Notification Center, click the Notification Center button, the right-most button of the menu bar. Its screen appears, as shown in Figure 6-14.

9. **Click the Share buttons at the top to write a Messages message (see Book II, Chapter 3) or post to your Facebook, Twitter, or LinkedIn account.**

You see buttons only for accounts to which you signed in in Internet Account preferences, as we explain in Book I, Chapter 3.

For Facebook or LinkedIn, open the pop-up menu to choose who you want to see your post.

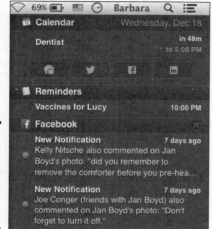

Figure 6-14:
See notifications from different apps in one place.

10. **(Optional) Click the Notifications Preferences button at the bottom-right corner to open the Notifications Preferences window and make changes.**

11. **Click the Desktop to close Notification Center.**

Using Your Mac's Accessibility Features

Not everyone has perfect eyesight, hearing, or eye-hand coordination. If you have trouble with your vision, hearing, or ability to use the keyboard, trackpad, or mouse (or all three), using a computer can be difficult. That's why every Mac comes with special Accessibility features that you can turn on and modify for your needs. These features fall under three categories — seeing, hearing, and interacting — all of which we introduce you to on the following pages. If you're interested in getting the most out of the Accessibility features, especially VoiceOver and Switch Control, we recommend that you read Apple's extensive instructions for all the Accessibility features on both the Help menu and online:

www.apple.com/support/accessibility/

Click the question mark button in the lower-right corner of any System Preferences pane to open help for that preference.

Mitigating vision limitations

Every Mac includes three options to help the visually impaired:

✦ **Display:** Inverts the color of the screen so you see white or light colored text on a dark background.

✦ **Zoom:** Sets up keyboard shortcuts so you can enlarge (zoom) the screen.

✦ **VoiceOver:** Allows your Mac to read text, e-mail, and even descriptions of the screen in a computer-generated voice. VoiceOver can speak more than 30 languages and analyzes text paragraph by paragraph, so the reading is more natural and, well, humanlike. You can set up preferences for specific activities: for example, reading headlines at a quicker speaking rate than the article itself. And there are special commands to make browsing web pages easier.

To modify the vision assistance features of your Mac, follow these steps:

1. **Choose ⌘⇨System Preferences and click the Accessibility icon.**

The Accessibility preferences pane, shown in Figure 6-15, opens.

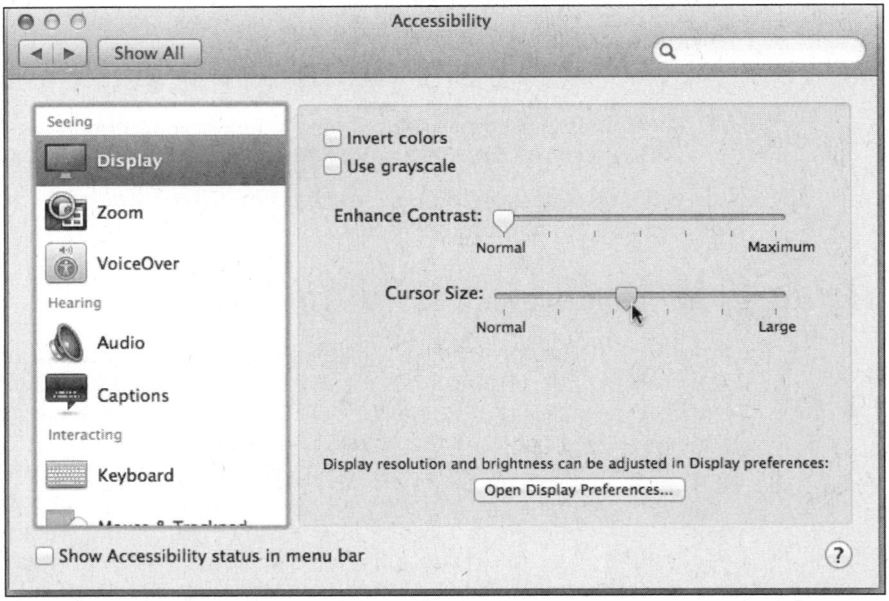

Figure 6-15:
Set options
for making
your Mac
easier to
use.

2. **Click the following tabs and select the options you want to activate:**

- *Display:* Select the Invert Colors check box to switch to display white text on a black screen or the Use Grayscale check box to eliminate all color and make your display look like the images in this book — black on white.

Use the sliders to change the contrast and cursor size. Although the Cursor Size slider is in the Seeing section, we find a larger cursor can also help if you have difficulty using the mouse or trackpad to insert the cursor in a precise position or click a specific item.

- *Zoom:* Select the options for how you want to zoom. Choose Use Keyboard Shortcuts to Zoom to use the commands listed and/or Use Scroll Gesture with Modifier Keys to Zoom to zoom by holding a modifier key while scrolling. Choose the Zoom Style from the pop-up menu to magnify the Fullscreen or a Picture-in-Picture. Click the More Options button to see additional choices for the selected Zoom Style. Figure 6-16 shows the Picture-in-Picture Zoom Style with a crosshair cursor style and the Window Position as Follow Mouse Cursor. Try the different options to see which one works best for you.

The zooming options can be particularly helpful when working with photo editing apps or when aligning several objects in a drawing or page layout app.

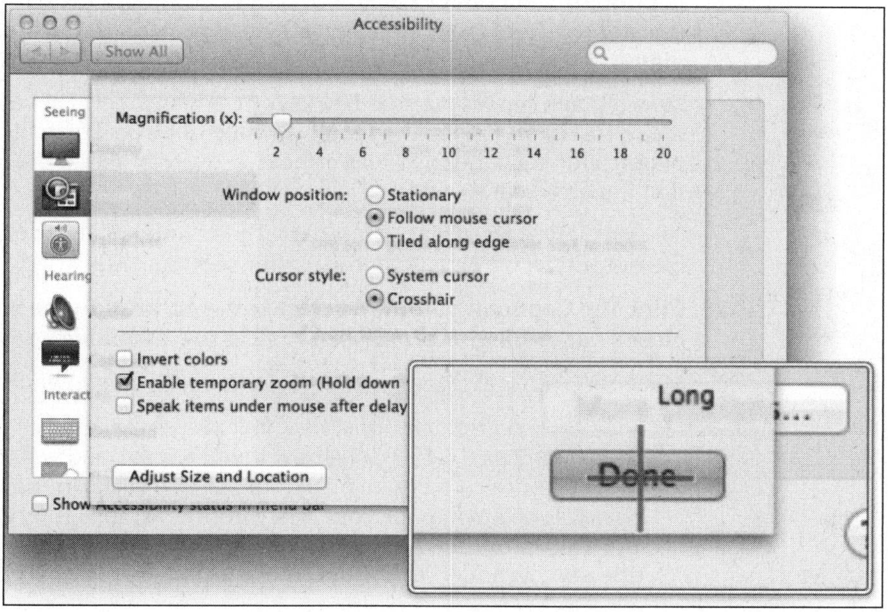

Figure 6-16:
Zooming options come in handy even if you have perfect vision.

- *VoiceOver:* Allows your Mac to describe what's onscreen and assist you in using the Macintosh menus. Click the Open VoiceOver Utility button to customize such options as how fast your Mac speaks and whether it speaks with a male or female synthesized voice. You find built-in support for many Braille tablets and verbosity settings, which allow you to specify how much information you want to receive about what's onscreen.

Click Show Accessibility Status in the Menu Bar to access an Accessibility menu that shows which features are activated.

3. **Click the Close button or press ⌘+Q to quit System Preferences or go on to the next section to set up other Accessibility functions.**

Compensating for hearing limitations

To adjust for hearing impairments, you can have your Mac flash the screen to catch your attention and set up subtitles and closed captioning to appear when those options are available. Follow these steps to manage these two Hearing options:

1. **Choose ⌘⇨System Preferences and click the Accessibility icon.**

2. **Click the Audio tab, and then select the Flash the Screen When an Alert Sound Occurs check box.**

3. **(Optional) Select the Play Stereo Audio as Mono check box to remove the stereo effect from music or other stereo-enabled sounds your Mac plays.**

Stereo plays separate audio tracks for each speaker. This effect mixes those tracks and plays the result through one speaker, which means that people who have hearing impairment in one ear get all the audio in the non-impaired ear.

Use the Sound Preferences to adjust the volume of alerts and other audible output, as we explain in the earlier section, "Adjusting Sounds."

4. **Click the Captions button to select how you want to see subtitles or closed captioning, when those services are available.**

Make the appropriate selections from the options shown in Figure 6-17.

- *Style for Subtitles and Captions:* Click one of the choices in the list, as shown in Figure 6-17, to see how it will appear and select it. Or click the plus button to create a custom subtitle style. In the window that opens, type a name for your new subtitle; choose the typeface, size, and color from the pop-up menus; and then click Done. The new subtitle style is added to the list.

- *Prefer Closed Captions and SDH (Synchronous Digital Hierarchy):* Select this check box if you want to see those types of captions rather than subtitles.

5. **Click the Close button or press ⌘+Q to quit System Preferences or go on to the next section to set up other Accessibility functions.**

If you're watching movies, TV shows, or other video in one of your Mac's media player applications (such as iTunes, QuickTime, or DVD Player), you may have closed caption options available, depending on the source of the video. Some apps have controls for subtitles and closed captioning within their menus.

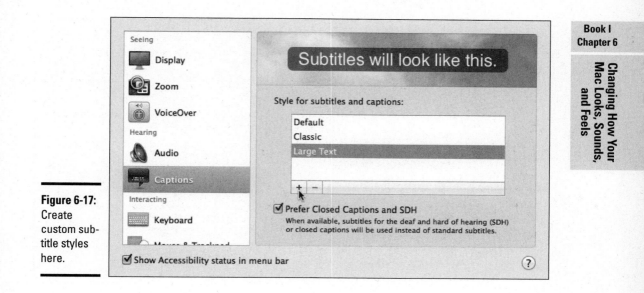

Figure 6-17:
Create
custom sub-
title styles
here.

Interacting with ease

If you have physical limitations or find eye-hand coordination challenging,
your Mac offers several options to improve your control of the user interface.
You find each of the following under the Interacting section of the Accessibility
preferences.

Easing keyboard limitations

If you have physical limitations using the keyboard, the Mac offers two solutions: Sticky Keys and Slow Keys. Sticky Keys can help you use keystroke
shortcuts, such as ⌘+P (Print), which usually require pressing two or more
keys at the same time. By turning on Sticky Keys, you can use keystroke
shortcuts by pressing one key at a time in sequence. Press the modifier key
first, such as the ⌘ key, and it "sticks" in place and waits until you press a
second key to complete the keystroke shortcut.

The Slow Keys feature slows the reaction time of the Mac every time you
press a key. Normally when you press a key, the Mac accepts it right away,
but Slow Keys can force a Mac to wait a long time before accepting the typed
key. That way, your Mac will ignore any accidental taps on the keyboard and
patiently wait until you hold down a key for a designated period before it
accepts it as valid.

To turn on Sticky Keys or Slow Keys, follow these steps:

1. **Choose ⬧System Preferences and click the Accessibility icon.**

2. **Click Keyboard in the Interacting section in the left pane of the
   window, as shown in Figure 6-18.**

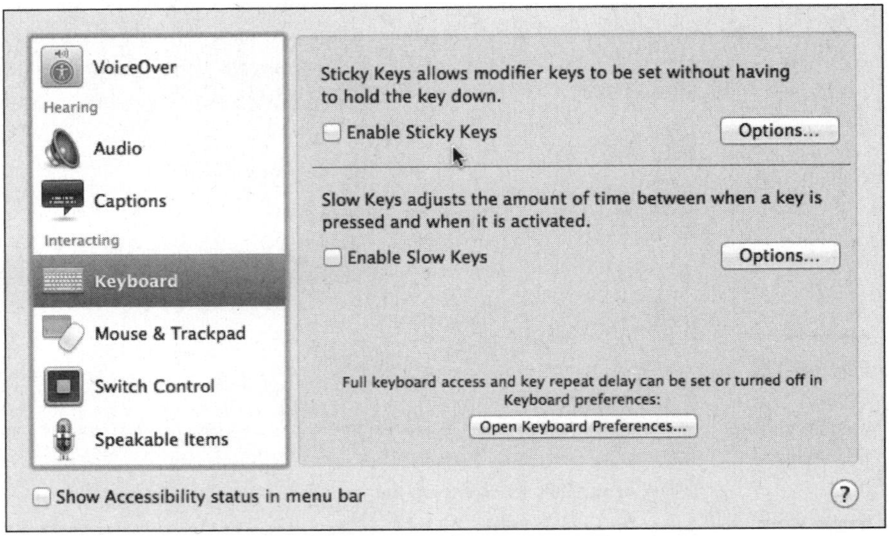

Figure 6-18: Keyboard preferences let you adjust keyboard behavior.

3. **(Optional) Select the Enable Sticky Keys check box and then click Options to select any additional options you want to activate.**

   When you enable Sticky Keys, you can press key combinations in a sequence instead of trying to hold down two or three keys at the same time. You can also make these adjustments here:

   - *Press the Shift Key Five Times to Toggle Sticky Keys:* You can turn the Sticky Keys feature on or off from the keyboard.

   - *Beep When a Modifier Key Is Set:* Alerts you when you press a so-called "modifier" key — a key such as Option or ⌘ — which is used in combination with another key to modify how that key works.

   - *Display Pressed Keys On Screen:* When activated, any modifier keys you press (such as the ⌘ or Option key) display onscreen in the corner you choose from the pop-up menu, so you can verify that you've pressed the right key.

4. **Click Done when you finish selecting your options.**

5. **(Optional) Select the Enable Slow Keys check box and then click its Options button.**

   When you enable Slow Keys, you can adjust the amount of time that passes from when you touch a key and when it's activated. Here are your choices:

   - *Use Click Key Sounds:* This option causes your Mac to make a clicking sound every time you press a key to give you audible feedback.

   - *Acceptance Delay:* Dragging this slider to the left lengthens the time it takes your Mac to recognize when you press and hold down a key; dragging the slider to the right shortens the time your Mac waits to recognize when you press and hold down a key.

6. **Press Done when you finish selecting your options.**

7. **Click the Close button or press ⌘+Q to quit System Preferences or go on to the next section to set up other Accessibility functions.**

Choosing mouse and trackpad options

If you have physical limitations using the mouse or trackpad, you can turn on the Mouse Keys feature, which lets you control the mouse through the numeric keys. Click the Accessibility icon in System Preferences and then click Mouse & Trackpad in the list on the left pane of the window (see Figure 6-19). Select the Enable Mouse Keys check box, which then activates the keys on the keyboard to function as shown in Table 6-1.

Table 6-1	Mouse Key Commands
Numeric Key	*What It Does*
9	Moves the pointer diagonally up to the right
8	Moves the pointer straight up
7	Moves the pointer diagonally up to the left
6 or o	Moves the pointer to the right
4 or u	Moves the pointer to the left
3 or l	Moves the pointer diagonally down to the right
2 or k	Moves the pointer down
1 or j	Moves the pointer diagonally down to the left
0	"Right-clicks" the right mouse button

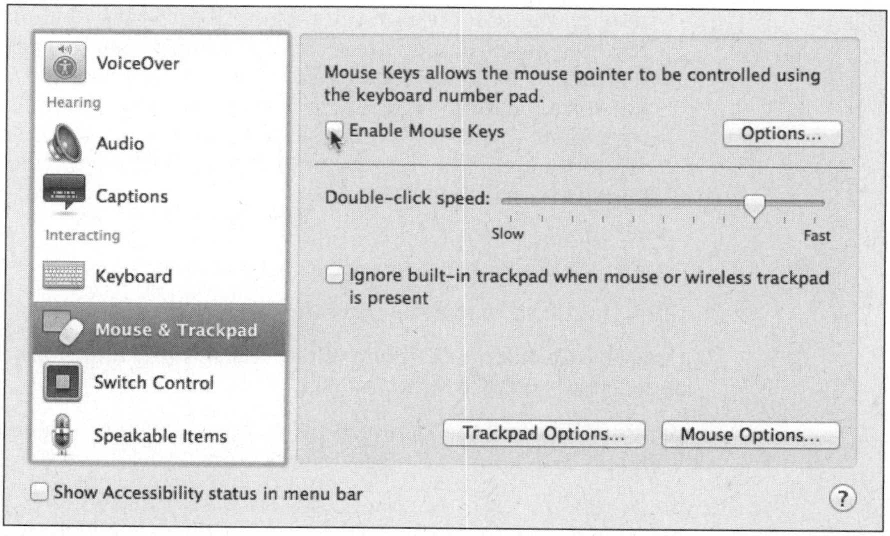

Figure 6-19:
Click the various options buttons and sliders to adjust how you use the mouse and trackpad.

When Mouse Keys is active, click the 5, i, or m key, which your Mac interprets as clicking the mouse key or trackpad, and then do one of the following to move the pointer. You may have to try all three of the 5, i, and m keys because which one works depends on your keyboard and Mac model.

The Mouse Keys feature is really designed for keyboards that have a separate numeric keypad. If you're using a laptop or other keyboard that doesn't have a separate numeric keypad, the numeric keys might be embedded in the regular typewriter keys. To control the mouse pointer, you have to turn on the Num Lock key to use the numeric keys to move the mouse pointer. Then you have to press the Num Lock key again to use the keys for typing ordinary letters.

MacBook and desktop Mac compact keyboards (without dedicated numeric keypads) do not have Num Lock keys and corresponding numeric key overlays on their keyboards. When Mouse Keys is turned on, you can use the letters as shown in Table 6-1, or you might want to consider buying an optional external numeric keypad or replacing it with an extended keyboard.

Use the various options and sliders to make the following adjustments to how the mouse and trackpad respond to your input (refer to Figure 6-19).

1. **Click the Options button and then make these choices:**

   - *Press the Option Key Five Times to Toggle Mouse Keys On or Off:* Lets you turn the Mouse Keys feature on or off from the keyboard.

   - *Ignore Built-In Trackpad When Mouse Keys Is On* (only Macs with trackpads): Disables the trackpad when you turn on Mouse Keys.

   If you select this check box, you will have to use the mouse keys to deselect it and use the trackpad again.

   - *Initial Delay:* Drag the slider to define how long the Mac waits before moving the pointer with the numeric key. A short value means that the Mac might immediately move the pointer as soon as you press a number or letter key. A long value means that you must hold down a key for a longer period before it starts moving the pointer. Choose a long value if you use a compact keyboard so you can type normally without moving the mouse and move the mouse without typing a series of the same letter.

   - *Maximum Speed:* Drag the slider to adjust how fast the Mouse Keys feature moves the pointer with the keyboard.

2. **Click the Done button to close the Mouse Keys options.**

3. **Drag the Double-click Speed slider to establish a double-clicking speed that's comfortable for you.**

4. **(Optional) Select the Ignore Built-In Trackpad When Mouse or Wireless Trackpad Is Present check box.**

Selecting this option tells your MacBook trackpad to ignore any touches and accept commands only from a mouse or wireless trackpad.

5. **Click the Trackpad Options button to set the following options:**

- *Scrolling Speed:* Use the slider to set the scrolling speed and then open the Scrolling pop-up menu to choose scrolling *with inertia* (scrolling continues after you lift your finger) or *without inertia* (scrolling stops when you lift your finger).

- *Enable Dragging:* Open the pop-up menu to choose Without Drag Lock, in which you place the pointer on the item, tap the trackpad twice, and then drag the item without removing your finger from the trackpad. Or, opt for With Drag Lock, in which you click and drag an item and even if you lift your finger from the trackpad, the item remains locked to the dragging maneuver until you tap the trackpad once.

6. **Click the Done button to close the Trackpad Options.**

7. **Click Mouse Options and drag the slider.**

   Dragging the slider sets the Scrolling Speed that occurs when you use the mouse to scroll through windows.

8. **Click Done to exit the Mouse Options.**

9. **Click the Close button or press ⌘+Q to quit System Preferences or go on to the next section to set up other Accessibility functions.**

To find different types of keyboards and mice designed to make controlling your computer even more comfortable, search for *ergonomic input devices* by using your favorite search engine, such as Google, Yahoo!, or Bing. Search results will contain a list of product reviews and websites selling everything from left-handed keyboards and mice to foot pedals and keyboards designed to type letters by pressing multiple keys like piano chords. For a little extra money, you can buy the perfect keyboard and mouse that can make your Mac more comfortable for you to use.

Enabling Switch Control

Switch Control allows you to command your Mac with a series of switches, which can be the mouse, a keyboard, or a separate dedicated device. Experience and space limit our explanation here but to give you an idea, Figure 6-20 shows the Switch Control Home row that appears when Enable Switch Control is selected. We advise you to consult the Apple Accessibility documentation or set up an appointment with a Genius at an Apple Store to best take advantage of these functions.

Figure 6-20:
Switch
Control
commands
your Mac
from the
mouse,
keyboard, or
dedicated
device.

Speaking with Your Mac

Your Mac offers voice command, dictation, and speech capabilities. The Speakable Items feature lets you control your Mac by using spoken commands, and the Dictation & Speech functions let you dictate to your Mac or have your Mac read text or alert you when something happens (for example, when a dialog pops up onscreen). Speakable Items are part of the Accessibility functions; Dictation & Speech share an icon in the System Preferences window. We talk about both here.

Your Mac's voice command, dictation, and speech capabilities can be useful for controlling your Mac or listening to text you've written to catch typos or other errors you might miss by only reading what you've written rather than hearing it aloud.

Setting up Speakable Items

To use the Mac's built-in voice recognition software, you have to define its settings and then assign specific types of commands to your voice. You define the Speakable Items settings to choose how to turn on voice recognition and how your Mac will acknowledge that it received your voice commands correctly. For example, your Mac may wait until you press the Esc key or speak a certain word before it starts listening to voice commands. When it understands your command, it can beep.

To define the Speakable Items settings, follow these steps:

1. **Choose System Preferences and click the Accessibility icon.**

2. **Click the Speakable Items button in the left pane of the Accessibility window and then click the Settings tab, shown in Figure 6-21.**

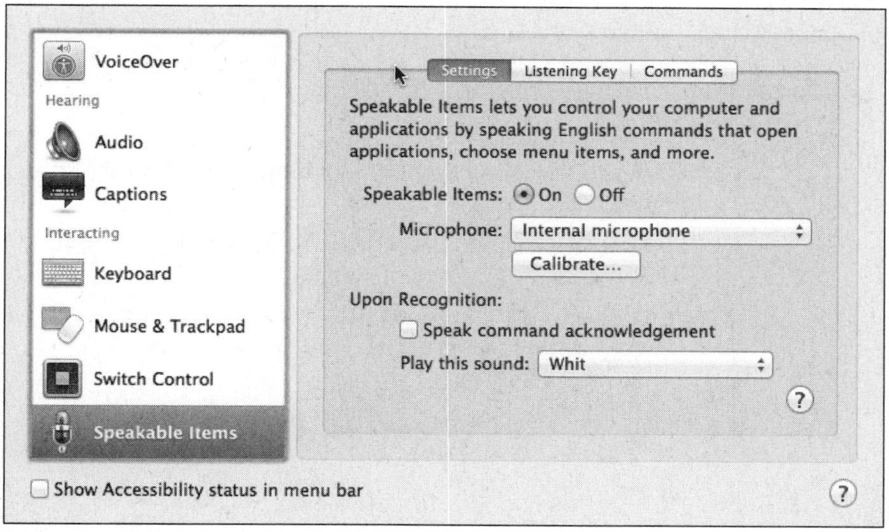

Figure 6-21: Define how your Mac recognizes spoken commands.

3. **Select the On radio button to turn on the Speakable Items feature.**

4. **Choose an appropriate device for accepting your spoken commands from the Microphone pop-up menu.**

   Internal Microphone would be an obvious choice here unless you happen to have an external microphone connected to your Mac.

5. **Click the Calibrate button to open the Microphone Calibration dialog, as shown in Figure 6-22.**

6. **Recite the phrases displayed in the Microphone Calibration dialog. If necessary, adjust the slider until your Mac recognizes your spoken commands.**

   Each command phrase in the listing blinks when your Mac successfully recognizes your phrasing of the command.

7. **When your Mac recognizes all phrases, click Done to return to the Speech Recognition preferences pane.**

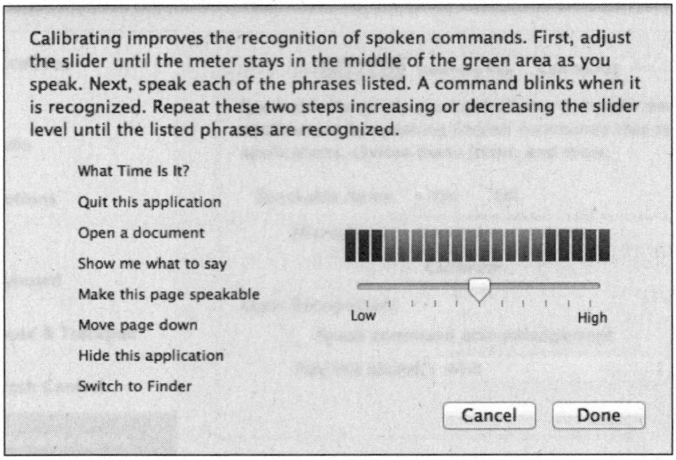

Calibrating improves the recognition of spoken commands. First, adjust the slider until the meter stays in the middle of the green area as you speak. Next, speak each of the phrases listed. A command blinks when it is recognized. Repeat these two steps increasing or decreasing the slider level until the listed phrases are recognized.

What Time Is It?

Quit this application

Open a document

Show me what to say

Make this page speakable

Move page down

Hide this application

Switch to Finder

Low   High

Cancel   Done

Figure 6-22: Train your Mac to recognize your voice.

8. **Click the Listening Key tab, click the Change Key button shown in Figure 6-23.**

   Pressing the Listening Key (Esc is the default) tells your Mac to begin listening for your spoken commands. You can change the default here.

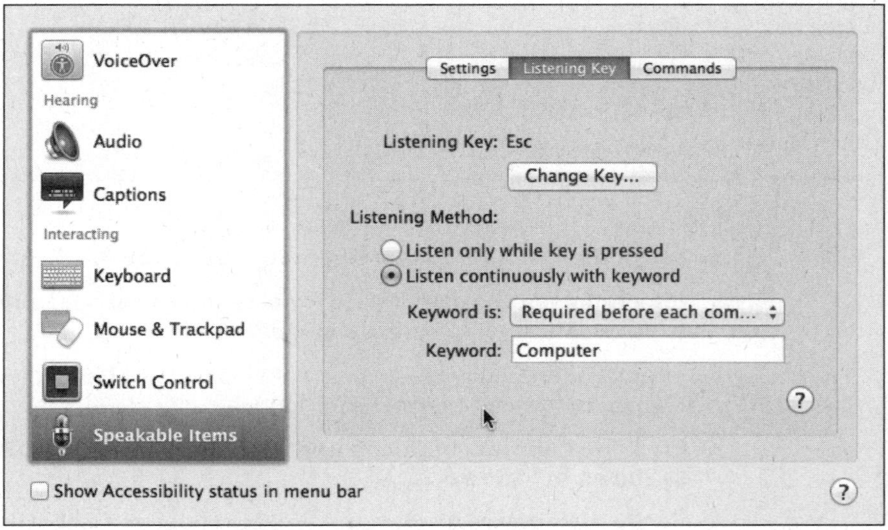

VoiceOver

Hearing

Audio

Captions

Interacting

Keyboard

Mouse & Trackpad

Switch Control

Speakable Items

Settings   Listening Key   Commands

Listening Key: Esc

Change Key...

Listening Method:

◯ Listen only while key is pressed

◉ Listen continuously with keyword

Keyword is: Required before each com... ⬍

Keyword: Computer

☐ Show Accessibility status in menu bar

Figure 6-23: Define a listening key to start giving spoken commands.

9. **Press a key and then click OK to return to the Speech Recognition dialog.**

   You might choose a key such as ` (the accent grave character) or one of your Mac keyboard function keys.

10. **Select one of the following radio buttons in the Listening Method category:**

- *Listen Only While Key Is Pressed:* Your Mac accepts only spoken commands as long as you hold down the Escape key, or a different listening key you defined in Step 9. If you select this radio button, go to Step 13.

- *Listen Continuously with Keyword:* Your Mac waits to hear a spoken keyword (such as "Computer" or "Yoo-hoo!") before accepting additional spoken commands. If you select this radio button, go to Step 11.

11. **Open the Keyword Is pop-up menu and choose one of the following:**

- *Optional before Commands:* Your Mac listens for spoken commands all the time. This can make it easier to give spoken commands, but it also means that your Mac might misinterpret the radio or background conversations as commands.

- *Required before Each Command:* You must speak the keyword before your Mac will accept spoken commands.

- *Required 15 Seconds after Last Command:* You must repeat the keyword within 15 seconds after each command.

- *Required 30 Seconds after Last Command:* Same as the preceding option except the Mac waits up to 30 seconds for the next spoken commands.

12. **In the Keyword text box, enter your keyword if you don't want to use the default keyword (Computer) to speak to your Mac.**

13. **(Optional) Make choices in the Upon Recognition area (under the Settings tab; refer to Figure 6-21).**

If you want your Mac to use the default sound (voice) Whit to confirm commands it successfully recognizes, select the Speak Command Acknowledgement check box. If you prefer to hear an alert sound rather than Whit's voice, open the Play This Sound pop-up menu and choose the alert sound you want.

14. **Click the Commands tab to open the Commands preferences pane, as shown in Figure 6-24.**

15. **Select the check boxes for one or more of the following command sets:**

- *Contacts:* Listens for names stored in your Address Book. Select Address Book and click the Configure button to specify which names in your Address Book you want recognized.

- *Global Speakable Items:* Listens for common commands applicable to any situation, such as asking your Mac, "What time is it?" or "Tell me a joke" — and that's no joke! Select Global Speakable Items and click the Configure button to turn off the Speak Command Names Exactly As Written. When this command is turned off, you can ask the same question in more than one way, such as asking "What is the time?" rather than "What time is it?"

Click the Open Speakable Items Folder to open a Finder window containing file icons of all the commands you can say to your Mac, as shown in Figure 6-25.

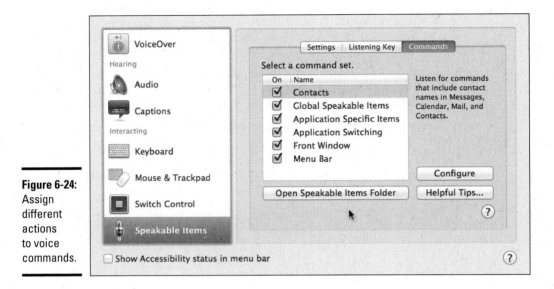

Figure 6-24:
Assign
different
actions
to voice
commands.

Figure 6-25:
Here are
all com-
mands your
Mac can
recognize.

- *Application Specific Items:* Listens for commands specific to each application. A word processor might have a Format menu, but an audio-editing application might not.

- *Application Switching:* Listens for commands to switch between, start, or quit applications.

- *Front Window:* Listens for the commands to control specific items in the displayed window, such as telling your Mac to click a button or check box.

- *Menu Bar:* Listens for commands to display pull-down menus and choose a command.

16. **Click the Close button or press ⌘+Q to quit System Preferences or go on to the next section to set up other Accessibility functions.**

Setting up Dictation & Speech

If you long for a secretary who takes dictation, your days of waiting are over. Follow the first set of steps to set up the dictation part of the Dictation & Speech preferences, and then read on to learn how your Mac can read text to you or alert you when something occurs, such as when you try to quit an application without saving a document.

To define the dictation capabilities of your Mac, follow these steps:

1. **Choose ⬤⇨System Preferences and click the Dictation & Speech icon.**

2. **On the Dictation tab, select the On radio button to activate Dictation.**

3. **Select the Use Enhanced Dictation check box.**

   Enhanced Dictation lets you dictate even when you don't have an Internet connection, as shown in Figure 6-26.

   The dictation dictionary for the default language, U.S. English, must be downloaded. The first time you turn on Enhanced Dictation, a dialog asks you to confirm the download of this dictation dictionary.

4. **(Optional) Open the Language pop-up menu and click Customize to add more languages.**

   a. *Select the check box for any language(s) you wish to dictate in.*

   b. *Click OK.*

   Your Mac downloads dictation dictionaries for the selected language(s).

5. **(Optional) Open the Shortcut pop-up menu to choose a key command for starting dictation.**

   Select Off to activate dictation with apps' Edit menus, or select Customize to specify a key command that isn't in the list.

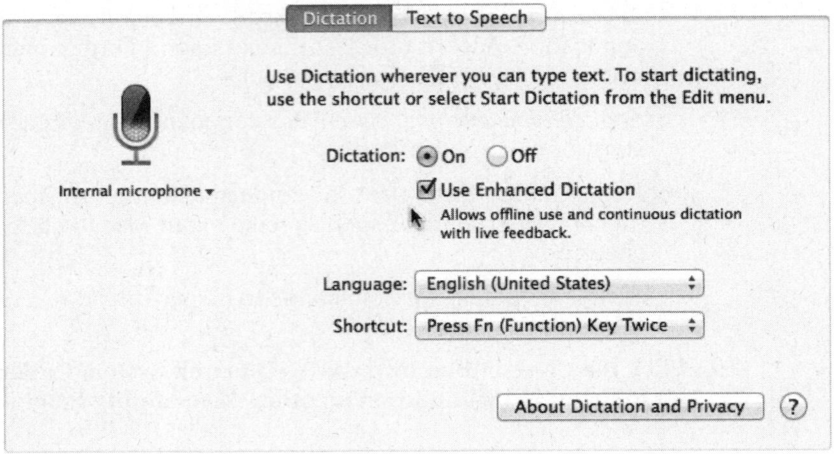

Figure 6-26:
Use
Dictation
without an
Internet
connection.

When you're in an app that you use to create written text, such as a word processor or an e-mail app, use your dictation shortcut or choose Edit⇨Start Dictation. The mini-window shown in Figure 6-27 appears, and you can begin speaking.

Figure 6-27:
Your Mac is
ready and
listening.

If you activated more than one language, use the arrows next to the language to switch to another.

Continue here to choose the voice that will read to you:

1. **Click the Text to Speech tab to open the Text to Speech preferences, as shown in Figure 6-28.**

2. **From the System Voice pop-up menu, choose Customize.**

The bundled voices are very computer-like and unnatural. We deselected all of them.

3. **Click a name and then click the Play button to hear a sample.**

Downloading additional voices lets you hear smooth, natural feedback, and you can choose different languages, too.

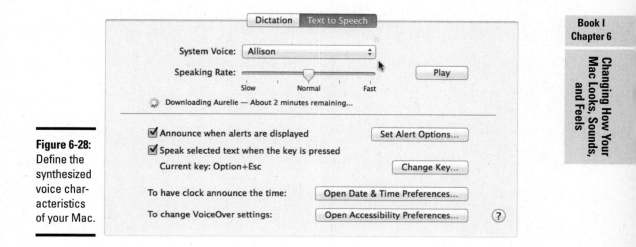

Figure 6-28:
Define the
synthesized
voice char-
acteristics
of your Mac.

4. **When you find one or more that you like, select the check box next to the name and then click OK.**

   The voices are downloaded. (You need an Internet connection to perform this task.)

5. **Choose the voice you want to hear from the pop-up menu.**

   If you choose a voice from a language that's different from the one you want read, such as a French speaker for English text, your text is read with a (charming?) accent.

6. **Drag the Speaking Rate slider to a desired speed and then click Play to hear your chosen synthesized voice at the specified speaking rate.**

7. **Select the check boxes for any of the following additional Text to Speech options you want to enable:**

   • *Announce When Alerts Are Displayed:* Makes your Mac speak when it needs your attention. It might say, "Attention!" or the name of the ailing app, for instance.

   • *Set Alert Options:* When you select Announce When Alerts Are Displayed, click this button to open a dialog and define how and when your Mac should speak an alert. Make any changes you want in the Set Alert Options dialog and then click OK to return to the Text to Speech preferences pane.

   • *Speak Selected Text When the Key Is Pressed:* Allows you to press a key combination (Option+Esc is the default) to tell your Mac when to start reading any text you select. Click the Change Key button to open a dialog where you can change the key combination to one that's easier for you.

8. **Click the Close button or press ⌘+Q to exit System Preferences.**

Book II
Online Communications

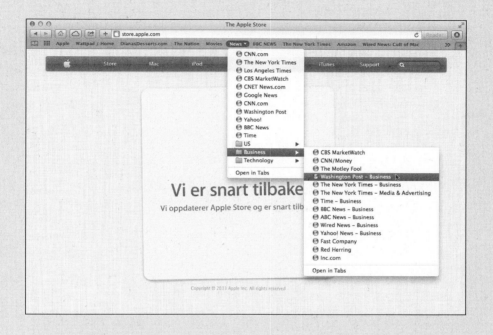

Contents at a Glance

Chapter 1: Browsing the Web with Safari

In This Chapter

✔ Browsing websites

✔ Managing bookmarks

✔ Creating a Reading List

✔ Securing your privacy

✔ Sharing web pages

✔ Viewing and playing multimedia files

✔ Downloading files

✔ Extending Safari's capabilities

The World Wide Web gives you entrance to a universe of fun facts, virtual museums around the world, and news from mainstream and obscure outlets, movies, radio stations, new apps, online shopping, local restaurants, and far-flung ferries. To access all this omnipresent goodness, you use a *web browser,* which is an app that lets you, well, browse, all the things stored on the web from around the globe.

In this chapter, we introduce you to *Safari,* which is the web browser app that comes with your Mac. We show you Safari's many features for browsing, searching, and reading on the Internet. Along the way, you'll find tips and tricks to make your surfing experience more fun and productive.

Browsing Websites

After you connect to the Internet (as explained in Book I, Chapter 3), you can run a web browser app to browse online. The most popular browser for the Mac is the one that comes with it: Safari. However, you can download and run another web browser, such as

✦ **Firefox:** www.mozilla.org/en-US/firefox/new

✦ **Google Chrome:** www.google.com/chrome

✦ **Internet Explorer:** http://windows.microsoft.com/en-us/internet-explorer/browser-ie - touchweb=touchvidtab1

✦ **Opera:** www.opera.com

In this section, we tell you how to explore the web with Safari.

Visiting websites

To visit a website, you use the website's *address* (also known as a *URL*, or Uniform Resource Locator). Most website addresses, such as `http://www.dummies.com`, consist of these parts:

✦ **`http://www:`** Identifies the address as part of the web that uses the HyperText Transfer Protocol (HTTP). Some websites omit the `www` portion of the name and begin with `http` or `https`, which is HTTP secure. Other websites use something else like `mobile`, which means the site is formatted for better viewing on mobile devices. Just keep in mind that `www` is common but not always necessary for many website addresses.

✦ **The domain name of the website (such as `dummies`):** Most website names are abbreviations or smashed-together names of the website, such as `whitehouse` for the White House website.

✦ **An identifying extension (such as `.com`):** The extension identifies the type of website, as shown in Table 1-1. Many websites in other countries end with a two-letter country address, such as `.uk` for the United Kingdom or `.ch` for Switzerland.

Table 1-1	Common Web Address Extensions	
Three-Letter Extension	*Type of Website*	*Examples*
`.com`	Often a commercial website, but can be another type of website	`www.apple.com`
`.gov`	Government website	`www.nasa.gov`
`.edu`	School website	`www.mit.edu`
`.net`	Network, sometimes used as an alternative to the `.com` extension	`www.earthlink.net`
`.org`	A nonprofit organization website	`www.redcross.org`
`.mil`	Military website	`www.army.mil`

When visiting different web pages on a site, you might see additional text that identifies a specific web page, such as

`www.dummies.com/how-to/computers-software.html`
`www.apple.com/iphone`

Opening a website you know

When you know the website address (URL) you want to visit, simply type it in to Safari. Follow these steps:

1. **Click the Safari icon (it looks like a compass) from the Dock or Launchpad to run Safari.**

2. **Click in the Search and Address field and type an address (such as www.dummies.com), as shown in Figure 1-1, and then press Return.**

   As you begin to type an address, Safari auto-completes it with a likely match, usually based on your viewing history, and then highlights the part it added. In Figure 1-1, we typed **dum**, and Safari filled in the rest. You can see, too, other potential matches listed below; as you type more letters, the choices narrow. Press the Return key if the highlighted address is the one you want. Otherwise, continue typing or choose from the pop-up list that appears (if the website you want is listed there).

   If you type a website address and see an error message, it might mean that you typed the website address incorrectly, your Internet connection isn't working, or the website is temporarily (or permanently) unavailable.

   Safari displays the website corresponding to the address you typed.

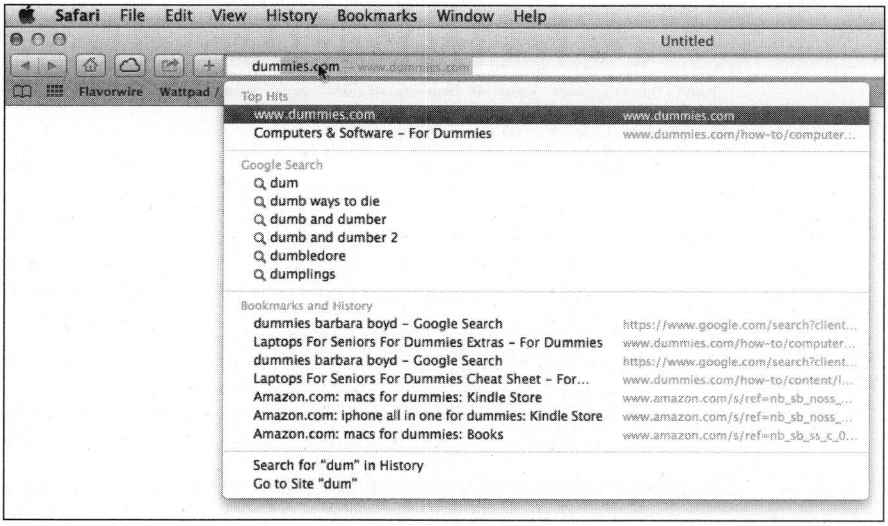

**Book II
Chapter 1**

Browsing the Web with Safari

Safari File Edit View History Bookmarks Window Help

Untitled

dummies.com

Flavorwire Wattpad /

Top Hits
 www.dummies.com   www.dummies.com
 Computers & Software – For Dummies   www.dummies.com/how-to/computer...

Google Search
 Q dum
 Q dumb ways to die
 Q dumb and dumber
 Q dumb and dumber 2
 Q dumbledore
 Q dumplings

Bookmarks and History
 dummies barbara boyd – Google Search   https://www.google.com/search?client...
 Laptops For Seniors For Dummies Extras – For Dummies   www.dummies.com/how-to/computer...
 dummies barbara boyd – Google Search   https://www.google.com/search?client...
 Laptops For Seniors For Dummies Cheat Sheet – For...   www.dummies.com/how-to/content/l...
 Amazon.com: macs for dummies: Kindle Store   www.amazon.com/s/ref=nb_sb_noss_...
 Amazon.com: iphone all in one for dummies: Kindle Store   www.amazon.com/s/ref=nb_sb_noss_...
 Amazon.com: macs for dummies: Books   www.amazon.com/s/ref=nb_sb_ss_c_0...

 Search for "dum" in History
 Go to Site "dum"

Figure 1-1:
Begin typing
an address,
and Safari
suggests
potential
matches.

3. **Move about the web page (mouse, trackpad, or arrow keys) to scroll up and down. Move the pointer over images, buttons, and bold text to click links that open other web pages.**

   Double-tap with two fingers on the trackpad or Magic Mouse to zoom in or out of the web page. This doesn't change the size of the Safari window but makes everything on the web page larger. Click and drag a corner or edge of the Safari window to resize it.

If you use a MacBook or a Magic Mouse or trackpad with a desktop Mac model, use the two- or three-finger swipe or two-finger scroll gesture to move back and forward between web pages that you visited. Choose ⌘⇨System Preferences⇨Trackpad⇨More Gestures. Click Swipe between Pages, and from the pop-up menu, choose which finger and gesture combination you want to use for that gesture.

You may encounter a web page that has fields where you type limited information, such as your name, address, and billing information to make an online purchase. Other fields are meant for typing in longer passages, such as comments about a blog post. Resize the second type of field by clicking and dragging the bottom-right corner, allowing you to see more of what you type.

4. **When you finish, click the Close button (the red circle in the upper-left corner) to simply close the Safari window.**

   Or choose Safari⇨Quit Safari to completely exit the application.

Identifying Safari's tools

As with any software, you can get the most out of Safari web browser when you're familiar with the tools it offers. Here we you tell you where to find each tool and give you a general idea of each tool's purpose. Throughout this chapter, we give you more information on how to use these tools.

Safari's Toolbar runs the width of the top of the browser. On the left side of the Toolbar, shown in Figure 1-2, you see the following tools:

✦ **Back:** Takes you to the previous web page (unless this is your first stop); click again to go back another page, and so on, until you wind up on the first page you viewed when you launched Safari.

✦ **Forward:** Moves you forward to a page you backed away from; click again to advance to the next page you backed away from, and so on, until you wind up on the last page you visited before you clicked the Back button.

✦ **Home:** Click Home to return to the web page that opens when you open Safari.

✦ **iCloud:** Opens iCloud Tabs, which shows the websites that are open in Safari on your other iOS devices.

✦ **Share:** Use this tool to easily grab the link to the page you're reading and send it to someone else or save it as a bookmark or on Reading List.

✦ **Add:** Open a new tab.

✦ **Search and Address:** Type a web address here or enter a search term.

✦ **Sidebar:** In the Sidebar pane, see your bookmarks, Reading List, and Shared Links..

✦ **Top Sites:** Your Mac keeps track of which sites you visit most frequently and helps you quickly return to them.

Back

Forward

Home

iCloud

Share

Add Search and Address

Figure 1-2:
Check out
your surfing
choices.

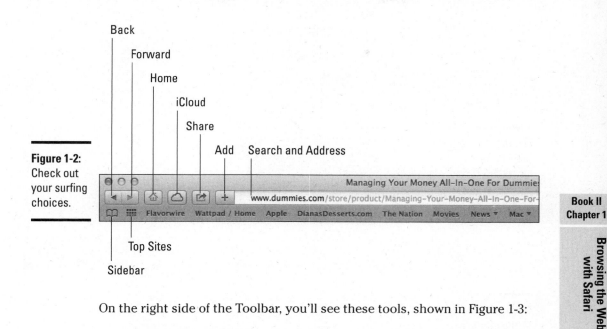

Top Sites

Sidebar

On the right side of the Toolbar, you'll see these tools, shown in Figure 1-3:

✦ **Private Browsing:** While this option is selected, Safari forgets your
browsing history when you leave Safari. This is a good choice if you want
to keep your online shopping secret from curious eyes that might use and
see your computer before the holidays.

✦ **Reload:** Clicking the little arrowed-circle icon on the right side of the
address bar reloads the current web page and displays any new information
that changed since you arrived on the web page (such as breaking news
on *The New York Times* home page). When Safari is loading or reloading a
web page, the arrowed-circle turns into an X icon. Clicking the X icon stops
Safari from loading or reloading the web page.

✦ **Reader:** If the Reader option is available, as explained in the section
"Reading in Reader," clicking this button will open the text in Reader.

✦ **Full Screen view:** Safari supports full-screen view. Click the Full Screen
button in the upper-right corner to take advantage of your entire screen. To
return to partial-screen view, press the Esc button or hover the pointer in
the upper-right corner until you see the Full Screen View toggle switch and
then click it once.

If Safari looks different on your Mac than Figures 1-2 and 1-3, you probably
have different options selected for the Toolbar (or are using a different version, in which case, upgrade and then return here). To add or delete the buttons on the Safari Toolbar, choose View➪Customize Toolbar. A pane opens,
as shown in Figure 1-4. Click and drag the icons to and from the toolbar and
the pane to create a toolbar that meets your browsing needs. We tell you
what each of the buttons do throughout the rest of this chapter.

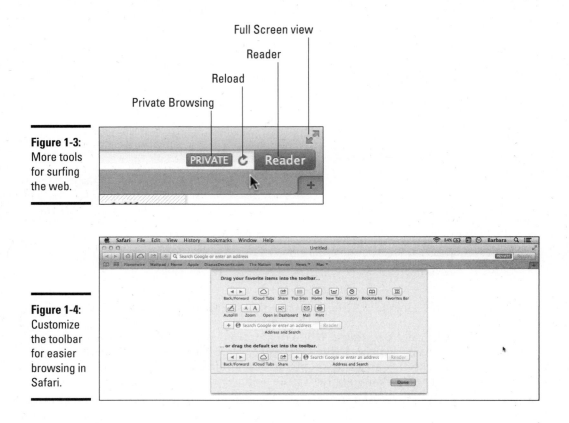

Figure 1-3:
More tools
for surfing
the web.

Figure 1-4:
Customize
the toolbar
for easier
browsing in
Safari.

Searching for websites

The real power of the web is searching for, and finding, websites you don't
know the address for. Whether you want to find the website for a specific
company or person or more general information about a topic, the answers
are literally at your fingertips. Just type a word or phrase that describes the
information you want, press Return, and a list of related web search results
(*hits* or *links*) appears, probably offering more than you ever wanted to know
about the subject of your search.

When you want to find something on the web, you usually go through a *search
engine,* which is a behind-the-scenes technology used by special websites that
can look for other websites and the information they contain based on a word
or phrase you enter. Google is probably the most well-known search engine
(and is Safari's default search engine), but others include Yahoo! and Bing,
which you can designate as the default search engine. Here's how to use Safari
to access search engines and then start your engine, um, er, search:

1. **Click the Safari icon on the Dock or Launchpad to run Safari.**

2. **Click in the Search and Address field (refer to Figure 1-2), enter a word
or phrase, and then press Return.**

The Safari window displays a web page of links your search engine found, as shown in Figure 1-5.

Click the website you want to visit or click one of the buttons at the top of the results web page to see results in other types of media, such as images, videos, shopping, news, or maps. Click the More button to see all the choices.

If you want to switch to Yahoo! or Bing, do the following:

1. **Choose Safari⇨Preferences, and then click the General tab.**

2. **Click the pop-up menu next to Default Search Engine and choose Yahoo! or Bing.**

3. **Click the Close button in the upper-left corner of the Preferences window.**

If you search for websites and find yourself wandering down a number of blind alleys because the web pages you navigate to aren't what you're looking for, return to your search results and start afresh. Choose History⇨Search Results SnapBack, and the results instantly replace whatever page you were viewing.

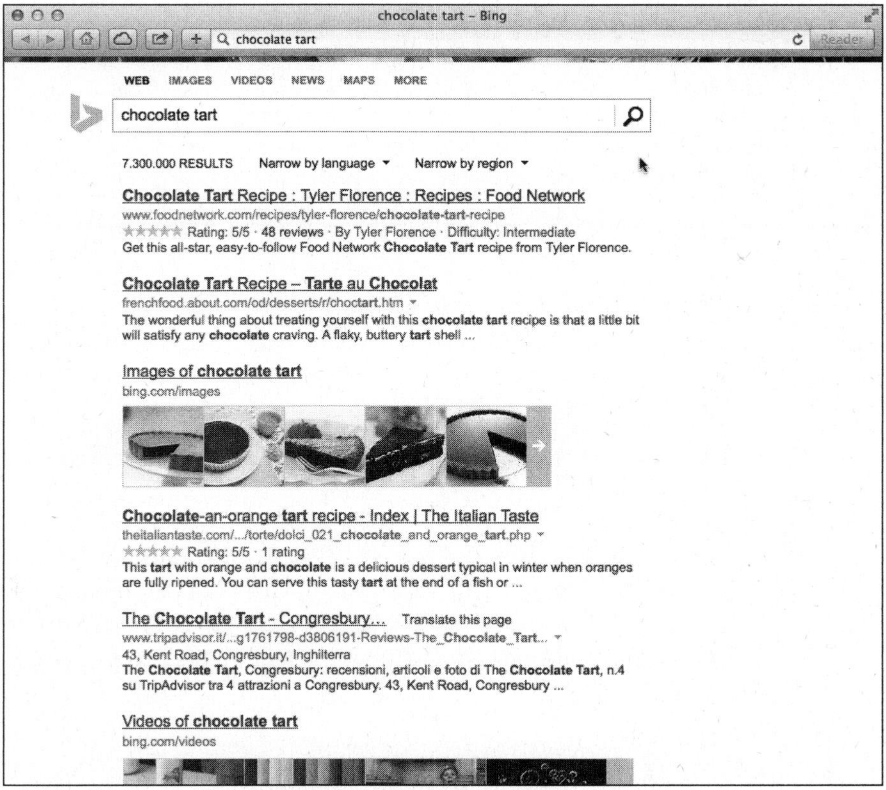

Figure 1-5:
Words or phrases you search for appear as web links in a new web page.

Searching tips

Given the billions of websites on the web, your search can turn up more exact results if you better define your search terms. Here are a few ways you can specify your search terms:

✔ Use quotation marks around a phrase to find the words exactly as you typed them. For example, if you type **John Quincy Adams** in the Search field, your result contains references for **John** Smith and Jane **Adams** in **Quincy**, Massachusetts, as well as references to the former president. If you type **"John Quincy Adams"**, your search results contain only websites that contain the name as you typed it.

✔ Use Boolean operations without quotes, for example, type **John AND Quincy AND Adams**.

✔ Confine your search to a specific website by adding `site:domain`. For example, if you want references to John Quincy Adams from the White House website, type **"John Quincy Adams" site:whitehouse.gov**.

✔ Exclude certain common usages by placing a hyphen before the word you want to exclude.

✔ Don't worry about using small articles and prepositions like *a, the, of, about;* or using capital letters.

✔ Check your spelling. If you mistype a word or phrase, the search engine might offer suggestions for the correct spelling and look for websites that contain that misspelled word or phrase, which probably won't be the website you really want to see.

Every time you type a word or phrase in the Search text box, Safari (and most other browsers) saves the last ten words or phrases you searched. To search for that same word or phrase later, just click the down arrow that appears in the left side of the Search text box to display a pull-down menu. Then click the word or phrase you want to search for again.

Going back in time

If you visit a website and want to visit it again, Safari stores a list of your visited websites in its History menu, even for one year if you choose that option in Safari➪Preferences➪General.

To view a list of the websites you visited, follow these steps:

1. **In Safari, click History on the menu bar.**

A drop-down menu appears, displaying the most recent websites you visited. Additionally, the History menu lists the past week's dates so you can view websites that you visited several days ago, as shown in Figure 1-6.

2. **Choose a website to have Safari display your selected site.**

History	Bookmarks	Window	Help
Show Top Sites			⌥⌘1
Show History			⌥⌘2
Back			⌘[
Forward			⌘]
Home			⇧⌘H
Search Results SnapBack			⌥⌘S

Reopen Last Closed Window
Reopen All Windows from Last Session

🔴 FoodNetwork TV EMEA – TV sho... & Schedule & Cooking shows
🔴 Amaretto Chocolate Tart with A...ntiis : Recipes : Food Network
🔵 Chocolate Tart Recipe : Tyler Florence : Recipes : Food Network
🅱 Bing – More
𝐼 Chocolate Tart – Opinioni, prezzi & offerte su Chocolate Tart
🅱 Bing Mappe
🅱 chocolate tart – Bing News
🅱 chocolate tart – Bing
🔵 Official Site of the ABC Network – ABC.com
🔵 Put Your Life on a Diet: Living the Simple Life
   How–To Help and Videos – For Dummies
🔵 Welcome to Diana's Desserts | DianasDesserts.com
🔵 dummies barbara boyd – Google Search
 Apple – iPhone
   Computers & Software – For Dummies
N The Nation
 Apple (United Kingdom)
🔲 Wattpad / Home

Earlier Today | ▶
Sunday, November 10, 2013 | ▶
Saturday, November 9, 2013 | ▶
Friday, November 8, 2013 | ▶
Thursday, November 7, 2013 | ▶
Wednesday, November 6, 2013 | ▶
Tuesday, November 5, 2013 | ▶

Clear History...

Figure 1-6:
The History menu lets you revisit previously viewed websites.

Book II
Chapter 1

Browsing the Web
with Safari

Although the History menu displays your web history from only the past seven days, you can choose History➪Show All History to view a list of all the websites you visited after the last time your history was deleted. To establish the length of time you want to keep your browsing history, go to Safari➪Preferences and click the General button on the toolbar. Choose a period specified by the Remove History Items pop-up menu, as shown in Figure 1-7.

You can also erase your web-browsing history at any time by choosing History➪Clear History.

Reading in Reader

If Safari perceives a readable article on the page you are viewing, the Reader button is active in the Search and Address field, and you have the option to open the article in Reader. Safari aims to be elegant and clutter-free, so Reader removes all the ads, buttons, bells, and whistles from the web page and shows you only the article as one continuous page. Even the scroll bar appears only when you hover the mouse pointer near the edge of the Reader "page," as shown in Figure 1-8.

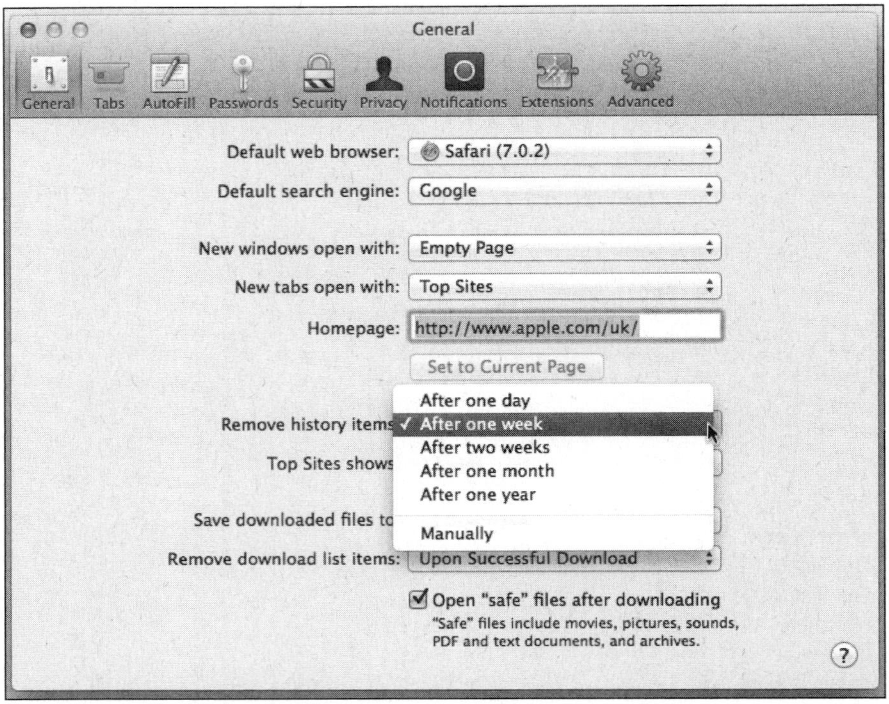

Figure 1-7:
Choose how often you want your browsing history erased.

To display an article in Reader, do the following:

1. **Click the Safari icon on the Dock or Launchpad.**

2. **Type in the URL for the website you want to visit.**

   For example, you might visit *The New Yorker* at www.newyorker.com.

3. **Click the article you want to read.**

   You see the article with various advertisements, banners, photos, links, and so on.

4. **Click the Reader button or choose View⇨Show Reader.**

   (Or press ⌘+Shift+R.)

   If the article runs over several pages, Reader displays it as one continuous page so you need only scroll down, not click from one page to the next.

If you need to adjust the size of the text, click the type buttons (the two A's) in the upper-left corner.

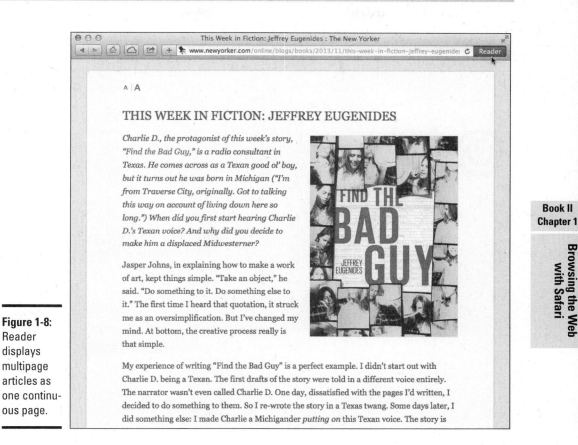

Figure 1-8:
Reader displays multipage articles as one continuous page.

To exit Reader, click the Reader button, choose View⇨Hide Reader. Or press the Esc key to exit Reader and return to the normal Safari view of the article. Click the Back button to return to the original site.

In both Reader and normal Safari view, press ⌘+= or ⌘+– to zoom in or out on the text. If you have a Magic Mouse or Trackpad or a MacBook that recognizes multitouch gestures, you can also pinch in or out to zoom.

Using tabbed browsing

When you want to keep track of more than one website while browsing a second, third, or fourth site, you could open two (or three or four) separate browser windows. However, here's a more handy way. Safari and most other browsers offer a *tabbed browsing* feature, which allows you to easily jump around among multiple web pages in a single window. This is similar to the tabbed Finder window we explain in Book I, Chapter 4. All you have to do is click the tab associated with the web page, as we discuss in these sections.

Book II
Chapter 1

Browsing the Web
with Safari

Creating new tabs

When you load Safari, you see a single web page displayed in a window. To add a tab, simply click the New Tab button (the plus sign on the right), and then open a website by typing a URL or search term in the Search and Address field.

Choose what type of tab you want to see when you click New Tab by going to Safari⇨Preferences and clicking the General button on the toolbar. Choose one of the four choices in the New Tabs Open With pop-up menu, as shown in Figure 1-9. We like to open in the Top Sites display, which we explain later in this chapter.

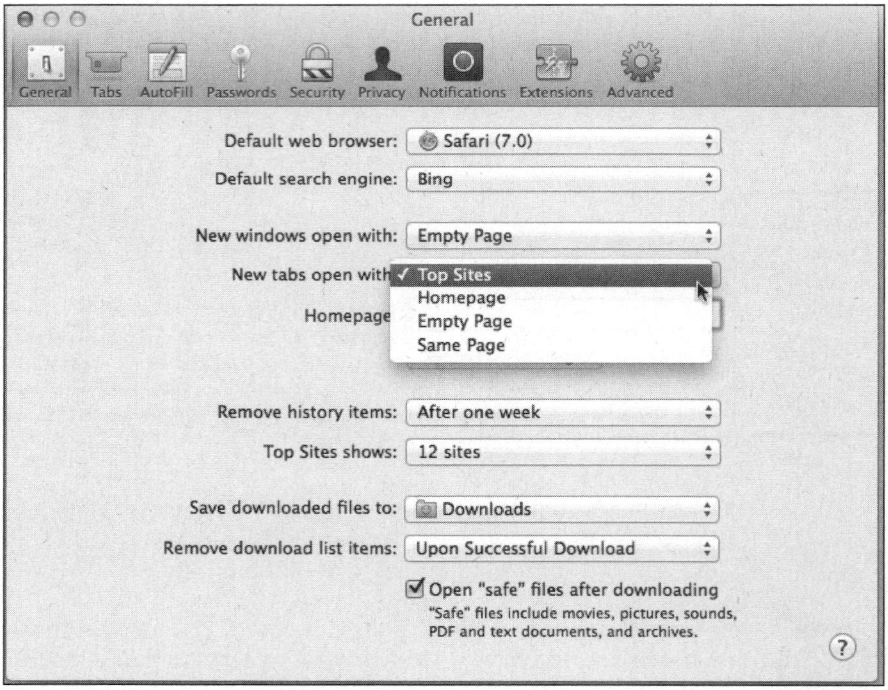

Figure 1-9:
Choose how you want to see new tabs.

Default web browser:	Safari (7.0)	
Default search engine:	Bing	
New windows open with:	Empty Page	
New tabs open with:	✓ Top Sites	
	Homepage	
Homepage	Empty Page	
	Same Page	
Remove history items:	After one week	
Top Sites shows:	12 sites	
Save downloaded files to:	Downloads	
Remove download list items:	Upon Successful Download	

☑ Open "safe" files after downloading
"Safe" files include movies, pictures, sounds, PDF and text documents, and archives.

General   Tabs   AutoFill   Passwords   Security   Privacy   Notifications   Extensions   Advanced

If you turn on Safari in iCloud on your Mac and one or more iOS device, you can access tabs opened on one device from another. On your Mac, click the iCloud button on the toolbar to see the tabs open in Safari on your iPhone, iPad, or iPod touch, as shown in Figure 1-10. See Book I, Chapter 3 to learn about iCloud.

Figure 1-10:
Access
tabs that
are open
on other
devices with
iCloud.

To work with tabs, set your preferences as explained here:

1. **Open Safari and choose Safari⇨Preferences.**

2. **Click the Tabs button on the toolbar.**

3. **From the pop-up menu shown in Figure 1-11, choose when you want
tabs to open instead of windows.**

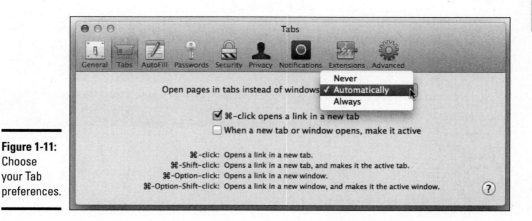

Figure 1-11:
Choose
your Tab
preferences.

4. **Select the check boxes to activate one or both of the two choices:**

   • *⌘-click Opens a Link in a New Tab:* Rather than leave the current
     web page and replace it with the linked page, a ⌘-click will open the
     linked page in a new tab and leave the current web page open.

   • *When a New Tab or Window Opens, Make It Active:* When you click the
     New button, the tab or window that opens becomes the active one.

5. **Click the Close button.**

Managing tabs

When you open multiple tabbed windows, as shown in Figure 1-12, you can rearrange how they're ordered, close them, or save a group of tabs as a bookmark that you can reopen all at once with a single click of your mouse or add them to your Reading List (which we explain shortly).

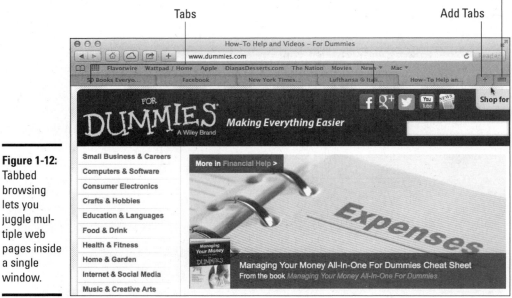

Tab view

Tabs

Add Tabs

Figure 1-12: Tabbed browsing lets you juggle multiple web pages inside a single window.

Some cool things you can try doing with tabbed windows include

✦ **Add a new tab.** Press ⌘+T or click the plus sign at the far right of the Tab bar.

✦ **Switch from tab to tab.** Press ⌘+Shift+→ or ⌘+Shift+←.

✦ **Close a tab.** Move your mouse over the tab and click the X that appears or press ⌘+W, although that will close the Safari window if you have only one tab open.

✦ **Rearrange the order of your tabs.** Drag and drop a tab to the left or right of another tab.

✦ **Move a tab to a new window.** Drag it below the Tab bar and then let go of your mouse button, or right-click a tab and choose Move Tab to New Window.

✦ **Save every currently loaded tabbed window as a bookmark.** Right-click any tab (or click the Bookmarks menu) and choose Add Bookmark for These Tabs.

✦ **Save the articles of every currently loaded tabbed window in the Reading List.** Right-click any tab (or click the Bookmarks menu) and choose Add These Tabs to Reading List.

✦ **Merge a bunch of open web page windows into a single web page with tabs for each window.** Choose Windows⇨Merge All Windows.

✦ **View tabs that get shoved off the row of visible tabs when you've opened too many tabs to display them all.** Click the double right-pointing arrows on the rightmost tab.

✦ **Open a contextual menu that displays all the tab options.** Right-click a tab.

Setting your Safari home page

The first time you open Safari, the Apple website appears because it's set as the default home page. Subsequent times you open Safari, the website you were browsing when you last closed or quit Safari (or shut down and restarted your Mac) reopens. You can change your Safari home page to whatever you want — even a blank page, if that's what you prefer.

Throughout this chapter, all step-by-step instructions are given for Safari. Just keep in mind that other browsers (Firefox, Chrome, Internet Explorer and so on) work in relatively similar ways.

To define a home page in Safari, follow these steps:

1. **Click the Safari icon on the Dock or Launchpad.**

2. **Click in the Search and Address field at the top of the Safari window and type the address of the web page you want to use as your home page.**

   If you have set the page as a bookmark, you can just click the bookmark to open the web page.

3. **Choose Safari⇨Preferences and click the General button on the toolbar.**

4. **Click the Set to Current Page button.**

   The website address of the page you are viewing automatically fills the Homepage field, as shown in Figure 1-13.

   You can also skip Step 2, go directly to Safari General preferences, and type the URL in the Homepage field.

   If you want Safari to open to your home page or a blank page when you restart or reopen Safari (instead of opening the most recent web page you visited), choose Homepage or Empty Page from the New Windows Open With pop-up menu.

5. **Close the Safari preferences pane.**

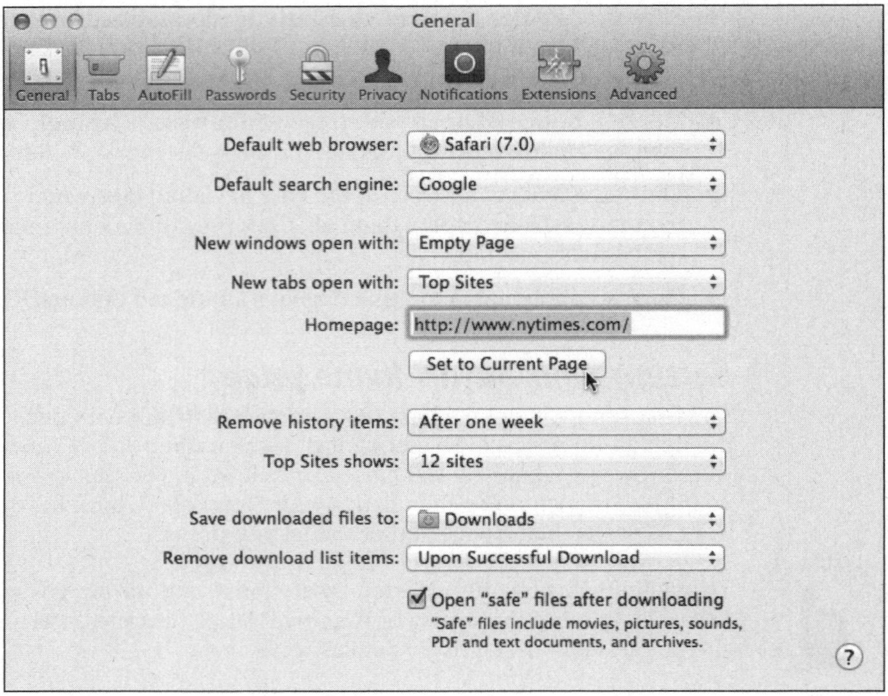

Figure 1-13:
Set your
home page
here.

Searching within a web page

You can search for a word or phrase within the text on a web page, and Safari
will find and highlight each occurrence of the word or phrase. Here's how:

1. **From the web page you want to search, choose Edit⇨Find⇨Find.**

   Under the toolbar, the Find Banner appears that has a search field and
   navigation buttons.

2. **Type in the word or phrase you want to find.**

3. **Click the small triangle next to the magnifying glass to choose whether
   you want to find text that starts with the word you entered or contains
   the word you entered.**

   The results are immediately highlighted in the text and the number of
   hits is shown to the left of the search field.

4. **Use the navigation arrows to go to the next or previous occurrence of
   the search term.**

5. **Click Done to close the Find banner or choose Edit⇨Find⇨Close Find
   Banner.**

Organizing Your Website Experience

You can use Safari just to browse new websites and read articles at the moment you find them, but that doesn't take advantage of all Safari can do to help you manage your web browsing adventure — it's not named Safari for nothin'! In this section, we tell you how to use the Safari features that organize favorite websites you want to revisit, manage the articles you want to read later, and list links to articles your friends have posted on social media sites you use — namely, Bookmarks, Reading List, and Shared Links. You access all three from the Sidebar, which opens when you click the Sidebar button (the open book) or choose View⇔Show Sidebar.

To make the Sidebar pane wider or narrower, move the pointer to the right edge of the Sidebar until it becomes a vertical line with an arrow on one or both sides, and then click and drag.

Using bookmarks

Bookmarks are links to websites, such as a favorite news outlet or a reference source. Click a bookmark, and Safari opens to the bookmarked web page. What's more, bookmarks let you group likeminded websites, such as news sites, book review sites, gadgets sites, or sites related to one project you're working on, together in folders.

The Favorites bar, as shown in Figure 1-14, gives you quick access to websites you visit most frequently.

**Book II
Chapter 1**

**Browsing the Web
with Safari**

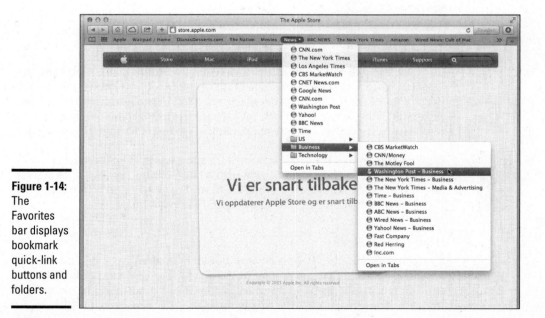

Figure 1-14:
The
Favorites
bar displays
bookmark
quick-link
buttons and
folders.

Use the Favorites bar for one-click access to your favorite or frequently visited websites. You can place as many bookmarks and folders as you like on the Favorites bar, but you will see only the number that fit in the width of the Safari window; you have to click the arrows at the right end of the Favorites bar to open a menu that displays bookmarks that don't fit. You can get around that problem by placing folders on the Favorites bar.

The Bookmarks menu and the Sidebar, as shown in Figure 1-15, show all your bookmarks and folders.

Figure 1-15: The Sidebar shows your bookmarks and folders.

Click the Sidebar button or choose View⇨Show Sidebar, and then click the Bookmarks tab. The Bookmarks section of the Sidebar displays the Favorites Bar and Bookmarks Menu folders that are fixed in the number one and two positions of the Bookmarks list. Clicking a folder displays the bookmarks within or collapses them if it's already open. Click a bookmark to open that web page.

Bookmarks behave the same whether they appear in the Sidebar, on the Bookmarks menu, or on the Favorites bar. Simply click the bookmark, and it opens the linked web page. Click and drag to open a bookmark in the Bookmarks menu or a folder on the Favorites bar.

Adding bookmarks

By default, Safari comes with several bookmarks already placed on the Favorites bar and Bookmarks menu, all of which you see in Bookmarks on the Sidebar. You'll probably want to add your own choices to bookmarks. To bookmark a website address, follow these steps:

1. **In Safari, visit a website that you want to store as a bookmark.**

A website is a collection of one or more web pages. If you want to book-mark a news website, for instance, you should use the top-level landing page as the bookmarked page instead of a web page that's linked to a specific article.

2. **Choose Bookmarks⇨Add Bookmark to open the dialog shown in Figure 1-16.**

Or you can right-click the plus-sign button that appears to the left of the address bar and choose Add Bookmark.

By default, the Name text box displays the current web page's title, which is typically the main website's name.

You can also add a bookmark by simply clicking the icon to the left of the URL and dragging it down to the Favorites bar or into a folder in the Bookmarks section of the Sidebar.

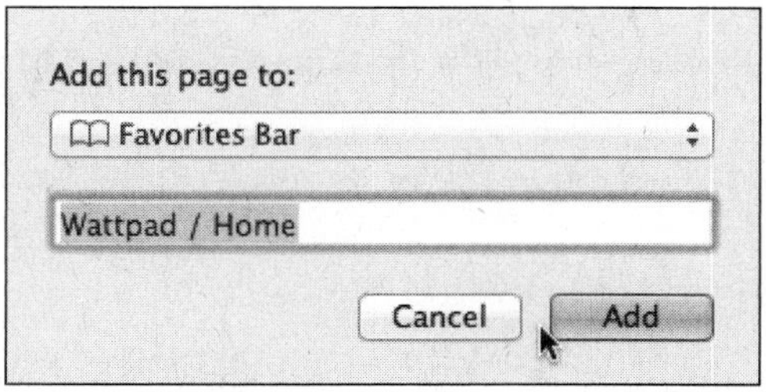

Figure 1-16:
Accept
or edit a
bookmark's
name.

Add this page to:

📖 Favorites Bar

Wattpad / Home

Cancel   Add

3. **(Optional) Type a new name for the bookmark if you don't want to keep the default name.**

4. **Click the Location pop-up menu and choose a location for storing your bookmark.**

You can choose the Favorites bar, the Bookmarks menu, or a specific folder stored on either. (You discover how to create a bookmark folder in the "Storing bookmarks in folders" section, later in this chapter.)

5. **Click the Add button.**

Your new bookmark appears where you placed it.

Turn on Safari in iCloud on your Mac and your iOS devices, or Safari on a Windows computer with iCloud, to sync your bookmarks across all devices. See Book I, Chapter 3 to learn about using iCloud.

Storing bookmarks in folders

After you save many bookmarks, they can start to clutter the Bookmarks menu or Favorites bar. To organize your bookmarks, you can store related bookmarks in folders. There are two ways to create a bookmark folder: The first steps work in the Sidebar, and the second steps work in the Bookmark Editor.

Follow these steps to work in the Sidebar:

1. **Click the Sidebar button (the open book) or choose View⇨Show Sidebar, and then click the Bookmarks tab.**

   You see a list of the bookmarks that came with Safari along with any you added. (Refer to Figure 1-15.)

2. **Click the Add Folder button (the plus side) at the bottom of the Sidebar.**

   An Untitled Folder is added to the bottom of the list.

3. **Type a name for the folder and press Return.**

4. **Click the icon next to the bookmark you want to add to the folder and drag it to the folder.**

   If you click the name, the web page opens.

Follow these steps to work in the Bookmark Editor:

1. **In Safari, choose Bookmarks⇨Edit Bookmarks to display your saved bookmarks.**

2. **Click the New Folder button at the bottom left of the window, as shown in Figure 1-17.**

   An untitled folder is added to the top of the list.

   Click Favorites Bar, Bookmarks Menu, or another folder in the left column if you want the new folder to be placed inside an existing folder.

3. **Type a name for the folder and press Return.**

4. **(Optional) Click the disclosure triangle to the left of a folder name to display the bookmarks and folders within that folder.**

5. **Click and drag the bookmarks you want to move into the new folder.**

6. **Choose Bookmarks⇨Hide Bookmarks Editor.**

Rearranging or deleting bookmarks

Safari saves your bookmarks and bookmark folders in the order you create them, adding them to the bottom of an ever-growing list. If you continue to add bookmarks to the Bookmarks menu without placing them in folders, you may find that you have a gazillion bookmarks listed willy-nilly and can't remember what half of them link to (guilty, as charged). As time passes, you probably have bookmarks you don't use anymore — some may not even work anymore. The procedure is the same whether you work in the Sidebar or the Bookmarks Editor. Follow these steps to put your bookmarks in a more logical order and delete any you no longer want:

1. **In Safari, choose Bookmarks⇨Edit Bookmarks.**

   Or click the Sidebar button and then click the Bookmarks tab.

**Book II
Chapter 1**

Browsing the Web
with Safari

Figure 1-17:
Add new
folders
in the
Bookmarks
Editor.

2. **Click the folder you want to move or delete (Sidebar) or click the disclosure triangle next to the folder name that contains the bookmark (Bookmarks Editor).**

   The contents, which might include bookmarks and additional folders that contain other bookmarks, are listed below.

   Click the additional folders to see the bookmarks contained within. You may need to repeat this step several times to find the bookmark you want.

3. **Click and drag the bookmark or bookmark folder you want to move up or down the list to a new folder or position.**

   Drag the bookmark or folder beyond the last item in a folder to move it out of the folder. A line shows where the item is being moved to; if you move it into a folder, the folder is highlighted.

   Safari moves your chosen bookmark to its new location.

4. **Click and drag bookmarks up and down within the collection or folder to change the order in which they are displayed.**

5. **In the Bookmarks Editor, click the bookmark that you want to delete and press Delete.**

   Or, in the Sidebar, control-click the undesired bookmark and choose Delete from the pop-up menu.

   You can also delete a folder this way, but all the bookmarks and folders within the deleted folder will be deleted.

   To restore a bookmark you mistakenly deleted, press ⌘+Z or choose Edit⇨Undo Remove Bookmark.

6. **Choose Bookmarks⇨Hide Bookmarks Editor to return to the most recent web page you viewed or click the Sidebar button to close the sidebar.**

Renaming bookmarks and folders

You may want to bookmark several web pages from the same website but have trouble differentiating them in the Bookmarks menu or Sidebar because the name that's displayed begins with the website and then the slashes and such to specify the web page. You can rename bookmarks and folders to something that's more meaningful to you, which will help you find your bookmarks more quickly. Here's how to rename in the Bookmarks Editor or the Sidebar:

✦ **Bookmarks Editor:** Choose View⇨Edit Bookmarks. The Bookmarks Editor opens (refer to Figure 1-17). Click the bookmark or folder you want to rename, and then click it again. The pause between the two clicks is more pronounced than in a double-click. The name of the bookmark or folder is highlighted. Type the new name you want to use or click the text to edit it, and then press Return.

✦ **Sidebar:** Click the Sidebar button, and then click the Bookmarks tab. Control-click the bookmark or folder you want to rename, and choose Rename Bookmark from the pop-up menu. The name of the bookmark or folder is highlighted. Type the new name you want to use or click the text to edit it, and then press Return.

Importing and exporting bookmarks

After you collect and organize bookmarks, you might become dependent on your bookmarks to help you navigate the web. Fortunately, if you ever want to switch browsers, you can export bookmarks from one browser and import them into another browser.

To export bookmarks from Safari, follow these steps:

1. **In Safari, choose File⇨Export Bookmarks to open the Export Bookmarks dialog.**

2. **(Optional) Type a descriptive name for your bookmarks if you don't want to keep the default of Safari Bookmarks.**

3. **Click the Where pop-up menu to choose where you want to store your exported bookmarks file.**

   If you click the arrow button that appears to the right of the Save As text box, a window appears displaying all the drives and folders that you can choose in which to store your bookmarks.

4. **Click Save.**

After you export bookmarks from one browser, it's usually a snap to import them into a second browser. To import bookmarks into Safari, follow these steps:

1. **In Safari, choose File⊏⇒Import Bookmarks to open the Import Bookmarks dialog.**

2. **Navigate to the folder where the exported bookmarks file is stored.**

3. **Click the bookmark file you want to use and then click the Import button.**

   Your imported bookmarks appear in an Imported folder that includes the date when you imported the folder. At this point, you can move this folder or its contents to the Bookmarks bar or Bookmarks menu to organize them. (See the earlier section, "Rearranging or deleting bookmarks.)

Creating a Reading List

Sometimes you find a great article that you really, really want to read but you just don't have time. Instead of bookmarking the page (we tell you all about bookmarks in the previous section), you can save the article to Reading List. And you can read those articles offline so you can get caught up on your reading while flying. Here's how to save and manage articles in the Reading List:

1. **In Safari, with the article or web page you want to read later open, click the One-Step Add button (the plus sign) at the left end of the Search and Address field.**

   The article is added to your reading list.

2. **When you're ready to read one or more of your saved articles, click the Sidebar icon in the toolbar (it looks like an open book) or choose View⊏⇒Show Sidebar.**

3. **Click the Reading List tab to see the articles you placed there.**

   The Reading List, down the left side of the Safari window, shown in Figure 1-18, shows the title of the article, its source website, and the first few words of the article.

   Scroll through the list to see articles further down.

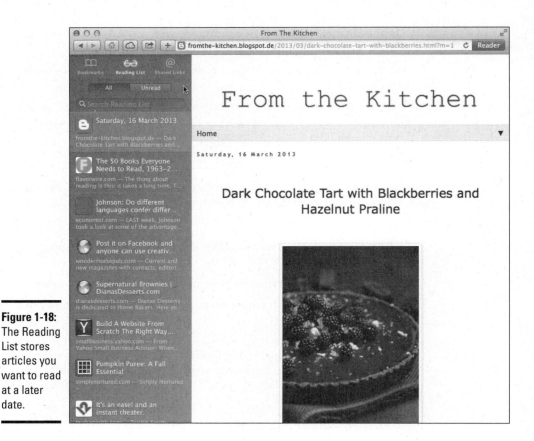

Figure 1-18:
The Reading List stores articles you want to read at a later date.

4. **Click the article you want to read.**

   It also could be a web page with more than one article, such as the cover page of a newspaper.

   The web page opens in the main part of the Safari window to the right of the Reading List.

   Click the Reader button for distraction-free reading.

5. **Click the All or Unread buttons to change which articles you see in the Reading List.**

6. **To delete an article from the list, click the article and then click the X in the upper-right corner near the name of the selected article.**

7. **To delete the whole list, click the Clear All button.**

8. **Click the Sidebar button again to close the Sidebar.**

Seeing what your friends are reading

The latest version of Safari (7.0 as of this writing) added a feature that's pretty neat if you use LinkedIn or Twitter. The Sidebar has a third tab called Shared Links, which displays the links posted by people you follow on LinkedIn and Twitter. Here are a few things you can do with this new feature:

✦ Click a link to see it in the Safari window on the right, as shown in Figure 1-19.

✦ Control-click to open a contextual menu, and then choose to open the link in a new tab or window, or on the source website (LinkedIn or Twitter).

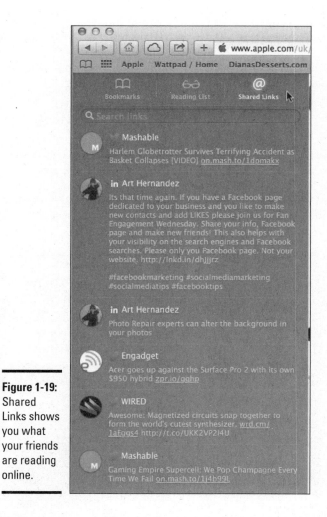

Figure 1-19:
Shared Links shows you what your friends are reading online.

✦ Choose View⇨Update Shared Links to refresh the list and see the latest additions.

✦ Click the Search field (pull down on the list if you don't see it at the top of the list) and type a word or phrase to find related links in the list.

Displaying favorites in Top Sites

While you browse the web and go from one site to another to another, Safari pays attention behind the scenes to which websites you visit most. By tracking the websites you visit most frequently, Safari can display a selection of Top Sites that you can browse through to return to what Safari deems to be your favorite websites.

To display the Top Sites view of websites you visited, that Safari believes are your favorite websites, follow these steps:

1. **In the Safari window, click the Top Sites icon (it looks like a grid) on the Favorites bar to open the Top Sites display window.**

   You see thumbnail views, shown in Figure 1-20, of the sites you visited most frequently. A star appears in the upper-right corner of the thumbnail of sites that have been updated since you last visited.

   You can modify the thumbnail view. Go to Safari⇨Preferences, click the General button, and then choose how many sites you want to see in Top Sites — 6, 12, or 24 — from the Top Sites Shows pop-up menu. When you change the size of the Safari window, the number of thumbnail images in Top Sites remains, but the size of each individual thumbnail changes to fit.

Figure 1-20: Add or remove Top Sites choices.

2. **Click a Top Sites thumbnail image of a website you want to visit.**

   Safari goes to that web page.

3. **(Optional) Hover the cursor over the upper-left corner to see the Top Sites editing options:**

   - *Exclude website.* To exclude a Top Sites selection that Safari deemed a favorite, click the X in the upper-left corner of that Top Sites thumbnail image. As you delete one thumbnail, a new one is added in the lower-right corner of the Top Sites display.

   - *Make a website permanent.* To mark a Top Sites selection as a permanent top site, click the pushpin icon next to the X in the upper-left corner of the Top Sites thumbnail image. The pushpin icon is highlighted to indicate that the website is a permanent top site. Click a highlighted pushpin icon to reverse the action: The page is no longer a permanent fixture in the Top Sites display and is replaced by a website you visit more frequently.

4. **(Optional) To rearrange the order in which your Top Sites thumbnail images appear, click a top site and drag and drop it to the location where you want it to appear.**

5. **(Optional) To add a new website to the Top Sites display window to Top Sites, do one of the following:**

   - Press and hold the Add button to the left of the Search and Address field and then choose Add to Top Sites from the pop-up menu.

   - Click the tiny icon to the left of the address, and then drag and drop it into the Top Sites display window where you want it to appear.

   - Click and drag the URL icon to the Top Sites button.

   - Drag a link from another source directly into the Top Sites display window, such as a website link in an e-mail message, or from another open Safari web page window.

6. **To exit the Top Sites display window, click one of the thumbnails to go to that website.**

   You can also type a web address in the Search and Address field and then press Return to go to that website or click a bookmark.

   You can choose the Top Sites display as the default for a new tab (refer to Figure 1-9).

Storing Personal Info and Keeping it Private

Safari and iCloud have terrific built-in features that help you remember user names and passwords and credit card information. And Safari has security and privacy features to keep that personal information to yourself — or to your Mac. Here we tell you how to use AutoFill so Safari remembers passwords for you, and then we explain how to keep your information safe.

Using AutoFill to track passwords and more

If you don't share your Mac and you visit a lot of websites that require usernames and passwords, Safari can remember and automatically fill in the username and password for you when you open those websites. Safari can also automatically fill in forms with your name and address, credit card information, and information you've completed on an online form in the past. Safari encrypts this information, so even though it's remembered, it's safe.

To use the AutoFill options, as shown in Figure 1-21, do the following:

1. **Choose Safari⬄Preferences and click the AutoFill button on the toolbar.**

2. **Select the Using Info from My Contacts Card check box.**

   Safari presents pre-filled drop-down fields in website forms that request information such as your address and telephone number, which will be taken from Contacts.

   Click Edit to open Contacts and view the information that will be accessed. (See Book V, Chapter 1 to learn more about Contacts.)

3. **Select the User Names and Passwords check box.**

   The first time you visit a website that requires a username and password, Safari asks whether you want it remembered. If you choose Yes, your username and password are filled in automatically the next time you visit the website.

4. **(Optional) Click the Edit button next to User Names and Passwords, or click the Passwords button on the AutoFill dialog toolbar, both of which open a list of websites and passwords you asked Safari to save. You can also do the following:**

   • Select the Show Passwords for Selected Sites check box to see the remembered password when you click a site in the list.

   • Select AutoFill User Names and Passwords if you want to override a websites' request and use AutoFill anyway.

   • Click a website (or Control-click multiple websites) and then click the Remove button to eliminate those user names and passwords from Safari's memory.

   Then click the AutoFill button to return to the AutoFill window.

5. **Select the Credit Cards check box and then click Edit to add your credit card number(s) and expiration date(s).**

   When you're making an online purchase and reach the credit card information fields, a drop-down field lets you choose which credit card you want to use from those you entered.

WARNING!

If you choose to use AutoFill for names, passwords — and especially credit cards — we highly recommend setting up your Mac to require a password whenever it is turned on or wakes from sleep. See Book III, Chapter 2 to learn more about Mac security features.

6. **Select the Other Forms check box, which will remember what you enter the first time you fill in a form and use it if the same website asks for the same information again.**

   Click the Edit button to see, and remove, websites for which AutoFill has been enabled.

Figure 1-21:
AutoFill
keeps track
of pass-
words and
fills in forms.

REMEMBER

If you turn on the Keychain option in iCloud, the information you let AutoFill manage is available across all devices signed in to the same iCloud account with Keychain activated. See Book I, Chapter 3 to learn about iCloud.

Protecting your web-browsing privacy

Safari encrypts your web browsing to help avoid Internet eavesdropping and potential digital theft. And, instead of letting websites access your information automatically when you fill out forms, Safari detects forms and presents your information in drop-down fields so you can choose which information to insert.

As a rule, Safari keeps track of your browsing history, but if you use Safari on a public Mac, perhaps in a library, you may not want to leave a trace of where you've been. Choose Safari⇨Private Browsing and Safari keeps your browsing secrets safe. In a nutshell, turning on the Private Browsing keeps your web-browsing history usage private by

✦ Not tracking which websites you visit

✦ Removing any files that you downloaded from the Downloads window (Window⇨Downloads)

✦ Not saving names or passwords that you enter on websites

✦ Not saving search words or terms that you enter in the Search and Address field

In other words, the Private Browsing feature gives Safari a case of amnesia when you turn it on, making Safari mind its own business until you turn off Private Browsing. You know when Private Browsing is active because you see the word `Private` in the Search and Address field. You can use the navigation buttons during the session, but when you close Safari, your viewing history is erased.

When Private Browsing is turned off, Safari goes back to thoughtfully keeping track of the websites you visit and the terms you type into the search box so you can easily return to those sites or searches later.

In addition to Private Browsing, Safari offers Security and Privacy preferences. Do the following to set these up:

1. **Choose Safari⇨Preferences and click the Security button on the toolbar.**

2. **Select the check box next to the options you want to activate:**

- *Fraudulent Sites:* When you open a website that Safari finds suspicious, you receive a warning that requires you to confirm or cancel opening the page.

- *Web Content:* JavaScript is a language used for buttons, forms, and other website content; if this check box is left clear, some website functionality may be lost. Pop-up windows often contain advertising, so you may want to leave this check box clear. That said, some website functionality may be lost if you don't enable this feature. In both cases, if necessary, you'll receive a message from the website prompting you to activate the feature.

- *Internet Plug-ins:* For the most part, plug-ins enable media playback on a website, such as videos, music, or slideshows. Some plug-ins track your browsing history. Click the Manage Website Settings button to see which plug-ins are installed on your Mac and which sites have been using them, as shown in Figure 1-22. You can read about the security-risk level and set specific settings for each plug-in.

  When a web page requires a plug-in that isn't installed, an arrow points to the object that requires the plug-in with a message that reads "Missing Plug-In." You can usually click to install the necessary plug-in.

3. **Click the Privacy button on the toolbar to open Privacy preferences, as shown in Figure 1-23.**

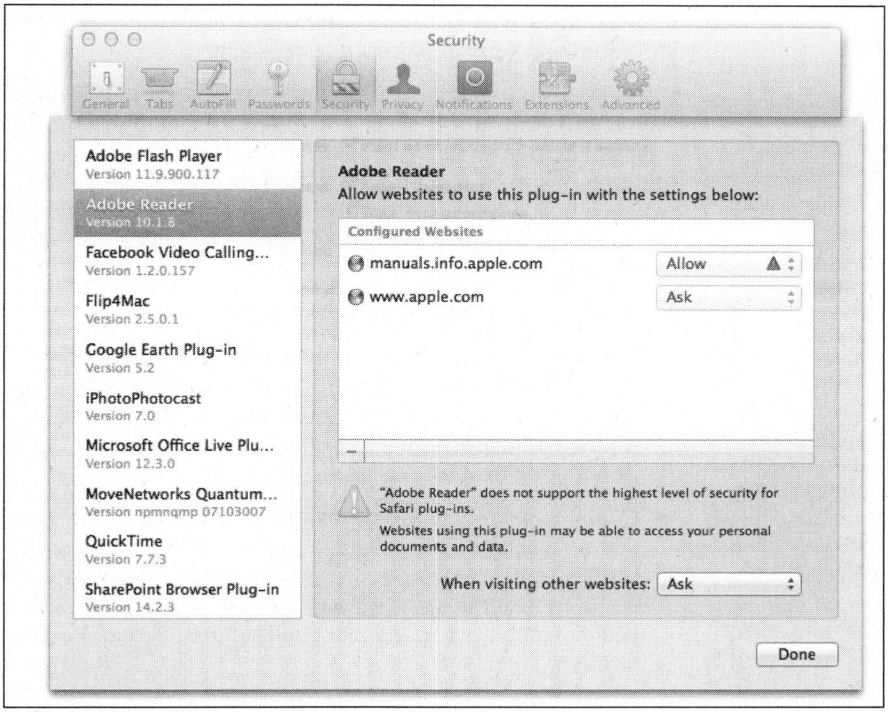

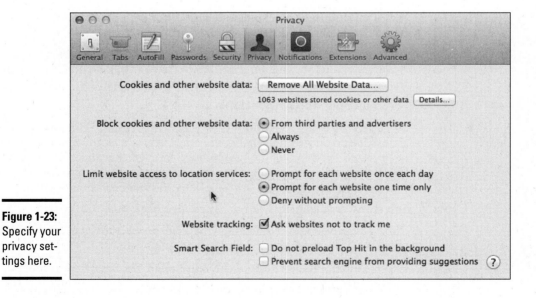

Figure 1-22:
Manage
your plug-
in settings
form the
Security
preferences.

Figure 1-23:
Specify your
privacy set-
tings here.

4. **Tighten your web-browsing security by clicking the Remove All Website Data button to remove cookies.**

   Safari keeps a list of websites that keep track of information about you. This data is stored on your Mac in different places and used in different ways. Clicking the Remove All Website Data button, deletes this data but that may lead to problems with loading your favorite web pages until Safari builds up the information again. You can click the Details button and see who's tracking what, and then select specific sites you would like to remove.

   The three basic types of information are

   • *Cache* is information, such as a web page address, your Mac stores and remembers about your Safari usage so Safari runs faster. You can empty the cache by choosing Safari⇨Empty Cache. A confirmation dialog will ask whether you really want to do this because it can slow down your browsing.

   • *Cookies* are pieces of information about you that websites you visit use to track your browser usage. Cookies may also be used for user authentication or specific information. When you sign up with a website, that site gives you a cookie so that the next time you go to that website, it recognizes you because it sees you have one of its cookies.

   • *Local storage* is information about you that's used by the websites you visit.

5. **Select an option to block cookies and other website data: Always, Never, or From Third Parties and Advertisers.**

   If you selectively block cookies by selecting the From Third Parties and Advertisers option, you are less likely to have trouble with online stores that use cookies to keep your shopping cart information.

6. **Select an option to limit location services.**

   Some websites ask to identify your physical location, which they can access based on your Internet connection. You can select when you want to be asked by selecting the Prompt for Each Website Once Each Day or the Prompt for Each Website One Time Only options; if you want to tacitly deny access to everyone, select the Deny without Prompting option.

7. **Select the Ask Websites Not to Track Me check box.**

   This is a request, not a demand, which means websites can continue to track you if they decide to deny (ignore) your request.

8. **Choose none, one, or both of the options for the Smart Search Field.**

9. **Click the Notifications button on the toolbar to see a privacy-related preference.**

We explain the Notification Center in full in Book I, Chapter 6. Within Safari, there are websites that would like to notify you when information is updated. The first time this happens, a dialog asks whether you want to allow the website to push notifications. You can allow or deny this action. Allowing it means you will receive a notification each time new information is added to the website and the website manager deems it worthy of telling you; denying means you will be left alone and will see the new information the next time you choose to visit the website. The Notifications preferences shows a list of websites that have asked for your permission to send notifications along with the response you gave.

10. **Click the Close button.**

If you have reason to believe that your Mac or your Internet browsing have been tampered with, you can reset Safari. To do this, choose Safari➪Reset Safari. A dialog opens with a series of check boxes, as shown in Figure 1-24. You can't undo this procedure; so *carefully* choose the items you want to reset.

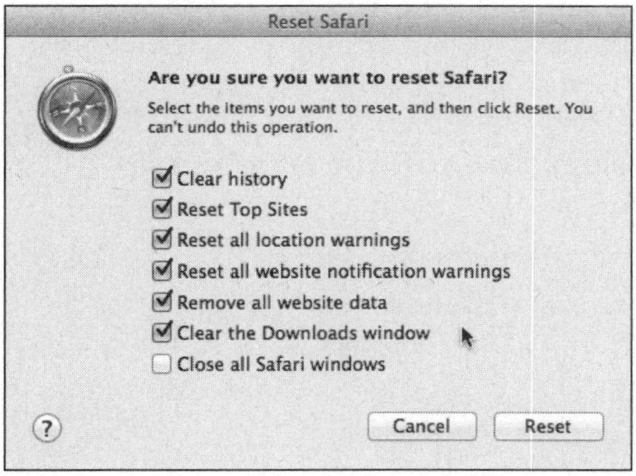

Figure 1-24:
Resetting
Safari
wipes out
all traces of
your brows-
ing history,
and then
some.

> **Reset Safari**
>
> **Are you sure you want to reset Safari?**
> Select the items you want to reset, and then click Reset. You can't undo this operation.
>
> ☑ Clear history
> ☑ Reset Top Sites
> ☑ Reset all location warnings
> ☑ Reset all website notification warnings
> ☑ Remove all website data
> ☑ Clear the Downloads window
> ☐ Close all Safari windows
>
> Cancel   Reset

Saving and Sharing Web Pages

When you come upon a web page containing a story or a recipe that you want to save for later reference, you can add it to the Reading List, as we explain previously, or you can save the file. If you want to share that great recipe with friends, you have many options so they can have a look at what you find so interesting. We explain both saving and sharing here.

Saving a web page as a file

When you save a web page as a file, you store the complete text and graphics of that web page as a file on your Mac's hard drive. Safari gives you three ways to save a web page:

✦ **As a Web Archive:** A *web archive* is meant for viewing a web page only in the Safari browser.

✦ **As an HTML Source File (called Page Source):** If you view a web page saved as Page Source, you won't see any of the graphics, but you will see text references to the graphics and each one's associated URL. Saving a web page as an HTML source file lets you view and edit that file in any browser or web page authoring application, which is helpful if you want to figure out how someone designed that particular web page.

HTML stands for *HyperText Markup Language,* which is a special language used to specify the layout and behavior of web pages.

✦ **As a PDF (Portable Document Format) file:** In simple terms, Safari saves the web page as an image and exports it at a PDF file, which can be viewed, but not edited, in many popular apps such as Preview, Adobe Acrobat Reader, Microsoft Word, and Pages.

PDF is a special file format for storing the layout of text and graphics so they appear exactly the same on different computers.

To save a web page as a file, follow these steps:

1. **In Safari, find the web page that you want to save and choose File⇨Save As.**

Or, choose File⇨Export as PDF.

The Save As dialog opens, as shown in Figure 1-25.

Figure 1-25: Choose the file format and location.

Export As:	Spray Painted Bananas – Wattpad.weba	▼
Tags:		
Where:	🗁 Downloads	⬍

Format: Web Archive ⬍
Saves text, images, and other content of this page.

Cancel | Save

2. **(Optional) Type a new descriptive name in the Save As or Export As field if you don't want to keep the one Safari automatically fills in for you.**

3. **(Optional) Add any tags you want to associate with the saved file.**

Tags are keywords that help you find your file at a later date. See Book I, Chapter 4 to learn about tags and tagging.

4. **From the Where pop-up menu, choose where you want to store your file on your Mac's hard drive.**

If you click the Expand (downward-pointing arrow) button to the right of the Export As field, the Save As dialog expands to let you choose more folders to store your file.

5. **If you choose Save As, open the Format pop-up menu, choose Web Archive or Page Source, and then click Save.**

After you save a file as a Web Archive, Page Source, or PDF, you can view it by double-clicking the file icon in the folder where you saved it.

Saving a photo from the web

Websites are full of graphics and photos. There are times when you want to save an image, and Safari makes it easy to do — just make sure that you keep the image to yourself if you don't have the rights to it. To save an image to iPhoto, do the following:

1. **In Safari, find the image on a web page that you want to save.**

2. **Right-click the image and choose Add Image to iPhoto Library, as shown in Figure 1-26.**

   Or choose one of the other saving options from the menu.

   Some websites "protect" against copying the images by using a transparent overlay that prevents your click from being on, and selecting, the image you want to copy.

Figure 1-26:
Right-click
to save an
image from
a web page.

3. **iPhoto opens automatically and the image is imported.**

   You can adjust, share, or print the image. (See Book IV, Chapter 3 for details on using iPhoto.)

Sharing a web page

If we had to choose one word to describe Apple apps, it would probably be "sharing." Whether it's text in Pages, an image in iPhoto, or a web page in Safari, the procedure for sharing is the same and as simple as a click.

To share a link to web page, do the following:

In Safari, click the Share button on the toolbar or choose File⇨Share; then choose one of these options, as shown in Figure 1-27:

✦ **Email This Page:** Sends a link to the web page in an e-mail message. The Mail application loads and opens a new e-mail message containing your web page link. Fill in the address and subject fields, write an accompanying message, and click Send. (See Book II, Chapter 2 to learn about Mail.)

✦ **Messages:** Sends a link to the web page that the recipient can click to open the web page with her web browser. A message bubble opens. Fill in the address field and click Send. (See Book II, Chapter 3 to learn about Messages.)

✦ **AirDrop:** Sends the link to other Macs on the same network with AirDrop opened.

✦ **Twitter/Facebook/LinkedIn:** Opens a form with the link attached. Type your tweet or status update and click Send or Post. If you aren't signed in to your account, you will be prompted to sign in or create a new account. (See Book I, Chapter 3 to learn about setting up Internet accounts.)

Figure 1-27: Share news and discoveries with people you know.

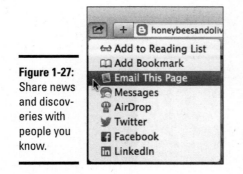

If you send a link to a web page and that web page or website is changed or is no longer available, someone who clicks the link will see an error message instead of the web page you wanted him to see.

Printing a web page

Rather than saving or sharing a web page as a file, you might just want to print it instead: for example, you might want to print a press clip that lauds your latest art installation and mail it to your grandmother who doesn't have Internet access. To print a web page, follow these steps:

1. **In Safari, find the web page you want to print and choose File➪Print to open the Print dialog.**

2. **Open the Printer pop-up menu and choose the printer to use.**

3. **Use the other pop-up menus to choose print quality, number of copies, and page range.**

   Leave Print Backgrounds and Print Headers and Footers unchecked as this usually prints unnecessary information that only wastes ink.

4. **Click the Show Details button to see more options, with regard to page size, scale, and layout. Click Hide Details to close these options.**

   If you click the PDF button, you can save your web page as a PDF file.

5. **Click Print.**

Book II
Chapter 1

Browsing the Web
with Safari

Viewing and Playing Multimedia Files

The most basic web pages consist of mainly text and sometimes graphics. However, most websites offer robust content beyond simple words and pictures, including content stored as video, audio, and other types of common files, such as PDF files. Usually, you can just click the playback button, and the audio or video begins to roll. Sometimes you might need additional software — a plug-in — to view content, and you will be prompted to download the appropriate plug-in.

Watching video

Many news sites offer videos that require *plug-ins,* which are special apps that can read specific types of media, such as Adobe Flash, Windows Media Player, or RealPlayer.

To download the necessary plug-in so you can play Windows Media video content, go to

`www.microsoft.com/mac/products/flip4mac.mspx`

and download Windows Media Components for QuickTime. This app allows the QuickTime Player that comes with your Mac to play most video files designed to run with Windows Media Player.

Some websites won't work unless you're using Microsoft Windows. In this case, you might need to run Windows on your Mac with one of the applications described in Book III, Chapter 5.

Besides downloading and installing the Windows Media Components for Quick Time, you could also download and install both

✦ The RealPlayer app (www.real.com)

✦ Adobe Flash (http://get.adobe.com/flashplayer/?promoid=JZ EFT)

After you have these three apps installed, you should be able to watch videos on most every website you visit.

Some users have reported problems between Adobe Flash and Safari and some websites. If you run into similar trouble, the solution is to install and use a separate browser, such as Chrome, for websites that use Adobe Flash.

Listening to streaming audio

Many websites offer audio that you can listen to, such as live interviews or radio shows. Such audio is often stored as *streaming audio,* which means that your computer downloads a temporary audio file and begins playing it almost instantly but doesn't actually save the radio app as a file on your hard drive.

Sometimes you can listen to streaming audio through the iTunes application, sometimes you need a copy of Windows Media Components, and sometimes you need a copy of RealPlayer.

Viewing PDF files

Many downloadable documents, booklets, brochures, e-book editions of *The New York Times* best-selling nonfiction and fiction titles, and user guides are offered as a PDF file. If a website offers a PDF file as a link you can click to open, you can view and scroll through it directly within Safari.

You can save a PDF document you're viewing to look at later by clicking the document displayed in the Safari web browser window and choosing File⇨Save As. You don't have to choose Export as PDF because the file already is a PDF. If you double-click a PDF file icon, you can view the contents of that PDF file by using the Preview application included with every Mac.

You can also view PDF files by using the Adobe Reader application — a free download from Adobe (www.adobe.com) — which offers the basic features of the Preview application plus extra features for opening and viewing PDF documents. If you have problems printing certain PDF files with the Preview application, try printing them with the Adobe Reader application instead.

Downloading Files

Part of the web's appeal is that you can find interesting content — music tracks, or free demos of apps you can try before you buy, for example — that you can download and install on your own computer. (When you copy a file from the web and store it on your computer, that's *downloading*. When you copy a file from your computer to a website — such as your electronic tax forms that you file electronically on the IRS's website — that's *uploading*.)

Download those files only if you trust the source. If you visit an unknown website, that unknown website might be trying to trick you into downloading a file that could do harmful things to your Mac, such as delete files, spy on your activities, or even bombard you with unwanted ads, so be careful. Safari has built-in protections that scan websites and downloads to warn you of potential dangers. To discover ways you can protect your Mac (and yourself) from potentially dangerous Internet threats, take a look at the earlier section on protecting your web-browsing privacy and consult Book III, Chapter 2.

**Book II
Chapter 1**

Browsing the Web with Safari

When you find a file you want to download, follow these steps:

1. **Click the Download link or button to begin downloading the file you want to save on your Mac's hard drive.**

   An arrow button appears next to the search field with a small progress bar. Clicking the progress bar opens a list of past and current downloads and their status. You can also view downloads from the Downloads stack on the Dock, and from there, open them in the Finder.

2. **When the file has completely downloaded, double-click the file icon in the Downloads progress list to open the file.**

   Alternatively, you can go to the Downloads stack on the Dock and open the file from there.

   If you downloaded an application, that application might start running or installing itself on your Mac, so follow the onscreen instructions. See Book I, Chapter 5 to read about the App Store and downloading apps.

   If you click the magnifying glass icon to the right of a file displayed in the Downloads progress window, Safari opens a Finder window and displays the contents of the Downloads stack.

By default, downloaded files are saved to the Downloads folder. To change the destination folder, choose Safari⇨Preferences and click the General button. From the Save Downloaded Files To pop-up menu, choose Other, and then click the destination folder in the chooser.

While the Safari Preferences are open, choose to open "safe" files, such as PDFs, photo, and movies, as soon as the download is finished by selecting the Open "Safe" Files After Downloading check box.

Using Extensions

You can enhance your Safari Internet navigation experience by adding *extensions,* which are add-on applets designed by developers and approved by Apple. To find and install extensions, follow these steps:

1. **Click the Safari icon on the Dock or Launchpad.**

2. **Choose Safari⇨Safari Extensions.**

The Safari Extensions Gallery on the Apple website opens, as shown in Figure 1-28.

Figure 1-28:
Safari
Extensions
automate
and add
features to
your web
browsing
activities.

3. **Search for extensions by scrolling through the extensions on the opening page or clicking a category and scrolling through the results.**

4. **When you find a useful or entertaining extension, click the Install Now button.**

The extension is installed in your Home directory's hidden Library folder to be accessed by Safari. (See Book I, Chapter 4 to learn more about the Library folder.) Depending on the type of task the extension performs, it may appear as a banner under the toolbar or as a button on the toolbar, or it might show up on-call: for example, as password manager.

Capturing Web Clips

Rather than view an entire web page, you might really care about only a certain part of a web page that's frequently updated, such as traffic reports on local highways, or breaking news. Safari lets you copy part of a web page and store it as a Dashboard widget called a *Web Clip.*

Dashboard widgets are applications that perform a single task and pop up whenever you choose the Dashboard from the Dock or press Fn+F12. You find out more about Dashboard widgets in Book I, Chapter 2.

To create a Web Clip, follow these steps:

1. **In Safari, go to the web page you're interested in and choose File⇨Open in Dashboard.**

The web page darkens and highlights a portion of the currently displayed web page.

2. **Move your pointer over the part of the web page that you want to view as a Dashboard widget, and then click the mouse to create a selection box.**

3. **(Optional) Click one of the selection box handles surrounding the selection box and drag your mouse to make the box bigger or smaller around the section of information you want to capture.**

4. **Click the Add button in the upper-right corner to save your Web Clip as a Dashboard widget.**

Dashboard automatically opens and displays your newly created Web Clip widget.

To delete a Web Clip, click the Dashboard icon on the Dock (or press Fn+F12 to display your Dashboard widgets or F4 on Apple keyboards from 2007 to 2012), hold down the Option key, move your pointer over the widget you want to delete, and then click the Close button that appears in the upper-left corner. *Adiós,* Web Clip.

5. To manage your extensions after you install them, choose Safari⇨ Preferences and click the Extensions tab.

6. Click the extension you want to manage and choose settings from the menus offered. Click Uninstall if you want to remove the extension.

7. Click a bookmark or enter a new URL in the Search and Address field when you're finished visiting the Extensions Gallery.

Chapter 2: Corresponding with Mail

In This Chapter

✔ **Configuring an e-mail account**

✔ **Writing e-mail**

✔ **Receiving and reading e-mail**

✔ **Organizing mailboxes and mail**

✔ **Cleaning up junk e-mail**

Some futurists say that e-mail, like its paper-based predecessor, is being replaced — in this case, by social networks and by text messages exchanged via mobile phones and other handheld devices. No doubt there are examples of a start-up receiving funding after a Facebook exchange. However — for now, anyway — e-mail remains the professional, not to mention private, secure, and trackable, method of electronic communication. E-mail is fast, (almost always) free, and accessible to anyone with a computer, smartphone, tablet, or e-reader and an Internet connection.

When you have an e-mail account, you have two choices for reading and writing messages:

✦ Through a web browser, such as Safari or Firefox (see the preceding chapter for the lowdown on Safari)

✦ Through an e-mail application, such as the Mac's free Mail application

Accessing an e-mail account through a web browser is simple because you don't need to know how to use another application, and you don't have to worry about knowing the technical details of your e-mail account. (You do need Internet access, though, to read or respond to messages.)

Accessing an e-mail account through an e-mail application lets you download messages so you can read or respond to them even if you aren't connected to the Internet. (Of course, you won't be able to send or receive any messages until you connect to the Internet again.)

If you plan to access your e-mail account only through a browser, such as Safari, you can skip this entire chapter because this chapter explains how to use Mail. If you want to use Mail, read on. In this chapter, we explain how to send and receive e-mail. First, though, we give you a quick review of how to set up an e-mail account. (You can find the full run-down in Book I, Chapter 3.) Then we take you through Mail, the e-mail application that came with your Mac. Mail not only sends and receives messages but is also a veritable filing cabinet for your documents; you can use it to organize and store your correspondence to make later searches easier when you need to find an old "letter" or contract.

Adding an E-Mail Account to Mail

We explain the down and dirty of connecting to the Internet and setting up Internet accounts with all those crazy acronyms like POP, IMAP, DNS, and ISP in Book I, Chapter 3. Here we briefly take you through adding an e-mail account from the Mail app. Before we begin, make sure you have the following information:

✦ **Username (or account name):** Typically a descriptive name (such as nickyhutsko) or a collection of numbers and symbols (such as nickyhutsko09). Your username plus the name of your e-mail or Internet Service Provider (ISP) defines your complete e-mail address, such as nickyhutsko@gmail.com or lilypond@comcast.net.

✦ **Password:** Any phrase that you choose to access your account. If someone sets up an e-mail account for you, he might have already assigned a password that you can always change later.

If you use one of the common Internet e-mail providers — such as Google, Yahoo!, AOL, or Apple's own iCloud — that's all you need. Mail takes care of the rest. And, if you use Apple's iCloud service and typed your icloud.com (or me.com) account name and password when you completed the Welcome setup process, Mail is already configured to access your iCloud e-mail account.

If you use another service provider, you may also need the following, which you can find on your ISP website:

✦ **Incoming server name:** This name is usually a combination of POP or IMAP and your e-mail account service provider, such as pop.comcast.net or imap.gmail.com.

✦ **Outgoing server name:** This name is usually a combination of SMTP (Simple Mail Transfer Protocol) and the name of the company that provides your e-mail account, such as smtp.gmail.com or smtp.comcast.net.

You can access your e-mail from Mail (or a different e-mail application) on your Mac, from a web browser on your Mac, or on another computer, such as at your friend's house or at an Internet café. You can also access your e-mail from handheld devices that have a Wi-Fi or cellular Internet connection. When you use a web browser, you go to the e-mail provider's website.

You can set up your Mail account when you first set up your Mac (as we explain in Book I, Chapter 3) or by setting up your e-mail account within the Mail application.

After you collect the technical information needed to access your e-mail account, you need to configure Mail to work with your e-mail account by following these steps:

1. **Click the Mail icon (the postage stamp with the soaring bird on it) on the Dock.**

The Add Account dialog prompts you to choose a service provider, as shown in Figure 2-1.

If you already added an e-mail account — for example, iCloud, during the initial setup of your Mac — you can still add additional accounts by choosing Mail⇨Add Account and following these steps.

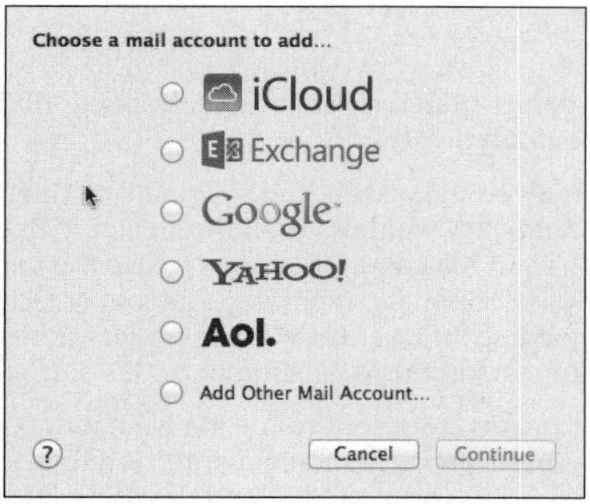

TIP

Figure 2-1:
The New Account dialog displays common e-mail service providers.

Choose a mail account to add...

○ ☁ iCloud

○ E⊠ Exchange

○ Google˙

○ YAHOO!

○ **Aol.**

○ Add Other Mail Account...

(?)   Cancel   Continue

2. **Select the radio button for the ISP you use — for example, Google — and then click the Continue button.**

If your ISP doesn't appear, select the Add Other Mail Account radio button and then click Continue.

3. **In the dialog that opens, enter your full name, e-mail address, and password in the text boxes, as shown in Figure 2-2, and the click the Set Up button.**

If you choose iCloud, use your Apple ID and password, and then click Sign In to add Mail to the iCloud services you use (see Book I, Chapter 3).

If you use Microsoft Exchange, click the Continue button (instead of Set Up).

Your full name is any name you want to associate with your messages. If you type Lily, friend of frogs in the Name text box, all your messages will include From: Lily, friend of frogs. Your e-mail address includes your username plus ISP name, such as lilypond@gmail.com. Your password might be case-sensitive (most are), so type it exactly.

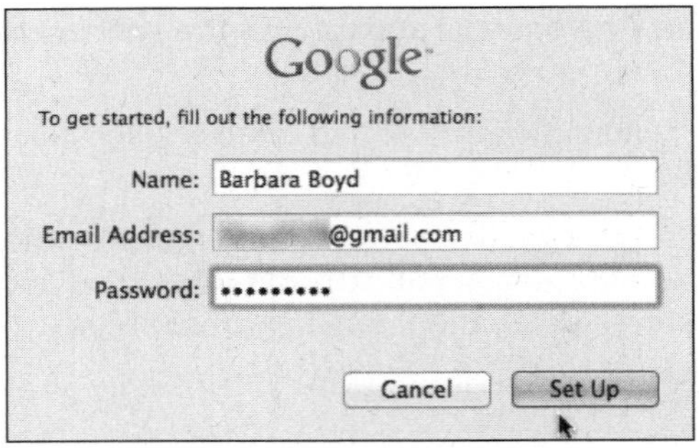

Figure 2-2:
Enter your
new account
info.

4. Mail connects to your e-mail account and attempts to fill in your account settings automatically.

If Mail succeeds in detecting your e-mail account's settings, Mail displays an account summary window, as shown in Figure 2-3. Select the check boxes if you want Mail and other apps to use the information associated with this account: for example, Contacts or Calendar. The options differ depending on what the service provider offers. Click Done, and the account appears in the Mail window.

If Mail doesn't automatically detect your e-mail account settings, continue following the onscreen steps to configure Mail to work with your e-mail account. You will be prompted to add the other information mentioned earlier: the incoming and outgoing mail server names.

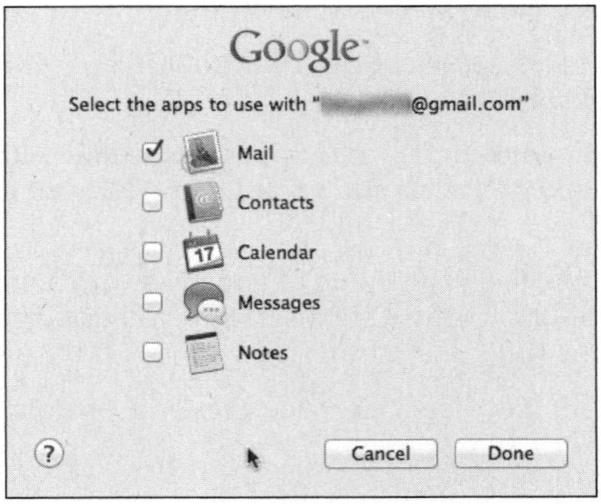

Figure 2-3:
Allow Mail
to set up
information
associated
with your
e-mail
account.

You can configure Mail to retrieve e-mail from multiple e-mail accounts. To add more e-mail accounts, choose File➪Add Account and repeat the preceding steps to add one or more additional e-mail accounts.

Looking at the Mail Window

Throughout the rest of the chapter, we refer to buttons and panes in the Mail window. At the top of the Mail window, you see two sets of tools, as shown in Figure 2-4:

Figure 2-4:
The Mail
window has
five parts.

✦ **Toolbar:** Runs across the top of the window and holds the buttons that you click to take an action, such as write a new message, send a message, or even throw away a message. You can customize the toolbar with the buttons you use most by choosing View➪Customize Toolbar to open the window shown in Figure 2-5. Click and drag the buttons until the toolbar has the tools you need. At the bottom, choose from the pop-up menu to show Icon and Text, Icon Only, or Text Only.

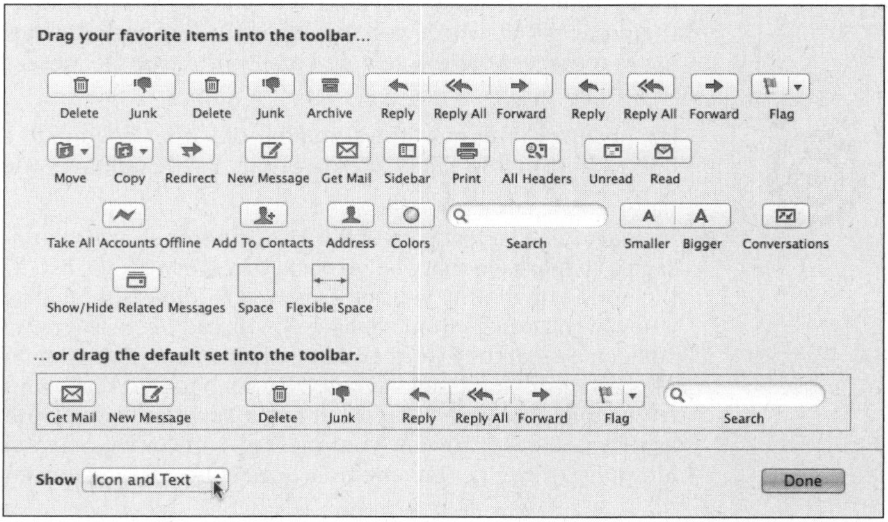

Figure 2-5:
Customize
the toolbar
to show the
buttons you
use most.

✦ **Favorites bar:** Here you find buttons that quickly open your favorite mailboxes. To customize the Favorites bar, drag the mailboxes from the Mailbox list to the Favorites bar; to delete a button from the Favorites bar, click and drag the undesired button out of the Favorites bar, and it disappears in a puff of smoke.

Take a look at Mail on your Mac's screen while reviewing the following parts of the Mail window.

✦ **Mailboxes:** The first column on the left shows a list of your mailboxes. *Hint:* If you don't see this column, click the Show button on the left of the Favorites bar. If you have more than one account, each account will have an item in the Inbox, Sent, Junk, and Trash sections. If you click the topmost button of the section — say, Inbox — you see all the messages in your Inbox listed in the center column. If you click Gmail in the Inbox section, you see only the messages on your Gmail e-mail account. If you have just one e-mail, you will see only the categories. Click the disclosure triangles to the left of the category names to show or hide the subcategories. For example, the Junk category is closed, but there are junk bins for Gmail, iCloud, and Libero in there.

✦ **Mail Activity pane:** Click the disclosure triangle at the bottom of the Mailboxes column to show or hide the Mail Activity pane. When you are sending or receiving messages, a status bar displays the progress of the action.

✦ **Message Preview list:** The second column (which is the first if the Mailboxes column is hidden) shows your messages. Click Sort By at the top of the column to choose how you want to sort your messages or choose View⇨Sort By. Choose View⇨Message Attributes and choose what information you want to see about each message in the preview.

If you prefer the classic layout from older versions of Mail (Mail⇨ Preferences⇨Viewing), you won't see the Message Preview pane but a list of messages for the selected mailbox above the Message pane, as described next.

Hover the pointer over the scroll bar on either column to show a vertical line with an arrow. Click and drag to make the columns wider or narrower.

✦ **Message:** The largest part of the Mail window shows your active message: the message that you've clicked in the Message list. Mail gives you the option of viewing your messages in a Conversation format. When you view a conversation, you see the thread of messages with the same subject, even if they were exchanged between more than one recipient. This way, you don't have to scroll through to find responses from different people on different days, but can follow the "conversation" exchanges as they occurred. To view your messages in conversation mode, choose View⇨Organize by Conversation. See Figure 2-6 for an example.

The number to the right of the preview in the Message Preview list shows how many exchanges make up the conversation. You can also see the "speakers" in the conversation by clicking the arrow next to the number; the active message in Figure 2-6 is expanded. To expand all the messages in Message Preview list, choose View➪Expand All Conversations. Choose View➪Collapse All Conversations to condense them again.

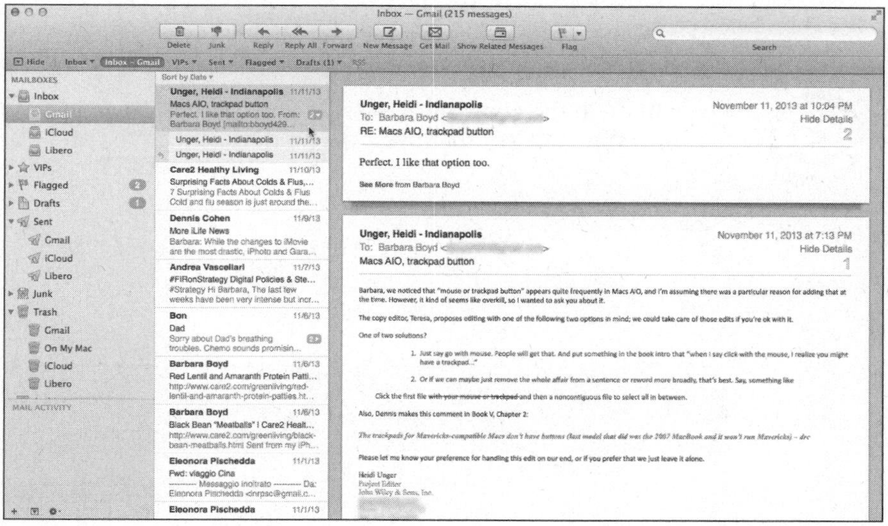

Figure 2-6: Viewing e-mail messages as a conversation makes it easy to follow the sequence of exchanges.

TIP To make adjustments to your view of the Mail window, choose Mail➪ Preferences and then click the Viewing button. Choose the "classic" version of Mail, with your messages displayed in a single line across the top and the active message below. Make other choices about how Mail displays unread messages and conversations.

REMEMBER Mail supports full-screen viewing. Just click the full-screen toggle switch in the upper-right corner and take advantage of your Mac's whole screen.

Writing E-Mails

After you configure your Mail account(s) and are familiar with the buttons and panes, you can start writing and sending e-mail to anyone with an e-mail address. In this section, we describe how to write and send an e-mail, attach files and photos, and customize the appearance of your messages.

Creating a new e-mail

When you write a message to someone for the first time, you have to create a new message. Follow these steps:

1. **In Mail, choose File⇨New Message or click the New Message button.**

   The New Message button looks like a piece of paper with a pencil on it (refer to Figure 2-4).

   A New Message window appears, as shown in Figure 2-7, in which all options are active — we tell you how to turn them on and off in the section, "Customizing your messages."

   Although the steps here instruct you to click in each field, you can also press the tab key to move from field to field.

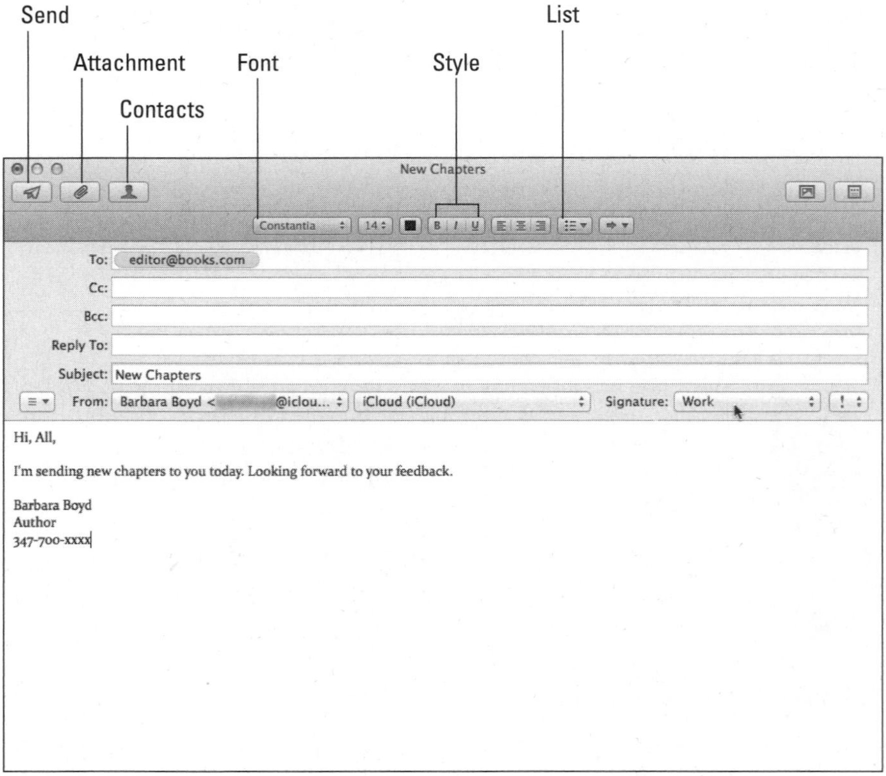

Send

Attachment   Font   Style

Contacts   List

To:	editor@books.com
Cc:	
Bcc:	
Reply To:	
Subject:	New Chapters
From:	Barbara Boyd < _____@iclou...	iCloud (iCloud)	Signature: Work

New Chapters

Constantia   14   B I U

Hi, All,

I'm sending new chapters to you today. Looking forward to your feedback.

Barbara Boyd
Author
347-700-xxxx

Figure 2-7:
Like a letter,
an e-mail
has a
recipient, a
sender, and
a message.

2. **Click the To text box and type an e-mail address or do one of the following:**

   - Click the Add button (the plus sign) at the right end of the field to open Contacts and select recipients from there.

   - Begin typing a name you have stored in Contacts, and Mail will automatically fill in that person's e-mail address (as long as it's part of the person's Contacts card). If a person has more than one e-mail address, click the one you want from the list that appears.

   - Click the Contacts button at the top of the message to open the Addresses window, which shows names and addresses from Contacts as well as any social networks that you activated contacts for (Book I, Chapter 3). Click the name(s) of the person(s) you want to send your message to and then click the To, Cc, or Bcc button.

   When working with lists, ⌘-click to select multiple, noncontiguous names.

   If you want to send the same message to several people, you can type multiple e-mail addresses (be sure to separate each with a comma) or add the addresses from Contacts.

3. **(Optional) Click the Cc and/or Bcc text box and add an e-mail address or addresses using one of the methods in Step 2.**

   - *Carbon copy (Cc):* The Cc field is where you type e-mail addresses of people who you want to keep informed, but who don't necessarily need to write a reply.

   - *Blind carbon copy (Bcc):* The Bcc field sends a copy of your message to e-mail addresses that you type here, but those e-mail addresses will not be visible to other recipients.

   When sending out a particularly important message, many people type the recipient's e-mail address in the To field and their own e-mail address in the Cc or Bcc fields. This way, they can verify that their message was sent correctly.

4. **(Optional) Type an e-mail address in the Reply To field if replies should be sent to an e-mail that's different than the address the message is being sent from.**

   For example, if you send 1,000 invitations to a big event, you could create an e-mail address specifically for the event on one of the common service providers. Although the invitation is sent from you, invitees respond to the special address, and your inbox isn't clogged with 1,000 responses.

5. **Click the Subject text box and type a brief description of your message for your recipient.**

**Book II
Chapter 2**

Corresponding
with Mail

6. (Optional) Open the From pop-up menu to send the message from a different e-mail account, if you have more than one.

7. (Optional) Open the Signature pop-up menu to choose a signature — if you created more than one — and use this option.

8. (Optional) Open the Priority pop-up menu to add urgency to your message.

9. Click in the Message field and type your message.

   Use the font, size, and style pop-up menus to change the typeface of your message, or use more than one typeface in a message. (This works only if you choose Rich Text in the Composing section of Mail⇨Preferences.) Click the List button to format your text with bullets or numbers.

   You can copy text from another message or another app like Notes or Pages, and then choose Edit⇨Paste to insert the copied text.

10. Click the Send button, which looks like a paper airplane, in the upper-left corner.

Replying to or forwarding a message

You'll often find yourself responding to messages others send to you. When you reply to a message, your reply can contain the text that you originally received so the recipient can better understand the context of your reply.

To reply to a message, you need to receive a message first. To receive messages, just click the Get Mail button (refer to Figure 2-4), which looks like an envelope. You find out more about receiving messages later in this chapter.

To reply to or forward a message, follow these steps:

1. In Mail, click the Inbox button on the Favorites bar.

   The left column lists all the messages stored in your Inbox folder.

2. Select a message in the Inbox that you want to reply to.

3. Click one of the following buttons on the toolbar.

   Or you can click buttons on the heads-up display, which is revealed when you hover the pointer over the center of the line between the address information and message. The heads-up display that contains the Trash, Reply, Reply All, and Forward buttons.

   • *Reply:* Opens a response message addressed to the sender only.

   • *Reply All:* If the message was sent to you and several other people, this option — the double left-pointing arrow — sends your response to everyone (except Bcc recipients who you don't know about) who received the original message.

- *Forward:* To send the message to another person, without replying to the sender or other recipients, click the Forward button, which is a right-pointing arrow.

  To both reply and forward the message, click Reply or Reply All. Then click in the To, Cc, or Bcc field, and type the e-mail address of the person you want to forward the message to.

4. **Write your reply in the message that appears with the cursor blinking above the text of the original message.**

5. **Click Send.**

Customizing your messages

Like other Mac apps, Mail offers preferences that let you customize and personalize your messages. You access many settings from the Mail Preferences window and one group of settings from a New Message. We explain both here.

Keeping up appearances

In this section, we talk about how your outgoing messages appear. Whether you write a new message, reply to a message, or forward a message to another person, you have several choices about how that message appears. Go to Mail⇨Preferences and set the following for your druthers:

1. **Click the Fonts & Colors button on the toolbar to choose the font for outgoing messages.**

2. **Click the Select button next to the Message Font field and scroll through the Fonts chooser to choose a Collection, Family, Typeface, and Size, as shown in Figure 2-8. Pull down the dot (by the cursor in Figure 2-8) to see what your font choice looks like.**

   You can also change the message font on individual messages using the pop-up menus above the message header (refer to Figure 2-7).

Minding your manners

Because of its electronic nature, e-mail can seem deceptively informal. However, since it has replaced much paper-based correspondence — personal and professional — some etiquette should be followed:

✔ When replying or forwarding a message, delete irrelevant content or select the part you want to include, then click the Reply button so only the selected part appears in the reply message.

✔ When answering multiple questions, place your responses in the text so the recipient understands the relevance.

✔ Even a quick "thanks" lets the sender know you received the message.

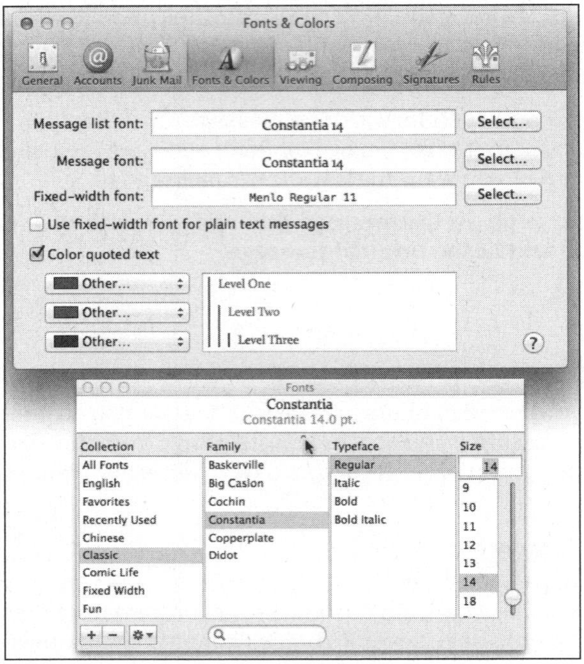

Figure 2-8:
Choose font styles and sizes in Mail Preferences.

3. **(Optional) Click the Select button next to Message List Font and Fixed-width Font to change those.**

4. **(Optional) Select the Color Quoted Text check box to change the color of text as it's quoted in an ongoing message conversation.**

   Click the color swatch pop-up menus to change the color used for each level of a conversation. Click Other to open a color selector and choose a custom color.

5. **Click the Composing button on the toolbar to make choices about the appearance of outgoing messages, as shown in Figure 2-9.**

6. **In the Composing section, choose the following:**

   - *Message Format:* Choose from Plain Text or *Rich Text,* which takes advantage of stylized text functions such as bold, italic, and underlining.

   - *Check Spelling:* Activate one of the spell checking options: As I Type, When I Click Send, or Never.

   - *Automatically Cc/Bcc Myself:* Select the check box to receive carbon copies (blind or viewed) for every message you send. The carbon copy will show up in your inbox in addition to the copy in your Sent messages folder.

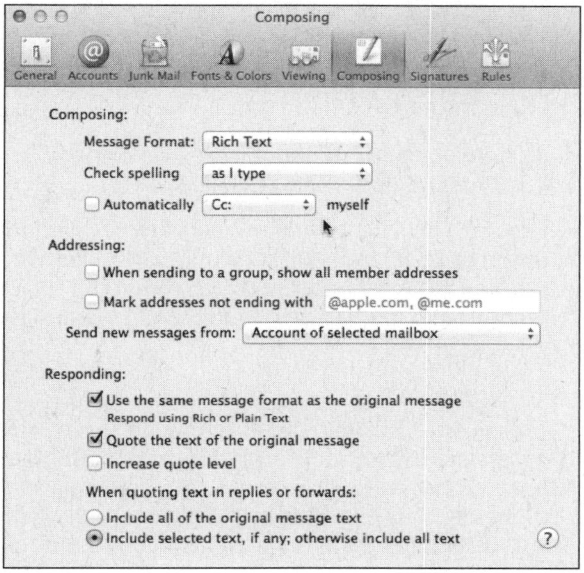

Book II
Chapter 2

Corresponding
with Mail

Figure 2-9:
Customize
how
outgoing
messages
look.

7. **In the Addressing section, make the following choices:**

- *When Sending to a Group, Show All Member Addresses:* If this check box is left clear, group members see only the group name, not the addresses of individual members.

- *Mark Addresses Not Ending With:* Select the check box and type e-mail address suffixes that you don't want marked. For example, if you type the suffix of your company e-mail, all other messages will be marked, but company messages will not.

- *Send New Messages From:* if you have multiple e-mail accounts, choose a specific account for sending all messages or choose Account of Selected Mailbox. You can always change the outgoing mailbox on individual messages as long as the From field is viewable. (See the upcoming section on showing and hiding address fields.)

8. **The five options in the Responding section affect how your replies appear:**

- *Use the Same Message Format as the Original Message:* We suggest selecting this so you don't risk sending a formatted, rich text message that the recipient can't view properly.

- *Quote the Text of the Original Message:* Select this check box to show the original message in your reply.

- *Increase Quote Level:* Select this check box, and the original text will be indented one level. If you have an ongoing conversation, the original text indents one more level with each response.

- *When Quoting Text in Replies or Forwards:* You have two choices here:

- *Include All of the Original Message Text:* The original text is included in forwarded messages as well as replies.

- *Include Selected Text, If Any; Otherwise Include All Text:* If you want to include only a portion of the original message, highlight the portion of the message you want to appear in your reply, and then click the Reply or Forward button. Only the highlighted text appears in your message.

Signing your message

The signature block at the bottom of an outgoing message or reply gives you an opportunity to give a little extra information to the recipient, such as your phone number and website, or express your personality and wit with an image or citation. If you have multiple e-mail accounts, you can assign a different signature to each account. You can also create multiple signature blocks and then choose which you want to use depending on the tone and occasion of your message. Here's how to create message signatures:

1. **Choose Mail⇨Preferences and then click the Signatures button on the toolbar.**

2. **As shown in Figure 2-10, click the account name in the first column and then click the + (plus sign) at the bottom of the second column.**

   Mail makes a signature suggestion, such as your first name or your first and last name with your e-mail address.

Figure 2-10: Create signature blocks for different types of messages.

3. **(Optional) To change the default signature that Mail chose, click the text to select it and retype what you want to appear as your signature block.**

   You can also copy and paste an image from another app.

   To insert a website link, leave the cursor in the Signature block but choose Edit⇨Add Link. Type the URL (or copy and paste or click and drag from Safari) and then click OK. Recipients can click the link, and the website opens in the recipient's browser. You can also select typed text or an image and then choose Edit⇨Add Link; the link is applied to the selected item (see Figure 2-10).

4. **Repeat Steps 2 and 3 to create other signatures: for example, a professional signature you use for work and another you use for messages sent to friends.**

   Hint: Double-click the signature name (Signature #1, Signature #2, and so on) to give the signature a more meaningful name.

5. **(Optional) Click All Signatures, and then click and drag signatures from the second column to a different account name to use the same signature for different accounts.**

   The number of signatures associated with each account is shown under the account name.

   When you show the signature field in outgoing messages, you see only the signatures associated with the account you're using to send the message.

6. **Click the Close button.**

Select and edit signature blocks within a message if it's not quite appropriate in that instance.

Showing and hiding address fields

Whenever you write a message, the To field is always visible because you need to send your message to at least one e-mail address. However, Mail can hide and display the Header fields — Cc, Bcc, Reply To, and From — because you don't always want or need them in every message you write. A Priority and Signatures menu can be added, too, if those are something you find useful. Follow these steps:

1. **Click the New Message button (refer to Figure 2-4) to open a new message.**

2. **Click the Header Fields button to the left of the From field.**

3. **Choose Customize.**

   The header appears, as shown in Figure 2-11.

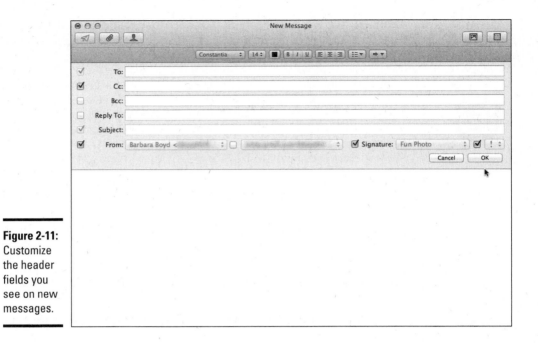

Figure 2-11:
Customize
the header
fields you
see on new
messages.

4. **Select the check boxes next to the fields you want to appear on your messages.**

   Those with a check mark appear in your new messages. Check the boxes next to Signature and/or Priority to see a menu for those items on new messages.

   The To and Subject fields are mandatory, but the From field is not. This doesn't mean that your messages will be mandatory, only that you won't see that field on the New Message window. If you have more than one e-mail address, you should leave it so you can confirm which address the message is being sent from.

5. **Click OK.**

   You will see only the fields you selected in this and future new messages, replies, or forwarded messages that you create.

   If you want to show or hide the header fields or the priority menu on a single message, click the Header Fields button and select, or deselect, the item you want to show or hide.

Sending a file or photo attachment

When you send an e-mail, you're sending text. However, sometimes you might want to send pictures, documents or videos. Anyone receiving your message and file attachment can then save the file attachment and open it later. Many people need to share files or digital images, and file attachments are one way to share files with others.

Your e-mail account may limit the maximum file size you can send, such as 10MB, and your recipients may have limits on the file size they can receive. If you have a file larger than 60 to 70 percent of the maximum limit, you might have to send your files through a free remote storage and file-sharing service, such as Hightail (www.hightail.com), SendThisFile (www.sendthisfile.com), or Dropbox (www.dropbox.com).

To attach a file to a message, follow these steps:

1. **In Mail, open a new Message window as described in one of the preceding sections.**

You can open a new Message window to create a new message, reply to an existing message, or forward an existing message.

2. **Choose File⇨Attach Files or click the Attach button, which looks like a paper clip.**

A browse dialog appears.

3. **Navigate through the folders to get to the file you want to send and then click it.**

To select multiple files, hold down the ⌘ key and click each file you want to send. To select a range of files, hold down the Shift key and click the first and last files you want to send.

4. **Click Choose File.**

If you have just one file, it is pasted into your message. If you paste multiple files, the file is particularly large or in a format that Mail can't display, such as FileMaker or ePub, you see an icon for the attached file in the message window.

To send a single file as a file or to facilitate sending multiple files, select the file(s) in the Finder, and then choose File⇨Compress. The Finder creates a ZIP file that comprises the selected files. Attach the ZIP file to your message.

5. **Choose Edit⇨Attachments and select one or more of the following to set rules for attachments:**

- *Include Original Attachments In Reply:* Attaches the original attachment to your reply to the message it came with. This option is usually best left not selected because it only creates bigger messages that take longer to send, and the person who sent you the attachment should have it, anyway.

- *Always Send Windows-Friendly Attachments:* Makes sure that Windows users can read your attachment. This option is best selected because you can never be 100 percent sure which operating system your recipient will use to read your attachment.

- *Always Insert Attachment at End of Message:* Inserts the attachment at the bottom, so the recipient may have to scroll down to get to the attachment. Whether you select this option is really a personal preference. If you want the attachment in the middle of the message — a photo, for example — don't select this check box.

6. **Click the Message text box and type your message.**

7. **Click the Send button.**

You could use the preceding steps to attach a photo to your message, or you can go directly to the Photo Browser, which shows photo previews instead of a list of names like DSC174 that don't mean anything to you until you open them. To use the Photo Browser, do the following:

1. **In Mail, open a new Message window, as described in one of the preceding sections.**

   You can open a new Message window to create a new message, reply to an existing message, or forward an existing message.

2. **Click the Photo Browser button, which has an image of a mountain with a tiny moon over it.**

   The Photo Browser opens, as shown in Figure 2-12. Click and drag the bottom-right corner to enlarge the browser.

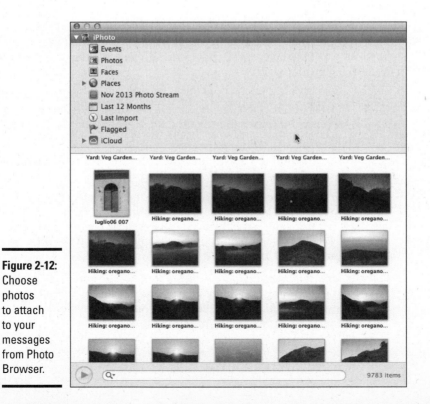

Figure 2-12: Choose photos to attach to your messages from Photo Browser.

3. **Scroll through thumbnails from your iPhoto and Photo Booth photos, events, and albums until you find the photo you want.**

4. **Double-click an event or album to see the photos in the event or album; double-click a photo to see an enlarged preview in the bottom half of the browser window.**

5. **To select multiple photos, hold down the ⌘ key and click each photo you want to send. To select a range of photos, hold down the Shift key and click the first and last photos you want to send.**

6. **Drag the selected photo or photos into your message.**

   The photos are pasted into your message.

7. **Adjust the image size by selecting Small, Medium, Large, or Actual Size from the pop-up menu on the bottom right of the new message window, as shown in Figure 2-13.**

   The larger the photo, the larger the message file will be, making it potentially slower to send and receive, although the better resolution is useful if the photo is destined to be printed.

Figure 2-13:
Adjust the
size of the
photo you
want to
send.

8. **Click in the Message text box to type in a message.**

9. **Click the Send button.**

In Book IV, Chapter 3, we explain how to send photos directly from iPhoto.

Using stationery

E-mail stationery consists of graphic designs and formatted text that you can edit to create e-mail messages that look more interesting than plain text. Keep in mind, however, that all those pretty accents increase the size of any e-mail messages you create with stationery and may not be legible if the recipient uses an e-mail application that doesn't support HTML. To use the Mail application's Stationery feature to create a new message, follow these steps:

1. **In Mail, choose File⇨New Message or click the New Message button to open a New Message window.**

2. **Click the Show Stationery button in the upper-right corner of the new message window.**

   A list of stationery categories (Birthday, Photos, and so on) appears in the upper-left pane, and a list of stationery designs appears in the upper middle of the New Message window.

3. **Click a Stationery category, such as Sentiments or Birthday.**

   Each time you click a different category, the Mail window displays thumbnail images of stationery designs in that category.

4. **Click the stationery design that you want to use.**

   Your chosen stationery appears in the main section of the New Message window.

5. **Click any placeholder text and edit or type new text.**

After you choose a stationery design, you can edit the text and replace it with your own message. If the stationery displays a photograph, you can replace the photograph with another picture stored in iPhoto or somewhere else on your hard drive.

To add your own pictures to a stationery design, follow these steps:

1. **Make sure that Mail displays a stationery design that includes one or more pictures.**

2. **Click the Photo Browser button.**

   The Photo Browser window appears, containing all the photographs you've stored in iPhoto and Photo Booth.

3. **Scroll to the folder that contains a photograph that you want to use in your stationery.**

4. **Click and drag your chosen photograph onto the picture in your stationery design.**

5. **Release the mouse button.**

   Your chosen picture now appears in your stationery, as shown in the lower part of Figure 2-14.

6. **Click the Close button of the Finder or Photo Browser window.**

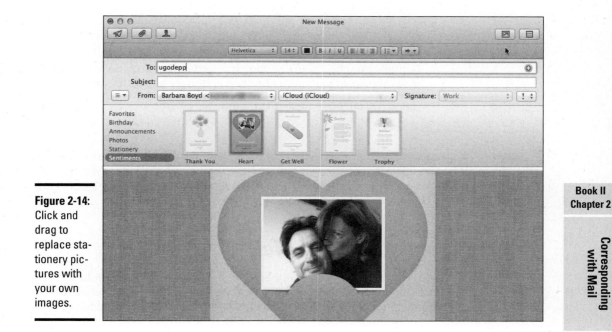

Figure 2-14:
Click and
drag to
replace sta-
tionery pic-
tures with
your own
images.

Spelling and grammar checking

Although e-mail is considered less formal than many other forms of communication (say, letters or a last will and testament), you probably don't want
your e-mail message riddled with spelling errors and typos that can make
you look bad. That's why Mail provides a spelling and grammar checker.

If you have spell checking turned on while you type (Mail➪Preferences➪
Composing), the spell checker will underline suspected misspelled words in
red to help you find potential problems easily. If you want to spell-check and
grammar-check your entire message, follow these steps:

1. **Open a New Message window as described earlier in this chapter.**

You can open a New Message window to create a new message, reply to
an existing message, or forward an existing message.

2. **Type your message.**

3. **Choose Edit➪Spelling and Grammar➪Show Spelling and Grammar.**

The spelling and grammar checker does it thing, with a Spelling and
Grammar dialog appearing each time Mail finds a potentially misspelled
word.

4. **Click one of the following buttons:**

• *Change:* Changes the misspelled word with the spelling that you
choose from the list box on the left

• *Find Next:* Finds the next occurrence of the same misspelled word

- *Ignore:* Tells Mail that the word is correct
- *Learn:* Adds the word to the dictionary
- *Define:* Launches Mac's Dictionary application and looks up and displays the word's definition in the Dictionary's main window
- *Guess:* Offers best-guess word choices

5. **Click Send.**

The spelling and grammar checker can't catch all possible errors (words like *fiend* and *friend* can slip past because the words are spelled correctly), so make sure that you proofread your message after you finish spell-checking and grammar-checking your message.

Receiving and Reading E-Mail

To receive e-mail, your e-mail application must contact your incoming mail server and download the messages to your Mac. Then you can either check for new mail manually or have Mail check for new mail automatically.

Retrieving e-mail

To check and retrieve e-mail manually in Mail, choose Mailbox⇨Get New Mail or click the Get Mail icon. The number of new messages appears next to the Inbox icon, and in a red circle on the Mail icon on the Dock and Launchpad.

Checking for new e-mail manually can get tedious, so you can configure Mail to check for new mail automatically at fixed intervals of time, such as every 5 or 15 minutes. To configure Mail to check for new messages automatically, follow these steps:

1. **In Mail, choose Mail⇨Preferences.**

2. **Click the General icon on the toolbar to display the General pane, as shown in Figure 2-15.**

3. **From the Check for New Messages pop-up menu, choose an option to determine how often to check for new messages.**

   Automatically will get your new mail whenever you open Mail and continuously as long as Mail remains open. Choose Every Minute, Every 5 Minutes, Every 15 Minutes, Every 30 Minutes, or Every Hour, to check at the chosen interval.

4. **(Optional) Choose a sound to play when you receive new messages from the New Messages Sound pop-up menu.**

   You can also choose None in case any sound bothers you.

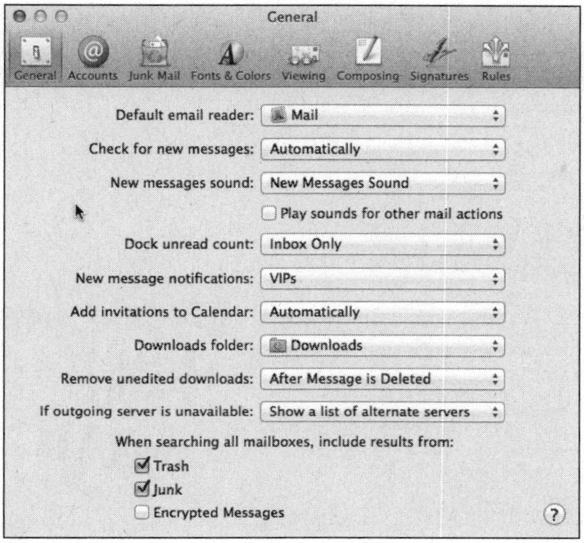

Figure 2-15:
Set how
often to
check for
new e-mail.

5. **Use the pop-up menus to select your preferences for the following options:**

   - *Dock Unread Count:* Choose whether the number in the badge on the Mail icon on the Dock reflects unread messages in your inbox only or in all mailboxes: for example, unread messages that went directly to Junk.

   - *New Message Notifications:* Indicate which types of communications you want the Notification Center to manage: Inbox Only, VIPs, Contacts, or All Mailboxes. (See Book I, Chapter 6 to learn about the Notifications.)

   - *Add Invitations to Calendar:* Invitations sent in the iCal file format can be added automatically to the Calendar app or never added, in which case you can add them manually.

6. **Click the Close button.**

Mail can check for new messages only if you leave Mail running. If you quit Mail, it can't check for new messages periodically.

Reading e-mail

After you start receiving e-mail, you can start reading your messages. When you receive a new message, Mail flags it with a dot in the Message Preview list, as shown in Figure 2-16. If you have the Mailboxes list showing, the number next to each mailbox indicates the number of unread messages.

Your Mac can read your messages aloud to you. Just open a message and then choose Edit➪Speech➪Start Speaking.

Figure 2-16:
Mail shows
you which
messages
you haven't
read yet.

To read a message, follow these steps:

1. **In Mail, click the Inbox button on the Favorites bar.**

   A list of messages stored in the Inbox appears in the Message Preview list.

2. **Click a message to read the message in the message pane, or double-click a message to display and read a message in a separate window.**

The advantage of the message pane is that you can scan your messages quickly by clicking each one without having to open a separate window. The advantage of reading a message in a separate window is that you can resize that window and see more of the message without having to scroll as often as you would if you were reading that same message in the message pane.

Viewing and saving file attachments

When you receive a message that has a file attachment, you see a paper clip next to the sender's name in the Message Preview list and also on the actual message. To save a file attachment, follow these steps:

1. **In Mail, click the Inbox button on the Favorites bar.**

   A list of messages stored in the Inbox appears.

2. **Click a message with an attachment icon (paper clip) in the Message Preview list.**

3. **Click the attachment icon within the message and then choose File⇨Quick Look Attachments, which shows you a preview of the file without actually opening it.**

A window appears, displaying the contents of your file attachment (or playing the file if it's a music or video file). If there are multiple images, click the arrows to move from one image to the next or click the thumbnail view button to see all the images at once. Click the Close button (the X in the upper-left corner) of the Quick Look window when you finish looking at its contents.

Double-click an attachment to open it in its originating app.

4. **Choose File⇨Save Attachments.**

   If the e-mail message contains more than one attachment, choose an individual attachment to save it but not the others.

5. **In the dialog that opens, choose the folder where you want to save the attachments.**

   By default, Mail saves your attachments into the Downloads stack on the Dock, unless you designate another folder in the General window of Mail preferences.

6. **Click Save.**

   You can also just click and drag attachments from the message body to the Desktop or a Finder window or folder. To do so, hold down the ⌘ key to select more than one attachment; then click and drag any one of the selected attachments to the Desktop or a Finder window.

**Book II
Chapter 2**

**Corresponding
with Mail**

Adding an e-mail address to Contacts

Typing an e-mail address every time you want to send a message can get tedious — if you can even remember the address. Mail searches your messages as well as Contacts for matches when you begin to type a name in an address field. Nonetheless, you may want to add the people behind those addresses to Contacts on your Mac so your addresses are all in one place.

When you receive an e-mail from someone whose name and address you want to remember, you can store that person's e-mail address in Contacts by following these steps:

1. **In Mail, click the Inbox button on the Favorites bar.**

2. **In the Message Preview list, select a message sent by someone whose e-mail address you want to save.**

3. **Choose Message⇨Add Sender to Contacts.**

   Although nothing appears to happen, your chosen e-mail address is now stored in Contacts.

To view your list of stored names and e-mail addresses, you can retrieve information from Contacts by choosing Window⇨Address Panel.

Organizing E-Mail

To help you manage and organize your e-mail messages, Mail lets you search and sort your messages. Spotlight (search) finds specific text stored in a particular message. When you find the messages you want, you may want to group them in a folder. You can also establish "smart mailboxes" so Mail automatically puts related messages in the same folder or establish rules for what mail goes to which mailbox. We also tell you how to use the Flag tool, which helps you sort e-mails related to specific tasks you'd like to attend to.

Searching through e-mail

To manage your e-mail effectively, you need to be able to search for one message (or more) you want to find and view. To search through your e-mail for the names of senders, subjects, or text in a message, follow these steps:

1. **In Mail, click the Spotlight Search box in the upper-right corner.**

2. **Type a word, phrase, or partial phrase that you want to find.**

   When you type, Mail displays a list of messages that match the text you're typing in the Message Preview list and indicates where the text was found (for example, People, Subject, Mailboxes, or Attachments), and the word Search appears next to the buttons on the Favorites bar, as shown in Figure 2-17.

3. **Click one of the buttons on the Favorites bar or the mailboxes in the Mailboxes list (click Show to see it) to narrow your search.**

   Your options are to search through All Mailboxes, the Inbox, or one of the account-specific inboxes or in Sent or one of the account-specific outboxes.

   To include the Trash, Junk, or Encrypted Messages in your search, choose Mail➪Preferences➪General and select the Trash, Junk, and/or Encrypted Messages check boxes.

4. **(Optional) Click the Save button in the upper-right corner to open a Smart Mailbox window, and then customize your search.**

   Type in a name for your new Smart Mailbox search, choose any options you want to customize your search, and then click OK to save your Smart Mailbox search.

   We explain smart mailboxes in depth in the "Automatically organizing e-mail with smart mailboxes" section, later in this chapter.

5. **Click a message to read it.**

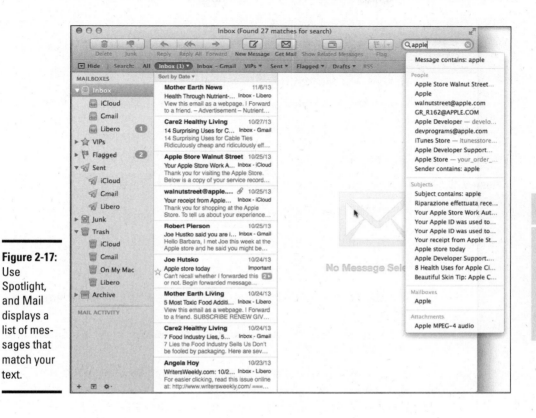

Figure 2-17:
Use
Spotlight,
and Mail
displays a
list of mes-
sages that
match your
text.

Organizing e-mail with mailbox folders

When you receive e-mail, all your messages are dumped in the Inbox. If you have multiple accounts, the Inbox shows messages from all accounts, and clicking a specific account on the Favorites bar or the Mailboxes list shows only the messages in that account. Organizing your messages by conversation (choose View➪Organize by Conversation) helps, but after a while, you might have so many messages stored there that trying to find related messages can be nearly impossible.

To fix this problem, you can create separate folders for organizing your different e-mails. After you create a folder, choosing to organize by conversation keeps related messages together so you can quickly find them later.

One common type of e-mail to organize is junk e-mail, which you can route automatically to the Trash folder, as we write about in the upcoming "Dealing with Junk E-Mail" section.

Creating a mailbox folder

To create a mailbox folder, follow these steps:

1. In Mail, choose Mailbox⇨New Mailbox.

A New Mailbox dialog appears, as shown in Figure 2-18.

New Mailbox

Enter name for new local mailbox to be created at the
top level of the "On My Mac" section.

Location: 🖥 On My Mac

Name: Wiley

Cancel | OK

2. Use the Location pop-up menu to choose a destination for your new folder.

3. In the Name text box, type a descriptive name for your mailbox folder and then click OK.

Your mailbox folder appears in the Mailboxes column of the Mail window.

4. (Optional) Drag the folder onto the Favorites bar if you want.

Storing messages in a mailbox folder

When you create a mailbox folder, it's completely empty. To store messages in a mailbox folder, you must drag those messages manually to the mailbox folder. Dragging moves your message from the Inbox folder to your designated mailbox folder.

To move a message to a mailbox folder, follow these steps:

1. In Mail, click the Inbox icon in the Mailboxes list or on the Favorites bar to view your e-mail messages.

2. Click a message and drag it to the mailbox folder you want and then release the mouse.

Your selected message now appears in the mailbox folder.

If you hold down the ⌘ key while clicking a message, you can select multiple messages. If you hold down the Shift key, you can click one message and then click another message to select those two messages and every message in between.

Deleting a mailbox folder

You can delete a mailbox folder by following these steps:

1. **In Mail, click the mailbox folder you want to delete.**

2. **Choose Mailbox⇨Delete.**

A confirmation dialog appears, asking whether you're sure that you want to delete your folder.

When you delete a mailbox folder, you delete all messages stored inside.

3. **Click Delete.**

Automatically organizing e-mail with smart mailboxes

Mailbox folders can help organize your messages, but you must manually drag messages into those folders or set up rules to automate the process. As an alternative, to make this process automatic, you can use *smart mailboxes*.

A smart mailbox differs from an ordinary mailbox in two ways:

✦ A smart mailbox lets you define the type of messages you want to store automatically; that way, Mail sorts your messages without any additional work from you.

✦ A smart mailbox doesn't actually contain a message but only a link to the actual message, which is still stored in the Inbox folder (or any folder that you move it to). Because smart mailboxes don't actually move messages, a single message can have links stored in multiple smart mailboxes.

Creating a smart mailbox

To create a smart mailbox, you need to define a name for your smart mailbox along with the criteria for the types of messages to store in your smart mailbox. To create a smart mailbox, follow these steps:

1. **In Mail, choose Mailbox⇨New Smart Mailbox.**

A New Smart Mailbox dialog appears.

2. **Click the Smart Mailbox Name text box and type a descriptive name for your smart mailbox.**

3. **Open the Match pop-up menu and choose All (of the Following Conditions) or Any (of the Following Conditions).**

4. **Open the first criterion pop-up menu and choose an option, such as From or Date Received, as shown in Figure 2-19.**

5. **Open the second criterion pop-up menu and choose how to apply your first criterion (for example, Contains or Ends With).**

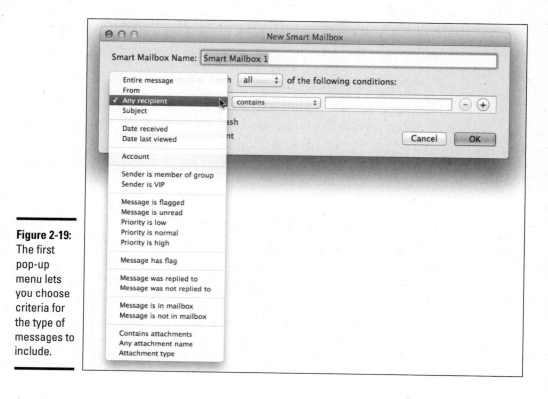

Figure 2-19:
The first
pop-up
menu lets
you choose
criteria for
the type of
messages to
include.

6. **In the Criteria text box, type a word or phrase that you want to use for your criterion.**

7. **(Optional) Click the Add Rule icon (the plus-sign button) and repeat Steps 3–6.**

8. **Click OK.**

    Your smart mailbox appears in the Mailboxes column of the Mail window. If any messages match your defined criteria, you can click your smart mailbox's icon to see a list of messages.

The messages stored in a smart mailbox are just links to the actual messages stored in your Inbox folder. If you delete a message from a smart mailbox, the message remains in the Inbox; if you delete a message from the Inbox, it is also deleted from the smart mailbox.

Deleting a smart mailbox

Deleting a smart mailbox doesn't physically delete any messages because a smart mailbox only contains links to existing messages. To delete a smart mailbox, follow these steps:

1. **In Mail, click the smart mailbox folder you want to delete.**

 2. Choose Mailbox⇨Delete.

  A confirmation dialog appears, asking whether you're sure that you want to delete your smart mailbox.

 3. Click Delete (or Cancel).

Automatically organizing e-mail with rules

Smart mailboxes provide links to e-mail messages that remain in your Inbox folder. However, you may want to actually move a message from the Inbox folder to another folder automatically, which you can do by defining rules.

The basic idea behind rules is to pick criteria for selecting messages, such as all messages from specific e-mail addresses or subject lines that contain certain phrases, and route them automatically into a folder.

To create a rule, follow these steps:

 1. Choose Mail⇨Preferences to open the Mail preferences window.

 2. Click the Rules icon on the toolbar.

  The Rules window appears.

 3. Click Add Rule.

  The Rules window displays pop-up menus for defining a rule.

 4. Click the Description text box and type a description of what your rule does.

 5. Open one or more pop-up menus to define how your rule works.

  For instance, you might define what to look for or which folder to move the message to, as shown in Figure 2-20.

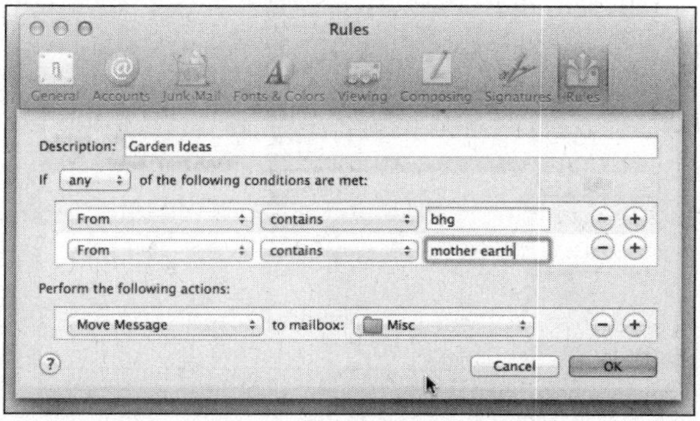

Figure 2-20:
Select mes-
sages to
sort by your
rule.

 6. (Optional) Click the plus sign button to define another sorting crite-rion for your rule and repeat Steps 5 and 6 as often as necessary.

7. **Click OK when you finish defining your rule.**

   A confirmation dialog appears, asking whether you want to apply your new rule to your messages.

8. **Click Apply.**

9. **Click the Close button of the Rules window.**

   Mail now displays your messages sorted into folders according to your defined rules.

To modify an existing rule, click an existing rule and click Edit.

Flagging your messages

Sometimes you receive a message that contains a task you must attend to later. You could print the message and hang it on a bulletin board in your office or on your refrigerator so you don't forget, or you can flag it in Mail. You can choose from seven colors so you can use different colors for different types of e-mails: say, all e-mails related to one project, or to give the task a priority. Here's how to work with flags:

1. **Click Inbox on the Favorites bar or Mailboxes list.**

2. **Select the message you want to flag.**

3. **Click the Flag pop-up menu on the toolbar, or choose Message⊏›Flag, and select the color flag you want to assign to that message.**

   A little colored flag appears next to the message in the Message Preview list and next to the From field in the message itself.

4. **To see your flagged messages all together, do one of the following:**

   • Click Flagged in the Mailboxes list. (Click Show to the left of the Favorites bar to see the Mailboxes list.)

   • Click the Flagged button on the Favorites bar. (If you don't see the button, drag it from the Mailboxes list.)

   • Choose Flags from the Sort By menu at the top of the Message Preview list to see the flagged messages all together in the mailbox that you're viewing.

5. **To remove the flag, select the message and choose Clear Flag from the flag pop-up menu.**

Flags are named by their color, but you can rename them; for example, name the red flag "Urgent" rather than "red." Click the disclosure triangle next to Flagged in the Mailboxes list. Double-click the flag name (the color) to select the word, and then type the name you want.

You can set up rules (choose Mail➪Preferences➪Rules) to automatically flag messages that meet certain criteria.

Dealing with Junk E-Mail

Just like you receive junk mail in your paper mailbox, soon after you get an e-mail address, you're going to start receiving junk e-mail (or *spam*). While you can't entirely stop it, Mail has filters that help limit the inevitable flow of junk e-mail so you can keep your e-mail account from getting overwhelmed, and — perhaps more important — limit the dispersion of your e-mail address and the personal information on your computer that can be accessed through your e-mail.

Most junk e-mail messages are advertisements trying to sell you various products, but some junk e-mail messages are actually scams to trick you into visiting bogus websites that ask for your credit card number or (worse) try to trick you into giving your bank-account info. This form of spam is called *phishing*. Other times, junk e-mail might contain an attachment masquerading as a free application that secretly contains a computer virus. Or, a junk e-mail might try to trick you into clicking a web link that downloads and installs a computer virus on your Mac. By filtering out such malicious junk e-mail, you can minimize potential threats that can jeopardize your Mac's integrity or your personal information.

Filtering junk e-mail

Filtering means that Mail examines the content of messages and tries to determine whether the message is junk. To improve accuracy, Mail allows you to train it by manually identifying junk e-mail that its existing rules didn't catch.

After a few weeks of watching you identify junk e-mail, the Mail app's filters begin to recognize common junk e-mail and route it automatically to a special Junk folder, keeping your Inbox free from most junk e-mail so you can focus on reading the messages that matter to you.

To train Mail to recognize junk e-mail, follow these steps:

1. **In Mail, click the Inbox button on the Favorites bar or click Show to reveal the Mailboxes list, and then click the Inbox button.**

   A list of messages appears in the Message Preview list.

2. **Click a message that you consider junk.**

3. **Choose Message➪Mark➪As Junk Mail or click the Junk button on the toolbar.**

   This tells the Mail application's filters what you consider junk e-mail. The message is moved to the Junk mailbox.

4. **Click the Junk mailbox.**

   Mail displays the messages in the Message Preview list and the message information is written in brown.

5. **Click the message you marked as Junk.**

   A banner runs across the top of the message, as shown in the top of Figure 2-21. If you accidentally marked the message as Junk, click the Not Junk button and drag the message back to the inbox it came from.

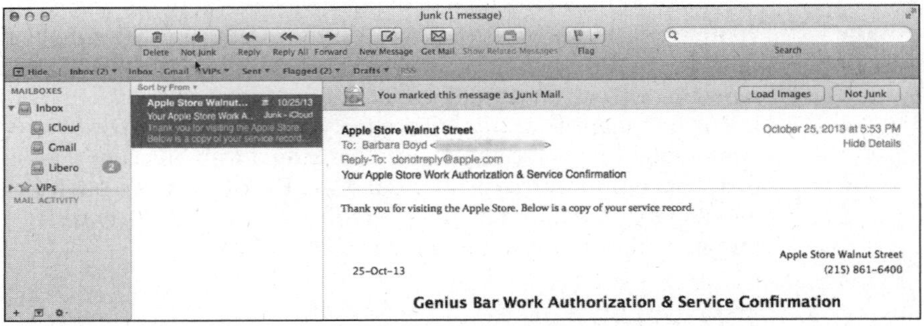

Figure 2-21:
Click Not
Junk for
legitimate
messages.

6. **Click the Delete icon (upper left).**

   This deletes your chosen message and "trains" Mail to recognize similar messages as junk.

Sometimes legitimate e-mail messages can wind up in Junk in Mail or in the Spam folders of web-based e-mail providers, such as Gmail, Yahoo! Mail, and Microsoft Live Hotmail. If there are messages in your Junk or Spam mailboxes that shouldn't be there, click the message. A banner runs across the top of the message, as shown in the bottom of Figure 2-21. Click the Not Junk button and drag the message to your Inbox. This way, Mail learns that messages from this sender are not junk mail.

The cleverness and prowess of spammers and phishers increases daily. Keep an eye out for these tipoffs to counterfeit requests:

✦ Misspelled words

✦ Logo design, colors, or type that is slightly different than that of the legitimate company

✦ Sender addresses that don't match the company name

Using advanced filter rules

If you find that you're still getting a lot of junk mail or that it arrives from a specific source, you can set the Junk mail preferences to better manage junk mail by following these steps:

1. **Choose Mail⟶Preferences and click the Junk button.**

The Junk Mail preferences window shown in Figure 2-22 opens.

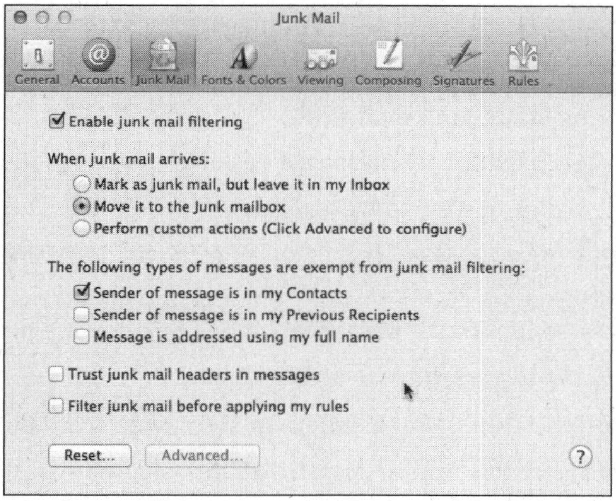

Book II
Chapter 2

Corresponding
with Mail

Figure 2-22:
Help Mail learn which messages are Junk by setting Junk preferences.

2. **Make sure that the Enable Junk Mail Filtering check box is selected.**

3. **Select one of the following choices to indicate where you want Junk mail to go when it arrives.**

- *Mark as Junk Mail, But Leave It in My Inbox:* Puts junk mail in with all your good mail.

- *Move It to the Junk Mailbox:* This option nicely separates junk mail for you and puts it in its own mailbox.

4. **(Optional) Select the Perform Custom Actions radio button to activate the Advanced button. Then click Advanced.**

A pane opens, as shown in Figure 2-23.

a. *Use the pop-up menus to set up rules for filtering incoming mail. Use the plus and minus buttons to the right of each rule to add or delete a rule.*

b. *Use the pop-up menus in the Perform the Following Actions section. Indicate what you want Mail to do when a message arrives that meets the established rules.*

c. *Click OK.*

Figure 2-23: Advanced Junk settings can better eliminate unwanted e-mail.

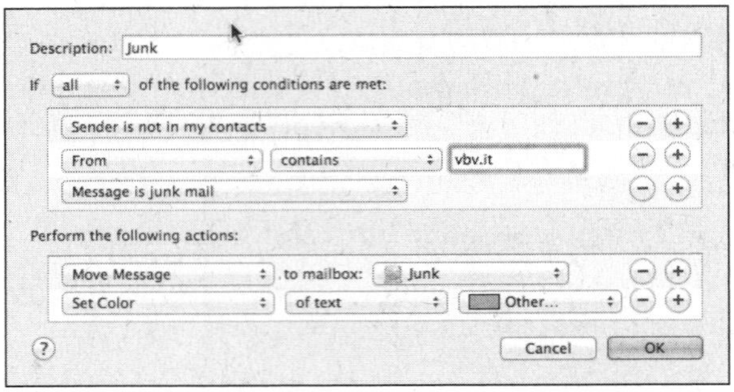

Description: Junk

If [all ⬍] of the following conditions are met:

[Sender is not in my contacts ⬍] ⊖ ⊕

[From ⬍] [contains ⬍] [vbv.it] ⊖ ⊕

[Message is junk mail ⬍] ⊖ ⊕

Perform the following actions:

[Move Message ⬍] .to mailbox: [📁 Junk ⬍] ⊖ ⊕

[Set Color ⬍] [of text ⬍] [Other... ⬍] ⊖ ⊕

(?)   [Cancel] [OK]

5. **Select one or more of the following choices for the types of messages to exempt from the junk mail filter.**

   This helps keep legitimate messages out of your Junk mailbox.

   - *Sender of Message Is in My Contacts*

   - *Sender of Message Is in My Previous Recipients*

     Even if the sender isn't in your Contacts, if you received a message from the sender in the past, it won't be considered junk.

   - *Message Is Addressed Using My Full Name*

6. **Select the Trust Junk Mail Headers in Messages check box.**

   When you select this option, Mail trusts the mail that your e-mail provider identifies as junk.

   Many web-based e-mail providers have special applications running on their e-mail servers that try to sniff out junk e-mail before it lands in your Inbox.

7. **Select the Filter Junk Mail before Applying My Rules check box.**

   This gives precedence to Mail's filter before applying your custom filter rules.

Although Mail's built-in junk e-mail filters can strip away most junk e-mail, consider getting a special junk e-mail filter as well. These e-mail filters strip out most junk e-mail better than Mail can do, but the Mail application's filters might later catch any junk e-mail that slips past these separate filters, which essentially doubles your defenses against junk e-mail. Some popular e-mail filters are SpamSieve (`http://c-command.com`) and SPAMfighter (`www.spamfighter.com`). Spam filters cost money and take time to configure, but if your e-mail account is overrun by junk e-mail, a separate junk e-mail filter might be your only solution short of getting a new e-mail account.

Deleting and Archiving Messages

After you read a message, you can leave it in your Inbox, delete it, or archive it for old time's sake. Generally, it's a good idea to delete messages you won't need again, such as an invitation to somebody's birthday party back in the summer of 2008. If you do delete a message that you shouldn't have, you can retrieve it, but only if the Trash folder hasn't been emptied.

Deleting messages

By deleting unnecessary messages, you can keep your Inbox organized and uncluttered — and if you're using an IMAP or Exchange account, free up space on the mail server where your e-mail messages are stored.

To delete a message, follow these steps:

1. **In Mail, click the Inbox button on the Favorites bar.**

   A list of messages stored in the Inbox appears.

2. **Click the message you want to delete.**

   To select multiple messages, hold down the ⌘ key and click additional messages. To select a range of messages, hold down the Shift key, click the first message to delete, click the last message to delete, and then release the Shift key.

   Sorting by From can make deleting messages from the same sender easier.

3. **Choose Edit➪Delete (or click the Delete button).**

Deleting a message doesn't immediately erase it but stores it in the Trash folder. If you don't "empty the trash," you still have the chance to retrieve deleted messages, as outlined in the next section.

Retrieving messages from the Trash folder

Each time you delete a message, Mail stores the deleted messages in the Trash folder. If you think you deleted a message by mistake, you can retrieve it by following these steps:

1. **In Mail, click the Trash folder.**

   A list of deleted messages appears.

2. **Click the message you want to retrieve.**

3. **Choose Message➪Move To➪Inbox.**

You can set up Mail to automatically move deleted messages to the trash and permanently erase those trashed messages after a month, a week, a day, or upon quitting Mail. To configure this option, choose Mail⇨Preferences, click the Accounts button, click a mail account in the Accounts column, and then click Mailbox Behaviors and adjust the settings for Trash to suit your e-mail housekeeping style.

Emptying the Trash folder

Messages stored in the Trash folder continue to take up space, so you should periodically empty the Trash folder by following these steps:

1. **In Mail, choose Mailbox⇨Erase Deleted Messages.**

A submenu appears, listing all the e-mail accounts in Mail.

2. **Take one of the following actions.**

- Choose In All Accounts to erase all deleted messages.

- Choose the name of a specific e-mail account to erase messages only from that particular account.

Archiving messages

If you want to reduce the number of messages you see in your mailboxes but not delete the messages — say, at the end of the year or when a project is complete — you can create an archive of those messages. Archived messages are kept in a folder in Mail but removed from active mailboxes. To archive messages, do the following:

1. **Click the mailbox that contains messages you want to archive.**

2. **Right-click the messages you want to archive or choose Edit⇨Select All if you want to archive all messages in the mailbox.**

3. **Choose Message⇨Archive.**

The selected messages are moved to the Archive file in Mail.

You can then click the Archive file, select the archived messages and choose Mailbox⇨Export Mailbox. Select a destination in the window that opens and then click Choose. Your messages are exported to a file in the selected folder on the chosen external drive or directory, and you can delete them from Mail to free up space on your Mac.

Chapter 3: Chatting with Messages and FaceTime

In This Chapter

✔ Setting up an account

✔ Chatting about other chat applications

✔ Adding your best buddies

✔ Chatting via text, audio, and video

✔ Saving chats

✔ Calling other Apple devices with FaceTime

The idea behind instant messaging (IM) is that you communicate with someone over the Internet by using text, audio, or video — and it's all free. (Well, it's sort of free, when you ignore the fact that you're probably paying your broadband Internet provider a pretty penny every month so you can access the Internet.)

Now you can swap messages with your friends, chat in real time across the planet, and even see each other through live video windows while you speak. Instant messaging offers another way for you to communicate with anyone in the world, using an Internet connection and your Mac.

By using your Mac's Messages app, you can exchange basic text chat messages with others instantly. And Messages also makes live video and audio chats and conferences, and file sharing, practically as easy as chatting over the telephone. If you have friends or family with a Mac or iPhone 4 or later, iPad 2 or later, or iPod touch (fourth generation or newer), you can use FaceTime to conduct a video chat from your Mac to your friend's Apple device.

In this chapter, we show you how to set up a Messages account and use Messages to have IM, audio, and video chats. We also explain how to share files, images, and even your Mac's screen with Messages. We give you all the tips and tricks to set up and use FaceTime, too.

Getting Started in Messages

Messages uses your Apple ID or the account name from another IM, such as Google Talk, AOL AIM, Jabber, or Yahoo! Messenger. Although each service offers its own app, Messages keeps all your accounts and contact information in one place so you don't have to have a separate app for each service and account.

Choosing a chat service

If you have an existing IM account with one of these services, you're ready to set up Messages and start chatting in a matter of minutes. If you don't have a chat account, you need to set up an account with at least one of the following services:

✦ **iMessage:** Use your Apple ID to communicate with friends who use iMessage on Macs and iOS devices.

✦ **AOL Instant Messenger (AIM):** Available free at www.aim.com, existing AIM account users and new users are warmly welcome to use their account name with Messages. You can also use your AOL e-mail account.

✦ **Google Talk:** Got a Google Gmail account? If so, you have a Google Talk account, which allows you to send and receive text messages or conduct video conferences with other Gmail account holders from your Gmail web page (http://gmail.google.com). Having a Google Gmail account also means that you can use it to set up Messages to send and receive text messages and connect with other Gmail account buddies with Messages audio and video chat, and screen-sharing feature. Google Talk usernames end with @gmail.com.

✦ **Jabber:** With this original IM service (based on *XMPP*, the open standard for instant messaging), you can create a Jabber account by visiting http://register.jabber.org or one of the other public XMPP services, and then use your Jabber account (which ends with @jabber.org) to log in and start chatting.

✦ **Yahoo! Messenger:** If you have a Yahoo! e-mail or Yahoo! Messenger account, you can set up an account for either in Messages as long as you have your username and password. Messages will take care of the rest. Set up an account at the Yahoo! website (http://messenger.yahoo.com).

As a general rule, you and the person you chat with have to have the same service, so you may want to have more than one account to chat with different people. To better understand which chat accounts can communicate with which other chat accounts, check out the nearby sidebar, "Can't we all just get along?"

You can install and run other chat applications to send and receive IM and conduct voice and video chats with your friends who use other chat accounts and chat applications.

Can't we all just get along?

You can use only some of Messages' livelier features — such as audio and video chatting and screen sharing — when you connect to friends using the same kind of account as you. You got it: iCloud account users can send text messages and video chat with one another and with AIM users, but they can't conduct video chats with Google Talk, Jabber, or Yahoo! users.

On the other hand, Google Talk accounts act as Jabber accounts, and Jabber accounts act as Google Talk accounts. That is, Google Talk and Jabber account holders running Messages

get to take advantage of Messages audio and video chat and screen-sharing features, in addition to text chat.

To get the most from using Messages with friends, you want to sign in with an account that matches the ones your friends are using. If your friends use Google Talk to sign in to Messages and you use Yahoo! Messenger, you might want to create a Google Gmail account and add your Google Talk account to Messages so you can audio chat and video chat with your friends who sign in with a Google Talk account name.

If your company uses a different IM system, ask your network administrator whether a profile is available for Macs. Install the profile on your Mac and then use Messages to chat with colleagues.

Setting up a Messages account

After you create a chat account, you can set up a Messages account by following these steps:

1. Click the Messages icon (the speech bubbles) on the Dock or Launchpad to launch Messages.

A window opens with the prompts for signing in with your Apple ID. This enables iMessage, which communicates with other Macs and iOS devices.

2. Log in:

- *Type in your Apple ID and password and click Sign In.*

    Messages opens, ready to start messaging.

- *Or, click Not Now and confirm that you want to skip this step.*

    Messages opens with the Add Account screen, as shown in Figure 3-1.

If you signed in with your Apple ID but want to add other instant message accounts, choose Messages⇨Add Account.

The Add Account screen opens (see Figure 3-1).

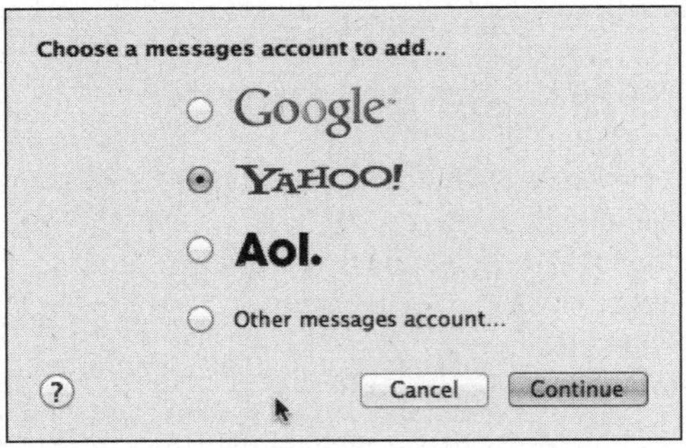

Figure 3-1:
Choose
the type of
account
you want
to add to
Messages.

Choose a messages account to add...

○ Google·

⦿ YAHOO!

○ Aol.

○ Other messages account...

⑦   Cancel   Continue

3. **Select the type of account you want to add and then click Continue:**

- For Internet messaging, select the Google, Yahoo!, or AOL radio button and then click Continue. A dialog opens with fields for your e-mail address and password. Enter those and click the Set Up button.

- Select the Use Other Messages Account radio button to add existing instant messaging accounts from AIM, Google Talk, Jabber, or Yahoo! and then click Continue. Click the Account Type pop-up menu and choose your account type. Type in your username and password and click the Create button, as shown in Figure 3-2.

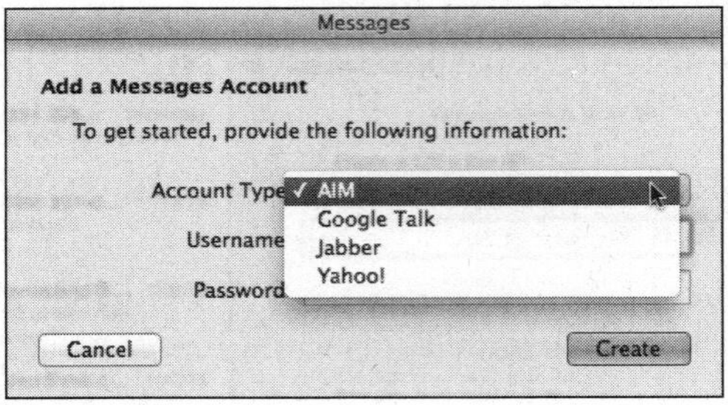

Figure 3-2:
Messages
prompts
you for your
account
information.

Messages

Add a Messages Account

To get started, provide the following information:

Account Type ✓ AIM
                Google Talk
Username   Jabber
                Yahoo!
Password

Cancel   Create

4. **Repeat to add other accounts.**

Messages opens, ready to start messaging.

If you want to use iMessage in the future to communicate with other Macs and iOS devices that use iMessage, go to Messages➪Preferences➪Accounts, click the iMessage icon in the Accounts list, and type in your Apple ID and password.

Keeping up appearances

You may be perfectly happy with how Messages looks, but check out the preferences that Messages offers for your chat window and for each individual account. Go to Messages⇨Preferences and do the following:

1. **Choose Messages⇨Preferences and then click the General button on the toolbar.**

2. **Peruse the choices. We suggest you consider a few:**

- *Message Received Sound:* Open the pop-up menu to choose the sound to indicate received messages.

- *Buddy List:* Select Show All My Accounts in One List to keep everything together, nice and tidy.

- *Account Status:* You have five choices here. In particular, we suggest selecting When I Quit Messages, Set My Status to Offline, and Set My Status to Away After the Computer Is Inactive. These automatically do what you'd probably do yourself.

3. **Click the Viewing button and use the pop-up menus to choose the background color, font color, and font style and size for you and the person you're chatting with (the Sender).**

4. **Click the Accounts button and do the following:**

- *Add or remove accounts.* Click the Add button (the plus sign) to add a new account, or click an account and then the Delete button (the minus sign) to remove one.

- *Manage individual account settings.* Click an account and use the check boxes, buttons, and menus to adjust the settings. Each account has different settings. For example, for your Apple iMessage account, you can add additional e-mail addresses where you can be reached. The others have account information and server settings. AIM offers additional Privacy settings, and Google has Chat settings.

5. **Click the Close button.**

 Choose View⇨Messages to change how your IM conversations appear: as balloons, boxes, or compact (a list form with the time stamps to the right instead of above each exchange). In that same menu, choose how your buddies' names appear by each exchange: name only, picture only, or name and picture.

Adding buddies to your account

If you're brand new to IM, setting up a chat account is only the beginning. Your next step is to contact your friends and other contacts you want to chat with, to exchange IM account names. Think of account names as telephone numbers; you can't call a friend without knowing her phone number, and you can't chat with someone if you don't know her account name.

Bonjour

Bonjour is another messaging service within Messages, and it allows you to exchange messages and files with other computers on your local network. When you activate Bonjour and enable IM, everyone on the network can see you. If you trust the folks with whom you share your local network, Bonjour offers a quick way to message and exchange files. If, however, your local network doesn't offer absolute security, you're better off using another IM option, if available. To activate Bonjour, choose Messages⇨Preferences and select the Accounts button. The window shown here opens.

Click the Bonjour button in the accounts list on the left and then select the options you wish to use. To see other people on your network who use Bonjour, open the Finder, choose Finder⇨Preferences, and then click the Sidebar button. Select the Bonjour Computers check box, in the Shared section.

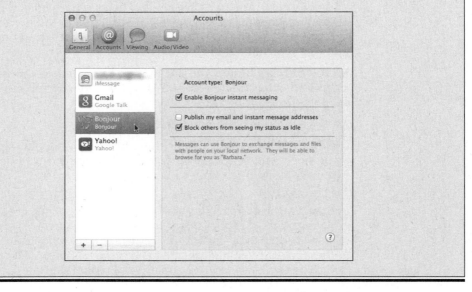

Chances are that you have IM account names in Contacts without even knowing it. As we mention earlier, Google Talk uses Google Mail (@gmail. com) addresses, and iOS devices can use mobile phone numbers as the identification for iMessages. You also want to store your friends' account names in *buddy lists,* which you use to initiate chats with all but the iMessage service

Storing names in a buddy list

In all IM accounts — except iMessage, which accesses Contacts — stored names automatically appear in your Messages buddy lists whenever your friends log in to their particular chat app (which can be an app other than

Messages, such as AOL Instant Messenger for Mac or Windows, or even a mobile chat app running on a smartphone).

If you use iMessage only, you can skip the buddy list section and go directly to the section "Chatting with Others."

To add a name to your buddy list, follow these steps:

1. **Click the Messages icon on the Dock or Launchpad to launch Messages.**

2. **Choose Window⇨Buddies or the name of the account you want to add buddies to, such as Gmail or AIM.**

You have to be online to add buddies; click Offline under your name to open the pop-up menu and choose Available.

3. **Choose Buddies⇨Add Buddy.**

Or click the Add (+) button in the lower-left corner of the Buddies window, and if the pop-up menu appears, select Add Buddy.

A dialog appears, as shown in Figure 3-3.

**Book II
Chapter 3**

Chatting with Messages and Facetime

Figure 3-3:
Add a buddy by chat account name or e-mail address.

4. **Fill in your buddy's chat account name and real name.**

You have two ways to do so:

- *Type your buddy's account name and real name in the text boxes shown in Figure 3-3.* Depending on the chat account your buddy has, the account name might be a single word or an e-mail address.

Filling in your buddy's first and last name is for your convenience only. If you don't know someone's first or last name, or if you prefer to see his chat account name rather than his real name in your buddy list, just leave the name fields blank.

- *Add contacts from Contacts.* Click the down-arrow button next to the Last Name field (refer to Figure 3-3) to expand the Add Buddy dialog and show names from the Contacts app. Use the search field or click the scroll arrows — both are visible in Figure 3-4 — to locate your buddy's contact card and then click your buddy's name to select him or her.

Your buddy's account name, first name, and last name automatically fill in the related fields of the Add Buddy dialog.

If Contacts holds many records, it might be easier to search for a name rather than scroll through your list. In the search field, type in the first few letters of the name of the person you want to add as a buddy. Potential matches appear in the names list. The more letters you type, the narrower the results.

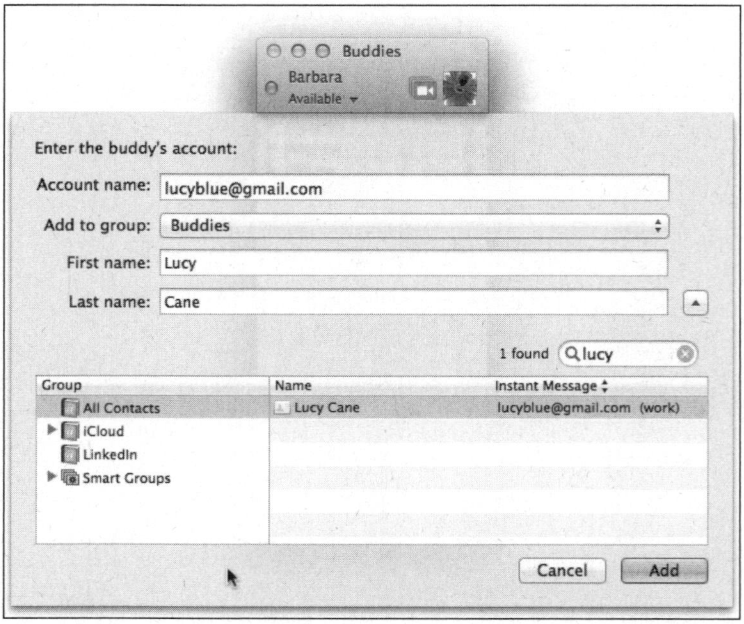

Figure 3-4: Clicking a buddy's contact card automatically fills in the blanks.

4. **(Optional) Click the column heading to the right of the Name column (named Instant Message in Figure 3-4).**

This opens a pop-up menu that lets you choose to display a contact's IM address, e-mail address, or phone number.

5. **(Optional) Open the Add to Group pop-up menu and choose the group category where you want to store your friend's name.**

   (See the upcoming section "Creating groups" to learn how to do that.)

   By default, new buddies go to the Buddies group. You can change which group your buddy appears in at any time.

6. **Click the Add button.**

   Your new buddy appears in your buddy list.

7. **Repeat Steps 2–6 to add other people to your buddy lists.**

   If a buddy has more than one account type, add a new buddy for each account. Each account will appear in the group where you store it.

Viewing your buddies

If you don't see your newly added buddy (or buddies you previously added) in your buddy list, you might have inadvertently chosen a Messages option to hide offline buddies from your buddy list. Messages gives you many options for viewing your buddies' status, all accessed from the View menu. When you see a check mark next to the item, it's active. You can choose one or more of the following:

✦ **Show Buddy Pictures:** Displays the image your buddy has assigned himself.

✦ **Show Audio Status:** Lets you know whether your buddy has audio capabilities.

✦ **Show Video Status:** Lets you know whether your buddy has video capabilities.

✦ **Show Offline Buddies:** Lists both online and offline buddies together; offline buddies' names are dimmed in the list.

✦ **Use Groups:** Divides the Buddies list by account. When deselected, all buddies are in one continuous list.

✦ **Use Offline Group:** Shows offline buddies in a group of their own and only online buddies in each account group. Use Groups must be selected to activate the Use Offline Group option.

✦ **Buddy Names:** From the submenu, choose how you want to see your buddies' names displayed: Full Names (Lucy Cane); Short Names (Lucy); or Handles (account names: Lucyblue).

✦ **Sort Buddies:** From the submenus choose

   • *By Availability:* Groups all buddies who are online and available for chatting when you are.

- *By Name:* Sorts buddies by name; use the lower part of the menu to choose *First Name, Last Name* (to sort buddies alphabetically by first name) or *Last Name, First Name* (to sort buddies alphabetically by last name).

- *Manually:* Allows you to drag names to sort them any which way you want. Select Use Groups to make this option active.

To see more information about a buddy, click the buddy and then choose Buddies➪Show Info or Buddies➪Show Profile (each gives you access to the other). You can lock the photo you want to see for your buddy, add or change information (such as a nickname or IM service), and, when you view the Profile, you can see which capabilities your buddy has for communicating with you, as shown in Figure 3-5.

Figure 3-5:
View your
buddy's
profile.

Creating groups

When you add a name to your buddy list, you see it in the Buddies list. If you choose View➪Use Groups, the buddies list is divided into groups — at the minimum, Buddies and Bonjour, and Offline if you choose View➪Use Offline Group. You can add other more descriptive groups — for example, Family or Golf Club — which are helpful if you have a lot of buddies or like to initiate group chats or broadcast a group message. You can always move or copy a buddy's chat account name to a different group or even create completely new groups, such as a group of people involved in a specific project. You can also grant a buddy membership in multiple groups simultaneously.

To create a group, follow these steps:

1. **Choose View➪Use Groups.**

2. **Click the Add (+) button in the bottom-left corner of the Buddy List window and choose Add Group from the pop-up menu.**

    A dialog appears, asking for a group name.

    You can rename a group by right-clicking the group name and choosing Rename Group from the shortcut menu that appears.

3. **Type a descriptive name for your group in the Enter Group Name text box and click the Add button.**

   Your new group appears in the buddy list, ready for you to copy or move names into your newly created group.

4. **Click the triangle to the left of the Buddies group in the window to reveal all your buddies added to date. Then do one of the following:**

   - *Move the name to a new group.* Click and drag a name from Buddies to the new group. The name leaves the Buddies group and shows up in the new group.

   - *Copy the name to a new group.* Hold down the Option key while clicking and dragging a name from Buddies to the new group. The name remains in Buddies and is copied to the new group.

When you add a buddy, choose the group where you want the name to appear.

Deleting names and groups in a buddy list

Eventually, you might want to prune names from your buddy lists to make it easier to keep track of people you actually chat with on a regular basis.

To delete a name from your buddy list, follow these steps:

1. **In the Buddies window, click the disclosure triangle next to a group to display the names in that group.**

2. **Click the name you want to delete.**

3. **Choose Buddies⇨Remove Buddy (or press the Delete key).**

   A confirmation dialog appears, asking whether you really want to delete the name.

4. **Click the Remove button (or Cancel if you suddenly change your mind before giving your buddy the axe).**

Rather than delete names one by one, you can also delete a group and all names stored in that group. To delete a group from your buddy list, follow these steps:

1. **In the Buddies window, right-click a group that you want to delete.**

2. **Choose Delete Group from the shortcut menu that appears.**

   A confirmation dialog opens, asking whether you really want to delete this group and all names in the group.

3. **Click Delete (or Cancel).**

Chatting with Others

You can chat with someone in five ways, and we tell you how in this section:

✦ **Text:** You type messages back and forth to each other. Anyone on your buddies list or in Contacts (who uses iMessages) can use text chatting — IM — because it requires only an Internet connection and a keyboard.

✦ **Audio:** You can talk to and hear the other person, much like a telephone. To participate in audio chatting, each person (there can be up to ten chat participants) needs a microphone and speakers or headphones. Most Macs come with a built-in microphone, but you might want an external microphone, such as one built into a headset, to capture your voice (and hear the other person's side of the conversation) more clearly.

✦ **Video:** You can talk to, hear, and see the other person in a live video window. Participating in a video chat with a buddy (or up to three buddies in a multiperson video chat) requires a video camera, such as the FaceTime video camera built in to all new and recent iMacs, MacBooks, and Apple displays. If your Mac is a model without a video camera (or if you want to connect a different kind of video camera to your Mac that has a built-in FaceTime video camera), you can buy and connect an external video camera that is USB Video Class (UVC), such as one of the models offered by Microsoft (www.microsoft.com/hardware), Creative Labs (www.creative.com), or Logitech (www.logitech.com).

✦ **Screen Sharing:** You can talk to and hear the other person while you take over her screen, mouse, and keyboard to fill your screen as though you're sitting in front of her computer. Likewise, your chat partner can take over your screen and control your keyboard or mouse as if she were sitting in front of your computer. iMessage and Yahoo! do not support screen sharing.

✦ **File Sharing:** You can talk and hear each other while you share a file (or files), such as a document, a Keynote presentation, or photos in your iPhoto library. The files you want to share appear on your chatting partner's screen. Likewise, if your chatting partner is sharing photos (or other files) with you, you see her on your screen.

If your Internet connection is too slow, Messages might refuse to let you start an audio or video chat.

Initiating a text chat

When you open Messages, the window has two parts (choose Window➪Messages if you don't see it). The left pane shows a list of your previous and active chats divided by account type (empty the first time you open Messages). Click a name in the left column, and the conversation appears on the right pane, as shown in Figure 3-6.

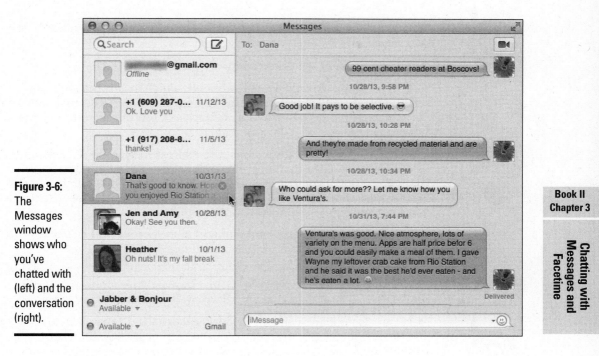

**Book II
Chapter 3**

Chatting with
Messages and
Facetime

Figure 3-6:
The
Messages
window
shows who
you've
chatted with
(left) and the
conversation
(right).

Just because someone is connected to the Internet doesn't necessarily mean
that he's in front of his computer and/or wants to chat. So if you find your
IMs falling on deaf ears (or fingertips) and the person isn't bothering to reply
to your messages or chat requests, chances are that the buddy you're trying
to chat with has gone fishing or is otherwise away from his computer.

To initiate a chat with someone, follow these steps:

1. **Click the Messages icon on the Dock or Launchpad.**

   Choose Window⇨Messages if you don't see the Messages window.

2. **Click the New Message button (looks like a pencil writing on a note
   pad) at the top of the chat list on the left side.**

   New Message appears at the top of the chat list, and a blank screen
   appears on the right.

3. **Begin typing the name of the person to whom you want to send an IM;
   potential matches from Contacts appear.**

   Or, do the following:

   Click the Add button (the plus sign) in the upper-left corner. This opens
   Contacts, which has a Buddies group in addition to the groups you have
   in Contacts. In Contacts, you can click Buddies to see those you added
   to Messages previously, and you can click All Contacts or one of the
   groups and scroll through to find the contact you seek.

A blue conversation bubble next to a name means that the contact uses iMessage.

4. **Click the name of the person with whom you want to chat.**

   It appears in the To field, in a blue bubble, which means that you can communicate with iMessage or the account associated with that contact. The account type appears in the message text box at the bottom of the screen, where you type your message.

   Unless otherwise specified as being an address for another IM account, Messages presumes that any phone number or e-mail in Contacts is iMessage-able. If you select it and the bubble is red, the number or address is not registered with iMessage, and clicking the disclosure triangle next to the address or number confirms that.

5. **(Optional) Repeat Steps 3 and 4 to add more people and create a group chat.**

   You can't add members to an iMessage chat after it begins (although you can with the other services). You can, however, have a one-on-one chat with a person and then chat with that same person in a group chat.

   You can also initiate a chat from your Buddies list. Choose Window⇨ Buddies. Double-click the name of the person or group with whom you want to chat, and a New Message window opens. Or click a name once and choose an action from the Buddies menu or click one of the buttons at the bottom of the Buddies window.

6. **Type a message in the text box at the bottom of the chat window and press Return to send your message; refer to Figure 3-6.**

   The recipient of your message will see something like Figure 3-7 on his Desktop (if he uses Messages). If he uses a different IM app, the user interface will probably be different — but that's his problem. If the recipient replies to your message, you see the response in the right pane of the Messages window, and you can start typing messages back and forth to one another. You type in the lower text box, and your dialogue with the other person appears in the main text box. You see an ellipsis while the other person writes the response.

Figure 3-7:
An invitation to chat.

> +1 ▢▢▢▢▢ ▢▢ ▢▢▢▢   [Reply]
> I haven't talked to her since she ca
> day

If you want to insert *emoticons* — those little smiley faces — in your text message, click the smiley face at the right end of the text-entry box (refer to Figure 3-6).

Choose Messages⇨Preferences⇨Viewing to change the colors and fonts used for your text chats. Choose View⇨Messages to choose how you see balloons, boxes, names, and pictures in text chats.

Initiating an audio or a video chat

To initiate an audio chat, everyone needs a microphone and speakers, which are standard equipment on iMacs and Macbooks (add-ons for Mac minis or MacPros) and on most Windows PCs (if that's what the person or people you want to chat with are using).

To initiate a video chat, everyone's computer needs a microphone and a video camera. Macs with a built-in FaceTime or iSight video camera can use that, but for Macs without a built-in FaceTime or iSight camera, you have three options:

**Book II
Chapter 3**

Chatting with Messages and Facetime

✦ Plug a digital video camcorder into your Mac's FireWire port (if your Mac model has a FireWire port; some don't).

✦ Buy a USB Video Class (UVC) video camera from Logitech (www.logitech.com), Creative Labs (www.creative.com), or Microsoft (www.microsoft.com/hardware), and plug it into your Mac.

✦ Conduct a one-way video chat in which you see the other person but the other person only hears your voice. If the person you're chatting with doesn't have a video camera but you do, the opposite occurs in which she sees you, but you only hear her.

Including you, up to ten people can participate in an audio chat. Video chats are limited to four people, and each must have a video camera connected to their computer along with a fast Internet connection (a minimum of 100 Kbps).

You can initiate an audio or video chat by following these steps:

1. **While in an IM chat, click the video icon in the upper-right corner and then choose Audio or Video.**

Or, choose Window⇨Buddies and then click the audio or video button next to the name of the person you want to initiate the chat with.

If you're chatting in iMessage, FaceTime opens, and a FaceTime call is initiated.

In AIM, Google Talk, Jabber, and Bonjour — which support Audio Chat (Yahoo! does not) — a message appears, informing you that your audio chat invitation is sent and that Messages is waiting for a reply.

If this feature is dimmed, you don't have a microphone on your Mac, or you don't have a fast enough Internet connection to support audio chatting.

If you don't see a Video Chat icon next to your buddy's name in the Buddy List window, your buddy does not have a video camera built-in or connected to his computer. If you see a Video Chat icon next to your buddy's name but it's dimmed, your buddy is currently in a video chat with another buddy or group of buddies.

2. **The buddy whom you invite to an audio or video chat clicks the Accept button.**

   Your chat begins, and you can both start talking as though you were speaking over a telephone or having a face-to-face conversation.

3. **Fine-tune your session:**

   - *Volume:* Drag the volume slider to adjust the sound level.

   - *More buddies:* If you click the plus-sign button, you can invite another person into your chat.

   - *Mute:* Click the Mute button (the microphone icon with a slash through it) in case you need to shout at your dog to stop barking at the cat, or whatever else you want to say but don't want your audio chat partner to hear.

   - *Move window:* You can click and hold on your live video-chat window and drag it to any corner in your buddy's live video window so you can see your buddy better.

4. **(Optional) Choose from these additional options for video chats:**

   - *Effects:* Click the Effects button in the bottom-left corner of the video chat window to open a window showing several different visual effects that you can choose to change how your live video appears on your buddy's screen. Click a visual effect to select it and then click the Close button to close the visual effects window.

   - *Zoom:* Click the Zoom button (double arrows) to make the video chat window fill your Mac's entire screen. Press the Escape key to close the full-screen view and return to the window view.

   - *Pause:* Choose Video⇨Pause Video to interrupt transmission of your side of the video; this also mutes the video.

   - *Snapshot:* Choose Video⇨Take Snapshot, which captures the moment onscreen.

   Here is another way to take a snapshot during a video chat: ⌘-click in the center of the video and drag the image out of the window. The file will be on the Desktop or in whichever folder you dragged it to, and is named `Image.tiff`.

   - Click and drag a file to the video window to send a file to the person you're chatting with.

Even if your Mac has a camera and a fast Internet connection, someone you want to connect with in a video chat might not. In that case, you might be limited to using an audio or text chat instead.

Sharing files, photos, and screens

While you're chatting either with instant messages, audio, or video, sharing files, documents, and photos is as easy as dragging the file to the Messages text field and pressing Return. If you're in the middle of a video chat, drag the file to the video screen, and off it goes.

When you're chatting on Jabber, AIM, Google Talk, or Bonjour (but not iMessage or Yahoo!) with another Mac user, you can share your screen and let your buddy control it as though it were her screen (or vice versa, if a buddy shares her screen with you). Here's how to do it:

Book II
Chapter 3

Chatting with Messages and Facetime

1. **Start a conversation with the buddy who you want to share your screen with or whose screen you want to share.**

2. **Choose Buddies⇨Share My Screen or choose Buddies⇨Ask to Share Screen.**

   • *Share My Screen:* Fills your buddy's screen with your screen, as though he's seated in front of your Mac, which he can now control with his mouse and keyboard.

   • *Ask to Share Screen:* Fills your screen with your friend's screen as though you're seated in front of his Mac and controlling it with your keyboard and mouse (assuming your buddy has granted you permission).

3. **After your buddy receives your request, she can respond by Accepting, Declining, or Replying to your request.**

4. **To end either type of the sharing session, press the X in the corner.**

Saving or deleting your conversations

Messages saves your conversations until you delete them. When they get particularly long, though, you might like to save them and start fresh with the same person. Do the following to save and delete your text chats:

1. **Click the Messages icon on the Dock or Launchpad.**

2. **Click the buddy with whom you have an ongoing conversation you want to save.**

   Your conversation appears in the right pane of the Messages window.

3. **Choose File⇨Print.**

4. **Click the PDF button at the bottom of the window and choose Save as PDF.**

5. **Type in a name for the file, choose a folder where you want to store it, and then click Save.**

6. **Choose File⇨Delete Conversation or hover the pointer over the chat list on the right end of the conversation you want to delete, and then click the X.**

Interpreting status indicators

When you look at your buddies list, you see different icons next to the names of your buddies. The colored bullets let you know your buddy's status; a phone or video icon tells you the type of chat her computer supports.

✦ **Red bullet:** Your buddy has an Away status and is unavailable to receive messages.

✦ **Yellow bullet:** Your buddy is available but hasn't used his computer for 15 minutes or more.

✦ **Green bullet:** Your buddy is available.

✦ **Gray bullet:** Your buddy's status can't be determined.

✦ **Telephone:** Your buddy's computer has a microphone, and she can have audio chats. If the telephone icon has depth, her computer supports multiperson audio chats.

✦ **Video camera:** Your buddy's computer has a video camera, and he can have video chats. If the video icon has depth, his computer supports multiperson video chats.

✦ **Wi-Fi:** Your buddy receives notifications of chat requests on her mobile phone.

Making Yourself Available (Or Not) for Chatting

As soon as you connect to the Internet, your Mac broadcasts your availability to all the friends in your buddy lists. The moment someone wants to chat with you, you'll see a window and maybe hear an audible alert. Choose how you want to be notified about incoming Messages requests from Notification Center (⌘⇨System Preferences⇨Notification Center), which we explain in Book I, Chapter 6.

Chat invitations can be fun to receive, but sometimes they can be distracting if you're trying to get work done and don't want to stop what you're doing to chat with someone. One thing you can do is change the status description others see next to your name in their own buddy lists. Changing your status description to Away or something that indicates you're not in a chatting mode can discourage others from sending you chat invitations until they see that you've set your status to Available again.

Changing your status

To let others know that you're busy, you can change your status message to indicate that you're out to lunch, on the phone, or revising a big book and not really in the mood to chat with others unless it's about something *really* important. (Otherwise, you might as well just exit Messages altogether.)

Although you change your status to indicate that you're away or unavailable to chat, you can still receive chat messages and invitations your buddies send if they choose to disregard your status message. Therefore, you still need to click Reply or Decline for each invitation you receive.

Alternatively, you can change your status to make yourself *invisible,* which means that you don't appear in your friends' Buddies windows. However, you still see your friends in your Buddies window (unless they choose to make themselves invisible, in which case neither of you can see the other).

To change the status that friends see about you in their buddy list, choose Window➪Buddies and then click the arrow button beneath your name in the Buddies window to open the My Status menu. (Alternatively, you can choose Messages➪My Status to open the My Status menu.) Choose a status line, as shown in Figure 3-8, and your chosen status now appears in your friends' buddy lists. The top half shows variations on Available (and displays) a green dot next to your name, and the bottom half shows different ways of explaining why you are unavailable or Away (and displays a red dot).

**Book II
Chapter 3**

Chatting with Messages and Facetime

Figure 3-8:
The My Status menu provides a variety of statuses you can display.

```
○ ○ ○          Buddies
  Barbara
○ should be working ▾

         Offline
       ○ Invisible

       ● Available
       ● Surfing the web
       ● Reading email
       ● At home
   ✓   ● should be working
       ● Emergencies Only
       ● Custom Available...

       ● Current iTunes Song

       ● Away
       ● Out to lunch
       ● On the phone
       ● In a meeting
       ● Custom Away...

         Edit Status Menu...
   ✓   Use Same Status for All Accounts
 +            A  ☺
```

If you have multiple accounts, you can choose a different status for each account; for example, on the account you use with colleagues and associates, you may want your status to read *Emergencies Only* or *On the Phone*. For your friends, you may want something clever like *Should be working*. You can also opt to use the same status for all accounts by choosing Use Same Status for All Accounts at the bottom of the My Status menu on the Messages Buddies window.

You can also choose a status that lets your buddies know you're available and what you're doing, such as surfing the web or reading e-mail. If you choose Current iTunes Song, people can see the name of the song you're listening to. If you choose Custom Available, you can type your own message that others will see. Choosing Custom Away lets you type your own Away message.

If you want to leave Messages running but sign out so that you are truly offline and unavailable, open the My Status menu beneath your name in the Buddy List window and choose Offline or Messages⇨Log Out.

Blocking chat invitations

Rather than block invitations from everyone by setting your status to Away or Invisible, you may want to accept chat invitations from some people but block them from others. For example, an old flame might be harassing you, so you want to block that person — but someone close to you, such as a family member or good friend, might need to reach you so you want that person to get through at any time.

Becoming invisible

The AIM and Apple iMessage accounts give you the option of making yourself invisible to your buddies. Being invisible lets you see who on your buddy lists might be available to chat, but when other people see your name on their buddy lists, your name appears as though you are offline.

To make yourself invisible in Messages, click the arrow beneath your name in the Buddy List window to open the My Status menu (see Figure 3-8) and select Invisible.

To make yourself visible again, open the My Status menu and choose a status that indicates you are online and available or away, such as Available or On the Phone.

For GoogleTalk, Jabber, and Yahoo! Messenger accounts, you must select Offline to be invisible to your buddies with Messages or go to the Google, Jabber, or Yahoo! websites to set your status to Invisible. If you choose one of the red statuses such as Away or In a Meeting, your buddies see you as unavailable but can still send you chat requests, and you can see their statuses.

1. **Choose Windows⇨Buddies.**

2. **Click the name of the person you want to block.**

3. **Choose Buddies⇨Block Person.**

If you use AIM, go to Messages⇨Preferences and click the Account button. Click AIM and then choose the Privacy tab to make the selections offered:

✦ *Allow Anyone:* Allows anyone to send you a chat invitation, close friends or complete strangers alike.

✦ *Allow People in My Buddy List:* Allows only people in your buddy lists to contact you.

✦ *Allow Specific People:* Allows you to create a list of specific people who have permission to contact you. Click the Edit List button to open the Allow Specific People window, and then click the plus sign and type in the name of the person you want to allow to contact you.

✦ *Block Everyone:* Stops all chat invitations from friends, family, co-workers, and everyone else in the world.

✦ *Block Specific People:* Allows you to create a list of specific people you always want to keep from contacting you. Click the Edit List button to open the Block Specific People window, and then click the plus sign and type in the name of the person you want to block from contacting you.

Note: If you select the Allow Specific People or Block Specific People radio buttons, you need to click the Edit List button and type the exact account names of the people you want to allow or block.

Making Calls with FaceTime

Instant messaging gives you rapid responses and quick input, but sometimes seeing a friendly familiar face makes an exchange that much better. With *FaceTime,* the video chat app that comes with your Mac, you can communicate with people who use the following devices with FaceTime installed:

✦ iPhone 4 and newer running iOS 4.1 or later

✦ iPod touch fourth generation and newer running iOS 4.1 or later

✦ iPad 2 and newer running (including iPad mini models) iOS 4.1 or later

✦ Intel-based Mac running OS X 10.6.6 or later with camera and microphone

FaceTime, like Messages, uses the Internet to communicate, so make sure you have a connection.

FaceTime uses the information in Contacts to call iPhone 4s and newer with a phone number and iPod touches, iPad 2s or newer, or other Macs with an e-mail address. Any edits you make to Contacts in FaceTime appear when you open Contacts on its own; addresses in FaceTime reflect the preferences you set up in Contacts. (See Book V, Chapter 1 to get a closer look at Contacts.) You also need an Internet connection and an Apple ID (your iTunes Store account or iCloud account work, too). If you don't have an Apple ID, you can set one up in FaceTime, or see Book I, Chapter 3 for detailed instructions.

In this section, we show you how to sign in to FaceTime, call your friends, and accept incoming calls. We also tell you how to add your favorites peeps so you can call them lickety-split.

Signing in to FaceTime

To use FaceTime to make or receive calls on your Mac, you have to turn on FaceTime and sign in to your account. To sign in to FaceTime, follow these instructions:

1. **Click the FaceTime icon, which looks like a video camera with an objective lens on the side, on the Dock or Launchpad.**

   The FaceTime window opens, and you see yourself in the video pane.

2. **Click the FaceTime button On or choose FaceTime⇨Turn FaceTime On.**

3. **Enter your Apple ID in the User Name field and the associated password in the Password field.**

   If you don't have an Apple ID, click Create New Account and fill in the form that appears to the right of the video window, and then click Next to finish setting up an Apple ID.

4. **Click Sign In.**

   FaceTime signs you in and asks for an e-mail address that other people with FaceTime can use to call you on your Mac.

5. **Type in the e-mail address associated with your Apple ID account.**

6. **Click Next.**

   The calling pane opens.

   You can close the FaceTime window, but you remain signed in so you can receive calls.

Making a call with FaceTime

After you turn on FaceTime and sign in to your account, you can make and receive calls. To make a call, follow these steps:

1. **Click the FaceTime icon on the Dock or Launchpad.**

   The FaceTime window opens, and you see yourself in the video pane.

2. **Click the Contacts button at the bottom of the pane.**

   Your Contacts information appears in the calling pane. If you have groups, you see a list of your groups. If your contacts are in one All Contacts group, you see an alphabetical list of your contacts, as shown in Figure 3-9.

Figure 3-9: FaceTime uses Contacts to make phone calls.

3. **Click the name of the person you want to call.**

   That person's info appears.

4. **Click the e-mail address to call the person on an iPod touch, an iPad, or a Mac. Click the person's mobile phone number to call the mobile phone.**

   The person you're calling must have FaceTime activated on her device (unless it's an iPhone) for the call to go through. If she doesn't have FaceTime turned on, you receive a message that she is unavailable.

   When the person accepts your phone call, you see her face in the main part of your screen. A small window appears where you see yourself, which is what the person you called sees, as shown in Figure 3-10.

5. **You have a few options while you're talking:**

   • Click the full-screen toggle in the top right corner of the FaceTime window or on the control bar at the bottom to see the person you called fill the whole screen.

Figure 3-10:
You see the person you're talking to in the large window and yourself in the picture-in-picture window.

- Click and drag any edge of the window to resize it.

- Click the Landscape/Portrait toggle (the curved arrow that appears when you hover the pointer over your image) on your image to rotate the image that the person you called sees. Landscape can be a better view if the person is using an iPad, iPod touch, or iPhone. You can also drag your image around to place it where it doesn't block your view of the person you called.

- Pause a call by choosing FaceTime⇨Hide or Window⇨Minimize. Click the FaceTime icon on the Dock to return to the paused call.

- Click the Mute button if you don't want the person you're speaking with to hear you. Click the Mute button again to unmute.

6. **When you finish your call, click the End button or close the FaceTime window.**

Receiving a FaceTime call

You can receive calls when you turn FaceTime on and sign in, as we describe in the first part of this section. If someone calls you, FaceTime automatically opens, and you see

✦ **Yourself in the video pane**

✦ **The name or phone number of the person who is calling you**

✦ **Two buttons that give you the option to accept or decline the phone call, as shown in Figure 3-11**

Click Accept to open the video call.

Figure 3-11:
You can
accept or
decline
incoming
calls.

If you don't want to receive FaceTime video call invitations, choose either
FaceTime⊅Turn Off FaceTime or FaceTime⊅Preferences and turn the switch
off or sign out.

Managing your Apple ID settings

You can make changes to your Apple ID settings in FaceTime or change the
country where you are located. To access your Apple ID settings, do the
following:

1. **Click the FaceTime icon on the Dock or Launchpad.**

The FaceTime window opens, and you see yourself in the video pane.

2. **Choose FaceTime⇨Preferences.**

   Your FaceTime Preferences appear, as shown in Figure 3-12, in the pane to the right of the video pane (replacing the Contacts list that usually appears there).

Figure 3-12:
Use
FaceTime
Preferences
to change
your country
location
and Apple
ID account
info.

3. **Click your account name in the Apple ID field.**

   The Apple ID pane appears.

4. **Click Change Location to change the country where you are using your Mac and FaceTime, and then click Save.**

5. **Click View Account to see your Apple ID account information, and do the following:**

   • Type the password and then click Sign In.

   • Click Manage Apple ID to open your account on the Apple website and make changes such as changing your password or your birthday. Follow the onscreen instructions to do so.

   • Click the FaceTime window and click Done, and then click the two Back buttons in the top left of the pane to return to the Preferences pane.

6. **Click Done to close Preferences.**

   The Contacts list appears again.

Adding contacts and favorites to FaceTime

FaceTime uses Contacts to make calls. Any time you add, delete, or edit a contact in Contacts, the information appears in FaceTime, too. You can also add a contact to Contacts from FaceTime by following these steps:

1. **Click the FaceTime icon on the Dock or Launchpad.**

   The FaceTime window opens, and you see yourself in the video pane.

2. **Choose the group you want to add the new contact to, or choose All Contacts if you don't have groups.**

3. **Click the plus sign in the upper-right corner.**

4. **Enter the person's first and last name, company name (optional), phone number, and e-mail (as shown in Figure 3-13).**

Figure 3-13:
Add new
people to
Contacts
from
FaceTime.

5. **Click Done.**

   The new contact is added to Contacts. If you want to add other pertinent information (such as a street address or birthday), go to Contacts to edit this contact's information (as explained in Book V, Chapter 1).

If you have people you call frequently, you may want to add them to your Favorites list so you don't have to scroll through the whole Contacts list to find them each time you want to call. To select a contact as a favorite, do this:

1. **In All Contacts or a Group, find the person you want to add as a favorite.**

   You can use the Search field to find a person quickly — scroll to the very top of the list of contacts to see it. Just type in the first letters of the first or last name. The more letters you type, the narrower the results in the list.

2. **Click the name of the person you want to make a favorite.**

3. **Click the Add to Favorites button, as shown in Figure 3-14.**

   A list of the person's phone numbers and e-mail addresses appears.

Figure 3-14: Make the people you call the most your FaceTime favorites.

4. **Click the phone number or e-mail address you use to call this person from FaceTime.**

   A star appears next to the phone number or e-mail address you chose.

5. **Click the Favorites button at the bottom of the pane.**

   The person is now in your Favorites list.

6. **To call someone from the Favorites list, click the Favorites button and click the name of the person you want to call.**

   To see more information about that person, click the arrow to the right of the name.

Chapter 4: Moving Around with Maps

In This Chapter

✓ **Finding your place**

✓ **Seeing the view from here**

✓ **Getting from here to there**

✓ **Sharing locations and directions**

Maps may seem an app that you just want on a mobile device such as an iPhone or iPad — and you find it there — but with Mac OS 10.9 Mavericks, Maps is available on your Mac, too, and with good reason. With an Internet connection, Maps can find your current location, provide directions between two locations, and calculate the travel time from where you are to your next appointment, taking traffic conditions into consideration, and give you that information in the Notification Center — talk about app integration. What's more, with its built-in search function, you can find specific types of businesses that are near a location, such as restaurants near your hotel.

In this chapter, we tell you how to find your present location and locate an address you know. We talk about how to get directions from one place to another, and then make those indications available on your mobile device. We also explain how to share or save the locations and directions you use.

Wherever You Go, There You Are

When you first open the Maps app (click the Maps icon on the Dock or Launchpad), a map of the United States appears in the window. (Look for the icon with a road map under a compass needle; that's the Maps icon.) In the following sections, we tell you how to find your location and use the Mac's gestures to navigate.

Finding your location

Maps uses network data to determine your location, and various apps, including Maps and Reminders, use a feature called Location Services to access your location to complete their tasks. If you want Maps to find your location, you have to enable Location Services by following these steps:

1. **Click the System Preferences icon on the Dock.**

Or choose System Preferences.

2. **Click the Security & Privacy button.**

3. **Click the Privacy tab at the top of the window.**

4. **Click Location Services, as shown in Figure 4-1.**

5. **Select the check boxes for Enable Location Services and then for Maps.**

   If the Location Services icons are dimmed and can't be selected, click the Lock button in the bottom-left corner, type an Administrator password for your Mac, and then select the check boxes. Click the Lock button again to prevent further changes.

   Learn more about the Security & Privacy preferences in Book III, Chapter 2.

6. **Click the Close button of the System Preferences window.**

When your Mac accesses Location Services, the Location Services icon appears on the status bar. Click the Current Position button in the upper-left corner, and a map of your neighborhood appears. Your exact location is the blue dot on the map, like you see in Figure 4-2. If there is a pulsing circle around the blue dot, your location is approximate; the smaller the circle, the more precise your exact (or nearly exact) location. A compass appears in the lower-right corner and points north.

Figure 4-1: Enable Location Services in the Security & Privacy preferences.

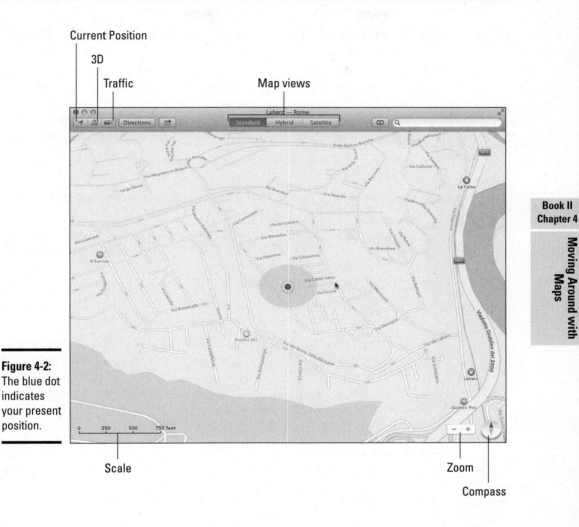

Current Position

3D

Traffic

Map views

Scale

Zoom

Compass

Figure 4-2:
The blue dot
indicates
your present
position.

Navigating the Maps interface

Maps has buttons and menus to change the view and navigate the map, but
Maps also takes advantage of the multitouch gestures offered by a trackpad.
To change the style of the map, click one of the three buttons at the top of
the window:

✦ **Standard:** Shows you a map. This is the default view.

✦ **Hybrid:** Shows the street names on a satellite view.

✦ **Satellite:** Shows a satellite view.

Click none, one, two, or all three of the following buttons:

✦ **Current Position:** Shows where you are presently located.

- ✦ **3D view:** Displays the map in three-dimensions, showing the highs and lows of mountains and buildings.

- ✦ **Traffic conditions:** Reveals any available information about traffic jams, roadwork, or smooth sailing. This service doesn't cover all areas.

Choose View⇨Show Scale if you want to place a scale on the map. Change the orientation and size of the map by doing the following:

- ✦ Click the plus and minus buttons next to the compass to zoom in and out of the map.

- ✦ Double-click the mouse or trackpad to zoom in; hold the Option key while double-clicking to zoom out.

- ✦ On a trackpad, use the spread and pinch gestures with your thumb and forefinger (or the two fingers that are comfortable for you) to zoom in and out of the map, respectively.

- ✦ On a trackpad, double-tap with one finger to zoom in or double-tap with two fingers to zoom out.

- ✦ Scroll to move the map up, down, or sideways.

- ✦ Click the compass or the 3D button at the top of the window to switch to 3D view, which just tilts the map in Standard view but becomes 3D in Hybrid and Satellite view.

- ✦ Click and hold the pointer on the compass and drag left or right to rotate the map.

- ✦ On a trackpad, use two fingers to rotate the map.

- ✦ Tap the Compass button that appears in the upper-right corner to return to a north-facing orientation.

Use the selections in the View menu as alternatives to Maps' buttons.

Asking For Directions

Even though you may not take your computer with you, or have Internet access while traveling, you can calmly plot your journey before grabbing your car keys. After planning your itinerary, print the directions or send them to your iPhone or iPad and be on your way, secure to find your way. First we show you how to find addresses or points of interest and store them in Maps, and then we show you how to get from one place to another.

Finding what you seek

You may know your way around your city or town but not know some of the street names — or perhaps you're headed to a city on business and want to find bookstores near your hotel. In these situations, you don't need directions as much as a location or information. Maps can work with a specific street name and number as well as inexact addresses, such as an intersection, a neighborhood, or a landmark. Use these steps to find either:

1. **Click Maps on the Dock or Launchpad.**

2. **(Optional) Click the Current Position button if you want to find something right in your neighborhood.**

3. **Click the Search field at the top right of the window.**

4. **Type one of the following in the search field. (If an address is already in the search field, click the X at the right end of the field to delete the text.)**

   - *An address* in the form of a street name and number or an intersection, with the city and state or just the name of a city or town

   - *A neighborhood, landmark, or service* such as SOMA (South of Market) San Francisco, Liberty Bell, or bookstores Philadelphia

   - *The name* of a person or business that's stored in your Contacts

   A list of potential matches from Contacts and the Maps database appears; when you type a word, the results list is divided by category such as Businesses (that contain those letters or word), Queries (potential words you could use to define your search), and Addresses (that contain those letters or word) as shown in Figure 4-3.

   After you search for addresses, Maps remembers them. In subsequent searches, a Bookmarks and History category appears.

Book II
Chapter 4

Moving Around with Maps

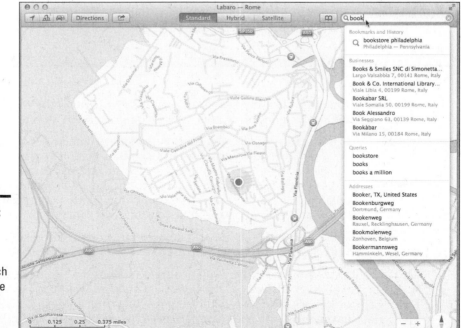

Figure 4-3: Type the first few letters of your search to generate potential matches.

5. **If you see the address you seek in the list, click it to open a map showing that location.**

   Otherwise, finish typing the complete search terms or address and press Return.

   A red pin on the map indicates the address you seek, and multiple results and pins appear if you searched for a service in a location, as shown in Figure 4-4. The address is written on a flag attached to the pin.

Figure 4-4: A red pin and flag indicate the sought-after address.

6. **(Optional) Click the Info button on the right end of the flag or double-click the item in the results list to see information about the location.**

   An information window opens that shows the distance of the location from your current location (determined by Location Services), along with information like the phone number and address of the selected site, the site's web address, or a link to Yelp!, as shown in Figure 4-5. When available, you'll also see Reviews and Photos buttons that give you reviews to read and photos to look at of the location.

   Click the web page address to find out more about the location you found, such as the menu of a restaurant or special exhibits at a museum.

   If you want to keep the found address in Maps for future use, click the Add Bookmark button in the information window or choose View➪Add Bookmark. Clicking the Add to Contacts button automatically opens Contacts and creates a new card with the address and associated information for the location.

Figure 4-5:
The Info
window
shows
details.

7. **Memorize what you found or go to the next section to learn how to save and share it.**

Sharing what you find

Often times, a glance at a map is all you need to orient yourself to a location. Other times, you want to keep the location information you found. Two easy ways to keep the information are

✦ Choose File➪Print to print a copy of the map and results list.

✦ Choose File➪Export as PDF to save a PDF of the map and results.

To share the map and location information with yourself to your iPhone or iPad or with someone else, do the following:

1. **Find the address you want to share with someone, either by searching or choosing from a bookmark or Contacts.**

2. **Tap the Share button at the top of the screen or at the top of the information window for a location.**

   Or choose File➪Share.

   The Share menu opens, as shown in Figure 4-6.

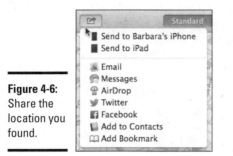

Figure 4-6:
Share the
location you
found.

3. **Click one of the sharing options:**

   • *Send to* iOS device: The location will be shared in the Maps' book-
     marks on your iOS device.

   • *Email or Messages:* Click one of these to open an outgoing message
     that contains the location. Fill in the address for one or more recipi-
     ents and then click Send. (See Book II, Chapters 2 and 3 to learn
     about Mail and Messages, respectively.)

   • *AirDrop:* Click to share the location with other people on your local
     network who use Macs with AirDrop access. (See Book III, Chapter 4
     to learn about AirDrop.)

   • *Twitter or Facebook:* Click to post to either of these social networks.
     You must be logged in to your account.

You can also click Add Bookmark or Add to Contacts to save the location in
either place.

Accessing a saved location

To view and use an address you've recently used or bookmarked, or from
your Contacts list, do the following:

1. **Click Maps on the Dock or Launchpad.**

2. **Click the Bookmarks button to the left of the Search field.**

   The window shown in Figure 4-7 opens.

3. **Do one of the following:**

   • *Click Recents* to use an address you've recently accessed.

     A list of recently used addresses opens.

   • *Click Bookmarks* to use a bookmarked location.

     A list of bookmarks opens.

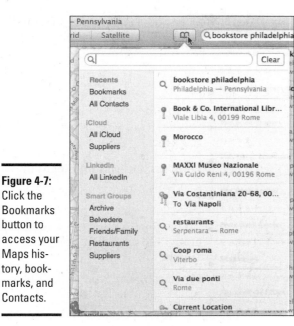

Figure 4-7:
Click the
Bookmarks
button to
access your
Maps his-
tory, book-
marks, and
Contacts.

- *Click All Contacts or one of the groups in Contacts to choose a person or business from Contacts.*

   Scroll through the list to open the Info screen that contains the address you seek.

4. **Tap the address you wish to use.**

   A map opens, and a red pin indicates the address or location you're looking for.

If you want a clean slate, you can clear your bookmarks by opening the list and clicking Edit, and then clicking the X to the right of the bookmark you want to delete. While you delete bookmarks one at a time, removing recent locations is an all-or-nothing deal. Click Recents and then click the Clear button, and the list is emptied. If you want to save a Recents address, open it and then save it as a bookmark or an addition to Contacts.

Dropping a pin

If there's no pin on the location you want to save or share, choose View⇨ Drop Pin. A purple pin shows up on the map with a flag that reads Dropped Pin. If the pin isn't exactly where you want it, click and drag it to the location you want. Click the Info button on the flag to display an information screen with the standard options.

To remove the pin, click Remove Pin. You can add a bookmark for the pin and use it as a starting or ending point when asking for directions, which we explain next.

Getting directions

Maps finds directions from your current location to where you're going or between two addresses that you provide or find. Follow these steps to ask Maps for directions:

1. **Open Maps and click the Directions button, if it isn't highlighted.**

The words Current Location appear in the Start field, and the End field is blank.

2. **Leave the Start field as your Current Location or click the X on the right end of the field to create an empty field as shown in Figure 4-8, and type a new address for the starting point.**

As you type, potential matches appear; click one or type the complete address.

A quick way to get directions from your current location is to click the Current Location button (refer to Figure 4-2), and then search for the address you want to go to. When the map is pinned, click the Info button on the right end of the flag and then click the Directions button. A route is immediately calculated.

Figure 4-8: Fill in the starting point and destination you want on the Directions screen.

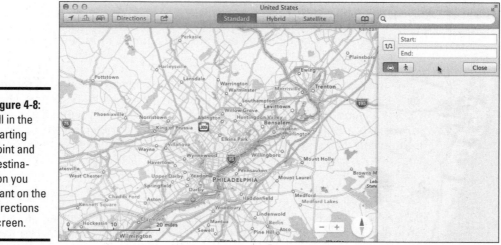

3. **Click the End field and type the address of where you want to go.**

   As you type, potential matches appear; click one or type the complete address.

   Swap the Start and End points of the directions by clicking the Swap button to the left of the Start and End fields.

   If you want directions and travel time for walking between destinations, click the Pedestrian button (next to the Driving button).

4. **Click the Directions button or click a match in the list.**

   A list of point-to-point indications appears, and the map shows the route from your starting point to your destination, as shown in Figure 4-9.

   The distance and estimated travel time are displayed above the directions. If more than one route is available, Maps displays alternate routes in light blue and the travel time for each. Click the route you want to follow to make it the main route.

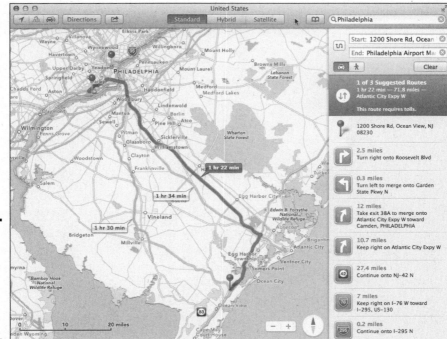

Figure 4-9:
Point-to-point directions are shown in a list and on the map.

5. **(Optional) Click the buttons at the top of the window to change the view.**

6. **(Optional) Click the Show Traffic button (refer to Figure 4-2).**

This feature is available in some locations only.

The roads on the map show you traffic conditions:

- *Red dashes* show where traffic is heavy and stop-and-go.
- *Orange dots* mean traffic is moving slowly.
- *White dash in a red circle* (Road Closed) icons mean what they show — road closed.
- *Men at Work* icons indicate road work.
- *Car bumper in a red square* indicate accidents.
- *Yellow triangles* (Yield icons) indicate general alerts.

7. (Optional) Print, save, or share the directions as we explain earlier.

Book III
Beyond the Basics

Check out the article "Finding and Adding Fonts to Your Mac" online at www.dummies.com/extras/macsaio.

Contents at a Glance

Chapter 1: Backing Up and Restoring Your Data

In This Chapter

✔ **Considering your options for backing up**

✔ **Using Time Machine to recover files**

✔ **Transferring your data to a new Mac with Migration Assistant**

✔ **Recovering files you've lost**

Backing up data is something that many people routinely ignore, like changing the oil in the car on a regular basis. The only time most people think about backing up their data is after they've already lost something important, such as a business presentation or a folder full of close-to-the-heart family photos. Of course, by that time, it's already too late.

Backing up your data may not sound as exciting as playing video games or browsing the web, but it should be part of your everyday routine. If you can't risk losing your data, you must take the time to back it up. The good news is that your Mac came with Time Machine, the application that makes backing up a routine that your Mac can do on its own.

In this chapter, we explain some of the different backup options. Next, we show you how to set up Time Machine to perform regular automatic backups. We also talk about recovering an individual file and restoring your Mac with the Time Machine backup in the unfortunate event that you lose all your files. We include a brief explanation of AutoSave and Versions, which you find in Apple apps such as Pages and Keynote. We explore storing your data online with third-party services. If you purchase a new Mac, you'll want to make a backup of your old Mac and then move all your stuff to the new one — we tell you how to do that, too.

Understanding Different Backup Options

Backing up is, essentially, duplicating your data — making a copy of every important file. You could duplicate each file as you create it and keep a copy on your hard drive, although this doesn't solve the problem if your hard drive crashes or your Mac is stolen. Ideally, you back up to one of the follow-ing external sources (we explain each of these in the following sections):

+ External hard drive — personal or networked, such as Time Capsule

+ Flash drive

+ Remote storage, such as Dropbox or SugarSync

+ CD-R or DVD-R

You must make sure to back up periodically, such as at the end of every week, or even every day if you update and create new files often. If you forget to back up your files, your backup copies could become woefully outdated, which can make them nearly useless.

Depending on the value of your files, you may want to consider using more than one backup method. For example, you may want to use Time Machine to completely back up your Mac on a weekly basis but depend on its hourly and daily backups for changes to the screenplay you're writing in Pages on iCloud. The idea here is that if catastrophe strikes and you lose your Mac, you can always replace the applications — *but* you can't retake family photos or rewrite your unfinished novel. The more backup copies you have of your critical files, the more likely it is that you'll never lose your data no matter what might happen to your Mac.

Backing up with external hard drives

To prevent the loss of all your data if your hard drive should suddenly bite the dust, you can connect an external hard drive to your Mac's USB or Thunderbolt port with a cable that's typically included with the hard drive.

USB and Thunderbolt ports connect peripherals to a computer. USB ports commonly connect a mouse, printer, or digital camera. Thunderbolt con-nects a display or storage device. The main advantage of using external hard drives is that copying large files is much faster and more convenient than copying the same files to CDs or DVDs. Additionally, external hard drives are easy to unplug from one Mac and plug into another Mac; plus, only one of the newest Mac models even has an optical disc drive.

You can also put an external hard drive on your network. For example, Apple's Time Capsule provides external storage and functions as a Wi-Fi hub so multiple computers can back up to the Time Capsule. (There are 2TB and 3TB (terabyte) versions, so you probably won't have to worry about storage space.) Any networked drive must use Apple File Protocol (AFP) file sharing.

Perhaps the biggest drawback of using external hard drives is that they can't protect against a catastrophe near your computer, such as a fire burn-ing down your house or a flood soaking your computer desk and office. If a disaster wipes out the entire area around your computer, your external hard drive may be wiped out in the catastrophe as well.

You can treat an external hard drive as just another place to copy your files, but for greater convenience, you should use a special backup application, such as Time Machine, which we get to in shortly, in the section "Blasting into the Past with Time Machine." Backup applications can be set to run according to a schedule (for example, to back up your files every night at 6 p.m.)

If the files haven't changed since the last time you backed them up, the backup application saves time by skipping over those files rather than copying the same files to the external hard drive again.

To retrieve files, you could just copy the files from your external hard drive back to your original hard drive — but be careful! If you changed a file on your original hard drive, copying the backup copy can wipe out the most recent changes and restore an old file to your hard drive, which probably isn't what you want. To keep you from accidentally wiping out new files with older versions of that same file, backup applications always compare the time and date a file was last modified to make sure that you always have copies of the latest file.

Storing backups on USB flash drives

Because of their low cost, fast copying speed, and ease of moving and plugging into any Mac, flash drives are a popular alternative for backing up files. Many USB flash drives have built-in key rings. Carrying one in your pocket or purse not only is convenient, but also ensures that your data is always safe and on your person should something happen to your Mac's hard drive at home or in the office, where your backup drive's original files are stored.

The biggest drawback of USB flash drives is their somewhat limited storage capacities, which typically range from 8GB to 128GB or sometimes more. USB flash drives in those capacity ranges can usually cost between $10 and $100, but a whopping 512GB model sold by Amazon (www.amazon.com) costs around $600 as of this writing. Whatever the capacity, USB flash drives are especially convenient for carrying your most critical files but not necessarily for backing up all your important files. In contrast to the hassles of writing (or *burning*) data to a CD or DVD, saving files to a USB flash drive is speedier and as simple as saving a file to a backup folder on your hard drive.

We found a 256GB flash drive for $3.50 (!), but it uses USB 2.0, which is the older transfer protocol. So you have a fair amount of storage but the transfer speed is s-l-o-w. Make sure the flash drive you choose uses USB 3.0, like the newest Macs. Of course, if you have an older Mac, you may have to use a USB 2.0 flash drive to match the USB port on your Mac.

Storing backups off-site

Backing up your Mac's important files to an off-site storage service virtually guarantees that you'll never lose your data. We explain how they work here but keep in mind that doing a complete remote backup will be slower than a

USB 2.0 flash drive and your ISP may limit file transfer sizes. You may want to use an external hard or flash drive for complete backups and then store particularly important documents on remote backup sites.

Low-cost (and even free) off-site storage options are available for Mac users. Many companies sell off-site storage space for a monthly fee. However, to entice you to try their services, they often provide a limited amount of free space that you can use for an unlimited period at no cost. To get your free off-site storage space, sign up with one or more of the following off-site data-backup sites, each of which offers a paid version with more storage space; most have a free option that offers from 2GB to 10GB of storage and then paid options for more storage or multiple users:

+ **Box** (`www.box.com`): Free 10GB storage space

+ **Dropbox** (`www.dropbox.com`): Free 2GB storage space

+ **ElephantDrive** (`www.elephantdrive.com`): Free 2GB storage space

+ **iDrive** (`www.idrive.com`): Free 5GB storage space

+ **Mozy** (`http://mozy.ie`): Free 2GB storage space

+ **SugarSync** (`www.sugarsync.com/free/`): Free 5GB storage space

+ **Syncplicity** (`www.syncplicity.com`): Free 2GB storage space

iCloud is fairly Apple-specific when it comes to online storage. Although iCloud offers 5GB of storage space free, plus up to 1,000 photos and any purchased media, apps, and books, it isn't a true Mac backup option. iCloud does automatically synchronize the contents of the Contacts, Calendar, Reminders, and Notes apps, as well as Safari bookmarks. iCloud also syncs documents created with an iCloud-enabled app, such as Pages or Numbers, and stored on iCloud between multiple Macs or between your Mac and your iPhone, iPad, iPod touch, or Windows PC. Even if you don't sync with another device, you can turn on the iCloud services and store your data remotely. However, iCloud doesn't backup apps not purchased in the App Store or Word documents or that 1,001st photo, so you should consider iCloud as a syncing tool for your Mac and a backup tool only for iOS devices.

Backing up to CDs or DVDs

With the advent of flash drives and remote storage, this section is almost obsolete. In fact, the newest Macs — even iMacs and Mac Pros — don't come with optical disc drives; you have to use an external drive to write files to CDs or DVDs. But perhaps the biggest drawback of backing up to a CD or DVD is the space limitation: CDs can store up to 700MB of data, single-layer DVDs can store 4.7GB of data, and dual-layer DVDs store up to 8.5GB of data.

A *dual-layer* disc employs a second physical layer within the disc, which the drive accesses by shining its laser through the disc's first, semitransparent layer.

If you need to back up only word-processor or spreadsheet files, a single CD should be sufficient. However, music, video, and digital photographs take up more space, which means that you may need to use several DVDs to back up all your files. The more discs you need to back up your files completely, the harder it is to keep track of all the discs — and the slower (and more tedious) your backups are to make. In view of all this hassle, you may not back up your data as often as you should; eventually, your backup files fall too far out of date to be useful, which defeats the purpose of backing up your data. So, if your data frequently exceeds the storage limits of a single CD or DVD, you should probably rely on a different backup method.

Blasting into the Past with Time Machine

One problem with traditional backup applications is that they store the latest, or the last two or three previous, versions of your files. Normally, this is exactly what you want, but what if you want to see an earlier version of a short story you began working on two weeks ago? Trying to find files created on certain dates in the past is nearly impossible, unless you do one of the following:

✦ **Keep a copy of the backup you made previously.**

✦ **Save different versions of the document.**

✦ **Work with applications that support Versions.** We explain this in the "Understanding Versions" section, later in this chapter.

Fortunately, that type of problem is trivial for your Mac's backup application, Time Machine. Unlike traditional backup applications that copy and store the latest or last one or two versions of files, Time Machine takes snapshots of your Mac's storage drive so that you can view its exact condition from two hours ago, two weeks ago, two months ago, or even farther back.

The external hard drive you use to back up your Mac with Time Machine should have oodles of storage space, and ideally, you use that drive *only* for Time Machine backups. The bigger the hard drive, the farther back in time you can go to recover old files and information.

By viewing the exact condition of what your Mac storage drive looked like in the past, you can see exactly what your files looked like at that time. After you find a specific file version from the past, you can easily restore it to the present with a click of the mouse.

Setting up Time Machine

To use Time Machine, you need to connect an external hard drive to your Mac with a USB or Thunderbolt cable, or you may have an additional hard drive installed in one of the additional drive bays inside an older Mac Pro desktop computer (the new 2013 Mac Pro models don't have multiple drive bays).

If you use an external drive that doesn't have its own power supply, connect your Mac to a power supply because your Mac supplies the juice to the external drive.

To set up Time Machine to back up the data on your Mac's primary hard drive to an external hard drive, follow these steps:

1. **Connect the external hard drive to your Mac.**

   When you plug in a new hard drive, the Time Machine backup feature typically starts automatically and asks whether you want to use the hard drive to back up your Mac. Another choice asks whether you want to encrypt the backup disk, which will scramble the data until you access it. Otherwise anyone who gets his or her hands on your external backup drive can read your data.

   If Time Machine automatically runs and prompts you as described, skip to Step 4. If Time Machine does not prompt you, continue to the next step.

2. **Choose ⌘⇨System Preferences and then click the Time Machine icon to open the Time Machine preferences pane, as shown in Figure 1-1.**

Figure 1-1:
To set up Time Machine, turn it on and choose an external drive to use.

> **Time Machine**
>
> OFF [ ] ON
>
> Select Backup Disk...
>
> Time Machine keeps:
> • Local snapshots as space permits
> • Hourly backups for the past 24 hours
> • Daily backups for the past month
> • Weekly backups for all previous months
> The oldest backups are deleted when your disk becomes full.
>
> ☑ Show Time Machine in menu bar   Options...   (?)

3. **(Optional) If you want to exclude files from your backup or your backup disk has limited storage, skip to the section "Skipping files you don't want to back up" and then return to Step 3 here.**

4. **Click the On button.**

   A dialog appears, listing all available external hard drives you can use, as shown in Figure 1-2.

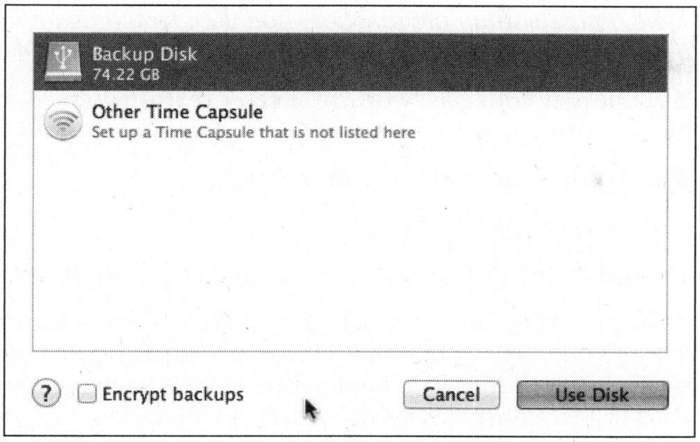

Figure 1-2:
You must
choose an
external
hard drive
to use
with Time
Machine.

5. **Select an external hard drive and, optionally, select the Encrypt Backups check box if you want to encrypt the files saved to your backup drive. (See Book III, Chapter 2 to discover more about encryption.)**

6. **Click the Use Disk button.**

   If you chose to encrypt your disk, the password creation screen opens. Do the following:

   a. *Click the key button if you want help creating a password or go directly to the next step.*

   Password Assistant (shown in Figure 1-3) opens and rates the security (quality) of your password. Manual lets you create your own password, or choose a type from the pop-up menu to see and select suggested passwords; drag the slider to define the password length. When you see a password you like, simply close the Password Assistant window and the selected password is assigned.

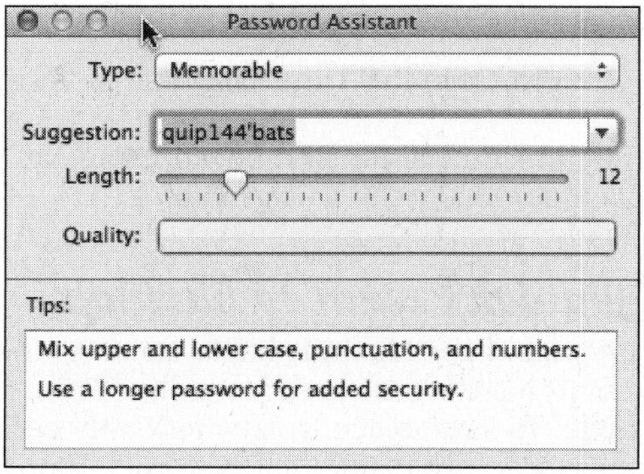

Figure 1-3:
Use
Password
Assistant
to create a
memorable,
secure
password.

b. *Type a password in the first field and then type it again in the second field to verify it.*

If you forget your password, you can't restore your Mac from your backup drive, so choose wisely.

c. *Type a password hint in the third field.*

d. *Click Encrypt Disk.*

Time Machine prepares your backup disk for encryption.

After preparing the drive, the Time Machine pane appears again, listing your chosen external hard drive, and after a short amount of time, the Time Machine application begins backing up your Mac's data to the external hard drive you selected.

7. **(Optional) Select the Show Time Machine in Menu Bar check box if it isn't already checked.**

With this option checked, the Time Machine icon on the menu bar animates with a twirling arrow whenever Time Machine is backing up your Mac's data. Clicking the Time Machine icon at any time (see Figure 1-4) is how you can keep tabs on the status of an active backup, start or stop a backup, and choose the Enter Time Machine command to run the Time Machine recovery application, as described in the upcoming section, "Retrieving files and folders."

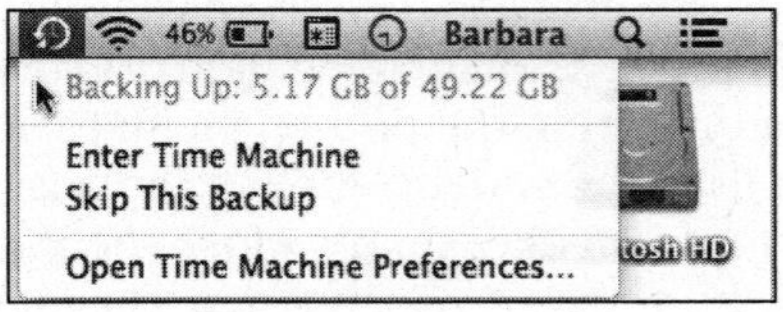

Figure 1-4:
Access
your Mac's
backup
options
from the
menu bar.

8. **Click the Close button to close the Time Machine preferences pane.**

Don't interrupt Time Machine during the first backup. You can continue working while Time Machine runs in the background.

Skipping files you don't want to back up

Unless you specify otherwise, Time Machine backs up everything on your Mac to which your account has access except temporary files, such as your web browser's cache. To save space, you can identify certain files and folders you're not concerned about losing that you want Time Machine to ignore. For example, you may not want to back up your Applications folder if you already have all your applications stored on separate installation discs or you purchased them through the App Store, which lets you download them again if necessary. Or you may choose to skip backing up media you purchased and downloaded from iTunes because if you lose them you can download them again, so there's no need to waste that precious space on your Mac's backup drive.

To tell Time Machine which files or folders to skip, follow these steps:

1. **Choose ⌥ System Preferences and then click the Time Machine icon to open the Time Machine preferences pane (refer to Figure 1-1).**

2. **Click the Options button to open the Exclude These Items from Backups dialog.**

3. **Click the plus sign (+) and then navigate through the mini-Finder window to the file or folder you want Time Machine to ignore.**

   You can select multiple drives, files, and folders by holding down the ⌘ key and then clicking what you want Time Machine to ignore.

4. **Click the Exclude button.**

   The Exclude These Items from Backups dialog appears again, as shown in Figure 1-5. Your backup disk appears first in the list. Next to each excluded item, you see the amount of storage it would occupy if you backed it up; below the list, you see the estimated size of your backup.

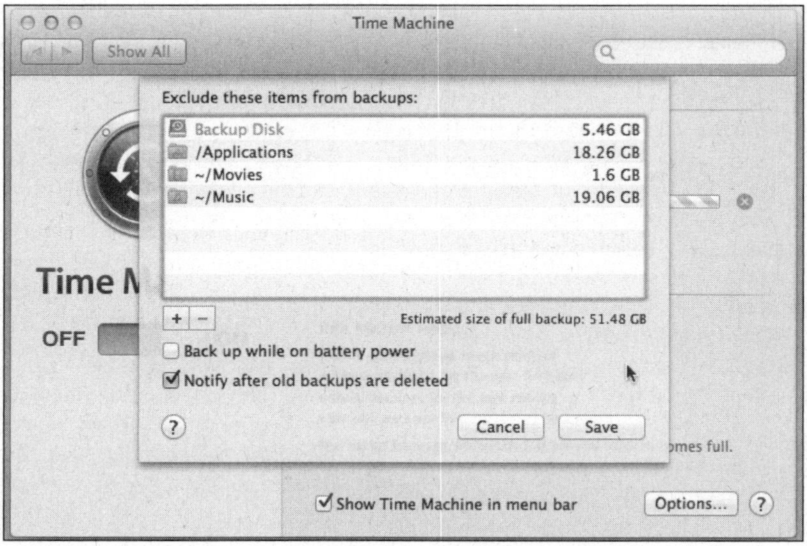

Figure 1-5:
Click the plus sign (+) to choose files you don't want to back up.

5. **Select or deselect these additional optional Time Machine features if you want:**

   - *Back Up While on Battery Power:* This option allows Time Machine to back up your MacBook when it's running on battery power. Turning on this option will drain your MacBook's battery faster.

   - *Notify After Old Backups Are Deleted:* Time Machine displays a dialog requesting your approval before it deletes any old backup files.

6. **Click the Save button.**

7. **Click the Time Machine On button, if it's not clicked already.**

   Return to Step 4 of the previous instructions to continue.

You may want to control the time and frequency of Time Machine back-ups — a feature that Time Machine itself doesn't offer. Although you could just connect your external backup drive only when you want to perform a backup or go into the Plist (pronounced *pea-list*) of your Mac (a place where technical information is kept) and rewrite the instructions, you may be better purchasing an app called Time Machine Backup Scheduler from the App Store ($3.99, Voros Innovation, `https://itunes.apple.com/us/ app/time-machine-backup-scheduler/`), which does the instructing for you.

How Time Machine does its backup thing

The first time you turn on and begin using Time Machine, it backs up the specified data from your user account on your Mac's hard drive (if you're the only user, it backs up everything), which can take a long time if your Mac's hard drive contains lots of applications and data. One thing you can do is start the Time Machine backup before going to bed so when you wake the next morning, your Mac will be completely (or almost completely) backed up — make sure PowerNap is on in ⇨System Preferences⇨Energy Saver so Time Machine works even if your Mac falls asleep.

After its initial backup of your Mac's hard drive, Time Machine automatically performs an incremental backup of any data changed on your Mac's hard drive (providing the backup drive is attached) every hour. Time Machine saves hourly backups for the past 24 hours, daily backups for the past month, and weekly backups for everything older than a month. Time Machine skips backing up files you create and then delete before the next hourly backup.

When your external backup hard drive starts running out of free space for more backups, Time Machine deletes the oldest files it finds in order to make room for the newer ones.

If you use a portable Mac, when the external drive isn't connected, Time Machine saves a snapshot on your Mac's internal drive; the next time you connect the external drive, the backup resumes.

Retrieving files and folders

Time Machine consists of two components:

✦ **The Time Machine preferences pane** (described earlier in this chapter; refer to Figure 1-1): Turn the Time Machine backup feature on or off, or adjust its settings.

✦ **The Time Machine restore application:** Recover files you deleted or changed from earlier backups. You run the restore application by clicking the Time Machine icon on the Dock or on the Launchpad, or by choosing the Enter Time Machine command from the Time Machine icon on the menu bar (refer to Figure 1-4).

After you configure Time Machine to back up your Mac, you can use the Time Machine recovery application to retrieve old files or information you deleted or changed after Time Machine backed them up. The two ways to use the Time Machine recovery application to recover files, folders, or other pieces of information, such as address cards, e-mail messages, or events from Calendar, are as follows:

✦ By running an application and then clicking the Time Machine icon on the Dock or Launchpad, or choosing the Enter Time Machine command from the Time Machine icon on the menu bar

✦ By opening a new Finder window and then clicking the Time Machine icon on the Dock or on the Launchpad, or choosing the Enter Time Machine command from the Time Machine icon on the menu bar

Recovering data from within an application

To use Time Machine to retrieve a specific piece of information from within an app (such as an address card from your Mac's Contacts app, which we use in this example), follow these steps:

1. **Click the Contacts icon on the Dock or on the Launchpad to launch Contacts.**

The Contacts app opens and displays the Contacts window, which lists all your contacts.

2. **Click the Time Machine icon on the Dock or Launchpad (or click the Time Machine icon on the menu bar and choose Enter Time Machine) to run the Time Machine restore app.**

Your Mac's screen will appear to space out while it launches the Time Machine restore app — into another dimension known as *The Time Machine Zone,* as shown in Figure 1-6.

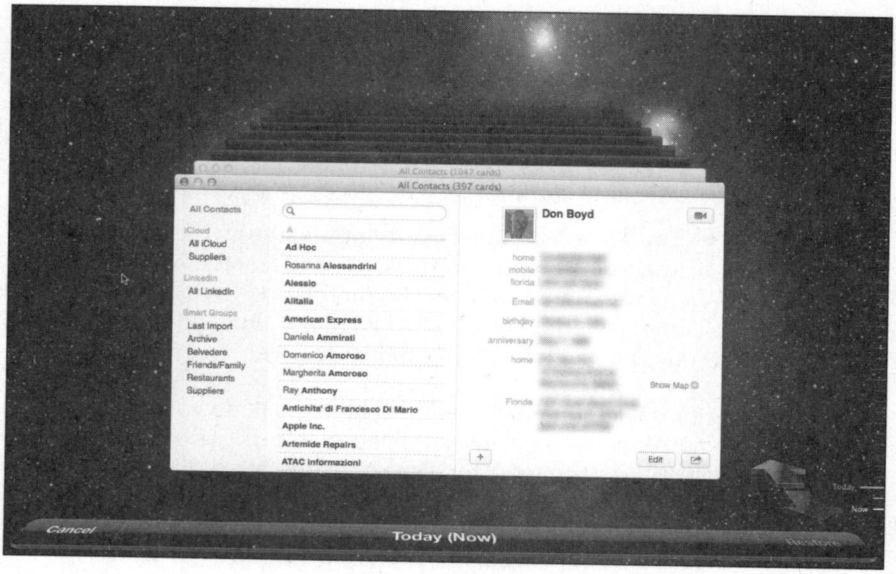

Figure 1-6:
The Time Machine restore application displays a far-out view of Contacts.

3. **Choose one of the following ways to select a contact card (or cards) that you want to restore from a past backup:**

   • *Click the Backward and Forward arrow buttons near the bottom-right corner of the screen.* Click the Backward button to move the Contacts window backward in time to earlier Time Machine backups. Click the Forward button to move forward to more recent Time Machine backups.

   • *Click a Contacts window in the stack of windows behind the frontmost Contacts window.* You can click the Contacts window directly behind the front Contacts window, or one behind it stretching farther back in time. Each time you click a Contacts window in the stack, Time Machine moves it to the front of the screen.

   • *Move the pointer to the Time Machine timeline along the right edge of the screen.* The timeline bars expand to display a specific date. To choose a specific date, click it.

4. **When you locate the contact card you want to retrieve, click it, click the Restore button in the lower-right corner, and then proceed to Step 6.**

   To select more than one contact card, hold down the ⌘ key and click each additional contact you want to recover.

5. **If the contact you want to restore is nowhere to be found in the Contacts windows — or if you change your mind and don't want to recover a backed-up contact — click the Cancel button in the lower-left corner (or press the Escape key).**

   Time Machine closes and returns you to the present.

6. **The Time Machine Contacts window zooms forward and then closes, returning you to the Contacts application window, which now includes the recovered contact card (or cards).**

   That's it — you've been saved!

You can search within Time Machine to locate the file you want to retrieve from a previous backup by typing in a search term in the search field. You can also use Spotlight Search from the Finder, and then click the Time Machine icon on the Dock or Launchpad. When you find the file you want, select it and click the Restore button. The item is placed in its original location.

Retrieving files and/or folders by using the Finder

To use the Finder window to retrieve files, folders, or a combination of both with the Time Machine restore app, follow these steps:

1. **Click the Time Machine icon on the Dock or on the Launchpad (or click the Time Machine icon on the menu bar and choose Enter Time Machine) to run the Time Machine restore app.**

2. **Choose one of the following ways to locate the file or folder from the past that you want to recover by using the Finder window:**

   - *Click the Backward and Forward arrow buttons near the bottom-right corner of the screen.* Click the Backward button to move the Finder window backward in time to previous Time Machine backups. Click the Forward button to work your way forward to more recent Time Machine backups.

   - *Click a Finder window behind the frontmost Finder window.* Each time you click a Finder window, Time Machine moves it forward to the front of the screen.

   - *Move the pointer to the Time Machine timeline along the right edge of the screen.* The timeline bars expand to display a specific date. To choose a specific date, click it.

To take a peek at the contents of a particular document, picture, audio track, or other file, click it and then click the Quick Look button on the toolbar (see Figure 1-7), which gives you a speedy way to view the contents of your selected file to make sure that it's the one you really want to recover. The file type needs to be one that Quick Look understands. Quick Look can't read some database applications, such as FileMaker and Bento, nor most CAD documents.

3. **When you locate the data you want to recover, select the file or folders, click the Restore button in the bottom-right corner of the screen, and then proceed to Step 5.**

To select more than one file or folder, hold down the ⌘ key and click each additional item you want to recover.

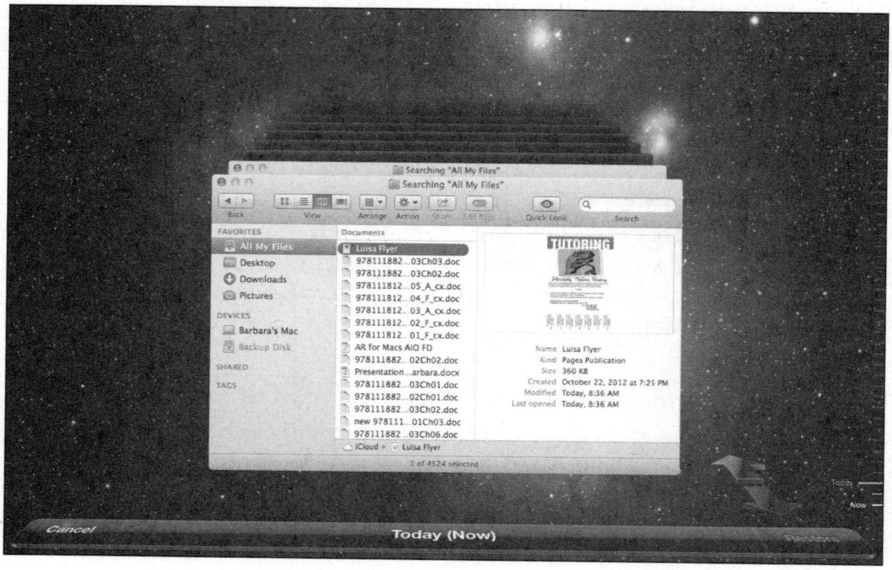

Figure 1-7:
Take a peek
with Quick
Look view.

4. **If the data you want to recover is nowhere to be found in the Finder windows — or if you change your mind and don't want to recover backup data — click the Cancel button in the bottom-left corner (or press the Escape key).**

The Time Machine recovery application closes, and you return to the present.

5. **The Time Machine Finder window zooms forward and then closes, safely returning you to a Finder window that now includes your recovered file or folder.**

Consider yourself saved!

Understanding Versions

Some apps — such as Apple's iWork apps, TextEdit, and Preview — have AutoSave and Versions functions, which automatically save your files while you work. AutoSave saves your document whenever you make changes. If you make a series of changes that you don't want to lose, you can choose to lock the document at that point. You have to unlock it to make future changes or use it as a template for a new document. To lock a document, hover the pointer near the file name at the top center of the window, click the disclosure triangle that appears and then click the check box next to Locked.

Versions takes a snapshot of your document when it's new, each time you open it, and once hourly while you're working on it. Versions keeps those hourly snapshots for a day, saves the day's last version for a month, and then saves weekly versions for previous months. If at some point you want to go back to an earlier version, choose File⇨Revert To⇨Browse All Versions, and Time Machine shows snapshots of that document, as shown in Figure 1-8. You can make side-by-side comparisons and cut and paste between them.

Figure 1-8: Versions is like having a mini Time Machine inside an app.

Restoring your entire backup

If your system or startup disk is damaged, you may have to restore your entire backup to your Mac. If you use Time Machine, you're worry free. Here's how to restore your Mac with Time Machine:

1. **Connect the backup drive to your computer.**

   If you use a networked drive, make sure that your computer and the drive are on the same network.

2. **Choose ⌘⇨Restart and hold down ⌘+R while your Mac restarts.**

   If you can't access the ⌘ menu — that is, your Mac is off and won't boot — hold down ⌘+R and press the On button. See Book III, Chapter 6 for more information about troubleshooting.

3. **Choose the language you use when the language chooser appears, and then click the arrow button (Continue).**

4. **Select Restore from a Time Machine Backup and then click Continue.**

5. **Choose the drive where your backup is stored:**

   • *Select the external drive and click Continue.*

   • *Select Time Capsule or the networked drive and click Connect to Remote Disk.*

6. **Enter the username and password if requested.**

7. **Select the date and time of the backup you want to use.**

   Time Machine begins copying your backup from the drive to your Mac.

8. **Breathe a sigh of relief that you back up regularly!**

Moving Your Backup from an Old Mac to a New Mac

Sooner or later, your Mac will be outdated, and you'll want to move your files to a new Mac. Apple has a handy Migration Assistant application to perform this task. You can transfer your files directly by connecting one Mac to the other with a Thunderbolt cable or over a network. If the old Mac is kaput, however, you can use your Time Machine backup. Follow these steps:

1. **On the new Mac, click the Launchpad icon on the Dock, open the Utilities folder, and then click Migration Assistant.**

   The Migration Assistant Introduction dialog opens, as shown in Figure 1-9.

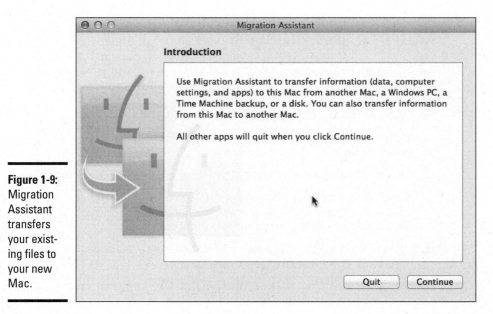

Figure 1-9: Migration Assistant transfers your existing files to your new Mac.

2. **Click Continue.**

   Migration Assistant automatically quits any open apps, the Desktop closes, and a Migration Assistant window opens.

3. **Select the From Another Mac, Time Machine Backup, or Startup Disk option and then click Continue.**

   Enter the password for your computer, if asked. The Select a Migration Method dialog opens.

4. **Choose the From a Time Machine Backup or Other Disk option button and click Continue.**

   Migration Assistant searches for external drives.

5. **Select the drive from which you want to transfer your backup.**

6. **Select the information you want to transfer.**

   - *Users* includes all the user's media, documents, messages, contacts, and calendars.

   - *Applications* transfers applications that are compatible with the new Mac.

   - *Settings* transfers personal settings. Check Computer to transfer your desktop image and other personal settings; check Network (not shown in the figure) to transfer your network settings.

7. **Click Continue.**

   Migration Assistant begins transferring the selected files.

If your new Mac has a newer operating system than your old Mac, applications that aren't compatible with the new operating system may not work or even be transferred. Choose ⇨Software Update to find and install any application updates that are compatible with the operating system of your new Mac.

Working with Data-Recovery Programs

Data-recovery apps work by taking advantage of the way computers store and organize files by physically placing them in certain areas, known as *sectors,* on your Mac's internal storage drive (or removable storage device). To find out more about the nitty-gritty of how hard drives manage files, check out the nearby sidebar, "Hard drive: A tale of control, corruption, and redemption."

Suppose you're a well-protected Mac user who backs up your data regularly. You're completely safe, right, and you never have to worry about losing files you can't retrieve? Not exactly. Here are three situations where backup applications can't help you, and you may need to rely on special data-recovery applications instead:

TECHNICAL STUFF

Hard drive: A tale of control, corruption, and redemption

To keep track of where each file is stored, your Mac maintains a directory that tells the computer the names of every file and the exact physical location where each file begins. Files are divided into blocks, and (typically) the end of each block contains a pointer to the next block of that file. This division is transparent to you, the user; when you open a file, you see all the blocks together. When different apps, such as word processors or spreadsheets, need to find and open a file, these apps depend on the Mac operating system to keep track of this directory so they know where to find a file.

When you delete a file, the computer simply removes that file's name from the directory. The blocks that make up your file still physically exist on the disk surface, but the computer can't find and assemble them again. Therefore data-recovery apps ignore the disk's directory listing and search for a file by examining every part of the entire storage device to find your missing files, locating the beginning of the first block and then following the pointers at the end of each block that indicate the beginning of the next one, creating a chain of blocks that make up the whole file.

If you didn't add any files since you last deleted the file you want to retrieve, a data-recovery app will likely retrieve your entire file again. If you saved and modified files since you last deleted a particular file, there's a good chance any new or modified files might have written over the area that contains your deleted file. In this case, your chances of recovering the entire file intact drops rapidly over time.

If a hardware failure corrupts a file, all or part of your file might be wiped out for good. However, in many cases, a hardware failure won't physically destroy all or part of a file. Instead, a hardware failure might physically scramble a file, much like throwing a pile of clothes all over the room. In this case, the file still physically exists, but the directory of the disk won't know where all the parts of the file have been scattered. So, to the computer, your files have effectively disappeared.

A data-recovery application can piece together scattered files by examining the physical surface of a disk, gathering up file fragments, and putting them back together again like Humpty Dumpty. Depending on how badly corrupted a file might be, collecting file fragments and putting them back together can recover an entire file or just part of a file, but sometimes recovering part of a file can be better than losing the whole file.

✦ **Accidental deletion from the hard drive:** The most common way to lose a file is by accidentally deleting it. If you try to recover your lost file through a backup app, such as Time Machine, you may be shocked to find that your backup app can recover only a version of your file from the previous hour or older, but not from the span of time between Time Machine backups. So, if you spent the last 45 minutes changing a file and accidentally deleted it before Time Machine could run its next automatic backup, you're out of luck if you want to recover the changes you made in the last 45 minutes.

Even if you format and erase your entire hard drive, your files may still physically remain on the hard drive, making it possible to recover those files.

✦ **Hardware failure:** Another way to lose a file is through a hardware failure, such as your hard drive mangling portions of its disk surface. If a power outage knocked out your Mac without properly shutting it down first, any open files that you were working on or that were stored may be corrupted. Such a failure can go unnoticed because the hard drive still works. As a result, your backup app copies and saves these mangled versions of your file. The moment you discover your file is corrupted, you also find that your backup app has been diligently copying and saving the same corrupted version of your file.

✦ **Deletion from removable media:** You may lose data by deleting it from removable media, such as a USB flash drive or digital camera flash memory card (such as a Compact Flash [CF] or Secure Digital [SD] card). Most likely, your backup apps protect only your hard drive files, not any removable storage devices, which means that you could take 20 priceless pictures of your dog doing midair back-flip Frisbee catches, only to delete all those pictures by mistake (and tanking your dog's chances at YouTube stardom). Because your backup app may never have saved those files, you can't recover what was never saved.

Some popular data-recovery applications include

✦ **Data Recovery for Mac** (`www.data-photo-recovery-tips.com/data-recovery-for-mac/`; **$90):** Specializes in recovering files from corrupted or reformatted hard drives.

✦ **Data Rescue 3** (`www.prosofteng.com`; **$99):** Recovers and retrieves data from a hard drive your Mac can no longer access because of a hard disk failure.

✦ **DiskWarrior 4** (`www.alsoft.com/DiskWarrior`; **$100):** Builds a new replacement directory, using data recovered from the original directory, thereby recovering files, folders, and documents that you thought were gone forever.

✦ **Klix** (`www.prosofteng.com`; **$20):** Recovers lost digital images stored on flash memory cards, such as SD or CF cards.

✦ **Softtote Data Recovery Mac** (`www.softtote.com`; $70): Retrieves lost, formatted, deleted, corrupted, and infected files.

The art of computer forensics

Most anything you store on your Mac can be recovered, given enough time and money. When most people lose data, they're thankful when a data-recovery app can retrieve their files. However, in the criminal world, people may want to delete files so that nobody can ever find them again, to hide evidence. To retrieve such deleted files, law enforcement agencies rely on *computer forensics.*

The basic idea behind computer forensics is to make an exact copy of a hard drive and then try to piece together the deleted files on that copy of the original hard drive. Some criminals have lit hard drives on fire, poured acid on them, and sliced them apart with a buzz saw — and law enforcement agencies still managed to read and recover portions of the files from the slivers of hard-drive fragments that contained magnetic traces of the original files.

The good news is that if you can't recover a file yourself by using a data-recovery application, you can often hire a professional service that can recover your data for you — but that data better be really important to you because data-recovery services are very expensive.

Chapter 2: Protecting Your Mac against Local and Remote Threats

In This Chapter

✔ Locking your Mac

✔ Adding passwords

✔ Encrypting your documents with FileVault

✔ Configuring Firewall and Privacy settings

✔ Adding other users to your Mac

One of the Mac's advantages is that it seems to be a minor target of viruses — but that certainly doesn't make it immune. With the world-wide connectivity of the Internet, everyone is vulnerable to everything, including malicious software *(malware)* and malicious people with above-average computer skills *(hackers)*. Worse are those hackers who like to use e-mail and websites to steal your personal identity information, such as credit card accounts or Social Security numbers *(phishing)*, or those who send out software masquerading as one thing but as soon as you open it, you discover it's harmful *(Trojan horses* disseminating malware). Although threats over the Internet attract the most attention, your Mac is also vulnerable from mundane threats, such as thieves who may want to steal your computer.

No matter how much you know about computers, you can always become a victim if you're not careful. Therefore this chapter looks at the different ways to protect your Mac from threats — physical and cyber, local and remote.

Locking Down Your Mac

Most people lock their cars and house doors when they're away, and your Mac should be no exception to this practice. To protect your Mac physically, you can get a security cable that wraps around an immovable object (like that heavy rolltop desk you have in the den) and then attaches to your Mac. You can attach it by threading it through a handle or hole in your Macintosh case, or if you have a MacBook Pro, by connecting it to your Mac's built-in security slot, which is a tiny slot that a security cable plugs into. If you have a MacBook Air, don't bother searching because there is no security slot, but Maclocks makes an unobtrusive "security skin."

Some companies that sell security cables are

✦ **Belkin:** www.belkin.com

✦ **Kensington:** www.kensington.com

✦ **Maclocks:** www.maclocks.com

✦ **Targus:** www.targus.com

✦ **Tryten:** www.tryten.com/categories/Mac-Computer-Locks

Of course, security cables can be cut, although a security cable deters a thief who forgot his bolt cutters.

After protecting your Mac physically, you have other ways to lock down your Mac and keep other people out. Use a password to stop intruders from sneaking into your computer if you step away from your desk, encrypt the files, and use a software or hardware firewall, or both, to stop intruders from sneaking into your computer over the Internet.

Anyone with enough time, determination, and skill can defeat passwords and firewalls. Security can only discourage and delay an intruder, but nothing can ever guarantee to stop one.

Using Passwords

Before you can ever use your Mac, you must configure it by creating an account name and password — an account on your Mac, not to be confused with your Apple ID. The Setup Wizard walks you through this when you turn on your Mac for the first time. If you're the only person using your Mac, you'll probably have just one account (although we encourage you to have two — one for admin and one for everyday use). If you disable automatic login, your password can keep others from using your Mac without your knowledge.

As a rule, your password should be difficult for someone to guess but easy for you to remember. Unfortunately, in practice, people often use simple — as in, lousy — passwords. To make your password difficult to guess but easy to remember, you should create a password that combines upper- and low-ercase letters with numbers and/or symbols, such as OCHSa*co2010alum! (which abbreviates a phrase: in this case, *Ocean City High School all-star class of 2010 Alumnus!*). When you create your user accounts, take advantage of the Password Assistant to have your Mac create a password for you. Of course, it may be harder to remember but also harder to guess.

One way to create passwords is to combine the first letters of the words in a phrase that you'll never forget with the name of a dearly departed pet. By picking a memorable phrase or lyric, such as "I'm walkin' on sunshine" and turning it into a nonsensical combination of letters, paired with the name of your long-gone pet hermit crab, Louise (Iw0sLou!se), you'll easily remember your password, but others won't easily guess it. Presumably, someone would have to know you very well to guess which phrase you use with which pet. Pairing these two things that are unique to you makes for a password that's easy for you to remember but hard for someone to guess.

Changing your password

Many online banking and credit card services require you to change your password every so often, some as often as once a month, which certainly keeps password-generating apps popular. Although it's a pain in the hindquarters, they have reason to require you to change — it increases security. To increase your file security, you should change the password on your Mac periodically, too. To change your password, follow these steps:

1. **Choose ⇨System Preferences.**

   The System Preferences window appears.

2. **Click the Users & Groups icon to open the Users & Groups preferences pane, as shown in Figure 2-1.**

   If the lock icon in the lower-left corner of the preferences window is locked, you must unlock it to make changes to your Mac's user account details. Click the lock icon, type your password in the dialog that appears, and then press Return to unlock your Mac's user account details.

REMEMBER

Book III
Chapter 2

Protecting Your Mac
against Local and
Remote Threats

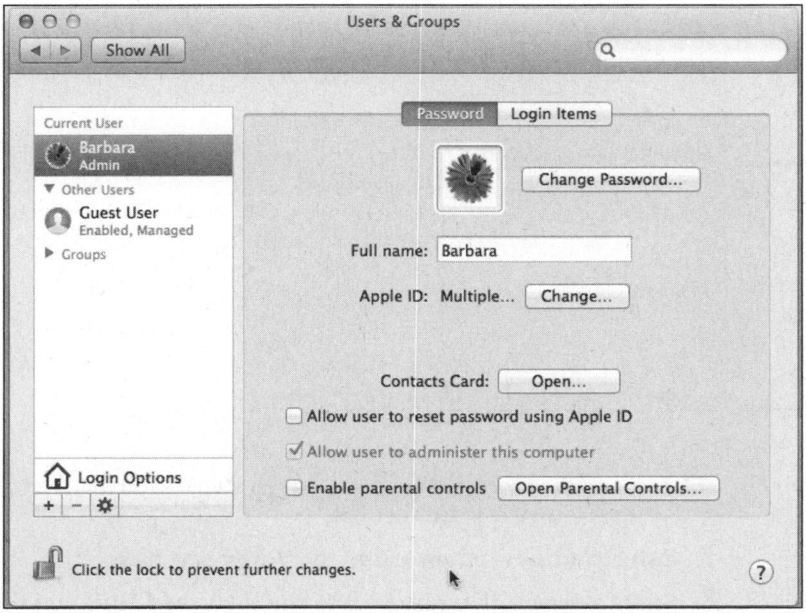

Figure 2-1:
Users &
Groups preferences let
you change
your user
account
details.

Users & Groups

Show All

Current User
Barbara
Admin

▼ Other Users
Guest User
Enabled, Managed
▶ Groups

Password | Login Items

Change Password...

Full name: Barbara

Apple ID: Multiple... Change...

Contacts Card: Open...

☐ Allow user to reset password using Apple ID

☑ Allow user to administer this computer

Login Options

☐ Enable parental controls Open Parental Controls...

Click the lock to prevent further changes.

3. **Click your username under Current User in the left pane (or another account name under Other Users that you want to modify).**

   If you haven't created any additional users, you see only yourself listed.

4. **Click the Change Password button.**

   A dialog appears, displaying text boxes for typing your old password and typing a new password twice to verify that you typed your new password correctly.

5. **Enter your current password in the Old Password text box.**

6. **Enter your new password in the New Password text box.**

   If you want your Mac to evaluate your password or invent a password for you, click the key icon to the right of the New Password text box. The Password Assistant opens.

   a. *Choose the type of password you want from the Type pop-up menu.* Manual lets you type in a password that you invent, and Password Assistant rates the security level of your password. The other five types offer various character combinations and security levels: Memorable; Letters & Numbers; Numbers Only; Random; or FIPS–181-compliant, which creates a password that meets federal standards.

   b. *Drag the Length slider to set how many characters you want your password to have.* The password appears in the Suggestion field, and the Quality bar shows how secure it is: the higher the quality, the safer the password. A 26-character Memorable password is of highest quality (see Figure 2-2).

Figure 2-2: Let Password Assistant help you choose a password.

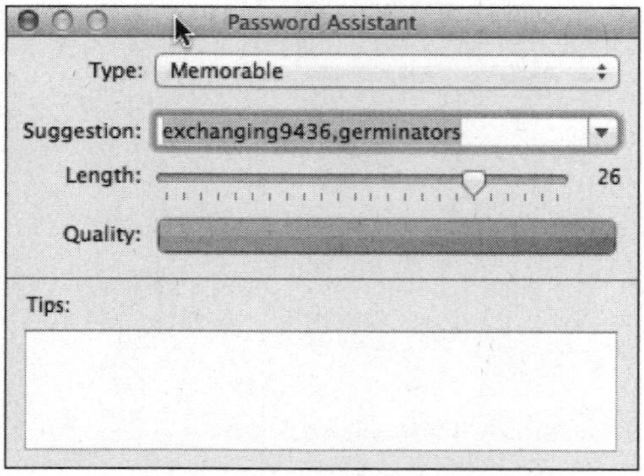

   c. *Click the Close button.* The chosen suggestion is inserted as bullets in the New Password text box.

7. **Enter your new password in the Verify text box.**

8. **Enter a descriptive phrase into the Password Hint text box.**

Adding a hint can help you remember your password, but it can also give an intruder a hint on what your password might be. Using our `Iw0sLou!se` example, you might use the phrase "favorite song crab." The intruder would have to know you pretty darn well to figure out that one!

9. **Click Change Password.**

   The password dialog disappears.

10. **Click the Close button to close the Users & Groups preferences window.**

Applying password protection

Normally, you need your password to log in to your account. As we mention earlier, we recommend creating an admin account that you use to make changes to your Mac, such as installing new software or changing certain settings, and a user account with a different username and password for your day-to-day Mac activities. The two account names and passwords should be different.

Of course, after you log in to either account, anyone can use your Mac if you walk away and don't log out. If you leave your Mac without logging out, your Mac will either go to sleep or display a screen saver. At this time, anyone could tap the keyboard and have full access to your Mac. To avoid this problem, you can password-protect your Mac when waking up from sleep or after displaying a screen saver.

For further protection, you can also password-protect your Mac from allowing an unauthorized person to make any changes to your Mac's various System Preferences. By applying password protection to different parts of your Mac, you can increase the chances that you'll be the only one to control your computer.

If you're the only person who has physical access to your Mac, you won't have to worry about password protection, but if your Mac is in an area where others can access it easily, password protection can be one extra step in keeping your Mac private.

All the choices here are optional, but we recommend choosing those that best meet your needs. To password-protect different parts of your Mac, follow these steps:

1. **Choose ➪System Preferences.**

   The System Preferences window appears.

2. **Click the Security & Privacy icon to open the Security & Privacy preferences pane.**

If the lock icon in the lower-left corner of the preferences window is locked, you must unlock it to make changes to your Mac's user account details. Click the lock icon, type your password in the dialog that appears, and then press Return to unlock your Mac's user account details.

3. **Click the General tab.**

The General preferences pane appears, as shown in Figure 2-3.

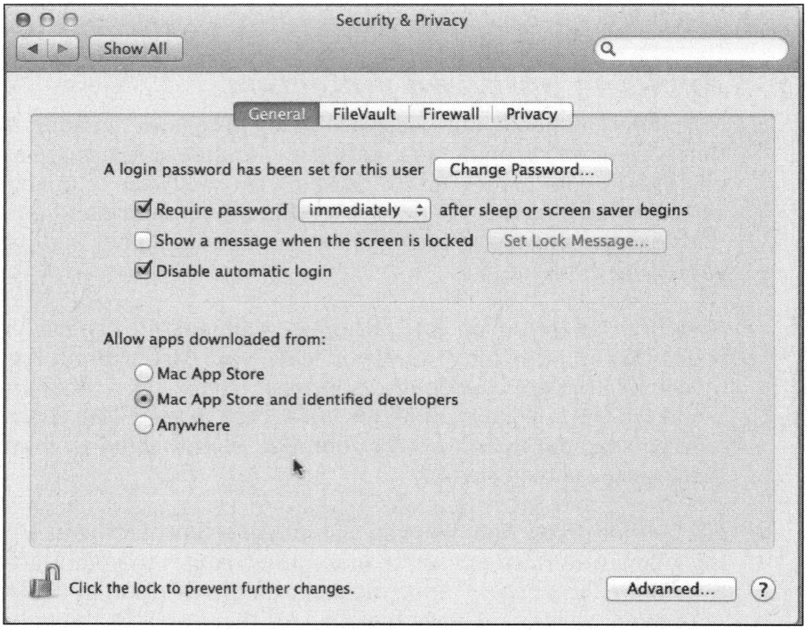

Figure 2-3: General Security & Privacy preferences let you choose different ways to password-protect your computer.

4. **Select (or deselect) the Require Password <*immediately*> after Sleep or Screen Saver Begins check box.**

You can also choose to require the password at an interval between 5 seconds and 4 hours after your Mac goes to sleep.

5. **Set a screen-lock message.**

   a. *Select the Show a Message When the Screen Is Locked check box.*

   b. *Click the Set Lock Message button.*

   c. *Type a message that will appear when your screen is locked, such as "Out to Lunch" or "Be Back at 2:30" or "Don't Even Think About Touching My Mac."*

6. **Select (or deselect) the Disable Automatic Login check box.**

If this check box is selected, your Mac asks for a user name and/or password before logging in to your account. If it's deselected, you don't enter a password to log in.

7. **Click one of the gatekeeper choices under Allow Apps Downloaded From:**

   - *Mac App Store:* Only apps from the App Store will be installed after being downloaded.

   - *Mac App Store and Identified Developers:* Only apps from the App Store or signed with an Apple Developer ID will be installed after being downloaded.

   - *Anywhere:* Downloads and installs any apps from any source, which opens you to risk from malware hackers.

   If you choose one of the first two choices and download apps from an unidentified source, when you try to install it, a warning tells you it's from an unidentified and potentially malicious source. Control-click the app to override Gatekeeper and install the app despite the warning.

8. **Click the Advanced button to select these two options:**

   - *Require an Administrator Password to Access System-Wide Preferences:* If this check box is selected, nobody can modify your Mac's System Preferences (such as the one you're adjusting right now!) without the proper password.

   - *Log Out after x Minutes of Inactivity:* If selected, this option logs off your account after the fixed period of time you set, so anyone trying to access your computer will need your password to log in to and access your account.

   Click OK after you make your choices.

9. **Click the Close button of the Security & Privacy preferences window.**

Encrypting Data with FileVault

Encryption physically scrambles your files so that even if people can access your files, they can't open or edit them unless they know the correct password. When you use FileVault, your Mac encrypts your entire drive, which means everything on your Mac is secure. If you have multiple users on your Mac, you must enable them so each can sign in with his password.

FileVault uses an encryption algorithm called Advanced Encryption Standard (AES), which is the latest U.S. government standard for scrambling data that even national governments with supercomputers can't crack — at least not in a realistic time frame.

Setting up FileVault

FileVault scrambles your files so that only your password (or the system's Master Password) can unlock the files so you — or someone you trust and give the password to — can read them. When you type in a password, you can access your files and use them normally, but as soon as you close a file, FileVault scrambles it once more. FileVault works in the background; you never even see it working.

FileVault uses your *login* password to encrypt your data. For added safety, FileVault creates a recovery key that can decrypt any encrypted files for all user accounts and the files for each account that you have stored on your Mac. If you forget your login password and your recovery key, your data will be encrypted forever with little hope of unscrambling and retrieving it again. You can opt to store your recovery password with Apple. If you lose it, you can retrieve it from Apple by giving the correct answers to three specific, pre-established questions.

To turn on FileVault, follow these steps:

1. **Choose ⌘⇨System Preferences and click the Security & Privacy icon.**

   The Security & Privacy preferences pane appears.

2. **Click the FileVault tab to open the FileVault preferences pane, as shown in Figure 2-4.**

   If the lock in the lower-left corner of the FileVault preferences pane is locked, click it, enter your password when prompted, and then click Unlock.

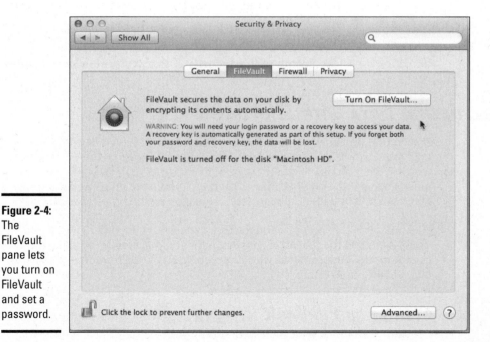

Figure 2-4:
The FileVault pane lets you turn on FileVault and set a password.

3. **Click the Turn on FileVault button.**

   The recovery key appears, as shown in Figure 2-5.

   If more than one person uses your Mac, a list of users appears. Click the Enable button next to the user(s) you want to give access to, enter the account password(s), click OK, and then click Continue.

   An enabled user who switches to his or her account must type in the password to access encrypted files. Users who forget their passwords will need the recovery key to gain access.

Figure 2-5: FileVault assigns a recovery key, which you use if you forget your password.

The recovery key is a "safety net" which can be used to unlock the disk if you forget your password.

Make a copy and store it in a safe place. If you forget your password and lose the recovery key, all the data on your disk will be lost.

OWHO-T5WB-36ZO-96UH-D8XF-HVEU

(?)   Cancel   Back   Continue

4. **Write down your recovery key and then click Continue.**

   The recovery key changes if you turn FileVault off and then on again.

5. **Choose whether to store your recovery key with Apple (see Figure 2-6):**

   - *No:* Select the Do Not Store the Recovery Key with Apple radio button.

   - *Yes:* Select the Store the Recovery Key with Apple radio button.

     Options for three questions appear, as shown in Figure 2-6. You must answer all three questions correctly for Apple to release your recovery key.

     Select a question from each of the three pop-up menus, type the answers for the questions in the text boxes, and then click Continue.

6. **In the dialog that opens, click the Restart button to begin the encryption process (or Cancel if you changed your mind).**

   Your Mac restarts and begins the encryption process. You can work while the encryption takes place. You can return to FileVault in System Preferences to check on the status.

FileVault also works with external hard drives, so your data is safe wherever it's stored.

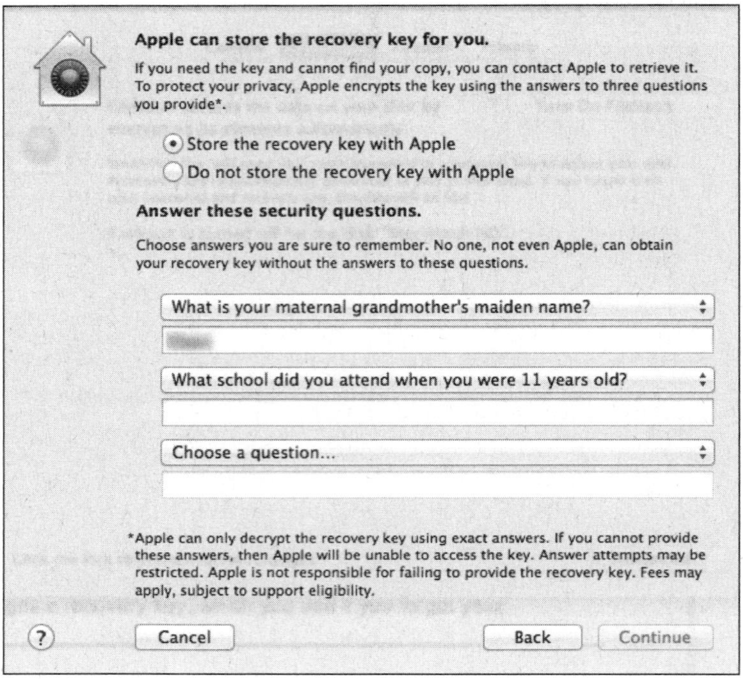

Apple can store the recovery key for you.

If you need the key and cannot find your copy, you can contact Apple to retrieve it. To protect your privacy, Apple encrypts the key using the answers to three questions you provide*.

- ● Store the recovery key with Apple
- ○ Do not store the recovery key with Apple

Answer these security questions.

Choose answers you are sure to remember. No one, not even Apple, can obtain your recovery key without the answers to these questions.

What is your maternal grandmother's maiden name?

What school did you attend when you were 11 years old?

Choose a question...

*Apple can only decrypt the recovery key using exact answers. If you cannot provide these answers, then Apple will be unable to access the key. Answer attempts may be restricted. Apple is not responsible for failing to provide the recovery key. Fees may apply, subject to support eligibility.

(?)   Cancel   Back   Continue

Figure 2-6:
Store your recovery key with Apple to protect against (your) memory loss.

Turning off FileVault

If you turned on FileVault and later change your mind, you can always turn it off:

1. **Choose ⌘ System Preferences and click the Security & Privacy icon.**

2. **Click the FileVault tab to open the FileVault preferences pane (refer to Figure 2-4).**

When FileVault is turned on, the Turn Off FileVault button appears.

3. **Click the Turn Off File Vault button, enter your login password, and then click OK.**

A confirmation dialog appears, informing you that you're about to turn off FileVault.

4. **Click the Turn Off FileVault button.**

If you decide to sell or give your Mac to someone, you can use FileVault's Instant Wipe function to completely *clean* your Mac's drive. Technically, Instant Wipe eliminates the FileVault key, making the data inaccessible, and then overwrites the data with an illegible pattern.

Using Firewalls

Padlocks and FileVault protect your Mac against local threats, but when you connect your Mac to the Internet, you essentially open a door to remote threats. A highly technical person (such as a hacker) situated anywhere in the world could access your computer, copy or modify your files, or erase all your data. To keep out unwanted intruders, every computer needs a special program called a *firewall*.

A firewall simply blocks access to your computer, while still allowing you access to the Internet so you can browse websites or send and receive e-mail. Every Mac comes with a software firewall that can protect you whenever your Mac connects to the Internet.

Many people use a special device — a *router* — to connect to the Internet. A router lets multiple computers use a single Internet connection, such as a high-speed broadband cable or DSL Internet connection. Routers include built-in hardware firewalls, and using one in combination with your Mac's software firewall can provide your Mac with twice the protection. For more about how to configure your router's firewall settings, refer to the router's user guide or look for more information in the support section of the router manufacturer's website.

Configuring the Mac firewall

Although the default setting for your Mac's firewall should be adequate for most people, you may want to configure your firewall to block additional Internet features for added security. For example, most people will likely need to access e-mail and web pages, but if you never transfer files by using FTP (short for File Transfer Protocol), you can safely block this service.

Don't configure your firewall unless you're sure that you know what you're doing. Otherwise, you may weaken the firewall or lock programs from accessing the Internet and not know how to repair those problems.

To configure your Mac's firewall, follow these steps:

1. **Choose System Preferences and then click the Security & Privacy icon.**

If the lock icon in the lower-left corner of the preferences window is locked, you must unlock it to make changes to your Mac's user account details. Click the lock icon, type your password in the dialog that appears, and then press Return to unlock your Mac's user account details.

2. **Click the Firewall tab.**

The Firewall preferences pane appears.

3. **Click the Turn On Firewall button to turn on your Mac's firewall (if it isn't already turned on).**

4. **Click the Firewall Options button to display the firewall's custom settings, as shown in Figure 2-7.**

    The dialog that appears offers three check boxes.

    In the center list box, you may see one or more sharing services you turned on by using the Sharing preferences pane (⌘⇨System Preferences⇨Sharing). Find out how to share in Book III, Chapter 4.

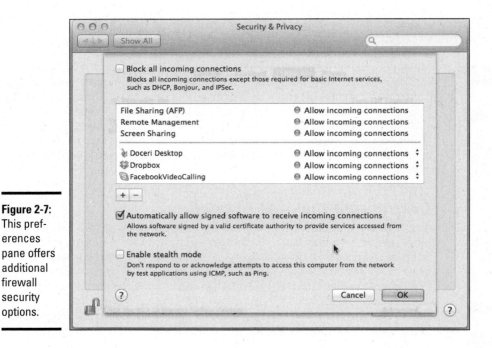

Figure 2-7:
This preferences pane offers additional firewall security options.

5. **Select (or deselect) the following check boxes:**

    • *Block All Incoming Connections:* Allows only essential communications for basic Internet and Mail access; also blocks sharing services, such as iTunes music sharing or Messages screen sharing. When you select this option, any services or applications listed in the pane disappear, replaced with a static warning that indicates all sharing services are being blocked.

    • *Automatically Allow Signed Software to Receive Incoming Connections:* Allows typical commercial applications such as Microsoft Word to check for software updates and Safari to access the web.

    • *Enable Stealth Mode:* Makes the firewall refuse to respond to any outside attempts to contact it and gather information based on its responses.

6. **Continue to Step 8 if you want to make additional adjustments to your Mac's firewall feature; otherwise, skip to Step 13.**

7. **(Optional) Click the Add (+) button to add applications that you want to allow or block from communicating over the Internet.**

   A dialog appears, listing the contents of the Applications folder.

8. **Click a program that you want to allow to access the Internet, such as Dropbox or Skype.**

9. **Click Add.**

   Your chosen program appears under the Applications category.

10. **(Optional) Click the pop-up button to the right of an application in the applications list and choose Allow Incoming Communications or Block Incoming Communications.**

11. **(Optional) To remove a program from the applications list, click the program name to select it and click the Delete (–) button below the program list.**

12. **Click OK.**

Beginning with Mac OS X 10.7 Lion, your Mac's security was enhanced with two features:

✦ **Advanced Space Layout Randomization (ASLR):** Makes your applications more resistant to malicious attacks

✦ **Sandboxing:** Limits the types of operations an application can do, thereby making it difficult for a threat to take advantage of an application and, consequently, affect the whole operating system. Think of it as strengthening a potential weak link.

Buying a more robust firewall

Although the built-in Mac firewall blocks incoming connections well, it allows all outgoing connections — meaning that a malicious program you may inadvertently download could communicate via the Internet without your knowledge. To prevent this problem, you need a firewall that can block both incoming and outgoing connections.

You should use only one software firewall at a time (although you *can* use one software firewall and a hardware firewall built into your router). If you use two or more software firewall programs, they may interfere with each other and cause your Mac to stop working correctly.

If you want a more robust firewall than the one that comes with the Mac (and the added security of antivirus and antimalware protection), consider one of the following:

✦ **ClamXav 2:** Available for free at www.clamxav.com

**Book III
Chapter 2**

Protecting Your Mac against Local and Remote Threats

✦ **Intego Mac Internet Security 2013:** Costs between $40 and $60; available at `www.intego.com`

One problem with a firewall is that in the normal scheme of things, you never really know how well it's working. To help you measure the effectiveness of your firewall, visit one of the following sites that will probe and test your computer, looking for the exact same vulnerabilities that hackers will look for:

✦ **Audit My PC:** `www.auditmypc.com`

✦ **HackerWatch:** `www.hackerwatch.org/probe`

✦ **ShieldsUP!:** `https://www.grc.com/x/ne.dll?bh0bkyd2`

✦ **Symantec Security Check:** `http://security.symantec.com/sscv6/WelcomePage.asp`

Because each firewall-testing website may test for different features, testing your Mac with two or more of these sites can help ensure that your Mac is as secure as possible.

Dealing with nasty malware and RATs

Two big threats exploit personal computers that aren't protected by properly configured firewall preferences or properly configured router firewall settings. The first of these threats — *malware* — consists of programs that sneak onto your computer and then secretly connect to the Internet to do merely annoying (and offensive) things (retrieve pornographic ads that appear all over your screen) or do more serious things (infect your computer with a virus that can erase your personal data). Or, they can keep track of every keystroke you type on your computer, which in turn is transmitted to a snooping program on a malevolent person's computer so the hacker can find out personal info such as credit card numbers, usernames, and passwords.

A second type of program that requires an outgoing Internet connection is a Remote Access Trojan (RAT). Malicious hackers often trick people into downloading and installing RATs on their computers. When installed, a RAT can connect to the Internet and allow the hacker to completely control the computer remotely over the Internet, including deleting or copying files, conducting attacks through this computer, or sending junk e-mail (spam) through this computer.

Although computer malware and RATs written and released by hackers typically target PCs running Windows, security experts agree that it's only a matter of time before the same digital nastiness begins infecting Macs. To guard against potential viruses, spyware, and RATs, your Mac displays a dialog that alerts you when you run a program for the first time. This feature can alert you if a virus, spyware, or a RAT tries to infect a Mac. For further protection, consider purchasing a router with built-in firewall features, or installing an antivirus and antimalware program. (See the "Buying a more robust firewall" section for recommendations.)

Selecting Privacy Settings

If you belong to a social network such as Facebook or LinkedIn, you may know a little bit about privacy settings and how confusing they can be. Seems like everyone wants to know where you are and what you're doing. Maybe that's okay with you, maybe it's not. Either way, you can set privacy settings on your Mac, too. Follow these steps:

1. **Choose ⌘➪System Preferences and then click the Security & Privacy icon.**

If the lock icon in the lower-left corner of the preferences window is locked, you must unlock it to make changes to your preferences. Click the lock icon, type your password in the dialog that appears, and then press Return to unlock your preferences.

2. **Click the Privacy tab.**

The Privacy preferences pane appears, as shown in Figure 2-8.

Figure 2-8: The Privacy preferences let you choose which apps access data from your Mac or other apps.

3. **Click each app in the list to allow other apps to access that app's contents.**

For example, click Contacts and then click the apps in the list on the right to give them access to Contacts. Each time an app requests access to information in another app, it will appear in the list for that app's Privacy preferences.

Two other choices to consider in particular:

- *Location Services:* Select the Enable Location Services check box, as shown in Figure 2-9, to allow applications that use your location to access it — for example, Safari and Maps. You can selectively allow access only to certain applications or deselect the check box and prohibit access altogether.

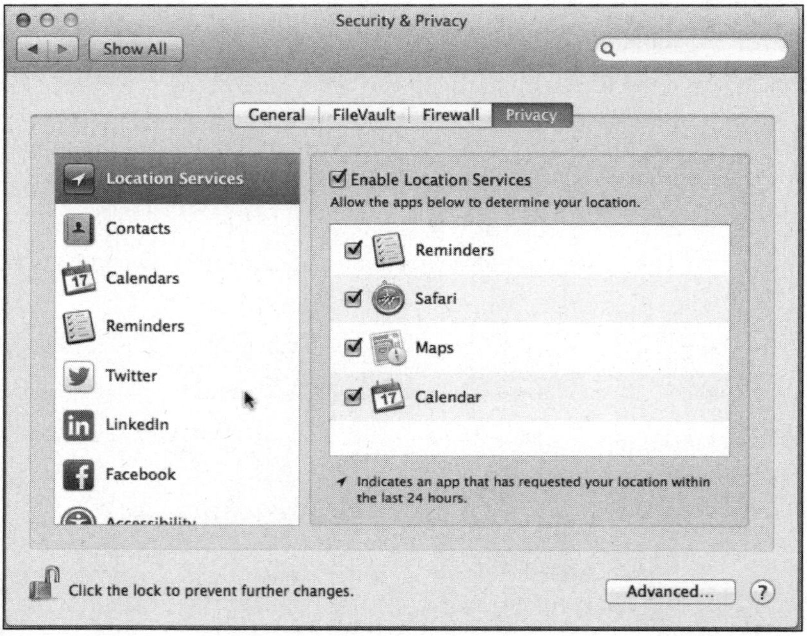

Figure 2-9:
Many apps use Location Services to complete their tasks.

- *Diagnostics & Usage (scroll down the list of apps to find it):* Select the Send Diagnostic & Usage Data to Apple check box if you want to send a message to Apple when you have a problem, such as Safari crashing, or to let your Mac send a message about how you're using it from time to time. The information is sent anonymously, so you don't have to worry about being spammed or anything.

4. **Click the Close button.**

Creating Multiple Accounts

Every Mac has at least one account that allows you to use your computer. However, if multiple people need to use your Mac, you probably don't want to share the same account, which can be like trying to share the same pair of pants.

One problem with sharing the same account is that one person may change the screen saver or delete an app or file that someone else may want. To avoid people interfering with each other, you can divide your Mac into multiple accounts.

Essentially, having multiple accounts gives your Mac a split personality. Each account lets each person customize the same Mac while shielding other users from these changes. So, one account can display pink daffodils on the screen, and another account can display pictures of Mt. Rushmore.

To access any account, you need to log in to that account. To exit an account, you need to log out. Although two users may be logged in at the same time, you see only one user's Desktop, Finder, and setup.

Not only do separate accounts keep multiple users from accessing each other's files, but creating multiple accounts also gives you the ability to restrict what other accounts can do. That means you — parents, for example — can block Internet access from an account, limit Internet access to specific times, or limit Internet access to specific websites. Such limits are *Parental Controls.*

Adding a new user account

To protect your files and settings, you should create a separate account for each person who uses your Mac. You can create four types of accounts:

✦ **Administrator:** Gives the user access to create, modify, and delete accounts. Typically, you have only one Administrator account; however, another user you trust implicitly, such as your partner, spouse, or job-share colleague may also have an Administrator account.

✦ **Standard:** Gives the user access to the computer and allows them to install programs or change their account settings, but doesn't let the user create, modify, or delete accounts or change any locked System Preferences settings.

✦ **Managed with Parental Controls:** Gives the user restricted access to the computer based on the Parental Controls defined by an Administrator account.

✦ **Sharing Only:** Gives the user remote access to shared files but not the access to log in or change settings on your computer.

Although each set of instructions begins with opening System Preferences and ends with closing System Preferences, you can open it once, go through each of the following sets of instructions, and then close System Preferences at the end.

You can set up a Managed with Parental Controls account from the Users & Groups System Preferences or directly from the Parental Controls System preferences. To set up a new user account, follow these steps:

1. **Choose ⇨System Preferences and click the Users & Groups icon Users & Groups preferences pane (see Figure 2-10).**

Book III
Chapter 2

Protecting Your Mac against Local and Remote Threats

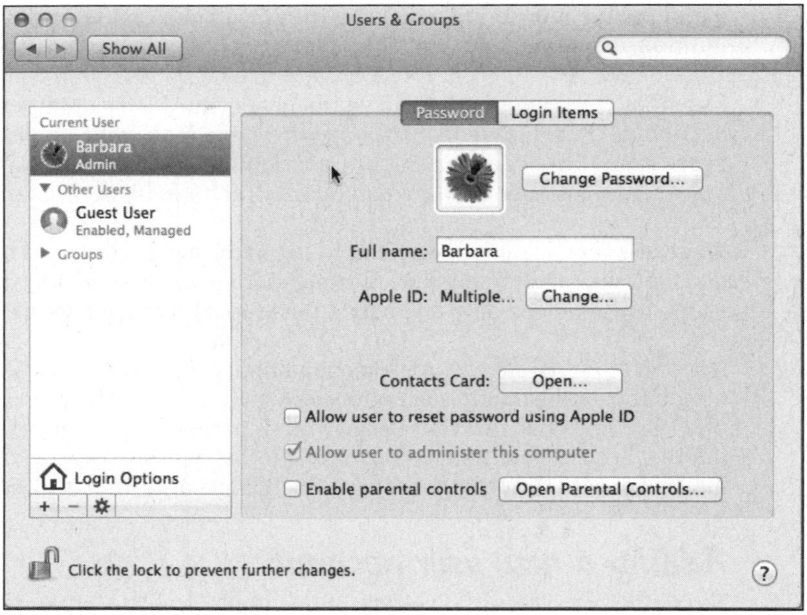

Figure 2-10:
Manage
all single
accounts
and groups
from the
Users &
Groups
preferences.

If the lock icon in the lower-left corner of the preferences window is locked, you must unlock it to make changes to your Mac's user account details. Click the lock icon, type your password in the dialog that appears, and then press Return to unlock your Mac's user account details.

2. **Click the Add (+) button in the lower-left corner (above the lock icon).**

    A New Account dialog appears.

3. **Choose the type of account you want to set up from the New Account pop-up menu, as shown in Figure 2-11.**

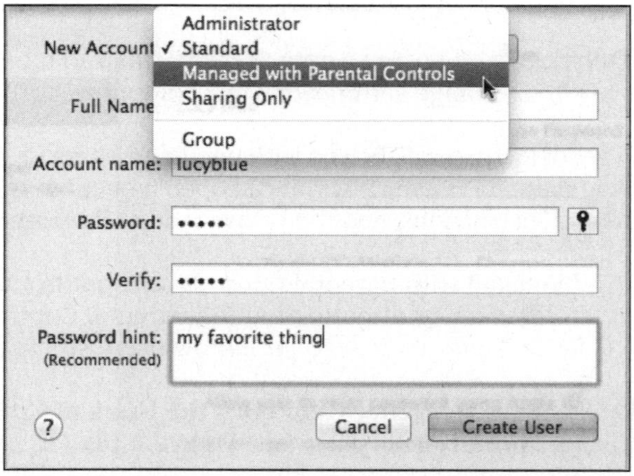

Figure 2-11:
The New
Account
dialog lets
you define
your new
account.

4. **Enter the name of the person who'll be using the account into the Full Name text box.**

5. **(Optional) In the Account Name text box, edit the short name that your Mac automatically creates.**

6. **Enter a password for this account into the Password text box.**

   If you click the key to the right of the password text box, your Mac will generate a random password that may be more difficult to guess but also harder to remember.

7. **Re-enter the password you chose in Step 7 in the Verify text box.**

8. **(Optional) In the Password Hint text box, enter a descriptive phrase to help remind you of your password.**

9. **Click the Create User button.**

   The Users & Groups preferences pane displays the name of your new account.

10. **(Optional) To assign an image to a user, follow these steps:**

    a. *Click the image (the Picture well) above the name to reveal a selection of images you can assign to that user.*

    b. *Click an image from the Defaults that are shown, click iCloud to choose a photo from Photo Stream, or click Camera to take a photo.*

    c. *Click Edit to zoom or add a special effect to the image or photo.*

    d. *When you have a photo you like, click the Done button to assign the photo to the user.*

11. **Click the Set button next to Apple ID to associate the correct Apple ID with this user.**

    The button will read Change if an existing Apple ID is already assigned.

12. **Select one or more of the choices in the pane, as shown in Figure 2-12:**

    • *Allow User to Reset Password Using Apple ID:* The user can go into the User & Groups panel on his Mac to set up and change the user password by identifying himself with his Apple ID.

    • *Allow User to Administer This Computer:* Change the account type to Administrator.

    • *Enable Parental Controls:* Click the Open Parental Controls button to assign the limits you want to apply to this user.

13. **Click the lock at the bottom of the window to prevent changes.**

14. **Click the Close button of the Users & Groups preferences window.**

Learn about Login Options later in this chapter, in the section "Enabling Fast User Switching."

Figure 2-12:
Associate
the Apple ID
and select
options for
new users.

Setting up a master password

If you have many user accounts set up on your Mac and each has a password, you should have a plan if someone forgets his password. By setting up a master password, the administrator of the Mac (probably you), can override any encrypting that the user may have set up and reset the password. To create a master password, follow these steps:

1. **Choose ☰⇨System Preferences and click the Users & Groups icon to open the Users & Groups preferences pane (refer to Figure 2-10).**

   Click the lock icon and enter your password to unlock the Users & Groups System Preferences.

2. **Click the Action button (it looks like a gear) at the bottom of the user list.**

3. **Choose Set Master Password.**

   A dialog opens, as shown in Figure 2-13.

4. **Type in a password in the Master Password text box.**

   If you want help inventing a password, click the key to the right of the text field.

5. **Retype the password in the Verify text box.**

6. **Type a hint to help you remember the Master Password.**

7. **Click OK.**

8. **Click the Close button of the Users & Groups preferences window.**

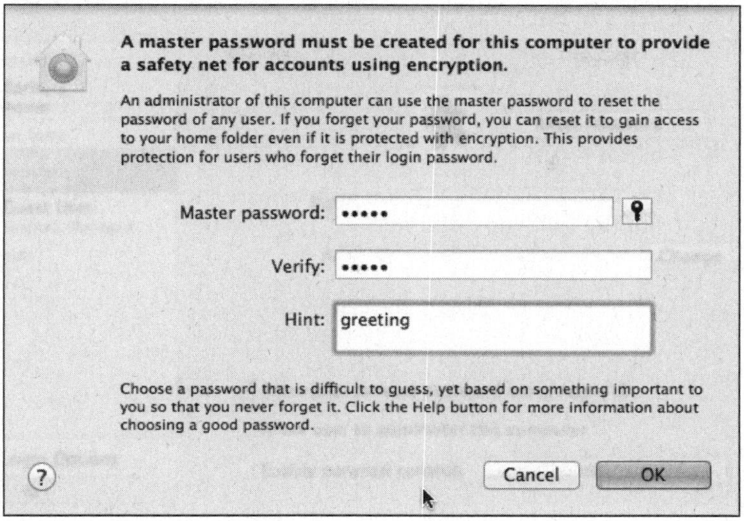

Figure 2-13:
Set a master password so the administrator can reset other users' passwords.

Defining Parental Controls

You may want to use Parental Controls not only to protect your children from seeing things they may not be mature enough to see, but also to restrict what guest users can do with your Mac. You apply limits or restrictions to a Managed with Parental Controls account even if the person who accesses that account isn't your child. You can place several types of restrictions on an account. Following are the categories of limits you find in the Parental Controls preferences:

✦ **Apps:** Limits the apps the user may use and offers an option to simplify the appearance of the Finder.

✦ **Web:** Limits which websites the account can access.

✦ **People:** Limits the account to sending and receiving e-mail and instant messages from a fixed list of approved people. You can also receive an e-mail when the user tries to exchange e-mail with a non-approved contact.

✦ **Time Limits:** Prevents someone from accessing the account at certain times or on certain days.

✦ **Other:** Select the associated check boxes to hide profanity, prevent modifications to the printers connected to the Mac, prevent saving data to a CD or DVD, or prevent changing the account password.

To apply Parental Controls to an account, follow these steps:

1. **Choose System Preferences and then click the Users & Groups icon.**

Click the lock icon and enter your password to unlock the Users & Groups System Preferences.

2. **Click the Parental Controls button.**

   The Parental Controls preferences window opens.

3. **Click the account to which you want to apply Parental Controls.**

4. **Click the Apps tab (if it isn't already selected).**

   The Apps preferences pane appears, as shown in Figure 2-14. Choose from the following options:

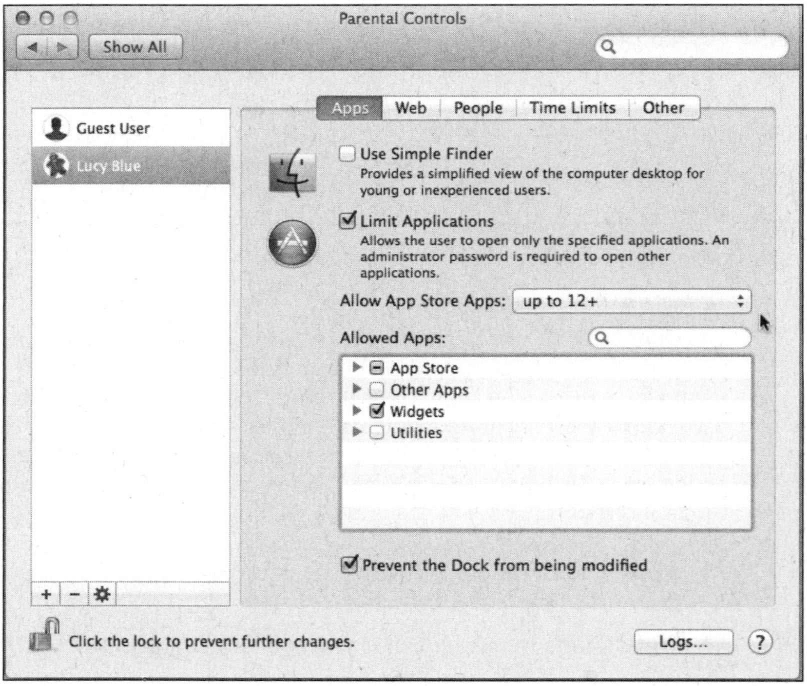

Figure 2-14: Choose which applications the user can use.

- *Use Simple Finder:* Select this check box to create a Finder that's easier for novice Mac users to work with.

- *Limit Applications:* Select this check box to restrict which apps the account can run. You can then do the following:

- *Allow App Store Apps:* From this menu, choose a specific age limit for the types of apps the App Store shows.

- *Allowed Apps:* Click the gray expansion triangle to the left of each Allowed Apps category to display a list of apps on your Mac for the selected category. Select or deselect the programs you want to allow or disallow the user from accessing.

   Selecting or deselecting the check box for an entire application category, such as App Store or Utilities, gives you a single-click way to allow user access to all or none of the programs in that selected category. A dash in the check box means that some of the apps within that category are selected, and the user is allowed to use the checked apps.

- *Prevent the Dock from Being Modified:* Choose whether this user may modify the Dock; this option isn't available if Use Simple Finder (earlier in this list) is enabled.

5. **Click the Web tab to open the Web preferences pane, as shown in Figure 2-15.**

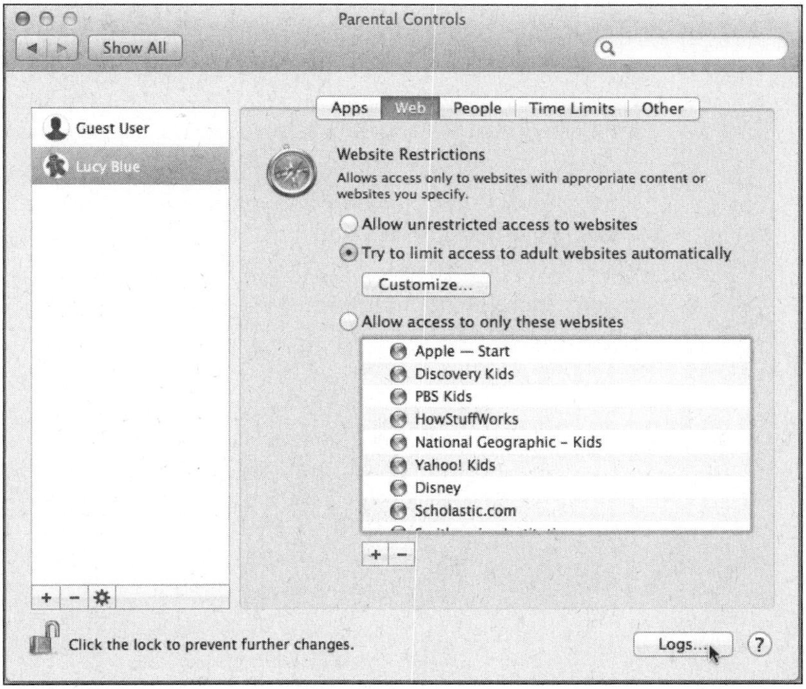

Figure 2-15:
Web preferences let you restrict what users can see.

**Book III
Chapter 2**

Protecting Your Mac against Local and Remote Threats

Select one of the following radio buttons under the Website Restrictions section:

- *Allow Unrestricted Access to Websites:* Selecting this option allows users to access any website they want to visit.

- *Try to Limit Access to Adult Websites Automatically:* If you select this option, you can click the Customize button so that you can type the websites the account can always access and the websites that the account can never access.

    In both cases, you must type the address you chose to allow or block. Although this option can attempt to block most adult websites automatically, you need to enter additional addresses for particular websites that slip past the adult website filter.

- *Allow Access to Only These Websites:* If you select this option, you can then specify which websites the user can access by clicking the "+" (plus-sign) button and adding websites you permit the user to visit. You can also remove websites you no longer want guest users to access by clicking the website in the list of allowed websites, and then clicking the "−" (minus sign) to remove the website.

TIP

Click the Logs button if you want to see a list of the apps or websites this user has used or visited in the past or contacts with whom Messages have been exchanged.

6. **Click the People tab.**

The People preferences pane appears, as shown in Figure 2-16, and you can do the following:

- *Game Center:* Select or deselect the Game Center options to allow multiplayer games and/or adding friends.

- *Limit Mail, Limit Messages:* Select one or both and click the Add (+) button under the Allowed Contacts box to open the dialog that allows you to add specific names or groups, as shown in Figure 2-17.

WARNING!

These controls don't limit who the user can use FaceTime with, so if you're concerned about that, don't give access to the FaceTime app (refer to Step 4).

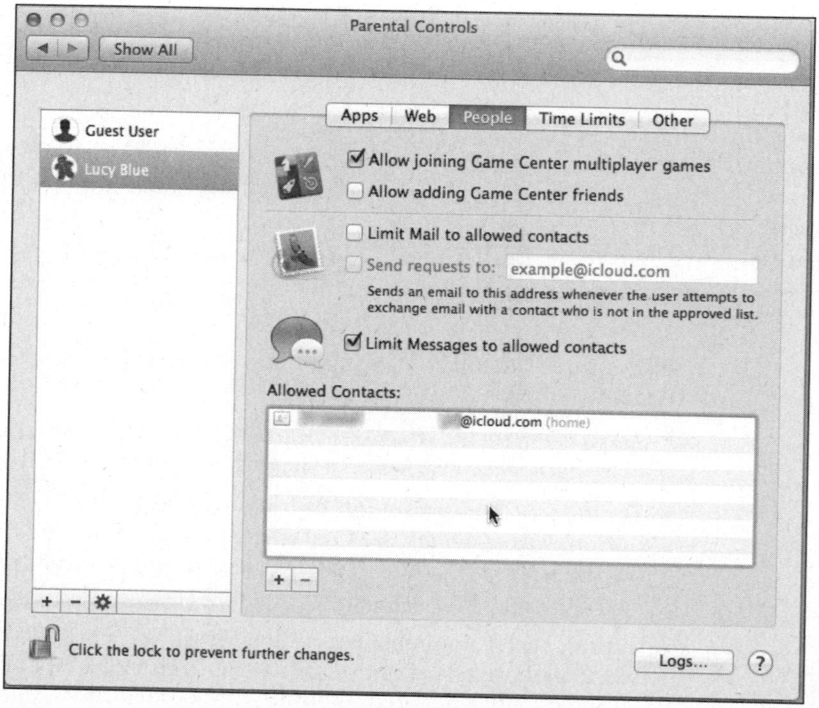

Figure 2-16:
People preferences lets you restrict who the user can contact.

[Screenshot of Parental Controls window]

Parental Controls — Show All

Guest User
Lucy Blue

Apps | Web | People | Time Limits | Other

☑ Allow joining Game Center multiplayer games
☐ Allow adding Game Center friends

☐ Limit Mail to allowed contacts
☐ Send requests to: example@icloud.com
Sends an email to this address whenever the user attempts to exchange email with a contact who is not in the approved list.

☑ Limit Messages to allowed contacts

Allowed Contacts:
@icloud.com (home)

+ − ⚙

Click the lock to prevent further changes.

Logs... ?

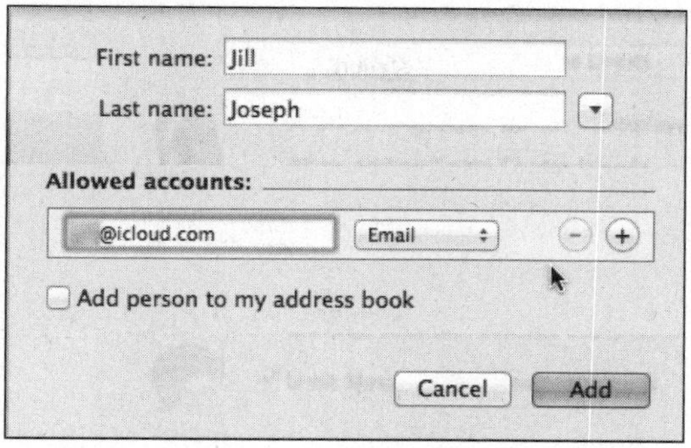

First name: Jill

Last name: Joseph

Allowed accounts:

@icloud.com   Email ⬍   ⊖ ⊕

☐ Add person to my address book

Cancel   Add

Figure 2-17:
Specify contacts you want to let the user access.

a. *Enter the first and last name of a person that you approve of into the First Name and Last Name text boxes.*

b. *Access your Contacts by clicking the triangle to the right of the Last Name field. Select multiple addresses by holding down the ⌘ key.*

c. *Enter an e-mail or IM address of the approved person in the Allowed Accounts text box.*

d. *Choose the account type (Email, AIM, or Jabber, for example) from the Allowed Accounts pop-up menu.*

e. *Select the Add Person to My Address Book check box, and the IM address and name of the approved person will be added to the Contacts app.*

f. *(Optional) Click the "+" button to specify another person and the associated e-mail or instant messaging chat account address.*

g. *Click Add.*

The dialog closes, and the names appear in the Allowed Contacts list.

If you want to remove someone from the Allowed Contacts list, click the name and press the Delete key or click the "–" button.

7. **Click the Time Limits tab to open the Time Limits preferences pane, as shown in Figure 2-18, and choose from the following:**

   • *Limit Weekday Use To:* Select this Weekday Time Limits option and drag the slider to specify how much time the account can use your Mac.

   • *Limit Weekend Use To:* Select this Weekend Time Limits option and drag the slider to specify how much time the account can use your Mac.

   • *School Nights and Weekend:* Select one or both check boxes under the Bedtime category and set the start and end times of when you don't want the account to use your Mac, such as between 9 p.m. and 9 a.m.

   The School Nights option defines Sunday–Thursday. The Weekend option defines Friday and Saturday; however, this option pays no mind to exceptions such as holidays, school vacations, snow days, and other potential non–school night calendar dates.

Book III
Chapter 2

Protecting Your Mac against Local and Remote Threats

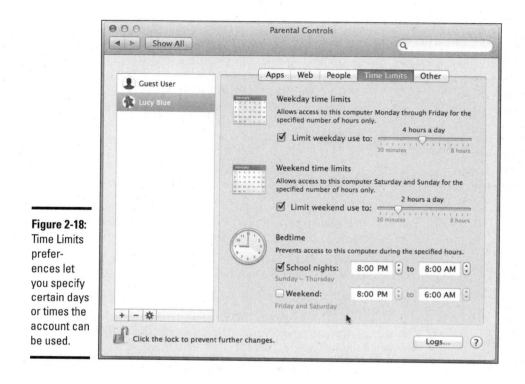

Figure 2-18:
Time Limits preferences let you specify certain days or times the account can be used.

8. **Click the Other tab to open the Other preferences pane.**

   Select the check boxes next to the limits you want to set. The effect each has is explained in the Other preferences window, as shown in Figure 2-19:

   - *Disable Built-In Camera*
   - *Disable Dictation*
   - *Hide Profanity in Dictionary*
   - *Limit Printer Administration*
   - *Disable Changing the Password*
   - *Limit CD and DVD Burning*

9. **Click the lock button at the bottom left of the window, and then click the Close button to quit System Preferences.**

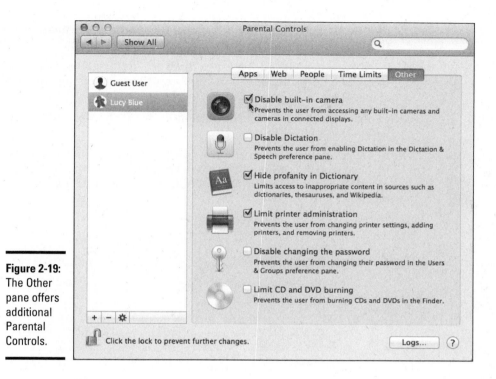

Book III
Chapter 2

Protecting Your Mac against Local and Remote Threats

Figure 2-19:
The Other pane offers additional Parental Controls.

Monitoring a Managed with Parental Controls account

After you create a Managed with Parental Controls account, you can view what that user has been doing on your Mac by reviewing *log files,* which keep track of all the websites the user visited and tried to visit (blocked by the Mac Parental Controls), the programs the user ran, and the people the user contacted through iMessages or e-mail. To view these log files, follow these steps:

1. Choose ▸System Preferences and then click the Parental Controls icon to open the Parental Controls preferences pane.

    If the lock icon in the lower-left corner of the preferences window is locked, click to unlock it, and then type your password in the dialog that appears. Press Return to unlock your Mac's user account details.

2. Click the account icon in the list on the left whose log files you want to examine.

3. Click the Logs button at the bottom right of the window.

4. Choose a period from the Show Activity For pop-up menu, such as viewing everything the user did in the past week or month.

5. **Choose Website/Application/Contact (depending on which log you want to view) or Date from the Group By pop-up menu.**

6. **Click Websites Visited, Websites Blocked, Applications, or Messages in the Log Collections list box to review the selected log, as shown in Figure 2-20.**

   Click the disclosure triangle to see more detail about the web pages within that website.

   Not all blocked websites are necessarily pornographic. Sometimes a blocked website could just be a blocked pop-up ad from an acceptable site, or an educational or reference site with keywords that trigger the block.

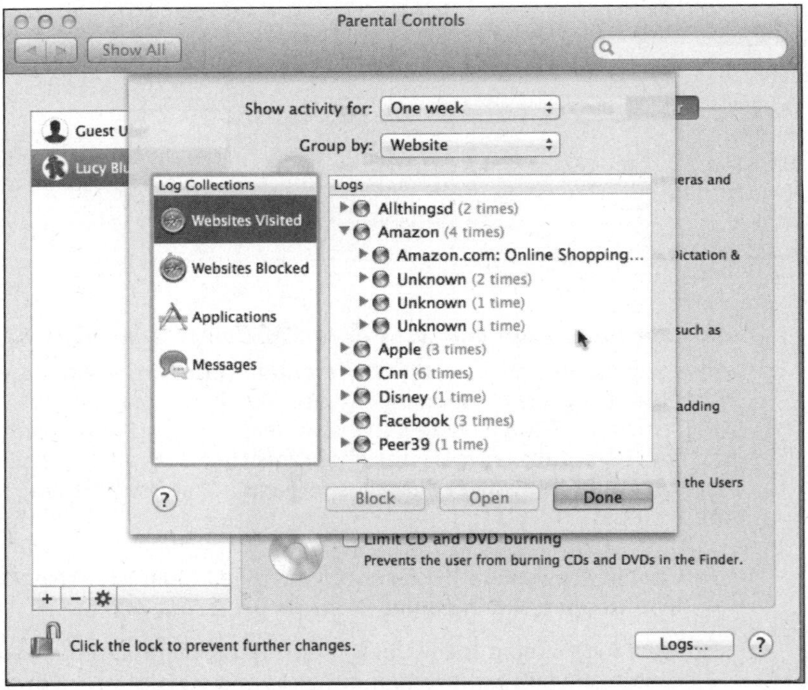

Figure 2-20:
See who's
been doing
what.

7. **Click the Close button to quit System Preferences.**

Activating a Sharing Only account

Your Mac comes with a pre-established Guest User account. This account lets friends or clients use your Mac temporarily, but nothing they do is saved on your Mac although it could be saved to a Shared file or to a remote storage site like Dropbox or an external hard or flash drive. By giving someone a Guest User desktop to use, your Desktop and everything you've so neatly organized doesn't get poked around or messed up.

Your Mac has only one Guest account because multiple users will access the same Guest account. To enable the Guest account, follow these steps:

1. **Choose ❤:System Preferences, and then click the Users & Groups icon.**

If the lock icon in the lower-left corner of the preferences window is locked, click to unlock it and then type your password in the dialog that appears. Press Return to unlock your Mac's user account details.

2. **Click the Guest User icon that appears in the list box on the left to open the Guest User dialog, as shown in Figure 2-21.**

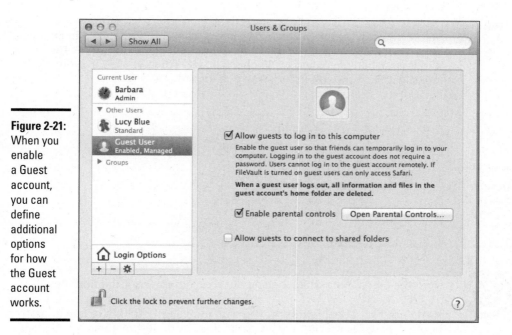

Figure 2-21: When you enable a Guest account, you can define additional options for how the Guest account works.

Book III
Chapter 2

Protecting Your Mac against Local and Remote Threats

3. **Select the Allow Guests to Log In to This Computer check box, which allows anyone to use your Mac's Guest account without a password.**

4. **(Optional) Click the Open Parental Controls button if you want to specify which programs guests can use (or not use) and whether they can access the Internet.**

Read about adjusting these settings in the earlier section, "Defining parental controls."

5. **(Optional) Select or deselect the Allow Guests to Connect to Shared Folders check box.**

If this option is selected, a Guest account can read files created by other accounts and stored in a special shared folder or the other users' Public folder.

6. **Click the Close button of the Accounts preferences window.**

Switching between accounts

The Mac offers several ways to switch between accounts. The most straight-forward way is to log out of one account and then log in to a different account. A faster and more convenient way is to use Fast User Switching, which essentially lets you switch accounts without having to log out of one account first.

To log out of an account, simply choose ⌘⇨Log Out (or press ⌘+Shift+Q). After you log out, the login window appears, listing the names and user icons of all accounts. At this time, you can click a different account name to log in to that account.

Before you can log out, a confirmation dialog appears as shown in Figure 2-22. Your open files and apps will be closed before logging out. Select the Reopen Windows When Logging Back In check box so when you log in, your Mac looks just like how you left it when you logged out.

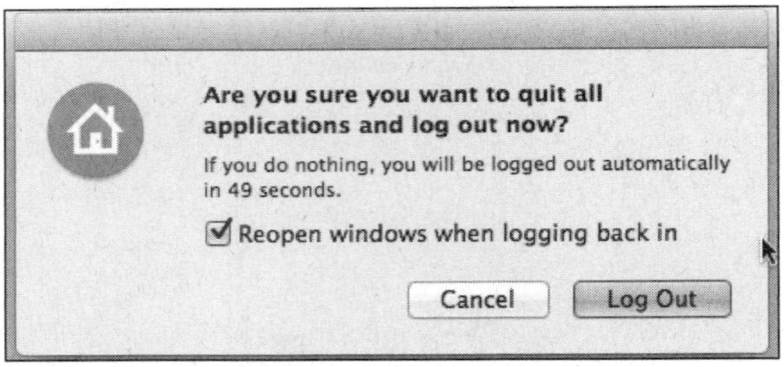

Figure 2-22:
Confirm that
you want to
log out.

> **Are you sure you want to quit all applications and log out now?**
>
> If you do nothing, you will be logged out automatically in 49 seconds.
>
> ☑ Reopen windows when logging back in
>
> Cancel   Log Out

Hold the Option key while logging out to avoid the confirmation dialog.

If you use Fast User Switching, you won't have to bother with any of that because Fast User Switching gives the illusion of putting the currently active account in "suspended animation" mode while your Mac opens another account.

Enabling Fast User Switching

Before you can use Fast User Switching, you have to turn on this feature. Log in as Administrator and then follow these steps:

1. **Choose ⌘⇨System Preferences, and then click the Users & Groups icon.**

   If the lock icon in the lower-left corner of the preferences window is locked, click to unlock it and then type your password in the dialog that appears. Press Return to unlock your Mac's user account details.

2. **Click the Login Options icon at the bottom of the list of users on the left side of the pane to display the Login Options pane, as shown in Figure 2-23.**

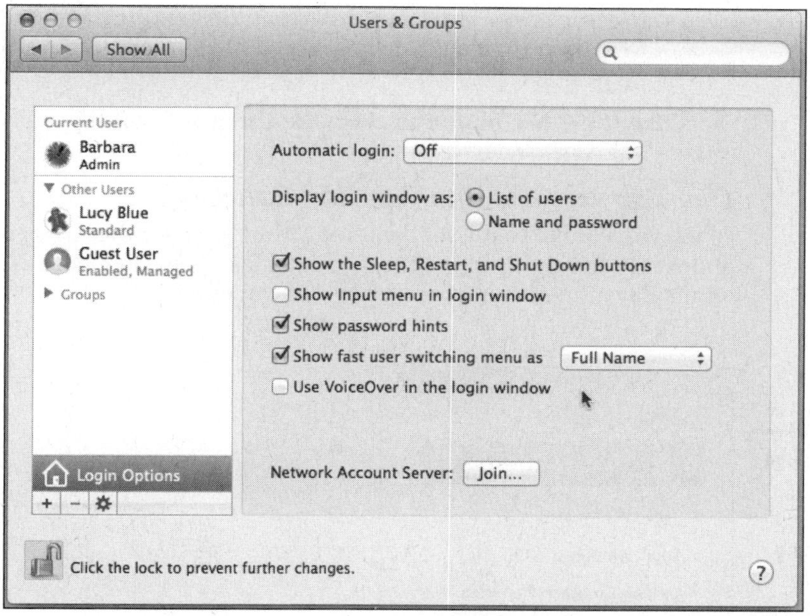

Figure 2-23:
Login
Options is
where you
can turn on
Fast User
Switching.

3. **Select the Show Fast User Switching Menu As check box, open the pop-up menu, and choose how you want to display the Fast User Switching Menu: Full Name, Short Name, or Icon.**

   These options display what appears on the menulet. Full Name displays full account names, Short Name displays abbreviated account names, and Icon displays a generic icon that takes up the least amount of space in the menu bar.

4. **Select other Login Options:**

   - *Automatic Login:* Leave this option Off or choose one user who will be automatically logged in when you restart your Mac, which is handy if you're the only user and your Mac is always in a safe place.

   - *Display Login Window As:* Choose List of Users (from which you click a user and then type in the password) or Name and Password (which requires you to enter both your user name and password).

   - *Show the Sleep, Restart, and Shut Down Buttons:* Select this if you want to see these buttons on the login screen.

   - *Show Input Menu in Login Window:* Allows users to choose the language they want to use when logging in.

   - *Show Password Hints:* Users can click the question mark on the login screen to see a password hint, which you set up when you created the user account name and password.

- *Use VoiceOver in the Login Window:* Select this if you want VoiceOver to work during login. Learn more about VoiceOver in Book I, Chapter 6.

5. **Click the Close button to close the Users & Groups preferences pane.**

Changing accounts with Fast User Switching

When you enable Fast User Switching, the Fast User Switching menulet appears in the right side of the menu bar, as shown in Figure 2-24. The menulet displays the names of accounts you can choose.

Figure 2-24:
The Fast
User
Switching
menulet.

To switch to a different account at any time, follow these steps:

1. **Click the Fast User Switching menulet on the right side of the menu bar and then click the account name you want to use.**

2. **Type the account password in the dialog that appears and press Return.**

   Your Mac switches you to your chosen account.

Deleting an account

After you create one or more accounts, you may want to delete an old or unused account. When you delete an account, your Mac gives you the option of retaining the account's Home folder, which may contain important files. To delete an account, follow these steps:

1. **Make sure that the account you want to delete is logged out and also that you're logged in to your Administrator account.**

2. **Choose ⇨System Preferences, and then click the Users & Groups icon or click the Fast User Switching menulet and choose Users & Groups Preferences (refer to Figure 2-24).**

   If the lock icon in the lower-left corner of the preferences window is locked, click to unlock it, and then type your password in the dialog that appears. Press Return to unlock your Mac's user account details.

3. **Select the account you want to delete in the accounts list and then click the Delete Account (–) button in the lower-left corner of the list.**

   A confirmation dialog appears, asking whether you really want to delete this account and presenting options to save the Home folder of the account, as shown in Figure 2-25. Select one of the following radio buttons:

   - *Save the Home Folder in a Disk Image:* Saves the home folder and its contents in a compressed disk image (DMG) file. This keeps the files compressed, so they take up less space on the hard drive than if you choose the next option (which does not compress the files contained in the Home folder). Choosing this option is like stuffing things in an attic to get them out of sight but still keeping them around in case you need them later.

   - *Don't Change the Home Folder:* Keeps the Home folder and its contents exactly as they are before you delete the account, so you can browse through the files contained within the folder at any time.

   - *Delete the Home Folder:* Wipes out any files the user may have created in the account. Click the check box next to Erase Home Folder Securely to encrypt the files when they're erased, making them irretrievable.

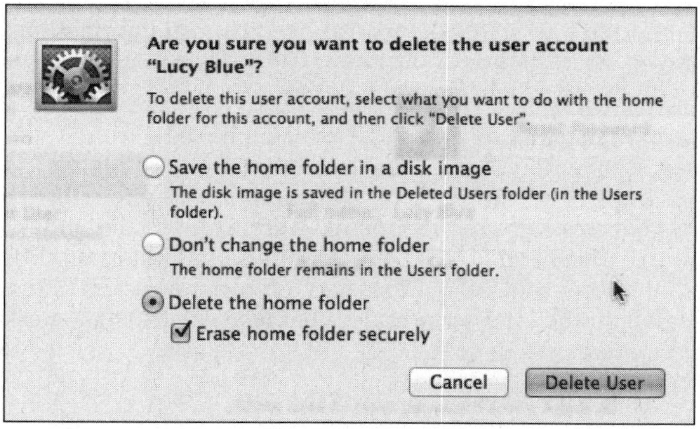

Figure 2-25:
Do you
really want
to delete?

4. **Click Delete User.**

   Your Mac deletes the specified account.

A Few Final Security Tips

We want to give you a few extra security tips to keep your Mac and your documents safe:

✦ **Really take out the trash.** From the Desktop, choose Finder⇨Secure Empty Trash when eliminating old files, especially if you have sensitive documents. This feature is more incinerator than simple trash can.

✦ **Avoid suspicious websites.** If you open a website and then a gazillion other pages open, quit Safari and re-open it. Then choose History⇨Clear History to wipe out any memory of the pages that you opened. Your Mac will screen downloads from Safari, Mail, and Messages and offers to move potential malicious files directly to the trash — usually a good idea.

✦ **Mix it up.** Resist the temptation to use the same password for everything. Use Password Assistant to generate passwords, and then track those passwords by using Keychain Access (choose Go⇨Utilities and click Keychain Access). See the section "Changing your password" at the beginning of this chapter to learn more about Password Assistant.

✦ **Put junk in its place.** If an e-mail arrives that *seems* to be from your bank or credit card provider, but the domain is @hotmail.com or @gmail.com or includes an overseas domain such as .es, don't respond! Mark it as Junk, and move on. Sorry to disappoint, but they really *didn't* find $14 million that belongs to you.

Banks don't send or ask for sensitive financial information via e-mail, maybe because they know that an ordinary e-mail message is about as secure as a postcard — as in, *not secure.*

Barbara recently received an e-mail supposedly from Apple asking to sign in to her iCloud account to confirm information. Even the domain was @apple.com, but something didn't look quite right. The misspellings in the web page that opened were a tip-off, and upon closer inspection, the logo and colors were very close but not exact. Hovering the pointer over the domain revealed the real, non-Apple URL and a quick search on the Internet revealed that fake Apple e-mail messages were in circulation!

Chapter 3: Networking Your Mac and Connecting Peripherals

In This Chapter

✔ Configuring wired and wireless networks

✔ Adding a printer to the network

✔ Using Bluetooth

Most households and small businesses have a few computers, a printer or two, a scanner, an Internet service, and maybe even an external drive where files are backed up from each computer. (Be sure to read about the importance of backing up in Book III, Chapter 1.) You can connect and disconnect *peripheral devices* (your printers, scanners, and such) to and from your computer when you want to use them — which would be a big hassle and time waster — or you can set up a network.

A *network* allows multiple computers to share files and devices, such as printers, modems, or back-up hard drives. Connecting two computers is the simplest of networks, but even a home setting today typically has a printer shared by two computers (more on that in the following chapter). And when multiple computers connect to a network, they can share files almost as quickly and easily as copying a file from one folder to another.

After you understand the concept of networking, networks aren't so difficult to set up. In this chapter, we show you how to set up a simple wired or wireless network — a few computers, a printer, and a modem. We then talk about another connectivity protocol — Bluetooth — which lets you connect peripherals (think keyboards and mice) wirelessly, as well as share files between devices. We delve into sharing in Book III, Chapter 4.

Creating a Wired Network

Setting up networks is easy with Macs because of *Bonjour*, Apple's implementation of zero-configuration networking, which is part of your Mac's operating system. With Bonjour, your Mac seeks and discovers the peripheral devices and servers on your local network and you don't have to do any complicated configuring. You may see the word Bonjour in some of the networking preferences windows or when you set up chats (see Book II, Chapter 3).

Sometimes you hear this referred to as *plug and play* — plug in your computer and peripherals and it just works!

The simplest wired network connects two computers, using either a USB or Thunderbolt cable or a cable that conforms to a networking cable standard called *Ethernet.* Your Mac has an Ethernet or Thunderbolt port or both. If you plug a cable into the ports of two Macs, you have a simple network, as shown in Figure 3-1.

Figure 3-1:
A simple network connects two Macs via Ethernet or Thunderbolt cable.

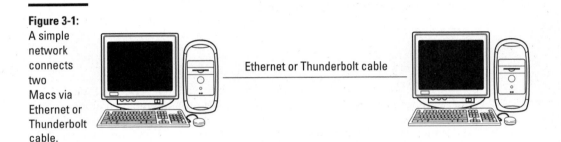

Ethernet or Thunderbolt cable

All recent Mac models have Thunderbolt ports. Thunderbolt offers two-way 10 Gbps connections, making it up to 2 times faster than USB 3. All desktop Mac models and the non–Retina MacBook Pro also have Ethernet ports. Other MacBook models without an Ethernet port rely on a wireless (Wi-Fi) connection, a USB-Ethernet adapter, or a Thunderbolt-Ethernet adapter.

Ethernet cables are often identified by the speeds at which they can send data. The earliest Ethernet cables were Category 3 (Cat 3) cables and could transfer data at 10 megabits per second (Mbps). The next generation of Ethernet cables was Category 5 and 5e (Cat 5/5e) cables, which could transfer data at 100 Mbps. Category 6 (Cat 6) cables transfer data at 1,000 Mbps or one gigabit per second (Gbit/s). With networking, speed is everything and Category 6a (Cat 6a) and Category 7 (Cat 7) transfer data at 10 Gbit/s. Category 7a supports transfer speeds of 100 Gbit/s.

Because it's physically impossible to connect more than two devices together with a single cable, wired networks use a *hub.* Each device connects to the hub, which indirectly connects each device to every other device also connected to the hub, as shown in Figure 3-2.

An improved variation of a hub is a *switch.* Physically, a hub and a switch both connect multiple devices in a single point (as shown in Figure 3-2).

With a hub, a network acts like one massive hallway that every computer shares. If many computers transfer data at the same time, the shared network can get crowded with data flowing everywhere, slowing the transfer of data throughout the network.

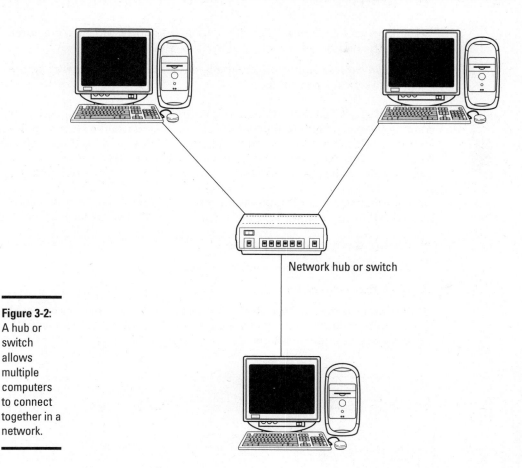

Network hub or switch

Figure 3-2:
A hub or
switch
allows
multiple
computers
to connect
together in a
network.

With a switch, the switch directs data between two devices. As a result, a switch can ensure that data transfers quickly, regardless of how much data the other devices on the network are transferring at the time.

A variation of a switch is a *router,* which often adds a firewall by using Network Address Translation (NAT) and Dynamic Host Configuration Protocol (DHCP). NAT uses one set of Internet Protocol (IP) addresses, which identify the computers and peripherals on the network for local network traffic, and another set for external traffic. This eliminates the risk of your device having the same address as another device. DHCP lets the router assign a different IP address to the same device each time it connects to the network.

Because routers cost nearly the same as ordinary hubs and switches, most wired networks rely on routers. So if you want to create a wired network of computers, you need

✦ Two or more devices — computers, printers, scanners, modems, external drives

+ A network switch or router with a number of ports equal to or greater than the number of devices you want to connect

+ Enough cables (and of sufficient length) to connect each device to the network switch or router

The speed of a wired network depends entirely on the slowest speed of the components used in your network. So, if you plan to use the fastest cables in your network, make sure your network switch is designed for those cables. If not, you'll have the fastest Ethernet cables connected to a slow network switch, which will run only as fast as the slowest part of your network.

After you connect your computers and peripherals to the hub or switch and turn everything on, follow these steps to make sure that your Mac is connected:

1. **Choose ⌘⇨System Preferences.**

The System Preferences window opens.

2. **Click the Network icon.**

3. **Beside Ethernet or Thunderbolt, or whichever type of network cable or connection you use, you should see a green light and the word** `Connected` **underneath, as shown in Figure 3-3.**

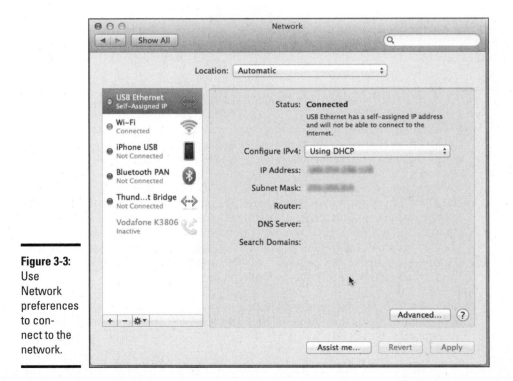

Figure 3-3:
Use Network preferences to connect to the network.

4. **To confirm that your printer is connected, click Show All or the Back button to return to the main System Preferences window.**

5. **Click the Printers & Scanners icon.**

   The Printers & Scanners preferences window opens, as shown in Figure 3-4. Printers and scanners connected to your network are listed on the left.

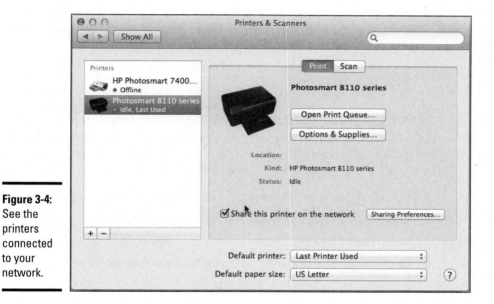

Figure 3-4:
See the printers connected to your network.

Book III
Chapter 3

Networking Your
Mac and Connecting
Peripherals

6. **Repeat these steps on other Macs and devices on your network.**

We explain how to set up file sharing in Book III, Chapter 4. After you set up sharing, you see other computers on your network in the Finder under the Shared heading.

When you set up a wired network, the router may have wireless capabilities. If so, you can use an Ethernet cable to connect to the router a computer or printer that stays in one place, and then connect to the wireless network connection on your MacBook to work from your lawn chair in the garden or connect from a desktop Mac in another room in the house. To do so, turn on Wi-Fi and select the network, as we explain in the next section.

Creating a Wireless Network

Essentially, a wireless network is no different from a wired network, except (of course) that there are no wires. Instead, radio waves take their place. Wireless networks can be a bit slower than wired networks, but unless you transfer big files, going wireless is probably a tidier and more cost-effective alternative because there are no cables to buy or tack along the baseboard.

We'd be remiss if we didn't mention two downsides to wireless networks:

✦ potential interference from cordless phones and microwave ovens

✦ less security because of the risk of others intercepting the signal

We show you how to create two types of wireless networks:

✦ A peer-to-peer (computer-to-computer) network that lets two or more Macs see each other without having to connect anything other than the computers themselves

✦ A wireless network that uses a wireless router and eventually a cable modem or DSL modem

Setting up a computer-to-computer network

Your Mac has a built-in AirPort Card, which lets it see other Macs and Wi-Fi–enabled devices just by turning on Wi-Fi and setting up a peer-to-peer (computer-to-computer) network. Do the following:

1. **Choose ⬆System Preferences and then click the Network icon.**

2. **Click Wi-Fi in the list on the left (refer to Figure 3-3).**

3. **Click Turn Wi-Fi On.**

4. **Click the pop-up menu by Network Name and choose Create Network.**

A dialog opens, as shown in Figure 3-5.

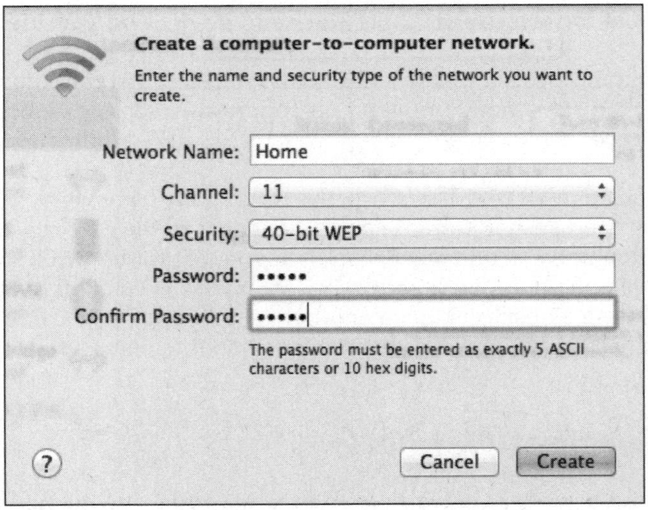

Create a computer-to-computer network.
Enter the name and security type of the network you want to create.

Network Name: Home
Channel: 11
Security: 40–bit WEP
Password: •••••
Confirm Password: •••••

The password must be entered as exactly 5 ASCII characters or 10 hex digits.

[Cancel] [Create]

Figure 3-5:
Create a computer-to-computer wireless network.

5. **Give your network a name, such as Home or Office.**

6. **Open the Security pop-up menu and assign a password to your network.**

We highly recommend you create a password to access your wireless network because wireless networks are easily viewed by other computers in the vicinity. You can choose a 40-bit WEP, which requires a 5-character password, or a 128-bit WEP, which requires a 13-character password. The longer the password, the harder it is for someone to guess what your password is.

Read more about WEP and WPA in the upcoming sidebar, "The hazards of wireless networking."

7. **Click Create.**

Your network now appears next to Network Name.

You have two ways to connect to your wireless network: from Network System Preferences or from the Wi-Fi menu on the menulet.

To connect to your wireless network from Network System Preferences, follow these steps:

1. **Click Wi-Fi in the list on the left.**

2. **Click the Turn Wi-Fi On button in the upper right of the window.**

3. **Open the pop-up menu by Network Name and choose the name of your network.**

4. **Enter the password, if you assigned one.**

5. **Click Join.**

The Wi-Fi icon on the menulet now shows a computer rather than the Wi-Fi bars.

To connect to your wireless network from the Wi-Fi menu on the menulet, follow these steps:

1. **Open the Wi-Fi pull-down menu on the menulet and drag to choose Turn Wi-Fi On.**

2. **Open the Wi-Fi pull-down menu again and choose your network.**

3. **Enter the password, if you assigned one.**

4. **Click Join.**

The Wi-Fi icon on the menulet changes to a computer.

Wireless printers also work on a computer-to-computer network. Follow the printer manufacturer's instructions for using a wireless printer on your network.

**Book III
Chapter 3**

**Networking Your
Mac and Connecting
Peripherals**

Setting up a wireless network with a router

When you use a computer-to-computer network, your Mac can't connect to the Internet with Wi-Fi. Because your Mac has wireless capabilities, though, you probably want to connect to both the Internet and your network wirelessly.

As with a wired network, you need a router for a wireless network. Instead of managing physical cables, though, a wireless router manages signals based on the wireless network protocols. The earliest wireless networks followed a technical specification called 802.11b or 802.11a. Newer wireless equipment followed a faster wireless standard called 802.11g, and the latest standard (at the time of this writing) is 802.11n. The faster, upcoming standard is 802.11ac.

When setting up a wireless network, make sure that your router uses the same wireless standard as the built-in wireless radio or wireless adapter plugged into each of your devices. All new and recent Macs connect to Wi-Fi routers that use one to five types of the wireless 802.11 network standards.

You can buy any brand of wireless router to create a network, including Apple's Airport Extreme Base Station or TimeCapsule. Any router you choose will come with specific software and instructions for setting up your network. The basic steps are to

1. Name your network and base station so devices on the network can then find and connect to your Wi-Fi network.

2. Set up a password.

   WPA2 provides the most security (see the nearby sidebar, "The hazards of wireless networking," for more information).

3. Define how you connect to the Internet.

   You may need information from your Internet Service Provider (ISP) for this step (see Book I, Chapter 3).

4. Add printers and/or external hard drives.

5. Configure your Macs for sharing, as we explain in Book III, Chapter 4.

Because of physical obstacles, wireless networks don't always reach certain parts of a room or building, resulting in "dead spots" where you can't connect wirelessly. Walls or furniture can disrupt the wireless signals. You can add a device called an *access point,* which picks up the signal and rebroadcasts it beyond the reach of the Wi-Fi router, extending your wireless network range. The newest (but not widely distributed) Wi-Fi protocol — 802.11ac — uses a technology that is better at penetrating walls, which will make this problem less troublesome in the future.

The difference between an access point and a router is that the router is at the center of the network, allowing the computers to share printers (see the next chapter), Internet connections, and external hard drives. The *access point* is what allows the devices with wireless capabilities to connect to the network from a greater distance.

The hazards of wireless networking

To access a wired network, someone must physically connect a computer to the network with a cable. However, connecting to a wireless network can be done from another room, outside a building, or even across the street. As a result, wireless networks can be much less secure because a wireless network essentially shoves dozens of virtual cables out the window, so anyone can walk by and connect to the network.

The practice of connecting to unsecured wireless networks with malicious intentions is *war driving* (also called *war flying, war walking,* or *war boating,* depending on how you move around). The basic idea behind war driving is to drive around a city and keep track of which areas offer an unsecured wireless network. After getting connected to an unsecured wireless network, an intruder can wipe out files, capture personal information, or interfere with the network's operation.

When you create a wireless network, you can make your network more secure by taking advantage of a variety of security measures and options. The simplest security measure is to use a password that locks out people who don't know the password. Three types of passwords are used for wireless networks:

- ✓ **Wired Equivalent Privacy (WEP)** is an older protocol and offers minimal (almost useless) protection. Because it's an older

protocol, it may not work on all your devices. Passwords use either 5 or 13 characters.

- ✓ **Wi-Fi Protected Access (WPA)** is better than WEP because it changes the encryption key for each data transmission.

- ✓ **Wi-Fi Protected Access 2 (WPA2)** is the best choice because it uses the more secure Advanced Encryption Standard (AES) to encrypt the password when it's transmitted.

For further protection, you can also use encryption. *Encryption* scrambles the data sent to and from the wireless network. Without encryption, anyone can intercept information sent through a wireless network (including passwords). Still another security measure involves configuring your wireless network to let only specific computers connect to the network. By doing this, an intruder can't gain access to the wireless network because his or her computer is not approved to access the network.

Ultimately, wireless networking requires more security measures simply because it offers potential intruders the ability to access the network without physically being in the same room, house, or building. Wireless networks can be as safe as wired networks — as long as you turn on security options that can make your wireless network as secure as possible.

Connecting and Choosing a Printer

Out of the box, Mac OS X comes with a number of special files called *printer drivers,* which tell your Mac how to communicate with most popular models of printer brands. When you buy a new printer, it often comes with a CD that contains a printer driver or a website address where you can download the appropriate driver. You can install the printer driver to unlock special features that the Mac's built-in drivers may not take advantage of.

Check the support section of the printer manufacturer's website to see whether a newer version of the printer installation software is available. After you run the installer, check the website every now and then to see whether a newer version (than the one you installed) is available. Some installers place a print utility on the Dock, and you may be able to set up the print utility to check automatically for updates.

Making your Mac work with your printer involves a two-step process:

1. You connect your printer to your Mac, either physically with a USB cable or network connection (such as a USB or Ethernet connection to a router) or wirelessly to a Wi-Fi–enabled printer that's connected to the same Wi-Fi network your Mac connects to.

2. You must install the proper printer driver on your Mac (if you don't want to use the supplied driver that comes with Mac OS X, or if your Mac doesn't have a driver for it). After you connect your printer to your Mac and install or select the correct printer driver, you can then print documents and control your printer's options.

You can download additional printer drivers (and drivers for other types of hardware, such as scanners and pressure-sensitive tablets) directly from the Apple website (www.apple.com/downloads/macosx/drivers) or from the printer manufacturer's website.

After you physically or wirelessly connect a printer to your Mac and install its printer driver, you may need to take one additional step and tell your Mac that this particular printer is connected. To get your Mac to recognize a connected printer, follow these steps:

1. **Choose ⌘➪System Preferences and then click the Printers & Scanners icon to open the Printers & Scanners preferences pane.**

2. **Click the Add (+) button.**

It's at the bottom of the printer list in the background window shown in Figure 3-6.

Note: Your Mac may list local printers (printers directly attached to your Mac) as well as printers linked to your Mac via a network. See Book III, Chapter 4 to learn more about sharing printers.

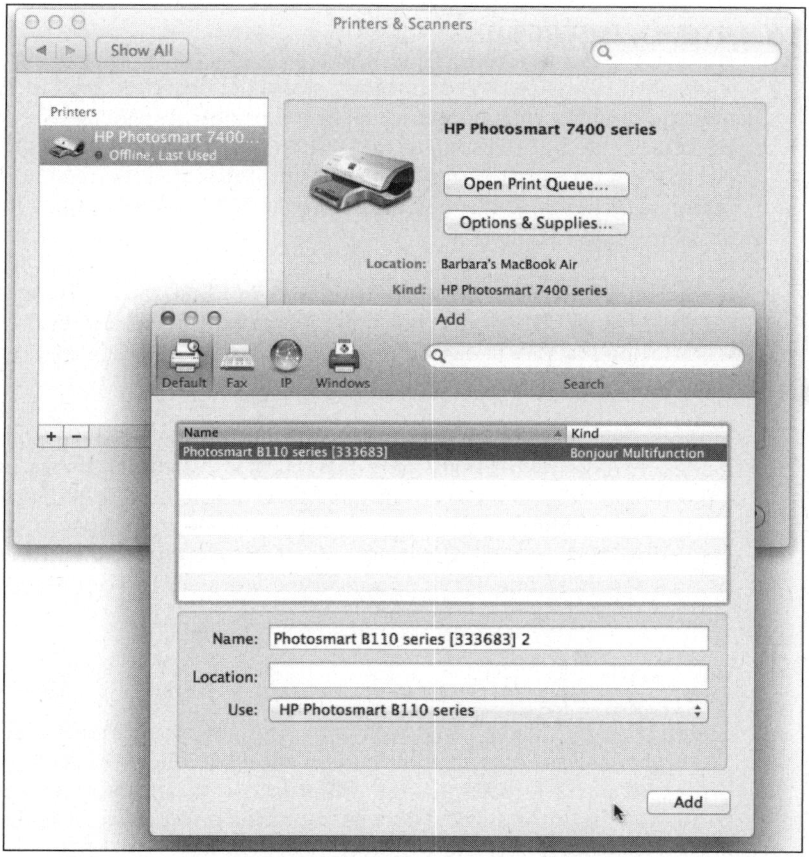

Figure 3-6:
Add or
delete print-
ers from the
Printers &
Scanners
preferences
pane.

3. **In the Add dialog that appears you see a list of printers that are available on the network.**

   Click the Default tab if you don't see the printers.

4. **In the list, click the printer you want your Mac's applications to always print to (unless you specify otherwise).**

5. **From the Use pop-up menu, choose the driver you want to use.**

6. **Click the Add button at the lower right of the Add window.**

7. **Click the Close button to quit System Preferences.**

Biting into Bluetooth

Bluetooth is a wireless technology standard designed primarily for connecting devices within a short distance of one another — up to 30 feet. Because of its short-range nature, Bluetooth is handy for connecting computers for short periods of time and for transferring small files, unlike faster wired or wireless (Wi-Fi) networks that connect computers on a more permanent basis.

If you think Bluetooth is a distant relative of Bluebeard or Babe the big blue ox, think again. Bluetooth was named after tenth-century Danish King Harald, who during his short reign improved communication and merged the Danish and Norwegian tribes.

Most mobile phones and tablets have built-in Bluetooth capabilities, which makes it easy to wirelessly sync calendars and address books between a hand-held device and a computer (as we explain in Book I, Chapter 3). Bluetooth-enabled input devices, such as wireless keyboards, mice, and game consoles, as well as wireless headsets for chatting with Messages or using Internet phone services like Skype, connect to your Mac by using your Mac's built-in Bluetooth feature.

Configuring Bluetooth on your Mac

The first step to using Bluetooth is to configure your Mac's Bluetooth preferences. For example, you may not want to allow other computers to browse your hard drive through Bluetooth without your express permission. Otherwise, someone could access your Mac and browse its hard drive from across the room, and you would never know it.

Although both your Mac and your iOS device (iPhone, iPad, iPod touch) have Bluetooth, you can't transfer files between them with Bluetooth — yet.

To configure how Bluetooth works on your Mac, follow these steps:

1. **Choose \u{f8ff}⇨System Preferences, and then click the Sharing icon.**

   Alternatively, right-click (two-finger click on a trackpad) the System Preferences icon on the Dock and choose Sharing from the menu that appears.

2. **Select the Bluetooth Sharing check box and make sure that Bluetooth Sharing is highlighted.**

   The Sharing window opens, as shown in Figure 3-7.

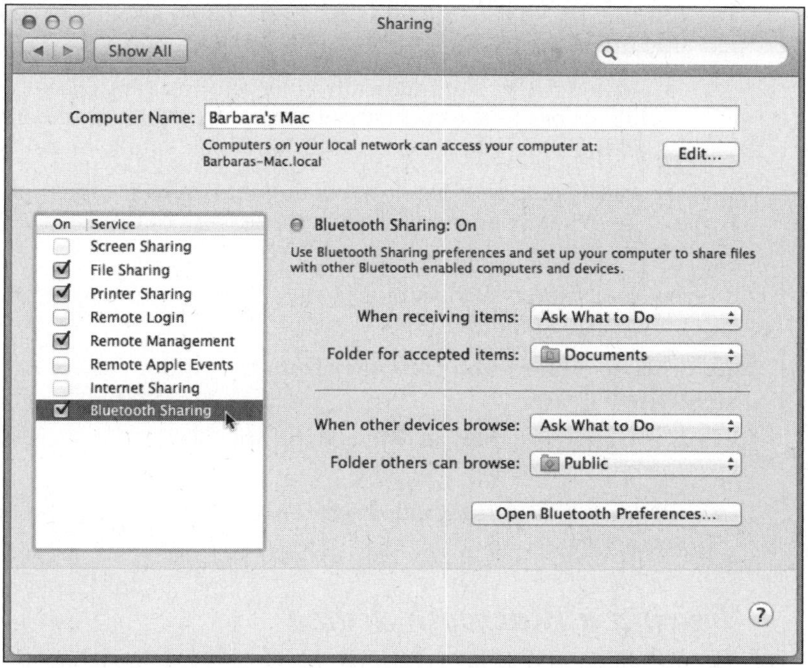

Figure 3-7:
The Sharing window lists preference choices for Bluetooth.

3. **Choose one of the following from the When Receiving Items pop-up menu:**

   - *Accept and Save:* Automatically saves any files sent to you through Bluetooth. (We don't recommend this option because someone can send you a malicious application, such as a virus or Trojan Horse, which can wipe out your files when opened.)

   - *Accept and Open:* Automatically saves and opens any files sent to you through Bluetooth. (We don't recommend this option because this — like the previous option — could automatically run a malicious application sent to your Mac through Bluetooth.)

   - *Ask What to Do:* Displays a dialog that gives you the option of accepting or rejecting a file sent to you through Bluetooth. This option is probably your best choice.

   - *Never Allow:* Always blocks anyone from sending you files through Bluetooth.

4. **Choose either Documents or Other from the Folder for Accepted Items pop-up menu.**

   If you choose Other, an Open dialog appears, letting you navigate to and click a folder where you want to store any files sent to you through Bluetooth.

5. **Choose one of the following from the When Other Devices Browse pop-up menu:**

   - *Always Allow:* Automatically gives another (any) Bluetooth device full access to the contents of your Mac. (Not recommended — this allows others to mess up your files accidentally or deliberately.)

   - *Ask What to Do:* Displays a dialog that gives you the option of accepting or rejecting another device's attempt to access your Mac through Bluetooth.

   - *Never Allow:* Always blocks anyone from browsing through your Mac by using Bluetooth.

6. **Choose either Public or Other from the Folder Others Can Browse pop-up menu.**

   If you choose Other, an Open dialog appears, letting you select a folder that you can share.

7. **Click the Open Bluetooth Preferences button and go on to the next section.**

Pairing a Bluetooth device

Pairing allows you to predetermine which Bluetooth-enabled devices can connect to your Mac. By pairing, you can keep strangers from trying to access your Mac without your knowledge. For additional security, paired devices require a password (also called a *passkey*) that further verifies that a specific device is allowed to connect to your Mac.

Pairing with your Mac

To pair a device with your Mac, follow these steps:

1. **Right-click (two-finger click on a trackpad) the System Preferences icon on the Dock and choose Bluetooth from the menu that appears.**

   Alternatively, choose ⌘↵System Preferences to open the System Preferences window and then click the Bluetooth icon.

   The Bluetooth preferences pane appears.

2. **If Bluetooth is off, click the Turn Bluetooth On button.**

   The Devices list shows Bluetooth-enabled devices in the vicinity and any devices you previously connected to.

3. **Click the Pair button next to the device you want to pair with your Mac.**

   A dialog shows a code that you should make sure matches the code on the device you're pairing. Click or tap Pair on the device to confirm, and the device appears as Connected in the Devices list, as shown in Figure 3-8.

Figure 3-8:
Bluetooth preferences let you pair a device with your Mac.

To unpair a device or remove a previously paired device from the list, make sure Bluetooth is turned on and then hover the pointer to the right of the device you want to remove. Click the X that appears (refer to Figure 3-8).

If you connect Bluetooth-enabled input devices to your Mac, such as keyboards, mice, or trackpads, you should consider a few advanced settings. Choose ⌘⇨ System Preferences and then click the Bluetooth icon or right-click (Control-click on a trackpad) the System Preferences icon on the Dock and choose Bluetooth. Click Advanced in the lower-right corner, and you see the window shown in Figure 3-9. Choose the settings that apply to the devices you use. For example, if you use a Bluetooth-enabled keyboard, you want to select the first and third options so that if your Mac doesn't see the keyboard, it opens Bluetooth Preferences automatically, and you can wake your Mac by touching the keyboard. For a wireless mouse, choose the second and third options.

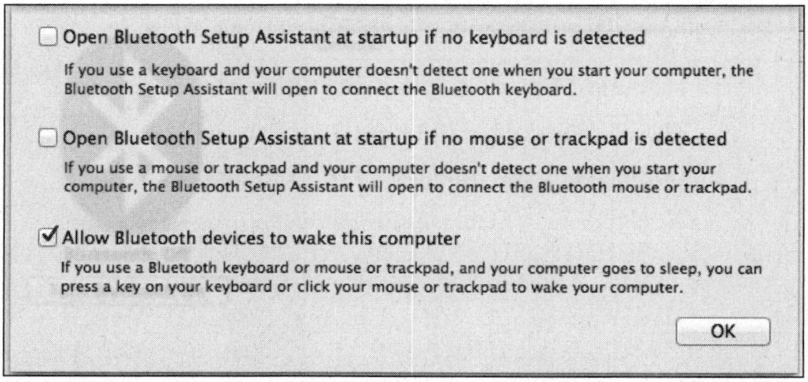

Figure 3-9:
Choose how your Mac interacts with input devices from the advanced Bluetooth settings.

☐ Open Bluetooth Setup Assistant at startup if no keyboard is detected

If you use a keyboard and your computer doesn't detect one when you start your computer, the Bluetooth Setup Assistant will open to connect the Bluetooth keyboard.

☐ Open Bluetooth Setup Assistant at startup if no mouse or trackpad is detected

If you use a mouse or trackpad and your computer doesn't detect one when you start your computer, the Bluetooth Setup Assistant will open to connect the Bluetooth mouse or trackpad.

☑ Allow Bluetooth devices to wake this computer

If you use a Bluetooth keyboard or mouse or trackpad, and your computer goes to sleep, you can press a key on your keyboard or click your mouse or trackpad to wake your computer.

OK

Troubleshooting connections with Bluetooth-enabled devices

Sometimes you pair a device with your Mac, but the connection doesn't seem to hold when your Mac goes to sleep. If you connect a keyboard or headset to your computer and experience problems with the Bluetooth connection, power down the device by following this procedure:

1. **Shut down your Mac.**

2. **Turn off the keyboard or headset and hold the power button for five seconds.**

3. **Turn on your Mac.**

4. **When your Mac says there is no keyboard connected, turn on the keyboard and hold the power button for 10 seconds.**

   Alternatively, turn on the headset and hold the power button for 10 seconds.

5. **Pair the device with your Mac as explained in the preceding section.**

Sharing through Bluetooth

Because Bluetooth lets you create a simple, short-range network between Macs, you can use a Bluetooth network to share files or even an Internet connection with others. Such a simple network isn't meant to share massive numbers of files or a long-term Internet connection, but it is handy for quick e-mail access or browsing a web page.

The speed of ordinary networks connected through Ethernet cables is 10, 100, or 1,000 megabits per second (Mbps), whereas the maximum speed of a Bluetooth network is only 1 Mbps.

When you want to copy a file from your Mac to another device, such as another Mac or a PC running Windows, you can set up a Bluetooth connection. Sharing files through Bluetooth allows you to transfer files to another device without the hassle of using connecting cables or mutually compatible removable storage devices like portable hard drives or USB flash drives. It's also a viable option when you're out of range of a Wi-Fi network.

To share files through Bluetooth, follow these steps:

1. **From the Finder, choose Go⊷Utilities.**

   The contents of the Utilities folder appear.

2. **Double-click the Bluetooth File Exchange icon.**

   A Select File to Send window appears.

Choose System Preferences⇨Bluetooth and then click Show Bluetooth in Menu Bar. Then to quickly transfer files, click the Bluetooth icon on the menu bar to choose Send File to Device and then proceed.

3. **Select a file.**

To select multiple files, hold down the ⌘ key and click each file you want to send.

4. **Click Send.**

A Send File window appears, listing all Bluetooth-enabled devices near your Mac, as shown in Figure 3-10.

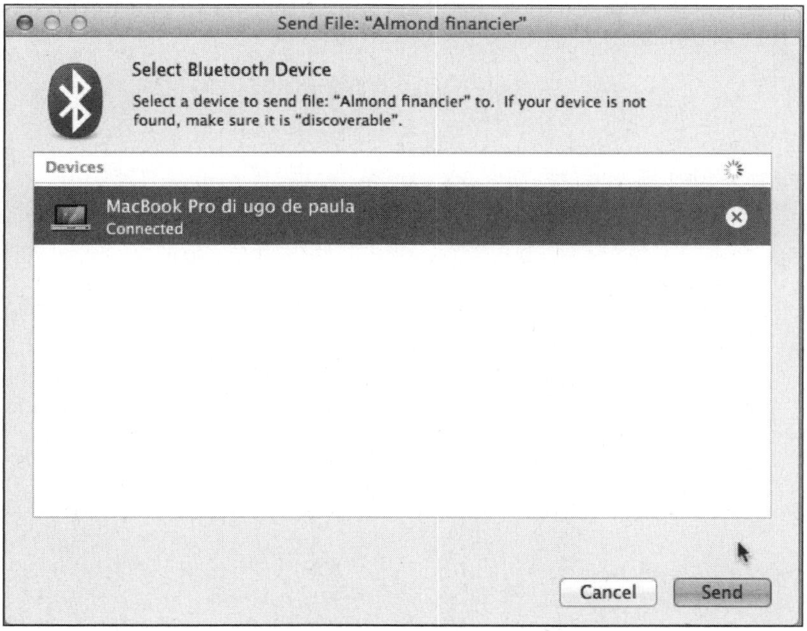

Figure 3-10:
The Send File window lets you choose a Bluetooth-enabled device to receive your file.

Send File: "Almond financier"

Select Bluetooth Device

Select a device to send file: "Almond financier" to. If your device is not found, make sure it is "discoverable".

Devices

MacBook Pro di ugo de paula
Connected

Cancel   Send

**Book III
Chapter 3**

Networking Your
Mac and Connecting
Peripherals

5. **Select a Bluetooth-enabled device and click Send.**

If you choose another Mac or mobile phone (but not an iPhone) to receive your files, a dialog may appear on the receiving device, asking the user to accept or decline the file transfer, as shown in Figure 3-11.

If the receiving device has been configured to Accept and Save or Accept and Open (transferred files), you won't see the dialog in Figure 3-11. The dialog in Figure 3-11 appears only if the user has selected Ask What to Do (the default option) when configuring Bluetooth settings.

Figure 3-11:
The receiving device can accept or decline a file transfer.

See Book III, Chapter 4 to learn about sharing an Internet connection with Bluetooth.

Chapter 4: Sharing Files and Resources on a Network

In This Chapter

✔ **Sharing files without having to e-mail them**

✔ **Sharing a printer on your network**

✔ **Sharing an Internet connection**

✔ **Letting other people see your screen**

The benefits of sharing over a network range from swapping files quickly and easily to sharing a single printer instead of having to buy a printer for every computer. Sharing files makes it easy for several people to work on the same project. Without a network, you could give someone a copy of a file, but then you may find yourself with three different versions of the same file, and deciphering which file contains the most accurate information would be difficult. (Read how to set up a network in the preceding chapter.)

Although networks allow others to share your files, other people connected to the network can't rummage through your Mac without your permission. Ideally, a network allows you to share files and equipment without risking the loss or corruption of crucial files on your own computer.

In this chapter, we talk about how to share files, printers, and Internet connections among computers on a network. We also show you how to access your Mac's screen from another computer with screen sharing.

Sharing Files with People Near and Far

If you want to share files with another Mac, you can set up a simple network, as we explain in the preceding chapter. Or, you can use *AirDrop,* which is a simple peer-to-peer (computer-to-computer) wireless network between Macs that sit near each other. An advantage of using AirDrop is sharing with many computers simultaneously without using a network hub.

Using AirDrop

AirDrop lets you set up a peer-to-peer network between two or more Macs that are near to each other — more or less in the same room — the caveat being that you must have a Mac that supports AirDrop and a Wi-Fi connection. It doesn't work with Macs connected with an Ethernet cable, nor does it transfer files with iOS devices, even thought they also have AirDrop. If your Mac is older than those listed here, AirDrop isn't for you:

✦ **iMac:** Early 2009

✦ **MacBook or MacBook Pro:** Late 2008

✦ **MacBook Air:** Mid-2010

✦ **Mac mini:** Mid-2010

✦ **Mac Pro:** Early 2009 with AirPort Extreme card or mid-2010

Don't despair, however — there are other solutions for peer-to-peer sharing even if you don't have AirDrop. Send files through Bluetooth or set up a peer-to-peer network (both explained in the preceding chapter), and then refer to the "Using a network" section in this chapter or use Messages, which we detail in Book II, Chapter 3.

You don't have to have any kind of network already set up; your Mac's internal Airport Extreme card sees other Macs. You do have to have OS X 10.7 Lion or later installed on any Macs you want to use AirDrop with. Here's how it works:

1. **From the Finder, choose Go⇨AirDrop.**

The AirDrop window opens, as shown in Figure 4-1. If you don't have Wi-Fi turned on, you're prompted to do so; when you do, you see the AirDrop window.

You see the contact photos of only those other Mac users who have AirDrop turned on; likewise, they only see you if you have AirDrop turned on. If your Mac goes to sleep, AirDrop disconnects.

2. **From the Finder, choose File⇨New Finder Window.**

3. **Scroll through the folders and files and then drag the file you want to transfer over the contact photo of the person you want to transfer the file to.**

4. **Click the Send button in the dialog, as shown in Figure 4-2.**

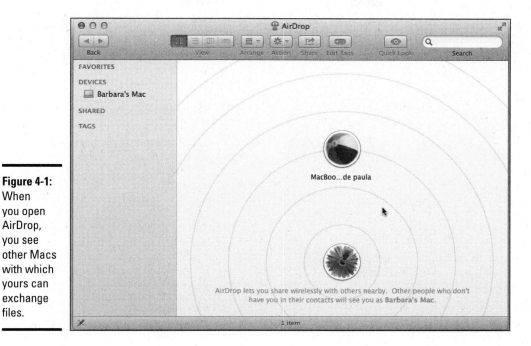

Figure 4-1:
When you open AirDrop, you see other Macs with which yours can exchange files.

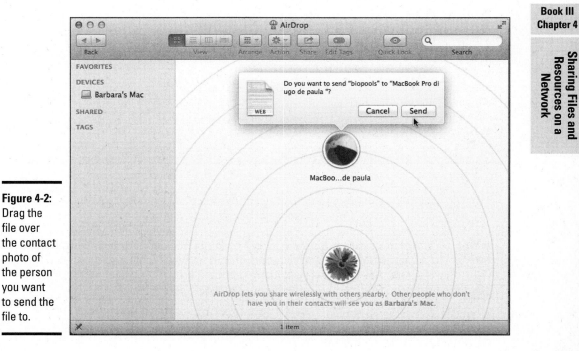

Figure 4-2:
Drag the file over the contact photo of the person you want to send the file to.

When you receive a file, a message appears asking what you want to do with the incoming file, as shown in Figure 4-3:

✦ **Save and Open:** This option opens the file and saves a copy of it to your Downloads folder.

✦ **Decline:** Choose this option if you don't want the file; the sender receives a notice that you rejected the file.

✦ **Save:** This option saves the file to your Downloads folder where you can open it later.

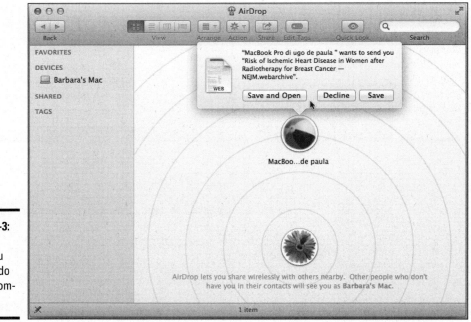

Figure 4-3: Choose what you want to do with incoming files.

If you begin a download and want to cancel, open your Downloads folder and click the X next to the icon of the incoming file.

In AirDrop, you don't have to worry about security. AirDrop automatically encrypts files and creates a *firewall* (an impenetrable barrier) between your Mac and the Mac you're sharing the file with. Other Macs on AirDrop can only see that you're on AirDrop; they can't peek into your Mac.

Using a network

Sharing files over the network is different from AirDrop in a few ways:

✦ On the network, your Mac can be in a different room, a different building, even in a different country.

✦ You set up the type of access you want others on the network to have.

✦ Your connection to the network runs in the background where you don't see it — even while your Mac is sleeping.

When your Mac is connected to a network, you have the option of sharing one or more folders with everyone else on the network. To share folders, you need to define different permission levels — *privileges* — that allow or restrict what users can do with a folder and the files inside it:

✦ **Read & Write:** Other users have the ability to see, retrieve, and add files to the folder.

✦ **Read Only:** Other users can see and open files, but they can't add files to the folder.

✦ **Write Only (Drop Box):** Other users can only place files in the folder; they can't see any files stored in that folder.

✦ **No Access:** Specified users are blocked from accessing files on your Mac.

You decide which folder(s) to share, who can access that folder, and what access level you want others to have in accessing your shared folder.

Each user on your Mac has his or her own Public folder that's created automatically when the user is added. By default, you can add and retrieve files to the Public folder (Read & Write privileges), and everyone can place files in the Drop Box folder (Write Only [Drop Box] privileges) stored within the Public folder. You can change the privileges for yourself or everyone, but you can delete neither user from the Public folder (although you can choose No Access for Everyone).

Turning on file sharing

The first step to sharing your files over a network is to turn on file sharing. Follow these steps:

1. **Choose ** **System Preferences, and then click the Sharing icon or right-click (two-finger click on a trackpad) the System Preferences icon on the Dock and choose Sharing from the menu that appears.**

2. **Select the File Sharing check box in the leftmost Service column.**

You see a list of Public folders on your Mac. If you have more than one user account set up on your Mac, you see the Public folders for each account (see Figure 4-4).

**Book III
Chapter 4**

**Sharing Files and
Resources on a
Network**

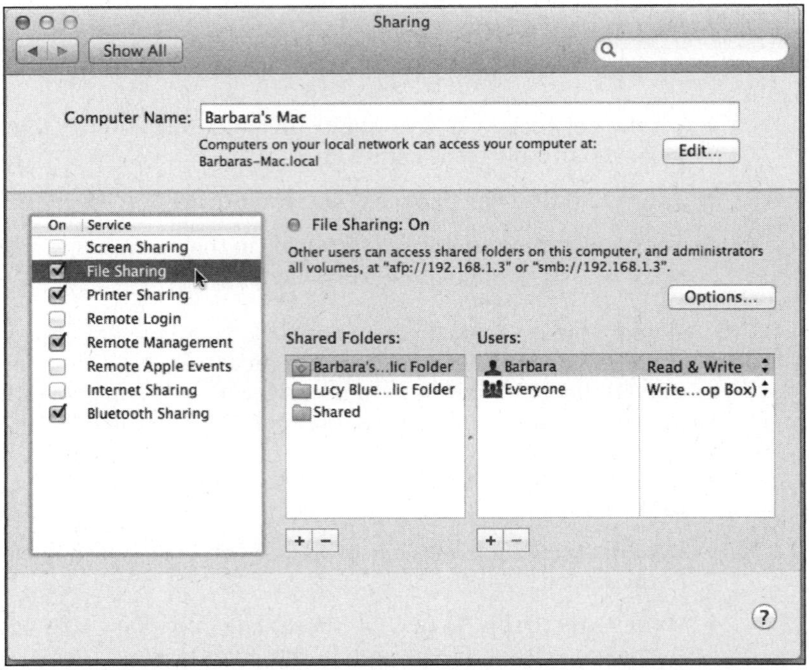

Figure 4-4:
See which
folders are
shared.

3. **Click the plus-sign button underneath the Shared Folders column.**

4. **From the dialog that appears, displaying all the drives and folders on your Mac, scroll through to find the folder you want to share.**

   The folder you want to share may be inside another folder.

5. **Click the folder you want to share, and then Click Add.**

   The folder appears in the list of Shared Folders.

6. **Repeat Steps 3–5 for each additional folder you want to share on the network.**

In the following section, you can see how to grant user privileges to your shared folders.

You don't have to share folders. If you don't turn on File Sharing, other people can't access your folders, but you can still use a network to access someone else's shared folders. You can also use devices, such as printers, that are on the network.

Defining user access to shared folders

After you define one or more folders to share, you can also define the type of access people can have to your shared folders, such as giving certain people the capability to open and modify files and stopping other people from accessing your shared files.

The three types of network users are

- ✦ **Yourself:** Gives you Read & Write access (or else you won't be able to modify any files in your shared folders)
- ✦ **Everyone:** Allows others to access your shared folders as guests without requiring a password
- ✦ **Names of specific network users:** Allows you to give individuals access to your shared folders with a name and a password

If you trust everyone on a network, you can give everyone Read & Write privileges to your shared folders. However, it's probably best to give everyone Read Only privileges and only certain people Read & Write privileges.

Defining access privileges for guests

To define access privileges for guests, follow these steps:

1. **If Sharing isn't open, right-click the System Preferences icon on the Dock and choose Sharing from the menu that appears, or choose ⬤⇨System Preferences and then click the Sharing icon.**

2. **Click File Sharing in the Service list.**

3. **Click a folder in the Shared Folders list.**

   The Users list enumerates all the people allowed to access this particular shared folder (refer to Figure 4-4). By default, every shared folder lists your name with Read & Write privileges.

4. **Click Unknown User (the guest account) to call up the access option pop-up menu and choose an access option, such as Read & Write, Read Only, Write Only (Drop Box), or No Access.**

5. **Repeat Steps 3 and 4 for each shared folder you want to configure.**

6. **Click the Close button of the System Preferences window.**

Giving individuals access to shared folders

The access level you give to the Everyone account for a shared folder means that anyone on the network has that level of access to your files — Read & Write, Read Only, Write Only. You probably want to give Everyone the minimum access to a shared folder and give specific individuals higher levels of access.

To define a username and password to access a shared folder, follow these steps:

1. **Right-click (two-finger click on a trackpad) the System Preferences icon on the Dock and choose Sharing from the menu that appears, or choose ⬤⇨System Preferences to open the System Preferences window and then click the Sharing icon.**

   The Sharing pane appears.

2. **Click File Sharing in the Service list.**

3. **Click a folder in the Shared Folders list.**

   The Users list enumerates all the people allowed to access this particular shared folder.

4. **Click the plus-sign button under the Users list, and then click the Contacts category or one of the groups from your Address Book in the left pane.**

   A dialog appears, shown in Figure 4-5, where you can either choose the name of a person stored in Contacts or create a new user.

   If the name of the person you want to add isn't a user in Contacts, add him to Contacts (see Book V, Chapter 1) or as a Sharing Only user (see Book III, Chapter 2).

Figure 4-5: Choose users from your Contacts who can access shared folders.

5. **Scroll through the list and click the name of the person to whom you want to grant privileges.**

   The Choose Password dialog appears, as shown in Figure 4-6.

Figure 4-6: Create the user's password.

6. **Enter a password in the Password text box.**

7. **Reenter the password in the Verify text box.**

8. **Click the Create Account button.**

9. **In the dialog that appears, type your user password (the one you use to sign in to your Mac) to approve the configuration change.**

   Your new user name appears in the Users list.

10. **Open the pop-up menu that appears to the right of the name you just added to the Users box, and choose Read & Write, Read Only, or Write Only (Drop Box) to assign access privileges, as shown in Figure 4-7.**

11. **Click the Close button to quit System Preferences.**

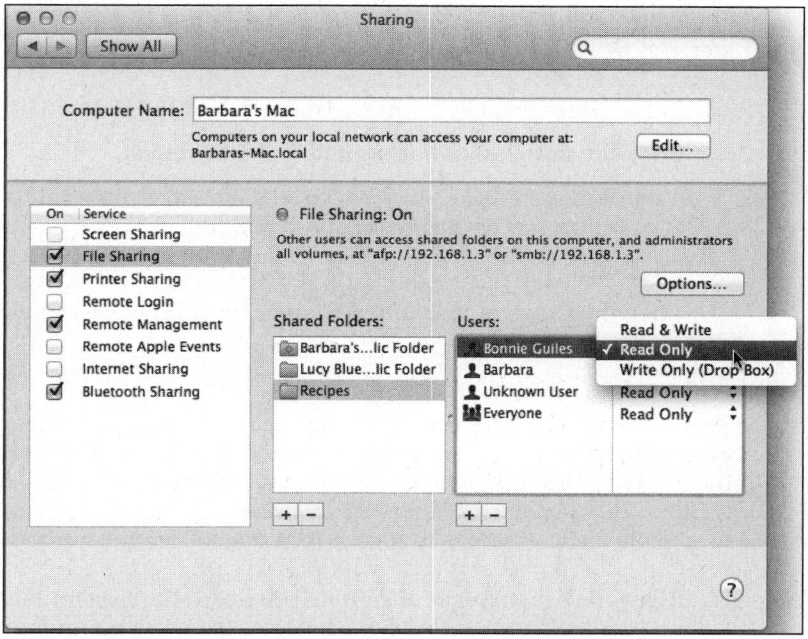

Figure 4-7:
New user
names in
the Users
list.

Removing accounts from shared folders

If you create an account for others to access your shared folders, you may later want to change their access privileges (such as changing their access from Read & Write to Read Only) or delete their accounts altogether.

To delete an account from a shared folder, follow these steps:

1. **Right-click (two-finger click on a trackpad) the System Preferences icon on the Dock and choose Sharing from the menu that appears, or choose System Preferences to open the System Preferences window and then click the Sharing icon.**

2. **Click File Sharing in the Services list.**

3. **Click a folder in the Shared Folders list.**

The Users list enumerates all the people allowed to access this particular shared folder.

4. **Click the name of the User for whom you want to change privileges.**

5. **Click the arrows next to the name to open the Privileges pop-up menu.**

6. **Select the new privileges you want the user to have.**

7. **Click the Close button of the System Preferences window.**

To delete a user, follow Steps 1–3 in the preceding list, and then follow these steps:

1. **In the Users list, click a name that you want to delete.**

2. **Click the minus-sign button under the Users list.**

   A confirmation dialog appears, asking whether you want to keep the account from accessing your shared folder.

3. **Click OK.**

4. **Click the Close button of the System Preferences window.**

File sharing in Sleep mode

Your Mac can share files even if you set up your Mac to sleep when it's inactive for a certain time. (You can use this feature if your wireless network supports the 802.11n or 802.11ac wireless protocol — see Book I, Chapter 3 or Book III, Chapter 3 for a brief explanation.) If you want your Mac to wake up when another user on the network wants to access your shared files, follow these steps:

1. **Right-click (two-finger click on a trackpad) the System Preferences icon on the Dock and choose Energy Saver from the menu that appears, or choose ⌘⇨System Preferences and then click the Energy Saver icon.**

2. **(MacBook model users) Click the Power Adapter tab.**

3. **Select the Wake for Wi-Fi Network Access check box.**

4. **Click the Close button of the System Preferences window.**

Accessing shared folders

You can share your folders with others on a network, and likewise, others may want to share their folders with you. To access a shared folder on someone else's computer, follow these steps:

1. **From the Finder, choose Go⇨Network.**

   A Network window appears, listing all the computers that offer shared folders, as shown in Figure 4-8.

   Choose the view you prefer from the buttons on the toolbar.

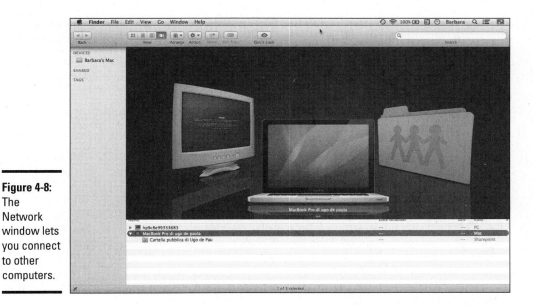

Figure 4-8:
The Network window lets you connect to other computers.

2. **Double-click the computer you want to access to open a connection window.**

3. **Click the Connect As button in the upper-right corner to display the dialog shown in Figure 4-9.**

Book III
Chapter 4

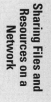

Sharing Files and Resources on a Network

Figure 4-9:
The Connect As dialog lets you access a shared folder with an account name and password.

4. **Select the radio button appropriate for your request:**
   - *Guest* gives you access to the folder, usually with Write Only privileges.
   - *Registered User* lets you sign in with your username and password.
   - *Using an Apple ID* lets you sign in with your Apple ID and password.

5. **With either of the last two choices, click in the Name text box and type the account name to use for accessing that shared folder.**

   The Registered User account name is the name that the computer's user created in the earlier section, "Giving individuals access to shared folders."

6. **Click the Password text box and type the corresponding password.**

7. **Click the Connect button.**

   Depending on your access to the shared folder, you may be able to copy, open, or modify files.

 You can also find the shared folder's Apple Filing Protocol (AFP) directly under the File Sharing: On text when you click a shared folder in the Sharing System Preferences window. Type the AFP address, such as `afp://192.168.1.3` (refer to Figure 4-7), in the URL address field of your browser and proceed from Step 4.

Sharing Printers

Instead of buying a separate printer for each computer on your network — which is expensive and space-consuming — connect a single printer directly to one computer, and then configure that computer to share its printer with any computer connected to the same network. Depending on your printer, some special functions may be limited to the connected Mac so connect the printer to the Mac that you use for the most diverse functions. To share a printer, follow these steps:

1. **Right-click (two-finger click on a trackpad) the System Preferences icon on the Dock and choose Sharing from the menu that appears, or choose System Preferences and click the Sharing icon.**

2. **Select the Printer Sharing check box.**

   A list of printers connected to your Mac — physically or wirelessly — appears, as shown in Figure 4-10.

3. **Select the check boxes of the printers you want to share.**

   Note that Everyone Can Print is the default in the Users column.

4. **(Optional) Add individual users just as you do for sharing files by clicking the plus-sign button beneath the Users column; choose No Access for Everyone and give selected users access to that printer.**

5. **Click the Close button to quit System Preferences.**

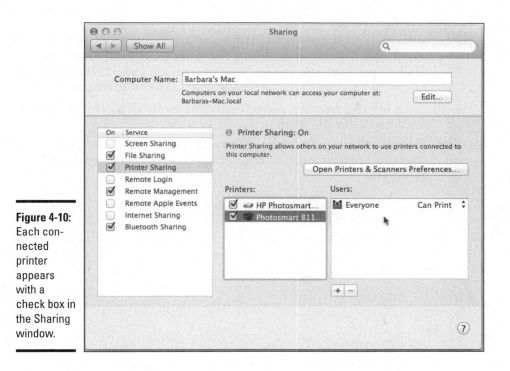

Figure 4-10: Each connected printer appears with a check box in the Sharing window.

**Book III
Chapter 4**

Sharing Files and Resources on a Network

When you choose File⇨Print in an application (say, Notes) to print a document or photo, a Print dialog appears. If you click the Printer pop-up menu, you see printers that you previously connected to your Mac. Choose Add Printer to choose a printer you haven't used, and a window appears (as we explain in Book III, Chapter 3), listing all the available printers connected directly to your Mac (USB) or shared over the network (Bonjour or Bonjour Shared). Click the Default tab if you don't see a list of printers.

Bonjour is Apple's implementation of a networking standard known as *zeroconf* (short for Zero Configuration Networking), used by most printers to connect to other computers through Ethernet cables (wired networks) or via wireless (Wi-Fi) connections (the number of the standard is 802.11a/b/g/n/ac). Printer companies have written software drivers to make their printers compatible with Bonjour/zeroconf. Windows users can download the Bonjour for Windows application for free, so Windows PCs can access shared printers on a network.

Sharing an Internet Connection

Although Wi-Fi and home networks seem universal, sometimes only one Mac has Internet access, and you'd like to tap into it from other Macs. Or one Mac may have access to the Internet through a wireless connection, but a second older Mac may not have a wireless or Ethernet adapter. With Internet Sharing turned on, though, the second Mac can access the Internet through the first Mac.

To share an Internet connection, follow these steps:

1. **Right-click (two-finger click on a trackpad) the System Preferences icon on the Dock and choose Sharing from the menu that appears, or choose ⌘⇨System Preferences and then click the Sharing icon.**

2. **Click Internet Sharing, without selecting its check box in the list box on the left, to highlight it.**

3. **From the Share Your Connection From pop-up menu, choose how your Mac is connected to the Internet, which could be any or all of the following:**

   - *iPhone USB*

   - *Bluetooth DUN*

     DUN stands for *dial-up network.* Your Mac is connected to the Internet through a cellular data connection on a smartphone or tablet.

   - *Thunderbolt Bridge*

   - *USB Ethernet*

   - *Wi-Fi*

   - *Bluetooth PAN*

     PAN stands for *personal area network.* You can create a personal area network between your Mac and other computers or handheld devices (such as smartphones and tablets) when your Mac is connected to the Internet through an Ethernet connection.

4. **In the To Computers Using list, select one or more of the check boxes that indicate how the other computer connects to your Mac:**

   - *Thunderbolt Bridge*

   - *USB Ethernet*

   - *Wi-Fi*

   - *Bluetooth PAN*

   Not all options will appear with every choice.

   To find out more about the different connection options for connecting your Macs to create a network, see Book III, Chapter 3.

5. **Select the Internet Sharing check box.**

   A warning dialog appears, as shown in Figure 4-11.

6. **Click the Start button.**

7. Click the Close button on the System Preferences window.

The second computer — connected to your Mac through Ethernet, Thunderbolt, Wi-Fi, or Bluetooth — can now access the Internet.

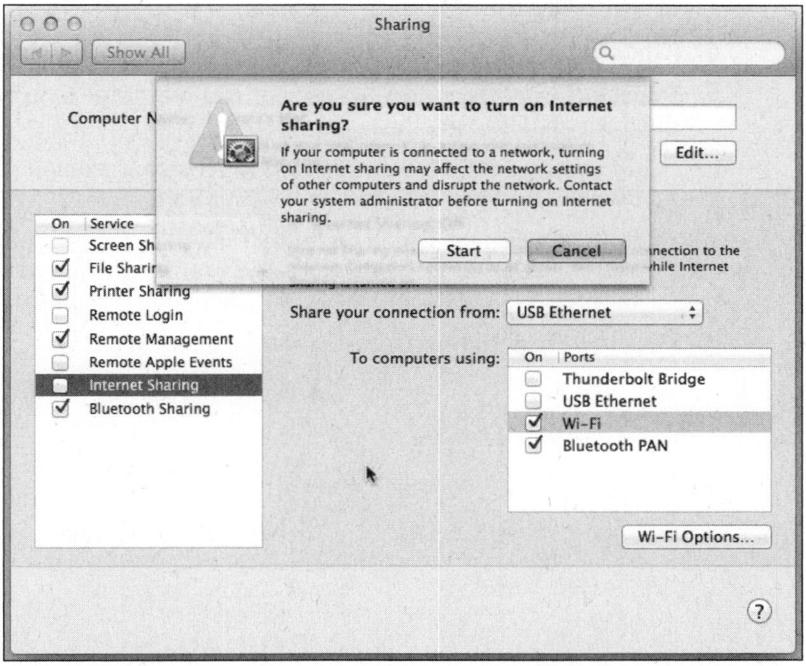

Figure 4-11: Define how to share your Internet connection.

Book III Chapter 4

Sharing Files and Resources on a Network

Seeing Your Screen from Afar

Wouldn't it be great if while you're away from your office you could access your Mac? Or if you have a problem with your Mac and want to consult an expert, you can share your screen to show exactly what's going on? Screen Sharing lets you do this.

Sharing your screen

For you or others to see and work on your Mac from another computer, you need to set up access on your Mac. Follow these steps to do so:

1. Right-click (two-finger click on a trackpad) the System Preferences icon on the Dock and choose Sharing from the menu that appears, or choose System Preferences and then click the Sharing icon.

2. **Select the Screen Sharing check box.**

   If you have Remote Management selected, deselect it, or Screen Sharing won't work.

3. **Take note of your computer's address under Screen Sharing: On, as shown in Figure 4-12.**

4. **(Optional) Click the Computer Settings button to add a password.**

5. **Select either of the Allow Access For radio buttons to grant screen sharing privileges to**

   - *All Users,* which allows anyone who sees your Mac on the network or uses the address to access your computer.

   - *Only These Users,* which limits access to the people you add to the list. Click the Add (+) button to add users to the list as you do for file sharing, as we explain earlier in this chapter.

6. **Click the Close button to exit System Preferences.**

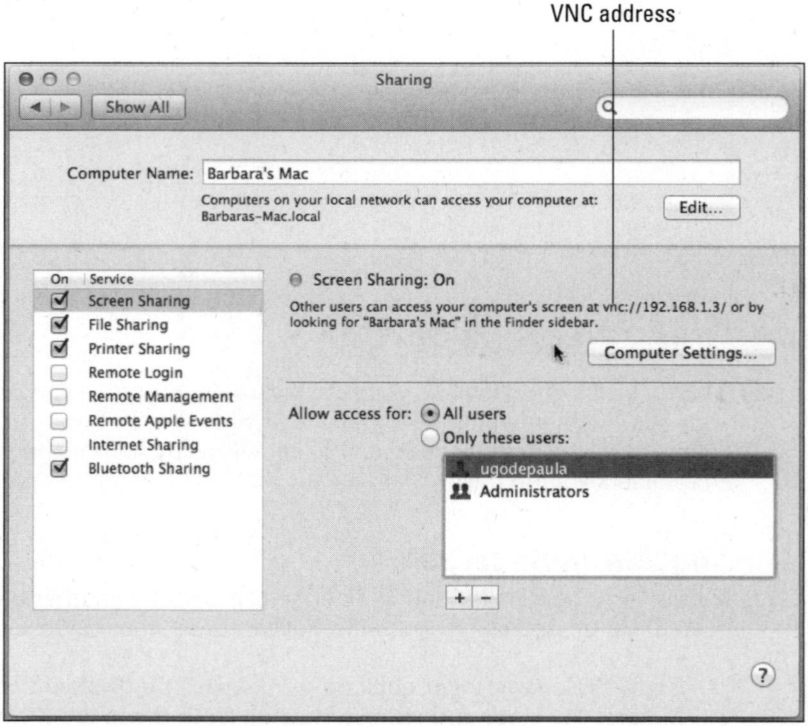

VNC address

Figure 4-12: Use your Mac's address to access the screen from another computer.

Accessing your Mac

To access your Mac from another computer — or someone else's Mac from yours — do the following:

1. **Open a web browser and type in the address of the Mac you want to view.**

This is `vnc://192.168.1.3/` in Figure 4-12.

or

Open a Finder window and click the other Mac's name in the Finder sidebar; or from the Finder, choose Go⇨Network and double-click the Mac you want to view in the list. Then click the Share Screen button at the top of the window, as shown in Figure 4-13.

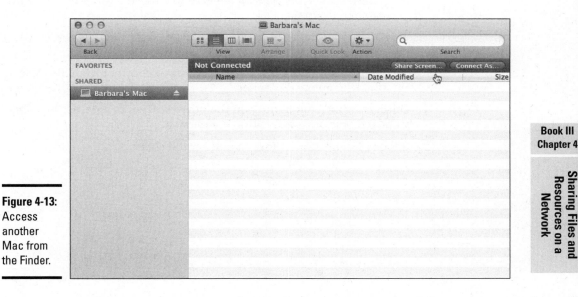

Figure 4-13:
Access another Mac from the Finder.

Book III
Chapter 4

Sharing Files and
Resources on a
Network

2. **Type in your username and password or use your Apple ID and password to access the screen of the other Mac.**

If you go through a browser, you can also ask permission to use the other Mac. After the shared Mac grants permission, as shown in Figure 4-14, the "asking" Mac shows the screen of the shared Mac as a window on the Desktop.

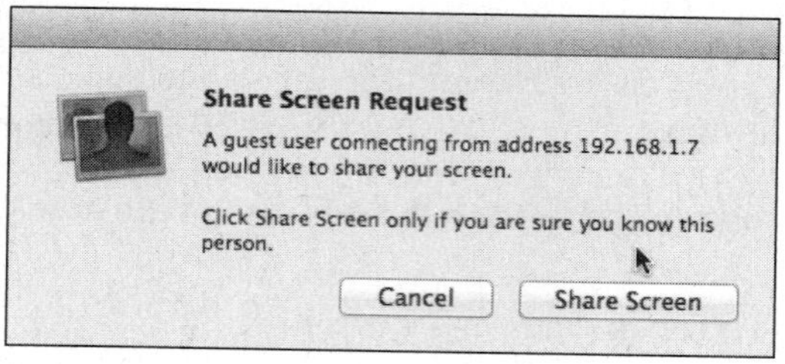

Figure 4-14:
Ask for
access
when you
aren't a
registered
user.

Share Screen Request

A guest user connecting from address 192.168.1.7
would like to share your screen.

Click Share Screen only if you are sure you know this
person.

Cancel   Share Screen

3. **Select the window of the shared Mac.**

   Screen sharing menus appear across the top:

   - *Choose Screen Sharing⇨Preferences* to choose how to interact with the shared screen.

   - *Choose View⇨Switch to Observe Mode* to only view the screen without being able to control it.

   - *Choose View⇨Switch to Virtual Display* to control the shared Mac from the remote computer.

4. **Observe what's happening on the other screen, or interact by using standard Mac and application commands.**

5. **Choose Connection⇨Close to end screen sharing.**

Chapter 5: Running Windows on a Mac

In This Chapter

✔ **Sending your Mac to Boot Camp**

✔ **Running virtual machines**

✔ **Tricking Windows apps with CrossOver Mac**

A s much as you may enjoy using your Mac, sometimes you may need to use an app that runs only on Windows. Many apps, particularly games, are Windows-only. Plus, you'll encounter Windows-only retail store point-of-sale (POS) system or stock-picking apps, as well as many custom apps developed by a company for in-house use.

You can access Microsoft Exchange services such as address lists, calendar events, and e-mail through Mail, Calendar, and Contacts, so you may not need to install Windows. And don't worry about wiping your hard drive and having to delete your Mac OS to run Windows. You can run Windows on your Mac and still use all the features that made you want to get a Mac in the first place.

If you do need to run Windows on your Mac, though, you have choices. In this chapter, we explain the second and third of those listed here:

✦ You can buy a Windows PC and use that computer just to run the Windows app(s) you need.

✦ You can install and run Windows 7 or 8 — in their various 64-bit iterations — on your Mac using the Boot Camp 5 utility app that comes as part of OS X 10.9 Mavericks.

✦ Use a virtualization app that makes your Mac think it's a Windows PC.

You can install and run earlier, 32-bit versions of Windows, but you must use a previous version of Boot Camp. The instructions in this chapter presume that

✦ You've never installed Windows on your Mac.

✦ You're using OS X 10.9 Mavericks.

If the Mavericks upgrade installation process discovers a previously installed, older version of Windows (XP, Vista, or 32-bit Windows 7), it leaves the prior version of Boot Camp 3 or 4 on your Mac so you can continue using those Windows operating systems. However, you can't upgrade to Boot Camp 5. *Boot Camp 5 works only with the 64-bit versions of Windows 7 or 8.*

Giving Your Mac a Split Personality with Boot Camp

To install Windows on a Mac, you use Boot Camp to split your storage drive in two parts — called *partitions.* Then you use one partition to install and run Windows, and a second partition to keep using OS X the way you've been using it. By having two different operating systems on your storage drive, you can choose which operating system to use every time you turn on your Mac.

Partitioning divides your hard drive in two parts: one part for OS X and the other part for Windows. Boot Camp uses *nondestructive partitioning,* which means that you resize your hard drive's partitions without losing data.

Before opening the OS X 10.9 Mavericks version of Boot Camp 5 to install Windows 7 or 8, make sure you have the following:

✦ **2GB (gigabytes) of RAM**

✦ **20GB of available storage drive space (Apple's recommended minimum)**

To find out how much free space you have on your storage drive as well as how much RAM, choose ➡About This Mac, click the More Info button, and then click the Storage tab and then click the Memory tab. Figure 5-1 shows the Mac HD as well as the Boot Camp partition.

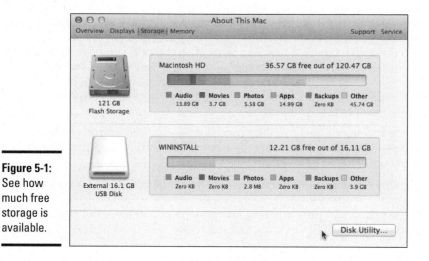

Figure 5-1:
See how much free storage is available.

✦ **Internet access**

✦ **Windows** (one of the following)

• *On disc:* An authentic, single, full-installation, 64-bit Microsoft Windows 7 (Home Premium, Professional, or Ultimate) or Windows 8 (Standard or Pro) disc and a built-in optical disc drive or a compatible external optical drive

- *On a flash drive:* A downloaded ISO disc image of one of the 64-bit versions of Windows 7 or 8 and an 8GB (or larger) USB flash drive (See Book I, Chapter 4 to learn more about ISO disc images.)

✦ **The Windows 25-digit product key**

✦ **An administrator account in OS X**

✦ **A USB flash drive**

You need this to install the downloaded drivers. If you plan to use the ISO image of Windows, though, you need only one USB flash drive with at least 8GB of storage.

As long as you meet these requirements, installing Windows on your Mac is like most things Mac: Just follow the onscreen instructions, and the procedure just works. Do the following steps, and you'll find you have two computers in one in no time:

1. **Open the Finder by clicking anywhere on the Desktop.**

2. **Choose Go⇨Utilities.**

3. **Double-click the Boot Camp Assistant icon.**

A Boot Camp Assistant task window appears, informing you of the things Boot Camp can help you with, as shown in Figure 5-2.

**Book III
Chapter 5**

Running Windows
on a Mac

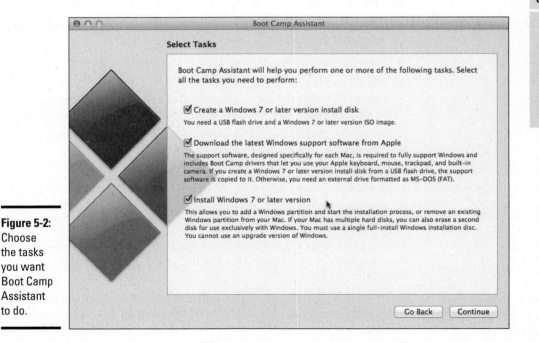

Figure 5-2:
Choose
the tasks
you want
Boot Camp
Assistant
to do.

4. **Select the check box(es) for the task(s) you want Boot Camp Assistant to perform:**

   - (Optional) *Create a Windows 7 or Later Version Install Disk:* If you downloaded Windows from the Internet, Boot Camp Assistant will copy it to a USB flash drive and then use it to install Windows on your Mac.

   - (Required) *Download the Latest Windows Support Software from Apple:* If you use a downloaded version of Windows with a USB flash drive, Boot Camp will format the drive, and the support software will be copied to that drive. If you plan to use a disc to install Windows, you must format a USB flash drive.

     a. *From the Finder, choose Go⇨Utilities and choose Disk Utility.*

     b. *Insert your flash drive in the USB port, select it in the drives list on the Disk Utility window, and then click the Erase tab.*

     c. *Choose MS-DOS (FAT) from the Format menu and click the Erase button.*

   - (Required) *Install Windows 7 or Later Version:* Select this check box regardless of whether you plan to use a single installation disc or an ISO image that will be copied to the USB flash drive.

5. **Click the Continue button.**

6. **(ISO image users only) Create a Bootable USB Drive.**

   If you're using an ISO image, the Create Bootable USB Drive for Windows Installation window opens, as shown in Figure 5-3.

   - *If the file path in the ISO image field is correct, click the Continue button.*

   - *Otherwise, click the Choose button, scroll through the folders and files to the ISO image file, click it, click Choose, and then click Continue.*

   Boot Camp Assistant copies the ISO image to the USB flash drive and installs the Apple support software and drivers necessary to use your Mac's keyboard and mouse or trackpad when running Windows.

   Type your user/administrator password in the dialog when asked.

   (Installation disc users only) Save Windows support software to the external drive.

   The window shown in Figure 5-4 appears. Confirm that the destination disk is the one you want to save the support software to and then click Continue.

   Boot Camp Assistant copies the Apple support software and drivers necessary to use your Mac's keyboard and mouse or trackpad when running Windows. Type your user/administrator password in the dialog when asked.

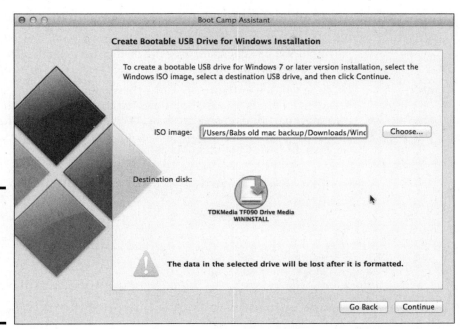

Figure 5-3:
The Create Bootable USB Drive for Windows Installation window.

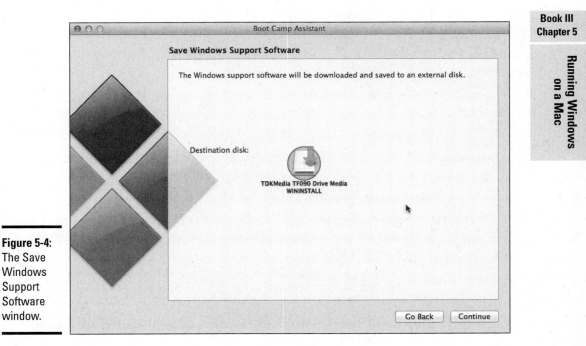

Figure 5-4:
The Save Windows Support Software window.

7. Create a Windows partition, as shown in Figure 5-5.

Boot Camp Assistant suggests the minimum size needed for the Windows partition. You can click and drag the divider between the OS X partition and the Windows partition left or right to change the partition size.

18GB, as you see in Figure 5-5, is the (bare) minimum Boot Camp Assistant suggests to install windows, although Apple recommends creating a partition no smaller than 20GB. We recommend that if you change the Windows partition side at all, don't go below the minimum suggested by the Boot Camp Assistant.

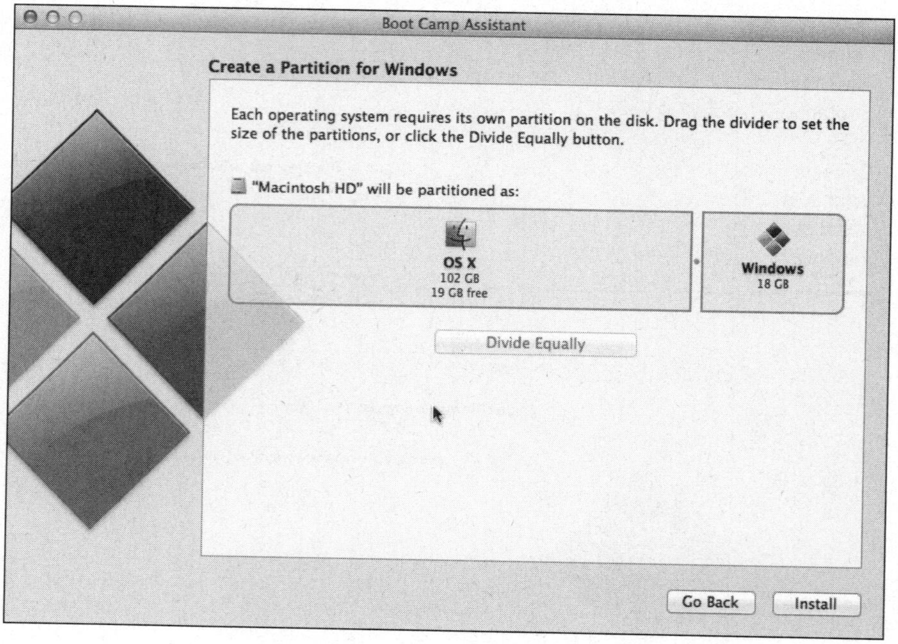

Figure 5-5:
Define how much hard drive space to allocate for Windows.

8. Click the Install button.

Boot Camp partitions your hard drive. (This process may take a little while.) When partitioning is complete, the Start Windows Installation window appears.

9. (Users with an installation disc or flash drive) Insert your Windows installation disc or flash drive in your Mac (or its external optical drive).

10. Choose your language and location from the pop-up menus and click Next.

11. **Enter your 25-digit product key and click Next.**

12. **Follow the Windows installation instructions on the screen. When the installation finishes, eject the disc or flash drive.**

Be patient. Installing Windows can take time. ***Note:*** Windows will reboot several times during installation, so don't panic if the screen suddenly goes blank.

If you see a message that tells you the software you're installing has not passed Windows Logo testing, click Continue Anyway. *Do not click Cancel in any of the installer dialogs.* Follow the instructions for any wizards that appear.

Choosing an operating system with Boot Camp

After you complete the Boot Camp installation process to install Windows on your Mac, you can choose which operating system you want to use when you start your Mac by following these steps:

1. **Restart your computer and hold down the Option key until two disk icons appear.**

One disk icon is labeled Windows, and the other is labeled Macintosh HD. (If you changed the name of your Mac's hard disk, you'll see this name displayed instead.)

2. **Click the Windows or Macintosh Startup Disk icon.**

Your chosen operating system starts.

Holding down the X key after you power-on your Mac tells your Mac that you want to load OS X. You can let go of the X key as soon as you see the OS X start-up screen.

To switch to a different operating system, you have to shut down the current operating system and repeat the preceding steps to choose the other operating system.

If you start your Mac without holding down the Option key, your Mac starts the default operating system. You can define the default operating system in OS X by following these steps:

1. **Within OS X, choose ⌘⟶System Preferences to open the System Preferences window.**

2. **Click the Startup Disk icon.**

The Startup Disk window opens.

3. **Click the OS X or Windows icon and then click the Restart button.**

Sharing Mac and Windows files

With Mac OS X version 10.6 and later, whether you're running the Mac or Windows operating system, you can open and view files from the other operating system's hard drive partition. To modify files, copy the file from the partition where the file is stored to the operating system partition you're using. For example, if you're in Windows and want to modify a file saved on your Mac partition, copy the file from the Mac partition to the Windows partition, and then make the changes.

Removing Windows from your Mac

If you want to wipe out the partition on your hard drive that contains Windows, you can do so by following these steps:

1. **From the Finder, choose Go⟹Utilities and then double-click the Boot Camp Assistant icon in the Utilities folder.**

   The Boot Camp Introduction window appears.

2. **Click the Continue button.**

3. **Select the Remove Windows 7 or Later Version check box, as shown in Figure 5-6.**

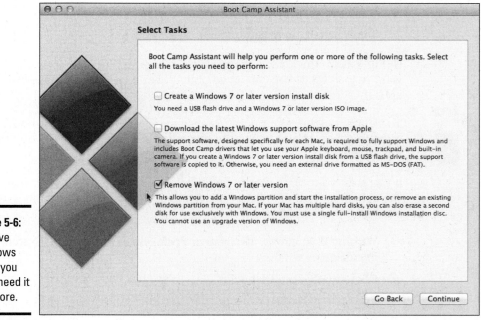

Figure 5-6: Remove Windows when you don't need it any more.

4. **Click the Continue button.**

   The Restore Disk to a Single Volume window appears.

   Wiping out your Windows partition deletes all data stored on that partition that you created by using Windows.

5. **Click the Restore button.**

   Type your user password in the dialog that appears.

Using Virtual Machines

Although you can share files between the Mac and Windows partitions (as we describe earlier in this chapter), you may still want to use a virtualization app to run Windows and OS X at the same time and switch between the two.

Virtualization is a technology that lets you run multiple operating systems at the same time, where each operating system "time-shares" the computer's hardware. Because the active operating system isn't really controlling the computer's hardware completely, it's dubbed a *virtual machine* — that is, a part of your computer that works like some other real machine, such as a Windows PC.

Here are some software choices that work on Macs with Intel processors (go to ⚫️About This Mac to confirm that your Mac uses one):

✦ **Parallels Desktop:** www.parallels.com, $79.99

✦ **VirtualBox:** www.virtualbox.org, free

✦ **VMware Fusion:** www.vmware.com, $59.99

Parallels Desktop, VirtualBox, and VMware Fusion work in similar ways by creating a single file on your Mac hard drive that represents a virtual PC hard drive — which contains the Windows operating system plus any additional Windows apps you install, such as Microsoft Office.

When you run Parallels Desktop, VirtualBox, or VMware Fusion, the app boots up from this virtual hard drive while your original OS X operating system continues to run. This lets you run another operating system, such as Windows, inside a separate OS X window, as shown in Figure 5-7.

Instead of requiring you to load Windows and then load a specific app within Windows, virtualization apps let you store a Windows app icon directly on the Desktop or on the Dock so that it behaves like a Mac app icon.

Clicking a Windows app icon loads Windows and the Windows app at the same time without showing the Windows desktop or the Windows Start menu.

Book III Chapter 5

Running Windows on a Mac

Figure 5-7:
The
Parallels
Desktop app
lets you run
Windows
inside a
separate
Mac
window.

Because the operating system stored on the virtual hard drive has to share the computer's processor and memory with OS X, operating systems running on virtual machines tend to run slower than when you run Windows and Windows programs within Boot Camp. In Boot Camp, the app has total access to your computer's hardware, meaning that the app runs as fast as it would on a standalone Windows PC.

To ease the migration from Windows to the Mac, virtualization programs can clone your existing Windows PC and duplicate it, with all your data and programs, on to the Mac. You can essentially use your old Windows PC as a virtual computer on your Mac.

Using CrossOver Mac

With Boot Camp, Parallels Desktop, VirtualBox, and VMware Fusion, you need to buy a separate copy of Windows. CrossOver Mac, though, lets you run many Windows apps without a copy of Windows. The app works by fooling Windows apps into thinking that they're really running on a Windows PC.

With CrossOver Mac, you can pop a Windows CD into your Mac and install the Windows app on a simulated PC that CrossOver Mac creates automatically on your Mac. After you install a Windows app, CrossOver Mac displays the normal Windows icons inside a Finder window. Double-clicking the Windows app icon runs that Windows app on your Mac, as shown in Figure 5-8.

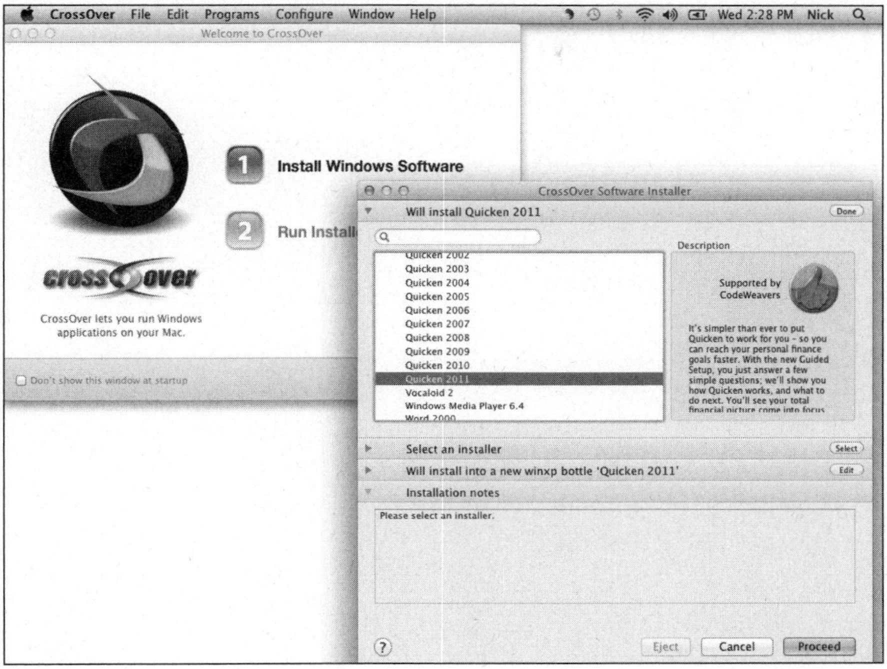

Figure 5-8:
CrossOver Mac lets you run a handful of Windows programs without running Windows.

Book III Chapter 5

Running Windows on a Mac

Like Parallels Desktop, VirtualBox, and VMware Fusion, CrossOver Mac runs only on Intel Mac computers. A more crucial limitation is that CrossOver Mac works with only a handful of Windows programs, so you can't run just any Windows app on a Mac with CrossOver Mac and expect it to run flawlessly.

To help you determine whether your favorite Windows app (such as Quicken or DirectX 8) or game (such as *Wizard 101, World of Warcraft,* or *Alien Swarm*), will work with CrossOver Mac, visit the product's website (www. codeweavers.com/compatibility/browse/name) to browse all known apps that have been tested and verified to work correctly.

If you need to run the latest Windows apps, a little-known Windows program, or a custom Windows program, CrossOver Mac probably won't let you run it. However, if you need to run only a handful of older or popular apps, CrossOver Mac may be the ideal solution.

Chapter 6: Maintenance and Troubleshooting

In This Chapter

✔ Taking care of application freezes and hang-ups

✔ Knowing what to do when you have trouble starting up

✔ Keeping your storage drives running smoothly

✔ Unjamming jammed CDs or DVDs

✔ Making your Mac perform routine maintenance

*N*o matter how well designed and well built a Mac is, it's still a machine, and all machines are liable to break down through no fault of yours. Many times, you can fix minor problems with a little bit of knowledge and willingness to poke and prod around your Mac. If your Mac isn't working correctly, you can check obvious things first, like making sure it's plugged in or that the battery is charged and that any connecting cables to your Mac are plugged in and secure. However, sometimes your Mac may be in more serious trouble than you can fix, so don't be afraid to take your Mac into your friendly neighborhood computer-repair store (one that specializes in repairing Macs, of course).

Before you rush your Mac to the emergency room of Mac repairs, do some simple troubleshooting yourself. At the very least, be sure to back up your important files — before you have any troubles — so you won't lose them if you wind up sending your Mac to the repair shop. (Read about backing up in Book III, Chapter 1.)

Luckily, Apple and third-party developers have created applications that analyze, diagnose, and repair problems on your Mac. In this chapter, we begin by addressing one of the most common problems: frozen apps. Then we get down to more serious problems related to your Mac not starting up properly or your hard drive acting strangely. We explain how to use the Recovery and Disk Utility applications that come with your Mac and give you suggestions for third-party applications to consider. We show you how to remove a jammed CD or DVD from the disc drive — in case you still have one of those. We close the chapter by giving you suggestions for preventive maintenance.

Open your Mac *only if you know what you're doing.* If you open the case and start fiddling around with its electronic insides, you may damage your Mac — and invalidate your Mac's warranty.

Shutting Down Frozen or Hung-Up Programs

Programs that always run perfectly may suddenly stop working for no apparent reason, and no matter which keys you press, where you click the mouse, or where you tap the trackpad, nothing happens. Sometimes you might see a spinning cursor (affectionately referred to as the "spinning beach ball of death"), which stays onscreen and refuses to go away until you take steps to unlock the frozen app.

Sometimes being patient and waiting a few minutes results in the hung-up app resolving whatever was ailing it as though nothing were wrong in the first place. More often, however, the spinning cursor keeps spinning in an oh-so-annoying fashion. To end the torment, you need to relaunch the Finder to refresh the Desktop or *force-quit* the frozen or hung-up app — basically, you shut down the app so that the rest of your Mac can get back to work. To force-quit an app, use one of the following methods:

✦ Choose ⌘➪Force Quit to display the Force Quit Applications dialog, as shown in Figure 6-1. Click the Finder and then click the Relaunch button.

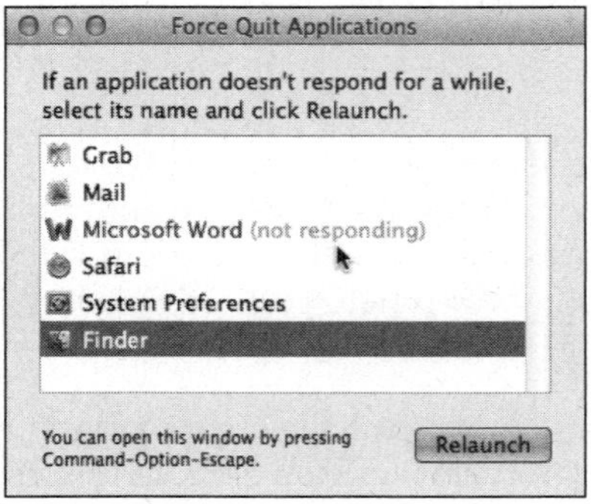

Figure 6-1:
Relaunch
the Finder
to unfreeze
your Mac.

> **Force Quit Applications**
>
> If an application doesn't respond for a while, select its name and click Relaunch.
>
> 🎞 Grab
> 📷 Mail
> W Microsoft Word (not responding)
> 🧭 Safari
> ⬜ System Preferences
> 📁 Finder
>
> You can open this window by pressing Command-Option-Escape.   [Relaunch]

✦ Right-click (two-finger click on the trackpad) the app's icon on the Dock and choose Force Quit from the menu that appears. If you use a trackpad, hold down the Option key and perform a two-finger tap on the app icon on the Dock and choose Force Quit from the menu.

✦ Choose ⌘➪Force Quit to display the Force Quit Applications dialog. Then select the name of the hung-up application and click the Force Quit button (in place of the Relaunch button you see in Figure 6-1).

✦ Press ⌘+Option+Esc to display the Force Quit Applications dialog. Then select the name of the hung-up application and click the Force Quit button.

✦ Load the Activity Monitor application (located inside the Utilities folder in the Launchpad), select the process name, and then choose View⇨Quit Process. From the Quit Process dialog that appears, click Force Quit.

One of the best ways to avoid problems with applications and the Mac operating system is to keep them updated. Set the App Store to check automatically for updates. Choose ⌘⇨System Preferences, and then click App Store to open the App Store preferences, as shown in Figure 6-2. Select the Automatically Check for Updates check box, and then choose any or all three options below. (See Book I, Chapter 5 for information about the App Store.)

Figure 6-2:
Keeping your operating system and applications updated helps avoid problems.

App Store

> The App Store keeps OS X and apps from the App Store up to date.
>
> ☑ Automatically check for updates
>   ☑ Download newly available updates in the background
>   You will be notified when the updates are ready to be installed
>   ☐ Install app updates
>   ☑ Install system data files and security updates
>
> ☐ Automatically download apps purchased on other Macs
>   You are signed in as barbaradepaula in the App Store
>
> Your computer is set to receive pre-release Software Update seeds [Change...]
>
> Last check was Thursday, November 21, 2013 [Check Now]

Handling Startup Troubles

Sometimes you may press the Power button to turn on your Mac, but nothing seems to happen. Other times, you may press the Power button and see the usual Apple logo on the screen — but *then* nothing happens.

Booting up in Safe Mode

If you turn on your Mac and you can't see the familiar Desktop, menu bar, and Dock, don't panic. The first thing to do is try to boot up your Mac in *Safe Mode,* which is a boot sequence that loads the bare minimum of the OS X operating system — just enough to get your computer running.

Many startup problems occur when nonessential apps, such as appointment reminders, automatically load at login time and wind up interfering with other startup apps, preventing your Mac from booting up correctly. Other startup apps load before you see the login screen or the Desktop (if you've set your Mac to bypass the login window automatically and go directly to the Desktop when it starts up). Booting up in Safe Mode cuts all the nonessential pre- and post-login apps out of the loop so that only your core apps load. A successful boot in Safe Mode at least tells you that your Mac's core system hasn't been compromised.

By booting up your Mac in Safe Mode, you can remove any applications you recently installed, turn off any startup options you may have activated, and then restart to see whether that fixes the boot-up problems. If you remove recently installed applications and deactivate startup options and problems persist, copy any important files from your hard drive to a backup drive to protect your crucial data in case the hard drive is starting to fail (see Book III, Chapter 1). Follow these steps to determine the cause of the problem:

1. **Turn on your Mac, and then immediately hold down the Shift key until the Apple logo appears on the screen, indicating that your Mac is booting up.**

   If your Mac is on but not responding, hold down the Power button until your Mac restarts, and then immediately hold down the Shift key until the Apple logo appears on the screen.

   If your Mac starts up, you know at least that the problem isn't with the Mac OS itself but with something else on your Mac. Move on to Step 2 to repair it.

2. **To turn off startup options, go to ➝System Preferences and click Users & Groups.**

   The Users & Groups window opens.

3. **Click your username in the column on the left.**

4. **Click the Login Items tab at the top of the right side of the window.**

   A list of the items that open automatically when you log in appears, as shown in Figure 6-3.

5. **Deselect a login item.**

6. **Click the Close button.**

7. **Choose ➝Restart.**

   If your Mac restarts without a problem, you know that the startup item you deselected was the problem.

   If your Mac doesn't restart, repeat Steps 1–5, each time deselecting the next login item on the list until your Mac restarts without a problem.

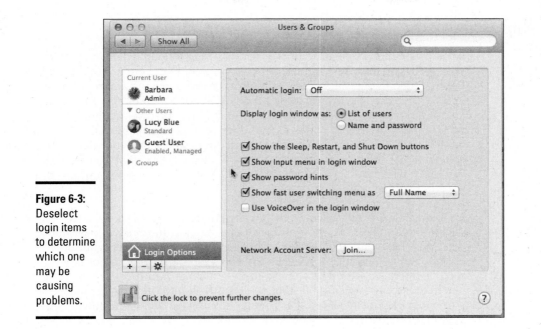

Figure 6-3:
Deselect login items to determine which one may be causing problems.

Uninstalling apps

If the problem isn't resolved by removing startup items, the next thing to try is to uninstall any apps you recently installed. Although sometimes uninstalling is as simple as dragging the app icon from the Applications folder to the Trash (we talk about that in Book I, Chapter 5), other times that's not the case. Just as there are *installers* that install apps on your Mac, there are also *uninstallers*.

When you install an app, you see the app icon in the Applications folder (and on the Launchpad), but there are also files associated with the app that the installer places in other folders on your Mac, such as the System and Library folders. To make sure that you throw away all the associated files, you need to run the uninstaller.

To find the uninstaller associated with the app you suspect is causing your problems, click the Spotlight Search button in the upper-right corner and enter **Uninstall**. Double-click the uninstaller you want to run. A window may open, asking for your login password or telling you that your Mac has to reboot. Either way, follow the onscreen instructions.

If your Mac reboots successfully afterward, you know that the removed app was causing the problems. At that point, before reinstalling, check the app in the App Store or visit the website of the problematic app to determine whether there's an update or information about incompatibility with your Mac model or operating system version. Try reinstalling from the disc if that's what you have; otherwise, try downloading the app anew and installing a new copy.

Repairing and Maintaining Storage Drives

If the problem isn't because of other apps trying to load when you turn on your Mac, you may have a more serious problem with your storage drive. Depending on your Mac model, your storage drive may be a hard drive or a flash drive (see Book I, Chapter 1 to learn about Mac models). Both can fail for a number of reasons. A minor problem may involve scrambled data on your hard drive that confuses your Mac and makes it impossible to read data from it. If data is scrambled, you can often reorganize your data with a special utility diagnostic and repair app — such as Disk Utility on your Mac, or DiskWarrior (www.alsoft.com/DiskWarrior) — to get your hard drive back in working condition.

A more serious problem could be physical damage to your hard drive. If a disk utility app fails to repair any problems on your hard drive, your hard drive's surface may be physically damaged. When this occurs, your only option is to copy critical files from the damaged hard drive (if possible), replace the drive with a new one, and then restore your most recent Time Machine backup (you *are* backing up, aren't you?) to the new hard drive so you're back in business again as though nothing (or almost nothing) went kaput in the first place.

To find out how to use Time Machine to back up your Mac's hard drive, check out Book III, Chapter 1.

The Disk Utility app that comes free with every Mac — tucked away in the Utilities folder inside the Applications folder or on the Launchpad — can examine your hard drive. However, to fix any problems it may find, you have to boot your Mac from a different hard drive or bootable USB flash drive, from the Recovery drive.

Empty the Trash every now and then to eliminate files that you throw away from the Trash's temporary storage. Control-click or right-click (two-finger tap on the trackpad) the Trash icon on the Dock and choose Empty Trash or choose Finder➪Secure Empty Trash.

You can't retrieve items thrown away with Secure Empty Trash, however, unless they were backed up with an application like Time Machine.

Verifying disk permissions

Disk permissions apply to your startup disk and define what each app's files are allowed to access and which users have access to which files. If permissions aren't correct, your files can become scrambled, which can cause your Mac to act erratically or prevent an app from launching.

Unlike repairing a hard drive, verifying and fixing disk permissions won't require you to boot up from a separate drive or partition. (We explain creating partitions in Book III, Chapter 5.)

To verify disk permissions, follow these steps:

1. **Load the Disk Utility app (stored inside the Utilities folder in the Applications folder).**

   The Disk Utility window appears.

2. **Select your Macintosh HD (or whatever you renamed your Mac's hard drive if you changed the name) from the left pane of the Disk Utility window.**

3. **Make sure that the window is on the First Aid pane. (If not, click the First Aid tab to call it up.)**

4. **Click Verify Disk Permissions.**

   If Disk Utility finds any problems, it displays a message to let you know. Otherwise, it displays a message to let you know all permissions are okay.

5. **Click Repair Disk Permissions.**

   Disk Utility displays any messages concerning permission problems it found and repaired.

6. **Choose Disk Utility⇨Quit Disk Utility.**

Verifying a disk

If you suspect that your hard drive may be scrambled or physically damaged, you can run the Disk Utility app to verify your suspicions.

The Disk Utility app can verify and repair all types of storage devices (except optical discs, such as CDs and DVDs), including hard drives, flash drives, and other types of removable storage media, such as compact flash cards.

To verify a disk, follow these steps:

1. **Load the Disk Utility app stored inside the Utilities folder on the Launchpad, or choose Go⇨Utilities from the Finder and then click the Disk Utility icon.**

   The Disk Utility window appears.

2. **Click the device (hard drive, flash drive, and so on) that you want to verify in the left pane of the Disk Utility window, as shown in Figure 6-4.**

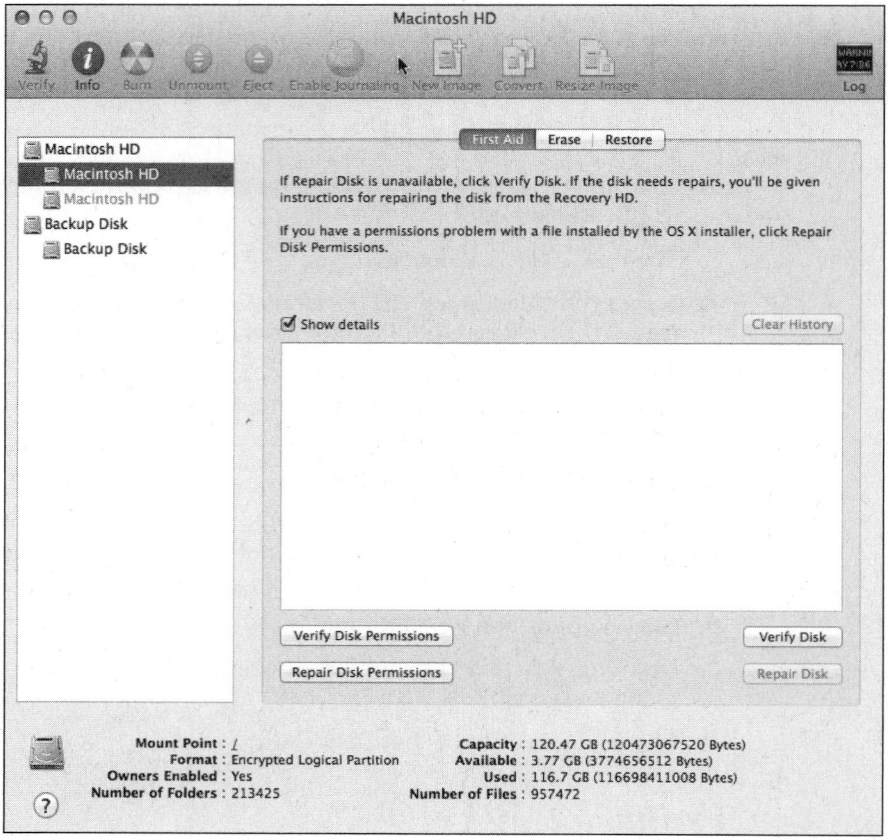

Figure 6-4:
Choose
a drive to
examine.

3. **Make sure that the First Aid pane is visible. (If not, click the First Aid tab to call it up.)**

4. **Click the Verify Disk button.**

   The Disk Utility application examines your chosen device and checks to make sure that all the files on that device are neatly organized. If Disk Utility can't verify that a device is working, you see a message informing you that First Aid feature of Disk Utility has failed.

5. **Click OK and then click the Repair Disk button.**

   You can do this step only with a non-startup disk. Otherwise, a message appears, as shown in Figure 6-5. To repair your Mac's startup disk, skip ahead to the next set of steps.

   Disk Utility tries to fix your device. If it succeeds, you see a message informing you that the device is repaired.

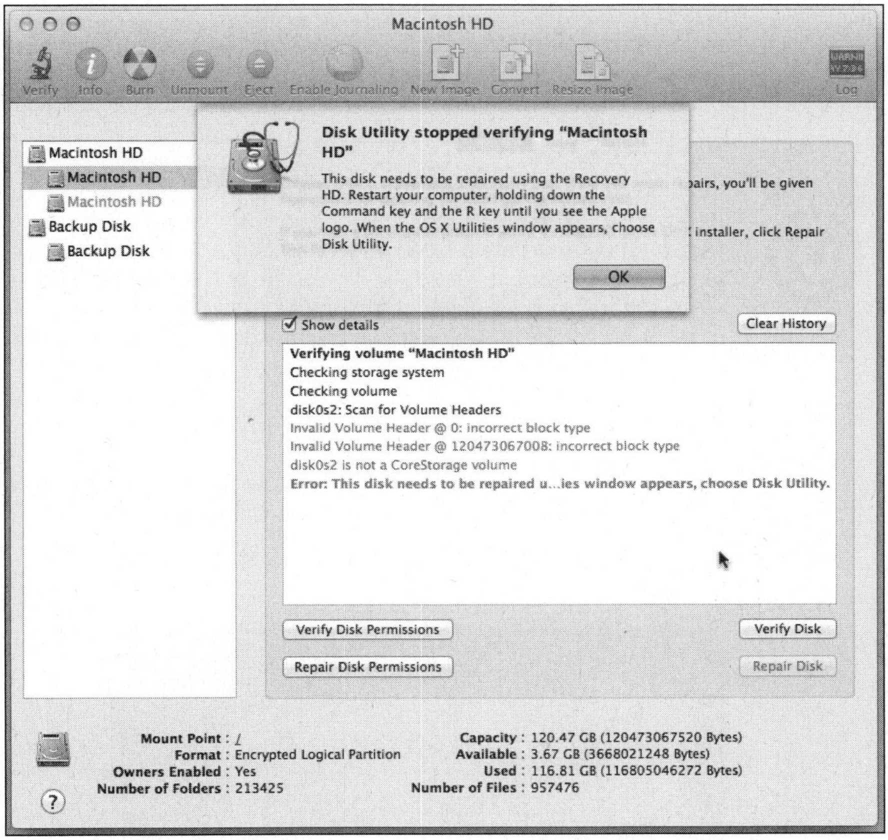

○ ○ ○   Macintosh HD

Verify   Info   Burn   Unmount   Eject   Enable Journaling   New Image   Convert   Resize Image   Log

Macintosh HD
   Macintosh HD
   Macintosh HD
Backup Disk
   Backup Disk

Disk Utility stopped verifying "Macintosh HD"

This disk needs to be repaired using the Recovery HD. Restart your computer, holding down the Command key and the R key until you see the Apple logo. When the OS X Utilities window appears, choose Disk Utility.

…pairs, you'll be given

…installer, click Repair

OK

☑ Show details   Clear History

Verifying volume "Macintosh HD"
Checking storage system
Checking volume
disk0s2: Scan for Volume Headers
Invalid Volume Header @ 0: incorrect block type
Invalid Volume Header @ 120473067008: incorrect block type
disk0s2 is not a CoreStorage volume
Error: This disk needs to be repaired u…ies window appears, choose Disk Utility.

Verify Disk Permissions   Verify Disk

Repair Disk Permissions   Repair Disk

Mount Point : /   Capacity : 120.47 GB (120473067520 Bytes)
Format : Encrypted Logical Partition   Available : 3.67 GB (3668021248 Bytes)
Owners Enabled : Yes   Used : 116.81 GB (116805046272 Bytes)
Number of Folders : 213425   Number of Files : 957476

Figure 6-5:
Disk Utility informs you whether a device may need repairing.

Book III Chapter 6

Maintenance and Troubleshooting

You can verify your hard drive to identify any problems, but you can't repair your startup hard drive by using Disk Utility stored on your startup hard drive. To repair your startup hard drive, you need to perform a Recovery Boot or reinstall the operating system, as described in the following sections or boot from another disk, as explained in the Tip.

Performing a Recovery Boot

If you can't boot up from your hard drive, even in Safe Mode, or you can boot in Safe Mode but can't boot in normal mode and any utility application you run can't fix the problem, you may have to boot from the Recovery drive. OS X creates two partitions on your Mac's hard drive:

✦ One is what you see as your Mac hard drive, where everything you do with your Mac is stored.

✦ The other is the unseen Recovery drive, which contains a copy of the operating system and the Disk Utility application (the grayed Macintosh HD in Figure 6-4).

When you have problems, you can boot your Mac from the Recovery drive, which can then run the Disk Utility Repair Disk feature on your Mac's primary hard drive, restore your hard drive from a Time Machine backup, or reinstall the operating system and return your Mac to its original out-of-the-box condition.

TIP

Rather than boot from the Recovery drive, you may want to download the Recovery Disk Assistant (http://support.apple.com/kb/dl1433), which lets you create a Recovery Hard Drive on an external USB drive with least 1GB of storage. We advise you to have a dedicated USB thumb drive to store the Recovery Ddrive. In the event that your Mac won't boot at all, not even in Recovery mode, you can try booting from the Recovery Disk on the external drive.

Here's how to boot from the Recovery drive:

1. **Press the Power button to turn on your Mac (or choose ⌘⟶Restart) and hold down ⌘+R until you see the Apple logo.**

   The OS X Utilities window opens, as shown in Figure 6-6.

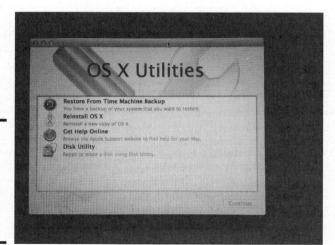

Figure 6-6: The Recovery drive may be able to repair your Mac.

2. **Select Disk Utility and then click Continue.**

3. **Select the Macintosh HD startup drive (or whatever your Mac's primary hard drive is named if you renamed it) in the left pane of the Disk Utility window.**

   The Mac OS X Base System is the Recovery drive, and you see that Repair Disk is gray because you can't repair the active system disk.

4. **Make sure that the First Aid pane is visible. (If it isn't, click the First Aid tab to call it up.)**

5. **Click the Repair Disk button.**

   The Repair feature of Disk Utility does what it can to fix any problems on your hard drive and informs you of its success — or failure.

6. **Choose Disk Utility➪Quit Disk Utility.**

   You see the Mac OS X Utilities window again.

7. **If the Disk Utility was able to repair your hard drive, choose ➪Restart.**

   Your Mac restarts, and you continue doing what you were doing before the problems began.

You can also use an app such as SuperDuper! (www.shirt-pocket.com) to clone your Mac's hard drive on an external drive, boot from that, and repair the internal hard drive with the Disk Utility on the external drive.

If Recovery Boot doesn't solve your problem, you can boot from a trouble-shooting disc that runs an app such as DiskWarrior (www.alsoft.com/DiskWarrior), Drive Genius (www.prosofteng.com), or Techtool Pro (www.micromat.com). By running any of these apps directly from the DVD or bootable USB flash drive, you can attempt to repair or resurrect any hard drive that fails to boot up on its own. Sometimes these troubleshooting DVDs can repair a hard drive, and sometimes they can't. If you have important files trapped on your hard drive, this option may be your only hope of retrieving your files to back them up before sending or taking your Mac to a repair service to repair or replace your Mac's hard drive.

You can use Safari to access the Internet from the Recovery disk. Before you go so far as reinstalling the operating system or erasing your Mac's hard drive, consult the Apple Support website (www.apple.com/support) and discussion boards (http://discussions.apple.com/index.jspa) to see whether someone else has had the same problem you're having — and maybe solved it.

Booting from another Mac through a Thunderbolt cable

You can also boot up from another Mac connected to your computer through an Ethernet or Thunderbolt cable. Either cable simply plugs into the respective ports of each Mac, connecting the two Macs. You may need a USB-Ethernet or Thunderbolt-Ethernet adapter if you have a MacBook model without an Ethernet port.

After connecting two Macs through a cable, you boot up the working Mac normally and boot up the other Mac in Target Mode. This makes the second Mac's hard drive appear as an external hard drive when viewed through the working Mac's Finder.

Using this approach, you can run a Disk Utility on the Target Mode Mac's hard drive (as described in the earlier section, "Verifying a disk") or you can run another hard-drive utility application (such as DiskWarrior, Drive Genius, or Techtool Pro) on the working Mac to rescue the hard drive of the defective Mac. This is much like jump-starting a car's dead battery by using a second car with a good battery.

To boot up from a second Mac connected by a cable, follow these steps:

1. **Connect the second Mac to your Mac with an Ethernet or a Thunderbolt cable.**

2. **Turn on the working Mac.**

3. **Turn on the Mac that's having startup troubles and hold down the T key.**

   When the defective Mac's hard drive appears as an external drive on the working Mac, you can copy your important files from the hard drive or run a utility application to fix the hard drive on the defective Mac. After copying files or repairing the hard drive, you need to disconnect the cable and restart both Macs.

Reinstalling the operating system

If neither Disk Utility nor a troubleshooting app solves your problem, the next thing to try is reinstalling the operating system from the Recovery drive. To reinstall the operating system, follow these steps:

1. **Press the Power button to turn on your Mac (or choose ⇨Restart) and hold down ⌘+R until you see the Apple logo.**

   The OS X Utilities window opens.

2. **Select Reinstall OS X and click Continue.**

   You must be connected to the Internet to reinstall OS X 10.9 Mavericks. Click the Wi-Fi icon in the menulet at the top of the screen to connect to your Wi-Fi network or connect via an Ethernet cable (see Book I, Chapter 3 to find out how to connect to the Internet).

3. **The installer verifies that you're a registered OS X Mavericks user.**

4. **Click Agree when the user agreement window appears.**

5. **Choose the hard drive where you want to reinstall and then click Install.**

6. **Follow the onscreen instructions and type in any requested information, such as username, e-mail, passwords, and so on.**

7. **When the installation is complete, your Mac restarts.**

Wipe out!

No one likes to reach this point, but if none of the procedures described in the earlier sections have solved your problem, you have to take drastic measures and *reformat* (completely erase) your hard drive, reinstall the operating system and apps, and restore your files from a backup. If you'd rather not take this step on your own, take your Mac to a trusted technician.

If you're ready to attempt to repair your Mac on your own by reformatting and starting over, here's how:

1. **Press the Power button to turn on your Mac (or choose Restart) and hold down ⌘+R until you see the Apple logo.**

   The OS X Utilities window opens.

2. **Select Disk Utility and then click Continue.**

3. **Select the Macintosh HD startup drive (or whatever your Mac's primary hard drive is named if you renamed it) from the left pane of the Disk Utility window.**

4. **Click the Erase tab at the top of the pane on the right.**

5. **Choose Mac OS Extended (Journaled) from the Format pop-up menu.**

6. **Click the Erase button.**

7. **When Disk Utility finishes erasing, choose Disk Utility⇨Quit Disk Utility.**

   The OS X Utilities window appears.

8. **Click Reinstall OS X and then click Continue.**

   Follow Steps 3–7 in the preceding section, "Reinstalling the operating system."

   When your Mac restarts, it's as new as when you took it out of the box, a tabula rasa.

9. **Connect the external drive where your Time Machine backup is stored.**

10. **Restore your Time Machine backup to your Mac (as we explain in Book III, Chapter 1).**

    Your Mac should be back to where it was before your problems began.

Erasing your hard drive and reinstalling the operating system from scratch will *also* wipe out any important files stored on your hard drive — *all* your files, in fact — so make sure that you're willing to accept this before erasing your hard drive. Ideally, you have a clone of your hard drive, or at least you should have all your important files backed up on a separate external drive, such as an external hard drive, flash drive, or remote storage site, before wiping out your hard drive completely.

Another occasion when you may want to erase your hard drive and reinstall the operating system is if you plan on selling your Mac or giving it away. For security reasons, you want to wipe out your data with one of the secure-erase options in Disk Utility and return the Mac to its original condition so someone else can personalize the Mac.

Removing Jammed CDs or DVDs

If a CD or DVD gets jammed in your Mac's internal or external CD/DVD drive, you can try one (or more) of the following methods to eject the stuck disc:

✦ If it has one, press the Eject key on your keyboard. (The MacBook Air, for example, does not have an Eject key, because it doesn't have an internal disc drive).

✦ Drag the CD/DVD icon on the Desktop to the Trash icon on the Dock. (The Trash icon turns into an Eject icon to let you know that your Mac wants to eject the disc but does not intend to delete the information on the disc.)

✦ Choose ⌘⇨Restart, and hold down the mouse or trackpad button while your Mac boots up.

✦ Click the Eject button next to the CD/DVD icon in the Sidebar of a Finder window. (Click the Mac-faced Finder icon on the Dock to open a new Finder window.)

✦ Click the Eject button next to the CD/DVD icon in iTunes.

✦ Choose Controls⇨Eject DVD from inside the DVD Player application.

✦ Load the Disk Utility application (located in the Utilities folder inside the Applications folder), click the CD/DVD icon, and click the Eject icon.

✦ Select the CD/DVD icon on the Desktop and choose File⇨Eject from the main menu.

✦ Select the CD/DVD icon on the Desktop and press ⌘+E.

✦ Control-click the CD/DVD icon on the Desktop and choose Eject from the menu that appears.

Although it may be tempting, don't jam tweezers, a flathead screwdriver, or any other object inside your CD/DVD drive to try to pry out a jammed disc. Not only can this scratch the disc surface, but it can also physically damage the CD/DVD drive.

Prevention is the best medicine, so here a few pointers on how to avoid getting discs jammed in the drive in the first place:

✦ Do not use mini or business card CDs/DVDs or any other non-119mm optical discs in slot-loading drives, which you slide the disc into a slot.

✦ Be careful of using discs with hand-applied labels in the drive. These labels can easily jam or make the disc too thick to eject properly.

✦ If your Mac's disc drive is repeatedly acting strange or not working properly when you try to play a music CD or watch a DVD, your disc drive may be on its last legs and may have to be repaired or replaced. Stop using the drive and take (or send) your Mac to Apple or an authorized service provider for a checkup.

If you purchase an external optical disc drive, instead of Apple's SuperDrive, you may be happier with a tray-loading drive. They tend to be faster, have fewer problems, and last longer.

Automating Preventive Maintenance

Your Mac has daily, weekly, and monthly maintenance tasks that it runs periodically early in the morning if you leave your Mac on at night. However, if your Mac is asleep during this time, it won't run these maintenance tasks. You can get out of bed before dawn every day and wake your Mac so it can run its maintenance tasks (ugh), or you can wisely set up your Mac to run its daily, weekly, and monthly maintenance tasks automatically.

To automate running your Mac's preventive maintenance apps, consider getting an application called MainMenu (`http://mainmenuapp.com/pro.php`).

To force your Mac to run its maintenance tasks automatically, follow these steps:

1. **Load the Terminal application (located in the Utilities folder inside the Applications folder or on the Launchpad).**

The Terminal window appears, as shown in Figure 6-7.

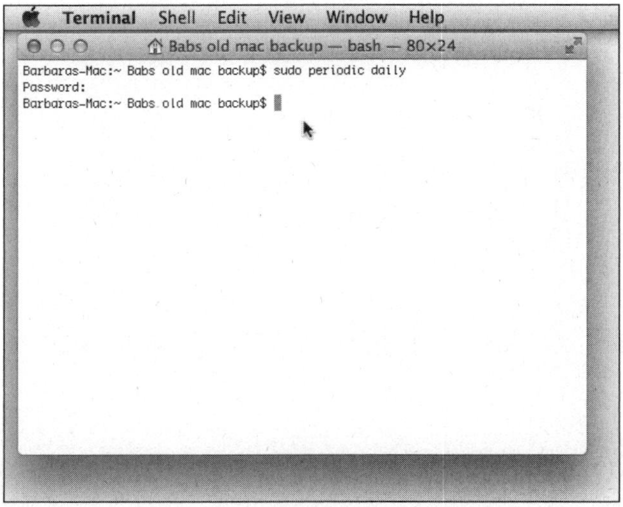

Book III
Chapter 6

Maintenance and
Troubleshooting

```
  Terminal  Shell  Edit  View  Window  Help
  ● ○ ○       ⌂ Babs old mac backup — bash — 80×24
Barbaras-Mac:~ Babs old mac backup$ sudo periodic daily
Password:
Barbaras-Mac:~ Babs old mac backup$ ▊

                          ▶
```

Figure 6-7:
Use
Terminal to
run maintenance tasks.

2. **Type** sudo periodic daily **and then press Return.**

   The Terminal window asks for your password.

   To make your Mac run weekly or monthly maintenance tasks, type **sudo periodic weekly** or **sudo periodic monthly**, respectively. Weekly and monthly tasks can take a long time to run. You'll know when a maintenance task is done when you see the cryptic-looking prompt (such as `mycomputer$`) reappear.

3. **Type your password and then press Return.**

   Wait until you see the Terminal prompt (such as `mycomputer$`) reappear.

4. **Choose Terminal⇨Quit Terminal.**

   The Terminal app lets you interact with the Mac operating system. Of course, you don't want to go messing around too much unless you know UNIX programming, but it can be useful to set up simple tasks like the one we explain here. In case you're wondering, *sudo* stands for substitute user do, as in take action.

Book IV

Your Mac as Multimedia Entertainment Center

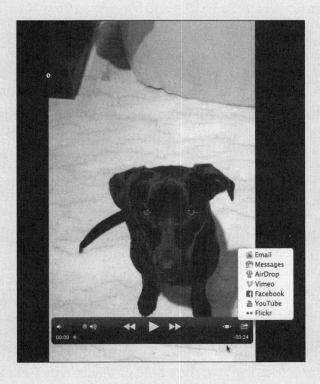

Contents at a Glance

Chapter 1: Tuning In and Listening with iTunes

In This Chapter

↙ **Looking at the iTunes window**

↙ **Setting your iTunes preferences**

↙ **Listening to audio in iTunes**

↙ **Creating playlists**

↙ **Tuning in to iTunes Radio**

↙ **Watching videos in iTunes**

↙ **Browsing and buying from the iTunes Store**

↙ **Sharing media**

Your Mac comes with the iTunes app, which you use to organize, play, and convert audio and video — and which also doubles as a disc-burning app. The most recent version of iTunes (at the time we wrote this), 11.1.3, contains iTunes Radio that lets you create custom stations based on music you feel like listening to — as long as you're connected to the Internet.

In this chapter, we tell you how iTunes is set up and how to listen to your music or iTunes Radio or watch a movie on iTunes. We show you how to set up playlists on your own or let iTunes do it for you with Genius. We also give you a tour of the iTunes Store so you can find out how to add other media to your Mac — so have your Apple ID handy. Finally, we explain how to share media with other people.

Getting to Know the iTunes Window

You can use iTunes to play music on your Mac, but iTunes shows its real strength when you use it to organize your media files. If you tend to have CDs stacked in the cupboard under your stereo and others sliding around under the passenger seat of your car and still more CDs in a desk drawer at work, moving all your music into iTunes helps you manage your music in one place. Before we get into listening, watching, and learning, we want to explain how iTunes manages your media.

You have many ways to customize your view of content you keep in iTunes. Figure 1-1 shows one of them.

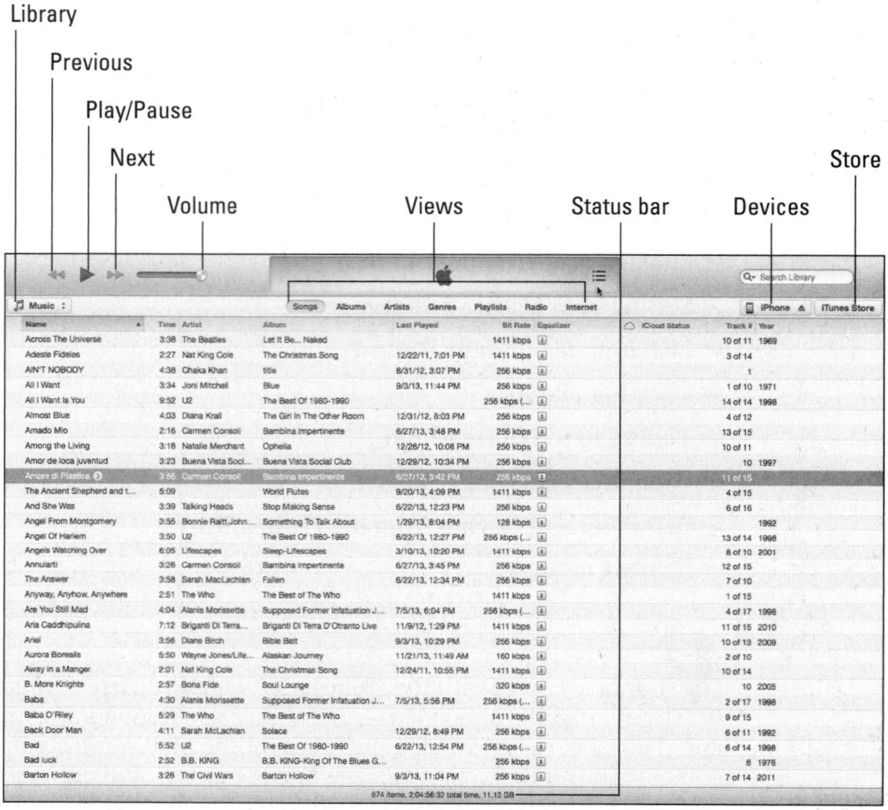

Library

Previous

Play/Pause

Next

Volume

Views

Status bar

Devices

Store

Figure 1-1:
Manage
your media
from the
iTunes
window.

+ **Toolbar:** Across the top, you find the playback and volume controls, the now-playing display, and the Search field.

+ **Library:** Displayed to the far left, just under the toolbar, is the Library button, which opens a pop-up menu that shows the media categories Music (which includes music videos), Movies, TV Shows, Podcasts, iTunes U, Audiobooks, Apps, and Tones, if you add any to the library. If your Library isn't divided by category, choose Files⇨Library⇨Organize Library. Select the Reorganize Files check box and then click OK. iTunes automatically divides your media by type. (If you select View⇨Show Sidebar this display changes and you see media categories listed in a sidebar instead of a pop-up menu.)

+ **View:** The buttons in the center, just under the toolbar, change the display choices. If you choose Music from the Library pop-up menu (or sidebar), you see the choices (as in Figure 1-1) for Songs, Albums, Artists, and so on. Should you choose Movies from the Library pop-up menu, the view buttons change according to that category.

To tweak the various views — for example, add or change the columns you see in Songs view — choose View⇨Show View Options, as shown in Figure 1-2, and select the things you want to see. Open the Sort By menu to change the order of the selections. Each view — Albums, Artists, Genres, Playlists, and Internet — has different view options except for Radio, which has no view options.

To narrow the choices the Songs or Playlists view displays, choose View⇨Column Browser⇨Show Column Browser and then click the columns you want to see. The selected columns appear above the list of songs, from which you then select specific genres, artists, albums, composers, or groupings.

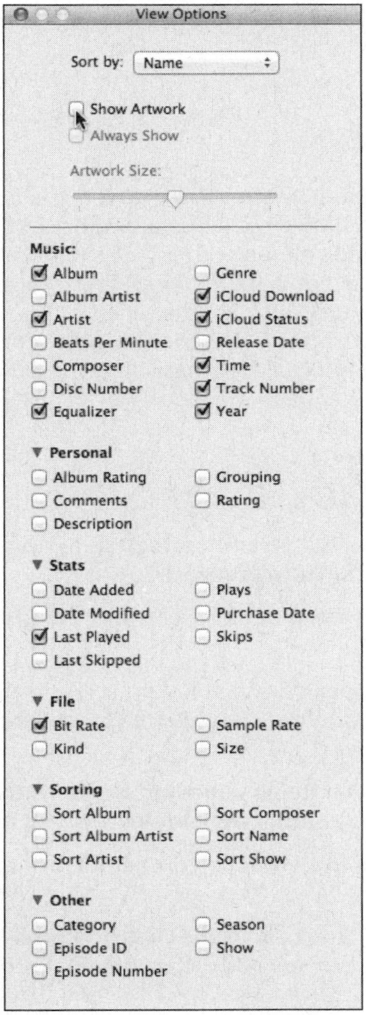

Figure 1-2:
Customize the information you see with View Options.

View Options

Sort by: Name

☐ Show Artwork
☐ Always Show

Artwork Size:

Music:
☑ Album ☐ Genre
☐ Album Artist ☑ iCloud Download
☑ Artist ☑ iCloud Status
☐ Beats Per Minute ☐ Release Date
☐ Composer ☑ Time
☐ Disc Number ☑ Track Number
☑ Equalizer ☑ Year

▼ **Personal**
☐ Album Rating ☐ Grouping
☐ Comments ☐ Rating
☐ Description

▼ **Stats**
☐ Date Added ☐ Plays
☐ Date Modified ☐ Purchase Date
☑ Last Played ☐ Skips
☐ Last Skipped

▼ **File**
☑ Bit Rate ☐ Sample Rate
☐ Kind ☐ Size

▼ **Sorting**
☐ Sort Album ☐ Sort Composer
☐ Sort Album Artist ☐ Sort Name
☐ Sort Artist ☐ Sort Show

▼ **Other**
☐ Category ☐ Season
☐ Episode ID ☐ Show
☐ Episode Number

**Book IV
Chapter 1**

**Tuning In and
Listening with
iTunes**

✦ **Devices:** When you connect a device (such as an iPhone or MP3 player) to your Mac, you see this button (or pop-up menu if more than one device is connected). Click that button or choose a device from the pop-up menu to open the options for syncing your device with iTunes; click the Eject button to remove the device from your computer safely.

✦ **iTunes Store:** Click this button to go to the iTunes Store, which we discus later in this chapter.

✦ **Status bar:** Choose View⇨Show Status Bar to see (across the bottom of the window) the number of items in a category, the playing time, and the amount of storage the media occupies.

If you're familiar with an older version of iTunes and prefer to see the Source list sidebar on the left side of the window, choose View⇨Show Sidebar, and the pop-up menu under the toolbar is replaced with the Source List sidebar.

Adjusting iTunes Preferences

Choosing how iTunes should respond when you insert a CD, what type of audio file format it uses to import your CD audio tracks, and which Library categories you want to display in the left-hand column of the iTunes application window are all options you can adjust by accessing the iTunes Preferences dialog. We go through the General and Parental Control preferences in this section, and throughout the chapter, we direct you to Preferences to adjust other aspects of iTunes. To open the iTunes Preferences dialog and adjust the settings, follow these steps:

1. **Choose iTunes⇨Preferences.**

The iTunes Preferences window appears.

2. **Click the General icon (if it isn't already selected) to display the General settings pane, as shown in Figure 1-3.**

3. **(Optional) Click the Library Name field if you want to give your library a different name.**

This is the name that will appear if you share your iTunes library through the iTunes Sharing preferences pane or Home Sharing, as explained later in this chapter.

4. **Select the check boxes for the items you want to see in the Library pop-up menu or sidebar, depending on which view you use.**

5. **Select the check boxes for the choices you prefer in the Views section.**

6. **Select or deselect the check boxes in the Notifications section to indicate whether you want to see song changes in Notification Center.**

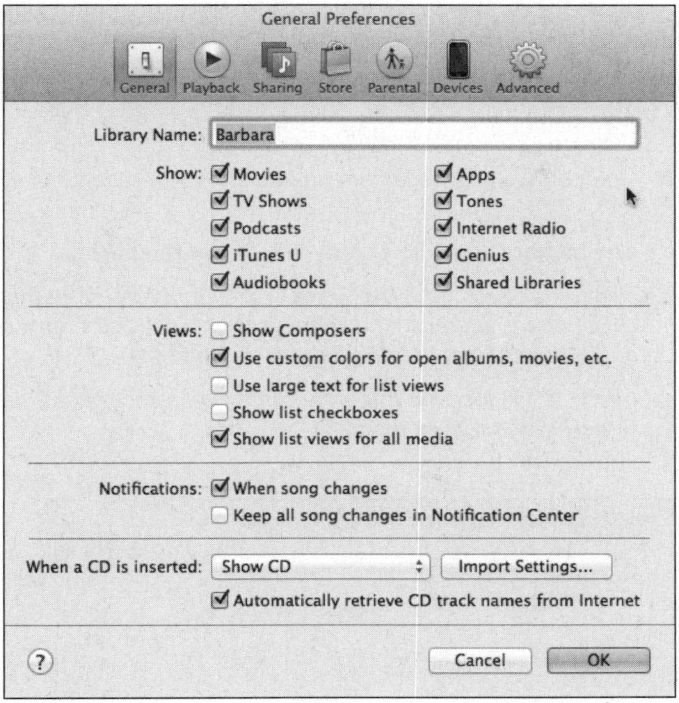

Figure 1-3:
Tailor iTunes
to your
liking.

7. **To specify what you want to happen whenever you insert an audio CD into your Mac, open the When a CD Is Inserted pop-up menu and choose one of the following:**

   - *Show CD:* Displays a list of audio tracks

   - *Play CD:* Displays a list of audio tracks and starts playing the first track

   - *Ask to Import CD:* Displays a dialog, asking whether you want to import all audio tracks from the CD (this is the default setting)

   - *Import CD:* Automatically converts all audio tracks into digital files

   - *Import CD and Eject:* Automatically converts all audio tracks into digital files and ejects the CD when it finishes without playing any tracks

8. **To specify the file format and audio quality of the audio files iTunes will create when importing CD audio tracks, click the Import Settings button.**

   The Import Settings preferences pane opens, as shown in Figure 1-4.

   a. *Open the Import Using pop-up menu and choose one of the following (see the nearby sidebar, "Understanding audio file compression formats" for more information):*

   AAC Encoder: Stores audio tracks as AAC files

   AIFF Encoder: Stores audio tracks as AIFF files

Apple Lossless Encoder: Stores audio tracks as a lossless compressed `.m4a` file

MP3 Encoder: Stores audio tracks as MP3 files

WAV Encoder: Stores audio tracks as WAV files

b. *Open the Setting pop-up menu and choose the audio quality for your files.*

The higher the audio quality, the larger the file size.

c. *(Optional) Select the Use Error Correction When Reading Audio CDs check box to increase the chances that iTunes can retrieve and convert audio tracks from a damaged or scratched CD.*

d. *Click OK to close the Import Settings preferences pane and return to the General Preferences pane.*

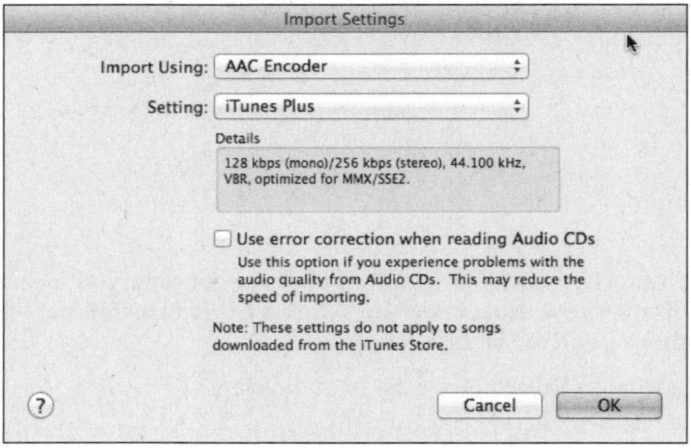

Figure 1-4:
Choose the file format iTunes uses to convert audio tracks from your CD.

Import Settings

Import Using: AAC Encoder

Setting: iTunes Plus

Details

128 kbps (mono)/256 kbps (stereo), 44.100 kHz, VBR, optimized for MMX/SSE2.

☐ Use error correction when reading Audio CDs

Use this option if you experience problems with the audio quality from Audio CDs. This may reduce the speed of importing.

Note: These settings do not apply to songs downloaded from the iTunes Store.

Cancel   OK

9. **Select the Automatically Retrieve CD Track Names from Internet check box if you want iTunes to try to identify audio tracks by their song titles.**

If this option isn't selected, each audio track will have a generic name (such as Track 1).

10. **(Optional) If you share your Mac with children, you may want to set up some Parental Control preferences which can limit the type of media that can be accessed in sharing or the iTunes Store. Click the Parental button at the top of the Preferences window, as shown in Figure 1-5, and do the following in the Parental Controls window that opens:**

- *Disable:* Select the check boxes for Podcasts, Internet Radio, iTunes Store, and/or Shared Libraries to deny access to those categories.

- *Ratings For:* Use the pop-up menu to change the country you want to see ratings for.

- *Restrict:* Choose limits you want to place on specific media, such as music, movie ratings, age ranges for TV shows and apps, or books.

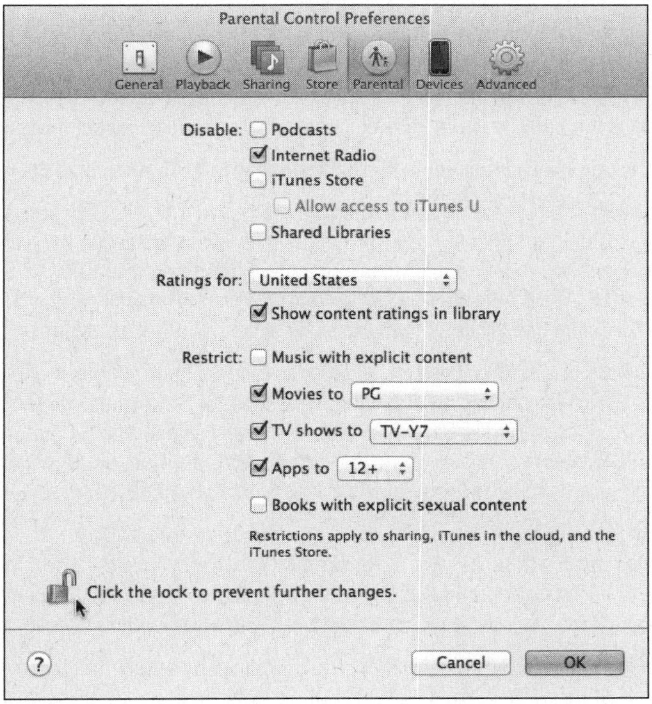

Figure 1-5:
Limit what media can be accessed in iTunes.

Then click the lock icon so changes can be made to the Parental Control preferences only after you enter your user password.

11. Click OK to close the iTunes Preferences dialog.

You return to the main iTunes application window.

Understanding audio file compression formats

Audio files offer tremendous advantages in storage and audio quality compared with previous forms of audio storage. However, dozens of different audio file compression types — the underlying conversion technology used to save audio as digital files — are out there. Therefore, to hear different audio files, you may need to use different applications. Think of having to buy two radios because one radio receives only AM stations, and the second radio receives only FM stations.

Different types of audio file compression formats exist because each file format offers certain advantages. The standard approaches to audio file compression are three schemes used for saving audio as digital files: lossless (no compression), lossless compression, and lossy compression.

Remember: Your Mac can play almost any audio file format as long as you install the right software.

✔ **Lossless audio files:** The highest-quality audio files are called *lossless* because they never lose any audio data. Lossless audio files offer the highest-quality sound, but they also create the largest file sizes. The two most popular lossless audio file formats are WAV (Waveform Audio File Format) and AIFF (Audio Interchange File Format). WAV files typically end with the `.wav` file extension, and AIFF files typically end with the `.aiff` or `.aif` file extension.

✔ **Compressed lossless audio files:** Lossless audio files take up large amounts of space, so compressed lossless audio files are designed to squeeze audio data into a smaller file size. Three popular compressed lossless audio file formats are FLAC (Free Lossless Audio Codec), Shorten, and Apple Lossless. FLAC files typically end with the `.flac` file extension, Shorten files typically end with the `.shn` file extension, and Apple Lossless files typically end with the `.m4a` file extension.

Remember: You can play Apple Lossless files in iTunes, but not FLAC or Shorten audio files. To play FLAC files, grab a free copy of flukeformac (`https://code.google.com/p/flukeformac/`) or VLC Media Player (`www.videolan.org/vlc`). To play Shorten files, use Audion (`www.panic.com/audion`), which is still available although not actively updated.

✔ **Compressed lossy audio files:** A *lossy* audio file compresses audio files by stripping certain audio data to shrink the file size. Think of pulling unnecessary clothing from a suitcase to lighten the load. The greater the audio quality, the more audio data the file needs to retain — and the bigger the file. The smaller the file, the less audio data the file can hold, but at a lower audio quality. As a result, most audio file formats strive for an optimal balance between audio quality and file size.

The amount of data an audio file format retains is measured in kilobits per second (Kbps). The higher the kilobits, the more data is stored and the higher the audio quality. The following table shows approximate kilobit values and the audio quality they produce.

Bit Rate (Kilobits per Second)	Audio Quality
32 Kbps	AM radio quality.
96 Kbps	FM radio quality.
128–160 Kbps	Good quality, but differences from the original audio source can be noticeable.

Bit Rate (Kilobits per Second)	Audio Quality
192 Kbps	Medium quality; slight differences from the original audio source can be heard.
224–320 Kbps	High quality; little loss of audio quality from the original source.

The most popular compressed lossy audio file formats are MP3 (MPEG-1 Audio Layer 3), AAC (Advanced Audio Coding), and WMA (Windows Media Audio). You can recognize MP3 audio files by their `.mp3` file extension.

The iTunes alternative to MP3 files is the AAC audio file format. AAC audio files offer greater audio quality and smaller file compression than equivalent MP3 files. The AAC format offers a Digital Rights Management (DRM) feature that allows copy protection; however, music you download today from iTunes is DRM-free. AAC files typically end with the `.aac` or `.m4a` file extension (if it doesn't have DRM) or the `.m4p` file extension (if it does have DRM).

Playing Audio with iTunes

iTunes turns your Mac into a stereo system and radio. You can play the most common audio files (MP3, WAV, AAC, and AIFF) on your Mac and connect headphones or external speakers to upgrade the playback quality and listening experience.

You don't have to use iTunes to play audio CDs and digital audio files on your Mac. You can always use another audio player on your Mac (such as RealPlayer, which you can get free at `www.real.com` or VLC Media Player at `www.videolan.org/vlc`). These other audio players can be especially useful if you want to play oddball audio formats like Ogg Vorbis or FLAC, but in most cases, you'll probably find that iTunes works just fine.

To launch iTunes, click the iTunes icon on the Dock or Launchpad.

Listening to CDs

You probably have audio CDs of your favorite albums, but rather than play them in a CD player, you can play them on your Mac — with an internal or external optical disc drive — by using iTunes. Much like a CD player, iTunes can play audio tracks on a CD in order or randomly. Even better, iTunes lets you choose which audio tracks you want to hear. To play an audio CD in iTunes, follow these steps:

1. **With iTunes open, insert an audio CD into your Mac.**

A dialog may appear (depending on the iTunes Preferences settings you choose), asking whether you want to import all audio tracks on the CD into iTunes. We discuss this process in the next section. For now, click No.

**Book IV
Chapter 1**

Tuning In and
Listening with
iTunes

If you're connected to the Internet, iTunes searches a website called Gracenote for information about the CD you inserted, based on multiple criteria, including the number, order, and length of tracks on the CD. If Gracenote finds a match for your CD, iTunes displays that information, which can include the album name and artist, track titles, and (if available in the iTunes Store), the album's cover artwork.

2. **Click the Play button or press the spacebar to start playing your selected audio tracks.**

   The Play button toggles to a Pause button (which you can click to pause the track you're listening to).

3. **When you finish listening to the CD, eject it by choosing Controls⇨ Eject Disc or by clicking the Eject Disc icon to the right of the CD icon.**

If you have a stereo, iTunes playback controls in the toolbar across the top of the window will look familiar (refer to Figure 1-1). You have a few extra options, which you access from the iTunes menu and preferences:

✦ **Volume slider:** Drag the volume slider to adjust the sound.

✦ **Adjust play:** Click one of the following buttons:

   • *Pause:* Temporarily stops playing audio. You can also press the spacebar to toggle the Play and Pause button.

   • *Previous:* Starts playing the selected audio track from the beginning. Clicking the Previous button a second time starts playing the previous audio track from the beginning.

   • *Next:* Skips the selected audio track and starts playing the next audio track.

✦ **Selective play:** Deselect the check boxes of any audio tracks you don't want to hear.

✦ **Random play:** Click the Shuffle button or choose Controls⇨Shuffle⇨ Turn On Shuffle to play your audio tracks in random order. Choosing the Shuffle command again toggles off random play.

✦ **Repeat-selection play:** Choose Controls⇨Repeat⇨All to play the selected audio tracks continuously on the CD or Repeat⇨One to repeat the same song. (Choose Controls⇨Repeat Off to toggle off the Repeat Play feature.)

✦ **Equalizer:** Choose Window⇨Equalizer and select one of the 22 preset frequency options closest to the type of media you're listening to, such as R&B, Classical, Small Speakers, or Spoken Word. You can also adjust the equalizer settings manually (see Figure 1-6).

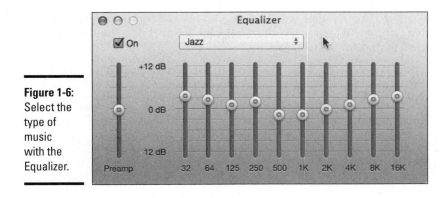

Figure 1-6:
Select the
type of
music
with the
Equalizer.

✦ **Preferences:** Choose iTunes⇨Preferences⇨Playback to adjust a few of
your playback options.

• *Crossfade Songs:* Move the slider to set the length of silence between
songs.

• *Sound Enhancer:* Move the slider from low to high to boost the sound
quality.

• *Sound Check:* Sometimes songs play at different volumes. Select the
Sound Check option so all songs are played at the same volume.

Control-click the iTunes icon on the Dock to bring up a playback controls
menu.

Importing a CD's audio tracks into iTunes

If you have a CD that you often listen to, just import the music into iTunes.
Converting audio tracks on a CD into digital audio files is *ripping.* After you
adjust the iTunes import settings (see the earlier section, "Adjusting iTunes
Preferences"), you're ready to rip.

By default, iTunes saves songs imported from your CDs as high-quality
iTunes Plus files in the 256 Kbps AAC format.

To convert an audio disc into digital files, open iTunes and follow these
steps:

1. **Insert an audio CD into your Mac's optical disc drive, internal or
external.**

Depending on how you set the iTunes preferences, a dialog may appear,
asking whether you want to import all audio tracks on the CD into
iTunes. Click Yes if you want to convert every audio track into a digital
audio file and import to iTunes. If you want to import only some of the
songs, click No and continue with the following steps.

If, in the iTunes Preferences dialog, you chose Play CD or Import CD, that action will take place automatically. If you chose Show CD, you see the window shown in Figure 1-7.

If the tracks of the CD don't appear in the central pane of iTunes, click the name of the CD in the Library pop-up menu.

2. **To choose which songs to import, deselect the check boxes of the tracks you don't want to import.**

   Check marks should appear in the check boxes of the audio tracks you want to import.

   If you don't see check boxes, choose iTunes⇨Preferences, click the General tab, and then select Show List Checkboxes in the Views section.

3. **Click the Options button and choose Get Track Names if you didn't select the automatic option in iTunes Preferences.**

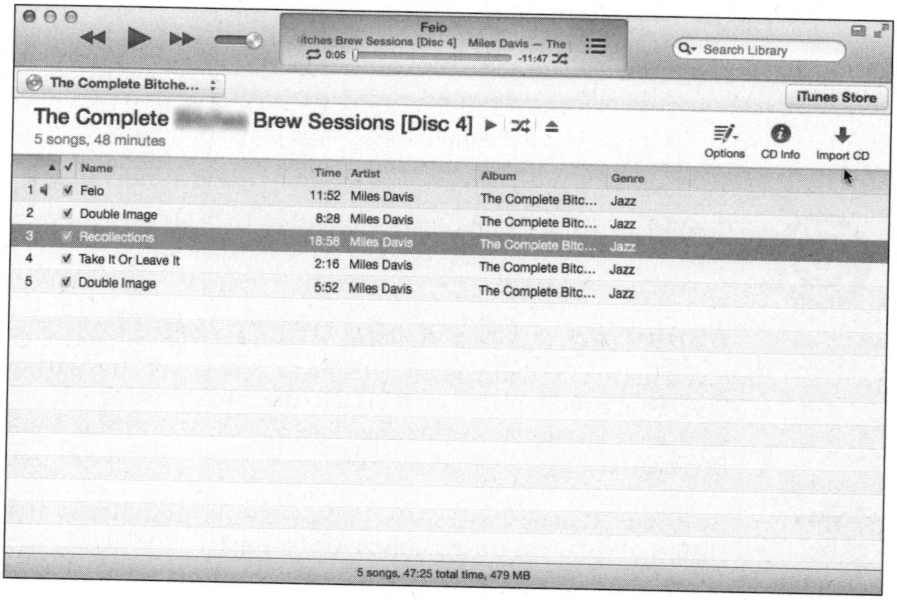

Figure 1-7:
Import all or some of the songs from a CD when you insert it.

4. **(Optional) Click the CD Info button to see information about the CD, such as the artist or year of publication.**

5. **Click the Import CD button in the upper-right corner of the iTunes window.**

   The Import Settings window opens (refer to Figure 1-7). AAC is the default encoding format; choose a different format from the pop-up menus if you prefer. Otherwise, click OK, and the iTunes app converts and copies all (or the selected) audio tracks into digital audio files and saves them to your Mac's hard drive in your Music folder.

The now-playing display indicates which track is being copied and how long it will take to copy. It takes about ten minutes to import a full CD. A white check mark in a green circle appears next to tracks that have been successfully imported.

6. **When iTunes finishes importing your CD's audio tracks, eject the CD by choosing Controls⇨Eject Disc or by clicking the Eject Disc icon to the right of the CD name in the Library pop-up menu.**

To download album cover artwork for CDs that you import to iTunes, choose File⇨Library⇨Get Album Artwork. You need an iTunes account or an Apple ID. If you have an iTunes account or Apple ID, choose Store⇨Sign In to sign in. To create an Apple ID, see Book I, Chapter 3. After you sign in, iTunes begins downloading album artwork. The now-playing display shows which album iTunes is working on and how much time remains.

Importing digital audio files

Besides ripping audio tracks from a CD and storing them on your Mac, you might also get digital audio files through the Internet or handed to you on a flash drive or an external hard drive. Before you can play any digital audio files in iTunes, you must first import those files, which essentially copies them into the iTunes folder inside your Music folder.

You can simply drag files into your iTunes library, or you can follow these steps:

1. **In iTunes, choose File⇨Add to Library to open the Add to Library dialog.**

2. **Navigate to and select the folder, audio files, or files you want to import into iTunes, and then click Choose.**

   iTunes imports the folder, audio files, or files into your Music folder.

If you download music from an online source other than iTunes, select the Automatically Add to iTunes option when selecting the destination for saving a downloaded a file, and the file shows up in your iTunes library.

What's more, if you have lower-quality audio files from various sources, consider subscribing to iTunes Match. For $24.99 per year (as of this writing), iTunes Match looks at your iTunes library and upgrades songs that you own and that are available in the iTunes Store to iTunes Plus quality. As an added bonus, with an iTunes Match subscription, iTunes Radio is ad-free. Choose Store⇨Turn On iTunes Match and follow the onscreen instructions to subscribe.

If you poke around in your Mac's folders and files and see two Library files in iTunes, don't delete one just because it *looks* like a duplicate. iTunes stores your media in two Library folders. One holds the actual media files, and the other makes media available to other apps, such as Keynote or iMovie.

Searching your iTunes library

After you copy music (and eventually other media) into iTunes, you may not be able to find what you're looking for in your library. To find a song, podcast, TV show, or any other media you store on iTunes, you can search by typing some or all of a song, album, or show title, artist name, and so on. To search iTunes, follow these steps:

1. **Click the library you want to search in — for example, Music or Podcasts.**

2. **Click the triangle next to the magnifying glass to choose which field you want to search, or select All to search all fields associated with the library you chose in Step 1.**

3. **Click the Search field in the upper-right corner of the iTunes window and then type part of the title, album, TV series, or other item that you want to find.**

   Each time you type a letter in the Search field, iTunes narrows the list of potential matches.

4. **Click the media you want to play.**

   Read the next section to find out more about playback.

Playing digital audio files

After you import one or more audio files into iTunes, you can view your list of audio files, as outlined in the beginning of this chapter in the "Getting to Know the iTunes Window" section. Refer to the earlier section, "Listening to CDs," for details on the playback controls. To play one or more audio files, follow these steps:

1. **Choose a view for displaying your audio file collection, such as Songs, Albums, or Artists.**

2. **Select songs with one of the following methods.**

   As you select songs, they're added to Up Next, which is a list of songs in the order in which they'll play. Click the Up Next button in the now-playing display to see the list of upcoming songs.

   • *Checkboxes:* If you use Checkboxes, select the check boxes of the audio tracks you want to hear and deselect the check boxes of audio tracks you don't want to hear.

     To deselect all audio tracks so you don't have to listen to them, hold down the ⌘ key and select a check box. To reselect all audio tracks, repeat the process.

   • *Menu:* If you don't use Checkboxes, click the disclosure triangle next to a song and choose Play Next from the pop-up menu. Continue to choose other songs but select Add to Up Next in the pop-up menu.

Choose another view, such as Albums, Artists, or Genres, click the album, artist, or genre you want to hear, and then click the Play button. Click the disclosure triangle next to the album, artist, or genre name to add all the songs on the album, by the artist, or in the genre to Up Next, as shown in Figure 1-8. You can also select songs singly from any of these views by hovering the pointer over the song, clicking the disclosure triangle that appears, and selecting Add to Up Next.

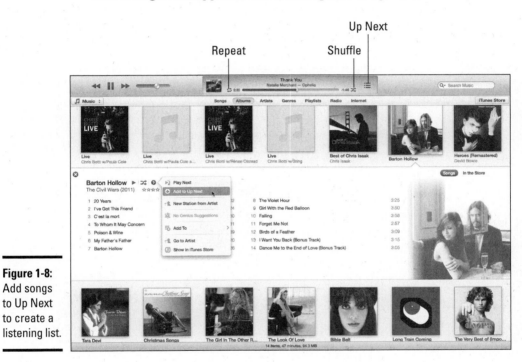

Figure 1-8: Add songs to Up Next to create a listening list.

3. **Click the Play button or press the spacebar to start playing your selected audio tracks.**

   The Play button toggles to a Pause button.

4. **Click the Repeat and/or Shuffle buttons in the now-playing display to use those options (see Figure 1-8).**

5. **To manage the Up Next list, click the Up Next button, and then choose what to do from the following:**

   • *To delete all songs in the Up Next list:* Click the Clear button.

   • *To show your listening history:* Click the Clock icon. Click it again to see the Up Next list.

- *To remove a song from Up Next:* Hover the pointer over a song and then click the X that appears on the left side.

- *To move a song to a new (higher or lower) position on the Up Next list:* Click and drag the song to its new position in the Up Next list.

- *To see more options:* Hover the pointer over a song and click the disclosure triangle for more options, as shown in Figure 1-9. Go To choices take you to the artist, song, or album in your iTunes library. New Station choices relate to iTunes Radio, which we talk about later. The Add To choice is for Playlist, which we talk about next.

If you have an iPhone, iPad, or iPod touch and a Wi-Fi network, you can download the Remote app from the App Store and control iTunes with your device.

Figure 1-9: Manage the Up Next list.

To reduce the playback controls to a small window, choose View⇨Switch to Mini Player, or click the Mini Player button at the top right of the window. To reduce the Mini Player to an even smaller window (both shown in Figure 1-10) that you can leave on the Desktop so you can listen and control your music while you're using your Mac to do other things, click the Up Next button.

For working with other media, see Book IV, Chapter 2, to learn about watching video and movies on your Mac and Book IV, Chapter 6, for information about reading e-books, listening to podcasts, and learning at iTunes U.

Figure 1-10: The Mini Player puts controls on your Desktop.

Burning an audio CD

Ubiquitous Wi-Fi, broadband cellular networks, and Apple's iCloud service make accessing and sharing digital files between your Mac and other iOS devices (such as an iPod touch or iPhone) quick and easy. However, if you find that you still want your music on a CD, you can use the iTunes disc-burning feature to copy your favorite audio files to a CD that you can play whenever you don't have the option of listening to music with iTunes on your Mac or iOS device.

CDs can hold approximately 70 to 80 minutes of audio. More stereos can recognize and play CD-Rs although newer stereos can recognize and play CD-RWs as well. (CD-Rs let you write to them only once, whereas CD-RWs allow you to erase and reuse them.)

To burn an audio CD, first create a playlist, and then instruct iTunes to copy all the songs in the playlist to an audio CD, as follows:

1. **Click the playlist you want to burn to CD.**

2. **(Optional) Deselect the check boxes of any songs you don't want to burn to the CD.**

3. **(Optional) Arrange the songs in the order you want them to play on the CD.**

   To arrange songs in a playlist, click in the first column (that displays the number of each song) and then drag a song up or down to a new position.

4. **Choose File⇨Burn Playlist to Disc.**

   The Burn Settings dialog appears, offering different radio buttons for choosing the type of CD you want to burn, such as Audio CD, MP3 CD, or Data CD, as shown in Figure 1-11. Audio CD is your best choice because some players don't recognize MP3 CDs, and Data CDs won't be playable.

Figure 1-11: Choose the type of CD you want to burn.

5. **Select a Disc Format radio button (Audio CD, MP3 CD, or Data CD).**

   If you choose Audio CD, consider these additional options:

   - (Optional) *Gap between Songs:* From this menu, choose None or from 1 to 5 Seconds to specify the amount of silence between song tracks.

   - (Optional) *Use Sound Check:* Select this check box to instruct iTunes to ensure that all the song tracks play from the CD at the same volume level.

   - (Optional) *Include CD Text:* Select this check box to display information about the CD on CD player models that offer a CD text information feature.

6. **(Optional) Open the Preferred Speed pop-up menu and choose a disc burning speed, such as Maximum Possible or 24x.**

   If the CDs you burn on your Mac don't play correctly on other CD players, choose a slower burning speed. Otherwise, use the Maximum Possible option.

7. **Click the Burn button.**

8. **When prompted, insert a blank CD-R or CD-RW into your Mac's internal or external optical disc drive.**

   The now-playing display of the iTunes window displays the progress of your disc burning. If you're burning more than one or two songs, you now have enough time to go get a cup of coffee, tea, or another beverage of your choosing.

Playing Around with Playlists

If you're a professional disc jockey or an event planner, you know how the sequence and mix of songs can set the mood of a crowd. Some songs provide background music that unconsciously stimulates calm conversation, while other songs grab your attention or inspire you to set foot on the dance floor. Rather than go through the hassle of selecting the same group of songs over and over, you can use iTunes to select a group of songs once and store that list as a *playlist*. When you want to hear the group of songs, just select the playlist rather than each song. You might choose calming New Age instrumentals when you're studying, a classic rock jam to keep you moving while housecleaning, and a jazz or blues mix to play in the background at a dinner party.

You create ordinary playlists or Smart Playlists, and iTunes creates Genius shuffles, playlists, and mixes — as long as you have an Internet connection.

✦ **Ordinary playlist:** A list of favorite songs you select to include in that playlist.

✦ **Smart Playlist:** You define rules for which songs to include, such as only songs recorded by a specific artist. As your audio file collection grows, a Smart Playlist can automatically include any new songs by that specific artist or by whatever other criteria you define for the particular Smart Playlist.

✦ **Genius playlist, shuffle, and mix:** iTunes creates Genius playlists based on a song you choose, but iTunes thinks for itself to create a Genius shuffle or Genius mix based on a genre that you choose.

All playlists are listed when you click the Playlist button. By default, iTunes already includes several Smart Playlists, including Recently Added, Recently Played, and Top 25 Most Played.

Creating an ordinary playlist

The simplest playlist to create is one that contains specific songs, such as a favorite album, a group of songs you want to listen to when you go for a run or workout, or perhaps every song by a particular artist. To create a playlist of particular songs you want to group, follow these steps:

1. **In iTunes, click the Playlists button at the top of the window.**

2. **Click the Add (+) button in the bottom-left corner and then choose New Playlist from the pop-up menu.**

Alternatively, choose File➪New➪Playlist.

An untitled playlist appears, highlighted, in a new pane on the right side of the window, as shown in Figure 1-12.

Book IV
Chapter 1

Tuning In and Listening with iTunes

Figure 1-12:
Click and
drag songs
to newly
created
playlists.

3. **Type a name for your playlist and then press Return.**

4. **Click the view you want to work in at the top of the window.**

5. **Click and drag songs, albums, or artists from the list on the left to the playlist on the right.**

6. **Click the Done button.**

TIP

To make a quick playlist, hold down the ⌘ key, click the songs you want in the playlist, and then choose File➪New➪Playlist from Selection. Your new playlist appears in the right pane with the name highlighted where you can type a more-identifying name.

Adding songs to a playlist

After you create a playlist, you can edit it. To add a song to a playlist, click the song and then click the disclosure triangle that appears to the right of the song name. Click the disclosure triangle next to Add To, and then choose the playlist you want to add the song to from the list that appears. The song you added appears in the playlist.

Alternatively, click the Playlists button and then click the playlist you want to add songs to. The playlist opens, displaying a list of the songs it contains. Click the Add To button in the upper-right corner and then drag songs from the Songs list to the playlist, as you do when creating a new playlist.

Putting a song in a playlist doesn't physically move the song from the folder. It's stored on your Mac's hard drive.

Deleting songs from a playlist

To delete a song from a playlist, follow these steps:

1. **In iTunes, click the playlist that contains the songs you want to delete.**

   Your chosen playlist appears onscreen.

2. **Click a song to delete and then press the Delete key.**

   A confirmation dialog appears, asking whether you really want to remove the song from your playlist.

3. **Click Remove.**

Deleting a song from a playlist doesn't delete the song from your iTunes library.

To delete a song from your music collection, choose Music from the Library pop-up menu, click a song you want to delete, and then press the Delete key. When a confirmation dialog appears, click Move to Trash if you want to delete the song track from your Mac's hard drive. Click Keep File if you want to keep the song track on your Mac's hard drive but no longer display it in your iTunes music library.

Creating a Smart Playlist

Manually adding and removing songs from a playlist can get tedious, especially if you regularly add new songs to your iTunes audio collection. Instead of placing specific songs in a playlist, a Smart Playlist lets you define specific criteria for the types of songs to store in that playlist, such as songs recorded earlier than 1990, or songs under a particular genre, such as Blues, Country, Hard Rock, or Folk. To create and use a Smart Playlist, you tag songs, define rules to determine which songs to include, and finally, edit existing playlists.

Tagging songs

To sort your song collection accurately into Smart Playlists, you can tag individual songs with descriptive information. Most songs stored as digital audio files already have some information stored in specific tags, such as the artist or album name. However, you might still want to edit or add new tags to help Smart Playlists sort your song collection.

To edit or add tags to a song, follow these steps:

1. **In iTunes, click a song that you want to tag and choose File⇨Get Info (or press ⌘+I) to display the song track's information.**

2. **Click the Info tab to display text boxes where you can type in or change the song track's associated information, as shown in Figure 1-13.**

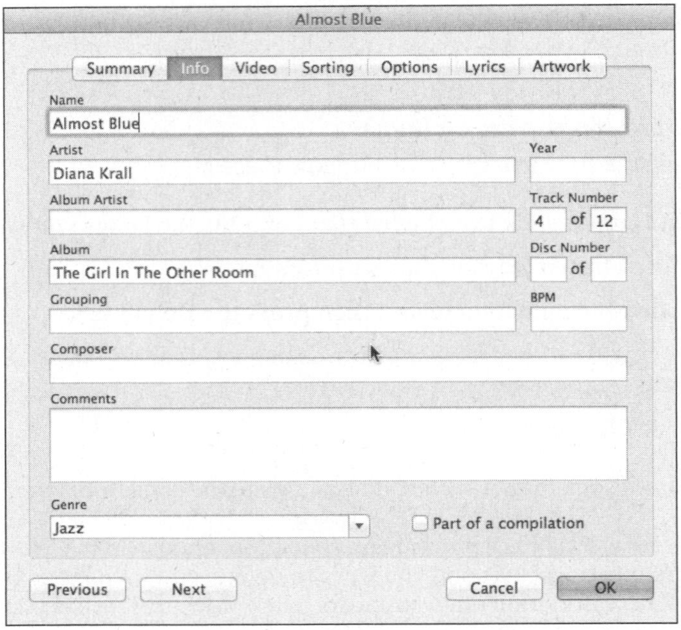

Almost Blue

Summary | Info | Video | Sorting | Options | Lyrics | Artwork

Name
Almost Blue

Artist
Diana Krall

Year

Album Artist

Track Number
4 of 12

Album
The Girl In The Other Room

Disc Number
of

Grouping

BPM

Composer

Comments

Genre
Jazz

☐ Part of a compilation

Previous | Next | Cancel | OK

Figure 1-13:
Edit or enter labels to identify a song.

3. **Click a text field and edit or enter information.**

4. **In the same Info pane, open the Genre pop-up menu to add or change the song's genre.**

5. **Click the song track's other tabs, such as Sorting or Options, shown in Figure 1-14, to make additional adjustments to your selected audio file.**

You can also set ratings by hovering over a song and clicking the disclosure triangle to the right of the name; click the dots at the top of the pop-up menu to rate the song to your liking.

6. **When you finish tagging the song track, click OK to close the dialog and return to the main iTunes window.**

Defining Smart Playlist rules

Smart Playlists use tags to sort and organize your song collection. You can use existing tags that are created for songs automatically (such as Artist and Album), as well as tags that you add to your songs to define the type of songs you want that Smart Playlist to store. A specific criterion for choosing a song is a *rule*.

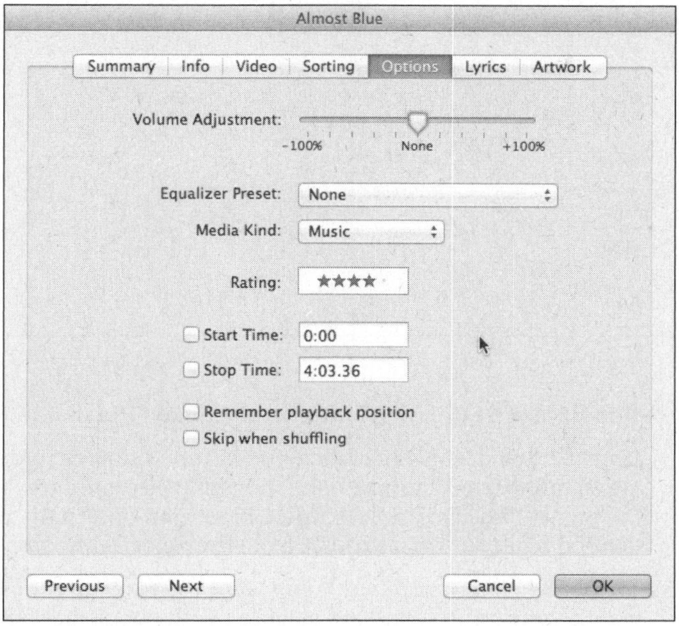

Figure 1-14:
Adjust
volume,
choose an
equalizer
setting, and
rate audio
files here.

To create a Smart Playlist, follow these steps:

1. **In iTunes, choose File⇨New⇨Smart Playlist. Or, in Playlists view, choose New Smart Playlist from the Add (+) pop-up menu.**

   A Smart Playlist dialog appears, prompting you to define a rule for specifying which songs to store in the playlist.

2. **Open the first pop-up menu on the left and choose a category, such as Artist or Date Added, for deciding which songs the Smart Playlist will automatically choose.**

3. **Open the second pop-up menu in the middle and choose how to use your chosen category.**

4. **Click the text box and type a criterion, such as a specific date or an artist name.**

5. **(Optional) Click the Plus sign to add another rule to the Playlist, as shown in Figure 1-15.**

   After you add a second rule, the All or Any menu appears next to Match in the first line.

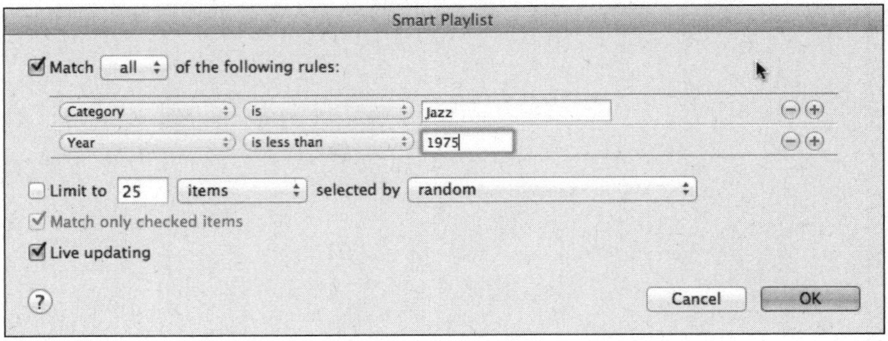

Figure 1-15:
Define a
rule for
choosing
songs.

Smart Playlist
☑ Match [all ⬍] of the following rules:
(Category ⬍) (is ⬍) [Jazz] ⊖ ⊕
(Year ⬍) (is less than ⬍) [1975] ⊖ ⊕
☐ Limit to [25] [items ⬍] selected by [random ⬍]
☑ Match only checked items
☑ Live updating
(?) [Cancel] [OK]

6. **(Optional) Make other selections in the Smart Playlist dialog:**

   • *Limit To:* Select this check box and enter a number to define the maximum number of (choose one) songs/file size/minutes/hours/items the Smart Playlist can hold; then choose an option that suits your desired Smart Playlist criteria from the Selected By pop-up menu.

   • *Match Only Checked Items:* If you want to store only those songs that match your criteria and are selected with check marks in the iTunes window, select this check box.

   • *Live Updating:* Select this check box if you want the Smart Playlist to update its list of songs automatically each time you add or remove a song from your iTunes song collection library or change a tag (on a song) that's used in the rule.

7. **Click OK.**

   Your Smart Playlist appears in the list of playlists in the Source List of the iTunes window. Smart Playlists have a gear icon to the left of the name.

To rename any playlist, double-click the name in the Playlist list to highlight the name, and then type in a new name to replace the existing name.

Editing a Smart Playlist

After you create a Smart Playlist, you can modify it, such as adding more rules or editing any existing rules. To edit a Smart Playlist, follow these steps:

1. **In iTunes, select the Smart Playlist that you want to edit from the iTunes Source list.**

2. **Choose File⇨Edit Smart Playlist or click the Edit button to the right of the playlist name.**

   The Smart Playlist dialog appears (refer to Figure 1-15).

3. **Make any changes to your Smart Playlist rule and then click OK.**

If you have a lot of playlists, the Playlists list can get pretty crowded. You can streamline your playlist list by filing similar playlists in folders. Choose File⇨New Playlist Folder. Double-click the folder to rename it with a meaningful name, and then click and drag the playlists you want to file to the folder.

Letting your Genius free

If your guests are already ringing the doorbell and you don't have time to create the background music for your party, you can let iTunes create a Genius shuffle, mix, or playlist for you with songs iTunes thinks go well together. iTunes automatically creates a Genius shuffle based on your existing collection, a Genius playlist is created based on a song you choose, and a Genius mix is based on a genre you choose. Genius also suggests new songs for you to purchase that it thinks you'll like based on your purchase history.

To create a Genius shuffle, simply choose Controls⇨Genius Shuffle, and iTunes goes to work. Click the Up Next button to see the songs in the shuffle. If you don't like the lineup, click Shuffle Again.

To listen to a Genius mix, click the Playlists button and then click Genius Mix in the list. Hover the pointer over the mix you want to hear and click the Play button that appears.

Here's how to create a Genius playlist:

1. **Choose Store⇨Turn On Genius.**

   iTunes asks you to sign in with your Apple ID if you haven't yet.

   You need an Internet connection for Genius to work.

   iTunes accesses the iTunes Store so it can analyze your interests in music, movies, and TV shows, see what other users who have similar tastes have in their collections, and then make informed suggestions about media you may like.

2. **Click a song you like in your music collection, click the disclosure triangle to the right of the song name, and then choose Create Genius Playlist.**

   A playlist is created from your music library with songs that iTunes thinks go well with the song you selected.

   The Genius playlist is automatically named with the song it's based on and saved in the playlist list.

3. **Click the pull-down menu next to 25 Songs under the playlist name to change how many songs you want in your Genius playlist: 25, 50, 75, or 100.**

4. **Click the Refresh button to update your Genius playlist after you add more music to your iTunes Music library.**

**Book IV
Chapter 1**

**Tuning In and
Listening with
iTunes**

Sometimes instead of Create Genius Playlist (as in Step 2), you see No Genius Suggestions. Genius seems somewhat limited if you have non-English, classical, or pre-1960 music. Tagging your songs, as we explain previously in the "Tagging songs" section, can help Genius create playlists because tagging gives iTunes more information to work with.

Deleting a playlist

You may want to delete a playlist or Smart Playlist you've created. To delete a playlist, follow these steps:

1. **In iTunes, click a playlist that you want to delete in the Playlists list and press the Delete key.**

A confirmation dialog appears, asking whether you really want to delete your playlist.

Deleting a playlist doesn't physically delete the audio files from your iTunes library.

2. **Click the Delete button.**

If iTunes created a Genius mix that you don't like, you can delete unwanted Genius mixes by using the same procedure.

Listening to the Radio

iTunes offers two types of radio listening:

✦ **iTunes Radio:** Creates a station based on a genre or song you choose

✦ **Internet radio:** Tunes in to radio stations through the Internet

We tell you about both here, but you have to be connected to the Internet to use either because the audio streams in real time.

Playing iTunes Radio

Although radio stations broadcast music and news programs within a category (such as country, classic rock, or conservative news), the playlists tend to be broad and flexible within the category. iTunes Radio, on the other hand, tends to offer more specific stations, and you can create your own stations based on songs, artists, and genres you want to hear. Follow these steps to use iTunes Radio:

1. **With iTunes open, click the Radio button at the top of the iTunes window.**

Across the top you see a row of pre-established station icons, such as iTunes Weekly Top 50 or Guest DJ stations, where an artist puts together a playlist of songs she likes, plus a few of her own recordings.

2. **Click one of the icons.**

   The music begins, usually with a brief spoken introduction about the station.

   Song information appears in the now-playing display, as in Figure 1-16. If you want to purchase the song from iTunes, click the price button. (Learn about purchasing from iTunes in the section, "Shopping at the iTunes Store," later in this chapter.)

   Just like broadcast radio, a 10- or 12-second advertisement plays between songs every now and then.

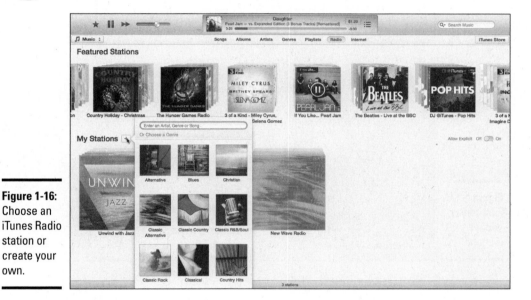

Figure 1-16:
Choose an iTunes Radio station or create your own.

3. **Click the add station button (+) to create your own iTunes Radio station (refer to Figure 1-16), and then do one of the following:**

   - *Click a genre icon.* From the subgenre list that appears, hover over one of the choices, click the Play button to the left to hear a sample, and then click the Add button to the right to add that station to your iTunes Radio selection. An icon appears in the My Stations section of iTunes Radio. Click another genre or subgenre to try a different music style.

   - *Type an artist, genre, or song in the Search field.* Click one of the choices from the list of matches that appears. An icon appears in the My Stations section of iTunes Radio.

4. **Click the Play button on one of the My Stations icons.**

   Songs begin to play from the same genre as the artist, song, or genre you selected.

**Book IV
Chapter 1**

Tuning In and
Listening with
iTunes

5. **Double-click one of the My Stations icons to tune the station and generate selections that better match your musical taste, as shown in Figure 1-17. Do the following:**

   • *Drag the tuning slider.* Choose the types of songs you want to hear related to your choice: *Hits* plays well-known songs similar to your base song, *Variety* plays some hits and some unknown songs, and *Discovery* plays songs you may not be familiar with but are similar to the base song.

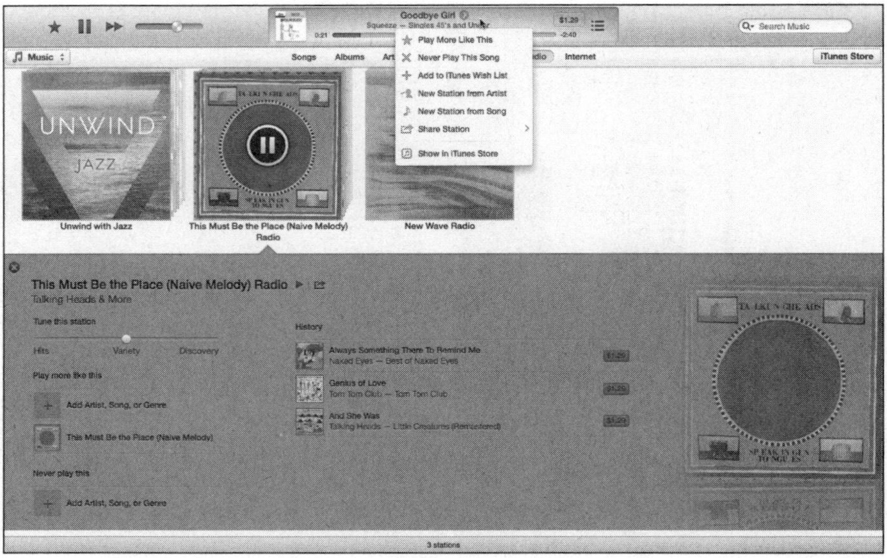

Figure 1-17: Fine-tune your stations.

   • *Click the Share button.* Send your station to someone by e-mail or Messages or post to Twitter or Facebook.

   • *Add/block other base songs.* Click the Add Artist, Song, or Genre button (+) to further define your station, or Click the Add button beneath Never Play This to block specific songs, artists, or genres from this station. The more artists, songs, or genres you add to or block from your station, the closer the iTunes choices will be to what you want to hear.

6. **From the toolbar, you can do the following:**

   • *Star button:* Click this to choose Play More Like This to add to the base songs, or click Never Play This Song to block it from your station.

   • *Next button:* Click to skip to a new song.

   • *Volume:* Drag the slider to increase or decrease playback volume.

- *Song-playing disclosure button:* Hover by the song-playing name and then click the disclosure button (refer to Figure 1-16) to add the song to the base, block the song, or create a new station from that song.

- *Up Next button:* In iTunes Radio, clicking this button reveals a playing history.

- *Price buttons:* Click the price button next to any song in the song playing or history list to purchase the song and add it to your iTunes library.

- *Mini Player button:* Click the Mini Player button (next to the full-screen button in the upper-right corner) to reduce the window. In the Mini Player window, hover over the album cover to reveal two arrows; click to open to a larger album cover view, as shown in Figure 1-18. Hover over the album to reveal playback controls, and click the small album icon to reduce the window again.

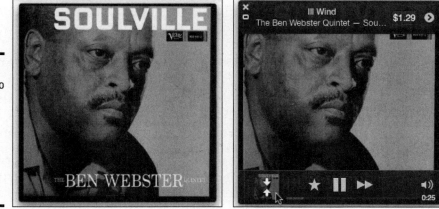

Figure 1-18: iTunes Radio Mini-Player window expands to an album view for the song that's playing.

Control-click an icon in My Stations to delete the station from your selections, or Control-click a Featured Stations icon to add it to My Stations.

7. **Click the Pause button to interrupt playback.**

8. **Choose iTunes⇨Quit iTunes (or press ⌘+Q) to leave the iTunes app altogether.**

Streaming Internet radio

Internet radio plays many of the same stations you listen to on your traditional radio plus many more stations from afar. Internet radio isn't limited to those stations within a broadcast range. For example, you can access the BBC or Radio Africa with far better reception than your short wave radio can provide.

Simply click the Internet button at the top of the iTunes window, and a list of categories appears. Click the disclosure button to the left of the category to see a list of all the stations within that category. To see a description of the station, choose View➪Show View Options and select the Comments check box. When you see a station you want to listen to, double-click it, and the audio begins to play. Use the playback and volume controls as you would to listen to other content.

If you know a specific station's call letters or name, type it in the Search field to see whether it's available. And, if you have a favorite station that's not listed, open Safari (or your favorite browser) and attempt to locate the station on the Internet to find out whether it provides an Internet stream. Open iTunes and choose File➪Open Stream. Select and copy the URL from Safari, and then paste the URL for the station in the URL field of the Open Stream window. It's now added to Internet radio.

Playing Digital Video Files

After you download movies, TV shows, lectures, or video podcasts, you want to watch them. To watch a video, follow these steps:

1. **Open the Library pop-up menu and choose the media you want to watch — for example, TV Shows.**

   The list of videos you have in your library in that category appears in the iTunes window.

   If you import media from non-iTunes sources, such as TV shows from Amazon, you find them in the Movies category. Click the item and then select File➪Get Info. Click the Options button and choose the appropriate media type from the Media Kind pop-up menu, and then they'll be in the right place.

2. **Click one of the view tabs to sort the contents of the library.**

   For example, TV Shows can be sorted by Unwatched, Shows, Genres, or List, which shows everything.

3. **Double-click the movie or episode you want to watch.**

   The video begins playing in the media pane.

4. **Move the pointer over the bottom of the video to see the playback controls.**

   You can also use the playback controls on the toolbar.

   Choose iTunes➪Preferences➪Playback, and select your Preferred Video Version in the pop-up menu: Standard or High Definition at 720p or 1080p.

Shopping at the iTunes Store

Despite its misleading name, the iTunes Store sells much more than music. You can also find music videos, movies, TV shows, audio and video podcasts, audio books, electronic books, iOS apps, and lectures from some of the best universities in the world. Think of it as a one-stop media megastore.

If you're a true music enthusiast or your tastes aren't exactly mainstream, picking through CDs — or long-playing vinyl records — in a music store is probably a thrilling and common activity. For the rest of us, digital downloads are where it's at, and iTunes meets a fair amount of our music purchasing requirements.

In this section, we accompany you down the virtual aisles of the iTunes Store, but don't stop at just music. The iTunes Store also offers movies, TV shows, audiobooks, podcasts, and lectures from some of the top universities in the country. And, while the iTunes Store has iOS apps, you find Mac apps in the App Store. The books you find in the iTunes Store, however, are the same you find in the iBooks Store.

Have your Apple ID on hand when you want to shop the iTunes Store because that's what you use to sign in. To create an Apple ID, choose Store⇨Create Apple ID.

For many purchases, you have to authorize your computer. This helps with copyright issues. You can authorize up to five computers, and you can also de-authorize computers, so don't worry about someone else using your Apple ID if you sell or give away your Mac. Other devices don't count as computers, so your iPad or iPhone aren't part of the five-computer limit. Choose Store⇨Authorize This Computer. That's it.

To open the iTunes Store, click the iTunes Store button at the upper-right side of the iTunes window. To return to your iTunes Library, click the Library button that appears where the iTunes Store button used to be.

With literally millions of digital media files to choose from, the initial impact can be overwhelming, but the iTunes Store organization helps you narrow your choices. When you first open the iTunes Store, the window you see is divided into sections that give you suggestions for different types of media to download, rent, or purchase (see Figure 1-19).

At the top, you see rotating banner ads for songs, TV shows, and movies. Scrolling down reveals other sections, such as Music, Movies, TV Shows, Apps, Books, Special Offers, and Free on iTunes. You also find one or two dividing strips, which advertise special iTunes offers. Clicking any of the ads or icons takes you to an information screen about that item.

Figure 1-19:
Browse the iTunes Store for music, movies, TV shows, and more.

In each section, you can use the scroll bar underneath the selection to scroll horizontally, or click See All to see the entire selection from that section.

Across the top of the window are tabs for each type of media: Music, Movies, TV Shows, App Store (see Book I, Chapter 5), Books, Podcasts, and iTunes U. To the left of the tabs, you see your Apple ID, which is a tab, too. (The Apple ID in Figure 1-19 is barbaradepaula.) When clicked, each tab opens a pull-down menu, as shown in Figure 1-20. The choices on the menus take you to selections of new releases, special offers, or specific categories or genres available in that type of media. The pull-down menu from your Apple ID tab gives you options for managing your account. The Home tab takes you back to the opening iTunes Store screen (refer to Figure 1-19).

Down the right side, you see two sections:

✦ **Quick Links:** This section is divided into two sections. The upper section is related to your Apple ID/iTunes account with buttons to access your account, your purchase history, redeem gift cards, or request support. The lower section lists options for searching, browsing, and buying.

✦ **Top Charts:** This section is divided into Singles, where you can view songs or music videos; and Albums, Movies, TV Shows, Apps, and Books. Click the chart title to see a full display of the list's contents.

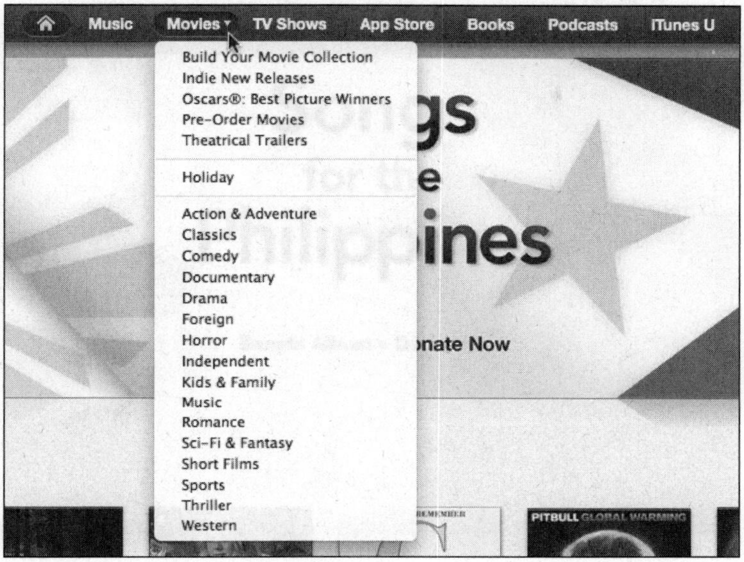

Figure 1-20: Click a media tab to open a pull-down menu with direct links to specific types of selections.

When you click an icon or name for any type of media from anywhere in the iTunes store, the information window opens. These are the parts of an information screen, as shown in Figure 1-21:

+ **Name**

+ **Genre**

+ **Release date**

+ **Buy button:** Click to download the media. Each option (for example, rent or buy, standard or high definition) has its own button. Songs can be purchased singly, or you can purchase the whole album. TV shows can be purchased singly or by season, and some movies have a rental option in addition to a buy option.

+ **Pop-up menu:** Click the triangle next to the price for a pop-up menu that has options to gift the app to a friend, add it to your own wish list, tell a friend about it, copy the link, or share the app info via Facebook or Twitter.

+ **Ratings:** For movies only. The ratings reflect the country where you're purchasing the film.

+ **Details:** The first few lines of the description are visible. If the description is longer, click More on the right side to expose the complete description.

+ **Ratings and Reviews:** Click the tab to see what others have said about this item. Users can give a simple star rating, from zero to five, or write a review. Reviews help you decide whether the item is worth downloading or purchasing.

+ **Related:** Click this tab to see other items similar to this one.

Figure 1-21:
Information about the media item is displayed in iTunes.

When you know what you're looking for

You might know exactly what you're looking for. Maybe you heard an old favorite song on the radio or a new singer you want to hear more of. A quick search through iTunes offerings, and you're one step closer to chilling with a great groove.

Type the name of the song or artist or a few key words — say, from a book title — in the Search Store field at the top right of the window. Press Return, and a list of matching results appears. The results are extracted from the entire iTunes Store but are divided by media category. If you click Music or Podcasts in the media type list on the right, you'll see only that type of media. Or click See All next to the media title to see all the items found that meet your search criteria in that type of media.

Click the Lists button to the left of the Library button to view items in your Wish List, songs you listened to on the Radio, and Previews you've looked at, as shown in Figure 1-22.

Downloading media from iTunes

When you find something you like, click the Buy button (Subscribe for Podcasts and iTunes U), and it's downloaded to iTunes on your Mac. If you have other Apple devices (such as an iPad or iPhone), you can automatically download your purchases to the other devices at the same time. Choose iTunes➪Preferences➪Store and choose the media you want to download simultaneously, as shown in Figure 1-23.

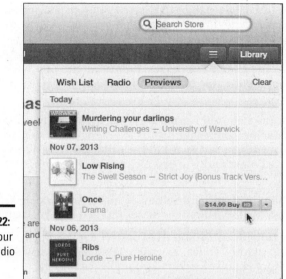

Figure 1-22:
Look at your
iTunes Radio
history.

When you rent a movie, you must begin watching it within 30 days and finish watching it within 24 hours of when you began. After either of those two deadlines pass, it's removed from your iTunes library.

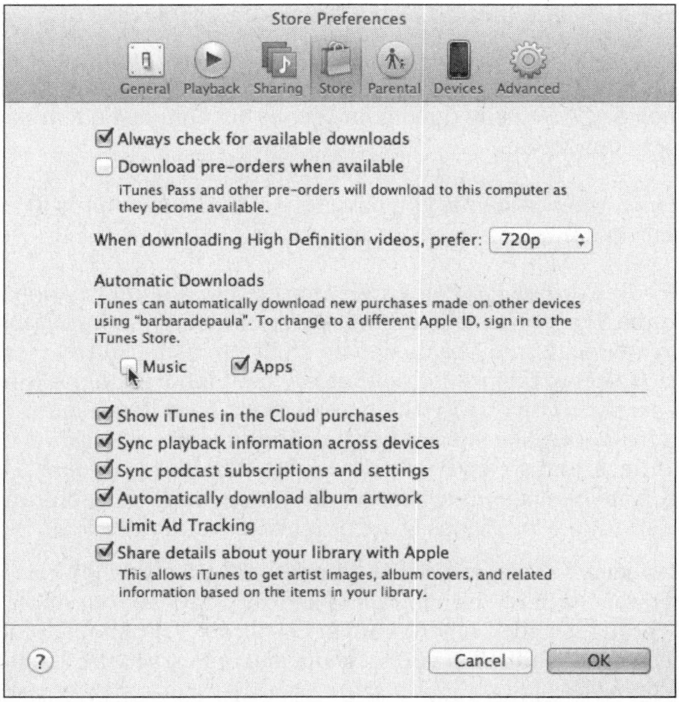

Figure 1-23:
Automatic
downloads
puts your
purchases
on all your
devices
simultane-
ously.

**Book IV
Chapter 1**

**Tuning In and
Listening with
iTunes**

From the choices in the lower half of the Store Preferences window, you can select how you want to sync downloads and play back across your devices. When selected, the following happens:

✦ **Show iTunes in the Cloud Purchases:** Items that are purchased but not yet downloaded to your Mac have an iCloud icon next to them in your iTunes library.

✦ **Sync Playback Information Across Devices:** If you begin watching a movie or listening to a podcast on your Mac or another device and then pause, the place you paused syncs to the other devices signed in to the same Apple ID account, and you can pick up where you left off on a different device.

✦ **Sync Podcast Subscriptions and Settings:** Choices that you make on one device or on your Mac sync to other devices signed in to the same Apple ID.

✦ **Automatically Download Album Artwork:** When you copy music from a CD or other source into iTunes, any associated album artwork available in the iTunes Store is downloaded to your iTunes library.

✦ **Limit Ad Tracking:** Apple developers can use a feature called iAd in their apps; ad tracking lets them send you targeted advertising based on your computer or device use. If you don't want them to use this information to send you targeted ads, select this check box.

✦ **Share Details about Your Library with Apple:** When selected, this option allows iTunes to provide Apple with information about media in your library.

Don't worry if you have to interrupt the download process or it's interrupted unexpectedly. iTunes remembers the point it reached, and it will resume downloading when you open your iTunes account again and have an active Internet connection.

Of course, when you buy, you have to pay from your Apple ID account. This happens in either of two ways:

✦ **Credit Card or PayPal:** Enter your credit card information into your Apple ID account. If you didn't enter credit card information when you created an Apple ID, you can do so by choosing Store⇨View Account and clicking Edit to the right of Payment Information. A window opens where you can choose the type of credit card you want to use and type in the necessary information: account number, expiration date, billing address, and so on. If you choose PayPal, click Continue. The PayPal website opens and by accessing your account, you confirm that you want to pay for iTunes Store purchases through PayPal.

✦ **Redeem:** You can redeem Apple or iTunes gift cards, gift certificates, or allowances (more on allowances shortly). Choose your Apple ID⇨Redeem. Type in the code from the card or certificate. The amount of the card or certificate is added to your account and appears to the left of the Apple ID account tab.

You can set up a monthly allowance for yourself or someone else. A set amount will be charged to your credit card or PayPal account and credited to the designated iTunes account. Choose your Apple ID⇨Account and type your password if requested. Scroll to the Settings section at the bottom of the window, and then click the Set Up an Allowance button. Follow the onscreen instructions to establish the recipient's name and amount.

All songs on iTunes are currently in iTunes Plus format, which is 256 Kbps AAC without DRM limitations. Songs cost 69 cents, 99 cents, or $1.29, and album prices vary depending on the number of songs. If you buy a few songs from the same album and later decide you want the whole album, choose the Complete My Album option, and iTunes deducts the cost of songs you already own from the album price. After you purchase and download media from iTunes, it's automatically downloaded to any other devices for which you set up the automatic downloads feature. Or you can sync and play it on any of your devices — your Mac, iPod, iPad, smartphone, or MP3 player.

Some albums on iTunes have an iTunes LP option. When you purchase an iTunes LP, you get liner notes, band photos, lyrics, and other bonus material along with the songs. You view everything in iTunes on your Mac.

If you want to build your video library, iTunes offers movies in both standard-definition (SD) and high-definition (HD) formats. If you're a passionate movie buff, you may like iTunes Extra, which includes extra video, such as director's comments or interviews with the actors along with the movie. Rentals have viewing time limits.

TV shows may be free — often to introduce a new series or season — or can be purchased singly or you can buy a season pass and download every episode. If not free, episodes start at $1.99, and you can choose standard or HD versions (HD begins at $2.99).

Like their paper and cloth counterparts, audiobooks and electronic books have a wide range of prices. You'll find some are free as well. For example, podcasts and iTunes U lectures may be downloaded for free. See Book IV, Chapter 6, to learn about enjoying books, podcasts, and iTunes U media.

After you download the item, close the iTunes Store by clicking the Library button in the upper-right corner. You return to your iTunes library. To confirm your purchases, look in the section of the library related to the type of media you downloaded. For example, if you purchased and downloaded songs, click Music; if you downloaded podcasts, click Podcasts.

To consult your past purchases on your iTunes account, choose Store⇨View Account. Sign in to iTunes with your Apple ID and choose Purchase History. You can also download purchases again and again because when you buy something in iTunes, it's yours forever.

If you ever have a problem with a purchase, choose Store➪View Account. Click Purchase History and click the Report a Problem button next to the item that isn't working.

Sharing the Wealth

You put together a terrific music and movie library on iTunes, and now you want your friends to know about the great new artist you heard or the quirky TV series you watch. You could just tell them or send them a link from the iTunes Store; however, iTunes gives you a few options for directly sharing the media with your friends or family.

Sharing over a network

If your Mac is connected to a network, you can let other computers on the same network stream media from your computer. Choose iTunes➪Preferences➪ Sharing. In the Sharing pane, shown in Figure 1-24, specify sharing your entire library or specific media and playlists in your library. You can add a password if you want to restrict who has access. Protected DRM content, such as movies and TV shows, can be viewed only on other "authorized" computers. (See the earlier section "Shopping at the iTunes Store" to lean about authorizing computers.)

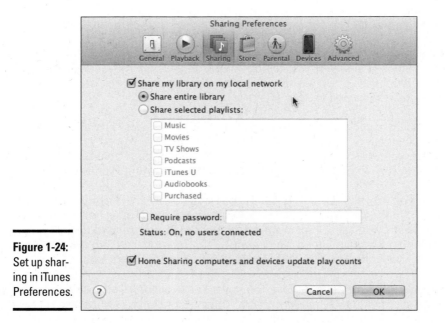

Figure 1-24:
Set up sharing in iTunes Preferences.

Enabling Home Sharing

If your household is like many today, it probably has more than one computer. Home Sharing lets you share the media you keep on iTunes — music,
TV shows, apps, and so on — among up to five computers in your house,
and you can copy content from one computer to another. Choose File⇨Home
Sharing⇨Turn On Home Sharing, and its dialog opens, as shown in Figure 1-25.
Enter the Apple ID you want to use for Home Sharing, and then repeat the process on the other computers, making sure to use the same Apple ID.

Figure 1-25:
Use Home
Sharing to
share your
media with
up to five
computers.

Media you add to one computer can then be shared with another computer
over the network. Choose the computer and media category from the Home
Sharing section of the Library pop-up menu, and then choose "Items Not in
My Library" from the Show menu. Select the items you want to import, and
click the Import button. If you want to automatically download iTunes Store
purchases made on a different computer using Home Sharing, after choosing the computer and media category from the Library pop-up menu, click
the Settings button, and choose Automatically Transfer New Purchases from
Library Name. Click OK.

Sharing from the iTunes Store

When you click the Buy button on an item in the iTunes Store, a pop-up
menu opens with sharing options in addition to the option to buy the
item. You can choose one or more of the following: Tell a Friend, Share
on Facebook, Share on Twitter, or even Gift This to purchase the item for
another person. Think how surprised and happy your friend, colleague, or
relative will be when the gifted item shows up in his or her e-mail inbox.

You can't use store credit to gift an item; you must pay for the item with a
credit card or PayPal.

Chapter 2: Watching Videos and Movies on Your Mac

In This Chapter

✔ **Understanding video disc formats**

✔ **Identifying digital video formats**

✔ **Playing digital video files**

✔ **Cozying up to QuickTime Player**

✔ **Playing a DVD on your Mac**

*L*ooking to unwind after a busy day of work? Feel free to kick back, relax, and cozy up to a movie on your Mac. Want to watch your favorite scene again? Your Mac can bookmark and store your favorite scenes so you can easily watch your favorite parts of a movie. And, you can watch them in slow motion so you don't miss one second of the action.

Although many full-length movies appear on DVD, with today's greater storage capacity and Internet connection bandwidth, many movies and videos — commercial or homemade — are stored entirely as digital video files either on your internal or external drive or the Internet. Your Mac can play many of them at your convenience.

In this chapter, we begin by explaining video disc formats and digital movie formats. Then we lay out the options your Mac offers for playing those formats — namely, QuickTime and DVD Player. You can read about the third option, iTunes, in Book IV, Chapter 1, and keep in mind that you can watch videos you capture in iPhoto, which we discuss in Book IV, Chapter 3.

Making Sense of Video Disc Formats

The most common video disc format is Digital Video Disc (DVD). However, DVDs aren't the only video disc format. An earlier video disc format is Video Compact Disc (VCD), which essentially stores video files on ordinary CDs. VCDs and SVCDs typically offer lower video quality than DVDs (comparable to videotape) and offer much less storage capability than DVDs. Other popular formats are DivX, xvid, and Matroska or mkv, which many DVD players can play.

Although DVD is the common video disc standard, Blu-ray is the dominant high-definition digital disc format. The main advantage of Blu-ray discs is that they can store much more data than standard DVDs (25GB for a Blu-ray disc versus 4.7GB for a DVD or 50GB versus 8.55GB for a *dual-layer* — that is, two layers recorded on the same side yet accessed separately — DVD). However, Blu-ray discs are more expensive to produce and purchase.

Your Mac's internal or external optical disc drive can play DVDs out of the box. If you want to watch Blu-ray discs, though, you need to buy a special Blu-ray disc drive and an application to use it or convert the file first by using an application like Pavtube (www.pavtube.com) to rip the Full Disc Copy and then HandBrake (http://handbrake.fr) to convert the file.

Only one current Mac, the non-Retina MacBook Pro, comes with an internal optical disc drive. You need an external optical disc drive to play DVDs on other current Mac models.

Understanding Digital Video Formats

Video discs are popular for storing and distributing videos, but with high-speed Internet connections and lower flash drive storage costs, storing full-length movies as a single digital video file has become both popular and practical. The biggest problem with digital video is the wide variety of digital video formats available. To play a digital video file, you need a video player application that accepts the type of video file you have. The following is a list of digital video file types and the applications you can use to play them:

+ **QuickTime (.mov):** Playable by the QuickTime Player that comes with every Mac.

+ **Audio/Video Interleaved (.avi):** An older video file format introduced by Microsoft in 1992, although still commonly used today.

+ **Windows Media Video (.wmv):** Playable on a Mac if you first install the Flip4Mac application (www.telestream.net), which allows the QuickTime Player to open and play DRM-free Windows Media Video files. (We explain DRM in Book IV, Chapter 1.)

+ **DivX (.divx):** A high-quality video format known for storing DVD-quality video images in a digital video file format. DivX files can play on a Mac with the free DivX player (www.divx.com) or the free VLC media player (www.videolan.org).

+ **Flash video (.flv):** A video file format commonly used on websites, such as news sites that offer video (CNN and Reuters) and YouTube, Myspace, and Yahoo! Video. You can play Flash videos with the free Adobe Flash Player (www.adobe.com).

+ **RealVideo (.rm):** A video file format often used for streaming video. You can play RealVideo files by using the free RealPlayer application (www.real.com).

✦ **Moving Picture Expert Group (MPEG;** `.mpg`**):** A video file format that consists of different versions, including

- *MPEG-1:* Used for storing video on VCDs

- *MPEG-2:* Broadcast-quality video used for storing video on SVCDs, DVDs, HD TV, HD DVDs, and Blu-ray discs

- *MPEG-3:* Originally designed for HD TV but now rarely used

- *MPEG-4:* For storing video on HD DVD and Blu-ray discs

You can view most MPEG-4 videos with the QuickTime Player; however, the free VLC media player (`www.videolan.org`) is a better solution because it reads all MPEG files as well as other video formats.

The QuickTime Player can't play audio stored as AC3 (Dolby Digital) files with MPEG video files; you can still watch the video albeit in silent movie mode. You can, however, play these files with an application such as VLC.

Most video players are free because the companies developing and promoting a specific video file format want as many people as possible to use (and rely on) their particular video file format. Then these companies can make money by selling applications that create and store video in their specific file format.

Playing a Digital Video File

Playing a digital video file is as simple as double-clicking that file, which opens the appropriate video player on your Mac and displays your video file onscreen. For a video file on a website, you can usually click the video file directly on the web page to see it play within your browser.

Occasionally, you may find a video file format that you can't play on your Mac. In this case, you have two choices:

✦ Download and install a video player for that particular video file format.

✦ Convert the video file into a format that your Mac can play.

In our opinion, it's simpler just to download and install (yet another) free video player to watch video encoded in a different video file format. However, downloading and installing multiple video players can be annoying, so you may prefer to convert digital file formats instead. To convert digital video files, you need a special digital video file format conversion application.

To convert non–copy-protected (and most copy-protected) DVD videos to MPEG-4, you can use a free application called HandBrake (`http://handbrake.fr`) as long as you also have VLC media player (`www.videolan.org`) installed. In case you need to convert one digital video file format into another one (such as converting a DivX file into a QuickTime file), grab a copy of the oddly named ffmpegX (`www.ffmpegx.com`) or MPEG Streamclip (`www.squared5.com`).

We won't go into how to use each application, but the gist is that you go to one of the aforementioned websites, download and install the conversion application, open the application, and then open the file you want to convert and choose something like Convert To and choose a file type for which you have a player.

Converting digital video files lets you store all your videos in a single file format, such as QuickTime, and avoid having to download and install half a dozen video players. It's your call which tactic you prefer.

Using QuickTime Player

Your Mac comes with QuickTime Player, which plays video and offers video-recording and -editing functions. In addition to QuickTime Movie (.mov), QuickTime Player supports MPEG-4 (.mp4, .m4v), MPEG-2, MPEG-1, 3GPP, 3GPP2, some AVI, and DV files.

Follow these steps to use the playing part of QuickTime Player:

1. **Open QuickTime Player by doing one of the following:**

    - *Drag the movie file over the QuickTime Player icon on the Dock.*

    - *Open QuickTime Player from the Dock or Launchpad and then choose File⇨Open File.*

      Choose the file you want to view from the Open dialog. You may have to sift through directories or folders to find the file you're looking for. Or click the Movies button in the Media section of the Finder sidebar to see all the movie files stored on your Mac, divided by app of origin, as shown in Figure 2-1.

    - *Choose File⇨Open Location.*

      An Open Location dialog appears, in which you can type the URL where the movie is located.

    - *Choose File⇨Open Recent and then choose a file you recently viewed from the pop-up menu.*

2. **When your selected movie opens, choose View and select one of the following viewing options:**

    - *Enter Full Screen:* Only your movie is seen, as large as possible, on the entire screen. No other windows or menus are visible.

    - *Float on Top:* Your movie plays on top of whatever else is on your desktop.

    - *Actual Size:* Displays movie closest to the size it was recorded as possible.

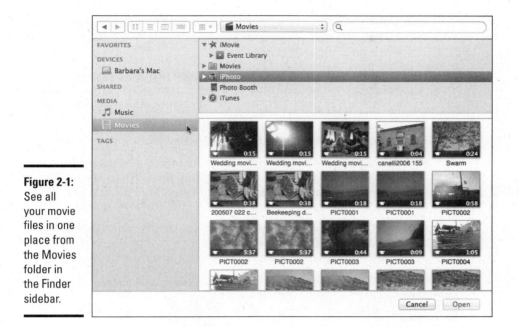

Figure 2-1:
See all
your movie
files in one
place from
the Movies
folder in
the Finder
sidebar.

- *Fit to Screen:* Your movie is adjusted to fit the screen while maintaining the height-to-width ratio. Other windows and the menu bar are visible.

- *Fill Screen:* Your movie is adjusted to fill the entire screen, without borders. Some of the image may be lost or distorted because the height-width ratio is ignored to fill the screen (only in full-screen mode).

- *Panoramic:* The movie is displayed with the outer horizontal edges compressed to avoid cropping (only in full-screen mode).

3. **(Optional) Choose other options from the View menu that may be available with your movie.**

    - *Languages* lets you choose a different language for the audio of your movie.

    - *Subtitles* displays a written translation in a language other than the spoken dialogue.

4. **(Optional) If your movie has chapters, you can choose View⇨Next Chapter or Previous Chapter to go to a different part of your movie.**

5. **Click the Play/Pause button to view your movie.**

6. **Use the other playback controls, shown in Figure 2-2, to view your movie.**

    - *Volume:* Move the slider left or right to decrease or increase the audio.

**Book IV
Chapter 2**

**Watching Videos
and Movies on
Your Mac**

- *Rewind or Fast Forward:* Click these buttons to go quickly ahead or back (respectively) in your movie. Clicking successively doubles the speed from 2 up to 32 times faster.

  Alternatively, drag the playhead slider left or right to go to another part of your movie. The time to the left of the playhead is how long your movie has played; the time to the right of the playhead indicates how much is left to play.

- *Play/Pause:* Click this toggle button to play or stop your movie.

- If you capture video with a smartphone or in a vertical position, the playback may take up less room than the entire screen (refer to Figure 2-2, which was captured with an iPhone). Clicking the Full Screen button changes the ratio but may distort the image.

- *Share:* Click this button to send the video to someone via Mail or Messages or post it to a social network. (See Book II, Chapters 2 and 3, to learn about Mail and Messages, respectively.)

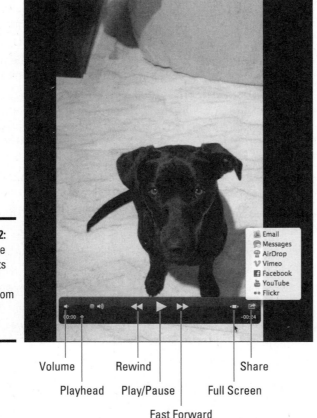

Figure 2-2:
QuickTime Player lets you view movies from many file formats.

Volume

Playhead

Rewind

Play/Pause

Fast Forward

Full Screen

Share

Playing a DVD

The most common video disc format is the DVD format. To play DVDs, just insert your DVD into your Mac's internal or external optical disc drive. DVD Player loads and displays your DVD's main menu, as shown in Figure 2-3.

Figure 2-3: When DVD Player starts, it displays the inserted DVD's main menu.

If you turn on Parental Controls by choosing Features➪Enable Parental Controls, you see a dialog that prompts you to enter your user password to watch the video. Likewise, if you previously watched the video and interrupted playback before the end, a dialog asks whether you want to start playback from the beginning or from where you left off.

Click the menu options to select them (or use your Mac's arrow keys to move through the DVD's menu options and then press Return or the spacebar to select them), such as Play Movie, or Special Features.

If you just want to watch a DVD from start to finish, you don't have to read the rest of this chapter. However, if you want to use some of the special features of DVD Player, keep reading.

Understanding full-screen mode and window mode

One of the simplest ways to enrich your viewing experience is to switch between full-screen mode and window mode. In full-screen mode, the video fills your entire computer screen. In window mode, the video fills only part of your computer screen while giving you access to the rest of your Mac Desktop, such as the Dock and other app windows, as shown in Figure 2-4.

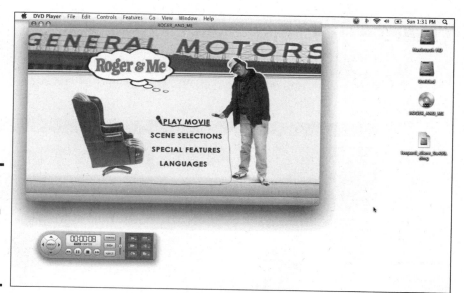

Figure 2-4:
DVD Player can shrink a video inside a window on your Desktop.

Exiting and returning to full-screen mode

The first time you insert a DVD into your Mac, DVD Player displays your video in full-screen mode. To exit full-screen mode, choose one of the following:

✦ Press Esc.

✦ Hover the pointer over the top-right corner to reveal the menu bar and then click the full-screen toggle button.

✦ Press ⌘+F.

✦ Click the Exit Full Screen button on the Controller, as shown in Figure 2-5.

Figure 2-5:
The Controller appears at the bottom of the screen in full-screen mode.

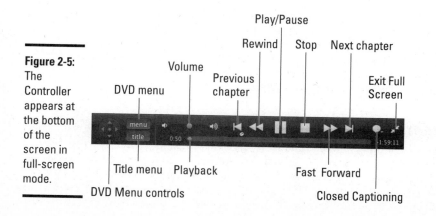

In full-screen mode, you can view the DVD Player menu bar by moving the pointer to the top of the screen. You can also view the DVD Controller in full-screen mode by moving the pointer to the bottom of the screen.

To return to full-screen mode, choose one of the following:

✦ Click the Full Screen button at the upper-right corner of the DVD Player window.

✦ Press ⌘+F.

✦ Choose View➪Enter Full Screen.

Viewing a video in a window

When you exit full-screen mode, your video appears in a window with the Controller displayed underneath the DVD window (refer to Figure 2-3). Choose the View menu, and you have the following options for displaying a video:

✦ Half Size

✦ Actual Size

✦ Double Size

✦ Fit to Screen

✦ Enter Full Screen

When viewing a video in a window, the Controller takes on a different *skin* (the display appearance), as shown in Figure 2-6. To open the drawer on the window-mode Controller, click and drag the handle down or toward the right (depending on how you choose to view the controller) or choose Controls➪Open Control Drawer.

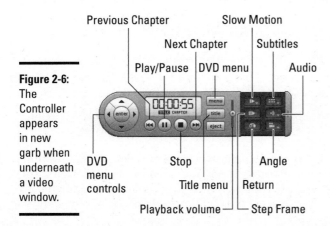

Figure 2-6: The Controller appears in new garb when underneath a video window.

Although the Controller in both full-screen and window mode allows you to control a DVD, each Controller offers slightly different features. You can access some features in both full-screen and window mode, but many features are available only in one mode or the other.

In either viewing mode, press Option+⌘+C to show or hide the Controller.

To avoid letting any other window cover up part of your video window, choose View⇨Viewer above Other Apps. To turn off this feature, choose the same command again.

Viewing the DVD and Title menus

Most DVDs include an initial menu that lets you choose what to watch, such as the feature presentation or extra content such as interviews with the director and actors. Some DVDs also offer a Title menu that lets you pick different episodes, such as a DVD containing multiple episodes from a single season of a TV show. DVDs may offer both an initial menu and a Title menu. To jump to the initial DVD or Title menu (and note that not all DVDs have one), try clicking the Menu button (DVD menu) or the Title button on the Controller.

If at any time you want to start the DVD from the very beginning, choose Go⇨Beginning of Disc. (In full-screen mode, move the pointer to the top of the screen to display the DVD Player menu bar.) Alternatively, click the Stop button twice.

Skipping through a video

Sometimes you may want to skip over or replay part of a video. To skip backward or forward through a video, follow these steps:

1. **In full-screen mode, click one of the following buttons on the Controller:**

   - *Rewind:* Plays the video quickly in reverse

   - *Fast Forward:* Plays the video quickly going forward

   In DVD Player window mode, click and hold the Previous Chapter button to rewind, or the Next Chapter button to fast-forward.

2. **Click Play or press the spacebar when you want to resume viewing the video.**

Hold down the ⌘ key and press the left- or right-arrow key to increase the rewind or fast-forward speed (respectively) incrementally by 2x, 4x, 8x, 16x, or 32x with each additional press of the arrow key. To stop rewinding/fast-forwarding and resume playing the video at normal speed, click the Play button or press the spacebar.

If you prefer menu commands, follow these steps:

1. **Choose Controls⇨Scan Forward (or Scan Backwards).**

   Your video continuously rewinds or fast-forwards.

2. **Change the scan rate by selecting Controls⇨Scan Rate⇨2/4/8/16/32x Speed.**

3. **Click the Play button or press the spacebar or choose Control⇨Play to resume playing the video at its normal speed.**

You can also drag the slider at the bottom of the Controller (in full-screen mode) to rewind or fast-forward a video.

Viewing frames in steps and slow motion

If you want to study a particular part of a video, the DVD Player lets you view individual frames one at a time or view your video in slow motion.

To view individual frames in steps, go into window mode. Then click the Step Frame button on the Controller.

Each time you click the Step Frame button, the video advances one frame.

To play the video at normal speed, click the Play button on the Controller or press the spacebar.

Stepping through a video one frame at a time can be tedious, so an easier way to step through a video is in slow motion. To view your video in slow motion, again in window mode:

1. **Choose Controls⇨Slow Motion or click the Slow Motion button on the Controller.**

2. **When the Slow Motion rate appears in the upper-left corner of the window, choose Controls⇨Slow Motion Rate⇨1/2, 1/4, 1/8 Speed to change how slow the video plays.**

   Clicking the Slow Motion button again changes the rate of slow motion.

Click the Play button on the Controller or press the spacebar to play the video at normal speed.

Skipping by chapters

Most DVD videos are divided into segments called *chapters,* which are usually listed somewhere on or inside the DVD case. If you want to view a favorite scene, just jump to the chapter that contains your favorite scene.

To move between chapters, choose one of the following:

✦ In full-screen mode, move your pointer to the top of the screen and then click the Chapters button (it looks like an open book) in the upper-left corner to open thumbnail images of the chapters. Click the chapter you want to skip to. Use the scroll bar to move forward and backward to other chapters.

✦ Click the Previous Chapter or Next Chapter button on the Controller.

✦ Press the left-arrow (previous) or right-arrow (next) key while the video is playing.

Placing bookmarks in a video

Sometimes your favorite parts of a movie don't correlate exactly to chapter sections on a DVD. In case you want to be able to jump to a specific part of a video, you can create a bookmark.

DVD Player saves your bookmarks on your Mac's hard drive, so if you pop the DVD out and back in again, your bookmarks are still preserved.

Creating a bookmark

To create a bookmark, follow these steps:

1. **Click the Pause button (or press the spacebar) to pause the video at the spot where you want to place a bookmark.**

2. **Choose Controls⇨New Bookmark or press ⌘+= to open a new bookmark dialog, as shown in Figure 2-7.**

Figure 2-7:
Enter a descriptive name for your bookmark.

> Bookmark: Bookmark 1
> Title: 1
> Time: 00:13:13
> ☐ Make Default Bookmark
> [Cancel] [Add]

3. **Enter a descriptive name for your bookmark in the text field and then click Add.**

If you select the Make Default Bookmark check box, you can jump to this bookmark in window mode by choosing Go⇨Default Bookmark.

Jumping to a bookmark

After you create at least one bookmark, you can jump to that bookmark by following these steps:

1. **Choose Go⇨Bookmarks.**

   A pop-up menu appears, listing all your saved bookmarks.

2. **Click the bookmark name you want to jump to.**

In full-screen mode, you can also click the Bookmarks button in the upper-left corner (under the Chapters button) and then click the bookmark you want to jump to.

Deleting a bookmark

After you create at least one bookmark, you can delete a bookmark by following these steps:

1. **Choose Window⇨Bookmarks.**

   A Bookmarks window appears.

2. **Click to select the bookmark you want to delete and then click the Remove bookmark button (minus sign).**

   A confirmation dialog appears, asking whether you're sure that you want to delete your chosen bookmark.

3. **Click OK (or Cancel) and then click the Close button to close the Bookmarks window.**

You can Control-click in the viewing screen to open a shortcut menu, as shown in Figure 2-8.

Figure 2-8:
Control-
click to
open a
shortcut
menu.

```
Half Size
Actual Size
Double Size
Fit to Screen
Enter Full Screen

DVD Menu
Beginning of Disc
Title               ▶
Chapter             ▶
Bookmarks           ▶

Add Bookmark...

Use Current Frame as Jacket Picture

Mute
Turn On Closed Captioning
```

**Book IV
Chapter 2**

**Watching Videos
and Movies on
Your Mac**

Viewing closed captioning

Many DVDs (but not all) include closed captioning and subtitles. *Closed captioning* displays written dialog onscreen in the same language that's being spoken — English, for example — whereas *subtitles* give you a choice of reading dialogue onscreen in a language other than what's being spoken, such as French and Spanish.

To turn on closed captioning, do one of the following:

✦ Choose Features⇨Turn On Closed Captioning, and then choose Separate Window or Over Video to set where you want to see the captions.

✦ In full-screen mode, click the Closed Captioning button on the Controller and then choose Turn On Closed Captioning. To view subtitles in different languages, do one of the following:

• Choose Features⇨Subtitles and then choose a language, such as French or Spanish.

• In full-screen mode, click the Closed Captioning button on the Controller and choose a language under the Subtitles category.

Some DVDs have subtitle options in the DVD's interactive menu, which you access by clicking the Menu button on the controller.

Viewing different camera angles

Some DVDs, such as those containing video of concerts, offer a choice of multiple camera angles. This gives you a chance to view a DVD and, at a certain spot, switch from looking at the drummer to looking at the lead guitarist.

To switch to a different camera angle, choose one of the following methods:

✦ Choose Features⇨Angle and then choose an angle.

✦ In window mode, click the Angle button on the Controller and then choose an angle. (If the DVD you're watching doesn't offer optional angles, the video will continue playing without changing the way it looks.)

✦ In full-screen mode, click the Streams/Closed Captioning button on the Controller and then choose an angle under the Angle category.

Choosing different audio tracks

Sometimes a DVD may offer multiple audio tracks, such as a default audio track and alternative audio tracks of foreign languages. To switch to different audio tracks, choose one of the following:

✦ Choose Features➪Audio and then choose an audio track.

✦ In window mode, click the Audio button on the Controller and then choose an audio track. (If the DVD you're watching has only one audio track, the audio will continue playing without changing how you're hearing the audio.)

✦ In full-screen mode, click the Streams/Closed Captioning button on the Controller and then choose an audio track under the Audio Streams category.

To reveal DVD Player menus in full-screen mode, move the pointer to the top of the screen.

Enhancing your viewing experience

DVD Player has a few options to take full advantage of both your Mac's capabilities and the DVD that you're watching. You can adjust the video color quality, screen size, and audio to better suit your viewing needs. Follow these steps:

1. Choose Window➪Video Zoom.

The Video Zoom inspector opens.

2. Select the On check box.

3. Open the pop-up menu next to Manual, as shown in Figure 2-9.

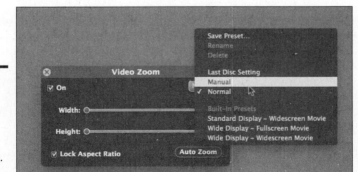

Figure 2-9:
Change
the display
setup for
watching
your movie.

4. Choose the preset zoom setting that you want.

The width and height sliders move according to the type of display you choose.

To adjust the color of your video, follow these steps:

1. **Choose Window⇨Video Color.**

   The Video Color inspector opens.

2. **Select the On check box.**

3. **Open the pop-up menu next to Manual, as shown in Figure 2-10.**

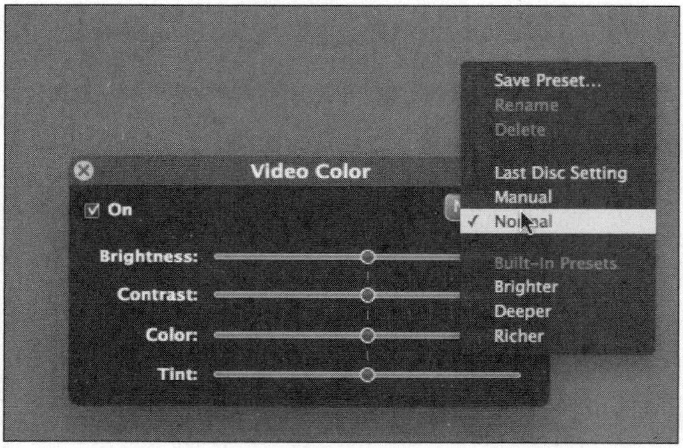

Figure 2-10: Use Video Color to brighten or enrich the color of your video.

4. **Choose the preset setting that you want: Brighter, Deeper, or Richer.**

   The Brightness, Contrast, Color, and Tint sliders move according to the type of color you choose.

You adjust the volume in DVD Player with the volume sliders on the controllers or by choosing Controls⇨Volume Up/Volume Down/Mute. You can control more than just the volume of the audio, however. For example, if you're watching a DVD on your Mac, you may want to set up the audio for small speakers. Follow these steps to adjust the audio:

1. **Choose Window⇨Audio Equalizer.**

   The Audio Equalizer inspector opens.

2. **Select the On check box.**

3. **Open the pop-up menu next to Normal, as shown in Figure 2-11.**

4. **Choose the preset setting that you want: Bass and Vocal Boost, Bass Boost, Small Speakers, Vocal Boost.**

   The equalizing sliders move according to the type of audio you choose.

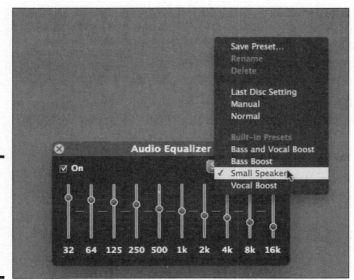

Figure 2-11:
The Audio Equalizer enhances the sound quality of your video.

Using the DVD Player Timer

If you're in the habit of falling asleep while watching a television show or film, you'll like the DVD Player Timer control. Like the sleep function on a clock radio, you set a time for how long you want your DVD to play and what action you want to take place when the time's up. Follow these steps:

1. **Choose Controls⇨Timer⇨Set Timer.**

   Note: Your DVD can be playing or stopped.

   The Timer Settings dialog opens, as shown in Figure 2-12.

2. **Set the time limit you want to set (30 minutes is the default), or select the At End of Current Title radio button.**

Figure 2-12:
Use the Timer to turn off DVD Player after a set interval.

Timer Settings

Action: Sleep

⦿ in [30] minutes
◯ at end of current title

[Cancel] [OK]

Use At End of Current Title if you want the action to take place when the DVD finishes playing (for example, so you don't have to get out of bed to turn off your Mac when the DVD finishes).

3. **Choose the action you want to happen when the time expires from the Action pop-up menu: Quit DVD Player, Sleep, Shut Down, or Log Out.**

4. **Click OK.**

The Timer appears briefly in the upper-left corner of the window. The other Timer options are activated in the Controls menu: Display Time, Resume, or Cancel Timer.

Ejecting a DVD

When you finish watching your DVD, you probably want to eject it from your Mac. Some Macs have an Eject key on the keyboard, which you can press to eject your disc. Otherwise, there are three ways to eject your DVD:

✦ From DVD Player, choose Controls⇨Eject DVD.

✦ In window mode, click the Eject button on the Controller.

✦ From the Finder, choose File⇨Eject *disc title*.

You can connect your Mac to a television, monitor, or projector, and watch your DVD on a bigger screen. First, see what kind of port your television, monitor, or projector has, and then look through the Apple Online Store or visit your local Apple reseller to find the cable and adapter that matches your Mac. Attach the adapter to your Mac and then connect an HDMI or VGA cable from the adapter to your television, monitor, or projector. If your movie doesn't appear automatically on the external device, choose ⌘⇨System Preferences⇨Displays and click Detect Displays to sync your Mac and the television, monitor, or projector.

Customizing DVD Player

Normally, you can pop a DVD into your Mac and watch it play right away. However, you may want to take some time to customize DVD Player to change how it plays.

Parental Controls

If you don't want your children watching certain DVDs, you can turn on DVD Player's Parental Controls. These controls are designed either to block certain types of DVDs from playing or to prevent certain objectionable scenes from appearing, while allowing the rest of the movie to be seen.

Because of the extra expense involved in adding Parental Control features to a DVD, many DVDs don't support these controls. If you turn on Parental Controls, it's entirely possible to watch an inappropriate DVD on your Mac if the DVD isn't programmed to implement such control features.

To turn on (or off) Parental Controls, follow these steps:

1. **Choose Features➪Enable Parental Control.**

   A dialog appears, asking for your password.

2. **Type your password and then click OK.**

3. **To see whether Parental Controls are enabled and set preferences, choose File➪Get Disc Info➪Parental Control.**

   The Parental Control pane appears, as shown in Figure 2-13.

Figure 2-13: Choose which DVDs your children can watch.

> Parental Control
>
> Info Jacket Picture Regions Parental Control
>
> **Parental Control is disabled.**
>
> When this media is opened while Parental Control is enabled:
>
> ⦿ Always ask for authorization
> ○ Always allow to be played
>
> 🔒 Click the lock to make changes   (?)
>
> Cancel   OK

4. **If the DVD has Parental Controls enabled, the first time a DVD is inserted, you have to authorize it with the administrator password in order to play the DVD.**

   In the confirmation dialog that appears, as shown in Figure 2-14, click the Play Once button if you want to require the administrator name and password each time the DVD is inserted, or click the Always Allow button to play the DVD whenever it's inserted.

Figure 2-14: Adjust Parental Controls.

> **Allow the media "MARTIAN_CHILD" to play?**
>
> Parental Control is on. To play this media, you will be asked to enter an administrator name and password.
>
> (?) Always Allow   Cancel   Play Once

If you want to change the authorization, when the DVD is playing, choose File⇨Get Disc Info and click Parental Control. Select Always Ask for Authorization if you want to require the administrator name and password to play the DVD or Always Allow to Be Played to let the DVD be played without being authorized again. You can also choose Features⇨Deauthorize Media. Enter the administrator name and password to immediately stop playback and eject the DVD.

To disable parental controls, choose Features⇨Disable Parental Controls.

Defining DVD Player preferences

Several things happen behind the scenes of the DVD Player app when you insert a DVD into your optical disc drive. You can select some options so DVD Player performs to your liking. Choose DVD Player⇨Preferences to open the window shown in Figure 2-15. Click through each tab at the top to do the following, and then click OK when you finish making adjustments:

✦ **Player:** Defines how DVD Player behaves when running, such as whether to start in full-screen mode and begin playing a disc as soon as it's inserted in the drive. If you watch videos when your Mac isn't connected to a power source, select the Put the DVD Drive to Sleep check box next to When Playing Using Battery.

✦ **Disc Setup:** Allows you to change the language used to display audio, subtitles, and DVD menus. If you connect external speakers to your Mac, select the preferred Audio Output here.

✦ **Windows:** Choose options for what you see onscreen.

✦ **Previously Viewed:** Defines how to handle a DVD that was ejected and inserted back into your Mac. For example, this option specifies whether to start playing the DVD at the beginning or at the last scene viewed before you ejected the DVD. You can also instruct the app to use the disc settings for the audio equalizer, video color, and video zoom.

✦ **High Definition:** Defines how to play high-definition DVDs.

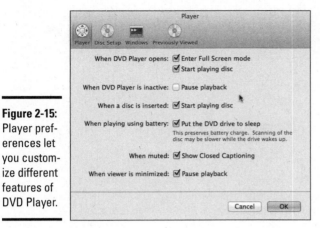

Figure 2-15:
Player pref-
erences let
you custom-
ize different
features of
DVD Player.

If you aren't sure which DVD Player features your Mac supports, choose
Help⇨Show Supported Features. A list appears on the screen; click the list
to close it.

Chapter 3: Importing, Viewing, Organizing, and Sharing Photos

In This Chapter

✔ Seeing how digital photography works

✔ Getting your digital images onto your Mac

✔ Capturing digital images without a digital camera

✔ Using iPhoto to organize your digital images

✔ Making your photos look better

✔ Sharing photos with your family and friends

More people are taking photos than ever before with digital cameras and mobile phones, and then using websites like Facebook, Instagram, and Flickr to share every moment and morsel. Of course, before you share your immortalized antics, you may want to edit the evidence with an image-editing app to make the subject or scene look better than it did in real life.

You can use iPhoto, which is part of the iLife suite, not only for image editing but also for managing (an important part of digital photography because it's so easy to accumulate hundreds, if not thousands, of photos in a short time) and sharing your photos. From start to finish, iPhoto can take care of organizing your photos so you can focus on taking even more photos. We explain all these tasks in this chapter, but first, we provide a brief introduction — or refresher — on digital photography.

Understanding Digital Photography

Instead of using film, digital photography captures images as a collection of tiny dots called *pixels*. A single photo can comprise millions of pixels. To help you understand the capabilities of different digital cameras and mobile phones with built-in digital cameras, manufacturers identify the gadgets by how many millions of pixels they can capture in each photo. This total number of pixels —the *resolution* — ranges from as little as less than 1 megapixel (MP; a megapixel equals one million pixels) to 16MP or more. Figure 3-1 shows how pixels create an image.

Figure 3-1:
Every digital image consists of hundreds, thousands, or millions of pixels.

When digital cameras were first introduced, the thought was, the greater the number of pixels used to create a photo, the sharper the overall image. In some cases, though, too many megapixels captured with a crummy lens can result in fuzzy images. What's more, those high-megapixel photos take up a lot of memory and storage space, which means sharing them electronically takes more Internet bandwidth and/or time. The truth is that lens quality, manageability, and flash and zoom features also affect image quality. And, image preference is subjective. After all, the photos you love from your honeymoon in the Himalayas may be considered poor by a National Geographic photographer.

Flash memory cards

Every time you snap a digital photo, your camera or mobile phone needs to save that photo somewhere. Some digital cameras and many mobile phones and tablets (such as the iPhone and iPad) come with built-in memory, which can store any digital images that you capture. However, to store large numbers of photos, most digital cameras and some mobile phones can also store photos on removable storage devices called *flash memory cards*.

In no particular order, here are a few things to keep in mind about flash memory cards:

✦ **Reuse:** Flash memory cards can be erased and reused. You can take as many photos as the flash memory card can hold, copy your photos to your Mac's hard drive or a remote storage site, and then erase the photos from the flash memory card so you can use it again.

✦ **Resolution versus storage:** The number of photos you can store on flash memory cards depends on the resolution of the photos you take. If you capture photos at a high resolution, you can store far fewer photos than if you capture those same photos at a lower resolution.

✦ **Storage and speed measurement:** Flash memory cards are often measured in terms of their storage size and speed. The amount of storage a flash memory card can hold is measured in megabytes (MB) and, most frequently today, gigabytes (GB), such as 512MB or 2GB. The greater the storage capability of a flash memory card, the higher the cost.

The speed of flash memory cards is often described as minimum read and write speeds, measured in megabytes per second (MB/sec) such as 10MB/sec. The higher the write speed of a flash memory card, the faster you can capture and store photos. Sometimes the speed of a flash memory card may also be described as a number — 60x, for example — which tells you the flash memory card is 60 times faster than the original flash memory cards.

✦ **Image recovery:** If you ever accidentally erase a photo from a flash memory card, don't panic (and don't store any more photos on that flash memory card). If you buy a special file-recovery application, such as MediaRECOVER (`http://freshcrop.com`) or PhotoRecoveryPro (`www.photorecoverypro.net`), you can often retrieve deleted photos from any type of flash memory card. However, if you delete a photo and then store more photos on the flash memory card, the new photos will likely wipe out any traces of your deleted photos, making it impossible to retrieve the deleted photos ever again.

Many different types of flash memory cards exist because each design is meant to set the "standard" for flash memory cards. Unfortunately, every flash memory card has its limitations, so companies keep coming up with newer designs to overcome these limitations. Because so many "standards" exist, the result is that there is no standard. The following are the most popular flash memory cards:

✦ **CompactFlash Type I (CFI) and CompactFlash Type II (CFII):** Introduced in 1994, CompactFlash cards were one of the first flash memory cards available and one of the largest. CompactFlash cards are available with up to 256GB of storage. There are two types of CompactFlash cards: Type I (3.3 mm thick), or CFI; and Type II (5.0 mm thick), or CFII.

Because of the thickness differences, make sure that you use the right CompactFlash cards for your digital camera and card reader. A digital camera and card reader that can use a CFII card can also use a CFI card, but the reverse isn't true.

✦ **Secure Digital (SD) and Plus Secure Digital (Plus SD):** SD cards are much smaller than CompactFlash cards and offer built-in encryption to prevent storing copyright-infringing materials, such as illegal songs, although this encryption feature is rarely used. Because of their small size, SD cards are slowly evolving into the standard for digital photography. Even smaller versions of SD cards include Mini and Micro SD cards, which are often the type of flash memory card used in mobile phones. Some formats of SD cards reach 2 terabytes of storage.

✦ **Memory Stick (MS), Memory Stick Pro (MS Pro), Memory Stick (MS Duo), Memory Stick Pro Duo (MS Pro Duo), and Memory Stick Micro (MS Micro):** The Memory Stick format was developed by Sony, and, as of this writing, only Sony devices (digital cameras, video camcorders, and PlayStations) use Memory Sticks for storing digital images. The original Memory Stick stores up to 32GB of data, whereas the Memory Stick Pro purportedly can hold up to 2TB (that's *terabytes,* as in "thousand gigabytes") of data. The Memory Stick Duo and Memory Stick Pro Duo look like an original Memory Stick cut in half. Sony also makes the Memory Stick Micro, which holds up to 16GB.

Despite Sony's backing, the Memory Stick format has never gained popularity with other manufacturers. If you buy a Sony camera, you'll probably be stuck with using Memory Sticks although some of the latest Sony cameras now use SD cards instead.

✦ **xD-Picture Cards (xD):** Olympus and Fuji invented the xD-Picture Cards to provide yet another standard. Fewer cameras use them — with the exception, of course, of Olympus cameras and some Fuji cameras. An xD-Picture Card is often more expensive than other flash memory cards and has a 2GB storage limit, making it less attractive.

Digital image file formats

When you take photos, your digital camera stores those photos in a specific graphics file format. The four most common file formats for storing digital photographs are

✦ **JPEG (Joint Photographic Experts Group):** JPEG is the most common file format because it is recognized by most computers and offers the ability to compress images to shrink the overall file size. (*Compressing* a JPEG file means decreasing the number of colors used in an image, which shrinks the file size but lowers the visual quality.)

✦ **PNG (Portable Network Graphics):** PNG images are used primarily for the Internet, not for print. Because PNG uses lossless compression and supports transparent pixels, images are sharper than JPEG. However, the files are larger.

✦ **TIFF (Tagged Image File Format):** If photo quality is more important than file size, save your photos as TIFF files. You can still compress TIFF files slightly, and TIFF files retain all colors unless you use JPEG compression. As a result, a compressed TIFF file is usually larger than an equivalent compressed JPEG file.

✦ **Raw (which doesn't stand for anything!):** Raw files offer greater visual quality, but there is no single Raw file format standard. As a result, every digital camera manufacturer offers its own Raw file format.

The biggest advantage is that Raw files allow for greater manipulation. As a result, professional photographers often use Raw files for greater control over manipulating their images. The biggest disadvantage is that Raw images take up a large amount of storage space, which means that you can't store as many images as photos captured in other formats.

Ultimately, there is no single "best" file format. If a digital camera lets you save images in different file formats, experiment to see which one you like best. You may prefer one type of file format, such as JPEG, for ordinary use, or PNG for images you want to post on your website, but prefer Raw for capturing images in special situations that don't require capturing images quickly, such as taking photos of a landscape.

Transferring Digital Images to the Mac

To transfer photos from a device — digital camera, mobile phone, or tablet — to your Mac, you have two choices:

✦ You can connect your device to your Mac by using a USB cable or wirelessly, if your device supports that option.

✦ You can pop the flash memory card out of your device and plug it into your Mac's built-in SDxD card reader (if your Mac has one) or a third-party card reader that connects to your Mac's USB port.

No matter which method you use, your Mac treats all the images stored on your device's flash memory card as just another external drive from which you can copy photos to your Mac's hard drive (such as into the Photos folder).

When you connect a device to your Mac, it can automatically load an app to retrieve those images. iPhoto and Image Capture, which both come preloaded on your Mac, can retrieve digital snapshots automatically.

If you organize photos in iPhoto, choose it as your default app to retrieve photos from a device. (You can specify another app as the external editor.) If you use a different app to organize your photos, such as Adobe Photoshop, you can make that app your default app. If you use more than one app to organize your photos, you can make Image Capture your default app and then use the Open With command to choose the app you want to use to edit your imported photos, deciding what to use on an image-by-image basis.

Defining a default app for retrieving photos

If you need to transfer digital images from a device to your Mac on a regular basis, you can define a default app to use for retrieving these images by following these steps:

1. **Double-click the Image Capture icon in the Applications folder or from Launchpad.**

   The Image Capture window appears.

2. **Connect your device to your Mac's USB port with the appropriate cable.**

   Your connected camera, smartphone, or tablet will appear under the Devices group in the left pane, as shown in Figure 3-2.

   You can also define a default application by running iPhoto and choosing iPhoto⇨Preferences.

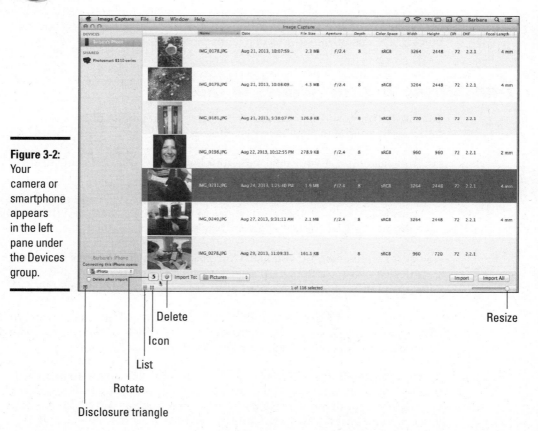

Figure 3-2: Your camera or smartphone appears in the left pane under the Devices group.

3. **Click the Connecting This [*your device name*] Opens pop-up menu in the bottom-left corner and then choose iPhoto or Image Capture (refer to Figure 3-2). (Click the disclosure triangle in the bottom-left corner if you don't see this pane.)**

   You can choose another application listed on the pop-up menu, or click Other to choose an application in your Mac's Applications folder that isn't listed in the pop-up menu so it can run automatically when you connect your camera to your Mac.

4. **(Optional) Choose the following options:**

   - *Delete after Import:* Selecting this check box copies your photos from your connected device to your Mac's hard drive, and then deletes the photos from your camera or smartphone, freeing memory on the device so you can take more photos.

   - *Import To:* Open the pop-up menu to the right of Import To to choose where you want Image Capture to save your imported photos.

5. **Choose File↪Quit to exit the Image Capture application, or go to the next section to learn more about using Image Capture.**

Retrieving photos using Image Capture

If you define Image Capture as the default application to run when you connect a digital camera to your Mac, follow these steps:

1. **Connect your device to your Mac with the appropriate cable.**

   The Image Capture window appears, displaying your devices in the right pane (refer to Figure 3-2).

   You can also use the Image Capture application to capture and copy images from a scanner, which will appear under the Devices menu if it's connected directly to your Mac or in the Shared menu (as in Figure 3-2), if it's on the same network as your Mac.

2. **(Optional) Before importing your photos, you can click the icons below the right pane of the Image Capture window (refer to Figure 3-2):**

   - Switch between List view (shows thumbnail images of your photos and information about each one) and Icon view (which shows a larger thumbnail image with just the file name).

   - Rotate a selected photo.

   - Delete a selected photo.

   - Choose the location to which you want Image Capture to save your imported photos (open the Import To pop-up menu).

3. (Optional) Click and drag the resizing slider in the bottom-right corner of the Image Capture window left or right to increase or decrease the size of your photo icons.

4. Click a photo that you want to transfer and then click the Import button, or click the Import All button to retrieve all photos stored on your camera or smartphone.

    To select multiple images, hold down the ⌘ key and click each photo you want to import.

5. Image Capture marks each photo with a check mark after it copies that photo to the location selected in the pop-up menu to the left of the Import button (refer to Figure 3-2).

6. Choose Image Capture⇨Quit Image Capture.

If you didn't select the Delete after Import check box, you have to erase the photos from your device or from the flash memory card after you import them to your Mac to open up space to store new snapshots.

Retrieving photos using iPhoto

iPhoto will import both photos and videos from your camera or phone to your Mac. If you want to use iPhoto as the default application to run when you connect a digital camera to your Mac, follow these steps:

1. Connect your device to your Mac with the appropriate cable (or plug your memory card into your memory card reader).

    iPhoto launches automatically if you chose it as your default (as explained in the section "Defining a default app for retrieving photos") and displays photos from your device in the right pane, as shown in Figure 3-3.

    If you're running iPhoto for the first time and didn't choose a default application, two dialogs will appear, offering these options:

    - *Do you want to use iPhoto when you connect your digital camera?:* Click Yes if you want iPhoto to open automatically whenever you plug in your digital camera or camera-enabled smartphone. Click No if you don't want iPhoto to open automatically — or click Decide Later if you'd rather make this momentous decision another time.

    - *Look up Photo Locations:* Click Yes if you want iPhoto to automatically add location information when it imports photos you snap with your GPS-capable camera or smartphone. Capturing the location is called *geotagging* and is much like the time-date stamp on traditional and digital photos.

Figure 3-3:
iPhoto displays the photos stored on a camera, smartphone, or memory card plugged into your Mac.

2. **(Optional) Before importing your photos, you can adjust or choose the following options in the upper area of the iPhoto window:**

   • *Event Name:* Click the text field and type a name for the batch of photos you're importing, such as **My Wedding Day** or **Summer Vacation.** Events without a specific name are identified by the date. See the section "Naming an event" to learn how to add a name after you import photos. If you use Photo Stream, each month is an event titled *month year Photo Stream.*

   • *Split Events:* Select this check box to make iPhoto automatically create separate event folders for photos you're importing based on the date you snapped the photos.

   • *Show All (number of) Photos (not shown in Figure 3-3; appears with some devices):* Click the arrow to the right to see all the photos that are still on your device but that you already imported to iPhoto.

3. **(Optional) Click and drag the Zoom slider in the bottom-left corner of the iPhoto window left or right to increase or decrease the size of your photo thumbnails.**

4. **Click a photo that you want to transfer and click the Import Selected button.**

   If you click Import All, iPhoto retrieves all photos stored on your camera or smartphone.

   To select multiple images, hold down the ⌘ key and click each photo you want to import.

5. **When iPhoto finishes importing your photos, a dialog appears asking whether you want to keep or delete the photos from your device.**

- *Delete Photos:* If you want to delete the photos from your device to make room so you can take more photos, click the Delete Photos button.

- *Keep Photos:* Otherwise, click the Keep Photos button to leave the photos on your camera or smartphone.

6. **Choose iPhoto⇨Quit iPhoto to exit iPhoto.**

Moving photos from other folders into iPhoto

If you have photos or image files in other folders on your Mac or on an external hard drive or flash drive, follow these steps to bring the photos and images into iPhoto:

1. **Click the iPhoto icon on the Dock or from Launchpad.**

2. **Choose File⇨Import to Library.**

   The Import Photos dialog appears, as shown in Figure 3-4.

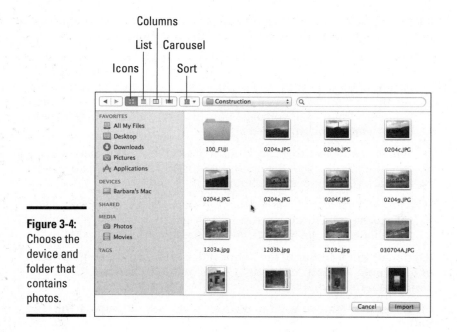

Figure 3-4: Choose the device and folder that contains photos.

3. **Click the drive or folder in the Source list that contains the photos you want to import.**

4. **Choose one of the following:**

   - *To import every photo file displayed on a drive or in a selected folder:* Proceed to Step 5.

   - *To import individual files from a drive or folder:* Click the photo file(s) that you want to import, or double-click a folder that contains the photos you want to import, and then click the photo files that you want to import.

     To select multiple photos, hold down the ⌘ key and click each photo you want to import. To select a range of photos, click the first photo you want to import, hold down the Shift key, and then click the last photo to include all the photos in between.

     To facilitate finding photos, click the view buttons at the top of the window to change how you see the folders and files: icons, list, columns, or carousel. Click the Sort button to arrange the contents by name, application, or date.

5. **Click the Import button.**

   iPhoto imports your photos and organizes them into an event, or several events if the photo files you import are tagged with information such as the date or location, and/or if you import the contents of two or more separate folders. Learn about tagging in the section "Tagging photos" later in this chapter.

Apple likes to use the term *Event* (note the capital), but we find that annoying after a bit. You can also create an event in Calendar/Reminders, so to save confusion and tedium, we just use *event*.

A fast way to import single photos into iPhoto is to drag and drop those photos to the iPhoto icon on the Dock, or to the Photos category under Library in the iPhoto Source list. Alternatively, Control-click a photo you see online or receive in an e-mail to open a contextual menu and then choose Add Image to iPhoto Library.

Retrieving photos by using the SDxD memory card reader

A second way to transfer digital images is to remove the memory card from your device and then plug it into the SDxD memory card reader port on your Mac, if your Mac has one. (You can also connect a card reader to a USB port and insert the card into the reader.) Your Mac displays the flash memory card icon on the Desktop and its contents in a Finder window the same way it displays an external hard drive.

Never yank a flash memory card out of the card reader port; doing so may cause your Mac to scramble the data on the memory card. Before physically removing a flash memory card from the port, choose one of the following ways to eject a flash memory card safely from your Mac:

✦ Drag the flash memory card icon to the Eject icon (where you usually find the Trash) on the Dock to eject it.

✦ Click the flash memory icon and choose File➪Eject.

✦ Click the flash memory icon and press ⌘+E.

✦ Control-click (right-click on a two-button mouse or two-finger click on a trackpad) the flash memory icon and choose Eject from the shortcut menu that appears.

✦ Click the Eject button that appears to the right of the flash memory icon in the Finder window Sidebar.

Capturing Photos from Other Sources

Maybe you don't have a digital camera or a handheld device. But, if you have a MacBook Air, a MacBook Pro, or an iMac, you have a built-in FaceTime digital camera in your Mac. You can also find a built-in FaceTime camera on Apple's Thunderbolt Display external monitor that can connect to your Mac desktop computer or act as a second display for your MacBook or iMac computer. To capture photos with this built-in camera, the simplest method is to use the Photo Booth app located in your Mac's Applications folder.

If you're the type who doesn't like taking photos, you may prefer to save photos you like from websites you visit or from friends' postings on social media networks such as Facebook, Pinterest, and Flickr. By copying photos from websites, you can find images that you wouldn't normally capture yourself, such as images of fighting in the Middle East or photos of mountain climbers scaling Mount Everest, unless of course you're a courageous-and-adventurous type.

Photos stored on websites are usually copyrighted, so you can't legally copy and distribute those photos for free or reuse them for commercial purposes.

Capturing photos with Photo Booth

If your Mac has a built-in FaceTime camera, you can capture photos of yourself (or whoever or whatever is stationed in front of your Mac) by using the Photo Booth application. Photos you snap with Photo Booth save as JPEG files in a Photo Booth folder tucked inside your Photos folder.

You can plug in an optional external webcam, such as one of the models sold by Logitech (www.logitech.com) or Microsoft (www.microsoft.com/hardware), or plug in certain camcorders, to capture photos with Photo Booth. You can also use one of these optional external choices to conduct live, two-way video chats with friends and family, as we write about in Book II, Chapter 3.

To capture photos with Photo Booth, follow these steps:

1. **Click the Photo Booth icon on the Dock or from Launchpad, or double-click the Photo Booth icon in the Applications folder.**

   The Photo Booth window appears, displaying the image seen through the FaceTime camera. Click the zoom widget in the upper-right corner to use Photo Booth in full-screen mode, as shown in Figure 3-5. That way you have those nice red theater curtains framing your image.

   If you click the Effects button, you can capture a photo by using visual effects (such as fish-eye) or in front of a background (such as the Eiffel Tower).

Figure 3-5:
Use Photo
Booth to
capture
photos with
your Mac's
built-in
FaceTime
camera.

2. **Use the three buttons on the lower-left side to choose from three formats:**

   - *Four-up photo:* Click the left button to take four successive photos, just like an old-fashioned photo booth.

   - *Single photo:* Click the middle button to take a single photo.

   - *Video:* Click the right button to record video.

3. **Click the camera button in the middle of the Photo Booth window (or press ⌘+T).**

   Photo Booth counts down from 3 (in seconds) before capturing your photo. If you choose Four-up, Photo Booth snaps four successive shots. If you chose Video, Photo Booth begins recording video. Click the camera button again to stop recording video.

   Each captured photo or video appears at the bottom of the Photo Booth window. Click a photo to see it in the Photo Booth viewing pane. Swipe left and right on the trackpad or with the Magic Mouse to move from one photo to the next.

If you hold down the Option key when you click the camera icon (or press ⌘+T), Photo Booth snaps your photo right away without going through the three-second countdown.

4. **(Optional) Click a photo from the preview filmstrip, and then click one of the following choices from the Share pop-up menu:**

- *E-mail or Messages* opens a new message in Mail or Messages (respectively) with your selected photo pasted in the message. Address and send the message as you normally would with either app.

- *AirDrop* makes your photo available to other AirDrop-capable Macs on the same network. See Book III, Chapter 4, to learn about AirDrop.

- *Twitter, Facebook, or Flickr* posts the photo to your account on those social networks.

- *Add to iPhoto* transfers the photo to your iPhoto library.

- *Change Profile Picture* opens a list of places where you can use the photo as your image on social networks, such as Facebook, Twitter, or LinkedIn, or as your Messages or Contacts image. Select the check boxes for where you want to use the photo, adjust the photo with the zoom slider, and then click the Set button, as shown in Figure 3-6.

Figure 3-6: Change your profile image directly from a photo taken in PhotoBooth.

5. **(Optional) Choose File➪Export to export your photo to another folder, and then click the disclosure triangle next to the Save As field to see the Finder. Scroll through the directories and folders to choose the location to which you want to save the image.**

6. **(Optional) To print your photo, click the photo you want to print in the preview filmstrip and then choose File➪Print. Adjust any necessary settings in the Print dialog that appears, and then click the Print button.**

7. **When you finish snapping and sharing photos, choose Photo Booth➪Quit Photo Booth or press ⌘+Q to exit Photo Booth.**

   Photo Booth stores its photos in a Photo Booth Library inside the Photos folder.

You can delete photos you take with Photo Booth as follows:

✦ **Single image:** In the preview filmstrip, click a photo that you want to delete, and then press the Delete key or click the "X" in the upper-left corner of the preview image.

✦ **All images:** To delete all your Photo Booth photos at one time, choose Edit➪Delete All Photos and click OK to confirm your choice.

When you choose the Delete All Photos command, you remove all photos stored in the Photo Booth folder inside the Photos folder.

Capturing photos from websites

By browsing through different websites, you can find a variety of images that you may want to use for personal use, such as adding them to an album in your iPhoto library of a movie star or public servant whose career you follow, or saving photos from the social network profiles of friends and relatives who live far away.

To save images from a web page, follow these steps:

1. **Launch Safari by clicking the Safari icon on the Dock.**

   You can use a different web browser for these steps if you prefer.

2. **Browse to a web page and Control-click a photo you want.**

   Doing so opens a shortcut menu, as shown in Figure 3-7.

   Generally, because of copyright rules, don't copy photos from websites for reuse on a commercial website.

**Book IV
Chapter 3**

Importing, Viewing, Organizing, and Sharing Photos

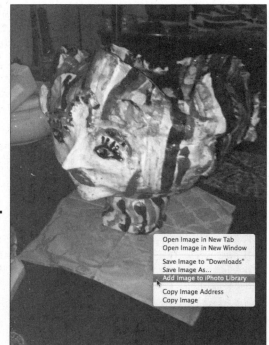

Figure 3-7:
Control-
click a web
page image
for a variety
of choices
for saving
the photo.

3. **Choose one of the following commands from the shortcut menu:**

   • *Save Image to "Downloads":* Saves the photo in the Downloads folder, stored inside your Home folder.

   • *Save Image As:* Lets you choose a name for your photo and a folder where you want to save the photo.

   • *Add Image to iPhoto Library:* Saves the image in your iPhoto photo library.

   • *Copy Image:* Copies the image to the Mac's invisible Clipboard so you can paste it into another document, such as an e-mail message or a letter to your mom.

The Save Image As option is the only one that lets you choose your own descriptive name for an image and specify the save location. All the other options save an image by using that image's original filename, which may be something cryptic like `wild_things_LJ-0187.jpg`, although you can always rename the file later if you want.

Clicking and dragging a web image to your Mac's Desktop, to the iPhoto icon on the Dock, to a Finder window, or directly to a document in apps such as Pages or Word is a quick way to capture photos from websites.

Organizing Photos with iPhoto

After importing your photos in one or more of the ways explained previously, you need to organize them so you can find the photos you want. Think of iPhoto as a place where you can dump all your digital photographs so you can browse them later. In iPhoto, your photos are sorted or grouped in different ways. The sorts or groups appear as follows in the Source list on the left side of the iPhoto window, as shown in Figure 3-8:

Figure 3-8: The Source list shows the different ways photos are sorted and grouped.

✦ **Library:** iPhoto comes with the following four libraries:

- *Events* typically contain photos captured on the same day, but you can also move photos from one event to another, split or merge events, and give events a name that means something to you.

- *Photos* holds all your photos in chronological order.

- *Faces* organizes your Library based on the faces of individuals you tag with a name. Over time, iPhoto tries to identify faces in new photos you import and automatically tag them with the name(s) of the person(s) in the photos.

- *Places* automatically tags and organizes your photos based on where you snapped them with your GPS-capable camera or mobile phone, like the Nikon Coolpix 6000 camera or the iPhone, both of which have built-in Global Positioning System (GPS) receivers. You can also manually tag photos with location information on an individual or group basis.

✦ **Recent:** Photos are grouped by those you most recently viewed, photos added in the last 12 months, photos added in the most recent import, flagged photos, and those you deleted. (When you delete a photo, it's placed in the iPhoto Trash until you click the Trash icon and then click the Empty Trash button.)

✦ **Shared:** Photos you share with others online appear here. For example, photos shared on iCloud or albums you create to post to Facebook.

✦ **Albums:** Construct iPhoto albums just like you create an album of printed photos by putting the photos you want together in a specific order. Create folders to hold and organize multiple albums, such as creating a single album for each vacation and then placing all the vacation albums together in one folder.

✦ **Projects:** Create printed objects such as photo books, calendars, and cards in iPhoto, and then send them electronically to the printer. In a few days, the printed piece is delivered to your doorstep.

✦ **Slideshows:** Create simple slideshows of your photos — from a library, an album, or a project — and then view the show on your Mac's screen or a larger monitor or projector.

If you work in full-screen view, the Source list items become buttons along the bottom of the screen. Click the full-screen button in the upper-right corner to switch to full-screen view, which is great for working in iPhoto because it takes advantage of all the real estate of your Mac screen — no matter how big or small.

Organizing the Events library

The iPhoto Library can store literally thousands of photos, which can soon become as disorganized as dumping a decade's worth of photographs in a box and then wondering why you can never find a specific photo easily.

When you import photos, iPhoto automatically distributes the photos into the libraries based on the *metadata* — data bits such as the date, time, and location — electronically imprinted on each photo. All the photos go singly into the Photos library but are grouped by date in the Events library, which gives you a head start on organizing the photos. You can then move the photos from one event to another, merge or split events, rename events, and even create new events. For example, iPhoto will divide your vacation photos by date, but you can merge all the dates to create one vacation event.

Two other ways you can organize and view photos are by using the *Faces* feature, which sorts photos by the faces of people in your photos, and by using the *Places* feature, which sorts photos based on the location where you capture them. We cover both of these ways of organizing and viewing photos in your iPhoto Library in later sections of this chapter.

Browsing through an event

Click the Events button in the Source list to see the Events chooser. Think of each event as a stack of photos, and you see the one on top. When you position the pointer over an event, iPhoto displays the date of the event and the number of photos it contains, as shown in Figure 3-9.

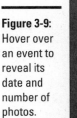

Figure 3-9: Hover over an event to reveal its date and number of photos.

An event can represent a single photo you capture on a particular day. More likely, though, an event represents several photos. To view thumbnail previews of all the photos stored in an Event, hover the pointer over the Event icon and then slowly move the pointer left or right (or press the left and right arrow keys) to step through a thumbnail preview of each photo contained in the event.

If you'd rather see individual thumbnails of all the photos stored in a single event, double-click the event to display them, shown in Figure 3-10.

Click the All Events button to return to the Events chooser.

Figure 3-10:
Double-
clicking
an event
expands all
the photos
in the iPhoto
window.

Naming an event

To make finding photos easier, you can give each event a descriptive name to jog your memory as to which photos are stored in each event without having to browse through them. To give your event a descriptive name, follow these steps:

1. **Click the Events category under Library in the Source list of the iPhoto window or click the Events button at the bottom of the screen if you're working in full-screen view.**

   iPhoto displays all your events. If you haven't named your events, each event may display the date when you captured those photos as its name.

2. **Click the event name, which appears directly under the event photo.**

   A yellow box highlights the event, and a text box appears along with the number of photos stored in that event.

3. **Type a new descriptive name for your event and then press Return.**

In addition to giving an event a meaningful, descriptive name, you can select a specific photo to represent the event in the Event chooser. Double-click an event to see all the photos contained within, click the photo you want to appear on the Event chooser for the open event, and then choose Events➪Make Key Photo.

Merging events

Even if you have photos stored as separate events, you may decide that the photos in both events really should be grouped as a single event. In this case, you can merge two events into a single event by following these steps:

1. **Click the Events category in the iPhoto Source list or on the toolbar along the bottom of the full-screen iPhoto window.**

   iPhoto displays all your events.

2. **Move the pointer over an event you want to move or merge into another event.**

3. **Click and drag the event to the event you want to merge it with.**

   The pointer turns into an arrow with a green plus sign.

4. **Release the mouse button when the pointer appears over an event.**

   Your two events now appear as a single event. If an event is untitled and referred to only as the date, then a date range (such as Jan. 28 – Feb. 15, 2014) appears under the event. If you merge two or more events with different names, the merged event will have the name of the event you dragged to. So if you drag an event named Baseball over an event named Summer Sports, the merged event will be named Summer Sports.

Splitting an event

Sometimes an event may contain too many, or unrelated, photos. In this case, you may want to store photos in separate events. To split an event, follow these steps:

1. **Click the Events category in the iPhoto Source list or on the toolbar along the bottom of the full-screen iPhoto window.**

   iPhoto displays all your events in the right pane.

2. **Double-click an event you want to split.**

   The photos in your event appear in the iPhoto window (refer to Figure 3-10).

3. **Hold down the ⌘ key and click each photo you want to add to your new separate event.**

   A yellow border highlights each chosen photo.

4. **Choose Events⇨Split Event.**

   Your chosen photos now appear in a separate event.

5. **Click the All Events button.**

   Your original and newly split events appear highlighted with a yellow border. Click the name to rename the new event as explained previously.

Moving photos from one event to another

If a photo appears in one event but you think it should appear in a different event, you can always move that photo. To move a photo from one event to another, follow these steps:

1. **Click the Events category in the iPhoto Source list or on the toolbar along the bottom of the full-screen iPhoto window.**

   iPhoto displays all your photos in the right pane.

2. **Click the event that contains the photos you want to move.**

3. **Hover the pointer over the photo(s) you want to move and click the Flag button in the upper-left corner of each one.**

4. **Click the All Events button to return to the Events chooser.**

5. **Click the event you want to move the flagged photos to.**

6. **Choose Events⇨All Flagged Photos to Selected Event.**

   Your chosen photo or group of photos now appears in the selected event.

7. **(Optional) Instead of moving the photos, you can create a new event that contains those photos by choosing Events⇨Create Event from Flagged Photos.**

Sorting events

The more events you create to store your photos, the harder it is to find what you need. To help keep you organized, iPhoto gives you five options for sorting your events. Choose View⇨Sort Events and then choose from

✦ **Date:** Sorts events chronologically.

✦ **Keyword:** If you add a keyword to the information about a photo, you can sort by that criterion. We explain keywords in the next section.

✦ **Title:** Lets you sort events by title.

✦ **Rating:** After you add ratings to photos, this sort option is active. Find out about ratings in the next section.

✦ **Manually:** Lets you sort events by clicking and dragging them to an order that you want.

Choose View⇨Sort Events again to choose Ascending or Descending. iPhoto sorts your events based on the sorting method that appears with a check mark in the Sort Events submenu.

Tagging photos

After you organize and name events, you can identify individual photos with a name, rating, or keyword, also known as a *tag*. These identifiers add information to photos that gives you another way to find or sort your photos and events. Click the Events button in the Source list and then double-click the event you want to work on.

To see all your photos in iPhoto, click the Photos button in the Library section of the Source list. Change how you view the Photos by choosing View⇨Event Titles to see all your photos sorted by event or View⇨Sort Photos and then choose Date, Keyword, Title, or Rating, and then Ascending or Descending, in the same way as we explain previously for events.

Naming photos

Devices that capture photos store them with generic filenames, such as DSC_846. Fortunately, you can replace these generic titles with more descriptive names. In iPhoto, you can give descriptive names to your events and descriptive names to individual photos. So an event may be named Spring Break, and photos stored in that event may be named Day 1: Arrival, Day 2: Imbibing, and Day 3: Recovering.

To name individual photos, do one of the following:

✦ Click Photos in the Source list to see all your photos.

✦ Click events in the Source list and then double-click an event to name the photos within that event. If you have a lot of photos, this may be the easier way to work with fewer photos at once.

Whether viewing all your photos or only those within one event, proceed as follows to name your photos:

1. **Choose View⇨Titles.**

   Note: If a check mark already appears to the left of Titles, skip this step.

   Titles appear underneath every photo.

2. **Click the title that you want to change.**

   A text box appears, as shown in Figure 3-11.

3. **Type a new name for your photo or use the arrow and Delete keys to edit the existing name.**

4. **Press Return.**

Figure 3-11: Descriptive titles can help you find photos.

If you want to give a group (batch) of photos the same base name (for example, the same name as the event with a number following), add a description, or change the date or time of the photo, ⌘-click to select multiple photos, and then choose Photos⇨Batch Change. Use the pop-up menus in the window that opens, as shown in Figure 3-12, to set the photo Title, Date, or Description.

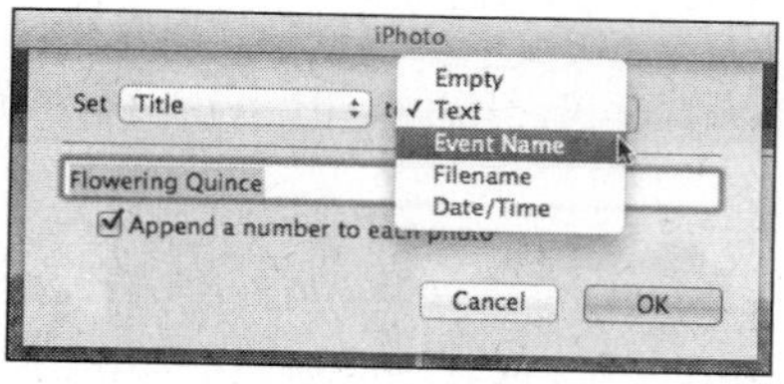

Figure 3-12: Change or add information to photos in batches.

Rating photos

Some photos are better than others, so another way to sort and organize photos is by rating them from zero to five stars. To rate photos, follow these steps:

1. **From the Source list, select either Photos or Events and then double-click an event.**

2. **Choose View⇨Rating.**

   Note: If a check mark already appears to the left of Rating, skip this step.

3. **Select the photo you want to rate or hover the pointer under it.**

   A row of five empty stars appears beneath your selected photo.

4. **Click the first, second, third, fourth, or fifth star to rate the photo with that number of stars, as shown in Figure 3-13.**

Figure 3-13: You can rate each photo with zero to five stars.

You can rate photos in the following ways, even without choosing View⇨Ratings:

✦ Click a photo — or ⌘-click several photos — and then choose Photos⇨My Rating and choose the number of stars you want to rate the photo(s) with from the submenu.

✦ Control-click a photo or click the disclosure triangle in the lower-right corner, and click the number of stars that corresponds to your rating.

✦ Click a photo and press ⌘+0 through ⌘+5 to rate a photo from zero to five stars, respectively.

Adding keywords to a photo

Keywords or *tags* help you organize photos based on categories, such as Cityscapes or Nature. By manually tagging photos by placing keywords on them, you can quickly find all your favorite outdoor photos or family photos.

To add a keyword to a photo, follow these steps:

1. **From the Source list, select either Photos or Events and then double-click an event.**

2. **Click a photo that you want to label with a keyword.**

If you hold down the ⌘ key, you can click two or more photos to assign the same keyword to all of them.

3. **Choose Window⇨Manage My Keywords.**

   The Keywords window appears, which displays several common keywords that iPhoto provides for you, as shown in Figure 3-14.

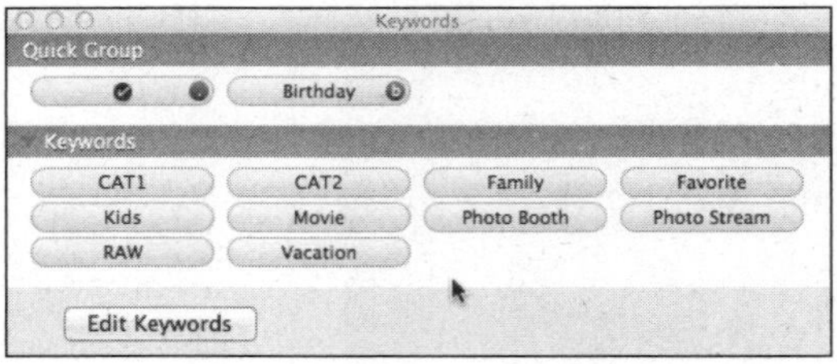

Figure 3-14:
The Keywords window displays a list of keywords you can use.

Keywords

Quick Group

Birthday

Keywords

CAT1	CAT2	Family	Favorite
Kids	Movie	Photo Booth	Photo Stream
RAW	Vacation		

Edit Keywords

4. **(Optional) To add your own keywords to the Keywords window, click the Edit Keywords button. When the Edit Keywords dialog appears, click the plus sign button to type your own keywords into the Keywords window, and then click the OK button.**

   - There is no limit to how many keywords you can create.

   - You can also click a keyword, and then click the minus sign button to remove a keyword from the Keyword window.

   Drag a keyword from the bottom part of the Keywords window to the top part to assign a key to represent a keyword. When the Keywords window is open, you can select a photo or photos and then press the shortcut key to add a keyword to that photo, or photos, quickly.

5. **Click a keyword.**

   Your chosen keyword appears briefly on the photo you select.

   If you click the same keyword in the keyword window, iPhoto removes the keyword from your chosen photo.

6. **(Optional) Click another keyword if you want to assign more than one to the photo.**

7. **(Optional) Click another photo and repeat Step 5.**

8. **Click the Close button on the Keywords window.**

9. **Choose View⇨Info and click the disclosure triangle next to Keywords to see the keyword(s) assigned to the photo.**

After you name, rate, and/or add keywords to photos, you can sort them by choosing View⇨Sort Photos and then choosing your sorting preference from the submenu. Then choose View⇨Sort Photos⇨Ascending (or Descending) to reorder the sort from beginning to end or vice versa.

Storing photos in albums and folders

Sorting and organizing photos into events can be cumbersome. For example, you may have dozens of birthday photos stored in separate events. Although you can store all these birthday photos in the same event, you may also want to keep them grouped with other photos in separate events that represent different years.

To keep photos stored in separate events while grouping them at the same time, you can create an *album* to group related photos without removing them from the events they're stored in. Essentially, a photo is in only one event, but that photo can be in as many albums as you want.

Creating albums and organizing photos manually

To create an album and store photos in it, follow these steps:

1. **Open the event that has some photos you want to put in the album.**

2. **Choose File⇨New Album.**

   An Untitled Album item appears under the Albums category in the Source list; above the pane where you see your Event photos, you see the title `Untitled Album`, as shown in Figure 3-15.

Figure 3-15: Name your album in the Albums category of the Source list or in the title above the photos.

3. **Click the words** Untitled Album **in the Source list or above the photos to rename the album you just created.**

    Your album name appears under the Albums category in the iPhoto Source List and at the top of the viewing pane.

4. **Click and drag photos you want to add to your album from other events to the album folder in the iPhoto Source list.**

    You can select multiple photos by holding down the ⌘ key and clicking each photo you want to add to an album.

5. **Release the mouse button to copy your photo(s) to the album.**

6. **Repeat Steps 4 and 5 for each additional photo you want to copy to the album.**

7. **To remove a photo from the album (but not from iPhoto), click the photo and choose Edit⇨Cut.**

    Now, if you click the album name in the iPhoto Source list, you can see all the photos in that album.

To access the menus from full-screen view, hover the pointer over the top of the screen.

Creating albums and organizing photos automatically

If manually dragging photos in and out of albums is too tedious, you can set up a *Smart Album* from within iPhoto that will store photos automatically.

To create a Smart Album that can store photos automatically, follow these steps:

1. **Choose File⇨New Smart Album.**

    A dialog appears, asking for a name for your Smart Album.

2. **Type a descriptive name for your album in the Smart Album Name text box.**

3. **Open the first pop-up menu and choose a criterion, such as Face or Rating, or a camera setting like Aperture or Camera Model.**

4. **Open the second and third pop-up menus to refine the criterion you choose in Step 3, such as choosing only photos with a rating of four stars or with the Birthday keyword.**

5. **(Optional) Click the plus sign button to define another criterion and repeat Steps 3 and 4.**

6. **Click OK.**

    Your Smart Album now stores photos based on your chosen criteria.

If you create too many albums, you can organize them into folders by choosing File⇨New Folder and dragging related albums into that folder.

Deleting photos, albums, and folders

Many times, you'll import photos into iPhoto and decide that the photo isn't worth saving after all. To keep your iPhoto library from becoming too cluttered, you can delete the photos you don't need.

Besides deleting individual photos, you can also delete albums and folders that contain photos you don't want. When you delete an album or folder (which contains albums), you don't physically delete the photos; you just delete the folder or album that contains the photos. The original photos are still stored in the iPhoto Photos library.

To delete a photo, album, or folder, click the photo (in Photos or Events) or the album or folder you want to delete and press the Delete key or drag it to the Trash icon in the iPhoto Source List. If you delete a photo from an album, it's deleted only from that album, not from iPhoto.

Press ⌘+Z or choose Edit➪Undo Delete right away if you want to recover your deleted items.

If you don't want to delete a photo but want it out of sight, hover the pointer over the lower-right corner of the photo you want to hide and click the disclosure triangle. Click the Hide button, and your photo is out of sight. To hide several photos at once, ⌘-click the photos you want to hide and then Control-click one of them. Click the Hide button, and all the selected photos are hidden.

To bring your photos out of hiding, choose View➪Hidden Photos. The hidden photos appear with an orange "X" in the upper-right corner. Choose View➪ Hidden Photos, again, and the photos disappear from view again. Or, click the disclosure triangle photos you want to see, and then click the Show button. The photo is back in its original spot.

Organizing photos with Faces and Places

Two more ways to organize and view photos in your iPhoto Library are the Faces and Places features.

**Book IV
Chapter 3**

Importing, Viewing, Organizing, and Sharing Photos

✦ **Faces:** Lets you add names to the faces of people in your photos. Over time, iPhoto automatically recognizes and labels the faces of people in new photos you import into your iPhoto Library.

✦ **Places:** Automatically tags and sorts photos you import that contain GPS information that your GPS-capable smartphone or camera adds to photos when you snap the photos with the GPS-tagging feature *(geotagging)* turned on.

You can use the Places feature even if you don't have a GPS-capable device by selecting and tagging individual photos, or a group of photos, with information that you type about the location where you captured the photos.

Using Faces to organize photos

You can organize photos in your iPhoto Library based on the faces of people in the photos.

To organize photos by using the Faces feature, follow these steps:

1. **Click Faces in the Source list and then click the Find Faces button on the toolbar at the bottom of the iPhoto window.**

A selection of faces to identify appears, as shown in Figure 3-16.

Figure 3-16:
Find Faces shows you a selection of faces to identify.

2. **Click in the field under the photo that reads `unnamed` and begin typing the name of the person.**

iPhoto displays a list of matches from Contacts, including your Facebook contacts if you have them linked to Contacts. The more letters you type, the narrower the results. If the name of the person of the photo appears, click that. If not, continue typing the correct name.

3. **Repeat Step 2 for the other photos.**

4. **Click Show More Faces to continue identifying people.**

When iPhoto finds a face that it thinks it recognizes, the name field reads `Is this that person?` ("Barbara Boyd" in Figure 3-16). Click the check mark if the name is correct. Click the "X" if the name is wrong and then enter the correct name. Faces has difficulty identifying profile or three-quarter headshots.

When you name a person in Faces, it automatically tags that person in Facebook when you share photos from iPhoto to Facebook, as explained in the "Sharing options" section.

5. **When you tire of playing the faces identification game, click Continue to Faces.**

    iPhoto displays a corkboard with the named faces of people you have identified so far. The more photos you identify for each person, the better iPhoto becomes at identifying faces correctly. Double-click the person's group of photos to see all your photos of that person. Click the All Faces button in the upper-left corner to return to the Faces view.

After you identify a good selection of faces, you can instruct iPhoto to search for matches by clicking the Events library and then choosing Photos➪Detect Missing Faces.

To view photos organized by Faces in your iPhoto library, click the Faces category under Library in the iPhoto Source list, and then double-click the snapshot of the person whose photos you want to look at.

Locating photos with Places

If your camera or smartphone has a GPS feature or geotagging turned on, photos you import into your iPhoto Library will automatically contain information about the location where you captured the photos. On iOS devices, you use Location Services to turn on geotagging. Check your camera or phone manual to find out how to activate geotagging. Otherwise, you can add location information to photos after importing them to iPhoto.

You view photos organized by the places where the photos were captured by clicking pushpins on a map of the world or by clicking a display listing photos by country, region, state, and city.

You must enable Places for iPhoto to assign locations to your photos. Choose iPhoto➪Preferences and click the Advanced tab. Select Automatically in the Look Up Places pop-up menu.

To view photos organized by the Places feature in your iPhoto Library, follow these steps:

1. **Click the Places category in the iPhoto Source list or click the Places button on the toolbar at the bottom of the window in full-screen view.**

    iPhoto displays a map of the world with red pushpins that indicate locations where your photos were captured. Moving the mouse pointer to a pushpin displays the name of the location where you captured the photos, as shown in Figure 3-17.

Book IV
Chapter 3

Importing, Viewing, Organizing, and Sharing Photos

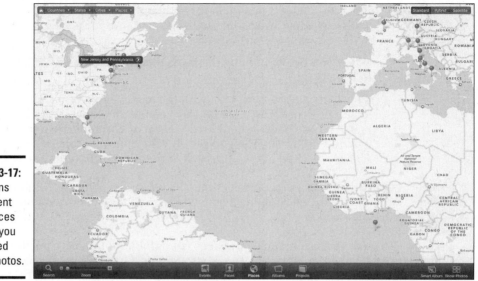

Figure 3-17:
Pushpins
represent
the places
where you
captured
your photos.

2. **Drag the Zoom slider to the right to zoom in on a region.**

As you zoom, more pushpins may appear. For example, in Figure 3-17, New Jersey and Pennsylvania photos are represented by one pushpin, but by zooming on the map, multiple push pins appear for photos taken in different cities in that region.

If you're using a mouse with a scroll wheel, you can zoom in and out on the map by rolling the scroll wheel forward and backward. If you're using a MacBook or a Magic Trackpad or Magic Mouse, you can zoom in and out on the map by pinching two fingertips together and apart on the trackpad.

3. **To view the photos for a location, move the mouse pointer to a pushpin to display the location name and click the arrow to the right of the location name.**

iPhoto displays the photos you captured (or manually tagged, as described in the next section) at the selected location.

4. **(Optional) From the World Map view, you can do these additional things:**

- *Standard, Hybrid, Satellite view:* Click one of these three buttons to change the World Map view. Standard shows roads and place names. Satellite displays an eye-in-the-sky view based on actual satellite imagery. Hybrid combines Standard and Satellite views into a single view.

- *Countries, States, Cities, Places view:* Click one of these four buttons, which becomes a pull-down menu, to narrow your view by location.

Manually adding information to photos

If your camera or smartphone doesn't have a GPS feature that automatically adds a location to photos you capture, you can still add location information to photos in your iPhoto collection by selecting and typing location names for your photos. You can also add keywords, ratings, and other information about your photos. Follow these steps:

1. **Click Photos in the Source list or Events and then a specific event to see the photo chooser.**

2. **Click a photo that you want to identify by location.**

   If you hold down the ⌘ key, you can click two or more photos to assign the same location to all of them.

3. **Click the Info button at the lower right of the window or choose View⇨ Info to display an information pane for the selected photo(s), as shown in Figure 3-18.**

Figure 3-18:
Add or
change
a photo's
location
information.

**Book IV
Chapter 3**

Importing, Viewing,
Organizing, and
Sharing Photos

4. **Click Assign a Place, or the pre-filled location name (*mara* in Figure 3-18), to put the cursor in that field, type or edit the name of the location where the photo was captured, and press Return.**

   While you type, a list beneath the location name appears with suggestions of locations that may match the location you want to assign to the photo.

5. **Edit other information for the photo(s) by clicking in the following fields:**

   • *Title:* Edit or type a title for the selected photo.

- *Rating:* Click the dots to choose the number of stars you want to give the photo (from one to five stars).

- *Description:* Edit or type a descriptive word or words to describe the photo so you can search for it when you want to find it again.

- *Faces:* The number of unnamed faces is indicated (refer to Figure 3-18). Click the "unnamed" text box in the photo and type the name of the person. If there are faces that haven't been detected, click Add a Face. A white box appears on the photo, which you click and drag to surround an undetected face. Click the Click to Name text box beneath the box and type the name of the person. As you type a name, a list of matches from Contacts appears; the more letters you type; the narrower your choices. Click the name when you see it. Click Add a Face again to identify additional undetected faces in the photo.

- *Keywords:* Click the Add Keyword field and begin typing an established keyword. Click the word you want from the list that appears. If you want to add a new keyword, choose Window⇨Manage My Keywords, and add the new word as explained previously.

6. **Click the Info button or choose View⇨Info to hide the Info pane.**

Editing Photos with iPhoto

Besides organizing your photos, iPhoto lets you edit them. Such editing can be as simple as rotating or cropping a photo, or it can be as intricate as removing red-eye from a photograph or modifying colors. When your photos look perfect, you can print them on your printer or through a printing service (which can actually cost less than what you may spend on ink cartridges and glossy photo paper!). And, because the digital format is universally World Wide Web–friendly, you can share your photos in a Messages or Mail message, or on a social network like Facebook or Twitter, or create a shared photo stream on your iCloud account.

First, you want to make those photos as flawless as possible. To edit a photo, follow these steps:

1. **Click Photos in the Source list or Events and then a specific event to see the photo chooser.**

2. **Click a photo and click the Edit button in the lower-right corner.**

   iPhoto displays your selected photo in the center pane, and an editing pane opens to the right of your photo, as shown in Figure 3-19.

Figure 3-19:
The editing
tools appear
in a pane to
the right of
your photo.

3. **Click the Quick Fixes tab at the top of the editing pane and click the buttons to do the following:**

   • *Rotate:* Rotates your photo 180 degrees clockwise or counterclockwise.

   • *Enhance:* Magically fixes brightness and contrast problems and improves your photo.

   • *Fix Red-Eye:* Gets rid of those vampiric red pupils that show up when the flash is too strong. Click the red pupils and drag the slider bar in the Edit pane to match the size of the pupil. Click Done when the redness is blackened.

   • *Straighten:* Changes the angle when you drag the slider. Perhaps you got a little too artistic or want to add an interesting angle to your photo. If you click the Decrease/Increase angle of photo icons that appear on opposite ends of the slider, you can adjust the angle of your photo by 0.1 degree increments. Click Done when the photo is in a position you like.

   • *Crop:* Lets you select only the part of the photo you want to keep. Grabber corners let you shift the border of the photo to show only the part you want. Use the Constrain pop-up menu to choose the photo proportions you want — for example, 2 x 3 or 4 x 6 for a postcard — and move the frame around on the image to crop that best part to the selected size. Click Done when you're satisfied.

   • *Retouch:* Gives you a tool to correct minor blemishes, scars, and wrinkles. Click and drag the tool over the discolored area to create a blemish-free photo. Click Done when you're pleased.

4. **Click the Effects tab of the Edit pane and click the effect you want, such as cooler colors, sepia tones, or a matte finish, as shown in Figure 3-20.**

Figure 3-20: The Effects tools let you choose a way to modify your picture.

5. **Click the Adjust tab of the Edit pane to adjust the following, as shown in Figure 3-21:**

- *Exposure:* Lightens or darkens a photo

- *Contrast:* Alters the differences between light and dark areas

- *Saturation:* Alters the intensity of colors in a photo

    Select the Avoid Saturating Skin Tones check box if you want to try to make skin coloration look more natural.

- *Definition:* Reduces haze and improves clarity without adding too much contrast

- *Highlights:* Increases detail in a photo by lightening or darkening areas

- *Shadows:* Lightens or darkens shadow areas of a photo

- *Sharpness:* Adjusts the focus of a photo

- *De-noise:* Alters the graininess of a photo

- *Temperature:* Alters colors by making them dimmer (colder) or brighter (hotter)

- *Tint:* Adjusts the red/green colors in a photo

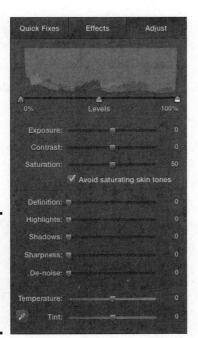

Figure 3-21: Improve your photo with the options on the Adjust tab.

Your image changes as you adjust any of these settings.

Click Undo to undo the last adjustment you made. And if you decide that your original photo looked better without any adjusted settings, click the Revert to Original button.

6. **(Optional) Choose Edit⇨Copy Adjustments to copy your adjusted settings so you can use the same settings to adjust another photo, which you can open and then choose Edit⇨Paste Adjustments to apply the adjusted settings.**

7. **Click the Edit button to close the Edit pane.**

Sharing Photos

For many people, there's no point in taking photos if they don't share them with others. If you fall in this camp, you can publicize your photos to the world by printing them; posting them on a web page; uploading them directly to Facebook, Twitter, or Flickr; sending them to others via Mail or Messages; or burning them to a CD/DVD. For an added fee, you can print your photos as books, calendars, or greeting cards. Here we give you the rundown for sharing in each and every way.

Printing photos

You can print individual photos or groups of photos on your home printer by following these steps:

1. **Click Photos in the Source list or Events and then a specific event to see the photo chooser.**

2. **Hold down the ⌘ key and click all the photos you want to print.**

3. **Choose File➪Print or click the Share button in the lower right of the window, and then click the Print button.**

   A Print dialog appears, as shown in Figure 3-22.

Figure 3-22:
Choose from different ways to print your photos.

4. **Click the print styles to the right.**

   The photo appears as it will be printed.

5. **Choose the printer, paper size, and quality from the pop-up menus.**

6. **Click the Print button.**

You can click the Order Prints button in the Share menu to have your photos sent to Apple for printing. The cost to print a 4-x-6 photo is less than what it would cost you in paper and ink on your printer, and the quality is as good as — usually better than — the top photo printers. You can also click the Book, Calendar, or Card button to create photo books, calendars, or greeting cards from your photos, which we briefly explain in the last section of this chapter.

Sending photos in a message

If you want to share photos with family members or friends who have an e-mail address or use Messages on a Mac, iPhone, iPad, or iPod touch, you can send photos by using the Mail or Messages app, which lets you send photos to people using AIM, Google, or other chat services even on non-Apple platforms. If you use a different e-mail app, such as Outlook, you can configure iPhoto to work with your e-mail app by following these steps:

1. **Choose iPhoto⇨Preferences.**

   A Preferences window appears.

2. **Click the General tab.**

3. **Open the Email Photos Using pop-up menu and choose your e-mail application or service.**

4. **Click the Close button of the Preferences window.**

After you configure your e-mail application to work with iPhoto, you can send a photo by following these steps:

1. **Click Photos in the Source list or Events and then a specific event to see the photo chooser.**

2. **Hold down the ⌘ key and click the photo you want to send. You can click up to ten photos to send in one e-mail.**

3. **Click the Share button and choose Mail or choose Share⇨Email.**

   Your photo appears in an e-mail message, as shown in Figure 3-23.

   You can apply one of the themes that appear in the chooser on the right side. Click the text placeholders to type in your own text. Choose Edit⇨Font to change the typeface.

   At the bottom of the chooser pane, open the pop-up menu to select the size image you want to insert in the e-mail. Or, choose Optimize so the e-mail file isn't too large to send.

Figure 3-23:
Sending a
photo from
iPhoto is as
simple as
sending an
e-mail.

4. **Enter an e-mail address or addresses in the To text box.**

   To add an e-mail address to iPhoto, choose iPhoto⇨Preferences and click the Accounts tab. Click the plus sign at the bottom of the pane, choose Email from the pop-up list, and click Add. Choose the type of e-mail service you use (such as Google Mail, iCloud, AOL, or Yahoo!), and click OK. Type in your account information in the appropriate fields, and click the Close button.

5. **Use the pop-up menu to choose the outgoing e-mail address (if you have more than one) and then click Send.**

To send a photo with Messages, open the photo you want to send. Click the Share button and then click the Messages button; a new message window appears with your photo attached to it. Address your message, type an accompanying note, and then click Send.

Posting your photos

You can upload your photos directly to iCloud, Flickr, Twitter, and Facebook from iPhoto by doing the following:

1. **Click Photos in the Source list or Events and then a specific event to see the photo chooser.**

2. **Hold down the ⌘ key and click the photo(s) you want to upload.**

3. **Click the Share button and choose Flickr, Twitter, or Facebook from the pop-up menu (or choose Share⇨Facebook/Flickr/Twitter).**

4. **Sign in to your account with your profile name and password.**

   Alternatively, choose iPhoto⇨Preferences and click the Accounts tab. Click the plus sign at the bottom of the pane, choose Facebook or Flickr from the pop-up list, and then click Add. Type in your profile name and password in the appropriate fields, and click Login.

5. **If you choose Twitter, a window opens with your photo attached. Type your tweet and click Send.**

   For iCloud, Facebook, or Flickr, choose the location where you want to use the photo — for example, for your profile or in an existing album.

   Figure 3-24 shows the locations for Facebook. See the next section to find out about creating shared photo streams on iCloud.

6. **A dialog asks you to select viewing privileges from a pop-up menu. If you choose New Album, you can type in a name for the album.**

7. **Click Publish.**

   Your photo or photos are uploaded to Facebook, Twitter, or Flickr. Comments made about your photo on Facebook appear in the Info pane of the photo in iPhoto.

You can also share your photos with yourself. Open a photo you like, edit it, and then choose Share⇨Set Desktop. The photo becomes the image on your Mac's Desktop.

Figure 3-24: Upload your photos to Facebook or Flickr directly from iPhoto.

Book IV
Chapter 3

Importing, Viewing, Organizing, and Sharing Photos

Using Photo Stream

Photo Stream is part of Apple's iCloud service. If you activate Photo Stream, 1,000 of your most recent photos are uploaded to Photo Stream for 30 days. If you reach the 1,000 photo limit and add more photos in a 30-day period, the new ones are uploaded, and the same quantity of old ones are deleted. To activate Photo Stream in iPhoto, choose iPhoto⇨Preferences and click the iCloud tab. Select the My Photo Stream and the Photo Sharing check boxes, as shown in Figure 3-25.

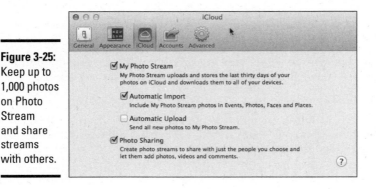

Figure 3-25:
Keep up to 1,000 photos on Photo Stream and share streams with others.

All the photos are synced to the devices you have connected to iCloud, such as your iPhone, iPad, or iPod touch. See Book I, Chapter 3, to find out more about using iCloud.

To share photo streams with others, do the following:

1. **Click Photos in the Source list or Events and then click a specific event to see the photo chooser.**

2. **Hold down the ⌘ key and click the photo(s) you want to upload.**

3. **Click the Share button and choose iCloud or select Share⇨iCloud.**

4. **Click New Photo Stream from the choices that appear.**

 A window appears, as shown in Figure 3-26.

5. **Type the names or e-mail addresses of the person(s) with whom you want to share your photos.**

 iPhoto accesses your Contacts. As you type a name, potential matches appear. If the address you want appears in the proposed list, click it. Type as many names as you like. Name the Photo Stream in the Name field and add any comments.

6. **Select the Subscribers Can Post check box so that others can interact with your photo stream by adding their own photos and comments.**

7. **Select the Public Website check box to make your stream available to the general public.**

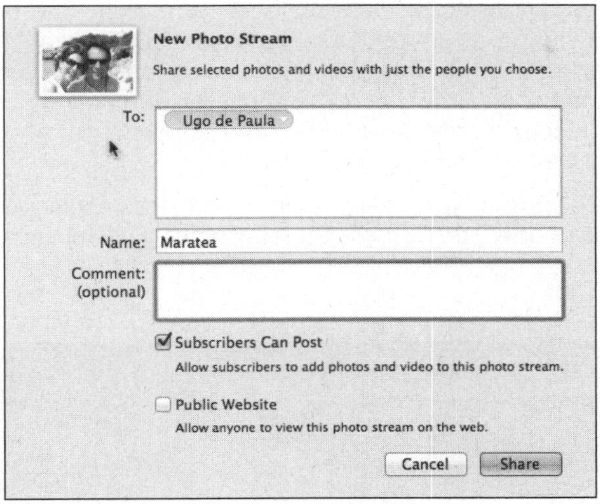

New Photo Stream

Share selected photos and videos with just the people you choose.

To: [Ugo de Paula]

Name: Maratea

Comment:
(optional)

☑ Subscribers Can Post

Allow subscribers to add photos and video to this photo stream.

☐ Public Website

Allow anyone to view this photo stream on the web.

[Cancel] [**Share**]

Figure 3-26:
Share Photo
Streams
with others.

8. **Click the Share button.**

The selected photos are posted on iCloud as a photo stream, and a message is sent to the people you invited to view that stream.

9. **After you create a shared photo stream, you can add more photos to it by clicking the Share button, then clicking the iCloud button, and finally, clicking the previously created photo stream.**

Your selected photos will be added to the selected photo stream.

Despite the confusing nomenclature, the photo stream that syncs up to 1,000 photos between your Mac and other devices is not the same as the photo stream you share, which is a specific group of selected photos that are accessed by other people from their devices.

Ordering books, calendars, and cards

For a fee, you can have your favorite iPhoto photos printed as books, calendars, or greeting cards. You will need your Apple ID and password when you reach the checkout, so keep it handy. To choose to print your photos in a book or calendar, or as a greeting card, follow these steps:

1. **Click Photos in the Source list or Events and then a specific event to see the photo chooser.**

2. **Hold down the ⌘ key and click all the photos you want to use or click an event.**

3. **Click the Share button at the bottom of the iPhoto window and choose Book, Calendar, or Card from the pop-up menu.**

The Carousel view appears, which you can "spin" through to see the printing options. Use the tabs at the top to choose format options of the printed material, such as hard cover, soft cover, or wire-bound for books or folder or flat for cards. Click the buttons near the Carousel samples to choose options, such as colors and size. The Card choice offers holiday cards, invitations, announcements, and blanks. The estimated price appears on the lower left. Scroll through the different styles or *themes* (or use the pop-up menu at the top) and see how your photos will look with each theme applied (see Figure 3-27).

If you plan to print cards, keep in mind that some themes accommodate up to four photos (six for baby announcements), while others have space for only one photo.

Figure 3-27: You can choose a specific style of book, calendar, or card to create.

4. **Click a style and click the Create button.**

   iPhoto distributes the photos you chose in the book, card, or calendar, as shown in Figure 3-28. Double-click a page to edit the photos in a book or calendar, and click and drag the photos to move them from one page to another. Use the buttons at the bottom to add pages or change the layout of a page or card. Photos on pages with *full bleed* fill the entire page and have no borders around the photos.

   iPhoto distributes the photos by using an Autoflow feature. iPhoto puts together photos that were taken on the same day and uses ratings to choose featured photos. iPhoto also detects faces and crops and frames the subject as it deems best.

Projects   untitled album 2 Book—62 pages   Change Theme

Double-click a page to edit

Cover

Slideshow   Zoom   Buy Book   Add Page   Layout   Options   Photos

Figure 3-28: iPhoto can automatically enter photos from an event.

5. **When you're satisfied with the layout of your book or calendar, click the Buy button.**

   A summary of your order appears with the total. Prices for books and calendars typically cost $10 to $30, and greeting cards cost $2 each. Apple's letter-pressed cards combine your digital photos with letter-press printing. Choose from 15 themes and order one card or a whole box of cards, which come with matching letter-pressed envelopes.

Photos that may not print well because of low resolution are marked with a warning that reads "Low resolution may result in poor print quality." Go to `http://support.apple.com/kb/HT1035?viewlocale=en_US& locale=en_US` to review the minimum and recommended resolution for each type of product.

6. **Click the Checkout button to proceed to pay online and enter your shipping information.**

   Your order goes directly to Apple, is dispatched to its service provider, and is delivered to your doorstep a few days later.

Even if you don't plan to print books, creating a book is a nice way to organize and view your photos on your computer. In full-screen view, click the Projects button at the bottom of the window to see all your projects arranged as books on a bookshelf. Double-click a project to open it, or click it, and then click the Slideshow button to view the book as an automatic slideshow.

Chapter 4: Making Movies with iMovie

In This Chapter

↙ **Discovering how iMovie works**

↙ **Importing and organizing videos**

↙ **Making your own iMovie project**

↙ **Adding special effects to your movie**

↙ **Deleting your movie**

↙ **Making a movie trailer**

↙ **Sharing your movie by e-mail, on YouTube, and more**

*N*ow that video capture is commonplace on both digital cameras and smartphones, making movies has descended from the realm of Super 8 aficionados to everyday use. If you have a digital video camcorder, digital camera, smartphone, or computer (like your Mac) that captures video, you can create movies with iMovie, the video-editing application that's part of Apple's iLife suite.

You can also use home (not commercial) video that someone gives you from a DVD, flash drive, or downloadable link. If, for example, you go river rafting or hang gliding, the company you go with may record your adventure and give or sell you the video on a DVD; you can then use the video footage (the *recording*) as part of your movie. Often when you make a presentation at a conference, the conference organizers record your presentation and give you a copy on DVD or flash drive, which you can then edit and incorporate into your professional curriculum or upload to your company's website.

With iMovie, you can edit your source video and even add a voiceover or background music, transitions, still images, and a few special effects to create a movie that tells a story and is compelling to watch.

The three buttons across the top of the iMovie window say it all — Import, Create, Share — and that's what we tell you how to do in this chapter.

Seeing How iMovie Works

To get the most out of iMovie, take a second to understand how the window is set up as well as some of the movie-making terms we use. When you first open iMovie, the *library* appears in a column on the left side of the window. The *toolbar* runs across the top, and two panes appear in the main section of the window. The lower *browser* pane shows clips from events, projects, or movies you import or create in iMovie (this will be empty if this is the first time you use iMovie), and the upper pane shows the preview of clips you select in the lower pane. When you're working on a project, the top pane is divided into two parts: the project pane and the preview pane. This will all make more sense when you start working in iMovie.

The *library* is where you see a list of projects or events, and the iMovie *browser* (not like your Safari Internet browser) is where you see the parts of your video, referred to as *clips.* Clips are made up of *frames.* Video speed is measured in *frames per second* (fps).

The basic steps for using iMovie, which we go through in detail in the subsequent sections, are

1. Import, store, and organize video in the Event Library.
2. Create a project, which is what iMovie calls your movie.
3. Add clips from your events to your project.
4. Rearrange and resize the clips.
5. Add transitions and effects.
6. Save your video as a digital video file for viewing and sharing with others.

Working with the Event Library

The Event Library holds all your source video, acting as your personal film vault. *Events* comprise one or more video clips, which you then use to construct movie projects. By storing videos in the Event Library, you have a handy place where you can choose footage from old videos to use in any new projects.

To store video in the Event Library, you must import video from one of the following sources:

✦ A digital video camera
✦ A smartphone or digital (still) camera capable of capturing video; the video can be imported into iPhoto and then brought into iMovie from iPhoto or imported directly into iMovie

✦ Video captured directly to your Mac by using the FaceTime HD camera with an app such as Photo Booth or iMovie itself

✦ Video captured and edited by using QuickTime Player (see Book IV, Chapter 2)

✦ A digital file downloaded from a website or accessed on a remote storage site

✦ A project created and saved using an earlier version of iMovie

✦ A digital video file stored on your hard drive, flash drive, or DVD

Importing video from a device

To *import* (that is, *copy*) a video that you captured with an external USB-enabled device, such as a digital camcorder, camera, or smartphone, to your Mac, follow these steps:

1. **Connect your device to your Mac with a USB cable.**

   The appropriate cable usually comes with the camera or smartphone and is often the one you use to charge the battery.

   If iPhoto or Image Capture opens, press ⌘+Q to quit the app.

   If you use a MiniDV or Digital-8 camcorder that captures video on tape, iMovie (version 10.0) may have left you, um, out of the picture. These types of camcorders use FireWire so if your Mac doesn't have a FireWire port, you need a FireWire to Thunderbolt adapter. Even with that, many users have reported problems getting iMovie to recognize the camcorder. The troubleshooting is longer than what we can address in this book, but if you're having problems, check out the discussions on the `https://discussions.apple.com`.

2. **Click the iMovie icon on the Dock or from Launchpad to open iMovie.**

   The Import window appears, displaying the various places you can import video from.

   If the Import window doesn't appear, click the Import button on the toolbar or choose File➪Import Media.

3. **Click the camera or device you want from the source list in the column on the left.**

   Any video on that device appears in the browser pane at the bottom of the window, as shown in Figure 4-1.

4. **(Optional) To view photos and video or only photos on a camera, open the pop-up menu in the upper-right corner and choose the type of media you want to see.**

   This menu doesn't appear when you click a device such as a flash drive in the Devices section.

Book IV
Chapter 4

Making Movies
with iMovie

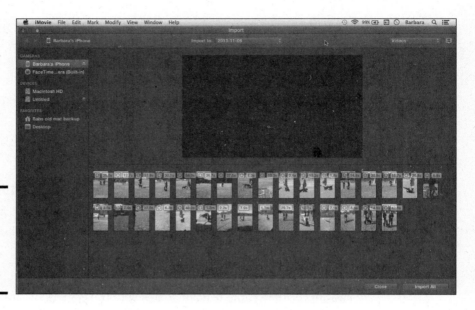

Figure 4-1:
Choose
where you
want to
save your
video file.

5. **Open the Import To pop-up menu to choose the destination in iMovie for the video clips.**

   You can create a new event, which is what you do if iMovie has no events yet, or choose to add the video to an existing event. This is a convenient choice if you want to import video related to the same event from several sources.

   When you choose New Event, a dialog opens with a field for typing a descriptive name for the event (the date and time is the default name). Type a name, if you like, and then click OK.

6. **To preview a video clip, click the thumbnail image and then drag the pointer across it. Or hover the pointer over the image in the preview pane to reveal playback controls, and then click the Play button.**

   An orange line — the *skimming line* — appears on the thumbnail, and a preview of the video plays in the preview pane.

7. **Select the clips you want to import by doing the following, or go to Step 8 if you want to import all clips.**

   • Shift-click to select contiguous clips.

   • ⌘-click to select noncontiguous clips.

8. **Click the Import Selected button if you selected some of the clips, or click the Import All button to copy all the clips to iMovie.**

   Your video is imported, and the iMovie window opens.

After you import a video, your original video footage remains on the device you imported from, so you may want to go back and erase it.

Importing a digital video file

Because iPhoto is usually the default destination for still and motion digital images, you probably have video files stored there. You can import the digital video file by connecting your device to your Mac, as we explain previously, or you can access the digital files from iPhoto and import them to iMovie. Likewise, if you have digital video files stored in QuickTime, MPEG-4, or digital video (DV) lying around on your storage drive, you can import them into iMovie. To import a DV file, follow these steps:

1. **Click the Import button or choose File⇨Import Media.**

   The Import window opens (refer to Figure 4-1).

   If the file you want to import is on a DVD, insert the DVD into the internal or external optical disc drive of your Mac and select the disc from the source list.

2. **Click the device (or a location in the Favorites section in the source list) where the video you want to import is stored.**

   The folders and files on that device appear in the browser at the bottom of the iMovie window.

   Check the Downloads and Movies folders on your Mac for video files saved from a website, e-mail, or QuickTime. You can access video and still photos in iPhoto from the Import window or directly in the iMovie window.

3. **Click and scroll through to find the DV file you want to import.**

   Double-click folders to view the contents.

   Click the Back button in the upper-left corner to go to a previously viewed folder or drive, as indicated in Figure 4-2.

4. **Open the Import To pop-up menu to choose the destination in iMovie for the video clips.**

   You can create a new event (which is what you do if iMovie has no events yet) or add the video to an existing event (which is convenient if you want to import video related to the same event from several sources).

   When you choose New Event, a dialog opens with a field for typing a descriptive name for the event, and the date and time make up the default name. Type a name, if you like, and then click OK.

**Book IV
Chapter 4**

**Making Movies
with iMovie**

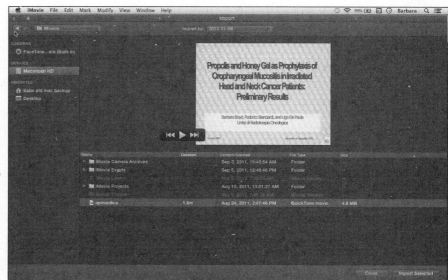

Figure 4-2:
Import files
from your
Mac or
other stor-
age drives.

5. **To preview a video clip, hover the pointer over the image in the pre-view pane to reveal playback controls, and then click the Play button.**

6. **Select the clips you want to import by doing the following:**

   • Shift-click to select contiguous clips.

   • ⌘-click to select noncontiguous clips.

   • Click a folder to import all the contents.

7. **Click the Import Selected button to copy the clips to iMovie.**

   Your video is imported, the Import window closes, and the iMovie window is again active.

If you try to click the iMovie window while the Import window is open, it doesn't work. You must close the Import window first to click anything on the iMovie window. If you open the Import window and then decide not to import anything, click the Close button in the upper-left corner to continue working in iMovie.

To capture video using the FaceTime HD camera on your Mac, click the Import button and then click FaceTime in the source list. The preview pane shows you (or whoever is seated in front of your Mac). Choose a destination for your soon-to-be-recorded video from the Import To pop-up menu. Click the Record button at the bottom of the preview screen, say or do the words or actions you want to capture, and then click the Record button again to stop recording. Click the Close button at the bottom right of the window, and the video is stored in the event you chose or created.

Organizing the Event Library

The more videos you store, the more crowded the Event Library becomes, and the harder it is to find what you want. When you import video to the Event Library, you choose to add the video to an existing event or create a new event.

The iMovie Library lists the titles of the video you see in the All Events browser, which contains your raw unedited video. Click the following:

✦ **All Events:** Your events appear as thumbnail images in the browser pane of the iMovie window. Double-click a thumbnail to see the clips in that event.

✦ **iMovie Library:** The events are listed singly. The items in the list match those you see in the browser when you select All Events.

You can manage, rearrange, and reorganize your events by clicking All Events and then double-clicking an event to open it, or by clicking the disclosure triangle next to iMovie Library to see a list of your events, and then doing the following:

✦ **Rename an Event:** Click All Events in the Libraries list and then click the name of an event under the thumbnail image in the Events browser. Or, in the iMovie Library events list, click the event name once to select the event, and then click again to highlight the name. Type a different name, and then press Return.

✦ **Merge Events:** Click and drag one event over another in the iMovie Library event list. The dragged event is added to the event underneath.

✦ **Move a Clip:** Click an event in the iMovie Library list to see the clips contained in the event. Click and drag across a clip to select the clip you want to split off from the main event: It will be outlined in yellow. Hover the pointer over the selected clip, and it becomes a hand icon. Click and drag the hand/pointer (which then becomes a filmstrip icon) to the event you want to move it to. The selected clip is moved from one event to another.

TIP

If you have video or still images in iPhoto that you want to move into an event, click the iPhoto Library item in the Libraries list, and then click and drag the video(s) or photo(s) to the event you want it in. You can then use the video in that event in any projects you create.

✦ **Split an Event:** Choose File➪New Event to create a new event in the iMovie Library. Rename the event, as we explain earlier in this chapter. Double-click the event you want to split to see the clips that it contains. After you click and drag across a clip to select the clip you want to split off from the main event, it will be outlined in yellow. Hover the pointer over the selected clip, and it becomes a hand icon. Click and drag the hand/pointer, which then becomes a filmstrip icon, to the new event. The selected clip is moved from the original event to the new one.

**Book IV
Chapter 4**

Making Movies
with iMovie

✦ **Delete an Event:** Click the event you want to delete in the iMovie Library events list, or click All Events and then click the unwanted event in the browser pane. Choose File➪Move to Trash or press ⌘+Delete. If you delete an event by mistake, immediately press ⌘+Z or choose Edit➪Undo to cancel the action.

Creating an iMovie Project

Projects contain still images or video clips from source video and images accessed from your Libraries, which includes your iPhoto library. Like events, Projects can be viewed by clicking All Projects in the Libraries list; you also see them listed under iMovie Library. A clapperboard icon next to the event name lets you know it's a project. Double-click a project or click and then click Edit Project to view the Project browser, which is where you edit your movie. To view (or hide) the Library list — so you have more room to work on your project — click the Hide button in the toolbar just above the Libraries column.

In the Project browser, you can rearrange, trim, and delete video clips to create your movie. This is where you add titles, transitions, audio, or special effects to your edited movie. If you accidentally erase or mess up a movie in the Project browser, just retrieve the original footage from the All Events Library and start over. You can copy and store the same video footage in two or more projects.

To create a project, follow these steps:

1. **Click the Create button on the toolbar at the top of the iMovie window and then choose Movie from the pop-up menu, or choose File➪New Movie.**

    The Themes chooser appears, as shown in Figure 4-3.

2. **Hover the pointer over a theme and click the Play button that appears to see a preview of the theme.**

    Themes provide stylized transitions and titles for your project. You can choose a theme and then manually add or change transitions, or change the theme itself. You can also add a theme when you're already in the middle of editing a project.

    Two themes offer particularly enhanced movie possibilities: Sports and CNN iReport. Sports has a Sports Team Editor where you type in the players' names and stats. CNN iReport prepares videos in CNN style so you can propose your stories to CNN's iReport segment.

Figure 4-3:
Choose a theme for your movie.

3. **Click the theme you want to use for your movie (or choose No Theme if you want to do the work yourself) and then click the Create button.**

   The Project Editor workspace opens, as shown in Figure 4-4. The Libraries column is hidden, and there are three panes:

   • *Project pane:* Where you place the clips and content of your movie

   • *Preview pane:* Where you can see how your movie will play

   • *Events pane:* Where you view clips to place in your movie

   Choose Window⇨Swap Project and Event to invert the positions of the Project and Event panes. To take advantage of your Mac's entire screen, click the Full Screen button in the upper-right corner of the window or choose Window⇨Enter Full Screen.

4. **(Optional) To instruct iMovie to insert transitions between clips automatically, choose Window⇨Movie Properties. Click the Settings button, and then select the Automatic Content check box (refer to Figure 4-4).**

   iMovie will automatically insert transitions — in a style that's part of the theme you chose — whenever it finds shifts from one piece of video to another. This is useful as a way to insert transitions quickly. You can then later deactivate this feature and manually delete or substitute transitions when you edit your video.

   To change your movie's theme, choose Window⇨Movie Properties and then click the Settings button. Click the theme name to open the Themes chooser. Select a different theme and then click the Create button.

Project

Events

Preview

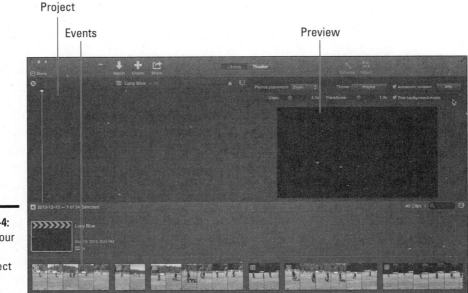

Figure 4-4:
Create your
movie in
the Project
pane.

Selecting video clips

At its simplest, a movie is a collection of video clips. When you create a
movie, you select clips in Events and place them in a project. Before you can
select a video clip to store in a project, you need to see exactly what part of
a video you want to use as a clip. To help you find any part of a video, iMovie
displays an entire video as a series of images — *frames* — that appear like
a filmstrip. To find a specific part of a video, you can skim through a video.
When you find the part of a video to use, just click and drag it into a project.

Skimming a video

Skimming a video lets you see the video footage just by moving the mouse
pointer over the video images. To view a video by skimming while working
on a project, follow these steps:

1. **Click All Events in the Libraries column.**

   If Libraries is hidden, click the Show button on the left of the toolbar.

   A thumbnail image represents each of your events in the Events pane.

2. **Double-click an event to see all the clips it contains.**

   You can click the iMovie Library item in the Libraries column to see a
   list of all events in your library, and then click an event name to see the
   clips in the Event browser.

3. **Click the Clip Settings button (the filmstrip icon), and then drag the
   sliders to choose how many seconds each frame represents and to
   zoom in or out of the clips, as shown in Figure 4-5.**

Clip Settings button

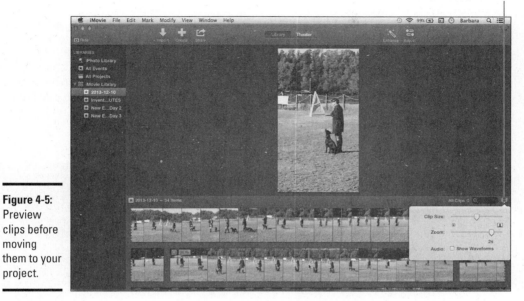

Figure 4-5:
Preview clips before moving them to your project.

4. **Move the pointer over any of the thumbnail images of a video file displayed in the Event browser.**

   An orange vertical line appears over the thumbnail image.

5. **Move the pointer left and right to watch your video in the Preview pane of the iMovie window.**

   Click the "X" in the upper-left corner of the Project pane to close it and give more window space to the Preview pane (refer to Figure 4-5).

   The faster you move the pointer, the faster the video plays. Moving the pointer to the left plays the video backward. Moving the pointer to the right plays the video forward.

   Click anywhere in a clip to place the playhead at a starting point, and then press the spacebar. Your video will play from that point forward. Press the spacebar again to stop the video.

   ### Placing a video clip

   After you identify some clips you want to include in your movie, you can begin placing them in your project.

   If you hid the Project pane, click All Projects in the Libraries column, and then click the icon related to your project in the All Projects browser.

**Book IV
Chapter 4**

**Making Movies
with iMovie**

To place a video clip in a project, follow these steps:

1. **In the Events browser, move the pointer to the beginning of the part of the video that you want to use.**

2. **Click and drag to the right.**

   A yellow outline defines the size of your clip, and an Add button appears, as shown in Figure 4-6. If you get more or less than you want, click outside the clip to start over or click and drag the left or right end to adjust the selection.

Figure 4-6: A yellow outline defines the size of a video clip.

3. **Release the mouse or lift your finger from the trackpad when you're happy with the portion of the video that your clip contains.**

4. **Click the Add button (+) in the lower-right corner of the selected clip.**

   Your selected video clip appears as a thumbnail image in the Project pane of the iMovie window.

5. **Repeat Steps 1–4 to add other clips to your movie project.**

   If you want to add clips from other events, click the All Events item in the Libraries column or click a single event in the iMovie Library. You can skim, preview, and select the clips in the Events browser.

Editing video clips in a project

After you place one or more video clips in a project, you usually want to edit those video clips to put them in the best order, trim unnecessary footage, and add titles and audio to create an entertaining or informative movie. In the following sections, we take you through movie-making basics; starting in the "Using Special Effects" section, we go a step farther and show you how to add special effects.

Rearranging the order of video clips

A project plays video clips in the sequence you specify, but you may want to change the order of your video clips. To rearrange the order of your video clips in a project, follow these steps:

1. **Click All Projects in the Libraries column, and then, in the Projects browser, double-click the project with which you want to work.**

2. **Click and drag the clip you want to move.**

As you move the clip, the other clips move to the left or right to provide a space to place the clip you're moving. A blue outline indicates where the clip will go.

3. **Release the mouse or lift your finger from the trackpad.**

Your video clip appears in its new location.

If you decide you don't want a clip, you can easily delete it from your project. Don't worry — deleting a video clip from a project doesn't delete the video clip from the All Events library. In the Project editor, click the video clip that you want to delete. Then choose Edit⇨Delete Selection (or press Delete).

Adjusting the size of a video clip

Sometimes a video clip contains a little too much footage that you need to trim. Other times, you may have trimmed a video clip a little too much and need to add more footage. In either case, you can fix this problem and change the size of your video clip by following these steps:

1. **Open the project as explained in the previous steps.**

2. **Drag the Frames per Second slider to the right to see more frames of your clip, which facilitates precise clipping.**

3. **Move the pointer over a video clip and click the left or right edge of the clip.**

To make a more precise adjustment, click the clip to select it and then double-click to open the Clip Trimmer window (or choose Window⇨Show Clip Trimmer), as shown in Figure 4-7, and then move the point to the left or right edge.

A two-headed arrow appears.

**Book IV
Chapter 4**

**Making Movies
with iMovie**

Frames per Second slider

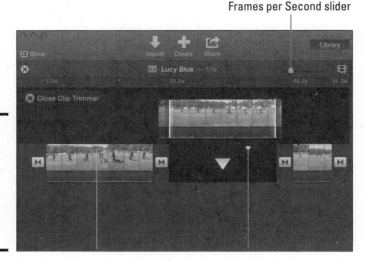

Figure 4-7:
The Clip
Trimmer
lets you
precisely
shorten or
lengthen a
clip.

4. **Click and drag the arrow left to shorten the clip or right to lengthen it.**

   The number of seconds that will be added or subtracted from the original clip appears above the clip. The seconds stamped on the clip indicate the total length of the clip.

   When you increase the video, the original footage from before or after
   the clip you're working on is added.

5. **Drag the *skimmer* (the orange vertical line) to view your edited video
   clip in the Preview pane.**

6. **Click the Close Clip Trimmer button (or choose Window⇨Hide Clip
   Trimmer) to close the Clip Trimmer window.**

You can also lengthen or shorten the playing time of a clip by changing the playback speed, which also adds a special effect to your movie. Select a clip and
then click once in the middle of the clip to open the Speed window, as shown in
Figure 4-8. Click a percentage to slow down the clip or a multiple to speed it up,
or type a value in the Custom field. You can also select the Reverse check box to
play the clip backward. You can change a clip's speed by choosing Modify⇨Slow
Motion⇨50%/25%/10% or Modify⇨Fast Forward⇨2x/4x/8x/20x.

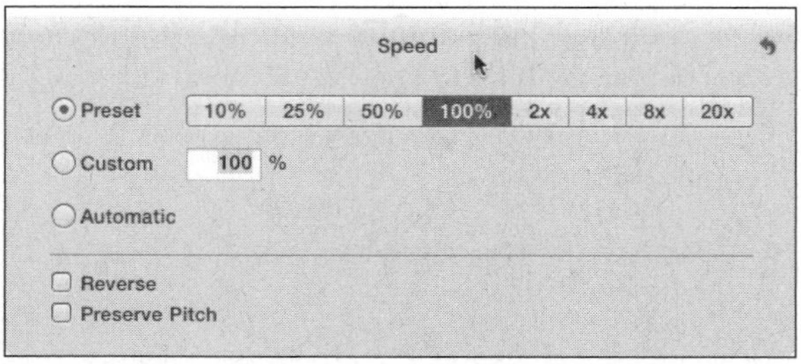

Figure 4-8:
Use the
Speed
window to
adjust play-
back speed.

Speed

| Preset | 10% | 25% | 50% | 100% | 2x | 4x | 8x | 20x |

Custom 100 %

Automatic

☐ Reverse
☐ Preserve Pitch

Adding and editing transitions

Normally, when you place video clips in a project, those video clips play one after another. To soften the shift from one clip to the next, add transitions between the clips. Themes come with stylized transitions that relate to the theme. You can change themed transitions if you want. To add or edit a transition, follow these steps:

1. **Click All Projects in the Libraries column, and then, in the Projects browser, double-click the project with which you want to work.**

   The Project browser shows thumbnail images of your selected project.

   As your project grows, choose Window⇨Swap Project and Event to move the Project pane to the bottom of the window, giving you more space to work.

2. **Click Transitions in the Content Library.**

   If you don't see the Content Library, either click the Show button to reveal the Libraries column or choose Window⇨Content Library⇨Transitions.

   The Transitions window opens, as shown in Figure 4-9.

   Some different types of transitions include Cube (which spins a cube on the screen where a different video clip appears on each side of the cube) and Page Curl (which peels away one video clip like a piece of paper).

3. **Click and drag the desired transition style to the space between two clips.**

   Use the skimmer to watch the transition in the Preview pane.

Figure 4-9: Use transitions to create unique visual effects between video clips.

Making Movies with iMovie

TIP

If you're using a theme, the theme transitions appear in the first row of the Transitions browser.

4. (Optional) To change the style of transition, drag a different transition from the browser to the transition icon in the Project pane.

5. (Optional) To change the duration of your transition, do the following:

    a. Choose Window⇨Show Adjustments Bar.

    b. Click the Inspector button (i).

    c. Click the transition icon within your project in the Project browser.

    d. Type a new value in the Transitions text box.

6. Click another item in the Libraries, such as an event, to open the associated browser in place of the Transitions browser.

Adding still images

You don't have to limit your movie content to video, titles, and transitions. Still images — such as photos, scanned documents, and graphics — can add depth to your subject matter. To add still images from iPhoto, follow these steps:

1. Click All Projects in the Libraries column, and then, in the Projects browser, double-click the project with which you want to work.

2. Click iPhoto Library in the Libraries column.

The iPhoto browser opens, as shown in Figure 4-10. If you use iCloud or link Facebook to iPhoto, you can access those libraries by clicking the leftmost tab (Events in Figure 4-10) to open a pop-up menu with other choices.

Figure 4-10:
Insert a photo from iPhoto.

3. **Scroll through your Events and Photos in the browser to find the photo you want to add to your movie.**

4. **Click and drag the image from the iPhoto Library browser to the Project pane.**

   If you drag the image over a part of a clip, a pop-up menu appears with choices of what to do with the image. The options are

   • *Replace:* Replaces the frame with the still image

   • *Insert:* Inserts the still image between the two frames of the clip where you placed it

5. **Choose the option you want, which is probably Insert.**

   Your clip is divided, and the still image now rests between the two parts of the clip.

   A still image is given four seconds of video time.

6. **Click another item in the Libraries, such as an event, to open the associated browser in place of the iPhoto Library browser.**

The photos you see in the Photos browser are in iPhoto on your Mac. If you want to use a scanned document or other image, drag the image into iPhoto so you can find it in the iPhoto Library browser in iMovie.

Adding titles

Titles tell your viewer what your movie is about. Opening titles can display the video's name and purpose, and closing titles can list the credits of the people who appeared in the video and put it together. Transition titles can indicate a time or subject change in the movie.

Titles can appear by themselves or be superimposed over part of your video. To create titles for a project, follow these steps:

1. **Click All Projects in the Libraries column, and then, in the Projects browser, double-click the project with which you want to work.**

2. **Click Titles in the Content Library or choose Window⇨Content Library⇨Titles.**

   The Titles browser opens, as shown in Figure 4-11. If you're using a theme, the name of the theme and the titles associated with it appear at in the first row. Otherwise, you see No Theme.

Figure 4-11:
The Titles browser shows title styles you can use.

3. **Click and drag a title from the Titles browser to a video clip or in between two clips.**

   If you're working with a theme and selected Automatic Content in the Movie Properties Settings (choose Window⇨Movie Properties and then click the Settings button), the title style will be superimposed on the theme style. Turn off Automatic Content to insert a title without the theme style. Any titles or transitions created by the theme remain in place. In a themed title, you can edit the text but not the appearance.

   Titles appear in a purple balloon above the filmstrip in the Project pane.

4. **Release the mouse or lift your finger from the trackpad.**

   If you release the mouse or lift your finger from the trackpad over a video clip, your title appears superimposed over the video image.

   If you release the mouse or lift your finger from the trackpad between video clips, your title appears as a separate video clip between those two video clips. A background chooser opens where you choose the texture or color of the background that appears behind your title — or, if Automatic Content is on with a theme, the theme background will be used.

5. **Click the title balloon that appears over a video clip.**

   Your chosen title format appears in the Preview pane.

6. **In the Preview pane, double-click the text you want to edit and type new text, or use the arrow and Delete keys to edit the existing title.**

7. **(Optional for nontheme titles only) Use the menus to choose a different color, font size, and typeface for your text.**

8. **Click the Play button to preview how your titles appear.**

9. **(Optional) To change the duration of time your title is onscreen, click the Inspector button (*i*), and change the number of seconds by typing a new number in the Duration text box.**

10. **Click another item in the Libraries, such as an event, to open the associated browser in place of the iPhoto Library browser.**

To delete a title, click the title balloon. Then press Delete or choose Edit⇨Delete.

Adding maps and backgrounds

Maps add visual interest to your movie, especially if you're making a movie about a journey or you just want to show where the events of your movie take place. iMovie comes with several maps and globes that you can place in your movie. To add a map or globe to your movie, follow these steps:

1. **Click All Projects in the Libraries column, and then, in the Projects browser, double-click the project with which you want to work.**

2. **Click Maps & Backgrounds in the Content Library or choose Window⇨Content Library⇨Maps & Backgrounds.**

   The Maps & Backgrounds browser opens. The first row shows four animated globes, the second row shows four animated maps, and the third row shows four still map images. Beneath those is a selection of background colors and styles.

3. **Click and drag the map or background you want to use to the place in your movie where you want it to appear.**

   A blue vertical line indicates where you can insert the map or globe. *Note:* You have to insert it before or after a clip; it can't replace a clip.

   Drag the map or background over a title to use it as the title background.

   Your map or background appears in the Preview window.

4. **(Optional) To change the duration of time your map or background is onscreen, choose Window⇨Show Adjustments Bar and then click the Inspector button (*i*). Then change the number of seconds by typing a new number in the Duration text box.**

5. **(Optional for globes or maps with routes) Click the Route button (it looks like a globe) on the Adjustments bar, which appears when you choose Window⇨Show Adjustments Bar, and do the following to specify the route's beginning and end points:**

   a. *Click the first field next to Route to open a list of cities, as shown in Figure 4-12.*

Figure 4-12:
The Map
Inspector
opens when
you insert
a globe or
map into
your movie.

b. *Click a city or type a city name or location (such as Grand Canyon) in the search field.*

This first field is where the journey begins.

c. *Click the Name to Display on Map field and type a different entry if you want other words to appear on the map, such as "Our Journey's Beginning."*

d. *Click Done.*

e. *Repeat Steps a–d for the second field.*

This second field is where the journey ends.

6. **Click the Style pop-up menu if you want to change the type of map or globe.**

7. **Click the Play button on the preview image to see how the map fits into your movie.**

The Map Inspector flips over, and you can type in the city you want to use as your starting point.

8. **Click the Maps and Backgrounds button to close the browser.**

You may have to split a clip to insert a globe or map exactly where you want it. Double-click at the point where you want to divide the clip. Choose Clip⇨Split Clip. Your clip is now divided into two parts, and you can insert a globe or map between the two parts of the clip.

When you insert still images or moving maps, you probably want to add a transition in the spaces between your video and the still image or map.

Adding audio files

To enliven your movie, you can add audio files that play background music or sound effects to match the video that's playing — a dog barking, say, or a telephone ringing. You can also record a voiceover directly in iMovie with your Mac's built-in microphone or an external microphone connected to the USB or line-in port.

To add an audio file to a project, follow these steps:

1. **Click All Projects in the Libraries column, and then, in the Projects browser, double-click the project with which you want to work.**

2. **Click iTunes, Sound Effects, or GarageBand from the Content Library, or choose Window⇨Content Library⇨iTunes/Sound Effects/ GarageBand.**

   Choose the source of the music or sound you want to add; Sound Effects are part of iMovie.

   A list of audio files appears in the browser, as shown in Figure 4-13. Note the time to the right of each audio file.

3. **Click and drag an audio file to a video clip in the Project pane.**

   A green bubble appears below the video clip to show you where the audio file will start playing.

4. **Double-click the audio file to open the Clip Trimmer.**

5. **Click and drag the left or right ends to shorten the audio file from the beginning (left) or the end (right).**

Figure 4-13: Audio files can add music or sound effects to your videos.

6. **Click the Close Clip Trimmer button to close the Clip Trimmer.**

7. **(Optional) To link an audio file to a specific clip — so if you move the clip the audio goes with it — click the audio file and then click a clip. Choose Edit⇨Connect.**

   The audio appears in a green bubble beneath the clip and linked to it.

If the audio file is longer than the clip, you may want to trim it, or it will continue to play when the movie flows to the next clip.

Adding background audio

Background audio plays throughout your movie, behind other audio. You can adjust the volume of the background audio so it doesn't disturb other audio in your movie, and you can have more than one background audio file so different background audio plays during different moments of your movie. For example, you may begin with background music to play during the opening title of your movie, and then the music may fade, a different song plays more quietly while there is talking, and at one point you may want to add a thunderstorm as background audio.

Here's how to add background audio:

1. **Click All Projects in the Libraries column, and then, in the Projects browser, double-click the project in which you want to work.**

2. **Click iTunes, Sound Effects, or GarageBand in the Content Library or choose Window⇨Content Library⇨iTunes/Sound Effects/GarageBand.**

3. **Click and drag the audio file you want to use for background to the drop well at the very bottom of the Project pane, where you see a field outlined by a dashed line with musical notes at the left end.**

4. **Double-click the audio file to open the Clip Trimmer.**

5. **Click and drag the left or right ends to shorten the audio file from the beginning (left) or the end (right).**

6. **Click the Close Clip Trimmer button to close the Clip Trimmer.**

7. **To add more background audio, click the audio in the browser, and then choose Edit⇨Append to Background Music.**

Adding a voiceover

Voiceovers can narrate the action in your movie or accompany still images, making them seem more "active." To add a voiceover to your movie, follow these steps:

1. **Click All Projects in the Libraries column, and then, in the Projects browser, double-click the project with which you want to work.**

2. **Choose Window⇨Record Voiceover.**

   The Voiceover tools appear in the Preview pane, as shown in Figure 4-14.

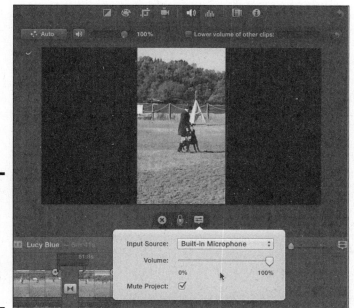

Figure 4-14:
Use the
Voiceover
feature
to add
narration to
your iMovie
project.

3. **Choose the device you want to use to record in the Input pop-up window and then adjust the volume.**

4. **Select the Mute Project check box if you want to silence the other audio while you speak.**

   If you deselect Mute Project, wear headphones so you hear the audio, but the microphone you're speaking into doesn't record it.

5. **Click the clip where you want the voiceover to begin, and then click the Record button (the microphone).**

   The clip begins playing in the Preview pane, a few seconds before where you want to begin your voiceover, and a countdown lets you know when to begin speaking. This way, you can watch your video while you're recording.

6. **Press the Record button again to stop recording.**

Adjusting audio and video clip volume

You can adjust the volume of either audio or video clips so that one is louder than the other — for example, if you have a voiceover that translates something spoken in a foreign language in the video clip. Adjust the volume on either type of clip by doing the following:

1. **Click to select the audio or video clip in the Project pane.**

2. **Choose Window⇨Show Adjustments Bar or click the Adjust button. See Figure 4-15 for the following steps.**

**Book IV
Chapter 4**

**Making Movies
with iMovie**

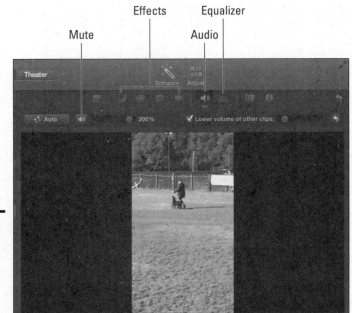

Mute Effects Equalizer Audio

Figure 4-15:
Adjust the volume of both audio and video clips.

3. **Click the Audio button (it looks like a speaker).**

4. **(Optional) Click the Auto button to let iMovie automatically improve the loudness of the selected clip for you.**

5. **(Optional) Click the Mute button to mute, or unmute, the playback of audio in the selected clip.**

6. **Drag the volume slider to adjust how loudly the selected clip will play.**

7. **(Optional) Select the Lower Volume of Other Clips check box, and then drag the volume slider to set the volume of clips that run simultaneously with the selected clip.**

This process is called *ducking* in video-editing language.

8. **(Optional) Click the Equalizer button and do the following:**

   • *Mitigate the background.* Select the Recue Background Noise check box and then drag its slider to the percentage that you want background noise reduced.

   • *Enhance the clip.* From the Equalizer pop-up menu, choose a style that will equalize and enhance your selected clip's audio, such as Voice Enhance or Bass Boost.

9. **(Optional) Click the Effects button, and then double-click an Audio Effect from the pop-up chooser.**

Using Special Effects

With iMovie, you can make your movie unique and memorable with special effects. We explain the audio effects earlier in this chapter, telling you how to slow down or speed up the playback rate of your clips in the section about adding clips. There are some other fine-tuning adjustments you can make, which we explain here. All are accessed by clicking the clip you want to adjust and then using the Adjustment Bar tools in the Preview pane.

✦ **Clip Adjustments:** In addition to changing the speed and direction of the clip, choose preset video and audio effects, and control stabilization and motion distortion.

✦ **Video Adjustments:** Make changes to brightness, contrast, exposure, and the like.

✦ **Cropping and Rotation:** Zoom in on a frame or frames of your clip to rotate or apply the Ken Burns effect. (See the nearby sidebar, "Who is Ken Burns?")

Applying special effects

To apply special effects to one or more clips in your movie, do the following:

1. **Click to select the video clip you want to adjust in the Project pane.**

The clip appears in the Preview pane.

2. **Click the Adjust button or choose Window⇨Show Adjustment Bar.**

3. **Click the Effects button, and then click a Video Effect from the pop-up chooser, such as Sepia, Dream, or X-ray.**

You see the effect you made in the Preview pane.

4. **Try other effects and click the one you want to choose.**

You find more effects from the iMovie Modify menu. These effects can be used singly or combined. Try these out to add pizzazz and professionalism to your video. Click a clip, place the playhead where you want the effect to begin or take place, and then from the Modify menu, choose one, or more, of the following:

✦ **Enhance** automatically corrects the clip as iMovie thinks best.

✦ **Fade To⇨Black and White/Sepia/Dream** adds a color effect to your clip as it plays.

✦ **Flash and Hold Frame** adds a white flash at the end of the clip and then displays the last frame as a still image with the Ken Burns zooming effect.

✦ **Add Freeze Frame** inserts a still image of the frame you select in the clip. The clip is divided so you can edit the frozen frame as a still and define the playback duration.

**Book IV
Chapter 4**

**Making Movies
with iMovie**

Who is Ken Burns?

Ken Burns is a documentary filmmaker. There are two Ken Burns effects:

✓ **Zooming and panning a still image**

Use this effect to make inanimate objects interesting in a documentary, bringing things like photos of Civil War memorabilia to life when motion film is unavailable.

✓ **The fame one gains after appearing in one of Mr. Burns' documentaries**

iMovie can help you with only the first Ken Burns effect.

✦ **Slow Motion**⇨**50%/25%/10%** plays your selected clip or selected frames at the fraction you select of the normal speed.

✦ **Fast Forward**⇨**2x/4x/8x/20x** plays the selected clip or frames at twice or more the normal speed.

✦ **Instant Replay**⇨**100%/50%/25%/10%** plays the selected clip or frames at the normal speed and then replays it at a percentage of normal speed, as you select.

✦ **Rewind**⇨**1x/2x/4x** plays the selected clip or frames at normal speed, then plays back the rewind at normal or two or four times the speed, and then plays it again forward at normal speed.

✦ **Reset Speed** cancels the speed changes you made and returns the clip to normal forward speed.

Adjusting the quality of a clip

The video effects change the appearance and motion of your clip; however, you can also adjust the quality of the video in your clip. Follow these steps:

1. **Click to select the video clip you want to adjust in the Project pane.**

The clip appears in the Preview pane.

2. **Click the Adjust button or choose Window⇨Show Adjustment Bar.**

The tools on the Adjustment Bar, as shown in Figure 4-16, do the following when selected, and show the results immediately in the Preview pane.

Color Balance: Click the buttons to adjust the color of the selected clip.

• *Auto* instructs iMovie to improve the color quality automatically.

• *Match Color* lets you match the color in the selected clip to the color in another clip. The Preview pane splits in two; your selected clip is on the right side. Click the clip you want to match, and it appears in the left side. Select the check mark when you like the results to save them.

- *White Balance* corrects the colors in relation to a spot in the image that should be white or gray. Because white is the reference point for all the other colors, changing the white point changes the colors. Choose a point with the dropper to use as the white point, and then select the check mark when you're pleased with the adjustments.

- *Skin Tone Balance* corrects the image colors based on skin tones. For each, follow the onscreen instructions to select a color to use as the base and then iMovie adjusts the clip. Choose a point with the dropper to use as the skin tone reference point, and then select the check mark to accept the changes.

Color Correction

Cropping

Color Balance | Stabilization

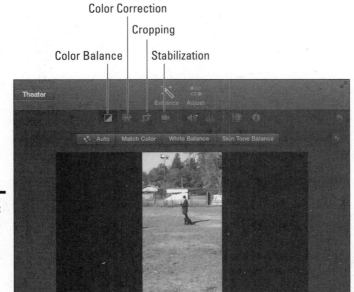

Figure 4-16:
Adjust the quality of the video in the Video Inspector.

After clicking one of these options and making adjustments, click the On/Off switch Off if you want to turn the function off. Click the "X" to leave the function on but cancel the most recent changes.

Color Correction: Use the sliders to change the following:

- *Brightness:* Affects the overall light level. Increasing brightness makes the image lighter.

- *Saturation:* Affects the amount of color in the clip. Dragging to the right intensifies color, and dragging to the far left makes a black-and-white image.

- *Temperature:* Makes the colors of the clip *warmer* (redder, more yellow or orange) or *cooler* (bluer or greener).

Cropping tools change the size and rotation of the clip. You can choose the following effects:

- *Fit:* iMovie adjusts the image to fill the screen size.

- *Crop:* Click and drag the corners to resize the image as you want.

- *Ken Burns:* Apply a zoom and pan effect to the image. The boxes on the image let you choose the start and end points and direction of the pan, as shown in Figure 4-17. Click the Swap button to change which area is the start and which the end.

- *Rotate counterclockwise or clockwise:* Click the buttons to rotate your clip.

  Click the Refresh button to cancel the changes you made or the check mark to accept the changes.

Stabilization: Use the feature to adjust the following:

- *Stabilize Shaky Video:* Select the check box to activate this function, which stabilizes shakiness in the clip. Move the slider to designate the percentage of correction you want to apply.

- *Fix Rolling Shutter:* Select the check box to activate this function, which corrects for some quick or side-to-side movements, and then choose the level of correction — Low, Medium, High, or Extra High.

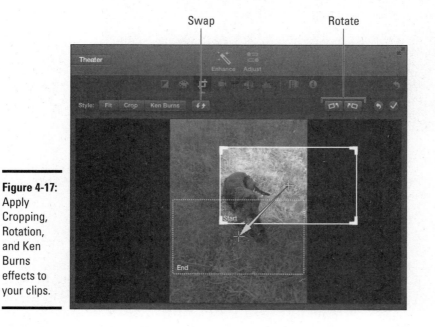

Figure 4-17:
Apply Cropping, Rotation, and Ken Burns effects to your clips.

Two-image video effects

iMovie's two-image video effects take your movie from good to fabulous. Sounds complicated, but it's not. Have two images in mind that would look great and have an awesome impact if they could be shown at once? Follow these steps:

1. **Click All Projects in the Libraries column, and then, in the Projects browser, double-click the project with which you want to work.**

2. **Add both clips to the Project, if you haven't yet.**

3. **Click and drag one clip above the other until a blue line connects the two clips.**

4. **Click one of the clips and then, referring to the Preview pane, click the Adjust button or choose Window➪Show Adjustments Bar, to see the adjustment tools.**

5. **Click the Overlay button.**

   The tools shown in Figure 4-18 appear.

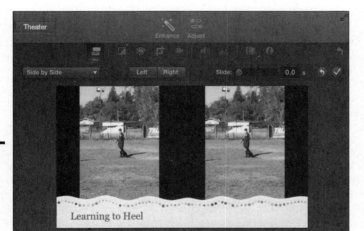

Figure 4-18: Choose from three two-image effects.

6. **Choose one of the options from the pop-up menu:**

   - *Cutaway:* The first clip cuts away to expose the second clip.

   - *Side by Side:* The two clips play next to each other in a split-screen effect.

   - *Picture in Picture:* The second clip plays in a box superimposed on the first clip.

   A fourth option, Green/Blue Screen, should be used if you capture action in front of a green or blue screen and then want to superimpose that video in front of another video. For example, you record someone dancing in front of a blue screen (or wall) and then connect that video to a video of open sea. Apply the Green/Blue Screen function to the two videos, and it appears as if the person is dancing on water.

7. **Hover the pointer over the Preview video and click the Play button.**

8. **Press the Pause button to stop playback.**

Deleting an iMovie Project

When you finish a project or decide you don't want it anymore, you can delete an entire project.

When you delete a project, you also delete any video clips stored inside that project. However, the original videos (from which you copied clips to add to the project) remain in the Event Library.

To delete a project, follow these steps:

1. **Click the project you want to delete from the Project Library list.**

2. **Choose File⇨Move Project to Trash.**

If you accidentally delete a project, you can retrieve it by pressing ⌘+Z or choosing Edit⇨Undo Delete Project (as long as you haven't emptied the Trash yet).

Making a Trailer for Your Movie

After you create the cinematic masterpiece of your summer vacation abroad, you may decide you want Thanksgiving dinner to be the opening night of your movie debut. To drum up interest and anticipation, you can create a *trailer* (a brief preview of the movie to pique people's interest) for your movie and e-mail it to your friends and family or post it on YouTube or Facebook. To create a trailer, follow these steps:

1. **Click the iMovie icon on the Dock or from Launchpad.**

2. **Click the Create button and choose Trailer.**

3. **Choose one of the Trailer themes in the chooser that appears.**

   Look through the previews to determine the kinds of clips required for the theme and choose one that appropriately matches your movie.

4. **Click Create.**

   The Trailer window opens, as shown in Figure 4-19.

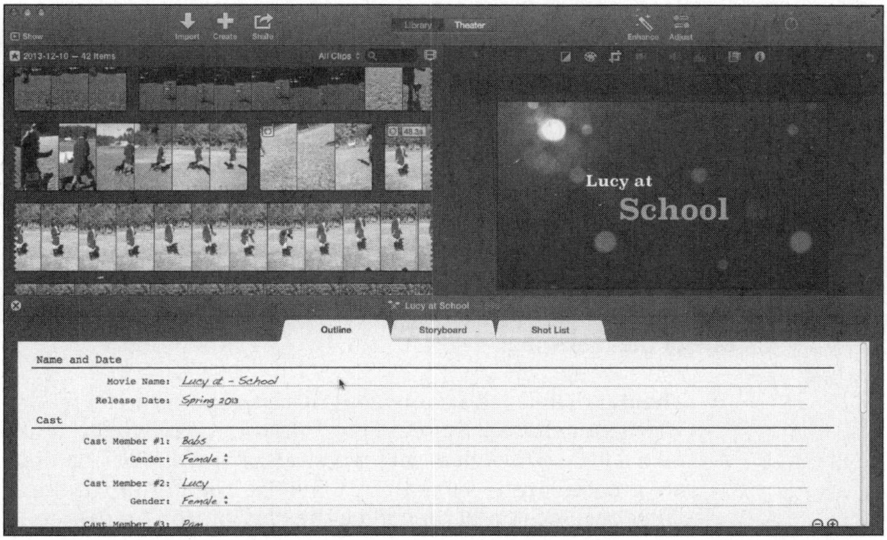

Figure 4-19:
Add your
own text to
your movie
trailer.

5. **Replace the text in the trailer outline with your own information.**

   Give your movie a name and a release date. Add actors. Make up a production company name. Fill in the credits with the names of people who
   helped make your movie.

6. **Click the Storyboard tab.**

   The Storyboard shows the sequence of the trailer. Empty drop wells
   show you the type of images or clips you should drag from the Event
   browser into the storyboard. (Click the Shot List tab to see all the types
   of clips you need for the trailer.) Text fields in between indicate the text
   that will play; double-click the text and retype your own.

7. **Click frames in the Event browser that correspond to the images in
   the Storyboard.**

   The frame you click is placed in the first drop well, the second frame
   goes in the second drop well, and so on, until all the drop wells are filled.
   iMovie adds transitions, titles, and effects.

8. **Click the Play button to see your trailer in the Preview pane.**

You can convert a trailer to a project and edit it as a normal project, but you
can't revert a project to a trailer. So, we recommend that you choose Edit⇨
Duplicate Movie to create a copy of your trailer before you convert it to a
movie. Then, when you're ready to convert the trailer, choose File⇨Convert
Trailer to Movie.

Sharing Your Movie

The point of organizing video clips in a project is to create a polished movie. With iMovie, you can save your project to view on a computer; in iTunes; on an iPod, iPad, or iPhone; or on a website, such as YouTube or Vimeo. You can save the same video project to different formats in case you want to view your video on your Mac but also want to post a copy on Facebook for other people to enjoy.

Instead of giving you a Save option, iMovie offers Share options. Click the Share button in the iMovie window or choose File⇨Share and then choose one of the following:

✦ **Theater:** This is the equivalent of saving your movie to view in iMovie. When you share your movie to Theater, the movie is created, which may take a little while given that versions that will work on different devices are created at the same time. Click the Theater tab at the top of the iMovie window, and then click the Play button on the icon that represents your movie to watch it. Click the iCloud button to sign in to your iCloud account and view the movie on your other devices, such as an iPad with the iMovie app installed.

✦ **Email:** Open the Size pop-up menu to choose to send a video that is Small, Medium, or Large. When you change the size, which reflects the screen size, the storage amount needed changes. For example, a large video may be more than 10MB — the recommended limit — so you may be better off sending a small- or medium-size video. Click the Share button. A blank e-mail message opens with your video attached. Address the e-mail (see Book II, Chapter 2) and click Send.

✦ **iTunes:** Choose the size in which you want to save the movie — SD (Standard Definition), Large, or HD (High Definition) 720 or 1080 — and then click Share. The movie is saved to iTunes.

✦ **YouTube/Facebook/Vimeo/CNN iReport:** Use the pop-up menus to choose the size, category (YouTube), and viewing privileges (all but CNN), and then click the Next button. Enter your account name and password in the dialog that appears, and click OK. Click the Publish button on the copyrights window that appears, and your movie is prepared and uploaded to your account.

✦ **File:** Click the arrows to the right of the format to choose the size you want to save the movie as, and then click the Compatibility menu, as shown in Figure 4-20, to see which computers and devices will be able to play your movie. You may have to save more than one file copy to share with different types of devices. Click the Next button, type a different name for your movie in the Save As field if you like, and then choose a destination from the Where menu. Click the disclosure triangle to the right of the Save As field to expand the window and scroll through your drives and folders to choose a destination. Click Save.

Figure 4-20:
Check the compatibility before saving your movie.

Select the Add to Theater check box in the sharing dialog windows if you want to automatically place a copy of your movie in the Theater. This saves you the step of Sharing to Theater and then sharing elsewhere.

**Book IV
Chapter 4**

**Making Movies
with iMovie**

Chapter 5: Making Your Own Kind of Music with GarageBand

In This Chapter

✔ **Recording your music**

✔ **Editing your recordings**

✔ **Saving your music**

✔ **Taking music lessons in GarageBand**

*W*hen you mention that you use a Mac to a group of non-Mac users, one of the first things you hear is, "Oh, yeah, Macs are great for graphics." And although that's true, your Mac is a pretty terrific music-making machine, too — and we're not talking iTunes here (although we do talk about iTunes at length in Book IV, Chapter 1).

With GarageBand, which is part of Apple's iLife suite, you can record and compose music and ringtones, as well as presentations and speeches. In its simplest form, GarageBand provides instruments (such as drums, keyboards, and guitars) and prerecorded tracks that you mix up to create a virtual one-person band. You arrange the separate audio tracks and put them together to create your own songs.

GarageBand really sings (bah-dum-dum) when you record your own music. You have the option of using your Mac's built-in microphone or connecting your instruments and hand-held microphone to your Mac and recording directly. After you lay down the individual tracks, you can clean up the sound, alter the rhythms and timing, and cut and splice the best performances to generate a CD or iTunes-quality recording.

If you want to learn to play an instrument or brush up on your childhood music lessons, GarageBand even offers guitar and piano lessons to get you started. You can play along, and GarageBand will evaluate your progress.

In this chapter, we introduce you to the most basic functions of GarageBand and provide an overview for using them. We recommend you learn the basics and then play around. The more you use it, the more you see how powerful and flexible an application GarageBand truly is.

Recording Audio

Because GarageBand works with audio, the first task is to record audio into GarageBand by using your Mac's built-in microphone, an external microphone, or audio input (such as a keyboard or guitar plugged directly into your Mac).

If you don't have a real instrument, GarageBand provides a variety of software instruments — virtual musical instruments, such as pianos, guitars, and drums — that you can play and control through your Mac. All you have to do is specify the notes to play and the tempo, and the software instruments let you hear your music played by the instruments you choose.

In this section, we show you how to create and record music with GarageBand's built-in software instruments first; then we show you how to use real instruments. We also explain the various GarageBand controls you find at the top of the window. Regardless of what type of instrument you record, you create one instrumental track at a time, gradually layering additional tracks until you've defined the parts for an entire band or orchestra.

Creating music with software instruments

To use software instruments, you specify the instrument you want to use, such as a baby grand piano or a steel-string acoustic guitar. Then you define the notes you want that instrument to play by using a virtual keyboard — using either the keyboard on your Mac or an external keyboard that you connect to the USB port — to play the notes.

 If your Mac came with an older version of GarageBand, the newest version 10.0.1, which this chapter refers to, can be downloaded for free at the App Store, but be prepared to wait up to an hour for the complete download to finish.

To create a software instrument, follow these steps:

1. **Open GarageBand by clicking the GarageBand icon on the Dock or from Launchpad.**

   The GarageBand chooser opens, as shown in Figure 5-1.

2. **Click the Empty Project icon. Or, if you want to jump directly to a specific genre or type of instrument, click one of the other icons (such as Keyboard Collection or Hip Hop) and then skip to Step 8.**

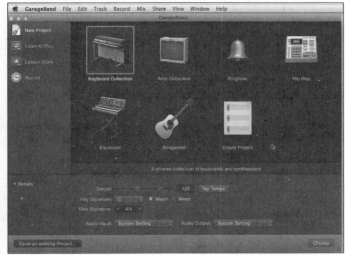

Figure 5-1:
Choose
the type
of project
you want to
create in the
GarageBand
chooser.

3. **Click the Details disclosure triangle to select a tempo, and then use the slider and pop-up menus to choose the following:**

   - *Tempo:* Drag the slider left and right to adjust the tempo of your new project.

   - *Key Signature:* From the pop-up menu, choose the key for your project and then select the Major or Minor radio button.

   - *Time Signature:* Click in the field to type the time signature you want to use or click the arrows to the left and right of the field to increase or decrease one fraction at a time.

     Without getting into a full-blown music lesson, the *key signature* indicates the key in which you play your music, such as C-sharp or A-flat. The key signature can be in different *scales* or a series of ascending or descending notes. The key signatures are built on major scales, for example the C major key begins and ends with the C note. In minor scales, some of the notes are raised a half-step. *Tempo* sets the pace for the entire piece, and *time signature* tells you how many beats of which type of note occur in each measure. A waltz's tempo may be *adagio*, which means play slowly, with a 3/4 time signature, which means three notes played with the beat on the quarter-note in each *measure*, which comprises the notes and rests between two bar marks — see it's already getting complicated, just go play!

   - *Audio Input and Audio Output:* If you connect an external mic or speakers, choose those from the respective pop-up menus. If you use your Mac's built-in mic and speakers, choose Built-In or leave System Settings.

**Book IV
Chapter 5**

**Making Your Own
Kind of Music with
GarageBand**

You can adjust these settings after you create your project, so don't worry if they aren't exactly right.

4. **Click the Choose button.**

The Recording Options window opens.

5. **Click the Software Instrument icon, as shown in Figure 5-2, and then click the Create button.**

A window appears, displaying a Musical Typing keyboard and a single audio track for a classic electric piano waiting to be filled with your recording.

Figure 5-2:
Choose Software Instrument to use sounds pre-loaded in GarageBand to create your song.

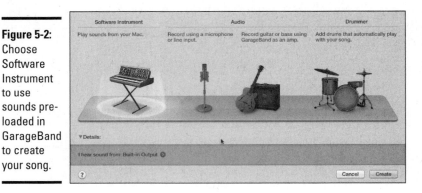

6. **To change the instrument you want to play and record, click an instrument category (such as Bass or Guitar) in the Library pane, and then click the specific effect to use (such as Upright Studio Bass or Classic Clean Guitar), as shown in Figure 5-3.**

The instruments and their effects are called *patches.* Two other terms you should be familiar with are *loops,* which are pre-recorded snippets of music or sound effects, and *tracks,* which contain the recorded music of each instrument or voice and can also hold loops. Many tracks together make up the song.

7. **Press the keyboard keys associated with the notes you want to hear to test the sound.**

For example, A plays a C note at the low end of the octave and K plays the C note at the high end. You can play one octave at a time; press the Z and X keys to move down or up an octave. The blue highlighted section on the keyboard at the top of the window indicates which octave you're playing.

8. **Click the Record button (the red dot inside a black circle at the top of the GarageBand window) and type on the Musical Typing keyboard to record the notes you play.**

If you don't see the Musical Typing keyboard, choose Window⇨Show Musical Typing.

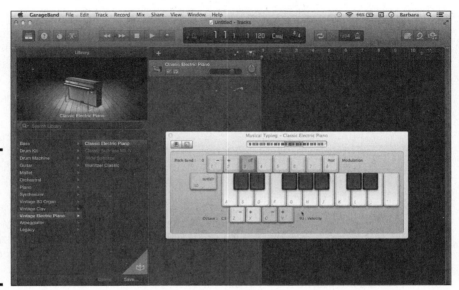

Figure 5-3:
The Library
pane dis-
plays a list
of different
instruments
you can
choose.

9. **Click the Stop button to stop recording.**

10. **Click the Locate button — it replaces (toggles to) the Stop button
    to the left of the Play button when the recording or playing has
    stopped — to return to the beginning of your recording, and then
    click Play to hear the notes you recorded.**

11. **Click the Save button at the bottom of the Library pane or choose
    GarageBand⇨Save.**

12. **Type a name for your project in the Save dialog that appears and then
    click the Save button.**

To add another software instrument, follow these steps:

1. **Click the Add Track button (+) at the top of the tracks list or choose
   Track⇨New Track.**

   The window shown earlier in Figure 5-2 appears.

2. **Click the Software Instrument icon, and then click the Create button.**

   The new instrument track appears in the GarageBand window.

3. **(Optional) Choose View⇨Show Library if you don't see the list of
   instrument patches**.

4. **Repeat Steps 8–10 in the preceding step list to record a track with the
   new instrument.**

5. **Repeat this procedure to record a song with an entire band of
   instruments.**

**Book IV
Chapter 5**

**Making Your Own
Kind of Music with
GarageBand**

GarageBand comes with a lot of sounds to choose from, but you may have noticed some of the selections are dimmed. The dimmed patches are available as a one-time, in-app purchase for $4.99, which you access by choosing GarageBand⇨Purchase More Sounds. As with any Apple purchase, you need your Apple ID, which we explain in Book I, Chapter 3.

Interpreting the Control bar

Consider the whole GarageBand window a music composition, mixing, and editing workspace. Depending on the task you want to perform, you can show or hide a pane, which displays the tools that control the desired task. GarageBand lets you show panes with menu commands or with the buttons on the Control bar.

The callouts in Figure 5-4 identify the Control bar buttons, and here we tell you what each does and what its menu counterpart is in case you prefer to use menus instead of buttons. For the most part, click a button to perform an action and then click it again to stop the action or do the reverse of what you did. For example, click the Library button once to show the Library, and click it again to hide the Library.

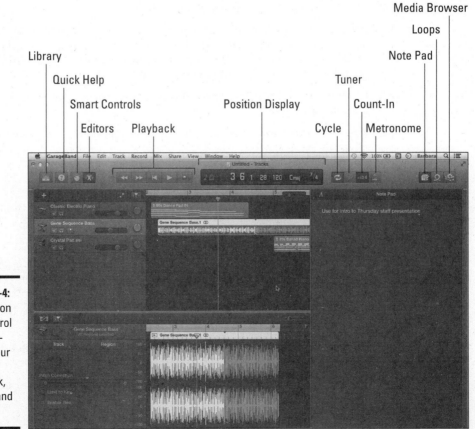

Figure 5-4: Buttons on the Control bar command your views, playback, tempo, and more.

The buttons are

✦ **Library (View⇨Show/Hide Library):** Reveals the *patch library,* which is where you choose the types of instruments you want to play in the tracks.

✦ **Quick Help (Help⇨Quick Help):** When selected, a Quick Help window appears. Then, you hover the pointer over a button, and the explanation appears in the Quick Help window.

✦ **Smart Controls (View⇨Show/Hide Smart Controls):** *Smart Controls* let you modify the sound of the selected patch. The appearance of the Smart Controls changes, depending on the patch, although for each you can tweak the tone, compression, and effects.

✦ **Editors (View⇨Show/Hide Editor):** Depending on the selected track type, you can edit audio, drums, piano, or the musical score.

You can view Smart Controls or Editors but not at the same time.

✦ **Playback controls (always in view):** These buttons work as those you may know from other recording machines or stereos: Rewind, Fast Forward, Stop/Locate (which moves the playhead back to the beginning of the track), Play, and Record.

✦ **Position Display (always in view):** The first button on the left in the display toggles between the Beats & Project view and Time view, which changes the information in the display and the ruler above the tracks. In Beats & Project view (as shown in Figure 5-5), the numbers and fields do the following:

• *Playhead Position* indicates the playhead position by Bars, Beats, Divisions, and Ticks, each being a fraction of the previous. Double-click any of the numbers to type a different value and move the playhead; this can be a precise way to position the playhead exactly where you want it.

• *Beats per Minute* indicates the tempo. Double-click to select the value and type a new one to change the tempo.

• *Key* tells you what key your music plays in; click to open a pop-up menu and choose a different key.

• *Time Signature* is the time your music uses. Drag the beat (top) number vertically to increase or decrease it; click the note value (bottom number) to open a pop-up menu with possible values. Or, double-click and type in new values.

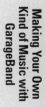

Book IV
Chapter 5

Making Your Own
Kind of Music with
GarageBand

Figure 5-5:
Beats &
Project.

In Time view (as shown in Figure 5-6), click any of the elements and drag vertically to change the value, or double-click and type a new value to move the playhead to that position.

Figure 5-6:
Move the
playhead in
Time view.

✦ **Cycle:** When you turn on Cycle mode, you replay the highlighted part of the project, allowing you to rehearse the section or record multiple takes. Click and drag the ends of the cycle to resize it; click in the center and drag left or right to reposition the cycle; click the Cycle button again to remove the cycle.

✦ **Tuner (active when instruments are attached to your Mac):** Click to open the tuner and tune your instrument.

✦ **Count-In:** When on, the metronome will count-in none, one, or two bars when you begin recording. Choose Record⇨Count-In to select One or Two Bars, or None.

✦ **Metronome:** Click to turn on a metronome that will knock to the tempo of your project. When Count-In is selected, you can use the metronome during the count-in bars only or throughout the project.

You can see one of the following at a time, and the Library pane is hidden when one of the following panes is open. If you choose View⇨Show Library, any of these panes that are open will close:

✦ **Note Pad (View⇨Show/Hide Note Pad):** Opens, or closes, a pane where you can jot down notes about your project.

✦ **Apple Loops (View⇨Show/Hide Apple Loops):** Opens, or closes, the pane where you can select Apple Loops (as explained a few sections further on).

✦ **Media Browser (View⇨Show/Hide Media Browser):** Opens, or closes, a chooser where you can browse and select media from other apps, such as iTunes or iPhoto, to use or refer to in your project.

Playing with a real instrument

The easiest way to record on GarageBand is to sing or to play an instrument within hearing range of your Mac's built-in microphone. For better quality, however, connect a hand-held microphone or instrument to your Mac's audio input or USB port. By playing with a real instrument, you can record yourself or your whole band, edit the sound, and save your recording. You can play or sing along with your own recording. Record other single tracks while playing different instruments and mix them together, and your recording sounds like a multipiece band or orchestra.

If you connect a MIDI (Musical Instrument Digital Interface) keyboard to your Mac's USB port, instead of using the Mac keyboard to play GarageBand's software instruments, you use the MIDI keyboard, which gives you more octaves and familiar keyboard playing, and turns your Mac into a synthesizer. If, instead, you want to use GarageBand to record what you play on your keyboard, plug it into your Mac's line-in port. Choose GarageBand⇨Preferences⇨Audio/MIDI to confirm that your keyboard is connected.

To record a real instrument connected to your Mac, follow these steps:

1. **Click the GarageBand icon on the Dock or from Launchpad.**

2. **Click the Empty Project icon.**

3. **Click the Details disclosure triangle, and select the tempo, key, and time for the project.**

4. **Click the Choose button.**

   The Recording Options window opens.

5. **Click either the Microphone or Guitar/Bass icon under Audio, as shown in Figure 5-7.**

Figure 5-7:
Record audio from a microphone or guitar connected to your Mac or with your Mac's built-in microphone.

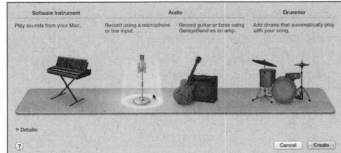

6. **Click the Create button.**

The recording window opens (refer to Figure 5-3).

Control-click by a track name and then choose New Audio Track or New Software Instrument Track from the contextual menu.

7. **Click one of the Voice or Guitar categories and patch choices in the Library.**

8. **Click the track you want to record.**

9. **Click the Smart Controls button, and then click the Inspector button (*i*).**

10. **Adjust the Recording Level by dragging the slider or clicking Automatic Level Control.**

11. **Choose the input source from the Input pop-up menu.**

12. **Click the Monitoring button to hear your microphone or instrument as you record.**

You can also click the Monitoring button by the track name to activate this feature. GarageBand may suggest using headphones if you select this option.

13. **Click the Record button on your track and then start playing away.**

When you finish playing, click the Stop button.

14. **(Optional) To record multiple takes of the same track, click the Cycles button.**

When you click the track to record again, a folder is created on the track that contains all the takes. You can then, later, listen to the different takes and select the best one, or use bits and pieces of different takes to create a track.

15. **(Optional) If you want to add more instruments, choose Track⇨New Track or click the Add Track button (the plus sign) at the top of the Tracks list.**

Repeat the steps for adding a Software Instrument or Audio.

You can combine real and software instruments in your recordings to create a custom sound.

16. **(Optional) To add a drum track to your song (you can add only one per project), click the Add Track button, click the Drummer icon, and then click Create.**

The Editors pane appears in the GarageBand window, as shown in Figure 5-8.

a. Click the menu above the drummer avatars to choose the genre.

b. Choose a drummer from the selection.

c. *Click a preset and then click the Play button to hear a sample.*

d. *Repeat to audition other drummers before deciding which one best suits your band, er . . . project.*

Figure 5-8:
Add a drum track.

For the best recording quality, connect an audio interface to your Mac's USB, Thunderbolt or line-in port. Then connect your instruments to the audio interface. Make sure that the audio interface is compatible with OS X.

Using Apple Loops

No, this section isn't about recording the sound of a certain cereal. *Apple Loops* are prerecorded snippets that you can use with video you post on your web page or use as background music in an iMovie production or Keynote presentation. (Find more on Keynote in Book V, Chapter 4.) Rather than play "Twinkle, Twinkle, Little Star" on your keyboard or shell out the bucks for a Fender Stratocaster to create an attention-grabbing riff, you can easily create your own little ditties with the loops that come with GarageBand. Combine several loops into short jingles or even full-length songs.

To create a song by using Apple Loops, follow these steps:

1. **Click the GarageBand icon on the Dock or from Launchpad.**
2. **Click Empty Project and then click the Choose button.**
3. **Click Software Instrument and then click Create.**

You can close the Musical Keyboard window by clicking the red Close button in the upper left of the window.

4. **Choose View➪Show Apple Loops, or click the Apple Loops button at the right end of the Control bar at the top of the GarageBand window.**

   The Loops browser opens, as shown in Figure 5-9.

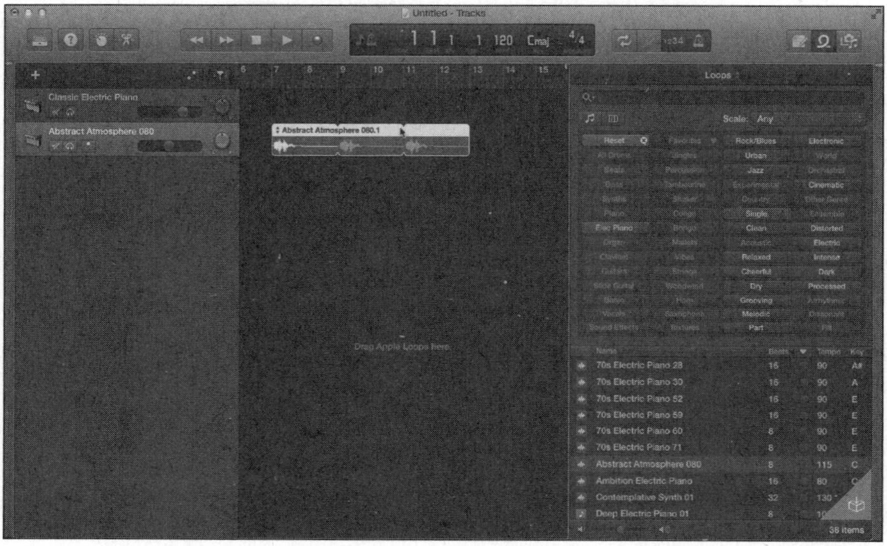

Figure 5-9: Use pre-recorded Apple Loops to create background music for presentations and videos.

5. **Choose instruments and styles from the Keywords buttons in the top half of the Apple Loops pane.**

   As you make your choices, some choices dim because they aren't compatible with those you made.

   Narrow your choices by doing one or more of the following:

   • *Loops pop-up menu:* From this menu, at the top of the pane, select a music genre.

   • *Scale pop-up menu:* Choose select Major, Minor, Neither, or Good for Both.

   • *Column view button:* See Figure 5-10; make successive choices to narrow the results.

   The loops that meet your criteria appear in the list on the bottom half of the pane, and show the name, beats, tempo, and key of the selection.

6. **Click the filenames to hear samples of the songs listed.**

7. **Click to deselect instruments and/or styles to see more, or different, samples.**

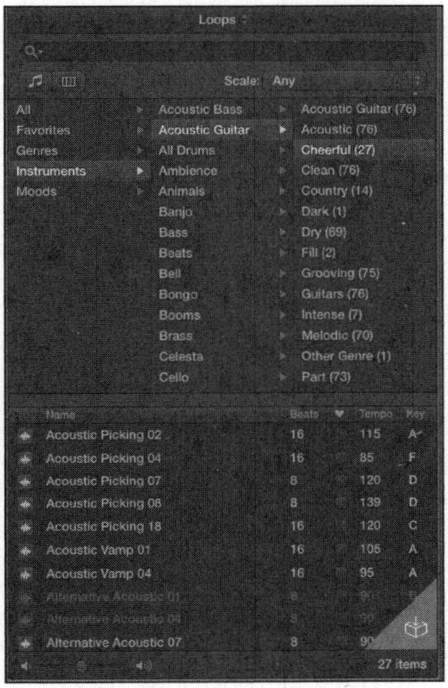

Figure 5-10:
Select criteria in the column view to see the number of choices you have.

8. **When you find one you like, click and drag the file to the Tracks pane in the middle of the window (refer to Figure 5-9).**

   Audio loops, which are single instrument loops, have a green icon next to them in the list at the bottom half of the pane and can be dragged into a software instrument or audio track or be used to create their own track.

9. **(Optional) To add other music clips and create a song with multiple instruments, click Reset and then repeat Steps 5–8.**

10. **(Optional) Click and drag the right end of the loop to repeat the loop one or more times.**

11. **Click the Play button to hear your composition.**

Editing Audio Tracks

One of the great things about recording with GarageBand is that you can edit your audio. If you lay down multiple tracks and find that the timing is off between them, you can use one as the base and correct the others. If you play a riff off-key, delete that section and even replace it with a riff from a different part of the track. If you want the song you recorded in your basement to sound like you were in a stadium, add a concert-hall sound effect. You get the idea — the options are virtually endless.

**Book IV
Chapter 5**

Making Your Own Kind of Music with GarageBand

In this section, we explain the editing basics, but we encourage you to be adventurous and play around with GarageBand to develop your own particular performing style.

Expanding track views

Whenever you add a software instrument, audio, drummer, or loop, a new track is added to your project. You can add editing tracks that help you manage and refine your project. Open the Track menu and choose to show, or hide, one or more of the following:

✦ **Arrangement Track:** Use to add a track at the top of the tracks where you can add markers to quickly rearrange parts of your project.

✦ **Movie Track:** When you're laying tracks to accompany a movie project, you can view thumbnails from the movie in this track to see at what point the music will play.

✦ **Transposition Track:** Change the pitch of parts of the project.

✦ **Tempo Track:** See all the tempo changes in the project.

✦ **Master Track:** Use the Master Track to control the overall volume of the project. This track always appears at the bottom of the track list.

From the Tracks menu, you can also choose which buttons to show in the *Track header,* which is where you see the name of the track. You can see some or all of the following buttons in the Track header:

✦ **Mute (always present):** When selected, the tracks audio is silent during playback.

✦ **Solo (always present):** When selected, the track will play alone, and other tracks will be muted. The Mute button on muted tracks blinks to let you know those tracks will be absent during the solo.

✦ **Track Lock (Tracks⇨Track Header⇨Show/Hide Track Lock Button):** When you create a track that's exactly how you want it, click the Track Lock button to avoid accidentally changing it.

✦ **Record Enable (Tracks⇨Track Header⇨Show/Hide Record Enable Button):** When activated, you can record the track. Record Enable can be activated on more than one track at a time.

✦ **Monitoring (Tracks⇨Track Header⇨Show/Hide Input Monitoring Button):** When activated, you can hear sounds on tracks that aren't Record Enabled. For example, before recording, you can perform a sound check and adjust the volume or other controls.

✦ **Volume:** Drag the slider left and right to decrease or increase the volume of the track.

✦ **Pan:** Click and drag the dial to the left or right to change or emphasize playback on a specific side.

If you have an iPad, download the free (Apple) app, Logic Remote, and use the iPad's touchscreen controls to manage GarageBand on your Mac.

Splitting a track

When you first record an instrument, GarageBand saves it as a single, long track. To make it easier to edit this track, you can split a track into parts that you can modify individually, save and reuse, delete, or rearrange in a new position. The parts of a track are *audio regions,* sometimes referred to as just *regions.*

To split a track, follow these steps:

1. **Select a track that you want to split.**

   GarageBand highlights your chosen instrument.

2. **Drag the playhead to where you want to split the track.**

   If you can't find the playhead, click the Locate button to move the playhead to the beginning of your track.

3. **Choose Edit➪Split Regions at Playhead or press ⌘+T.**

   GarageBand splits your track.

4. **Double-click any track, or select a track and click the Editor button on the Control bar, to bring up the Track Editor pane.**

   The Track Editor zooms in on an audio region of the track so you can split a more defined point, as shown in Figure 5-11.

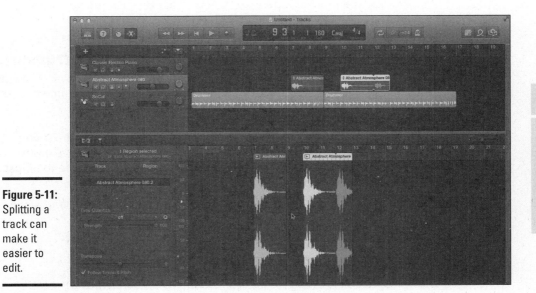

Figure 5-11: Splitting a track can make it easier to edit.

Joining a track

Even if you split a track, you can always rejoin the parts. To join two audio regions of a track, click and drag them so they're adjacent and then follow these steps:

1. **Click the first part of the track that you want to join.**

2. **Hold down the Shift key and click the second part of the track you want to join.**

3. **Choose Edit⇨Join Regions or press ⌘+J.**

   GarageBand connects the two parts.

Moving tracks

After you record two or more tracks, you may want to adjust how each track plays relative to one another. For example, you can make one track play before or after a second track to create interesting audio effects. To move tracks, follow these steps:

1. **Click the track that you want to move.**

   GarageBand highlights your selected instrument track.

   For more flexibility, split a track into multiple regions so you can move each region separately.

2. **Click and drag the track to the left or right to adjust the relative positions of the two tracks.**

3. **Release the mouse button when you're happy with the new arrangement of the tracks and regions.**

Quantize the times of real and Software Instruments

You can *quantize,* or automatically correct and regularize, the timing of regions of the tracks in recordings done with both real and Software Instruments. The sequence is slightly different between the two types of instruments:

✦ **In tracks recorded with real instruments either connected to your Mac's line-in port or directly through the Mac's microphone or an external mic connected to your Mac, you can use Flex Time to adjust the timing of individual notes.**

   a. *Click the Flex button (the wave form in the top left of the Editors pane) to turn on Flex Time.*

   b. *Move the pointer over the zoomed track in the Track Editor.*

      It becomes a wave symbol.

   c. *Click and drag to shorten or stretch notes within the track.*

    d. *Click the Flex Time button to see the difference between the two versions.*

✦ **With a Software Instrument, you can set the Time Quantize before recording, in which case the region is quantized automatically.**

    To quantize after you record

    a. *Click the Software Instrument track you want to quantize.*

    b. *Click the Editors button (if the Track Editor pane isn't open).*

    c. *Choose the note value you want from the Time Quantize pop-up menu.*

You can change the beat, tempo, and key of your project with the buttons in the Beats & Project Display on the Control bar.

Groove matching

When you record your instruments separately, the timing within each may be fine, but they still aren't synchronized. GarageBand saves you from painstakingly matching each track or re-recording by letting you designate one of the tracks as the Groove Track. To do so, follow these steps:

1. **Choose Tracks⇨Track Header⇨Show Groove Track.**

2. **Identify the track you want to use as the groove standard for your song.**

3. **Hover the pointer over the left side of the track name until you see the outline of a star, and then click that track.**

    Check boxes appear to the left of the other track headers.

4. **Select the check boxes next to each track you want to match to the Groove Track.**

5. **To make a different track the Groove Track, repeat Step 3 by a different track header.**

You can't use groove matching if a track is automatically quantized.

Saving Music

After you finish arranging and modifying your song, choose File⇨Save to save your GarageBand project (so you can edit it later). If you want to share your creation with others, you can do one or more of the following:

✦ Save as a song or ringtone in the iTunes library.

✦ Upload to your SoundCloud account. (More on SoundCloud in a bit.)

✦ Export to an optical disc.

We show you the steps for each in the following sections.

Saving a song in iTunes

If you create a song that you want to save and play later, you can store that song in iTunes by following these steps:

1. **Choose Share⇨Song to iTunes.**

   A dialog appears, as shown in Figure 5-12.

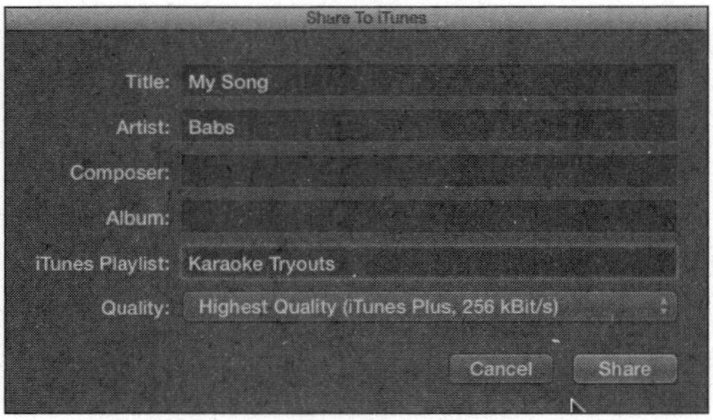

Figure 5-12: Choose a playlist, artist name, and audio setting for your song.

> Share To iTunes
>
> Title: My Song
> Artist: Babs
> Composer:
> Album:
> iTunes Playlist: Karaoke Tryouts
> Quality: Highest Quality (iTunes Plus, 256 kBit/s)
>
> Cancel   Share

2. **Click the Title, Artist, Composer, Album, and iTunes Playlist text boxes and enter any information you want to store.**

   Choose GarageBand⇨Preferences and click the My Info tab to enter default information that will be used whenever you share your projects.

3. **Choose a setting from the Quality pop-up menu.**

4. **Click the Share button.**

   Your song appears in your iTunes library.

Saving a song as a ringtone

Any of the songs you create can be used as ringtones for your iPhone — or as a FaceTime notification on your Mac, iPod touch, or iPad, or as a text tone with iMessage on any iOS device or the Messages app on your Mac. Just follow these steps:

1. **Choose Share⇨Send Ringtone to iTunes.**

   Ringtones can't be more than 40 seconds. If your selection is too long, a dialog asks whether you want to adjust it — if you don't, GarageBand will truncate the selection for you. Click Adjust, and then drag your selection left or right so the start and end points for your selection include the segment you want to hear as a ringtone (or notification or text tone).

2. **GarageBand automatically converts your song and opens the iTunes application.**

3. **Your song appears in the Ringtones library on iTunes, ready to be synched to your iPhone.**

You can also create a ringtone from scratch by clicking the Ringtone icon in the GarageBand Project window and then click the Choose button. Create a tone from Apple Loops or by adding new tracks of your own, just as you would if you were recording a song.

Sharing your song on SoundCloud

SoundCloud lets you share songs you create with others on a social network, and you can listen to others' musical creations too. If you use the SoundCloud social network, you may want to send your songs directly from GarageBand so others can hear your recordings and creations. Choose Share⇨SoundCloud, and then sign in to your SoundCloud account. (If you don't have an account, you can use your Facebook or Google account information or click Sign Up to create a SoundCloud account.) After you sign in, GarageBand can access your SoundCloud account, and songs will be automatically uploaded when you next choose Share⇨SoundCloud.

Saving a song to your storage drive

If you don't want to store your song in iTunes, you can save your song as a separate audio file that you can store anywhere, such as on an external hard drive or a USB flash drive. To save your song as an audio file, follow these steps:

1. **Choose Share⇨Export Song to Disk.**

   The Export Song to Disk dialog appears.

2. **Type a name for your project in the Save As field.**

3. **Choose a setting from the Quality pop-up menu.**

4. **Choose a location for storing your project from the Where pop-up menu.**

   The GarageBand folder is the default location. Click the disclosure triangle to expand the Save dialog and scroll through the directories to save your project in a different drive or location.

5. **Click Export.**

Burning a song to CD

If you create a song that you want to share with others, you can burn it to a CD and then give the CD away. To burn a song to a CD, follow these steps:

1. **Choose Share⇨Burn Song to CD.**

   A dialog appears, telling you that it's waiting for a blank CD-R or CD-RW.

2. **Insert a blank CD-R or CD-RW into your Mac and click Burn.**

Learning to Play the Guitar and Piano

You can learn piano or guitar basics with GarageBand music lessons. GarageBand provides 40 free lessons for learning piano and guitar.

Your first two free lessons are preloaded in GarageBand; you can download the remaining 38 free lessons by clicking the Lesson Store in the GarageBand chooser window, and then clicking the Basic Lessons tab and clicking each additional lesson you want to download. Additionally, you can click the Artist Lessons tab to purchase and download lessons taught by distinguished musicians, including Sting, Norah Jones, John Fogerty, and Sarah McLachlan.

You can follow the lesson with your free-standing piano or guitar or with a keyboard or guitar hooked up to your Mac. To take a music lesson, follow these steps:

1. **Click the GarageBand icon on the Dock or from Launchpad.**

   The GarageBand chooser appears.

2. **Click Learn to Play in the sidebar on the left.**

3. **Click the Guitar Lessons, Piano Lessons, or Artist Lessons tab at the top of the window.**

4. **Click a lesson in the list that appears, and then click the Choose button.**

   A full-screen window opens with an instruction video and a keyboard or guitar, and the lesson begins, as shown in Figure 5-13.

Figure 5-13:
Learn to play an instrument with GarageBand.

Notice the buttons in the top-right corner of the lesson window:

- *Glossary* gives you a reference tool for musical words and definitions.
- *Tuner* helps you tune your guitar.
- *Mixer* lists options for what you hear while you're taking the lesson.
- *Setup* lets you customize your learning interface.
- *Notes* lets you choose what kind of musical notation you see on the lesson window.

5. **Click the Play button in the playback controls.**

   The lesson begins. Click the Play button again to stop the lesson.

   - *Chapters:* At the bottom of the lesson window, a bar is divided into the lesson chapters. You can click on their titles to jump from one section of the lesson to the next, or drag the slider to the point you want to review.
   - *Cycle button:* Click the Cycle button (the two arrows chasing each other in a circle) to highlight the chapters. With the Cycle button on, you can highlight a chapter, and the Rewind button takes you back to the highlighted chapter if you move to a different point in the lesson. When the Cycle button is off, clicking the Rewind button takes you to the beginning of the lesson. You can also adjust the speed of the lesson with the slider to the left of the playback controls, although with slower speeds, the instructor's voice is muted.

6. **After you take the lesson, you can play along. Hover with the pointer to the left of your instructor to see two chapters: Learn and Play. Click Play.**

7. **If you're using an acoustic instrument, position yourself near your Mac so the microphone picks up your practice. If you're using an electronic keyboard or guitar, plug it in to the USB port on your Mac.**

8. **Click the Record button and play along.**

   GarageBand records your practice and tells you the percentage you got right with the How Did I Play? feature. GarageBand also keeps a history of your practices so you can track your progress. Click the My Results or History buttons in the lower-right corner to see how you did.

Chapter 6: Reading, Listening, and Learning on Your Mac

In This Chapter

✓ **Reading iBooks**

✓ **Attending iTunes U**

✓ **Enjoying podcasts**

We talk about iTunes and the iTunes Store in Book IV, Chapter 1. You may have noticed there's much more in the iTunes Store than just music and movies. iTunes offers a warehouse of podcasts, books, and university courses, too. In this chapter, we walk you through the stacks of the iBooks Store and show you how to use your Mac as an electronic reading device (also known as an *e-reader*).

We also flip through the course catalog of iTunes U, the online Apple learning institution that gives you free access to the virtual ivy-covered walls of some of the world's most prestigious universities. iTunes U also offers professional development courses, as well as K–12 materials and classes.

We close the chapter with *podcasts,* which are free audio and video broadcasts that used to be limited to iPods (hence, the name) but can be enjoyed on your Mac, too. The iTunes Store offers a seemingly endless assortment of podcast categories and topics.

Thumbing through iBooks

When you first open iBooks, you see the iBooks welcome screen that invites you to Get Started. Click the Get Started button, and then sign in to your iTunes account with your Apple ID and password (unless you're already signed in, in which case you won't be prompted to do this). For a refresher on how to get an Apple ID, see Book I, Chapter 3.

Any e-books (although not audiobooks) you previously purchased from iTunes will be automatically represented in iBooks, as you see in Figure 6-1. Books that have been downloaded to your Mac are accessible from iBooks. Books that you purchased but didn't download to your Mac have a cloud icon in the right corner of the book icon, which means they're available for download.

Figure 6-1:
iBooks automatically accesses any e-books you've purchased from the iTunes Store.

If you have no e-books, or you want to acquire more, click the iBooks Store button in the upper-left corner, and go to Step 2 in the next section.

Finding something to read at the iBooks Store

Like other popular online bookstores (whose names we won't mention), the iBooks Store offers fiction and nonfiction books on just about any subject you can think of and for readers of all ages. To shop for books and look for free books, just follow these steps:

1. **Click the iBooks icon on the Dock or from Launchpad.**

Your Library opens (refer to Figure 6-1) although you won't see any book icons if you haven't downloaded any books. Books you keep in iTunes, even if downloaded from other sources, will appear.

2. **Click the iBooks Store button in the upper-left corner.**

The iBooks Store opens, as shown in Figure 6-2, and has the same layout as the iTunes and App Stores with promotional banners and icons filling the main part of the screen. The tabs at the top of the window — Featured, Top Charts, NYTimes, Categories, and Top Authors — help you narrow your search. Use the Search field to look for a book by a specific title or author, or on a specific subject. The list running down the lower right of the window has Quick Links that access your Apple ID account and the short list of the most-downloaded paid and free books in the iBooks Store and the *New York Times* bestsellers. At the very bottom, you can find the More to Explore section, which gives you quick access to groups of books, such as Fiction Essentials or Popular Teen Series.

Figure 6-2:
The iBooks Store looks like the other Apple stores.

3. **Click a tab that interests you to narrow your choices and then click a book that you might like to read, or click a promotional button on the Featured screen.**

   The info screen opens (see Figure 6-3) and shows the usual information: Details, Ratings and Reviews, and Related tabs; and Price and Get Sample buttons to either purchase the book or download a sample, respectively.

4. **After you find something you want to try or purchase, click one of the following:**

   - *Get Sample:* Click this button to download a sample to your Mac. If you like it, you can purchase it later.

   - *Price button:* Clicking this button confirms that you want to purchase the book. Then enter your Apple ID and password.

   As items are downloading, you can continue browsing. After the book downloads to your Mac, the book has a New or Sample banner across it in your Library (refer to Figure 6-1).

   When an update for a book is available, the download button appears (the arrow, as shown in Figure 6-3); click it to download the updated material.

5. **(Optional) Do one of the following:**

   - *Click the Read or Read Sample button to open your recently downloaded item.*

   - *Click the Back button (to the right of the Library button) to return to the category or chart you were perusing.*

   - *Click another tab at the top to go to a different category or chart.*

**Book IV
Chapter 6**

Reading, Listening, and Learning on Your Mac

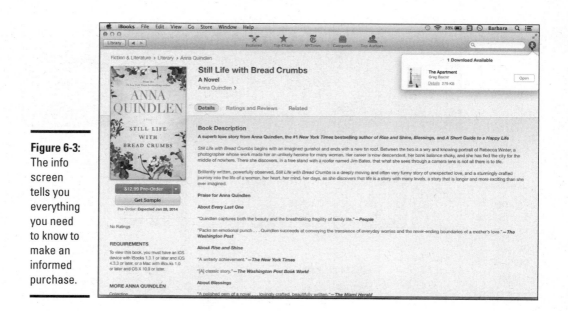

Figure 6-3:
The info
screen
tells you
everything
you need
to know to
make an
informed
purchase.

As long as you sign in to the same Apple ID on all your devices, iBooks syncs purchases from the iBooks or iTunes Store across your iOS devices and Macs. Choose iBooks➪Preferences and then click the Store button. Select the Download New Purchases Automatically check box so that purchases you make on another device are automatically downloaded to your Mac. On an iOS device, choose Settings➪iTunes & App Store, and tap Books to the On position in the Automatic Downloads section to simultaneously download books purchased on your Mac to your other devices.

Shopping for books at the iTunes Store

Although iBooks has its own iBooks Store, you can also shop for e-books in the iTunes Store. The Books layout mimics the other media categories: banner ads, sections by category, and top charts down the right side. The iTunes top downloads are divided into paid and free; the *New York Times* bestsellers are divided by fiction and nonfiction. The Books section of iTunes comprises electronic books and audiobooks, which you listen to via iTunes on your computer or, more likely, on your iPhone, iPod, or iPad in the device's Music app. To switch between electronic books (which iTunes refers to simply as "books") and audiobooks, click one of the subheads in the Books or Audiobooks section to open that department of the iTunes Store.

If you download a book into iTunes and then want it to appear in iBooks, choose File➪Move Books from iTunes.

Adding books and files from other sources

iBooks neatly keeps your digital reading material such as e-books in the ePub format and PDFs together in one place. To add your PDFs to iBooks, you can simply drag them into the iBooks window or iBooks icon on the Dock. To add either PDFs or e-books in the ePub format that you obtained from sources other than the iBooks Store, do the following:

1. **Click the iBooks icon on the Dock or from Launchpad.**

2. **If iBooks opens to the iBooks Store, click the Library button in the upper-left corner.**

3. **Choose File➪Add to Library.**

   Click and scroll through the chooser window or use the Search field to find the PDF or ePub e-book you want to add.

4. **Click the Add button.**

   The file is added to iBooks.

   To view only your PDF files, click the Collections tab at the top of the window and then click PDFs in the list on the left.

When you click to open a PDF in iBooks on your Mac, iBooks defaults to Preview, or another PDF reading app such as Adobe Reader, to open the file. iBooks does, however, read PDFs on iOS devices.

Reading by screenlight

After you download one or more books, the joy begins. Click the Library button in the upper-left corner, and then click the book you want to read. The book opens in a separate window, usually to the cover but sometimes (as with a sample) to a random page. You can use the following tools:

✦ **Library:** Click the Library button to return to the Library window.

   To quickly open a book you recently read, choose File➪Open Recent and select the book you want from the submenu.

✦ **Table of Contents:** Click the Table of Contents button, which opens the table of contents as a pop-up menu. Click the chapter or section you want to go to.

✦ **Navigation:** Click the right side of the page to go forward one page; click the left side to go back one page. Or swipe left or right on the trackpad to turn the pages.

✦ **Readability:** Click the Font Size button in the upper-right corner, and a window opens as shown in Figure 6-4.

   • *Click the small or large A to adjust the size of text on the page.*

   • *Click one of the color choices to change the page and type colors.*

   • *Click a font name in the list to change the typeface.*

Library

Table of Contents

Notes

Bookmarks

Search

Font sizes

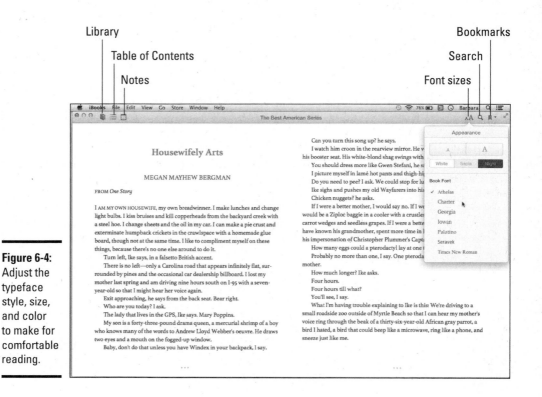

Figure 6-4:
Adjust the typeface style, size, and color to make for comfortable reading.

✦ **Search:** Click the Search button to look for a specific word or phrase or jump to a page number.

✦ **Bookmarks:** Click the Bookmarks button to virtually dog-ear a page so you can find it later; click the disclosure triangle next to the bookmark to see a list of bookmarked pages.

✦ **Resizing:** Click the full-screen button to use your Mac's entire screen or click and drag one of the window edges or corners to resize the window.

✦ **Definitions:** Double-click a word to open a definition of the word.

✦ **Notes:** Create a note. Click and drag to select a phrase or section of text. When the contextual menu opens, as shown in Figure 6-5, do the following:

   • *Choose a color to highlight the selected text or click the underlined* a *to underline it.*

   • *Click Add Note to open a virtual sticky note where you can type your thoughts.*

   • *Click Copy to temporarily save the selection to your Mac's Clipboard, and then paste it somewhere else.*

   • *Click More to see additional options (see Figure 6-5), such as searching the web or sharing the passage on a social network.*

   • *Click the Notes button to see sections you highlighted or notes you added to the book.*

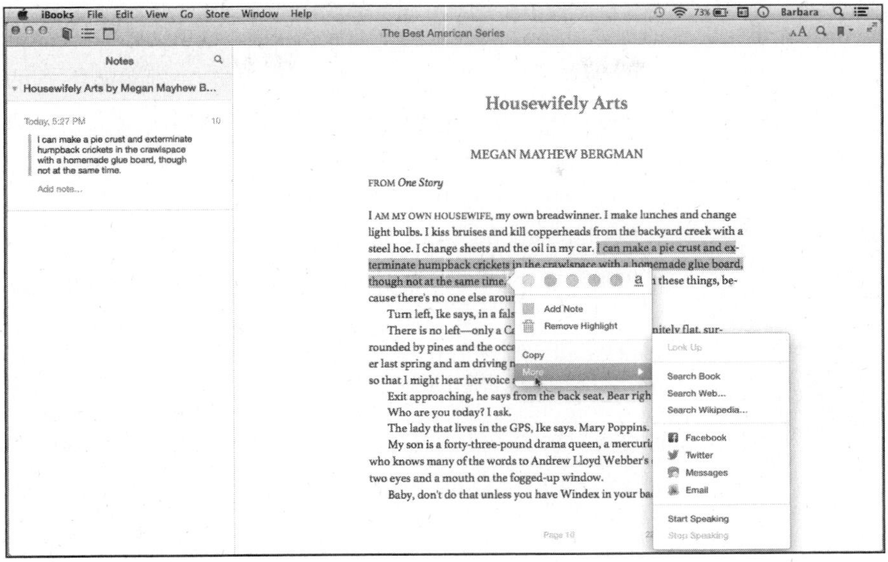

Figure 6-5:
Highlight
text and
take notes;
click the
Notes
button to
see them.

◆ **Preferences:** Choose iBooks⇨Preferences, and then click the General
button to turn on options, such as auto-hyphenation and justified text,
as well as to turn on syncing bookmarks, highlights, and collections on
your other devices.

TIP

Enhanced or interactive books may have multimedia capabilities, such as
clicking a three-dimensional item and then rotating it to view different
angles, or watching a video that correlates with the book. These types of
books can be read only on iBooks on Macs and iPads.

Sorting your books

iBooks gives you choices of how you want to sort and view your books
in your library. Access commands for sorting the books and seeing more
information in the View menu:

◆ Choose View⇨Sort By to re-order your books by Most Recent (those
opened most recently), Title, or Manually, which lets you click and drag
the books to the order you want.

◆ Choose View⇨Show Title and Author to see that information beneath
the book cover icon.

◆ Choose View⇨Show Purchases in iCloud to see books that haven't yet
been downloaded to your Mac.

The tabs across the top of the window change your point of view:

✦ **All Books:** Shows you the covers of all your books.

✦ **Collections:** A pane appears on the left of the window that lists three collections initially:

- Purchased, which shows books you purchased

- Books, which shows only books

- PDFs, which shows any PDFs you've copied into iBooks

Collections are a great way to group and sort your books. Choose File↪ New Collection, and then type in a new name in the highlighted item in the Collections list. (iBooks switches to Collections view automatically when you choose New Collection.) Click and drag books from the Purchased or Books collection into the newly created collection.

✦ **Authors:** A list of authors appears down the left of the window (refer to Figure 6-1). Click an author's name in the list to see books only by that author, or click All Authors to see all your books.

✦ **Categories:** A list of categories for which you have books appears down the left of the window. Click a category to see the books within it.

✦ **List:** The icons disappear, and you see a spreadsheet-style list of your book titles, authors, and other information such as when you last read the book and the date it was added.

Continuing Education at iTunes U

Divided into 16 genres (think academic departments), iTunes U features audio and video lectures from seminars and courses at universities around the world. iTunes U isn't limited to university, however. You find lectures and presentations from professional meetings and conferences, such as TED and the Prostate Health Conference, as well as K–12 and professional certification material. Aside from the vast selection of topics and the quality of the presentations, the best part is that the lectures are free!

Choosing courses

Here we briefly explain how the iTunes U course catalog is organized in the iTunes Store. As with the other iTunes Store departments, iTunes U lets you look at its offerings overall, by genre, by most popular, and, of course, by searching, which we explain in Book IV, Chapter 1.

The iTunes U offerings differ a bit from Music and Movies. The selections are divided into "courses" and "collections." Courses have a syllabus, study materials, which may be e-books or worksheets, and the lectures themselves as either audio or video files to be followed in chronological order as you build upon gained knowledge from one lesson to the next. Collections often run less than 15 minutes and are standalone lectures related to a similar topic; you don't need to listen to or watch all of them to gain full knowledge.

In addition to downloading single lectures, you can subscribe to a whole course or series and manage subscription preferences. Here, we briefly repeat how to reach iTunes U in the iTunes Store, to lead in to subscription management:

1. **Click iTunes on the Dock or from Launchpad, and then click iTunes Store in the upper-right corner.**

2. **Click the iTunes U tab at the top of the iTunes Store window.**

3. **Browse as you would for any media in iTunes by clicking through the categories that appear in the iTunes U pop-up menu or through the banners, icons, and lists.**

4. **Click the course or collection that interests you to open the info screen.**

5. **When you find a course or collection you want to watch or listen to, you have the following options, as shown in Figure 6-6:**

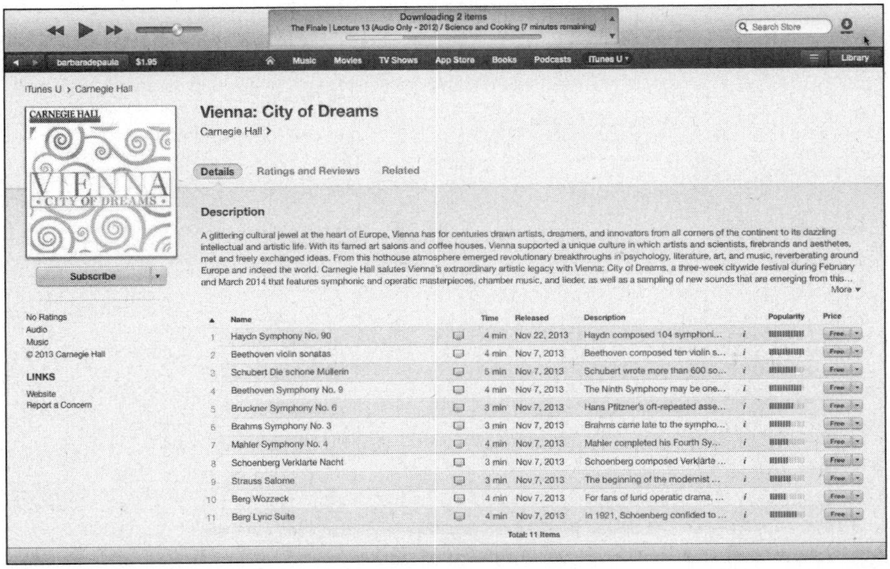

Figure 6-6: iTunes U offers lessons and lectures from universities around the world.

- *Click Subscribe* to subscribe to the entire course. Links to the materials are added to your iTunes U Library in iTunes, and updates are added as they become available. (This is the default setting that we show you how to change later.)

- *Click the Free button (in the Price column)* next to a single episode or material. The icon next to the name indicates the type of file it is: A monitor icon means video, and a speaker icon indicates audio. Some courses also have a syllabus to download as a PDF file.

Course materials are often available only through the iTunes U app on an iOS device, such as an iPad or iPhone.

6. **Click the Back button in the upper left to return to the iTunes U screen where you were before.**

Click the Library button in the upper right of the iTunes Store window to return to your iTunes Library.

Attending class

After you subscribe to a course or download single lectures, you find them in the iTunes U library, which you access by clicking iTunes U in the Library pop-up menu in the Library window. You can view all your courses by clicking the Courses tab, as shown in Figure 6-7. See those added most recently by clicking the New tab or see a list view by clicking — you guessed it — the List tab.

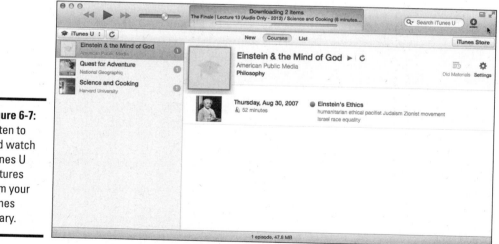

Figure 6-7: Listen to and watch iTunes U lectures from your iTunes library.

Click a course to display the lectures available so far. The icon next to the lecture indicates if it's audio or video. When you subscribe to a course, the most recent lecture — called Episode(s) — begins to download, and future episodes will be downloaded automatically when available. Until an episode has completed downloading, an iCloud icon appears next to it.

To download previous episodes, click the Settings button to choose how you want to manage the episodes, as shown in Figure 6-8. To download previous episodes, open the pop-up menu next to Download and choose All Episodes.

Click the Defaults button to select settings that will be applied to all courses, or use the settings for individual courses to differentiate between them. Click Done when you finish.

To listen to or watch an episode, click the Play button on the toolbar or next to the course title. Use the playback controls as you would for listening to music or watching a video (see Book IV, Chapter 2).

Video lecture   iCloud

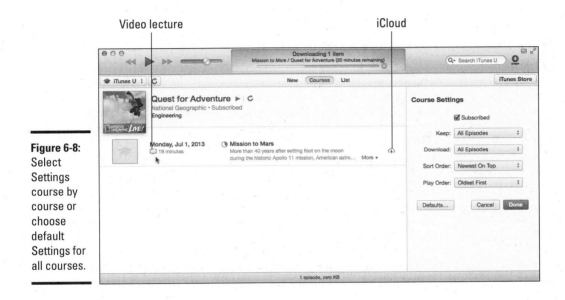

Figure 6-8: Select Settings course by course or choose default Settings for all courses.

Finding and Playing Podcasts

The iTunes Store offers both audio and video podcasts in 16 categories (at the time of publication), and you can view the podcasts by audio or video only, by category, or by new releases. Apple's recommendations show up under the Staff Favorites link, and Top Charts lists the most popular episodes.

As with iTunes U, you can listen to, or watch, a single episode of a podcast or subscribe, in which case iTunes automatically downloads new episodes to your podcast library. You can also *stream* a podcast — that is, listen to it while it's downloading. If you prefer to download and listen later, click the Pause button after clicking the download button; the podcast will download into the Podcast library, and you can play it at a later time. And, as with iTunes U, podcasts are free.

The iTunes Store isn't the only place to find podcasts. You may find others on the web and you can import them into iTunes with the Add to Library function described in Book IV, Chapter 1.

Managing your podcasts

Whether you download a single episode or subscribe to a series, you find the podcast in the Podcasts library of iTunes. Click the tabs across the top of the window to see different views:

✦ **Unplayed** displays all the podcasts you have downloaded or subscribed to but haven't listened to yet.

✦ **My Podcasts** shows you a list of the podcast series title on the left. When you click one of the series, a list of episodes appears on the right. You can access settings for a series from this view, which are explained in the upcoming List bullet.

If you want to see old episodes and even download some, click the Old Episodes button and then click Add All to add all the old episodes shown, or click the circle next to those you want to add and then click Done. Click the iCloud button next to the added episode to download it.

✦ **My Stations** sorts your podcasts by station categories that you create. Click the Add button (+) at the bottom of the My Stations view window and click the Untitled Station text box to rename your station. Then, click the circle to the right of the podcasts you want to be played on that station from the list on the right of the window, as shown in Figure 6-9. By default, the most recent unplayed episodes will be added to the station as they become available. You can adjust the order, number of episodes, and media type in the Station Settings, above the podcast list on the right. By putting several podcasts in a station, you can listen to a mix of similar podcasts — sort of like creating your own talk radio channel.

The icons next to the podcasts indicate the download status. A filled-in circle means the podcast has been downloaded, and a partially filled circle means the download is in progress.

✦ **List** shows a list (imagine that!) of the podcast episodes you downloaded or series you subscribed to. Click a specific podcast and then the Settings button at the bottom of the window. Click the Defaults button to select the default settings, as shown in Figure 6-10. After you select your default settings, click OK, and then click Done to close the settings. After you close Settings, the view switches to My Podcasts.

To set the same defaults for all podcasts, click the List tab, and then the Settings button directly, without choosing a specific podcast. The Podcast Defaults window opens (refer to Figure 6-10). Select your settings and click OK.

Downloading

Downloaded

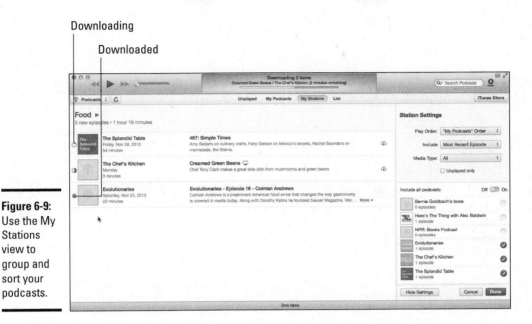

Figure 6-9:
Use the My
Stations
view to
group and
sort your
podcasts.

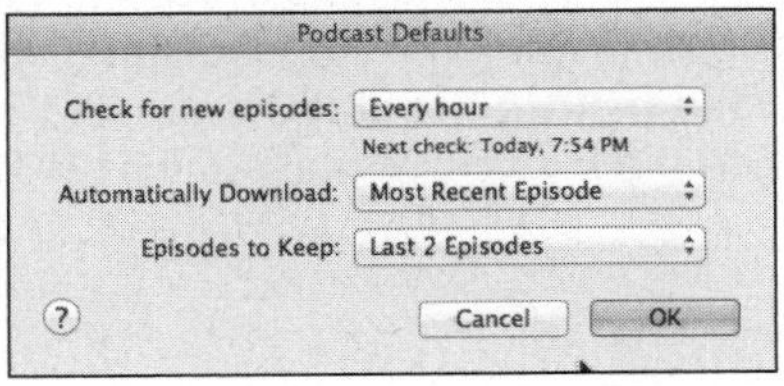

Figure 6-10:
Choose
default
podcast set-
tings from
List view.

Choose your default settings first, and then make any changes for any single podcast series. Done in the reverse order, the default settings will override the single series podcast settings.

Use the pop-up menus to select options for the selected podcast series, as shown in Figure 6-11. Click Done when you finish making your choices. Click the Refresh button to update your podcasts to replace the settings you chose.

If you want to subscribe to a podcast for which you downloaded just a single episode, choose List view, click the podcast you want to subscribe to, and then click the Subscribe button. Should you ever want to unsubscribe, do the same but click the Unsubscribe button.

Choose iTunes⇔Preferences, click the Store button, and then select the Sync Podcast Subscriptions and Settings check box to sync your preferences across all Macs and devices signed in to the same Apple ID.

Refresh

Figure 6-11:
Specify
different
podcast
settings for
individual
podcast
series you
subscribe to.

Listening to or watching podcasts

After you download or subscribe to a podcast, you'll want to enjoy it. In any
of the views, click a podcast and then click the Play button. If you click My
Stations, just click the Play button next to the station name to hear all the
podcasts on that station, back to back. Control playback as you would for
audio or video in iTunes.

Book V
Taking Care of Business

Contents at a Glance

Chapter 1: Managing Contacts

In This Chapter

✔ **Setting up Contacts**

✔ **Editing, searching, deleting, and grouping contacts**

✔ **Sharing contacts**

Your Mac comes with a contact management app called (surprise!) Contacts. Here you store names of people and businesses along with all sorts of information about them: phone numbers; street addresses; virtual addresses, such as those used for e-mail, instant messaging, or websites; social network usernames; and more intimate information, such as birthdays, anniversaries, and relations. Besides storing contact names and related contact information, Contacts can display contact information from more than one source, and it syncs with your iOS or Android devices — meaning that if you make a change to contact information on one device or computer, it's automatically updated on all your devices. Contacts also connects with other applications on your Mac so you can click someone's e-mail address and immediately

✦ Write and send an e-mail or message to that person.

✦ Open a FaceTime conversation.

✦ Click a street address and see it in Maps.

If by chance you still send letters or gifts the old-fashioned postal way, you can also print envelopes and mailing labels, and even the entire contacts list directly from Contacts.

Contacts is integrated with the other applications on your Mac that use addresses, including Mail (see Book II, Chapter 2), Messages (Book II, Chapter 3), and Calendar (Book V, Chapter 2). When you enter or search for a physical or virtual address in those applications, they refer to Contacts. This way, you have to enter contact information only once.

In this chapter, we explain how to set up Contacts by customizing the contact template with fields you use most frequently. Then we outline three ways to enter information: manually, importing data from another contact management app, and syncing with other accounts. In the second half of the chapter, we show you how to set up groups of contacts as well as how to print and export your contacts.

Setting Up Contacts

Contacts acts like a an electronic Rolodex. You save information about a person on a contact card so you can find that information again.

Each card contains information associated with one contact — be it a person or a company — such as telephone numbers and postal addresses, e-mail addresses, URLs, birthdays, profile usernames, and photos. And most contact information links to something else. For example, click an address, and Maps opens to show you a map of that address. Or click an e-mail address and open an outgoing e-mail message addressed to that person or start a FaceTime conversation. Click a URL, and the website opens in Safari. You get the picture.

Viewing Contacts

When you open Contacts, the window is divided into two or three columns, as shown in Figure 1-1. From left to right, the first column displays the Accounts list, which shows the sources and groups of your contacts although you can hide this column by choosing View➪Hide Groups. Clicking an item in the Accounts list then displays in the second column an alphabetized Contacts list of all contacts in the selected account or group. Click a contact in the Contacts list, and you see its card in the third column.

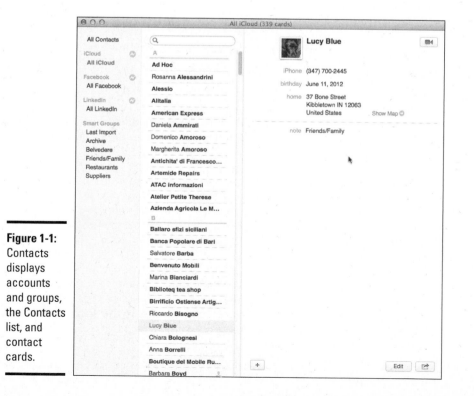

Figure 1-1: Contacts displays accounts and groups, the Contacts list, and contact cards.

You have a few options for how the name on a contact card is displayed:

✦ **Organize by company name.** When you create a contact card, Contacts assumes that you want to display that card in the alphabetized Contacts list by a person's name. To list a card by company name instead, click the card and choose Card⇨Mark as a Company. (Or, you can select the Company check box when you're creating a new contact card; I mention this later in the upcoming "Creating a contact" section and show it in Figure 1-4.) Your chosen card now displays a company name and icon. To change from a company name back to a person's name, choose Card⇨Mark as a Person.

✦ **Sort by first or last name.** To set whether your cards are sorted by first or last name, choose Contacts⇨Preferences⇨General and then select the sort and display options you prefer.

✦ **Change the display name of an individual card.** To change the first name/last name order for one card only, choose Card⇨Show First/Last Name Before Last/First. That one card only will change, regardless of the General Preferences you set.

You can view multiple cards by clicking a name in the Contacts list, and then choose Card⇨Open in Separate Window. Repeat until all the cards you want to see are open.

Designing your Contacts template

Each time you add a new contact, Contacts displays a contact card with blank fields that represent a piece of information to fill in about that person or entity, such as first and last name, company, title, and e-mail address. You may not want or need to store all that information about everyone, so you can define your Contacts card template to list only the fields you want to use, such as just name and e-mail address. Remember that you can always add more fields to an individual card as needed.

To modify the Contacts template, follow these steps:

1. **Click the Contacts icon on the Dock or from Launchpad.**

2. **Choose Contacts⇨Preferences.**

A Preferences window appears.

3. **Click the Template tab.**

The Template pane appears, as shown in Figure 1-2.

4. **Remove or add fields as you want.**

• *Remove a field.* Click the minus sign to the left of the field and repeat for every field you want to remove.

• *Add a field.* Open the Add Field pop-up menu (see Figure 1-3) and choose a field to add, such as URL or Birthday, repeating for each field you want to add.

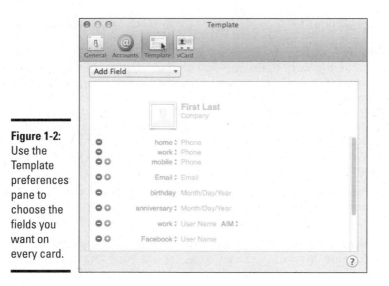

Figure 1-2:
Use the Template preferences pane to choose the fields you want on every card.

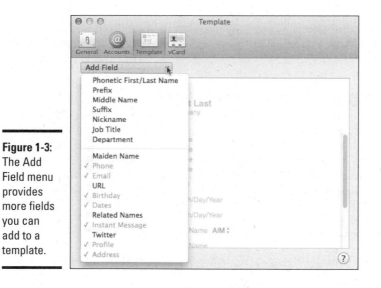

Figure 1-3:
The Add Field menu provides more fields you can add to a template.

Click the plus sign next to an existing field to add another field in that category — for example, the plus sign next to Mobile (refer to Figure 1-2) to add a field for another type of phone number, such as fax.

5. **(Optional) Click the label arrows next to the field name to change it or create a custom field name.**

For example, click Work or Home and choose Change Address Format to select the address format of a particular country. Doing so affects the address format of your entire Contacts. You can make this change on individual cards, though, as we explain in Step 2 in the "Creating a contact" section.

Or click Twitter, which is the default, and choose Facebook to set that as the default social network username field, as shown in Figure 1-3.

6. **Click the Close button of the Template preferences pane.**

Entering contacts

After you define a Contacts card template, the next step is to enter actual names and information by creating cards for new contacts.

Contacts comes with two contact cards: one for Apple Inc. and one for you. The card that's for you is called My Card, and this contact card always represents you. It contains your e-mail address, phone number, address, photo or representative image, and any other information you want to put on it. If you want to send your information to someone — say, a new business associate — you send this card by clicking the Share button at the bottom of the contact card. When you edit My Card, you see a check box next to each field you fill in. Just deselect the check box next to any information you don't want to send out when you share your card.

✦ **To define a different card to represent you:** Click that card and choose Card⇨Make This My Card.

✦ **To view your card at any time:** Choose Card⇨Go to My Card.

There are three ways to add contacts, which we explain in the upcoming subsections:

✦ Create contacts and manually enter information.

✦ Import contacts from an older address book application.

✦ Access other cloud or remote accounts.

Creating a contact

Follow these steps whenever you want to add a contact, either when you're populating Contacts for the first time or when you want to add a contact to your existing Contacts.

1. **Choose File⇨New Card, or click the plus sign at the bottom of the Contacts window and choose New Contact.**

The third column of the Contacts window displays a blank card for you to fill in, as shown in Figure 1-4.

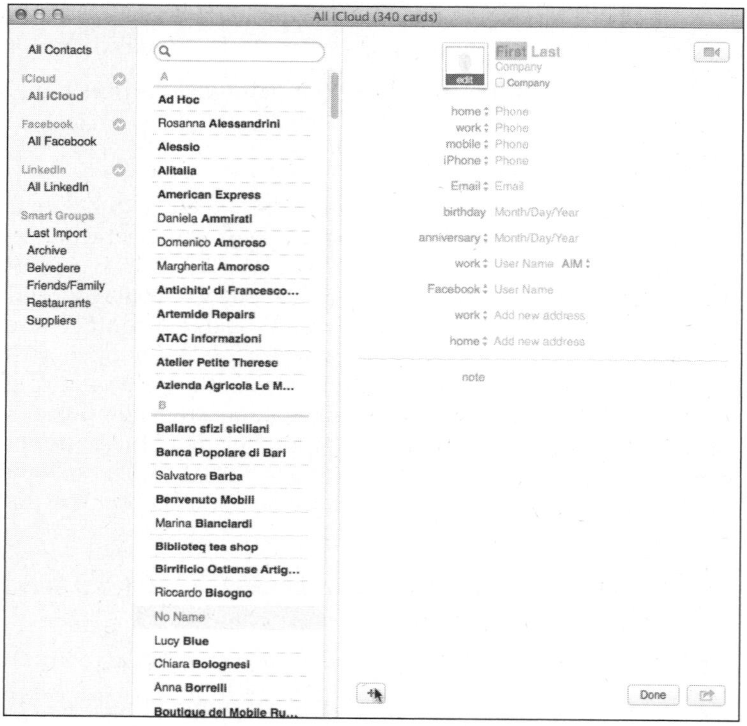

All iCloud (340 cards)

Figure 1-4:
Fill out a
card to add
a contact.

2. **Click the text fields (such as First, Last, or Home) and enter the information you want to save for your contact.**

   You don't have to fill every field. And some fields — Birthday, for example — can have just one entry; others, such as those for phone numbers or addresses, can have many entries. When you enter data in the existing field, a new blank field appears beneath the completed one.

   If you want a contact to be sorted by its business name instead of a person's name, click the checkbox next to Company.

   To change the address field format, click the field name — Home, Work, or Other — and choose Change Address Format from the pop-up menu. Choose the country for that address, and the card changes to reflect that country's address format.

   When you make changes to a field name or format on a card, the changes apply to that card only. To apply changes to *all* your contact cards, make the changes from Contacts⇨Preferences⇨Template.

3. **(Optional) To add a photo of your contact, double-click the photo icon to the left of the contact's name or choose Card⇨Choose Custom Image.**

   A photo pane opens, as shown in Figure 1-5. Use one of the following options to choose an image:

- *Defaults:* Choose an image that's included with Contacts.

- *iCloud:* Open a chooser that shows photos on your iCloud photo stream. Scroll through the photos to find the one you want, click it once to select it, and then click Done to insert your chosen photo into the photo box of the pane.

- *Faces:* Insert a Face from iPhoto. (See Book IV, Chapter 3 to find out more about iPhoto.)

- *Camera:* Take a photo with your Mac's built-in iSight camera (if it has one) or a third-party camera you have attached to your Mac.

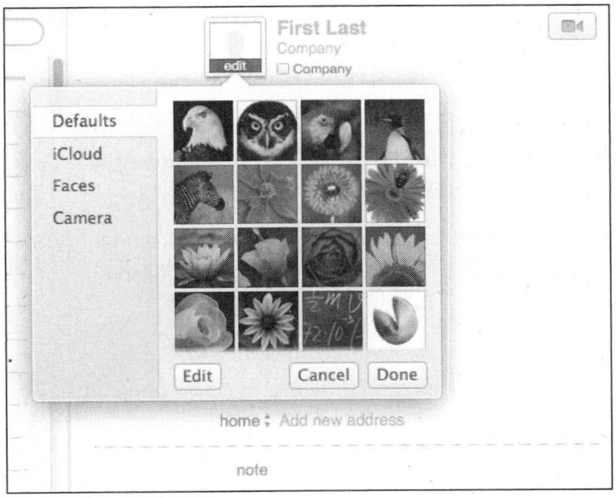

Figure 1-5:
Add a photo
to a contact
to connect
names with
faces.

4. **(Optional) After you choose a photo, you can edit it as follows:**

   - *Enlarge:* Use the zoom slider to enlarge the photo you want to use.

   - *Position:* Move the pointer over the photo until it becomes a small hand, which you use to click and drag the photo around in the photo box until it's where you like.

   - *Embellish:* Click the Special Effects button (it looks like a fan) to add special effects, such as sepia tone or a controlled blurring of the photo.

5. **Click Done when you're happy with the photo.**

   The photo now appears to the left of the contact's name.

6. **(Optional) If you want to add a field to this card only, choose Card⇨Add Field. Or click the plus sign at the bottom of the card, and then from the menu, choose a field to add to the card, as shown in Figure 1-6.**

   After you add a field to a card, you need to type information into that field.

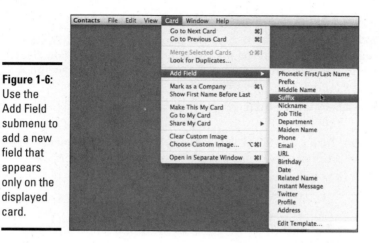

Figure 1-6:
Use the
Add Field
submenu to
add a new
field that
appears
only on the
displayed
card.

7. **To change the name of a field, click the name of the field and choose from the menu or scroll down to Custom.**

   The Add Custom Label dialog appears, as shown in Figure 1-7. Type in the name you want for the field and then click OK.

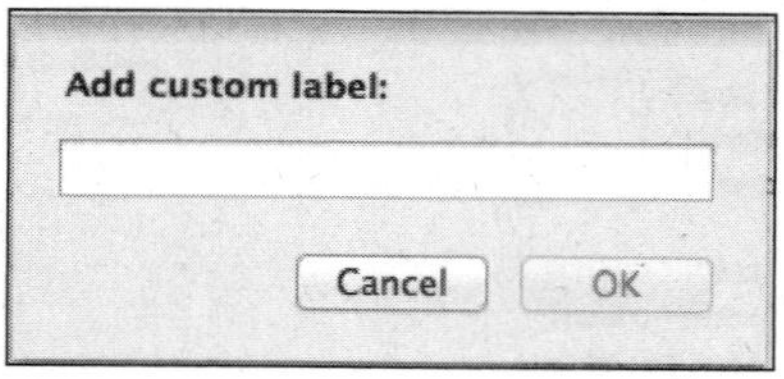

Figure 1-7:
Create
custom
names for
fields.

Add custom label:

Cancel   OK

8. **Click the Note field (refer to Figure 1-4) and type in any additional information that doesn't have an associated field.**

   Barbara uses this field to add a tag that she uses to create groups, which we explain later in this chapter.

9. **Click the Done button at the bottom of the Contacts window to save your new card.**

To help you remember how to pronounce names in unfamiliar languages, Contacts has a Phonetic First/Last Name field (refer to Figure 1-6). And the Related Names field gives you a place to enter the name of a contact's spouse, child, or assistant. Click the field name to reveal a pop-up menu of options.

Importing contacts

If your contacts are already in another application, no need to retype all that data. Just import the data into Contacts. Contacts understands the following four file formats:

+ **vCard:** Standard file format used to store contact information; used by applications on different types of computers.

+ **LDIF:** Standard data interchange file format.

    LDIF stands for Lightweight Directory Access Protocol (LDAP) Data Interchange Format.

+ **Text file:** Tab-delimited or comma-separated value (CSV) format; comes from a database, spreadsheet, or contact application.

+ **Contacts Archive:** Standard Contacts file format useful for transferring data between Macs with Contacts. Contacts can also read older Address Book archive files.

To import a contact's data file into Contacts, follow these steps:

1. **Choose File⇨Import.**

    A dialog appears.

2. **Select the file you want to import and then click Open.**

    Leave Text Encoding set to Automatic.

3. **Accept or review duplicate cards:**

    • *To automatically accept duplicates:* Click Import.

    • *To see duplicates and resolve differences between the two:* Click Review.

4. **Click Next.**

    If you're importing a text or CSV file, make sure that the correct field labels are associated with the data being imported. You can change the field labels if necessary.

    When the import is finished, Contacts contains the new contact cards.

In applications that use the vCard format, you can export the contents to a vCard file and then e-mail the file to yourself. Save the attached vCard file and then double-click it to import the contact into Contacts automatically without having to bother with the preceding steps.

Your newly imported contacts will appear in both the All Contacts group and the Last Import group under the Smart Group heading.

Accessing contacts from another device or server

We explain iCloud syncing in Book I, Chapter 3, but it deserves attention here as well. If you have a mobile phone and keep contact information on a cloud server (such as iCloud or Google) or a social network (such as Facebook or LinkedIn), you can add that information to Contacts on your Mac, too. The accounts you add to Contacts are listed in the Accounts list.

Likewise, you may have access to address books on network servers — perhaps, the company directory at your place of employment. By adding the cloud or remote account information to Contacts, you can access the information. ***Note:*** Because the data is in a *remote* location (not on your Mac), you need to be online to access the information, and you may or may not have editing privileges. To add an account, follow these steps:

1. **Choose Contacts⇨Add Account.**

2. **Complete one of the following step lists:**

   a. *Select the radio button next to the service you want to add, such as iCloud or Facebook (as shown in Figure 1-8), and then click Continue.*

   b. *Type in your username and password.*

      Your account is verified.

   c. *Select the Contacts radio button (if it isn't already) selected and then click Done.*

      Or

   a. *Select the Other Contacts Account radio button and then click Continue.*

   b. *Choose CardDAV or LDAP from the pull-down menu.*

   c. *Enter the requested information.*

      You may have to ask the network administrator or a techie in your group for the information.

   d. *Click Create.*

      Your access is verified.

   That account is added to the Accounts list on the Contacts window.

Figure 1-8:
Add an account to access address books stored on cloud or remote servers.

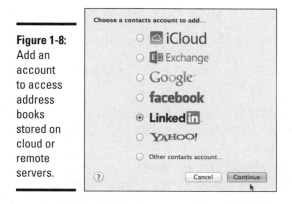

Choose a contacts account to add...

- ○ 🔲 iCloud
- ○ 🄴 Exchange
- ○ Google·
- ○ **facebook**
- ● **Linked** 🄸🄽·
- ○ YAHOO!
- ○ Other contacts account...

?   Cancel   Continue

When you access multiple accounts, Contacts does its best to merge cards from different accounts onto one card. When a contact card contains information from more than one account, at the very bottom of the card you see a Cards field, which lists the accounts the card references.

Working with Contacts

There's no reason to add names and numbers to Contacts if you don't plan to use them. In this section we explain all the different things you can do with Contacts: how to search for an number, edit a card when contact information changes, and create groups to make communicating with many people at once easier.

Searching contacts

The more contact cards you store in Contacts, the harder it is to find a particular contact you want. Instead of scrolling through every contact card to locate a certain one, you can search for specific contacts by following these steps:

1. **Click All Contacts or click the account or group you want to search from the Accounts list.**

2. **Click the Spotlight search field above the Contacts list.**

3. **Type a word or phrase that you want to find, such as a person's name or the company that person works for.**

   The Contacts displays a list of contacts that match the text you typed.

4. **Click a contact to display the card for that person or company.**

To search for the occurrence of a contact's name on your Mac, Control-click the name of the contact in the Contacts list and choose Spotlight from the shortcut menu.

Editing a card

Life is dynamic; things change. When you need to update information on a card — a change of address, phone number, or company, for example — edit a card by following these steps:

1. **Find and open the card for the contact for whom you have new or updated information.**

You can edit contacts that are part of your personal accounts but probably not those you access through a company server. You can also add information to Facebook and LinkedIn contacts, although you can't edit the information pulled from the contact's profile.

2. **Click the Edit button at the bottom of the window.**

3. **Do one of the following:**

   - Click the field in which you want to edit information, such as an out-of-date e-mail address or phone number. The existing information is highlighted, and you can simply type the updated information to replace the existing information.

   - Click an empty field and enter new information.

   - Click the plus sign at the bottom of the page and select a field you want to add from the menu. (Click More Fields if you don't see what you're looking for and then choose from that expanded menu.) Type in the new information in the added field.

4. **Repeat Step 3 to add additional information.**

5. **Click the Done button.**

   Contacts saves the updated contact information.

You can add or edit notes in the Notes field without being in Edit mode. Just click in the Notes field and type what you want.

Deleting a contact

Again, life is dynamic. When it's time for a little housekeeping, prune the contact cards you don't need any more.

You can delete only those contacts that are stored directly on your Mac or accounts that you access directly, such as via iCloud or Google. For example, you can't delete Facebook contacts or those on your company's server.

To delete a name from your Contacts, just click the contact and choose Edit⇨Delete Card. If you accidentally delete a contact, press ⌘+Z or choose Edit⇨Undo to restore it.

To choose multiple contacts to delete, hold down the ⌘ key and click at will. If you hold down the Shift key, you can click two contiguous cards — or, select two noncontiguous cards, which selects all cards in between as well.

Creating groups

To help you organize your contacts, use Contacts to create groups of contacts, such as for your co-workers, friends, family members, restaurants, and so on. For greater convenience, you can even store the same contact in multiple groups. Although you don't have to use groups, this feature can help you manage your list of important contact cards. It's also a great way to send e-mails to a group of people without having to type in each name singly — just Control-click the group name and choose Send Email to *group name*.

Using shortcut menus

Contacts has many more options than meet the eye. Most are revealed in pop-up or shortcut menus. Clicking field names in the Contact Card brings up shortcut menus, which present the options listed here:

✔ **Telephone Number:** Show in Large Type, Send Message, and FaceTime. If you have Skype installed and configured to link with Contacts, you see two more options: Call with Skype and Send SMS with Skype.

✔ **Address:** Open in Maps, Copy Address, and Copy Map URL.

✔ **E-mail:** Send Email, FaceTime, Send Message, Send My Card, and Search with Spotlight.

✔ **Twitter Profile:** Tweet and Show Tweets.

✔ **Facebook Profile:** View Profile and View Photos.

✔ **LinkedIn/Myspace/Profile:** View Profile.

✔ **Flickr:** View Photostream.

✔ **Sina Weibo:** Post and View Posts.

✔ **Tencent Weibo:** Send Message and View Profile.

✔ **Related:** Show "relation's name" and Search with Spotlight.

Your Contacts initially contains one group: All Contacts. The All Contacts group automatically stores all contacts you've saved in Contacts. Even when a contact is assigned to a group, the contact remains in All Contacts.

If your Mac is connected to a local area network (LAN), you may see a second group: Directories. The Directories group contains a list of contacts of everyone connected to that LAN. If you're using a Mac at home without a LAN, you won't see the Directories group.

Adding a group

You can create as many groups as you want, but for groups to be useful, you need to add contacts to that group. To create a new group, follow these steps:

1. **Choose File➪New Group, or click the plus sign at the bottom of the screen and choose New Group from the pop-up menu.**

2. **Replace *untitled group* with a more descriptive name in the Accounts list, as shown in Figure 1-9, and then press Return.**

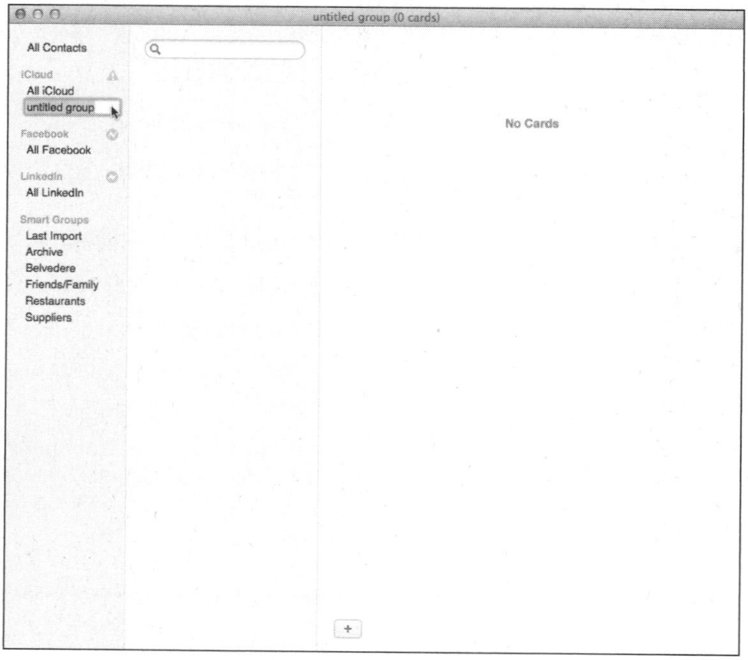

Figure 1-9:
Groups are
subsets
of your
contacts in
Contacts.

To add contacts to a group, follow these steps:

1. Click All Contacts in the Accounts list to see all the contacts stored in Contacts.

When All Contacts is selected, the Contacts list displays contacts from all the accounts, so you may see duplicate names.

2. Move the cursor over a contact, hold down the mouse or trackpad button until you see a contact card icon, and then drag the cursor over the group name where you want to store your contact.

If you hold down the ⌘ key, you can click and choose multiple contacts. If you hold down the Shift key, you can click two noncontiguous contacts to select those two contacts and all contacts in between as well.

3. Release the mouse or trackpad button when the group name appears highlighted.

Your chosen contact appears in your newly created group and in the All Contacts group.

To see which groups a contact belongs to, click a name in the Contacts list and then hold down the Option key. The groups to which that contact belongs are highlighted in the Accounts list on the left.

Creating a group from a selection of contacts

If you already have a group of contacts selected that you want to organize, you can create a new group and store those contacts at the same time. To create a new group from a selection of contacts, follow these steps:

1. **Click All Contacts in the Accounts list to see all the names stored in Contacts.**

2. **Hold down the ⌘ key and click each contact you want to store in a group.**

   You can select a range of contacts by holding down the Shift key and clicking two noncontiguous contacts. Doing so selects those two contacts and all contacts in between.

3. **Choose File⬦New Group from Selection.**

   The group appears in the Accounts list with the moniker *untitled group.*

4. **Type a more descriptive name for your group and then press Return.**

   Your group now contains the contacts you selected in Step 2.

To send an e-mail to a group, Control-click the group name and choose Send Email to *group name.*

Editing a distribution list

Say you have more than one phone number, e-mail, or street address for the same person. To choose which fields to use for each contact in a group, edit the distribution list. For example, you can choose the same type of address for all members of the group — for example, using the work address — or you can select the information for each member of the group. Follow this procedure:

1. **Choose Edit⬦Edit Distribution List.**

2. **Select the group you want to edit.**

3. **Click the column header to open a pop-up menu that lets you choose which type of data you want to manage: Email, Phone, or Address.**

4. **Select the corresponding information you want to use for each member who has more than one entry.**

Adding contacts automatically with Smart Groups

Adding contacts manually or selecting them for a group is fine, but what if you frequently add and delete contacts? Doing all this manually can get old. To keep your group's contacts accurate and up to date more easily, you can use the Smart Groups feature.

With a Smart Group, you define the types of contacts you want to store, such as contacts for everyone who works at a certain company. Then the Smart Group automatically adds any contacts to the group from your Contacts.

To create a Smart Group, follow these steps:

1. **Choose File⇨New Smart Group.**

    A dialog appears, asking for a contact and rule for storing contacts in the group. A *rule* lets you group contacts based on certain criteria. For example, you may want to group the contacts of all people who work for Apple and live in Texas.

2. **Click the Smart Group Name text box and type a descriptive name for your Smart Group.**

3. **Click the first pop-up menu and choose the criteria for including a contact in your Smart Group, such as Company or City, as shown in Figure 1-10.**

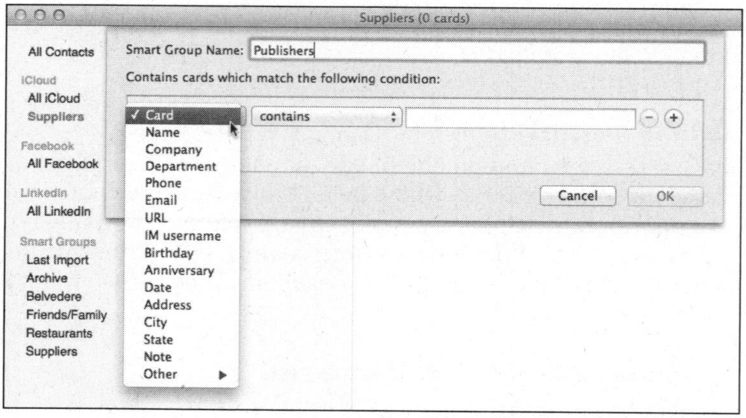

Figure 1-10: This pop-up menu defines the criteria for storing contacts in your Smart Group.

4. **Click the second pop-up menu and choose how to use the criteria you defined in Step 3, such as Contains or Was Updated After.**

5. **Click the text box and type a word or phrase for your criteria to use.**

    For example, if you want to create a Smart Group that stores only contacts of people who work at Apple, your entire Smart Group rule may look like *Company Contains Apple*.

6. **(Optional) Click the plus sign to the right of the text box to create any additional rules.**

If you create any additional rules and later decide you don't want them, you can always remove them by clicking the minus sign that appears next to the rule.

7. **Click OK.**

Creating a Smart Group from search results

Defining the criteria for storing names automatically in a Smart Group can be cumbersome when you aren't quite sure whether the defined criteria will work exactly the way you want. As an alternative, you can use Spotlight to search for the types of contacts you want to store, and *then* create a Smart Group based on your Spotlight search results. Using this approach, you can see exactly which types of contacts appear in your Smart Group.

To create a Smart Group from Spotlight search results, follow these steps:

1. **Click the Spotlight search field, type the text you want to find (such as the name of a company or part of an e-mail address), and press Return.**

The Contacts list shows the contacts that Spotlight found based on the text you typed in.

2. **Choose File➪New Smart Group from Current Search.**

A Smart Group appears in the Group category, using the text you typed as the group name.

You can edit a Smart Group by Control-clicking the name and choosing Edit Smart Group.

Deleting a group

If you create a group and no longer need it, you can delete it. When you delete a group, you delete only the group folder; you do not delete any contact cards stored in that group. To delete a group, click the group and choose Edit➪Delete Group.

You can delete a contact from the group by selecting the group, clicking the contact you want to delete, and then choosing Edit➪Delete Card. The contact remains in All Contacts. However, if you delete a contact from All Contacts, that contact is also deleted from all groups of which it was a member.

If you have both Contacts and Calendar open, from Contacts or a Group list, you can click and drag a contact (⌘-click to select more than one invitee) to the hour of an event to which you want to invite them. See Book V, Chapter 2 to find out more about inviting contacts to an event by using Calendar.

Sharing Your Contacts

Sometimes you may need to share contact information with others. Contacts makes it easy to share one card or a group in the vCard format. A *vCard* is a standard format that many applications use to store contact information. By sharing contact data as a vCard, the information can be accessed by another application and computer, such as a Windows PC running Outlook.

Sending one contact at a time

To share a single card, click the Share button in the bottom-right corner of the contact card and select one of the following:

✦ **Email Card:** Opens a blank e-mail message that contains a vCard attachment. Address the message to one or more recipients and click Send.

✦ **Message Card:** Opens a blank Messages message with a vCard attachment. Address the message and click Send.

✦ **AirDrop Card:** Makes the vCard available on AirDrop to other Macs on your network that have AirDrop turned on.

If you want to send your own card, choose Card⇨Share My Card and then choose one of the preceding options from the submenu.

Exporting multiple cards

You have three choices for sharing multiple cards from Contacts:

✦ Export contact data in the vCard format, which most contact management apps can import.

✦ Export as an archive, which most Macs can read.

✦ Export as a PDF, which most computers and hand-held devices can read.

Consider both the recipient's computer system and how the data will be used when exporting the cards. After the file is imported to another contact management app, either from the vCard or archive format, it can be edited. However, a PDF file is an image of the data, so it can be viewed or printed — but the data cannot be manipulated.

When exporting contacts for use in another application, the application you're importing may not recognize every detail for the contact, such as a person's picture or notes you've added to a person's contact card.

Whichever file type you choose, the process is as follows for exporting contacts from Contacts:

1. Select the names you want to export by doing one of the following:

- Click All Contacts.

- Click an account or group name.

  To quickly export a group, Control-click a (non-Smart) group name and choose Export Group vCard.

- Select contacts from the Contacts list by holding the ⌘ key and clicking each one.

2. Choose the file type to which you'd like to export the contacts.

- *To export a PDF:* Choose File⇨Export as PDF.

- *To export as a vCard or an Archive:* Choose File⇨Export, and then choose Export vCard or Contacts Archive from the submenu.

A Save As dialog appears.

3. Type a descriptive name for your file in the Save As text box.

4. Choose the location to store your file; this can be an external drive or a folder on your Mac.

5. Click Save.

You can then treat the file as you would any other file you want to share: Send it to someone as an e-mail attachment; copy it to a flash drive; or upload it to a cloud server, such as Dropbox.

Although your best bet for backing up Contacts is using iCloud, as explained in Book I, Chapter 3, you can also use one of the sharing options to create a backup that you store on an external drive, a CD, or a remote storage server.

Printing your Contacts

You can export Contacts to a PDF file and then print the document, or you can print directly from Contacts. In addition to printing in list form, Contacts lets you print all or some of your contact information in different formats, such as mailing labels or cards that you can carry with you. To print your Contacts, follow these steps:

1. Use one of the following methods to select the names you want to print:

- Click a single contact card.

- Hold down the ⌘ key and click multiple contacts.

- Hold down the Shift key, click a contact, and then click another contact elsewhere in the list. Selecting these two contacts highlights them both and all contacts in between.

- To print all contact cards stored in an account or group, click the account or group name and then choose Edit➪Select All or press ⌘+A.

- Use Spotlight to find names that meet a certain criteria.

2. **Choose File➪Print.**

   A Print dialog appears, as shown in Figure 1-11.

3. **Click the Printer pop-up menu and choose a printer to use.**

4. **Click the Style pop-up menu and choose one of the following:**

   - *Mailing Labels:* Prints names and addresses on different types of mailing labels

   - *Envelopes:* Prints names and addresses on envelopes fed into your printer

   - *Lists:* Prints your Contacts as a long list

   - *Pocket Address Book:* Prints your Contacts in a condensed form suitable for carrying with you

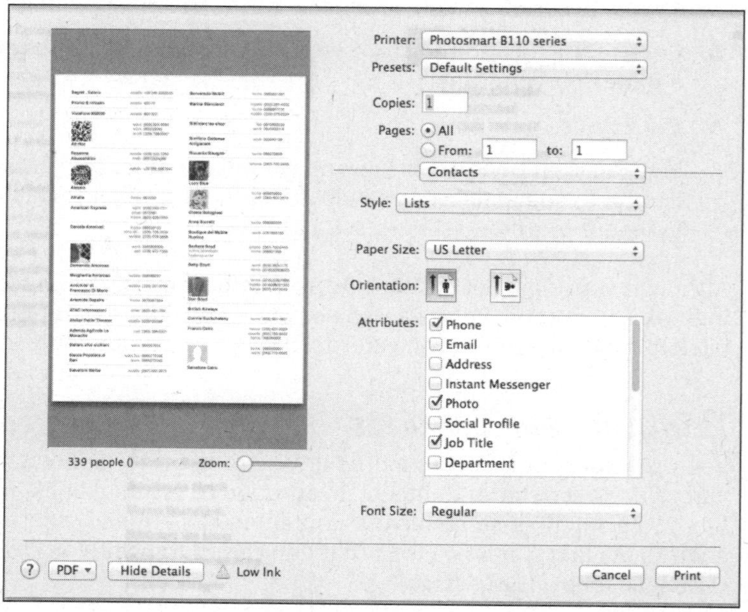

Figure 1-11: The expanded Print dialog lets you choose how to print your selected contacts.

Depending on the style that you choose in this step, you may need to pick additional options, such as defining the specific size of your mailing labels or choosing whether to print names in alphabetical order. You can also adjust other settings and options, such as number of copies and the font you want to use for your printed output.

5. Click Print.

Chapter 2: Staying on Schedule with Calendar

In This Chapter

✔ **Navigating the Calendar window**

✔ **Viewing calendars**

✔ **Creating and storing events**

✔ **Finding the events you're looking for**

✔ **Organizing tasks with Reminders**

You're busy. You may rely on a planner, random scraps of paper, or your memory to keep track of obligations, appointments, and commitments. Your Mac comes with an alternative: Calendar, which is Apple's calendar application. Calendar helps you track appointments and reminds you of tasks or deadlines.

In this chapter, first we introduce the Calendar interface. Then we show you how to create calendars and access them from different sources. Next, we explain how to put *events* (what Calendar calls anything such as an appointment, a birthday, or whatever else that requires a time/date reference) on your calendar(s). We talk about sharing your calendar with your other devices and with other people, both online and in print. And while we're on the subject of remembering, we present the task management app Reminders, which you use to create To Do lists and assign a time- or location-based alert to each task.

Getting Acquainted with Calendar

The Calendar toolbar displays the following items, as shown in Figure 2-1:

✦ **Calendars:** This button hides or reveals the Calendars list to the left of the calendar itself.

✦ **Add (+) button:** Clicking this button adds an event.

✦ **Inbox:** Displays how many invitations you have.

✦ **Views:** The buttons in the center give you access to the four Calendar views: Day, Week, Month, and Year.

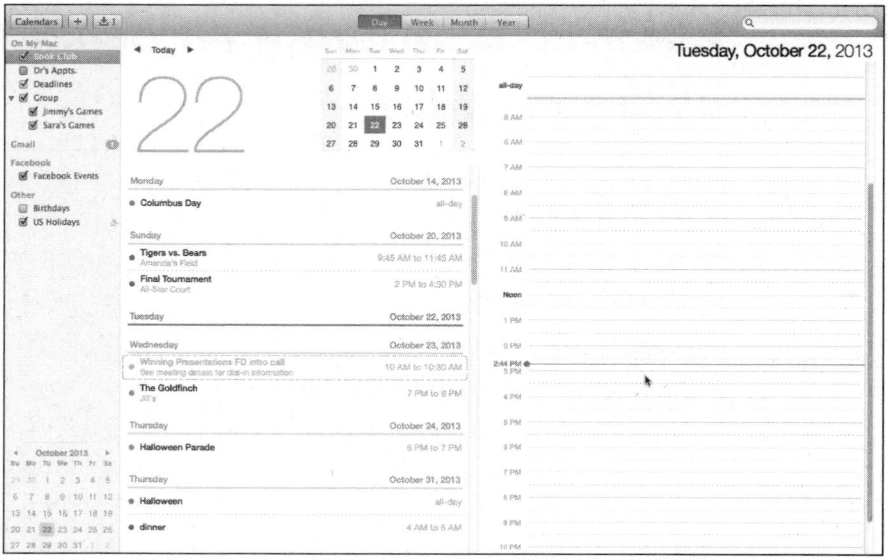

Figure 2-1:
The Calendar toolbar helps you view different calendars and choose the view you want.

- ✦ **Spotlight Search:** Calendar looks for matches of text typed in the search field.

- ✦ **Full-screen:** The button takes you to a full-screen view of Calendar.

- ✦ **Today:** In the upper-left corner, just under the toolbar, the Today button takes you to the current day in the view you're using. The arrows to the left and right move one unit (day, week, month, or year) into the past or into the future (respectively) from the date where you are.

Any scheduled activity, such as a doctor's appointment, a business meeting, or your kid's soccer practice, is an *event*.

Calendar offers four types of calendar views, each an electronic version of a familiar paper-based layout:

- ✦ **Day:** Shows a mini-month at the top, a list of eight to ten upcoming events on the left, and a day-at-a-glance for the active day on the right (refer to Figure 2-1).

- ✦ **Week:** Displays a week-at-a-glance version of your calendar, as shown in Figure 2-2. A column for each day is divided into half-hour time slots. You establish how many hours of the day you want to see.

   When viewing the current day in Day or Week view, a line with a red ball at the left end indicates the current time of day.

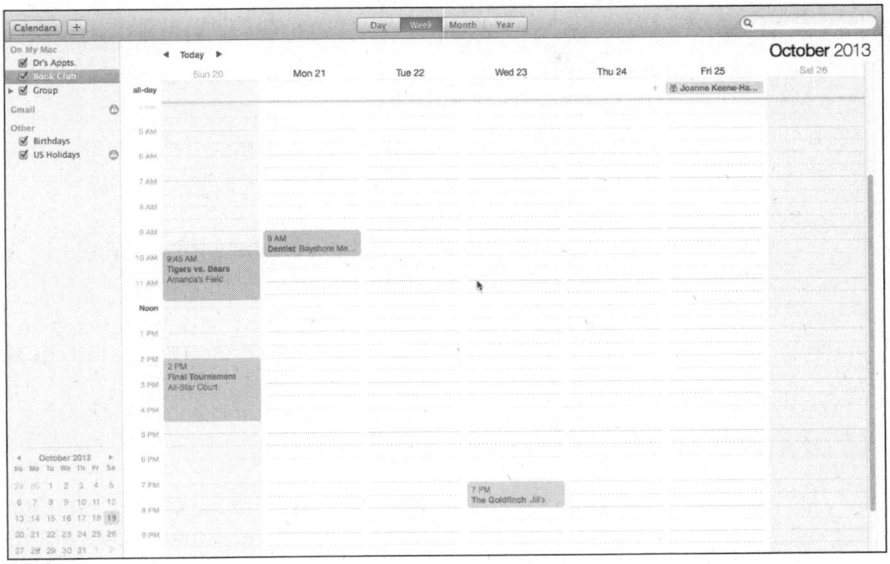

Figure 2-2:
Days are
divided into
half-hour
segments in
Week view.

+ **Month:** Shows a month-at-a-glance with as much of the text of your
events as possible on each day.

+ **Year:** Displays the whole year in one pane, as shown in Figure 2-3. The
days are color-coded according to how full they are. The current day
is blue. The other days are white, yellow, gold, orange, or red. White is
the color for a day with no events. Colors ranging from yellow through
orange to red are for days with appointments: Yellow days have the
fewest appointments, and red days have the most.

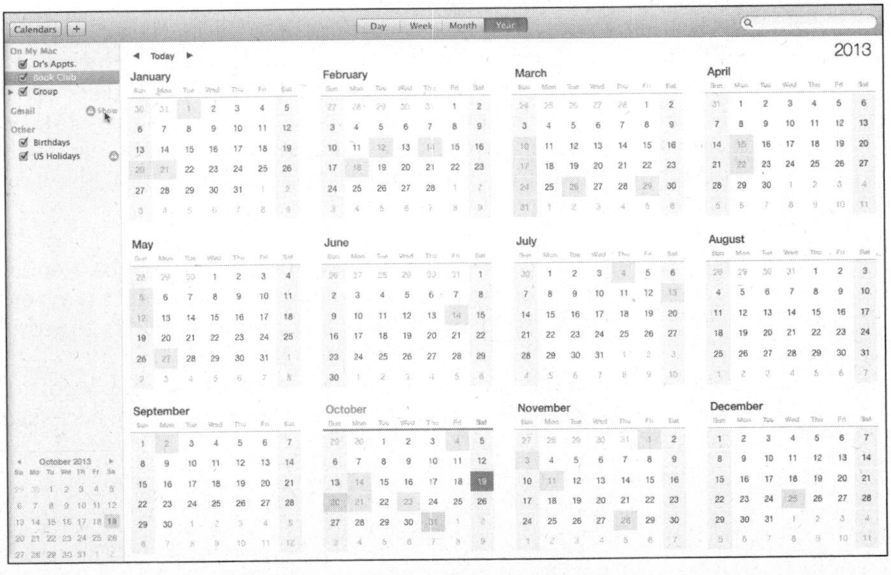

Figure 2-3:
Days are
color-coded
in Year view
to show
which are
busiest.

You can move from one view and date to the next in the following ways:

✦ **Mini-month:** Click a date in the mini-month in Day view to go to the date clicked, remaining in Day view.

✦ **Month:** Double-click a date in Month view to open that date in Day view. You must double-click the actual number; if you double-click in the space, a new event is created.

✦ **Week:** Double-click a date — again, the actual number — in Week view to open that date in Day view.

✦ **Year:** Double-click a date in Year view to open that date in Day view. Double-click a month in Year view to open that month in Month view.

Working with Multiple Calendars

The great thing about Calendar is that calendars from different sources can be viewed in one app. Calendar accesses and manages multiple calendars from multiple sources or accounts, including

✦ Your Mac or your iCloud account

You can activate one or the other but not both simultaneously.

✦ Online accounts where you keep (and perhaps share) calendars, such as Google or MS Exchange

✦ Social network calendars, such as Facebook or LinkedIn

✦ Calendar subscriptions

You can also import calendar data from another calendar or time management app.

When you click the Calendars button on the toolbar (refer to Figure 2-1), the Calendars list on the left side of Calendar displays the accounts you have activated. The calendars from each account are listed below its name. You can expand or collapse the list of calendars stored on each account by hovering the cursor to the right of the account name until Show or Hide appears and then clicking it.

By selecting or deselecting the check box next to each calendar in the Calendars list, you can selectively view specific events (say, only business events), or you can view business and personal events together.

Here we explain how to create a new calendar on your Mac or from iCloud, and then how to add calendars from other sources by accessing the related accounts.

Creating a new calendar

Calendar opens with a calendar to get you started. In the Calendars list, you see an On My Mac heading with Calendar listed under it. If you turned on Calendar in iCloud, you see iCloud — and any calendars you created on another device that use the same iCloud account — in the Calendars list. You may want or need to create additional calendars for other purposes. To create a new calendar, follow these steps:

1. **Click the Calendar icon on the Dock or from Launchpad.**

2. **Choose File⇨New Calendar.**

If you don't add other accounts, that's all you have to do. If you do add other accounts, you have to drag the cursor one notch further to the right and choose On My Mac (or iCloud, if you use iCloud) or one of the remote servers where you keep calendars (if you use remote servers).

An *Untitled* calendar appears in the Calendars pop-up list, as shown in Figure 2-4.

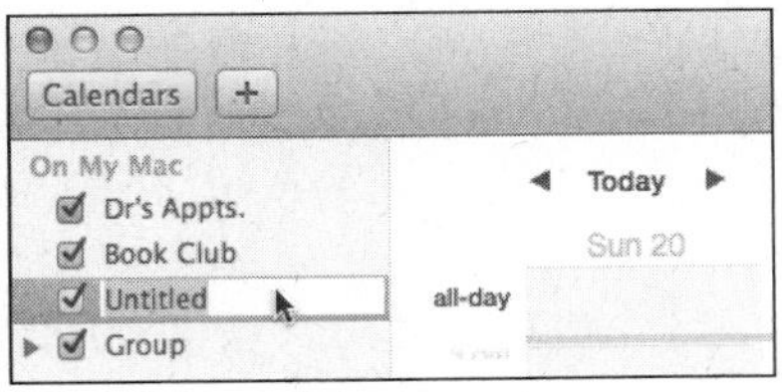

Figure 2-4:
New calendars are added to your Mac or iCloud account.

3. **Type a descriptive name for your calendar and then press Return.**

4. **Click a calendar in the Calendars list and choose Edit⇨Get Info.**

5. **In the Info dialog that appears, click the color pop-up menu, choose a color, and (if you like) type a description of the calendar in the Description field.**

6. **Click OK.**

Events stored on that calendar appear in the color you chose.

If you want to share or publish your calendar, refer to the section "Sharing your calendars" later in this chapter.

Accessing calendars from other accounts

With Mac OS X 10.9 Mavericks, Apple has made adding calendars from other accounts super easy. You can also add CalDAV or Exchange accounts, which are the formats most often used for shared corporate calendars. Events that you create or change at work with your company's calendar application, or events you create or change by using your Google or Yahoo! account, are added automatically to your calendar, and vice versa.

1. **Choose Calendar⇨Add Account.**

2. **Complete one of the following steps lists:**

   a. *Select the radio button next to the account you want to add (such as iCloud or Facebook, as shown in Figure 2-5) and then click Continue.*

   b. *Type in your username (it may be an e-mail address) and password, and then click Create or Continue.*

   Your account is verified.

   c. *Select the radio button next to Calendar (if not already selected) and then click Done.*

   Or

   a. *Select the radio button next to Add CalDAV account and then click Continue.*

   b. *Choose the account type from the pull-down menu: Automatic, Manual, or Advanced.*

   We suggest leaving Automatic selected.

   c. *Type the e-mail address and password you use to access this calendar.*

   d. *Click Create.*

   Your access is verified.

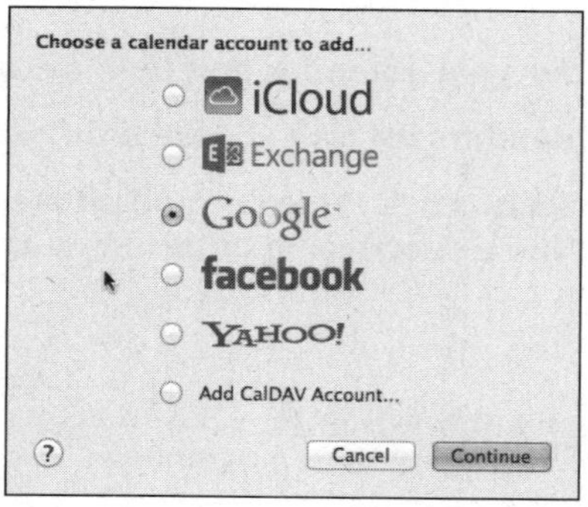

TIP

Figure 2-5:
Adding
Calendars
from other
accounts
takes just a
few clicks.

Choose a calendar account to add...

○ ☁ iCloud

○ 🄴 Exchange

⦿ Google

○ **facebook**

○ YAHOO!

○ Add CalDAV Account...

(?)   Cancel   Continue

That account is added to the Calendars list, and your online calendar's events appear in your Calendar window.

3. **After the account is set up, choose Calendar⇨Preferences and then click the Accounts tab.**

**Book V
Chapter 2**

Staying on Schedule
with Calendar

4. **Click the name of the account you added.**

5. **From the Refresh Calendars pull-down menu, choose the interval at which you want Calendar to retrieve information from the account or update information you add on the server, as shown in Figure 2-6:**

   • *Push*: The calendar is updated as soon as a change occurs.

   • *Every Minute/Hour*: Calendar checks the server and fetches any changes or sends changes you made.

   • *Manually:* Choose View⇨Refresh Calendars to fetch and send changes. If you use a MacBook and often run on battery power, this helps save the charge a bit.

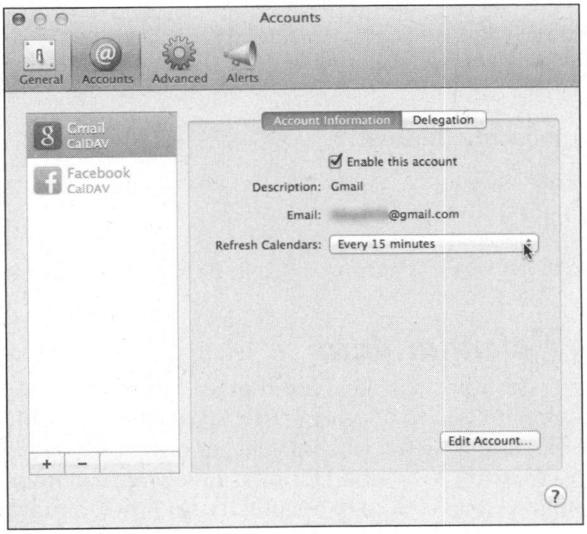

Figure 2-6:
Choose how often you want Calendar to refresh information for each account.

6. **(Optional) Repeat to add more accounts.**

When you use iCloud or another account-based online calendar (such as Google or Facebook), you can sign in to the same account, or accounts, on your smartphone, tablet, or from another computer. Your calendars are always at your fingertips.

Subscribing to online calendars

Another source of calendars for Calendar are those you can subscribe to online, such as a calendar of holidays, sports team schedules, bridge tournaments, or new DVD releases. Calendars you subscribe to appear under the Other category in the Calendars list. Events that appear in these calendars are added, deleted, and modified by whoever maintains the online calendar, which you can view but not change.

To subscribe to an online calendar

1. **Choose File⇨New Calendar Subscription to open the URL dialog.**

2. **Type the website URL for the calendar you want to subscribe to as shown in Figure 2-7. For example, the link to U.S. Holidays online calendar is** `https://p06-calendars.icloud.com/holiday/US_en.ics`**.**

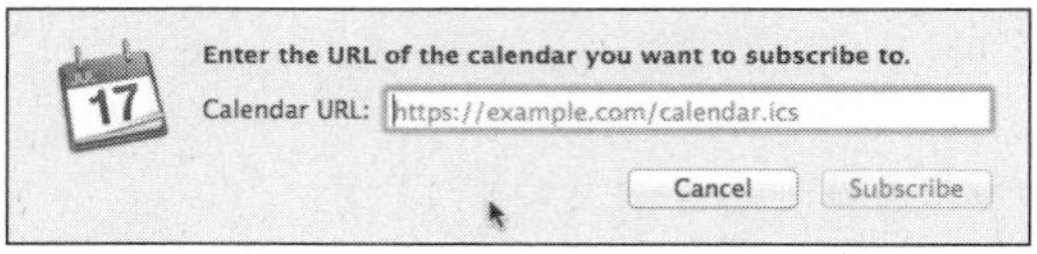

Figure 2-7:
You can subscribe to an online calendar.

Enter the URL of the calendar you want to subscribe to.

Calendar URL: | https://example.com/calendar.ics |

Cancel Subscribe

3. **Click the Subscribe button.**

The name appears in the Calendars list under Other, and the calendar's events appear in the Calendar window.

Visit iCalShare (`www.icalshare.com`) to find calendars you can subscribe to.

Importing Calendar data

If you store calendar information in another application, or on another operating system and you're migrating to a Mac, you can export that data as a Calendar file or a vCalendar (`.vcs`) file, and then import that file into Calendar. If you're using Microsoft Outlook, save your calendar information as a separate file (as opposed to exporting it), and then import that file into Calendar.

After you save calendar data from another application, you can import that file into Calendar by following these steps:

1. **Choose File⇨Import and then choose Import or Import from Entourage.**

Although Outlook replaced Entourage in MS-Office for Mac 2011, if you use MS-Office 2008, you still have Entourage. When you choose Import from Entourage, Calendar scans your Mac's hard drive for your existing Entourage calendar data and imports those calendar events into Calendar, and you can skip the remaining steps.

2. **Click the drive and/or folder that contains the file you want to import.**

3. **Click the file you want to import and then click Import.**

Calendar imports your chosen calendar file's data into Calendar. You can then rename the calendar if you want, and add events or edit existing ones, as explained just a bit further along in this chapter.

Creating a new calendar group

Rather than create a bunch of separate calendars, you may want to organize multiple calendars in a group. For example, if you have separate calendars to schedule events for your son's and daughter's school and sporting events and your father's doctor's appointments, you could put all those calendars into a Family group. You may wonder, "Why not just create one Family calendar?" The reason we suggest creating separate calendars is because you can then print each one for the person it pertains to, and you can give your children access to their unique calendars. A calendar group doesn't store events; it simply stores one or more calendars.

One caveat, however: Groups work only if you keep calendars on your Mac. That means if you use iCloud, you can't create groups. You may want to skip this section if that's your way of working with Calendar.

To create a calendar group, follow these steps:

1. **Click the Calendar icon on the Dock or from Launchpad.**

2. **Choose File⇨New Calendar Group.**

You won't see this option if you turn on Calendar in iCloud. What's more, you may have to sign out of your other online calendars, such as Google or Facebook, create your groups, and then sign back in to the online calendars.

3. **Type a descriptive name for your group and press Return.**

A disclosure triangle appears to the left of the group name in the calendars list; click the triangle to hide or show the calendars in the group.

Adding a new calendar to a group

After you create a group, you can add new calendars to the group by following these steps:

1. **Choose File⇨New Calendar⇨On My Mac.**

An Untitled Calendar appears in the On My Mac section.

2. **Type a descriptive name for your new calendar and press Return.**

3. **Move the pointer over the new calendar.**

4. **Click and drag the new calendar to the group you want to place the calendar in, and then release the mouse or trackpad button.**

   The name of your calendar now appears indented under the group.

Follow Steps 3 and 4 to move existing calendars to a group.

Moving a calendar out of a group

In case you don't want a calendar in a group, you can move it out of a group by following these steps:

1. **Click the Calendars button to open the Calendars list.**

2. **Move the cursor over the calendar you want to remove from a group.**

3. **Click and drag the calendar toward the left and up (or down) until it's out of the group.**

4. **Release the mouse or trackpad button.**

   Your existing calendar now appears outside any groups.

Moving a calendar or group

To help organize your calendars and groups, you may want to rearrange their order in the Calendar list by following these steps:

1. **Move the cursor to the calendar or group you want to move.**

2. **Hold down the mouse or trackpad button and drag the mouse or trackpad pointer up or down.**

   A thick horizontal line appears where your calendar or group will appear in the Calendar list, as shown in Figure 2-8.

3. **Release the mouse or trackpad button when you're happy with the new location of your calendar or group.**

Figure 2-8:
A horizontal line shows where your calendar or group will land.

Renaming and deleting calendars and groups

At any time, you can rename a calendar or group, whether it's on your Mac or on one of the online services (such as iCloud, Google, and Yahoo!). The name of a calendar or group is for your benefit and has no effect on the way Calendar works. To rename a calendar or group, double-click a calendar or group name, which highlights that name. Type a new name and press Return.

If you no longer need a particular calendar or group, click the one you want to delete and choose Edit➪Delete. If you have any events stored on a calendar, a dialog appears, asking whether you really want to delete that calendar or group. Click Delete. If you delete a calendar or group by mistake, choose Edit➪Undo or press ⌘+Z.

When you delete a calendar, you also delete any events stored on that calendar. When you delete a group, you delete all calendars stored in that group along with all events stored on those calendars. Make sure that you really want to delete a calendar or group of calendars. You can also archive a copy before deleting so you have the reference without cluttering your calendar.

Creating and Modifying Events

An *event* is any occurrence that has a specific time and date associated with it. Some common types of events are meetings, appointments with clients, times when you need to pick up someone (as at the airport), or recreational time (such as a concert or a two-week vacation). If you know that a particular event will occur on a specific date and time, you can store that event in Calendar so you won't forget or schedule a conflicting activity at that time.

Viewing events

As we list at the beginning of this chapter, Calendar lets you display time frames by day, week, month, or year, and shows all the events you've scheduled for the day, week, month, or year you choose to view. The amount of detail varies, depending on the view you choose. To change the time frame of your displayed events, click the Day, Week, Month, or Year button at the top of the Calendar window.

Creating an event

To create an event, start by deciding which calendar to store the event on, the date and time to schedule the event, and the event's duration. You also have options to create an event alert and whether to invite others to the event. Here, we show you how to create an event; in the next section, we explain your options.

There are two types of events — Quick Events, which let you quickly type a date, time, and event without much description such as "movie with Jim, Thursday at 7 pm," and full-blown Events, which have addresses, travel times, and other helpful information to get you to the right place at the right time. You have several ways to create an event:

✦ **To create a Quick Event:** Click the Add Event button (the plus sign on the toolbar) or choose File➪New Event. Then type in a phrase that defines your event in the Create Quick Event dialog that opens, as shown in Figure 2-9.

Calendar understands common phrases, such as "dinner on Tuesday" or "staff meeting Thursday from 9:00 a.m. to 1:00 p.m." Calendar uses the current date as the point of reference, and the default duration for an event is one hour. "Breakfast" or "morning" starts at 9:00 a.m. "Lunch" or "noon" begins at 12:00 p.m. "Dinner" or "night" starts at 8:00 p.m.

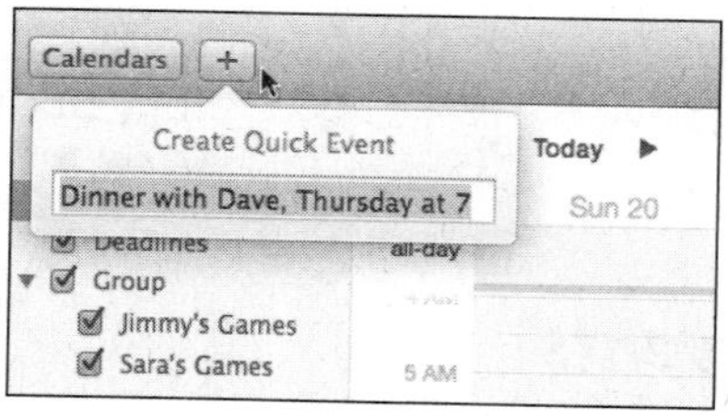

Figure 2-9:
Quickly
create an
event.

+ Calendars

Create Quick Event

Dinner with Dave, Thursday at 7

Today ►

Sun 20

Deadlines   all-day

▼ ☑ Group

   ☑ Jimmy's Games

   ☑ Sara's Games   5 AM

✦ **In Day or Week view:** Double-click the hour you want the event to begin, and then type in a title for your event. Or, click and drag from the starting time to the ending time, and then type a title for your event.

✦ **In Month view:** Double-click the date of the event, and type in the title and time, such as **Movie 7:00 p.m. – 9:00 p.m.**

✦ **In Week or Month view:** Click and drag from the beginning to ending date for a multi-day event.

You can change the start and end time of an event by moving the pointer to the top or bottom of an event until it turns into a two-way-pointing arrow. Then hold down the mouse or trackpad button and move it up or down to change your start and end times by 15-minute increments.

Editing an event

Sometimes a title, time, and date are enough descriptors for an event. Other times, you want to add more information, or something changes and you have to change the date or time of an event. Editing an event lets you change the time, the date, or the description of an event. You can also add features to an event, such as setting an alert, inviting people to your event, or automatically opening a file.

Changing the description of an event

Each time you create an event, you type in a description of that event. To modify this description, follow these steps:

1. **Double-click the event you want to modify and then click the Edit button.**

Alternatively, click the event and choose Edit⇨Edit Event or press ⌘+E. The Edit pane opens, as shown in Figure 2-10.

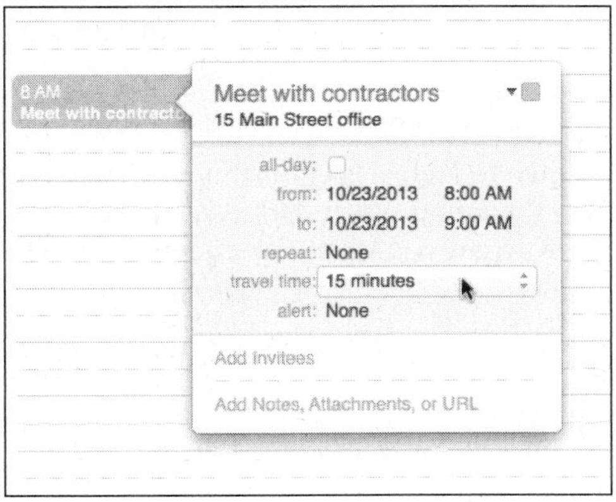

Figure 2-10:
Define
details for
your event,
create
alerts,
and invite
others.

8 AM	**Meet with contractors** ▾ ▣
Meet with contract...	15 Main Street office
	all-day: ☐
	from: 10/23/2013 8:00 AM
	to: 10/23/2013 9:00 AM
	repeat: None
	travel time: 15 minutes ↕
	alert: None
	Add invitees
	Add Notes, Attachments, or URL

2. **Click the event description. (In Figure 2-10, this is *Meet with contractors*.)**

A text box appears around the event description.

3. **Use the arrow and Delete keys to edit the event description; type any new text in the fields.**

- Click the Location field to type a location where the event takes place.

- Click the date and time to expand the options there, and then select the All-Day check box to create an event that lasts all day, like a birthday or vacation day. The From and To fields disappear if All Day is selected.

4. **Click the Travel Time pop-up menu to block out the necessary additional time to reach your appointment.**

Choose the amount of time necessary from the listed options or click Custom to fill in a specific quantity.

Choose View⇨Show Travel Time to see it reflected on the calendar. This helps you avoid scheduling appointments back to back.

5. **Click outside the event editing dialog when you're finished or make it a repeating event and add alerts, as we explain in the next two sections.**

Creating a recurring event

For an event that occurs regularly, such as every Monday or on the same day every month, you can create an event one time and then tell Calendar to display that event on a recurring basis. To create a recurring event, follow these steps:

1. **Double-click the event you want to modify.**

   Alternatively, click the event and choose Edit⇨Edit Event or press ⌘+E.

2. **Click the time interval to expand the options.**

3. **Click the Repeat pop-up menu and choose an option, such as Every Day or Every Month.**

4. **(Optional) In the Repeat pop-up menu, click Custom.**

   A dialog appears, shown in Figure 2-11, letting you define specific days for the recurring event, such as every Monday or the first Wednesday of every month. Click OK when you finish creating your custom recurring event.

   If you share the calendar you create in Calendar with other iOS devices, use the Custom option on your Mac because the other iOS devices don't offer the same flexibility.

Figure 2-11: Define parameters for a recurring event.

5. **Click the Ends pop-up menu to choose when the repeating should stop.**

   • *Never:* If you want the event to repeat in perpetuity.

   • *After:* Click in the field to the right and type the number of times you want it to repeat.

   • *On Date:* Type in the date you want the repeating event to end.

6. **Click outside the editing dialog to close it.**

   Calendar automatically displays your recurring event throughout the rest of the calendar until you modify the event.

If a particular event occurs two or three times, you can set it up as a repeating event or you can just duplicate it, which is sometimes easier. To duplicate an event, click it and choose Edit⇨Duplicate, or press ⌘+D (or hold down the Option key and then drag the event to the new time slot). When the duplicate appears, move the cursor to it, drag the event to a new date, and then release the mouse button.

Indicating your availability

If you share your calendar with others, you may want to indicate your availability during certain events. You can choose Busy or Free by selecting the pop-up menu next to Show As. Usually Calendar considers you Busy when you have an appointment, but if you show your attendance for three days at a conference, for instance, you may want to choose Free so those who view your calendar know that you're at the conference but free for appointments during that time.

Setting an alert for an event

Scheduling an event is useless if you forget about it. That's why Calendar gives you the option of setting two types of alerts that can notify you of upcoming events:

✦ A message with or without an audible sound that shows up on your Mac, and looks like a dialog in the upper right corner, and, if you use iCloud, on your other devices

✦ A message that can be sent to you as an e-mail or as a file that can be opened

You can choose more than one type of alert — or all of them — for each event.

To set an alert for an event, follow these steps:

1. **Double-click the event you want to be reminded about.**

   Alternatively, click it and then choose Edit⇨Edit Event, or press ⌘+E.

2. **Click the date and time to expand the Edit dialog.**

   An Edit dialog appears (refer to Figure 2-10).

3. **Click the Alert pop-up menu (you may see two; click either).**

   You can choose any of the following options:

   • *None:* You remove any alerts you've already set for the event.

   • *Message:* Click one of the time intervals that appear, and a message will be displayed that amount of time in advance of the event.

4. **For other options, click Custom and then choose the alert type.**

   - *Message:* Calendar sends a reminder message to you.

   - *Message with Sound:* Select the alert sound you want from the pop-up menu that appears beneath the alert type menu.

   - *Email:* If you have more than one address, choose the one (from the pop-up menu) you want the alert sent to.

   - *Open File:* The default choice opens the Calendar app. To open a different file, such as a report that you can review for an upcoming meeting, choose Other in the pop-up menu beneath the alert type menu and then scroll through the directories and folders of your Mac to select the file you want to open.

5. **Click the quantity field and enter how many minutes, hours, or days before or after the event you want the alert to trigger — for example, 15 minutes or 1 hour or 3 days before or after the event.**

6. **Click the pop-up menu to the right to choose the before or after interval (minutes, hours, days) or choose At Time of Event.**

7. **Scroll down to choose On Date and type in a specific date and time you want to receive the alert.**

8. **(Optional) Add another alert by hovering the cursor over the alert and then click the plus button that appears to the right.**

   You can add another alert (or many additional alerts) to an event by editing a new or existing alert.

9. **Click outside the event-editing dialog to close it.**

Moving an event to another calendar

You can always move an event from one calendar to another, such as from your Work calendar to your Home calendar. To move an event to another calendar, follow these steps:

1. **Double-click an event that you want to modify. Or click it once and then choose Edit⇨Edit Event, or press ⌘+E.**

2. **Click the colored square in the upper right of the dialog to open the Calendar pop-up menu and then click the calendar name you want the event to appear in.**

   Your event is moved.

Adding information to an event

To prepare for an event, you can also store information about that event's location, attendees, any important files related to the event (such as a presentation), a website URL, and any additional notes you want to jot down.

To add information to an event, follow these steps:

1. **Double-click an event that you want to modify. Or click it once and then choose Edit⟹Edit Event, or press ⌘+E.**

2. **Choose one or more of the following:**

   - *Location:* Click and type an address to remind yourself where the event will take place. When you first start typing, a list of names from Contacts that match what you're typing appears, and you can click a name to enter the related address.

   - *Note:* Type any additional notes about your event.

   - *Attachments:* Click to open the chooser that shows the directories and folders on your Mac. Select a file to attach to the event, such as a business presentation that you need to give at the event.

   - *URL:* Type a website address that's relevant to your event, such as a restaurant's website for an upcoming dinner.

3. **Click outside the event-editing dialog to close it.**

Inviting people to your event

Invitations for events ranging from staff meetings to birthday parties are often communicated electronically. Rather than type out a separate e-mail with the details of your event, you can send the invitation directly from Calendar. And Calendar keeps track of the responses so you can see who has accepted, declined, or is still deciding. Follow these steps:

1. **Click an event that you want to invite people to and then choose Edit⟹Edit Event or press ⌘+E.**

2. **Click Add Invitees and begin typing a name.**

   If the person you want to invite is in Contacts, Calendar automatically shows you a list of possible matches.

   The more you type, the narrower the list becomes.

3. **Choose the e-mail of the person you want to invite.**

4. **(Optional) Type in other names after the first one if you want to invite more than one person.**

5. **Click Send.**

   An invitation is sent in the Calendar or ICS file format. If the person has Calendar or another calendar application associated with the e-mail address, the invitation is sent directly to Calendar or the calendar application.

ICS is the standard file type for exchanging calendar information. Calendar, Outlook, Google Calendar, and Calendar (on iOS devices) support the ICS standard. (Unfortunately, Eudora, Entourage, Mailsmith, and others do not.) When you send or receive an e-mail with an invitation attached, the invitation probably has the `.ics` filename extension. To add the event automatically to Calendar or the calendar application currently in use, you or the recipient simply click that attachment in the e-mail message.

6. **The recipients have the option to Accept or Decline, or say Maybe.**

   You receive an e-mail when recipients respond: A white check mark in a green circle appears next to the recipients who accept, a question mark in an orange circle indicates a Maybe response, and a red circle-with-slash means the recipient declined the invitation.

If you have both Contacts and Calendar open, you can click and drag a contact (⌘-click to select more than one invitee) from a Contacts or Group List to the hour of the event to which you want to invite them. See Book V, Chapter 1 to discover more about Contacts.

Responding to invitations

If someone sends you an invitation in Mail and you accept, it's added to your calendar automatically. Invitations appear in the Inbox on the toolbar. The number indicates the number of invitations you have. A badge with a number appears on the Calendar icon on the Dock, which also indicates the number of invitations you have in your Inbox.

When you click the Inbox, the invitations appear, as shown in Figure 2-12. Click Maybe, Decline, or Accept. The sender will be notified of your response. If you Accept, the event is added to Calendar.

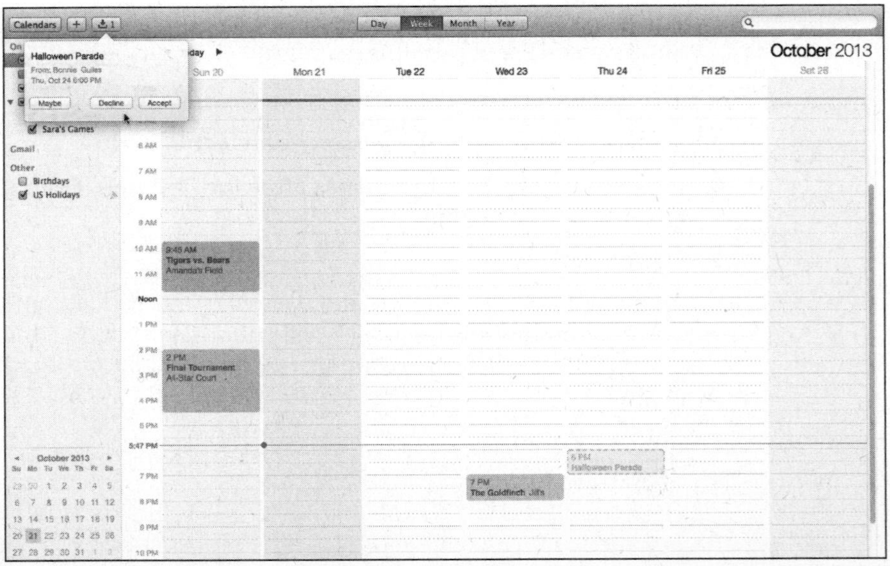

Figure 2-12:
Invitations appear in the Inbox on the toolbar.

Moving an event

In case you store an event at the wrong date or time, you can change the date and time in the Edit Event dialog, or move it to a new date and time by following these steps:

1. **Move the cursor to the middle of the event box.**

2. **Hold down the mouse button and drag the cursor to a new time or date.**

   The event moves with the cursor; the duration doesn't change.

3. **Release the mouse button when you're happy with the new date and time of the event.**

Deleting an event

When you no longer need to remember an event, you can delete it. Just click it and choose Edit⇨Delete. If you delete an event by mistake, press ⌘+Z or choose Edit⇨Undo to retrieve your event.

Finding Events

Storing events is useful only if you can view upcoming events so you can prepare for them. To help you find and view events, Calendar offers several different methods that include using colors to identify different types of events and letting you search for a specific event by name.

Color-coding events

Events in a calendar reflect the color you assign to the calendar when you create the calendar. So if you assign the color blue to your Home calendar and the color red to your Work calendar, you can quickly identify which events on your calendar are home related (blue) or work related (red).

Use contrasting colors for multiple calendars to make it easy to tell which events belong to which calendar.

Selectively hiding events

Normally, Calendar displays all events, color-coding them so you can tell which events belong to which calendars. However, if you have too many events, you may find mixing Home and Work events too confusing. If you want to see only events stored on a specific calendar (such as Home or Work calendars), you can hide the events that are stored on other calendars.

To hide events stored on other calendars, deselect the check box of any of those calendars in the Calendar List. To view events stored on a calendar, make sure that a check mark appears in the check box of that calendar, as shown in Figure 2-13.

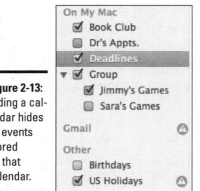

Figure 2-13: Hiding a calendar hides all events stored on that calendar.

Checking for today's events

Probably the most important events you need to keep an eye on are the ones you've scheduled for today. To see all events scheduled for today, click the Today button at the top of the Calendar window.

Another quick way to review any upcoming events for today is to use the Calendar widget in Dashboard. To display today's events in the Calendar widget, click the current date (which appears in the left pane of the Calendar widget) until the events pane appears. (For more information about using widgets and the Dashboard, see Book I, Chapter 2.)

Checking events for a specific date

Sometimes you may need to know whether you have any events scheduled on a certain date. To check a specific date, choose View⇨Go to Date (or Go to Today if you're looking for that) or double-click the date in one of the calendar views.

The Month view can show you the events scheduled for a particular date, but the Day and Week views can show you the specific times of your events for that day.

Searching for an event

If you scheduled an event several days ago, you may forget the exact date of that event. To help you find a specific event, Calendar lets you search for it by typing all or part of the information stored in that event — for example, the event name, the attendee names, or any notes you stored about the event.

To search for an event, follow these steps:

1. **Click the Spotlight text box in the upper-right corner of the Calendar window.**

2. **Type as much text as you can remember about the event you want to find, such as an attendee's name or the location of the event.**

The Calendar application displays a list of events that match the text you type. The list appears in a column on the right of the calendar window, as shown in Figure 2-14. If you have a recurring event, every instance that matches the search will appear. If the event you seek is on a hidden calendar (one that isn't selected), its contents won't appear in the search.

Figure 2-14: Spotlight can help you search and find events.

3. **Double-click an event that Spotlight found.**

Your chosen event appears.

4. **Click the Clear button in the Spotlight text box to remove the list of matching events.**

Exporting Calendar data

To share your calendars with other applications (even those running on other operating systems, such as Windows or Linux), you need to export your Calendar file by following these steps:

1. **Choose File⇨Export⇨Export.**

A dialog appears, giving you a chance to choose a filename and location to store your Calendar data, as shown in Figure 2-15.

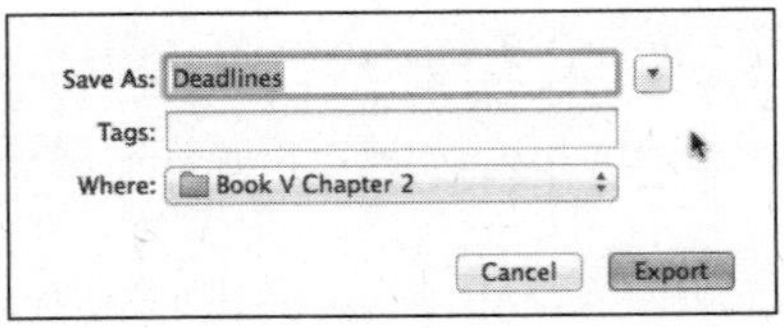

Figure 2-15:
Export your
calendars.

2. **In the Save As text box, type a name for your file.**

3. **Choose the location to store your file from the Where pop-up menu or click the disclosure triangle to expand the window and view the directories and folders on your Mac.**

4. **Click Export.**

Sharing your calendars

You can print your calendar and give a copy to people, but an easier way to share is to give others access to your calendar online. Your calendar will be a read-only file; the people who have access can view your calendar, but they can't change it. To share your calendar, follow these steps:

1. **Click the Calendar button to open the calendar list if it isn't in view.**

2. **Click the calendar you want to share.**

   You can share calendars only from On My Mac or iCloud.

3. **Choose Edit⇨Publish for a calendar on your Mac. Or, if you want to publish a calendar that's on iCloud, choose Edit⇨Share Calendar.**

   A dialog opens, as shown in Figure 2-16 for Mac calendars and as Figure 2-17 for iCloud calendars.

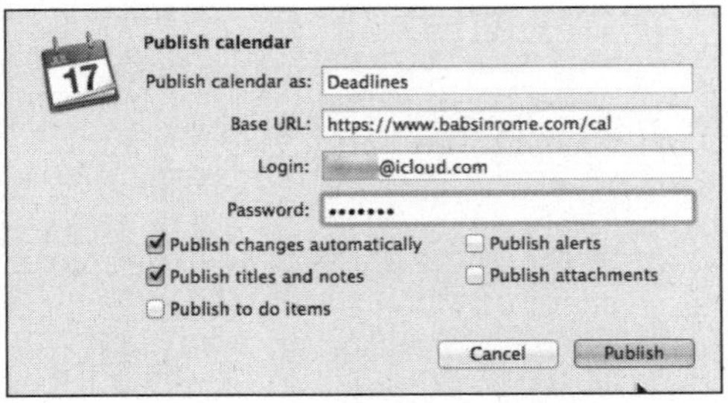

Figure 2-16:
Publish
calendars
stored on
your Mac so
other people
can refer to
them.

Share

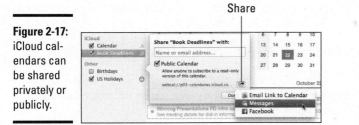

Figure 2-17:
iCloud cal-
endars can
be shared
privately or
publicly.

REMEMBER

4. **For calendars on your Mac, you can type a name for your calendar that will help those who have access understand what the calendar represents.**

   This name is only for the shared calendar; it doesn't change the name of the calendar in Calendar.

   Shared iCloud calendars use the name they have in Calendar, so you should give your calendar a recognizable name.

5. **Do one of the following to publish your calendar:**

   - *For calendars on your Mac* (refer to Figure 2-16): Type the URL web address of the server along with your login and password in the related fields. Select the options you want from the check boxes at the bottom of the dialog. Then click the Publish button.

   - *For calendars on iCloud* (refer to Figure 2-17): If the people you want to share your calendar with are in Contacts, type the names and then choose the correct e-mail addresses from the matches that appear. Otherwise, type the e-mail addresses of the people you want to share the calendar with.

     If you want to make the calendar public, select the Public Calendar check box, and then share the URL by clicking the Share button (the curved arrow next to the URL). A pop-up menu gives you three ways to share the link — e-mail, Messages, or Facebook. Click one and proceed as you would to send anything with those apps.

     Click Done. You can also click the URL to select it, and then copy and paste somewhere else, such as on your website.

Backing up Calendar data and restoring a backup file

Because Calendar can store all your upcoming events (appointments, meetings, and so on), disaster could strike if your hard drive fails and wipes out your Calendar data. The best way to avoid this is to use the Calendar option in iCloud. If you prefer not to use iCloud, you should keep a backup copy of your Calendar data. To do so, follow these steps:

1. **Choose File⇨Export⇨Calendar Archive.**

   The Save dialog appears.

2. **In the Save As text box, type a descriptive name for your Calendar backup file.**

3. **Choose the location for storing your file from the Where pop-up menu.**

4. **Click Save.**

Save your Calendar backup file on a separate drive, such as an external hard drive or a flash drive. That way, if your Mac hard drive fails, you won't lose both your original Calendar data and your backup file at the same time. (For more details on backing up files, see Book III, Chapter 1.)

To retrieve your schedule from a backup file that you created earlier, choose File⇨Import⇨Import. In the Open dialog that appears, click the drive and folder where you saved your backup Calendar file. Then click Import. Calendar imports the backed-up file; any changes you made since the last backup will be lost.

Printing a Calendar file

Even if you have a laptop, you can't always have your computer with you, so you may want to print your calendar in the Day, Week, or Month view. To print a calendar, follow these steps:

1. **Choose File⇨Print.**

   A Print dialog appears, as shown in Figure 2-18.

2. **Click the View pop-up menu and choose Day, Week, Month, List, or Selected Events.**

   Selected Events shows only the event(s) you select by Shift-clicking to select a series of contiguous events or ⌘-clicking to select noncontiguous events.

3. **(Optional) Change any other settings, such as the paper size, time range, or calendars, and select the options you want.**

4. **Click Continue.**

   Another Print dialog appears.

5. **Click the Printer pop-up menu, choose a printer, and then click Print.**

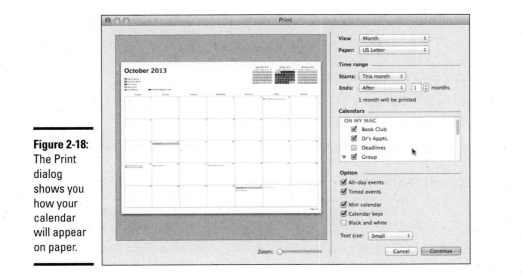

Figure 2-18:
The Print dialog shows you how your calendar will appear on paper.

Organizing Tasks with Reminders

Although you can put an event on your calendar in Calendar and then set an alert so you don't forget it, not everything you need to remember is an event. For these items, which you may think of as to-do's with deadlines, you record in the Reminders app. (If you're familiar with earlier versions of Mac OS X, these items were part of iCal as the To Do or Reminders functions.)

A typical Reminders list contains goals or important tasks that you want to accomplish, usually by a specific date or time or based on when you leave or arrive at a location. You can create multiple Reminders lists and categorize them however you want. Like Contacts and Calendar, Reminders is also part of iCloud, so your tasks can be synced across all your devices signed in to the same iCloud account.

Creating new Reminders tasks

Reminders is a catch-all for your To Do lists, neatly divided into categories you establish. Here's how to create new Reminders:

1. **Click the Reminders app icon on the Desktop.**

The Reminders app opens. The first time you open Reminders, you have two lists: Reminders and Completed.

2. **Click the Reminders list and then click the lined piece of "paper."**

   The cursor appears on the first line, and a check box is to the left of the cursor.

3. **Type the task you want to remember.**

   The task appears in the list with an info button to the right.

4. **Click the info button to open the Details screen.**

5. **Click each item to specify how you want Reminders to help you remember this task, as shown in Figure 2-19.**

   - *Remind Me On a Day:* Select the check box, and then click the date to open a calendar that allows you to specify the date. Click the hour and minute fields, and enter the time you want to be reminded on that date.

     Click the Repeat pop-up menu to choose an interval at which you want the alert to repeat.

   - *Remind Me At a Location:* Select the check box, and then enter the name of a person or business that's in Contacts or type a street address. Then, select either the Leaving or the Arriving radio button to hear an alert when one of these actions occurs.

     A summary of when the alert will take place is written beneath the Leaving and Arriving radio buttons.

   - *Priority:* Click the pop-up menu to give the task low, medium, high, or no priority.

   - *Note:* Type any additional details about the task in this field.

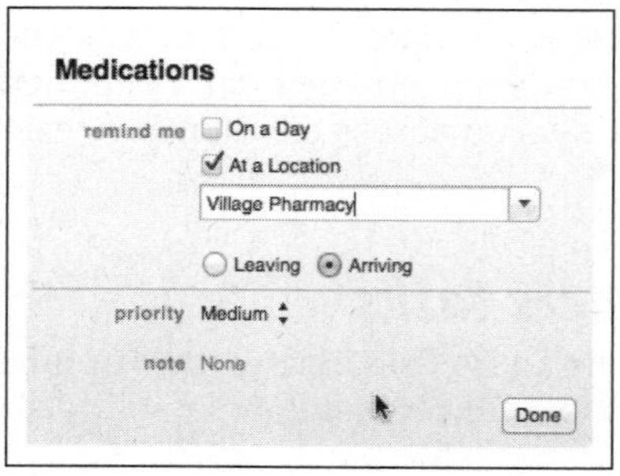

Figure 2-19:
Choose
when and
where
Reminders
should prod
you to your
task.

6. **Click Done to return to the list.**

7. **Choose ⌂System Preferences⌂Notifications to choose the alert style you want Reminders to use, and click Sounds in System Preferences to select your preferred alert sound.**

To rearrange, edit, or delete items in a list, do the following:

✦ **To rearrange the order of items in your list:** Click and drag each item to move it up or down in the list.

✦ **To edit a task:** Click the item and then click the info button to the right of the task to open the Details screen. Edit the task following the steps you use to create a task.

✦ **To delete an item:** Click it and then choose Edit➪Delete.

There are a few options for changing the view:

✦ **All tasks:** To view all your tasks for a certain day, click a date in the calendar, and a list by date appears. A dot under the date lets you know whether there are deadlines that day.

✦ **Hide or show:** Click the related buttons at the bottom of the window (see Figure 2-20) to hide or show the list of Reminders lists or calendar.

✦ **New window:** Double-click a list title either in the list of Reminders lists or on the list itself to open the list in a separate window. You can leave this window open on your Desktop and close the main Reminders window.

When you complete a task, select the check box to the left of the task on the list as shown in Figure 2-20. The completed tasks are moved to the Completed list, but you can also view them by scrolling up to the top of the originating list to see the completed section.

Making new lists

Keeping all your tasks on the existing Reminders list somewhat defeats the purpose of the app, which is to divide your tasks by subject. There are three ways to create new lists:

✦ Click the New List button (refer to Figure 2-20) at the bottom of the window.

✦ Choose File➪New List.

✦ Press ⌘+L.

When you create a new list, the name is highlighted; type a new name and then press Return or click elsewhere on the screen (such as on the list) to add tasks to it. To edit the list name later, click it once, and then click the text once to highlight it, and type a new name.

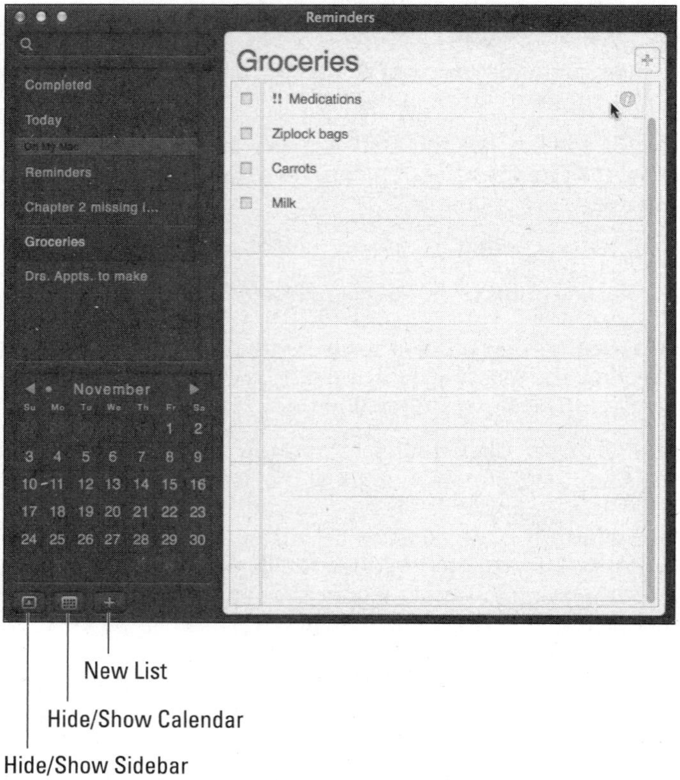

Figure 2-20:
Hide or show completed tasks on your lists.

New List

Hide/Show Calendar

Hide/Show Sidebar

When you have more than one list, choose Reminders⇨Default List and select the list that you want to set as default. Then when you create new tasks outside of a list — for example, in Outlook or another app that syncs with Reminders — those tasks are added to the chosen list.

To delete an entire list, click it in the list of reminders and then choose Edit⇨Delete. A dialog confirms whether you're sure you want to delete the entire list; click Delete to proceed, or click Cancel if you change your mind.

You can move from one list to the next (one day to the next if you're viewing tasks by date) and back by swiping with two fingers across the trackpad or Magic Mouse.

Adding Reminders from other accounts

If you keep To Do lists on other online services such as Exchange or Yahoo!, you can add those lists to Reminders and keep all your lists in one app. The procedure is pretty much the same as that for adding calendars from different services, as we describe earlier in this chapter. Choose Reminders⇨Add Account, select the radio button next to the account you want to add, and then click Continue.

Then type the required account name and password and click Continue. Your account is verified and added to the list of lists on the Reminders window. You may need to ask your network administrator for information if you want to add a CalDAV account.

Chapter 3: Creating Documents with Pages

In This Chapter

✔ Using document templates

✔ Working with photos

✔ Creating and formatting text

✔ Saving time with formatting styles

✔ Adding text boxes, charts, and tables

✔ Putting the finishing touches on your document

✔ Saving your document

✔ Printing, exporting, and e-mailing your document

Pages is the word-processing and page-layout app of Apple's iWork suite. In Pages, you can type, edit, and format text to produce stationery-style documents, such as letters, envelopes, and business cards as well as longer text-heavy documents, such as reports and résumés. But Pages doesn't stop there. You can add and arrange graphics and text boxes on a page to create colorful newsletters, brochures, menus, flyers, and the like.

In this chapter, we take you through the basics of Pages. Whether you choose to work on a simple letter or an eye-catching brochure, the functions and features are the same, so the instructions we give here apply to both. First, we introduce working with templates and then we explain formatting the document and the text within. We walk you through the procedures for inserting text boxes, photos, charts, and tables. At the end of the chapter, we show you how to save, print, and share your document.

In Book V, Chapter 6, we present some of the iWork features that apply to all three apps in the suite, including Pages.

Pages is part of the iWork suite. Your Mac may have a trial version of Pages that lets you play with the application to see whether it meets your needs. You can purchase and download Pages from the App Store for $19.99 from the Apple online store or your local Apple Store or authorized reseller. There's also a free iOS version of Pages that's available for the iPhone, iPad, and iPod touch.

Working with Document Templates

To help you start writing, Pages supplies a variety of document templates. When you choose a document template, you just enter new text and customize the appearance of the template so you don't have to create everything from scratch. The following sections tell you how to get started.

Choosing a template

Pages offers 63 templates although you find many more on the web, and we give you suggestions for websites to visit in Book V, Chapter 6. Some templates, such as those for reports or letters, are designed mostly for writing (relatively) plain and simple documents, with the emphasis on content. In these templates, you type continuous text directly on the page in the document and can insert images or charts. Other templates, such as flyers or newsletters, are designed for mixing text and graphics when content and presentation have almost equal importance. The text in these templates goes into text boxes. When choosing a template, you want to select one that's closest to the type of document you want to create.

Text on a page versus text boxes

You can quickly and easily create colorful, interesting documents on your Mac, but choosing the correct template can be confusing. For example, if you have to write a 100-page report, choose a report template that uses continuous text — not newsletter, which uses text boxes. Likewise, to publicize your garage sale, choose a flyer template, not letter.

In continuous text documents (also known as word-processing), you type directly on a page with, um, continuous text. You can insert photos or tables if you want, but they complement the text and aren't the main focus of the document. In documents with text boxes (also known as *page layout*), you have to create a text box first and then place that text box somewhere on your page.

The advantage of continuous text is that you can keep typing, and Pages creates new pages automatically while you type. The disadvantage

of this approach is that it's harder to define exactly where the text will appear on the page.

The advantage of using text boxes is that you can move those text boxes anywhere on a page (or to a different page). The disadvantage of typing text in text boxes is that they can display only a limited amount of text. If you need to type a larger chunk of text, you may need to link text boxes so that when your text overflows one text box, it flows automatically into another one.

Another difference between continuous text and text box documents is that you must manually add (or delete) pages when you use a template with text boxes (by choosing Insert➪Pages or Edit➪Delete Page). With a continuous text template, Pages adds pages automatically while you type and deletes pages as necessary when you delete text.

WARNING!

After you create a document by using a template, you can't switch to a new template. If you want to use a different template, you have to create another document.

To choose a document template, follow these steps:

1. **Click the Pages icon on the Dock or Launchpad.**

Or choose File⇨New if Pages is already running.

A dialog appears, displaying different templates you can choose, as shown in Figure 3-1.

Figure 3-1:
Pages provides various templates to help you create a document quickly.

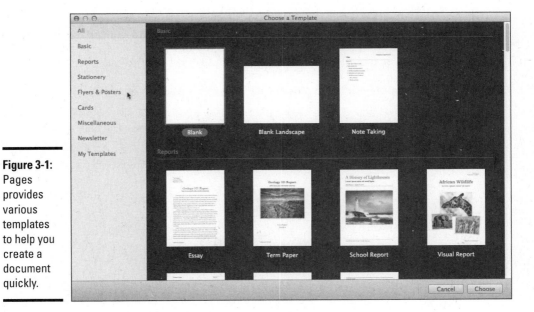

2. **Click a template category in the list on the left to narrow your choices or scroll through the center pane.**

If you want to start with a blank document, click the Blank portrait or landscape template, whichever best suits the type of document you want to create. Most of, but not all, the instructions apply to blank documents; we let you know when they don't.

3. **Select a template and then click the Choose button.**

Or double-click the icon for the template you want to use.

Pages opens your chosen template as a new, untitled document.

4. **Choose File⇨Save.**

The Save As dialog opens. Type a name for your document and choose the folder where you want to store it. Pages supports Versions, which keeps a running backup of your document each time you change it. (We explain this feature in Book I, Chapter 4, and Book III, Chapter 1.)

To keep things simple, these instructions are for saving and storing the document on your Mac. You can also save and store your iWork documents on iCloud, which is a great option if you work from different devices. See the section "Saving Your Documents on Your Mac or iCloud" later in this chapter for details.

Replacing placeholder text

Nearly every template, except for Blank, contains placeholder text (a mix of pseudo-Latin and gibberish that's been used in typesetting as dummy text since the sixteenth century), which you replace with your own text. To change placeholder text in a template, follow these steps:

1. **Double-click the placeholder text you want to change.**

Pages selects the entire placeholder text, which can be as short as the company name in the logo at the top of a letter or as large as several paragraphs, as shown in the newsletter text selection in Figure 3-2.

2. **Type any new text you want to replace the placeholder text.**

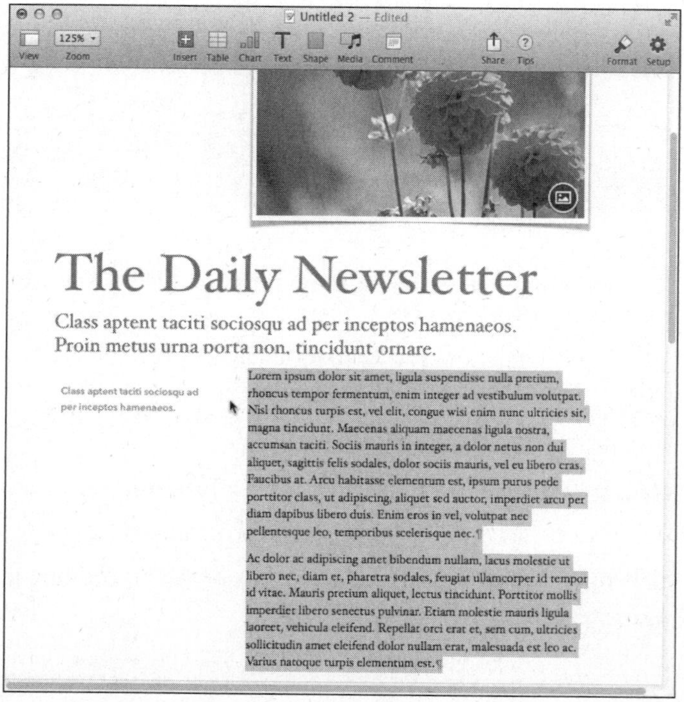

Figure 3-2:
To replace placeholder text, double-click it and type new text.

Replacing placeholder photos and graphics

Many templates display placeholder photos and graphics. Unless you happen to like the image included with a template, you'll probably want to replace it with one of your own. Here we explain how to place photos from iPhoto; how to place images from other places on your computer; and how to insert a chart or table from Numbers, iWork's spreadsheet application.

Inserting photos from iPhoto

These steps work with both templates and blank documents to add or replace photos in Pages documents with photos from iPhoto:

1. **Click the photo icon on the placeholder image; Media Browser appears.**

2. **Click the Photos tab in the Media Browser to view all the photos stored in iPhoto, iCloud (if you're connected to the Internet), and your Photo Stream photos.**

   See Book IV, Chapter 3, to learn about iPhoto.

   If, like us, you have thousands of photos, click one of the subheads under Events in the Library list to narrow your choices. This makes it easier to find the photo you want to add to your document.

3. **Click the photo you want to insert.**

   Pages replaces the placeholder image with the photo you choose from the Media Browser, as shown in Figure 3-3. The Media Browser closes automatically after the image is placed. In the next section, we explain how to manipulate photos in your documents.

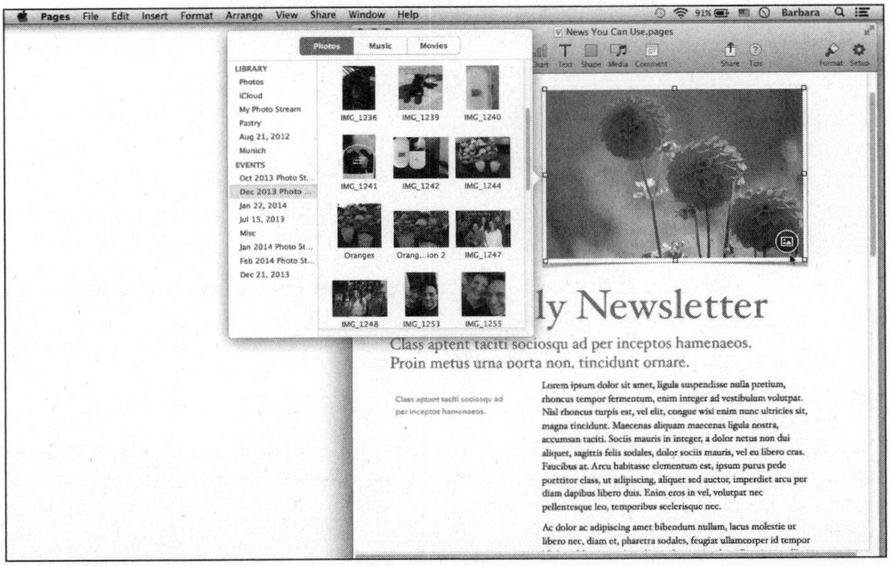

Figure 3-3:
Use the
Media
Browser
to insert
photos
directly.

TIP

To insert a photo without a placeholder, click the Media icon on the toolbar at the top of the Pages window, and repeat the previous Steps 2 and 3. The photo is added to your document. Move and resize as in the next section.

Moving and resizing a photo

After you place a photo in a document, you can move or resize it.

To move a photo, follow these steps:

1. **Drag the photo to a new position.**

   If your document has continuous text, the paragraphs shift while you move the image so that the text runs before and after the image. If you're using a document with text boxes, the image moves directly over the text box.

2. **Release the mouse button or lift your finger from the trackpad when you're happy with the new location of the photo.**

To resize a photo, follow these steps:

1. **Click the photo you want to resize.**

   Handles appear around your chosen picture.

2. **Move the pointer to a handle until the pointer turns into a two-way pointing arrow.**

3. **Drag the handle to resize your photo.**

   The photo maintains its original aspect ratio.

4. **Release the mouse button or lift your finger from the trackpad when you're happy with the new size of the photo.**

Inserting other images

If the image you want to insert isn't stored in iPhoto, do the following:

1. **Choose Insert⇨Choose.**

   A chooser opens, showing the folders and files on your Mac (as in Figure 3-4).

2. **Scroll through your folders and files until you find the image you want to insert.**

3. **Double-click the file.**

   Your image is added to your document.

4. **(Optional) To replace the placeholder image, click it, press Delete, and then drag the inserted image to the placeholder location.**

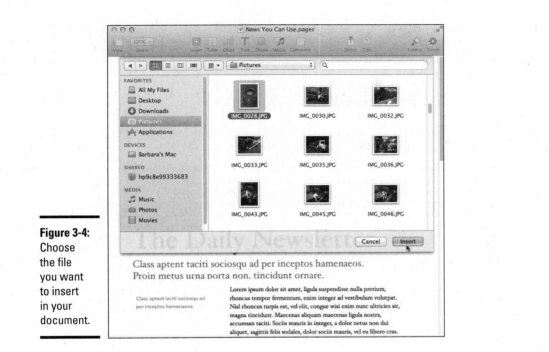

Figure 3-4:
Choose
the file
you want
to insert
in your
document.

Inserting charts and tables from Numbers

You can insert charts or tables from Numbers (iWork's spreadsheet app, which we explore in Book V, Chapter 5) directly in a document. (In the later section, "Creating Charts and Tables," we explain how to create a chart or table in Pages.)

1. **Open the Numbers document that has the chart or table you want to insert.**

2. **Select the chart or table you want to insert.**

3. **Choose Edit⇨Copy or press ⌘+C.**

4. **Return to your Pages document.**

5. **Choose Edit⇨Paste or press ⌘+P.**

6. **Drag the selection handles to resize the placeholder as needed to accommodate the table or chart.**

Adding pages or sections to your document

In continuous text documents, no matter how much text you type, pages are added. Each page has the same layout although some elements may be slightly changed. For example, when a second page is added to a letter, it has reduced header information (such as a smaller logo) and a page number instead of the address in the footer. In some documents, you may want to manually add a page break or create a section that has different margins than the rest of the document or begins a new chapter. For example, a financial report may have a cover page as one section, a table of contents for the second section, and third section containing descriptive text with charts and graphs.

To add different pages to your document, follow these steps:

1. **Place the cursor at the end of the page that you want the additional page to follow.**

2. **Click the Insert icon on the toolbar and choose the type of addition you want to make.**

   Available options will be bold; unavailable options will be dim in the pop-up menu.

   - *Page Break:* Appears in continuous text documents; creates a new page immediately after where you placed the cursor, which could be between two paragraphs or at the very end of your text.

   - *Column Break:* Appears if your document has columns; adds a column immediately after where you placed the cursor.

   - *Page:* Appears in documents that use text boxes; adds a blank page after the selected page. The text boxes, images, or other elements on the page remain unchanged.

You can add a new *section* to a document at any time without affecting the existing pages. Or, add a *section break* within an existing page, and then anything after the section break will move to the new section.

To add a new section to your document, simply choose Insert⇨Section, and a new section is added to the end of the document.

To add a section break, do the following:

1. **Click to place the cursor at the beginning of the text you want to move to the new section.**

2. **Choose Insert⇨Section Break.**

   The new section begins with the text that comes after where you placed the cursor.

3. **To see all the pages of your document, choose View⇨Show Page Thumbnails from the toolbar or the menu bar.**

   A left Sidebar opens, showing thumbnails of the pages or sections in your document, as shown in Figure 3-5. When you click a thumbnail, a yellow border surrounds all the pages that are in the same section. The first page of a section is flush left, and subsequent pages in the section are indented to the right.

Zoom

Section

Word Count

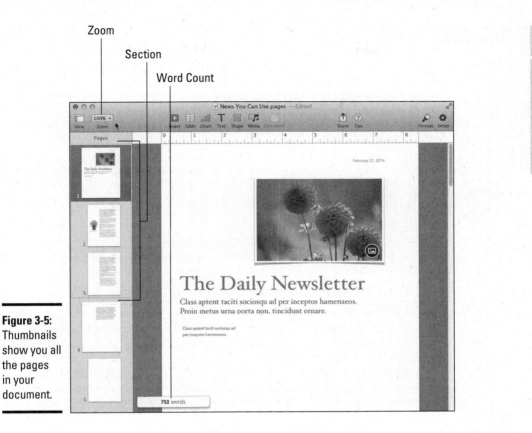

Figure 3-5:
Thumbnails
show you all
the pages
in your
document.

Moving around your document

The page thumbnails not only show you how many pages are in a section,
but they're also a way to jump from one page to another. Just click a thumbnail to move to that page.

Two other tools (as shown in Figure 3-5) help you manage your document:

+ **Zoom:** Click the pop-up menu, which lets you zoom in or out of your
  document to views that range from 25% to 400%. You can also choose to
  view one or two pages at a time.

+ **Word count:** Choose View➪Show Word Count to display the number of
  words in your document.

Choose View➪Hide Page Thumbnails/Hide Word Count to remove either of
those from view.

Working with Text

Text can appear directly on a page or inside a text box. Although you type text directly on a page in continuous text documents (such as those created with the Blank template, letters, or reports), you can add text boxes and type text inside those text boxes, which you may choose to do if you want to insert a sidebar. In some templates, such as newsletters, posters, and business cards, you can type text *only* inside text boxes.

In some ways, text boxes behave like other objects placed in your document, such as photos or charts, and have a few different options than continuous text. We explain adding text boxes later in this chapter in the "Creating and Placing Text Boxes" section.

Either way, after you type your text, you probably want to make some changes. In the following subsections, we explain how to edit, format, and adjust the spacing of your text.

Editing text

Whether you're typing text directly on a page or inside a text box, you can edit text by adding, deleting, or rearranging it.

+ **Adding text:** Any new text you type appears wherever the cursor is located. To add text, just place the cursor where you want the new text to appear, click, and then type away.

  If you want to start your text on a new page or section of a continuous text document, choose Insert⇨Page Break or Insert⇨Section/Section Break, as we explain previously.

+ **Deleting text:** You can delete text in two ways:

  • *Move the cursor to the right of the characters you want to erase and press Delete.* The Delete key appears to the right of the +/= key.

  • *Select text and press Delete.* Select text by holding down the Shift key and moving the cursor with the arrow keys or by clicking and dragging the mouse over the text to select it, and then press Delete.

+ **Rearranging text:** After you write some text, you may need to rearrange it by copying or moving chunks of text from one location to another. You can copy and move text between two text boxes or from one part of a continuous text page to another part of the same page — or to another page all together.

  To copy and move text, you can use the Cut, Copy, and Paste commands on the Edit menu, but you may find it quicker to select and drag text with the mouse. Here's how it's done:

  a. *Select the text you want to copy or move.*

  b. *Drag the selected text to a new location.*

If you want to copy text, hold down the Option key while dragging the selected text. If you want to move text, you don't need to hold down any keys.

c. Release the mouse button or lift your finger from the trackpad to finish copying or moving your text.

Formatting text

The text styles and images you choose for your document create the tone of what you want to communicate — businesslike, fun, weird, and so on. You can format text by using fonts, styles, sizes, and colors. (Later in this chapter, in the "Using Styles" section, we tell you how to apply formatting in a different way.)

To give you fast access to the formatting options, Pages displays a Format pane (see Figure 3-6) down the right side of the Pages window. To view (or hide) the Format pane, click the Format icon on the toolbar or choose View⇨Inspector⇨Format.

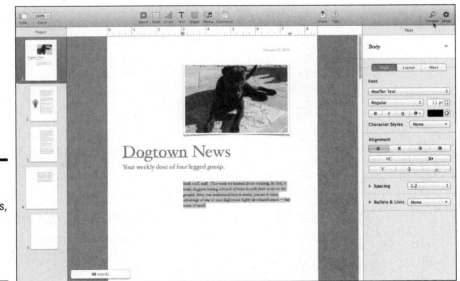

Figure 3-6: Choose fonts, styles, and sizes, text spacing, and alignment.

To change the selected text to another style included in the template, click the disclosure button next to the current style (*Body,* in the figure) to open the Paragraph Styles menu, and then click a different style, such as Title or Caption.

To format text in a way that isn't included in the template, select the text you want to format and then click the Style tab of the Format pane. Then, in the Font section, do any of the following:

✦ **Click the typeface (*Hoefler text*, in the figure).** Then choose a typeface from the menu that appears. Pages has "what-you-see-is-what-you-get" (affectionately known as WYSIWYG, pronounced *wizzy-wig*) menus so you see what the font looks like in the pop-up menu.

✦ **Click the style (*Regular*, in the figure).** Then choose a style, such as Regular or Italic. You can also click the style buttons below this menu or make a selection from the Character Styles pop-up menu.

✦ **Click the size arrows or type a number for the size you want (*11*, in the figure).**

✦ **Click the color swatch or picker.** A color menu appears when you click the swatch, or a choice of color pickers appears when you click the color circle next to the swatch. Click a color to change the color of your selected text.

For more info on choosing colors, see Book V, Chapter 4, where we tell you how to use these tools in Keynote. These tools are similar to each other in Pages and Keynote.

✦ **Click the gear button to open the Advanced Options menu, as shown in Figure 3-7.** Use the pop-up menus to fine-tune character spacing, ligatures, and capitalization, or add a background color. When you select the Shadow check box, additional menus appear to adjust how your selected text will be shadowed.

To adjust text in a text box, you can also select the entire text box and then click the Text tab of the Format pane. However, if the text box contains more than one type of formatted text, making changes with these tools will make all the text in the text box the same.

Adjusting line spacing, justification, and margins

You can change how characters look by playing with the font, but you can also change the way a block of text looks by changing how it's spaced on the page. In concrete terms, this means changing

✦ **Alignment:** Define how text aligns within the left and right margins, in text boxes, and also between the top and bottom.

✦ **Spacing:** Define how close together lines in a paragraph appear and how much space is between paragraphs.

✦ **Margins:** Define the left and right boundaries that text can't go past.

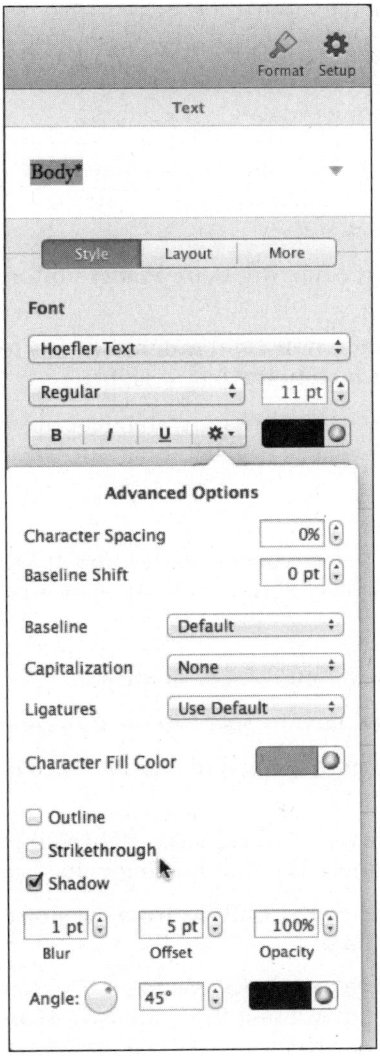

Figure 3-7:
Use
Advanced
Options to
fine-tune
your text.

Changing alignment

You may be more familiar with the term *justification*, which means how the text appears on the left and right edges. The Pages tools that adjust justification of your selected text are in the Alignment section of the Format pane, as follows:

✦ **Align Left:** Text appears flush against the left margin but ragged along the right margin.

✦ **Center:** Each line of text is centered within the left and right margins so that text appears ragged on both left and right margins.

✦ **Align Right:** Text appears flush against the right margin but ragged along the left margin.

✦ **Justify:** Text appears flush against both the left and right margins, but extra space appears between words and characters.

To align, or *justify,* your selected text, follow these steps:

1. **Select the text you want to modify.**

2. **Click the Align Left, Center, Align Right, or Justify buttons of the Format pane.**

3. **(Optional) Click the left outdent or right indent buttons to move the selected text about half an inch to the left or right.**

   The left outdent button is active only after you indent the selected text. Click the buttons more than once to further indent or outdent.

Changing line spacing

Line spacing used for most purposes typically varies from 0.5 to 2.0. (A value of 1.0 is single spacing, and a value of 2.0 is double spacing.) To change line spacing, follow these steps:

1. **Select the line or lines of text you want to modify.**

2. **Click the disclosure triangle next to Space to open those options.**

3. **Click the pop-up menu under Spacing and choose Lines if it isn't selected.**

4. **Click the up and down arrows for the spacing field to the right of the Spacing pop-up menu to choose the line spacing value, such as 1.5.**

5. **(Optional) Choose one of the other options from the pop-up menu and then choose a value accordingly:**

   • *At Least:* Sets a minimum of points for each line. This should be a minimum of the font size. For example, if you use a 10 point (pt) font, a 10 pt spacing is equal to a single-spaced paragraph.

   • *Exactly:* Sets the points to the exact number you choose. Oddly, if you set a 10 pt font to an exact 10 pt spacing, the lines almost overlap.

   • *Between:* Sets the number of points for the space between lines of text. The minimum is 1 pt and is equal to single spacing. A value equal to your font points creates double-spacing.

   The changes to your selected text occur immediately so you can try different solutions and see the effect they have on your text.

6. **Click the up and down arrows next to the value fields for Before Paragraph and After Paragraph to set the amount of blank space that occurs there.**

7. **Click the Format icon on the toolbar to close the Format pane.**

Defining margins for the whole document

The left and right margins define a document with only continuous text. Documents that use only text boxes are limited by the edges of the page.

To define the margins for the whole document, do the following:

1. **Click the Setup icon on the toolbar or choose View⇨Inspector⇨ Document Setup from the menu bar.**

2. **Click the Document tab, as shown in Figure 3-8.**

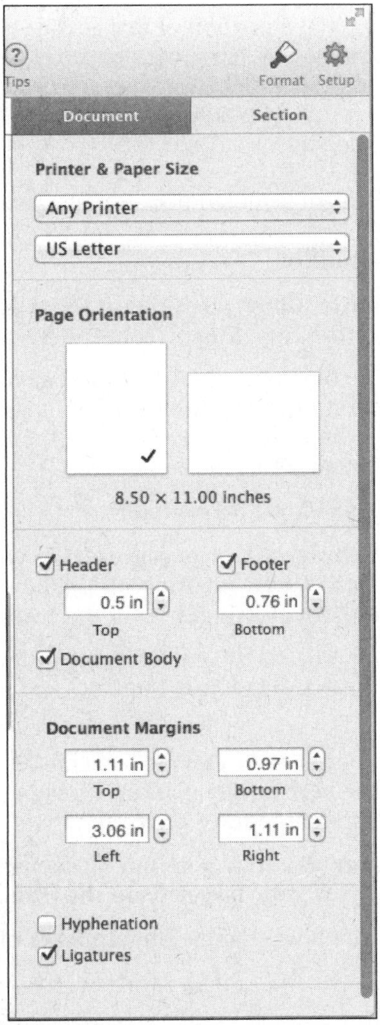

Figure 3-8:
Set the margins for the entire document.

3. **Choose a paper size, such as US Letter or Legal, from the pop-up menu in the Printer & Paper Size section.**

4. **(Optional) Change the page orientation.**

5. **In the Document Margins section, type in the values you want for your left, right, top, and bottom margins.**

   Or use the up and down arrows to choose a value.

To set the units of measure for your rulers, choose Pages⇨Preferences and then click Ruler. Use the pop-up menu next to Ruler Units to choose Inches, Centimeters, Points, or Picas.

Defining margins for a portion of text

To define the left and right margins of a portion of text — say a long citation from a book — you can use the ruler, which appears at the top of the Pages window when you choose View⇨Show Ruler. The ruler lets you define an exact location for your margins, such as placing the left margin exactly 1.5 inches from the left edge of the page.

To define the left and right margins of selected text, follow these steps:

1. **Select the text you want to modify.**

2. **Drag the Left Margin marker to a new position on the ruler and then release the mouse button or lift your finger from the trackpad.**

   The Left Margin marker is the blue triangle that appears on the left side of the ruler. If only the first lines of your paragraphs move, you've selected the Indent marker, which is at the very top of the Left Margin marker; grab the Left Margin marker from the bottom.

   If the ruler isn't visible, choose View⇨Show Rulers.

3. **To indent the first line of a paragraph or paragraphs in your selected text, drag the Indent marker to a new position on the ruler and then release the mouse button or lift your finger from the trackpad.**

   The Indent marker is the thin blue rectangle that appears over the Left Margin marker. Figure 3-9 shows the Left and Right Margin markers and the Indent marker.

   If you drag the Left Margin marker after you move the Indent marker, the Indent marker moves with the Left Margin marker; dragging the Indent marker, however, moves the Indent marker by itself.

4. **Drag the Right Margin marker to a new position on the ruler and then release the mouse button or lift your finger from the trackpad.**

   The Right Margin marker is the blue triangle that appears on the right side of the ruler.

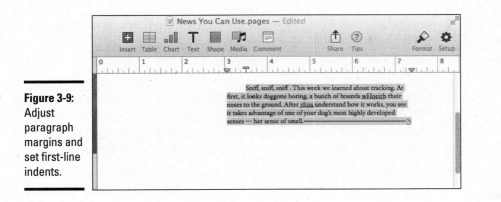

Figure 3-9:
Adjust
paragraph
margins and
set first-line
indents.

Creating precise tabs and indents

Dragging the Left Margin and Right Margin markers on the ruler is a fast way
to adjust the margins or first-line indents of a text selection. For a more precise way, follow these steps:

1. **Select the text you want to modify or click anywhere in the continuous text to apply the tabs to the entire document.**

2. **Click the Format icon on the toolbar or choose View⇨Inspector⇨
   Format.**

3. **Click the Layout tab.**

4. **Click the disclosure triangle next to Tabs.**

   The Text Inspector controls shown in Figure 3-10 appear.

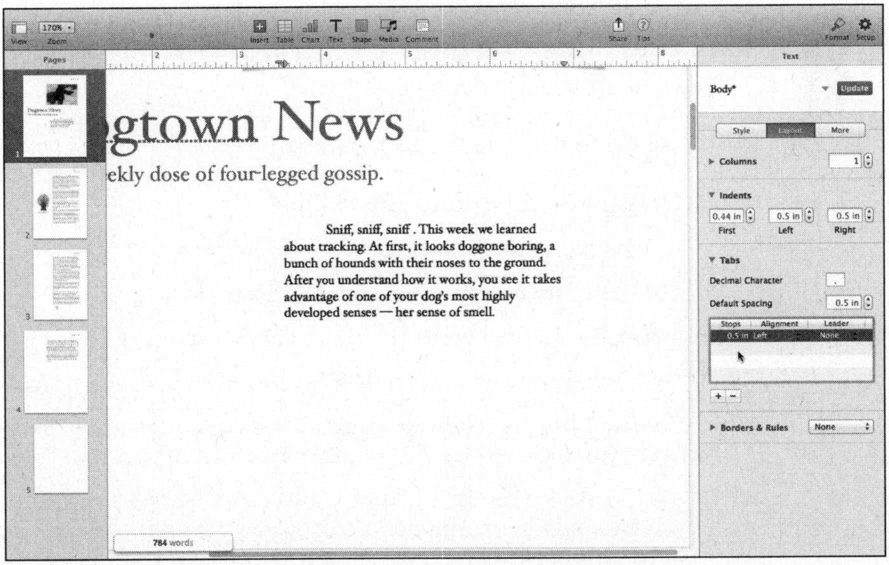

Figure 3-10:
Choose pre-
cise values
for adjust-
ing text
margins.

5. **(Optional) Click in the Decimal Character field if you plan to use the tab for numbers with decimals.**

   For example, you could change a decimal to a comma if you're creating a European document.

6. **Enter a value or click the up and down arrows to choose a value in the Default Spacing field.**

7. **(Optional) If you want to add tab stops, click the plus button at the bottom of the window in the Tabs section and do the following:**

   a. *Click the number under Stops and indicate a precise position for the tab.*

   b. *Click the type of tab you want in the menu under Alignment: Left, Center, Right, or Decimal.*

   c. *Choose a Leader style from the pop-up menu: none, dashes, dots, a line, or arrows.*

   If you want to delete a tab, click the tab and then click the minus sign to delete it.

Click the disclosure triangle next to Indents to establish precise indent measurements for the first lines of paragraphs and also for the left and right margins of your selected text.

Adding headers and footers to a continuous text document

The header and footer is the space between the top (header) and bottom (footer) margin and the document body where you type your main text. The header and footer are where you usually place the date, page number, or document title; they contain information that repeats on each page. As with margins, documents that use text boxes don't have headers or footers.

If you use a template, the headers and footers are predefined, but that doesn't stop you from changing them if you want.

Here's how to use headers and footers:

1. **Click the Setup icon on the toolbar.**

   Or, choose View➪Inspector➪Document Setup.

2. **Click the Document tab (refer to Figure 3-8).**

3. **Select the Header and/or Footer check boxes.**

   Text boxes for one or both will be added to your document.

4. **Choose how far from the edge of the page you want the header and footer to appear; type in a number or use the up and down arrows.**

   The header or footer text box moves according to value you set. The top and bottom margins must be greater than the header and footer distance; otherwise, the document text will cover the header and footer.

If your header is 1 inch, your top margin should be at least 1.5 inches. The header will begin 1 inch from the top of the page, and the main text — also known as the *document body* — will begin 1.5 inches from the top of the page or one-half inch below the header.

5. **Leave the Document Body check box selected.**

   Deselecting this box will convert your document to a page layout (text box only) document and may cause you to lose some of your work.

6. **Move the pointer near the top or bottom of the page, more or less where the header or footer should be, until an empty box appears, as shown in Figure 3-11.**

Figure 3-11: Enter header information.

7. **Click in the empty box.**

   The cursor flashes in the empty box, and a comment tells you where the header will be used.

   Notice the three header text boxes; you can enter distinct information in each and press Return independently in each one so text appears on different lines.

8. **Type the text you want to appear at the top or bottom of each page.**

   Format the text as you would any other text, setting the typeface, size, and style or choosing a style associated with the template.

9. **To add the date or page number automatically, position the cursor where you want the text to appear, and then choose Insert⇨Page Number/Page Count/Date & Time from the Pages menu bar.**

To format the Date & Time, double-click the inserted text. A window opens, as shown in Figure 3-12, giving you format choices and the option to update the date whenever the file is opened.

To format the page numbers, click the Section tab in the Setup pane and then click the Format pop-up menu to choose the number style (Arabic, Roman, or letters).

If your document has multiple sections that you want numbered separately, click the first page of a section in the Page Thumbnails, and then click the Section tab. Select the Start At radio button (which automatically deselects the Continue from Previous Section radio button) and then type the page number with which you want the section to begin, as shown in Figure 3-13.

If you don't want headers to appear on the first page — for example, you create a report that has a cover page — click the Setup icon on the toolbar and then click the Section tab. Select the Hide on First Page of Section check box.

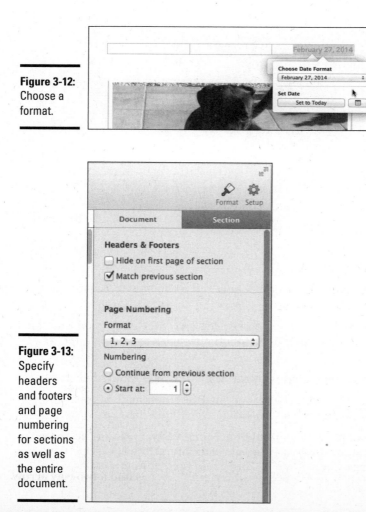

Figure 3-12: Choose a format.

Figure 3-13: Specify headers and footers and page numbering for sections as well as the entire document.

Creating and Placing Text Boxes

As we mention earlier, text boxes hold text that you can place anywhere on a page (even in the middle of other text). You can create and place text boxes on any Pages document, whether created from a blank document or a template.

Creating a text box

To create a text box, follow these steps:

1. **Click the Text icon on the toolbar and choose the paragraph style you want to use for the text in the text box, as shown in Figure 3-14.**

Figure 3-14:
Choose the paragraph style for your new text box.

2. **Type new text inside the text box.**

   Pages keeps your text within the boundaries of the text box.

You can also choose Insert⇨Text Box. The new text box will use the Body paragraph style.

Moving a text box

After you create a text box, you can move it. Simply drag the text box to a new location, even to a different page. If your document is lengthy, you can click the text box, choose Edit⇨Cut, click the destination page in the Pages pane (choose View⇨Show Thumbnail Pages if you don't see it), and then choose Edit⇨Paste to place your text box on the selected page.

Resizing a text box

Sometimes a text box is too large or small for the text you type inside. To fix this problem, resize the text box:

1. **Click anywhere inside the text box.**

2. **Move the pointer to a handle until the pointer turns into a two-way arrow.**

3. **Drag a handle to resize the text box.**

   Handles on the sides resize vertically, making the box longer, or horizontally, making the box taller. Handles on the corners resize proportionally in both directions, making the overall box bigger.

4. **Release the mouse button or lift your finger from the trackpad when you're happy with the size of the text box.**

Uniting text boxes

If you type more text than a text box can display, you see a Clipping Indicator icon, which appears as a plus sign inside a square at the bottom of the text box. When you see the Clipping Indicator at the bottom of a text box, you have two choices.

+ **Enlarge the text box.** You can resize the text box so it can display more text, as we describe in the preceding section. This may not always be practical because your page layout may not accommodate an expanded text box.

+ **Unite two text boxes.** If your text box is limited by the page margins, create another text box on the next page. Click one of the text boxes and then click the Arrange tab in the Format pane. Shift-click both text boxes, and then click the Unite button that appears at the bottom of the Format pane (when Arrange is selected). The two text boxes come together and your text flows from one to the next.

Depending on how much text you have, you can (and may need to) unite multiple text boxes.

Using Styles

You may have a favorite way to format text. Although you could manually change each formatting feature, you may find it faster and easier to use styles instead. Formatting styles store different types of formatting that you can apply to text. The Pages templates have formatting styles stored already. When you create your own documents, you can create formatting styles, too. By using formatting styles, you can format text quickly and consistently with minimum effort.

The following are the types of styles you can apply to text:

+ **Paragraph Styles:** Affect an entire paragraph (or many paragraphs) where the end of a paragraph is defined by a line that ends where you press Return.

+ **Image Styles:** Affect inserted images, applying special effects, borders, fill, and shadows.

+ **Text Box Styles:** Affect text inside a text box. There may be multiple paragraph styles inside a text box, in which case you want to follow the instructions for paragraph styles to apply them to each one in the text box.

Using a paragraph style

To apply a paragraph style, follow these steps:

1. **Drag to select the text you want to modify.**

2. **If you don't see the Format pane, click the Format icon on the toolbar.**

3. **If you're working with text in a text box, click the Text tab. If you chose continuous text, go to Step 4.**

4. **Click the disclosure triangle at the top of the Format pane to open the Paragraph Styles menu, as shown in Figure 3-15.**

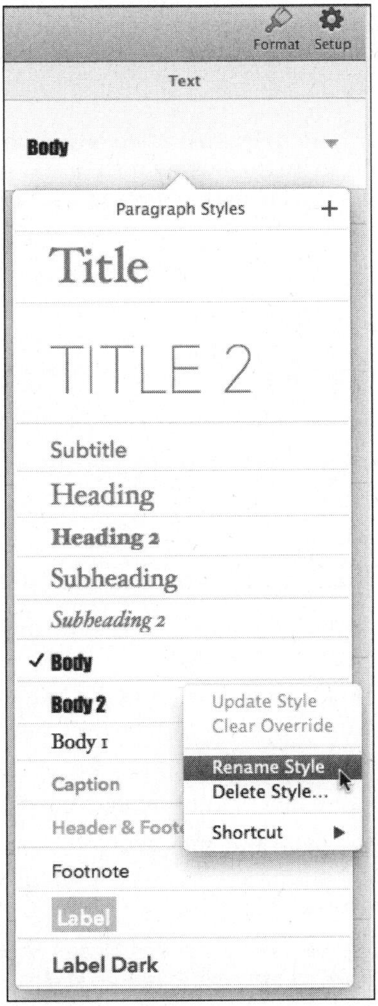

Figure 3-15:
See the paragraph, character, and list styles used in the document.

5. **Choose a style that you want to use for your selected text.**

Pages formats your selected text.

6. **(Optional) Use the Font tools (as we explain in the earlier section "Formatting text") to make changes to the paragraph style, click the disclosure triangle to open the Paragraph Styles menu, and then do one of the following to save the changes:**

- *Create a new paragraph style.* Click the plus sign next to Paragraph Styles. A new style is added to the menu with the name of the original style followed by a number 2. Click this new name in the menu and then click the arrow to the right to open a submenu. Choose Rename Style; the name is highlighted allowing you to type a new name.

- *Save the changes to the existing paragraph style.* Click the name of the original style and then click the arrow to the right to open a submenu. Click Update Style.

From the same pop-up menu, you can delete the style or assign a Hot Key so when you want to apply the style, instead of using the Format pane, you can just select the text and then press the Fn key associated with the style.

Using an image style

To apply a style to an image, follow these steps:

1. **Click the image you want to modify.**

2. **If you don't see the Format pane, click the Format icon on the toolbar.**

3. **Click the Style tab and then click one of the Image Styles, as shown in Figure 3-16.**

Pages formats your selected image.

4. **(Optional) Use the tools to make changes to the image style:**

- *Border:* Surrounds your image with a Line or Picture Frame; define the width, color, and scale of your choice.

- *Shadow:* Creates one of three types of shadows — Drop, Contact, or Curved — behind the entire image. Blur, offset, and opacity settings add more special effects.

- *Reflection:* Adds a mirrored effect of your image under it.

- *Opacity:* Affects the entire image and changes the intensity of all components: the text, fills, and borders. This is a good tool if you want to use the image as a backdrop behind text.

5. **Click the left or right triangle to open a second Image Styles chooser, and then click the plus sign to create a new image style.**

A new style is added to the chooser and the icon shows the effect.

Figure 3-16:
Choose from effects you can add to your images.

Using a text box style

When you create a text box, you can format the text (as we explain in the earlier section, "Formatting text"), and you can format the box itself, adding a background fill color, border, and shadow. Follow these steps:

1. **Click the text box you want to modify.**

   These actions apply to the text box and its contents so if there's more than one text style within the text box, you want to format those individually and then format the text box to apply a fill and/or border.

2. **If you don't see the Format pane, click the Format icon on the toolbar.**

3. **(Optional) Click the Style tab and then click one of the Text Box Styles, if there's only one text style in the text box.**

4. **Use the Fill, Border, Shadow, and Opacity tools to make changes to the image style:**

   With the Fill tool, you can choose the color and style of the color you want behind your text.

   Refer to the previous steps for using Border, Shadow, and Opacity.

5. **Click the left or right triangle to open a second Text Box Styles chooser, and then click the plus sign to create a new text box style.**

   A new style is added to the chooser and the icon shows the effect.

Creating Charts and Tables

As we mention earlier in this chapter, you can insert charts and tables directly from Numbers, which is great when you already have the charts and tables prepared or if you have complex data that's more easily worked with in Numbers. If you're starting from scratch, it may be quicker to build your chart or table directly in Pages. *Charts* are pie charts or bar charts that graphically represent data. *Tables* comprise rows and columns of information where the intersection of a row and a column is a *cell.*

Adding and removing a chart

Sometimes presenting your information as a chart makes your information easier to understand. To add a chart to a Pages document, follow these steps:

1. **Choose Insert⇨Chart⇨*Chart Type* or click the Charts icon on the Pages toolbar, and then choose the type of chart you want to create — bar, pie, 2-D or 3-D, for example.**

   A chart appears.

2. **Click the Edit Chart Data button at the bottom of the chart.**

   The Chart Data Editor appears, as shown in Figure 3-17.

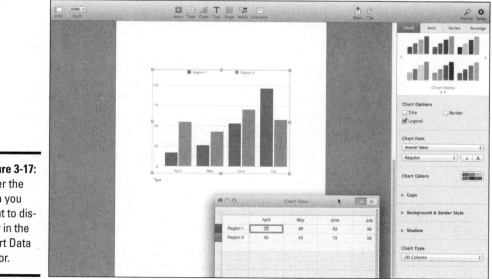

Figure 3-17: Enter the data you want to display in the Chart Data Editor.

3. **Double-click the Row and Column field headers of the Chart Data Editor to select the placeholder text and enter the information you want on your chart.**

4. **Click the cells below the headers to enter the number values you want the chart to show.**

   The data entered appears in the chart and titles.

5. **Click the Switch Axis buttons in the upper-right corner of the Chart Data Editor to invert the axis.**

6. **Click the Format icon to open the Format pane and then click the following tabs to choose how you want the data to appear:**

   - *Chart:* Change the chart color scheme (Chart Styles), the typeface, and size; add gaps between columns; add backgrounds, borders, and shadow; and even change the chart type.

   - *Axis:* Edit the axis options and value labels on the axis.

   - *Series:* Edit value labels on the bars and add trendlines.

   - *Arrange:* Wrap text around the chart and align and distribute its position among other objects on your document, such as text boxes and images.

     See Book V, Chapter 5, where we present Numbers. Read that chapter for detailed instructions about formatting charts.

To remove a chart, click it and press Delete.

Adding a table

Tables in Pages are *calculable*, which means that you can write formulas or insert functions in much the same way you would in Numbers. These are the steps for adding a table to your document:

1. **Choose Insert⇨Table⇨*Table Type* or click the Table icon on the Pages toolbar.**

   A blank table appears on your document.

2. **Edit the size of the rows and columns of your table by clicking the row and column headers and dragging to change their sizes.**

3. **Click the add rows or add columns button next to the far ends of the row and column headers and use the up and down arrows on the pop-up menu to set the number of rows and columns, as shown in Figure 3-18.**

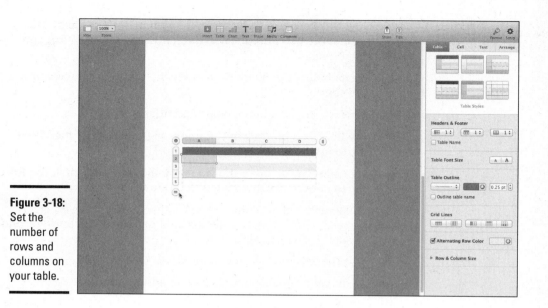

Figure 3-18:
Set the number of rows and columns on your table.

4. **Click the Format icon on the toolbar to see the Format pane, if it's not open.**

5. **Click the tabs to edit the table as follows:**

   • *Table:* Change the table color and layout scheme (Table Styles), and use the menus to set the number of header rows and columns and footer rows, select the table font size, and add a table outline and grid lines.

   • *Cell:* Select all the cells or a portion of them and then choose the data format you want to use to fill the cells and add fill and border to the cells.

   • *Text:* Edit the font and text alignment.

   • *Arrange:* Wrap text around the table and align and distribute its position among other objects on your document, such as text boxes and images.

6. **Set up functions and conditional formats by entering numerical data in a row or column of cells.**

   Type an equals sign to open the Functions pane and then assign a function — for example, sum or average — to the cell at the end of the row or column.

   See Book V, Chapter 5, where we present Numbers. Read that chapter for detailed instructions about formatting tables and writing formulas and using functions.

Adding shapes

Shapes add interest to your documents and make a good alternative to using background fill and border for your text. For example, you can create an interesting shape and then place a text box over it. (See the next section, "Arranging objects," to learn about positioning the two.) So rather than have a boring rectangle of text with a colored background, you can have a polygon with the text on it. If you use the Wrap Text tool that follows the contours of the shape, your text takes on the polygon shape, too. With your document open to the page where you want to insert a shape, follow these steps:

1. **Click the Shape icon on the toolbar and click the left and right arrows to flip through the color selections, as shown in Figure 3-19.**

2. **Choose the shape you want.**

   Your selected shape appears on the page with active resizing handles.

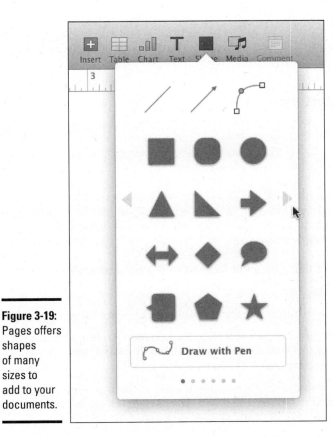

Figure 3-19:
Pages offers
shapes
of many
sizes to
add to your
documents.

Most shapes have green grabber dots that you drag to change the shape or size of the shape. Hover the cursor over one of the green dots until it changes from an arrow to a plus sign, and then drag to see how the shape changes. For example, dragging clockwise or counter-clockwise on the star or polygon increases or decreases the number of points on the star and the number of sides on the polygon. The grabber dot on the quote bubble or square moves the direction of the angle that points to another object.

3. **Click the shape and grab a *resizing handle* — one of the squares on the box that surrounds the shape — to enlarge or reduce the shape to the size you want.**

4. **Drag the shape to better position it on the page.**

5. **Click the shape, click the Format icon on the toolbar, and click the Style tab in the Format pane.**

6. **Click the options you see to change the color of the shape or add special effects, such as fill, shadow, and borders to the shape.**

To add text to your shape, create a text box (as we explain earlier) and drag it over your shape. Then edit the text. See the next section to learn about aligning objects.

Arranging objects

In your documents, you often have multiple shapes, objects, and images that may overlap. Sometimes one object even hides another and you almost go crazy trying to find it. Arranging and aligning objects can help keep everything in view and neatly . . . well . . . arranged.

Think of the shapes, objects, and so on as a stack of paper. If the bigger or darker sheet is on top, it hides what's underneath. You have to rearrange the order of your objects in order to see them all. To reveal objects that may be hidden by others, follow these steps:

1. **Click the object that you want to send to the bottom of the stack.**

2. **Choose Arrange⇨Send to Back.**

   Anything that was hidden by that object now appears on top of it.

3. **Click the other objects one at a time and choose Arrange⇨Send Back, Arrange⇨Bring to Front, or Arrange⇨Bring Forward until you're satisfied with the appearance of your page.**

   Text boxes are most useful when positioned as the top item on the stack, so most of the time, you want to choose Arrange⇨Bring to Front so your text boxes rest on top of other shapes or images.

After you have the objects in the positions you like, you can create groups or lock the objects.

4. **To create a group of objects, select your objects and then choose Arrange⇨Group.**

   The objects stay together and move together.

5. **To lock objects, select a single object, a group, or multiple objects, and then choose Arrange⇨Lock.**

   The locked objects or group are unmovable, undeleteable, and uneditable. (You can, however, copy or duplicate the locked object.) To unlock the objects, choose Arrange⇨Unlock.

Alignment refers to how objects are placed in relationship to each other. To align your shapes or objects, do the following:

1. **Hold down the Shift key and click the objects you want to align.**

   Resizing handles appear around each selected object.

2. **Choose Arrange⇨Align Objects or Arrange⇨Distribute Objects.**

   - *Align Objects:* Lets you align the left, right, top, or bottom sides of the objects, or the vertical or horizontal centers.

   - *Distribute Objects:* Evenly distributes the selected objects between the two farthest objects; choose horizontal or vertical.

Wrapping text around an object

When you insert a text box, photo, or chart inside continuous text or a text box, it sits on top of the existing text. To neatly separate the text and object, you want to *wrap* the text around the object. Follow these steps:

1. **Click the object, be it a text box, photo, or chart.**

2. **Click the Format icon on the toolbar or choose View⇨Show Inspector⇨Format.**

3. **Click the Arrange tab, as shown in Figure 3-20.**

4. **Click a text-wrap pop-up menu and choose one of the following:**

   - *Automatic:* Pages determines the best distribution for the object in the text.

   - *Around:* The text surrounds all sides of the object.

   - *Above and Below*: The text appears above and below the object, but the space to the left and right is clear.

   - *None:* The object will sit on top of the text.

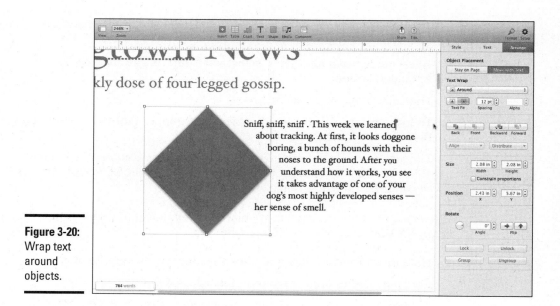

Figure 3-20: Wrap text around objects.

5. **If you choose any of the choices in Step 4 except None, click one of the Text Fit buttons to have the text create a rectangle around the object (left button) or flow around the contours of the object (right button).**

6. **Type in the Spacing field or use the up and down arrows to indicate the amount of space between the object and the text.**

Polishing Your Document

When you finish designing your document, you're ready to show it to the world. Of course, before you show your document to others, you should proofread your document for grammar and spelling. Fortunately, Pages is happy to help you check a document's spelling.

Spell-checking a document

Pages can spell-check your entire document, including text trapped inside text boxes and shapes. To spell-check an entire document, follow these steps:

1. **Choose Edit⇨Spelling and Grammar⇨Show Spelling and Grammar.**

    If you choose Edit⇨Spelling and Grammar⇨Check Document Now, Pages underlines words it thinks are misspelled, but it doesn't offer any suggestions.

A dialog appears, highlighting misspelled words and offering possible corrections, as shown in Figure 3-21.

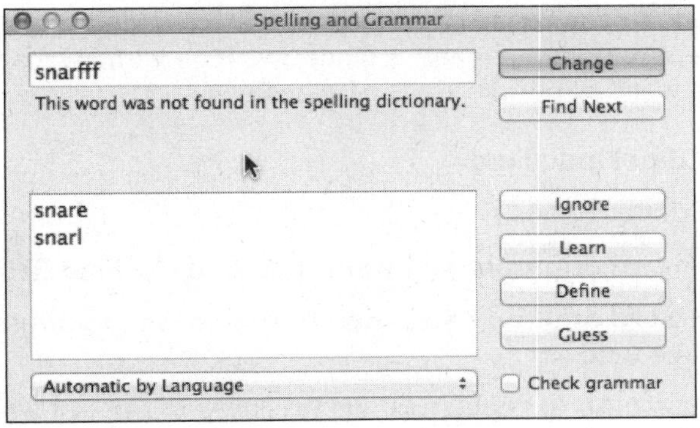

Figure 3-21:
Check spelling and grammar.

2. Click one of the following:

- *Change:* Changes the misspelled word with the word selected in the list box

- *Find Next:* Looks for the next misspelled word

- *Ignore:* Skips the misspelled word

- *Learn:* Stores the selected word in the Pages dictionary

- *Define:* Launches Mac's Dictionary application and displays the word's definition in the Dictionary's main window

- *Guess:* Offers best-guess word choices

3. Click the Close button of the Spelling dialog at any time to make it go away.

By default, Pages checks your spelling while you type. When Pages identifies a misspelled word, it underlines it with a red dotted line. If you Control-click any word underlined with a red dotted line, Pages displays a shortcut menu of correctly spelled words that you can choose. If you want to turn off spell-checking while you type, choose Edit⇨Spelling and Grammar⇨Check Spelling While Typing to clear the check mark for this command.

Proofreading your document is a good idea, even after spell-checking, because the spell checker only makes sure that the word is correctly spelled. If you type, "I have to dogs," when you really meant to type, "I have two dogs," no spell checker is going to flag that.

Finding and replacing text

Pages can also find and replace words or phrases. Say you're writing an article about a person named Swanson, only to realize that just before you send the article to your editor that the name is spelled Swansen. Pages will search your entire document and replace Swanson with Swansen. To find and replace a word or phrase, do the following:

1. **Choose Edit⊃Find⊃Find.**

The Find dialog opens.

2. **Type the word or phrase you want to find in the Find field.**

3. **Type the word or phrase you want to replace the found text with in the Replace field.**

4. **Click Replace All to replace all occurrences of the old word with the new word, or click Next to find the first occurrence of the word or phrase, and then do one of the following:**

- *Click Replace* to replace the old word with the new one. You have to click Next to highlight the next occurrence.

- *Click Replace & Find* to replace the highlighted word and find the next occurrence. (This saves you from having to click Replace and then click Next.)

5. **Continue reviewing the occurrences by repeating Step 4.**

Clicked the Advanced button (it looks like a gear) to see the following options:

✦ **Match Case:** Select this check box to have Pages distinguish uppercase and lowercase letters and find text *exactly* as you type it.

✦ **Whole Words:** Select this check box to ignore whole words that contain your text. If, for example, you search for *place* and select this option, *placemat* or *placement* won't be highlighted.

Saving Your Documents on Your Mac or iCloud

A handy feature of the iWork suite is that you can save your documents to iCloud and then access them from the apps on other devices where you have the Pages app installed and iCloud activated or from the iCloud website on other computers. This saves you from copying your document to a flash drive or e-mailing it to yourself.

Before you can use this feature, you have to turn on Pages in iCloud preferences by doing the following:

1. **Choose ⌘⊃System Preferences and click the iCloud icon.**

2. **Scroll down, select the Documents & Data check box, and then click the Options button.**

3. **Select the Pages check box.**

4. **Click Done and then click Close to exit System Preferences.**

To save your documents, choose File⇨Save. In the Save As window that opens, type a name for your document, and then click the Where pop-up menu, as shown in Figure 3-22, to choose iCloud or another destination folder, drive, or server. Click the disclosure triangle next to Save As to expand the window and scroll through your folders and directories.

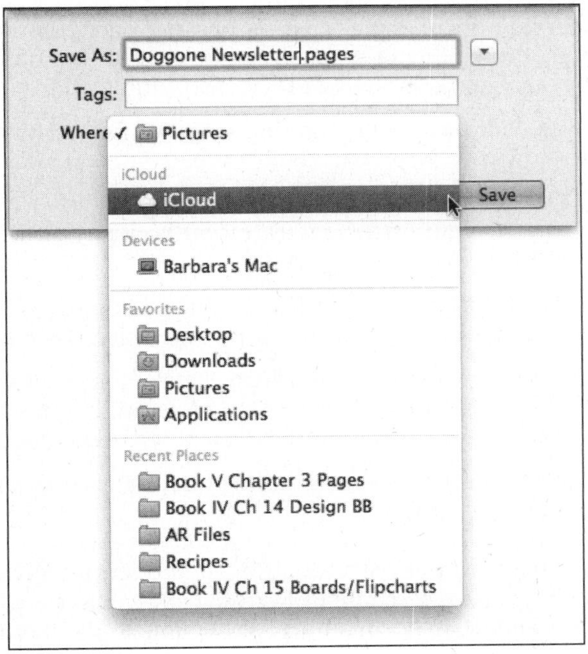

Figure 3-22:
Save your
documents
to your Mac
or to iCloud.

Printing Your Documents

You can print and distribute your document in the traditional way — as good old-fashioned hard copy — by following these steps:

1. **Choose File⇨Print.**

2. **Choose your printer, settings, number of copies, and page range.**

3. **Click the Print button.**

When your document comes out of the printer, you can hand it to someone, hang it up, or put a stamp on it and drop it in your local mailbox.

Exporting to a Different File Format

Chances are that you'll want to share your document electronically, too. However, as much as you love your Mac and Pages, not everyone uses the same types of computers or applications. Don't let that stop you from sharing your document files, though, because Pages can export files in diverse formats.

Although Pages saves documents in its own proprietary file format when you choose File⇨Save, if you want to share your Pages documents with others who don't have the Pages application, you can export your document into another file format by using these options:

✦ **PDF:** Saves your document as a series of static pages stored in the PDF Adobe Acrobat file format that can be viewed (but not necessarily edited) by any computer with a PDF viewing application.

✦ **Word:** Saves your document as a Microsoft Word file, which can be opened by any word processor that can read and edit Microsoft Word files.

✦ **Plain Text:** Saves your document as text without any formatting or graphic effects.

✦ **ePub:** Saves your document in a format that can be read in iBooks on an iPad, iPod touch, or iPhone as well as on many electronic readers.

✦ **Pages '09:** Saves your document a Pages '09 document. If you're sharing your document with someone who hasn't upgraded to the latest version of Pages, this is a way to be sure they can access your document.

✦ **ZIP Archive:** Compresses your document and saves it as a file that can easily be shared or stored.

The PDF file format preserves all formatting, but it doesn't let anyone edit that file unless they use a separate PDF-editing application, such as Adobe Acrobat Pro. If someone needs to edit your document, the Word option preserves Pages documents well. The Plain Text option is useful only if you can't transfer your Pages document to another application as a Word file.

To export a Pages document, follow these steps:

1. **Choose File⇨Export To⇨*File Type*.**

   A dialog appears.

2. **Select an option, such as Word or ePub, and then click Next.**

3. **In the dialog that appears, enter a name for your exported document in the Save As text box.**

4. **Select the folder where you want to store your document.**

   You may need to switch drives or folders until you find where you want to save your file.

5. **Click Export.**

When you export a document, your original Pages document remains untouched in its original location.

You can also share your documents as a Mail or Messages attachment or make them available on iCloud or AirDrop, not to mention social networking sites. See the end of Book V, Chapter 4, to learn about sharing. It works the same for Pages as for Keynote.

Chapter 4: Presenting with Keynote

In This Chapter

- ✔ Creating a presentation
- ✔ Adding, editing, and formatting text
- ✔ Working with shapes, charts, and tables
- ✔ Inserting photos and movies
- ✔ Changing the order of slides
- ✔ Using transitions and effects
- ✔ Customizing themes with masters
- ✔ Giving a presentation

*P*resentations used to be confined to the realm of professional conferences and shareholder meetings. With or without a projector, the combination of your Mac and Keynote ($19.99 at the App Store), makes it cost effective and time efficient to give presentations at weekly staff meetings, set up an interactive kiosk at the local small-business fair, or even post your presentation on your website. Keynote syncs with iCloud so you can access your presentations on all your devices such as an iPhone or iPad or on another computer from the iCloud website. Keynote enhances your creativity with ready-made templates so you can concentrate more of your time on talking to an audience and less of your time fumbling around with jammed slide projectors, whiteboards, and felt markers that stain your fingertips.

Best of all, you can spice up your presentation with tables, charts, and audio and visual effects, from playing music and movies to showing visually interesting effects — stuff like text sliding across the display or dissolving away into nothingness. Such effects help get your point across and hold an audience's attention.

In this chapter, we begin our presentation (pardon the pun) with the Keynote basics: working with themes and slide layouts, replacing placeholder text and media with your text and media, and adding charts, tables, and animation. At the end of the chapter, we give you tips for practicing your presentation and tell you about the options you have for running the presentation even without being present. When you're up to speed on the basics, check out Book V, Chapter 6, which shows you some nifty tricks that work across all three iWork applications.

Keynote is part of the iWork suite. If you bought a new Mac after November 2013, the iWork apps are included. If you have an older Mac, you can purchase and download Keynote from the App Store for $19.99.

Creating a Presentation

A Keynote presentation consists of one or more slides, where typically each slide displays information to make a single point. Although our sample slide in Figure 4-1 shows only text and a graphic, a slide can include charts, graphics, photos, video, and audio as well.

Figure 4-1: The appearance of a typical slide.

To make your presentation even more interesting to watch, you can add *transition* effects that appear when you switch from one slide to another. To emphasize the information on a particular slide, you can add individual visual effects, known as *builds,* to specific items, such as making text rotate or making a graphic image glide across the screen and halt in place.

We explain how to add all these embellishments to your presentation in the sections that follow; however, the basic steps to creating a presentation in Keynote are:

1. Pick a theme to use for your presentation.

2. Create one or more slides.

3. Type text or place graphics and images on each slide.

4. (Optional) Add an audio or video file to each slide.

5. (Optional) Add visual effects to animate an entire slide or just the text or graphics that appear on that slide.

Of course, you have to open the Keynote app to begin. Click the Keynote icon in the Dock or on the Launchpad. One of the following happens:

✦ If you didn't turn on Keynote in iCloud, the themes chooser opens and you can skip ahead to the next section.

✦ If you turned Keynote on in the Documents & Data section of iCloud, (refer to Book III, Chapter 2) you have to first choose where you want to work: iCloud or Mac. When you open Keynote to create a new document or work on an existing one, the window shown in Figure 4-2 opens.

   Click iCloud or On My Mac to choose where you want to save your document, and then click New Document to open the Choose a Theme dialog and proceed as explained in the next section.

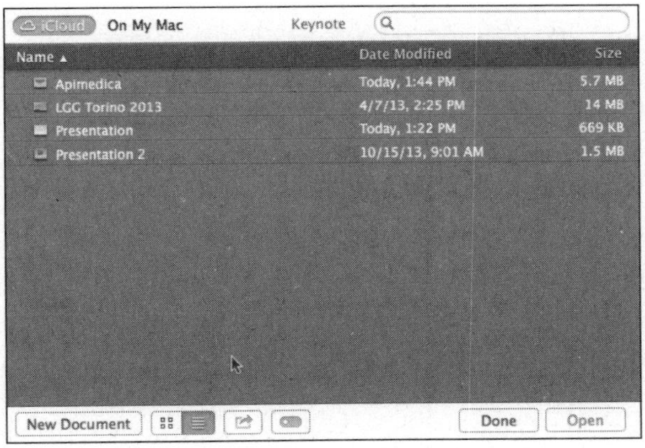

Figure 4-2:
Save your
Keynote
presenta-
tions on
iCloud or On
My Mac.

Choosing a theme and saving your presentation

A presentation consists of multiple slides. Although a black-and-white presentation can be elegant in a retro sort of way, color helps attract and keep your audience's attention. To make the creation of your presentation easier, Keynote provides *themes* that give your slides a consistent appearance, such as the font, size, style, and background color. Within each of the 30 themes, there are multiple *slide layouts,* which are templates for your slides. Each slide layout in a theme is a *master slide,* which defines the look of each slide you create based on the layout. We explain how to work with, and create, master slides in the section "Using Masters" later in this chapter. Most themes have the following slide layouts:

✦ Title, top or center

✦ Title and subtitle

✦ Title and bullets

✦ Title, bullets, and photo

✦ Bullet list

✦ Photo (horizontal, vertical, three-up, or full-page photo)

✦ Quote

✦ Blank

Each theme offers a standard and wide (HD) format. Make sure you decide which you want to use before creating your presentation.

If you want to create a presentation without using a theme — say you want your presentation to reflect your corporate color scheme and font family — pick a simple theme, such as Black or White, to start so you have multiple slide layouts to which you can apply your desired color scheme, fonts, and so on.

To pick a theme, follow these steps:

1. **Open Keynote from the Dock or Launchpad.**

   (If you use Keynote in iCloud, choose the destination for your presentation, and then click New Document.)

   The Choose a Theme dialog opens, as shown in Figure 4-3.

2. **Choose the slide format from the tabs at the top of the window: Standard (4:3) format or Wide (16:9) format.**

   Standard size slides echo traditional, square-ish 35mm slides and work well if you connect a projector to your Mac. Choose the Wide format when you plan to connect your Mac to a wide-screen HD monitor. If you're not sure which you'll be using, choose Wide as most projectors can accommodate wide but you don't risk having black horizontal borders on your slides when projected on a wide-screen monitor.

Figure 4-3:
Keynote provides a variety of themes for your presentations.

3. **Click a theme and click the Choose button or double-click a theme.**

   Keynote creates the first slide of your presentation, using your chosen theme. At this point, you can add text, graphics, audio, or video to the slide or you can add new slides.

4. **Choose File⇨Save.**

   A Save As dialog opens.

5. **Type a name for your presentation.**

6. **Type any tags you want to attach to the file or choose existing ones from the pop-up menu.**

   You can use tags to find files in Spotlight Search.

7. **Click the Where pop-up menu if you want to switch the destination between Mac and iCloud or choose another destination folder or volume. If you don't see the folder where you want to save your presentation, follow Step 8.**

8. **(Optional) If you're saving to your Mac, click the disclosure triangle next to the Save As field to see the directories and folders on your Mac or local network and choose the location where you want to store the file.**

9. **Click Save.**

If you want to save a copy of your presentation to another location, choose File⇨Save and then select where you want to save a copy from the pop-up menus.

If, instead, you want to move the presentation from your Mac to iCloud or vice versa, or to an external disk or flash drive, choose File⇨Move To and then select the new location from the pop-up menu. This action removes the presentation from its original location and places it on the new one.

Opening an existing file

If you're working on a document on one source, such as your Mac, and you want to open a document from another source, such as iCloud or an external drive, choose File⇨Open, and do one of the following:

✦ **From iCloud:** Click iCloud, click one of the documents in the list, and then click Open. (You need an Internet connection to work on iCloud documents.)

✦ **From your Mac or external drive:** Click On My Mac, scroll through the directories and folders to find an existing document you want to work on, click it, and then click Open. Choose On My Mac to access external drives and volumes shared on your local network, too.

You can also use Keynote to open a presentation created in another presentation app, and then use it as is, make changes, even save it as a Keynote file. To open a non-Keynote presentation, such as Microsoft's PowerPoint, drag the file you want to open over the Keynote icon in the Dock or follow the steps outlined in the preceding paragraphs.

Finding your way around Keynote

After you create a presentation, the Keynote slide editor window opens as shown in Figure 4-4. Across the top of the Keynote window, you see the Toolbar, which holds buttons for the most frequently used functions. Below the Toolbar is the Format bar, which has pop-up menus for formatting the text and objects on your slides. We explain both the Toolbar and Format bar functions throughout this chapter.

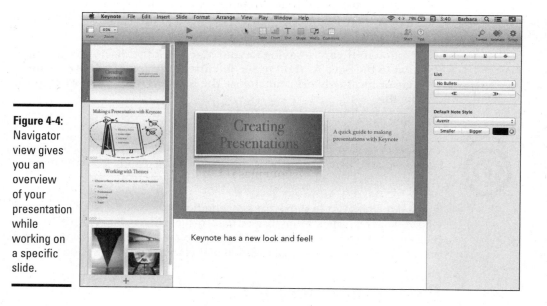

Figure 4-4: Navigator view gives you an overview of your presentation while working on a specific slide.

The window can have between one and three panels in the four available views. To switch to a different view, choose the View icon on the Keynote toolbar and then choose Navigator, Outline, Slide Only, or Light Table.

This is what you see in each view:

✦ **Navigator:** Useful for editing individual slides and manipulating all the slides in an entire presentation. Referring to Figure 4-4, you can see that thumbnails of your slides are displayed in the Slide Navigator in the left pane, the slide you're editing is in the center panel, and the Format pane is on the right.

✦ **Slide Only:** Useful for editing the text and graphics of a single slide. The Slide Navigator pane closes, but you still have all the formatting tools available in the Format pane.

✦ **Light Table:** You see all your slides together, as in Figure 4-5. You can click and drag slides to a new position or change the slide layout by choosing a new one from the Format pane. Move the slider at the bottom of the left pane to show more, but smaller, slides or fewer, larger slides. When you double-click a slide in Light Table, it opens in the most recent of the three other views you used. This view is particularly useful for manipulating a large number of slides in a presentation,

In both Navigator and Light Table views, slides with audio or movie media have three empty circles in the lower-left corner of the slide thumbnail image.

Audio/video indicators

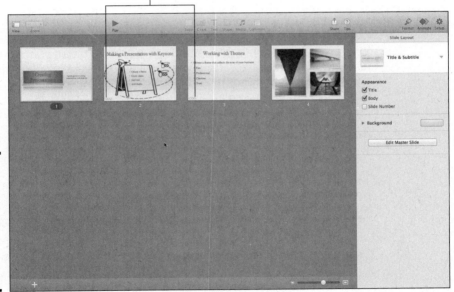

Figure 4-5:
Light Table
view dis-
plays slides
in rows and
columns
for easy
rearranging.

✦ **Outline:** Similar to Navigator view but instead of seeing thumbnail images in the Slide Navigator, you see the text of each slide, which you can edit, and the edits are reflected on the slides. Choose Keynote➪Preferences➪General to choose the font size you want to use in Outline View.

In addition to the presentation views, you can choose additional items you may want to see in the window. Choose View and then choose from these options:

✦ **Show/Hide Rulers (not available in Light Table view):** Use the rulers as a reference when working with objects on your slide.

✦ **Show/Hide Comments:** This is useful if other people comment on your presentation before or after you give it.

✦ **Show/Hide Presenter Notes (not available in Light Table view):** These are notes that you can view when giving your presentation. You see the notes on your computer below the slide preview, which helps you remember what you want to say, but the projected presentation displays only your slides. When you select Show Presenter Notes, you can type your speech or reminders on each slide.

To change the font or create a list format of notes, click the Presenter Notes section, and then click the Format icon in the toolbar (refer to Figure 4-4); make your choices from the buttons and menus you see.

Adding slides

When you create a new presentation, that presentation starts out containing just one slide. Because getting your idea across usually needs more than one slide, you probably want to add more slides. If you go overboard and add too many slides, you can always winnow a few.

Adding a blank slide

To add a blank slide to a presentation, do one of the following:

✦ Choose Slide⇨New Slide on the menu bar (any view). The new, blank slide appears at the end of the presentation.

✦ Control-click a slide, and choose New Slide (all but Full Slide view). The new blank slide appears after the slide you clicked.

✦ Click a slide in the Slide Navigator or Light Table view and press Return. The new blank slide appears after the slide you clicked.

Adding predefined slides

Each Keynote theme has a selection of slide layouts that you can use to build your presentation. When you use a slide layout, you need only insert your text and images in the existing placeholders, and that makes presentation creation a snap. The slide layout structures are more or less the same for each theme, but the colors, style, and fonts that have been applied make each theme different.

To create a new slide with a slide layout, click the slide before the location where you want to insert a new slide, and then click the New (+) icon in Slide Navigator, Light Table, or Outline view. Choose the slide layout you want, as shown in Figure 4-6. You can change the slide layout later, even after you add your own text and images — we tell you how in just a bit.

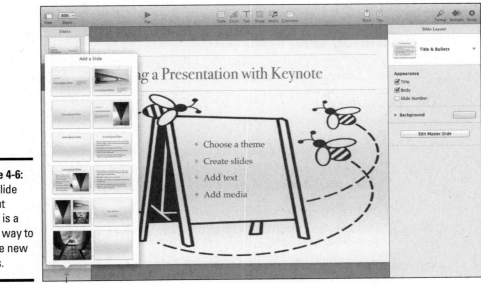

Figure 4-6:
The Slide
Layout
menu is a
quick way to
create new
slides.

New

Making duplicate slides

Making duplicate slides is helpful if you want to use the exact same header or layout on multiple slides. Even if you use slide layouts, you may tweak them and want to duplicate your efforts. Here's how:

+ **Duplicate one slide.** Click the slide you want to duplicate and choose Edit⇨Duplicate, or Control-click and choose Duplicate. The new, duplicate slide appears immediately after the original.

+ **Duplicate multiple slides.** To duplicate more than one slide at once, hold down the Shift key and click the first and last slides of a series you want to duplicate, or hold the ⌘ key and click individual, noncontiguous slides; then do either of the previous commands to duplicate all the slides you chose. The dupes will be inserted after the last selected slide.

If you want to create a duplicate of your entire presentation, choose File⇨Duplicate.

Manipulating Text

Whether it's a title, subtitle, bulleted list, quote, or descriptive paragraph, text on a slide is written in a text box — although the box borders can be invisible. Most slides contain at least one text box that holds the title of the slide. Other text may be free-flowing or even a bulleted list that's inserted in a graphic, like you see earlier in Figure 4-1.

Entering text

When you create a new slide, unless you choose the blank slide, the slide layout has text placeholders in text boxes and perhaps placeholder media, depending on the layout you choose. You replace the placeholders with your own words and images. For now, we're going to talk about text. To place text on a slide, follow these steps:

1. **Choose View⇨Navigator on the menu or toolbar.**

2. **In the Navigator, click the slide that you want to edit or create a new slide using one of the methods we outlined previously.**

   Your chosen slide appears.

3. **Double-click the placeholder text that appears in the Title, Subtitle, or Bullet Point text box.**

4. **Type text or use the arrow keys and Delete key to edit existing text.**

   The text style matches that shown in the placeholder text.

Inserting text boxes

Even when you work with a slide layout that contains text boxes, you can add your own. Click the slide where you want to place the text box. Click the Text icon in the Toolbar, and then click the text style you want to use. A text box appears on the slide in that style. Click and drag the text box to the position you want on the slide. Resize the text box by clicking and dragging the resizing handles (those small boxes that appear on the corners and in the middle of each edge). Double-click the word *text* to erase it, and then type the text you want on your slide.

If you want to delete a text box, click it once and then press the Delete key on the keyboard.

Editing text

To edit text that you've already entered, you have two choices:

+ **In Outline view:** Select the text you want to edit in the Slide Navigator, as shown in Figure 4-7. You can change the titles, and add and delete bullets. Select a bulleted item and click and drag it by the bullet to move it up or down in the list or move it to another slide. Double-click the slide icon to collapse and hide the text.

✦ **In Navigator or Slide Only view:** Double-click a word to highlight and change it or click and drag to select blocks of text you want to edit within the text boxes on the slide. Make the changes you want.

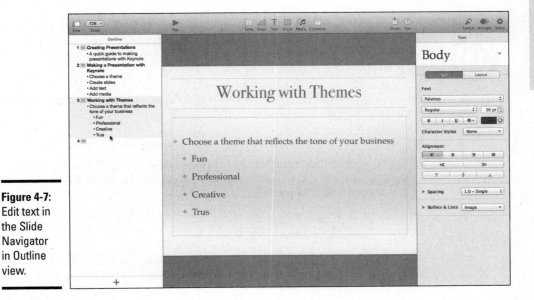

Figure 4-7:
Edit text in the Slide Navigator in Outline view.

To ensure that you don't give a presentation filled with typos and misspelled words, check the spelling in your presentation by choosing Edit⇨Spelling and Grammar⇨Check Spelling While Typing.

Formatting text and text boxes

Themes have predefined fonts, font sizes, and colors that create a coordinated design throughout the presentation and, quite frankly, make creating a presentation a snap. Nonetheless, you can format the text if you want by changing fonts, font sizes, or colors.

Use fonts and colors sparingly. Using too many fonts or colors can make text harder to read. When choosing text colors, make sure that you use colors that contrast with the slide's background color. For instance, light yellow text against a white or light-colored background is nearly impossible to read.

Any time you want to edit or change the style of an object, be it text, a shape, photo, chart, or table, click the object, and then click the Format icon in the toolbar. Click the tabs in the Format panel to see the editing and style options you can apply to the selected object. See the following sections for more details on formatting fonts, paragraphs, bullets, and backgrounds.

Changing fonts

Most likely, you've changed fonts in other programs, and the procedure in Keynote is fairly similar. If you'd like to select a different font, and/or change the font size or color, follow the instructions here.

Changing a font on a slide will change only that slide. If you want to make the same change to all slides in your presentation, you want to change the Master Slide, and we dedicate a section to that topic further along in this chapter.

After you've selected the text, you can edit fonts with the Format menu or follow these steps:

1. **Click the Text tab and then the Style button in the Format pane.**

2. **If you want to use a different font style that's part of your chosen theme, click the disclosure triangle next to the sample font to open the Paragraph Styles menu.**

   A list of styles appears from which you can choose a different one.

   Or

3. **If you want to change the typeface, size, or style, in the Font section, scroll through the Family menus to select the options you want.**

   The Family menu shows the typefaces as they are to help you imagine your presentation using that font.

4. **Click the font family when you find it, and then click the Typeface, Size, and Style menus and buttons to make those changes to your type.**

   The text on your slide changes to reflect the typeface, style, and size.

5. **(Optional) Click the gear icon to open the Advanced Options menu, as shown in Figure 4-8.**

6. **(Optional) Click the Colors icon to change the color of the font.**

   The color swatch opens a chooser that displays colors used in the theme. The color-wheel icon next to the color swatch opens the Colors window, as shown in Figure 4-9. Here's how to choose colors in the Colors window:

   a. *Click the color picker you prefer: Wheel, (which is the default), Slider, Palette, Spectrum, or Crayons. The color pickers give you different ways to choose colors. Click through to see which you're most comfortable using.*

   b. *Click the desired color in the color picker that appears in the Colors window.*

   c. *(Optional) In the color wheel, make the color lighter or darker by dragging the slider on the right side up and down.*

   d. *(Optional) In any of the color pickers, adjust the opacity by dragging the opacity slider left and right or type in a precise percentage in the text box to the right.*

   e. *When you have a color you like, drag the color from the color box at the top to the color palette at the bottom. Your color is saved in the palette for future use.*

   f. *Click the close window button or choose View⇨Close Colors.*

Keynote immediately uses your selected color to color the text you selected in Step 3. You can play around until you find a color you like.

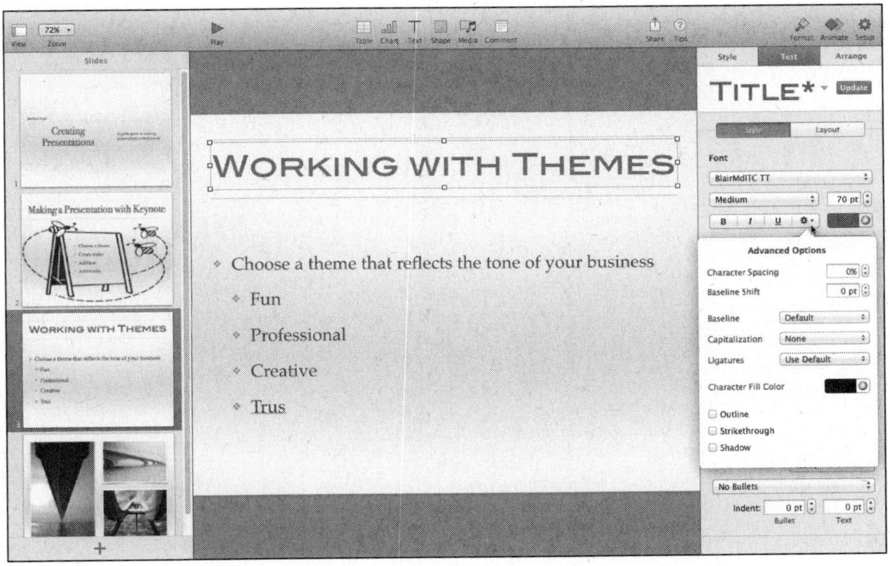

Figure 4-8:
The Text section of the Format panel lets you modify text.

The name in the Paragraph Styles menu changes to reflect the new settings you choose and an asterisk appears next to the name along with an update button (refer to Figure 4-8). You can take the following actions:

✦ **Click Update.** All slides that use that layout will reflect the changes you made.

✦ **Click somewhere else.** Only the slide where you made the change will be changed.

✦ **Click the name in the Paragraph Styles menu.** Choose the original style from the menu to revert to that style, or choose Edit⇨Undo to cancel your change.

Color pickers

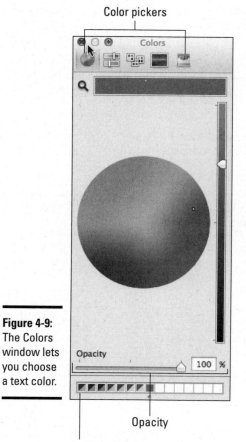

Figure 4-9:
The Colors
window lets
you choose
a text color.

Opacity

Color palette

Fonts aren't part of your presentation, but they reside on the computer from which you give the presentation. If you intend to use your presentation on a different computer, make sure that the fonts you use in your presentation are installed on the other computer, or Keynote will choose what it considers the closest font. So not only could the substitute font be ugly, but words may not fit within text boxes and may be cut off or dropped to a second line that could push lower text off the slide. If you use symbols or special characters, and they aren't available in the substitute font, they'll be replaced by a different symbol or an empty square.

Formatting paragraphs

Although you may not create paragraphs with your text, Keynote considers even a single line a paragraph as far as formatting alignment and vertical spacing of the text in your text boxes. Select the text you'd like to modify and follow these steps:

1. **Click the Text tab and then the Style button in the Format pane.**

2. **Click the horizontal and vertical alignment buttons in the Alignment section and choose one of the following**

   - *Left Alignment* (default): Text is aligned on the left and has a ragged edge on the right.

   - *Center Alignment:* Moves your text to the center, but any bullets you have remain at the left edge of the text box.

   - *Right Alignment:* Aligns your text on the right, and the left edge is ragged; bullets remain on the left edge of the text box.

   - *Justified:* Adjusts the text to have straight edges on the left and right.

   - *Minor adjustment:* Those two buttons below the alignment buttons shift the text one space at a time to the left or to the right.

   - *Upper Alignment:* Moves the text to the top of the text box.

   - *Middle Alignment:* Moves the text to the middle of the text box.

   - *Lower Alignment:* Moves the text to the bottom of the text box.

3. **To change the vertical spacing between the lines of your text, click the disclosure triangle next to Spacing to see the menus shown in Figure 4-10, and choose the distance you want between the lines and before and after paragraphs, if your text box has more than one paragraph.**

TIP

Giving your presentation that something extra

Capitalizing whole words or phrases in your presentation, especially in titles, is EYE-CATCHING. With Keynote, you don't have to use Caps Lock and retype everything if you change your mind. Click Format➪Font➪Capitalization (or choose Capitalization in the Advanced Options window), then choose one of the following

✔ **Title:** Capitalizes the first letter of each word in your selected text, including articles and prepositions.

✔ **All Caps:** Capitalizes all the letters in your selected text.

✔ **Small Caps:** Capitalizes all the letters in your selected text — but in a small size. Any letters you type while holding the Shift key will be big capital letters.

If your text is just a little too long for the space it's in, you can scrunch it together, just barely, so that it fits without using a smaller font size. Choose Format➪Font➪Character Spacing➪Tighten. For more precision, choose Character Spacing in the Advanced Options window and pick a specific percentage to tighten. If the typeface has a condensed variant, choose that for the best results.

Finally, **turn on font smoothing.** Choose ➪System Preferences➪General and select the Use LCD Font Smoothing when Available option. Font smoothing makes the curves and lines of fonts seem less pixelated so they're more recognizable and easier on your eyes.

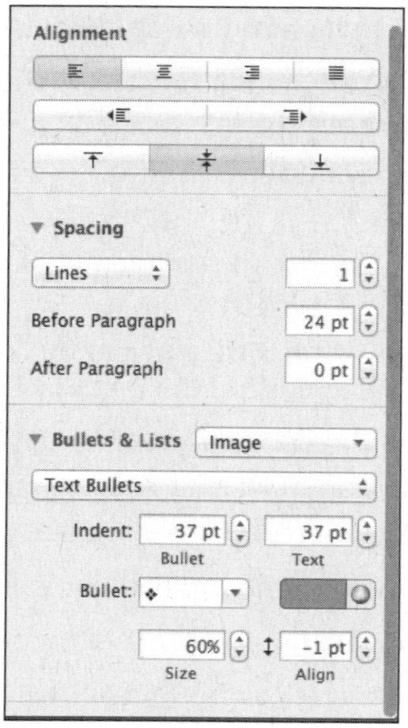

Figure 4-10:
Choose the
distance
between
lines with
the spacing
menu.

Text boxes adjust to the amount of text you type, so if you type more text than space allows, the text box grows as much as it can and then the font size begins to shrink to accommodate the text; delete text, and the font size grows again.

Formatting bullets

As we mention earlier in this chapter, themes come with predefined fonts, colors, styles, and bullets as part of the package. But Keynote offers such a variety of bullets, you may want to have some fun and change them. Select the text and follow these steps to change bullets:

1. **Click the Text tab and then the Style button in the Format pane.**

2. **Click the disclosure triangle next to Bullets to see your choices (refer to Figure 4-10).**

3. **Click the Bullets & Lists pull-down menu to choose the list style you want: Bullet, Image, Lettered, or Numbered.**

4. **Click the next menu to choose the bullet style: None, Text, Image, or Numbers.**

5. **Use the other pop-up menus to make adjustments; menus differ
slightly from one bullet style to another:**

- *Bullet/Number Indent:* Adjusts the distance from the outer edge of the text box and the bullet. The text moves with the bullet.

- *Text Indent:* Adjusts the distance from the outer edge of the text box and the text. The greater the difference between the bullet indent and the text indent, the farther the text is from the bullet.

- *Align:* Sets the vertical position of the bullet in relation to the text.

- *Size:* Alters the size of the bullet.

- *Color/Image:* Lets you edit the color of text or number bullets and the icon used for image bullets.

- *Numbered bullets:* Lets you choose from Arabic, Roman, and outline format, with and without parentheses.

Changing backgrounds and borders

Some text boxes have a background color that's different from the slide background or the box may be outlined by a border or frame. Again, the preset styles are in keeping with the theme you choose, but if you want to change them or you're creating your own custom theme, select the text and follow these steps:

1. **Click the Style tab in the Format pane.**

2. **Click the disclosure triangles next to each option and then choose the options you want from the pop-up menus.**

You see a preview of your choices on the slide, as shown in Figure 4-11.

- *Fill:* Puts a color, gradient, or image behind your text. Depending on the choice, you're presented with tools for choosing the color, the spectrum and direction (gradient), and scaling (image).

- *Border:* Surrounds your text with a Line and Picture Frame; define the width, color, and scale of your choice.

- *Shadow:* Creates one of three types of shadows — Drop, Contact, or Curved — behind the entire text box. Blur, offset, and opacity settings add more special effects.

- *Reflection:* Adds a mirrored effect of your text box under it.

- *Opacity:* Affects the entire text box and changes the intensity of all components: the text, fills, and borders.

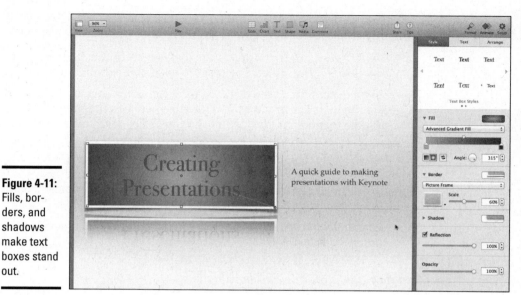

Figure 4-11:
Fills, borders, and shadows make text boxes stand out.

Adding Shapes, Charts, and Tables

One basic principle of a good presentation is giving the audience something interesting to look at. Here's where you get a look at how to use the visual-aid options offered in Keynote.

Inserting predrawn shapes

Shapes can help draw your viewers' eyes to the thing you want them to notice. An arrow can connect your first point to your second; a star makes a key success stand out visually. Keynote comes with three types of simple, straightforward lines, and 12 ready-to-go shapes that you can stretch, shrink, and twist like Silly Putty. If you're an artistic type, there's also a tool for drawing your own shape. Each theme offers the three lines and 12 shapes in a selection of colors associated with the theme, as well as clear. Follow these steps to insert a shape on your slide:

1. **Create a new slide or select the slide you want to put the shape on.**

2. **Click the Shape icon in the Toolbar and click the left and right arrows to flip through the color selection. Choose the shape you want, as shown in Figure 4-12.**

Your selected shape appears on the slide with active resizing handles.

Most shapes have green grabber dots that you drag to change the shape or size of the shape (the cursor in Figure 4-12 points to the grabber dot). Hover the cursor over one of the green dots until it changes from an arrow to a plus sign, and then click and drag to see how the shape changes. For example, dragging clockwise or counter-clockwise on the star or polygon increases or decreases the number of points on the star and the number of sides on the polygon. The grabber dot on the quote bubble or square moves the direction of the angle that points to another object.

3. **Click the shape and grab a resizing handle — one of the squares on the box that surrounds the shape — to enlarge or reduce the shape to the size you want.**

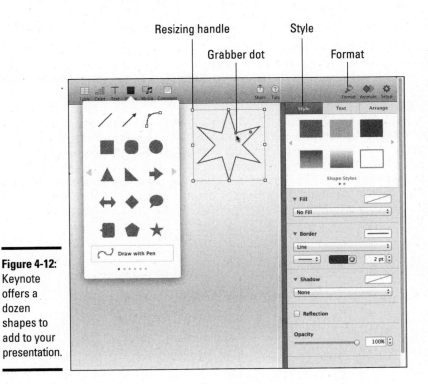

Figure 4-12: Keynote offers a dozen shapes to add to your presentation.

4. **Click and drag the shape to where you want it on your slide.**

5. **Click the shape and then select the Format icon in the Toolbar and the Style tab in the Format pane.**

   Click the options you see to change the color of the shape or add special effects such as fill, shadow, and borders to the shape.

To add text to your shape, create a text box as explained previously and drag it over your shape, and then edit the text. See the next section to learn about aligning objects.

Aligning and arranging objects

When working with multiple shapes, objects, images, and text boxes, you may want to align or overlap them. To align your shapes or objects, do the following:

1. **Hold down the Shift key and click the objects you want to align.**

Resizing handles appear around each selected object.

2. **Choose Arrange⇨Align Objects to align the left, right, top, or bottom sides of the objects, or the vertical or horizontal centers.**

Do it twice to choose the vertical alignment and then the horizontal alignment.

3. **Choose Arrange⇨Distribute Objects to evenly distribute the centers of the selected objects (whatever their size) between the two farthest objects; choose horizontal or vertical.**

Think about the objects on your slide as single pieces of paper, one on top of the other. If the largest piece is on top of the others, you can't see the others. On the other hand, if the largest piece is transparent, you can see what's underneath. You have to rearrange the order in which overlapping objects are stacked. For instance, in Figure 4-13, you can see that you'd want the text box object on the top of the stack. If, instead, the shape were on the top of the stack, you wouldn't see the text — unless, of course, the shape were transparent.

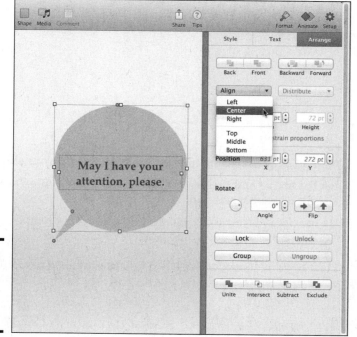

Figure 4-13:
Rearrange and group objects to your liking.

To reveal objects that may be hidden by others, follow these steps:

1. **Click the object that you want to arrange on the bottom of the stack.**

2. **Choose Arrange⇨Send to Back.**

   Anything that was hidden by that object now appears on top of it.

3. **Click the other objects one at a time and choose Arrange⇨Send to Back or Arrange⇨Bring to Front, or Arrange⇨Bring Forward until you're satisfied with the appearance of your slide.**

   Text boxes work best as the top item on the stack, so most of the time you want to choose Arrange⇨Bring to Front for text boxes that rest on top of other shapes or images.

4. **After you have the objects in the positions you like, you can create groups or lock the objects.**

   You have these options:

   • *Select your objects, and then choose Arrange⇨Group.*

     The objects stay together and move together.

   • *Select a single object, a group, or multiple objects, and then choose Arrange⇨Lock.*

     The objects become unmovable, undeletable, and uneditable. You can, however, copy or duplicate the locked object.

Choose Arrange⇨Unlock to unlock previously locked objects.

Instead of using the menus, click the text boxes and shapes you want to work with and then click Format in the toolbar and the Arrange tab in the Format pane. Use the buttons and menus to make adjustments to how the objects are aligned and arranged, as shown earlier in Figure 4-13. You can also resize, reposition, rotate, or flip the objects.

Adding a chart

Sometimes presenting your information as a chart makes your information easier to understand. Essentially, you choose a chart type and then input the information you want to represent. To add a chart to a presentation, follow these steps:

1. **Create a new slide or open an existing slide.**

2. **Click the Chart icon in the Toolbar and click the left and right arrows to flip through the color selection. First click a tab for the type of chart you want (2D, 3D, or Interactive); then choose the chart you want, as shown in Figure 4-14.**

   The chart appears on your slide.

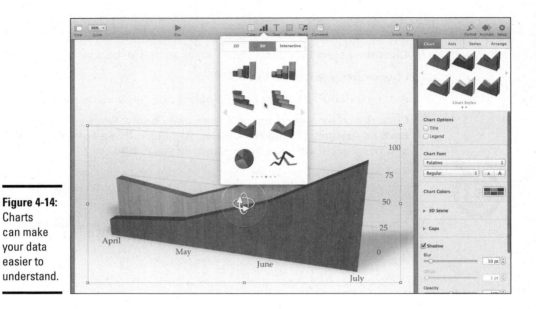

Figure 4-14:
Charts
can make
your data
easier to
understand.

3. **Click the chart on the slide, and then click the Edit Chart Data button.**

   A grid appears where you enter the data for your chart.

4. **Double-click the Row and Column field headers of the Chart Data Editor to select the placeholder text and enter the information you want on your chart.**

5. **Click the cells below the headers to enter the number values you want the chart to show.**

   The data entered appears in the chart and titles on the slide.

   Interactive charts are created the same way as 2D or 3D charts but during the presentation, the data is animated. While preparing the animated chart, use the slider at the bottom to see how each part will be displayed. Click the Play button in the toolbar to preview the animation; press Return when the slide presentation opens and press Esc to return to the Keynote editing screen.

6. **Click Format in the toolbar and then go through the tabs in the Format pane to edit the appearance and position of the chart and data:**

   • *Chart:* Gives you tools for changing the colors and fonts of the chart, as well as adding special effects such as shadow or opacity and a title and/or legend. At the bottom of the panel you find a Chart Type menu; click to change to a different type of chart — any data you entered will appear on the new type.

   • *Axis:* Lets you name the axes and change the scale. (This tab is available for all charts except pie charts.) Here you also find the menus for defining the value labels with percentage, currency, or others.

- *Series:* Offers menus for naming the value labels on charts, excluding pie charts.

- *Wedges:* Shows check boxes and menus for adding labels and defining the value data format in pie charts only. You can move the labels off the chart itself and separate the pieces of the pie by setting a greater distance from center with the respective slider bars.

- *Arrange:* Lets you reposition the chart in relation to other objects on the slide or align it on the slide itself. This doesn't change parts of the chart. (Refer to the previous section "Aligning and arranging objects" to understand how this works.)

- *Axis/Wedge Labels:* Double-click any of the text on the chart and the Axis or Wedge Labels tab appears in the Format panel. Here you can define the label (number, percentage, and so on) and also change the font family, size, style, and color.

7. **(Optional) If you decide that you want to remove a chart, click it, and then press Delete.**

Adding a table

When you add a table in Keynote, it's a fully functioning, calculable table, much as if it had been created in Numbers. These are the steps for adding a table to a slide in your presentation:

1. **Click the Table icon in the Toolbar and click the left and right arrows to flip through the color selection. Click the table you like, and it appears on your slide.**

2. **Change the size of your table by clicking the table and then doing the following:**

   - *Resize the table.* Click and drag the Resize button in the upper-left corner to resize the table. This doesn't add rows and columns but proportionately changes the table size.

   - *Add a row or column.* Click the add button (it has two parallel lines in a circle) at the bottom-left corner to add rows or the upper-right corner to add columns. A mini menu appears. The number indicates the current number of rows or columns; use the up and down arrows to increase or decrease the number. Rows and columns are added to the chart automatically.

   - *Insert or delete a row or column.* Hover the cursor over the row or column identifier (letters for columns, numbers for rows) of the column to the left of, or above, where you want to insert a new row or column. Click the disclosure arrow that appears to open a menu that gives you choices to insert a row or column before or after the one you selected. You can also delete the row or column you selected.

- *Adjust row height or column width.* Follow the steps for inserting, but choose Fit Height/Width to Content to adjust the height or width of the row or column to accommodate the contents of the cells in that row or column. Or, click the column or row and then hover the cursor over one of the edges of the row or column header until the cursor becomes a double-sided arrow. Click and drag the cursor/arrow to adjust the height or width of the row or column.

3. **Edit the appearance of your table with the fields in the Format pane. Select the cells, rows, or columns you want to edit and click the tab for the things you want to change:**

    - *Table:* Has menus and buttons to adjust the color, font size, grid lines and number of header and footer cells. These changes affect the entire table.

    - *Cell:* Makes changes to the cells, rows, or columns you select either singly or in multiples. Define how the data is formatted, such as currency or percentage, and assign fill and border colors and styles.

    - *Text:* Lets you define the text color, style, and alignment of text in selected cells, rows, or columns.

    - *Arrange:* Lets you reposition the table in relation to other objects on the slide or align it on the slide itself. (Refer to the previous section Aligning Objects to understand how this works.)

4. **To place formulas or functions in a cell, press the equals (=) key.**

    The functions menu appears in the Format pane.

5. **(Optional) If you decide that you want to remove a table, click the Resize button, and then press Delete.**

You can also use the Keynote menu to add objects to your slides. Choose Insert➪Table/Chart/Shape/Line, and then choose the specific type from the submenu that opens.

Adding Media Files

Text by itself can be as monotonous and confusing to read as the flight arrival and departure displays at an airport. Adding sound, still images, and movies makes your presentation appealing and communicative. Sound can be an audio recording of a song stored in iTunes or edited in GarageBand; photos can be digital photographs stored in iPhoto; and movies can be short video clips you've edited and stored in iMovie.

Adding sound

You can add any audio file stored in iTunes or GarageBand to a slide in your presentation or to the entire presentation. To add sound to a slide, follow these steps:

1. **Click the slide with which you want to play an audio file.**

2. **Click the Media button on the Keynote toolbar.**

   The Media Browser appears.

3. **Click the Music tab.**

   The Media Browser displays your iTunes library, as shown in Figure 4-15. (You see GarageBand, too, if you have music stored there.)

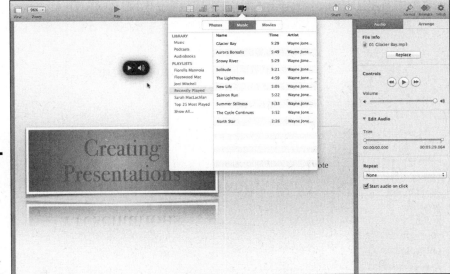

Figure 4-15:
The Media
Browser
lets you
choose an
audio file
from iTunes.

4. **Click the library, playlist, or folder where your audio resides.**

   The Media Browser displays all the available files you can choose.

5. **Click the audio file you want to use.**

   Keynote displays an audio icon directly on your slide to let you know audio is inserted here.

6. **Click the audio icon on the slide and then select or deselect Start Audio On Click in the Format pane.**

   When deselected, the audio will begin as soon as the slide appears in the presentation; when selected, you have to click any key to start playback.

In the Format pane, you can also replace the audio with a different file, set the playback volume, and trim the audio file so only a portion plays with your slide.

7. **To delete the audio, click it, and then press the Delete button.**

To add background audio that plays during the entire slideshow, do the following:

1. **Click the Setup icon in the toolbar.**

2. **Click the Audio tab in the Setup pane, shown in Figure 4-16.**

Figure 4-16: Add background audio to your entire presentation.

3. **Click the Add Music button at the bottom right of the Soundtrack section.**

The Media Browser opens.

4. **Select the audio you want, as explained in the preceding steps list.**

5. **Choose Play Once or Loop from the pop-up menu next to Soundtrack.**

- *Play Once:* The track stops playing if the audio ends before the presentation is over.

- *Loop:* Plays the audio again from the beginning if the track ends before the presentation is over.

You can add voiceover to accompany your presentation so when people view it without you, they have the benefit of hearing what you want to say about each slide. Choose Play⇨Record Slideshow and begin speaking. Click the right arrow to move to the next slide. Click the Esc key when you finish. Choose Play⇨Play Slideshow to hear how you did.

Adding photos or movies

If you store digital photos in iPhoto, you can place those photos on any slide in a Keynote presentation by following these steps:

1. **Create a new slide or click the slide where you want to insert a photo.**

2. **Open the Media Browser.**

   - *If you're replacing a placeholder image, click the Photo icon in the lower-right corner of the image to open the Media Browser.*

     Or

   - *Click the Media icon on the Keynote toolbar.*

   The Media Browser appears.

3. **Click the Photos or Movies tab.**

   The Media Browser displays all the pictures stored in iPhoto or all the movies stored in iPhoto or iMovie. Click an album or event to narrow your choices and more easily find the image or movie you want, as shown in Figure 4-17.

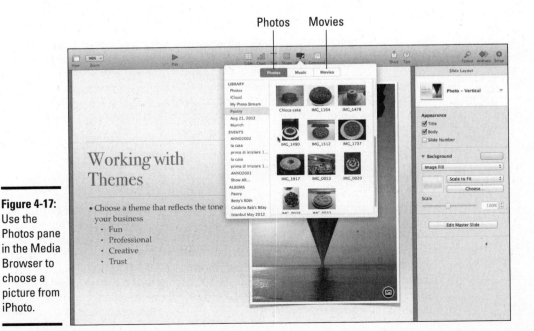

Photos   Movies

Figure 4-17:
Use the Photos pane in the Media Browser to choose a picture from iPhoto.

4. **Click the photo or movie you want from the Media Browser.**

   It immediately replaces the placeholder image, maintaining any border, shadow, and fill styles.

   If there is no placeholder media, the photo or movie fills your slide. Resize the photo or movie by clicking it, and then dragging the resize handles. Click and drag to position the photo where you want.

   With movies, you may be asked if you want to optimize the file (depending on your preferences in Keynote⇨Preferences⇨General). Optimizing the file will make adjustments so it displays nicely on a iOS device — if you plan to show your presentation on an iPad, this is a good idea, otherwise it's a step you can probably skip.

   Holding down the Shift key while resizing a photo or movie retains the height and width proportions.

5. **Edit the photo or movie by clicking it and then clicking Format in the toolbar. Click the tabs as follows:**

   - *Style:* Offers menus to choose one of the predefined image styles associated with the theme or change the borders, shadows, opacity, and reflection in the same way as explained for text boxes.

   - *Image:* Gives options for replacing the photo, masking and adjusting it, which we explain in Book V, Chapter 6 because it's a task that is the same for all iWork apps.

   - *Movie:* Lets you replace the movie, adjust the volume, or trim the movie. You can also select or deselect Start Movie On Click. When deselected, the audio will begin as soon as the slide appears in the presentation; when selected, you have to press any key to start playback.

   - *Arrange*: With text boxes, charts, and tables, gives you options to position the image in relation to other objects and the slide itself.

If you plan to use your presentation on a different computer, choose Keynote⇨Preferences⇨General. Next to Saving, select the Copy Audio and Movies into Document check box so your media files are part of the presentation.

Rearranging Slides

After you create your slides, chances are, they aren't in the exact order you want to give your presentation, or you may have a few that you aren't sure you want to use but aren't ready to delete. Keynote displays slides in the order they appear in the Navigator, Outline, or Light Table view. In Navigator and Outline view, the top slide appears first, followed by the slide directly beneath it, and so on, whereas in Light Table view, they're arranged left to right in a grid. After you create two or more slides in a presentation, you may want to rearrange their positions.

To rearrange slides in a presentation, follow these steps:

1. **Choose one of the following:**

   • View⇨Navigator or Outline (displays slides vertically in the Slide Organizer pane.)

   • View⇨Light Table (displays slides in rows and columns.)

2. **Click and drag a slide in either the Slide Navigator, Outline, or Light Table to its new position.**

   In Light Table view, Keynote moves slide icons out of the way to show you where your new slide will appear, but a grayed rectangle remains in the original position until you release the mouse button or lift your finger from the trackpad.

3. **Release the mouse button or lift your finger from the trackpad when you're happy with the new position of the slide in your presentation.**

Creating groups of slides

Keynote offers you the possibility of creating groups of slides within your presentation. You may want to create a group of related slides, much like an outline that has topics and subtopics. Groups make editing your presentation easier because you can move a group of related slides from one place to another without losing the order of the individual slides within the group.

To create a group, follow these steps:

1. **Choose View⇨Navigator.**

2. **Click the slide you want to be the first of the group.**

3. **Add a new slide. Or, if you want to group existing slides, arrange them in the order you want with the head of the group first and subsequent slides below, and then click the first slide you want to be in the group.**

4. **Press Tab or click and drag the slide toward the right.**

   The slide is indented to the right, and a disclosure triangle appears next to the head of the group. You can also have subgroups, as shown in Figure 4-18; Slide 2 is the head, Slide 3 is in the group, and Slide 4 is the first of a subgroup of Slide 3.

5. **Repeat for other slides.**

   Clicking the disclosure triangle opens and closes the group.

To move a slide out of a group, click and drag the slide to the left or click the slide, and then hold down the Shift key and press Tab; the slide moves to the left.

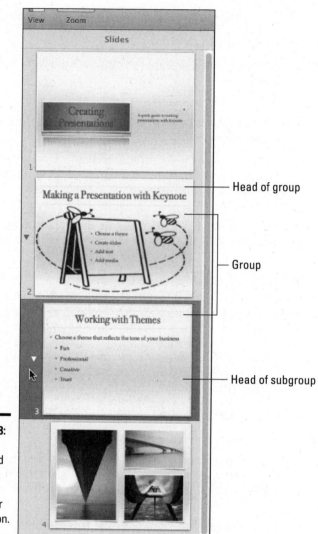

Figure 4-18:
Create
groups and
subgroups
of slides
within your
presentation.

Deleting a slide

Eventually, you may find that you don't need a slide anymore. Deleting a slide is easy, and deleting a slide group is, perhaps, too easy.

In groups, if you delete the head slide when the group is closed, the entire group is deleted. If you delete the head slide when the group is open, only that slide is deleted; slides in the group or subgroups move one step to the left.

To delete a slide, go to the Navigator, Outline, or Light Table view, select the slide(s) that you want to delete, and then do one of the following:

✦ Press Delete.

✦ Choose Edit⇨Delete on the menu bar.

✦ Control-click a slide and choose Delete.

If you delete a slide by mistake, choose Edit⇨Undo Delete on the menu bar (or press ⌘+Z).

Skipping a slide

You may use the same presentation multiple times but with different audiences or time allowances, so you may not want to use every slide every time. You can suppress slides without deleting them, which gives you the flexibility of using the same presentation in different settings. To skip a slide, go to Navigator, Outline, or Light Table view, select the slide(s) you want to skip, and then Control-click the slide and choose Skip Slide. To add the skipped slide back in the presentation, Control-click the slide and choose Don't Skip Slide.

Creating Transitions and Effects

To make your presentations visually interesting to watch, you can add transitions and effects. *Slide transitions* define how a slide appears and disappears from the display. *Text and graphic effects* define how the text or graphic initially appears on or disappears from the slide and how it moves around a slide. You can also add hyperlinks to your presentation.

Creating a slide transition

To create a slide transition, follow these steps:

1. **Choose View⇨Navigator on the menu bar.**

2. **In the Slide Navigator, click the slide that you want to display with a transition.**

3. **Click the Animate icon to open the Transitions pane.**

4. **Click the Add an Effect button to see the Transitions menu (as shown in Figure 4-19).**

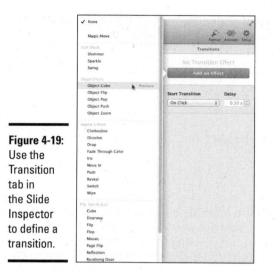

Figure 4-19:
Use the
Transition
tab in
the Slide
Inspector
to define a
transition.

5. **Choose an effect, such as Shimmer or Confetti.**

   Depending on the transition effect you choose, you may need to define other options, such as the direction or duration of your transition.

   The Magic Move effect lets you add animation to your presentation without hiring a designer. It animates an object, moving it from its location on one slide to a new location on the next slide. The object must be the same on both slides. Place the object at the starting point on the first slide and then on the end point on the second slide. The Magic Move feature moves the object when the slide transitions from the first slide to the second slide.

   A preview of your transition in action appears in the central slide pane.

   Click the Change button to use a different transition or add another one; choose None in the Effect pop-up menu to remove a transition.

6. **Click the Animate button to close the Transitions pane.**

Creating text and graphic effects

Sometimes you want your bullets to show up one at a time. Instead of creating separate slides — the first with one bullet, the second with two bullets, the third with three, and so on — create your slide with the bullets you want, and then choose how Keynote "builds" your slide during your presentation. Keynote offers three ways to create text and graphic effects in over 25 types of transitions:

✦ **Build In:** Defines how text and graphics enter a slide. (If you choose the Build In transition, initially, the text and graphics won't appear on the slide.)

✦ **Build Out:** Defines how text and graphics exit a slide.

✦ **Action:** Defines how text and graphics move on a slide.

Creating builds

To define an effect for text or graphics, follow these steps:

1. **Choose View⇨Navigator on the menu or toolbar.**

2. **In the Navigator, click the slide that contains the text or graphic you want to display with a visual effect.**

3. **Click the text or graphic you want to modify; for example, a text box with a bulleted list or a table with several rows.**

   Choose animated charts to add action to those.

4. **Click Animate in the toolbar.**

5. **Click the Build In or Build Out tab.**

6. **Click Add an Effect and choose an option from the pop-up menu.**

7. **Set the Delivery options to build your bullet list, chart, or table, one item at a time.**

8. **Click Preview to see how the build will display during your presentation.**

9. **Click Change to use a different effect or delete the effect (None).**

10. **(Optional) Click another object and assign a build to that object as in Steps 6 and 7.**

    a. *Click the Build Order button to open the Build Order window (refer to Figure 4-20).*

    b. *Click and drag the objects in the list to set the order they'll be added to the slide.*

    c. *Choose when to start the builds and the delay between each object.*

    d. *Click Preview to see how it will look during your presentation.*

    e. *Click the close button to exit the Build Order window.*

11. **Click Animate in the Toolbar to close the Builds pane.**

Making text and graphics move on a slide

If you choose the Action button for text or graphics, you can choose the Move Effect, which lets you define a line that the text or graphic follows as it moves across a slide. To define a line to move text or graphics on a slide, follow these steps:

1. **Follow Steps 1 through 4 in the preceding section for creating builds.**

2. **Click the Action tab.**

3. **Click Add an Effect.**

4. **Choose Move from the Effect pop-up menu.**

   Keynote displays a red line that shows how your chosen text or graphic will move, as shown in Figure 4-21.

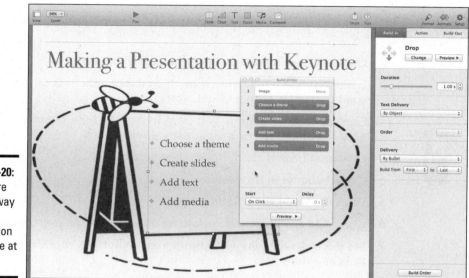

Figure 4-20:
Builds are
a great way
to show
information
one piece at
a time.

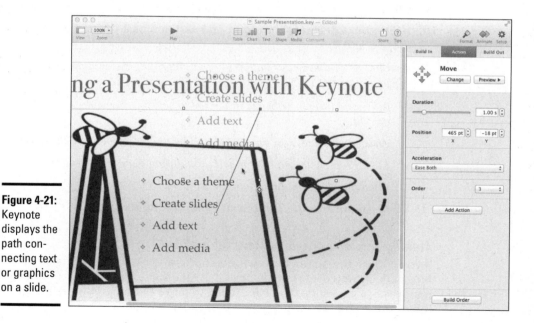

Figure 4-21:
Keynote
displays the
path con-
necting text
or graphics
on a slide.

5. **(Optional) Click and drag the handle at the beginning or end of the red line to move the line or change the line length.**

Moving the red line changes the direction your chosen text or graphic moves. Changing the line length determines how far your chosen text or graphic moves.

6. **(Optional) Click the Add Action button to add another action to the same object.**

7. **(Optional) Click another object to add an action or build to that object.**

   For example, you could have an easel slide across the slide, bounce or jiggle, and then the bulleted list appears on the easel, building one item at a time with the blur effect. Use the Build Order window to adjust the order in which the action and builds take place (refer to Figure 4-20).

The Action feature moves an object or text on a slide. The Magic Move feature animates objects or text from one slide to the next during the slide transition.

Adding hyperlinks to your presentation

Like links in a web page, hyperlinks within your presentation connect to another point in the presentation, connect to a website, or open an outgoing e-mail message. They're particularly useful for creating presentations that a viewer will watch alone — say, at a kiosk or even on your website. You don't have to be present for the viewer to see your presentation. Hyperlinks are also helpful if you want to access media stored remotely, such as a video that would take up storage on your computer.

Here's how to create a hyperlink:

1. **Choose View⇨Navigator on the menu or toolbar.**

2. **Click the slide that contains the text or graphic you want to use as the departure point for the hyperlink.**

3. **Select the text or graphic that will act as the hyperlink button.**

4. **Click Format⇨Add Link.**

   The Hyperlink window opens.

5. **Click the Link To pop-up menu, as shown in Figure 4-22, to choose what you want the hyperlink to link to:**

   - *Slide:* Use the check boxes to choose another slide within the presentation, or fill in the slide number.

   - *Webpage:* Type in the URL of the web page you want to link to.

   - *Email:* If the hyperlink is for an outgoing e-mail message, type in the address to whom the message should be sent, along with a subject line.

   - *Exit Slideshow:* Clicking the hyperlink will close the presentation.

To delete the hyperlink, click the hyperlink button on the object, and then click Remove.

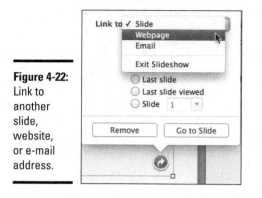

Figure 4-22:
Link to
another
slide,
website,
or e-mail
address.

Using Masters to Customize Themes

Instead of tweaking a slide layout and then duplicating the slide or duplicating a whole presentation and then redoing the text and images, you can
make changes to the slide master or create a new Keynote theme. *Masters*
are the templates used to create new slides based on the slide layout. When
you change a master, you can then update all slides that use that master
within the presentation. Changes you make to slide masters within a presentation only affect that specific presentation. See the tip after these steps
about how to create a new theme. To edit masters, follow these steps:

1. **In any view, click the Edit Master Slide button in the Format pane.**

   In the same view, you see the master slide and the format tools. We find
   Navigator view easiest for editing masters because you can see all the
   slide layouts in the left panel.

2. **Click the slide you want to edit.**

3. **Click the part you want to change (text or image), and then make the
   changes you want in the Format pane.**

   For example, you can simply choose a different predefined style for
   that placeholder by clicking the menus in the Format pane, or you can
   change the font itself, the color, size, and alignment.

   For text, you can also add new styles to the list or rename or delete
   existing styles, and then use those new or renamed styles on subsequent
   slide masters. Click text on any slide, and then click the Text tab in the
   Format pane. Click the text name to open the paragraph styles menu and
   then click the plus sign at the top to add a new style or click a style to
   delete or rename it, as shown in Figure 4-23.

   For text boxes or image placeholders, you can change the borders and
   shadows. Click and drag to change the position of placeholders.

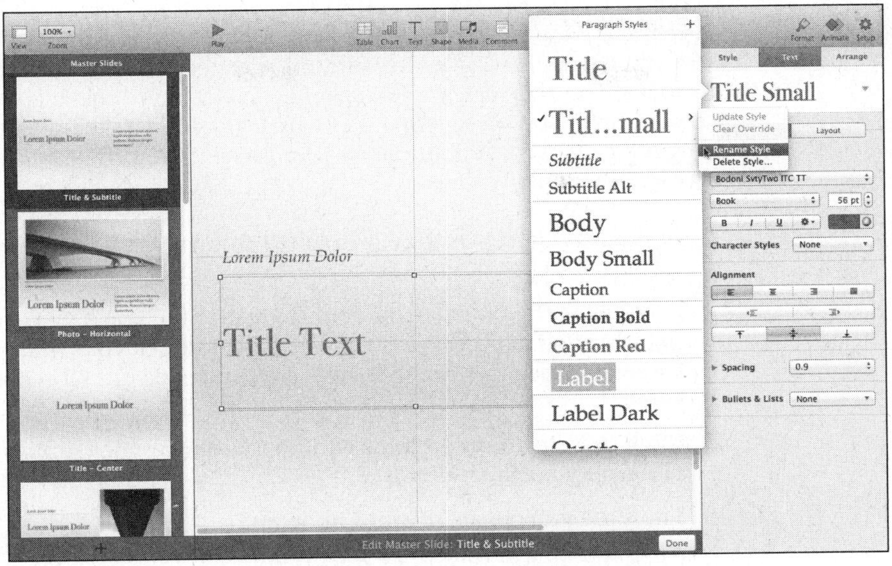

Figure 4-23:
Create
your own
slide layout
masters.

4. **Repeat Steps 2 and 3 for other slides.**

5. **Rename the slide by clicking to select the name in the Master Slide navigator and type a new name.**

6. **Add or duplicate Master Slides in the same way as you would for regular slides, and then edit them.**

   For example, if you frequently use a specific type of chart, you could add a Master Slide to the theme you use most often and insert a chart on that Master Slide.

7. **Click Done when you finish.**

TIP

To make your own personalized theme, create a new presentation from a plain theme or one that's similar to the end result you want. Edit the master slides, and then save it as a new theme by choosing File➪Save Theme. If you're creating a theme you'll use often, consider putting your company name or logo in the theme so it's one less task you have to do when creating presentations.

Polishing Your Presentation

When you finish modifying the slides in your presentation, you need to show your presentation to others. You may give a presentation in person or post it on YouTube or your website so people can view it at their leisure.

Viewing a presentation

After you finish creating a presentation, you need to view it to see how it actually looks. The slide order or visual effects may have looked good when you put your presentation together, but when viewed in its entirety, you may suddenly notice gaps or repetitions in your presentation. To view a presentation, follow these steps:

1. **In the Navigator, Outline, or Light Table view, click the first slide you want to view.**

   If you click the first slide of your presentation, you'll view your entire presentation. If you click a slide in the middle of your presentation, your slide show begins from that slide and proceeds until it reaches the last slide.

2. **Click the Play icon on the Keynote toolbar or choose Play⇨Play Slideshow on the menu bar.**

   The slide you chose in Step 1 appears.

3. **Click the mouse button or trackpad, press the spacebar, or use the right arrow key to view each successive slide — the left arrow key takes you back a slide.**

   If you're at the last slide of your presentation, click the mouse button or trackpad, or press the spacebar, to exit your presentation.

4. **(Optional) Press Esc if you want to stop viewing your presentation before reaching the last slide.**

If you don't want to click through the presentation, click the Setup icon in the toolbar and choose Self-Playing in the Presentation Type pop-up menu.

Rehearsing a presentation

Viewing a presentation lets you make sure that all the slides are in the right order and that all effects and transitions work as you expect. Before giving your presentation, you may want to rehearse it and let Keynote approximate how much time you spend on each slide.

Rehearsing can give you only a general estimate of the time needed to give your presentation. In real life, various conditions — for example, an impatient audience sitting in a stuffy conference room where the air conditioning suddenly breaks down — may make you nervous or speed up your timing.

To rehearse a presentation, follow these steps:

1. **In the Navigator, Outline, or Light Table view, click the first slide you want to view.**

2. **Choose Play⇨Rehearse Slideshow on the menu bar.**

Keynote displays your slides. Click the tool button in the upper right and you see the tools windows, as shown in Figure 4-24. We activated all the viewing options except the clock, so you see how much time has elapsed, the current and upcoming slide, the slide navigator, and presenter notes.

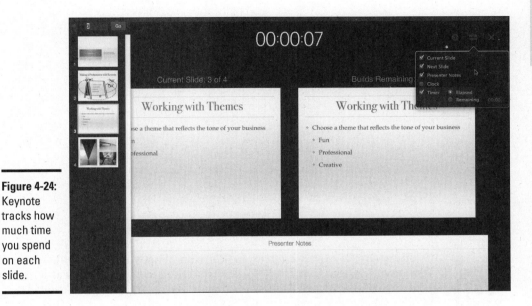

Figure 4-24:
Keynote
tracks how
much time
you spend
on each
slide.

3. **Practice what you're going to say when presenting each slide and press the spacebar or click the mouse button to advance to the next slide.**

Preparing for your big event

When the day arrives that you have to give your presentation, Keynote has some tools to help you there, too. As long as your presentation will be presented with a second projection system — that is, not viewed directly on your Mac while you're giving it — you can display your notes and stopwatch next to your slides on your Mac while the audience sees only your slides.

To set up the Presenter Display, follow these steps:

1. **Choose Keynote⇨Preferences.**

2. **Click the Slideshow tab.**

3. **Click Enable Presenter Display.**

   When your computer is connected to a projection system, you see the presenter display, which looks like Figure 4-24.

4. **Select the items you see onscreen, such as the pointer, in the Interacting section as shown in Figure 4-25.**

5. **Click the close button on the preferences window.**

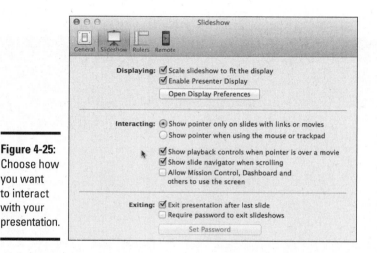

If you use an iOS device such as an iPhone or iPad, you can download the iOS version of Keynote from the App Store and then use your device as a remote control for Keynote presentations on your Mac. If you use an Android or Windows handheld device, you'll find remote control apps in their stores too.

Letting others run your presentation

When you give a presentation, you'll probably do it directly from your Mac. However, there may come a time when you need to save your presentation to run on a different type of computer or you want to give others the opportunity to see your presentation on your website, on YouTube, or on one of the presentation sharing websites like SlideShare (www.slideshare.net). Fortunately, Keynote lets you *export* a Keynote presentation in six different formats and share your presentation in several ways, such as by e-mail or on social media sites.

Exporting your Keynote presentation

To export a Keynote presentation, follow these steps:

1. **Choose File⇨Export To on the menu bar.**

2. **Click one of the following options:**

   • *PDF:* Saves your presentation as a series of static images stored in the Adobe Acrobat Portable Document File (PDF) format that can be viewed by any computer with a PDF viewing application. Any interesting visual or transition effects between slides will be lost.

- *PowerPoint:* Saves your presentation as a PowerPoint file that you can edit and run on any computer that runs PowerPoint. (Certain visual effects and transitions may not work in PowerPoint.)

- *QuickTime:* Saves your presentation as a movie that can play on a Windows PC or Mac computer that has the free QuickTime player. This movie preserves all transitions and visual effects.

- *HTML:* Saves each slide as a separate web page. Any interesting visual or transition effects between slides will be lost.

- *Images:* Saves each slide as a separate graphic file.

- *Keynote '09:* Saves your presentation as a file that's compatible with the previous version of Keynote.

TIP

If you want to preserve your visual effects and transitions, save your presentation as a QuickTime movie, which also allows you to play your presentation on a TV connected to an iOS device. If you want to preserve and edit your presentation on a Mac or Windows PC running Microsoft PowerPoint, save your presentation as a PowerPoint file.

3. **(Optional) The Export Your Presentation dialog opens, as shown in Figure 4-26. Depending on the option you choose in Step 2, you may see additional ways to customize your presentation.**

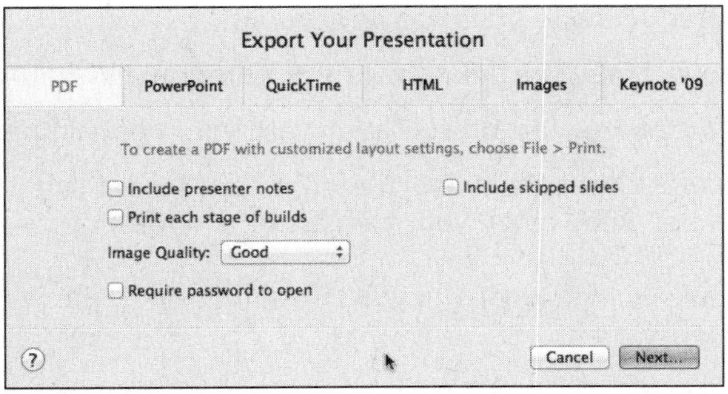

Figure 4-26:
Choose a format in which to save your Keynote presentation.

> Export Your Presentation
>
> | PDF | PowerPoint | QuickTime | HTML | Images | Keynote '09 |
>
> To create a PDF with customized layout settings, choose File > Print.
>
> ☐ Include presenter notes   ☐ Include skipped slides
> ☐ Print each stage of builds
> Image Quality: Good ⬍
> ☐ Require password to open
>
> ⑦   Cancel   Next...

4. **Click Next.**

   Another dialog appears, showing all the drives and folders on your hard drive.

5. **Click the folder where you want to store your presentation.**

   You may need to switch drives or folders until you find where you want to save your file.

6. **Click the Export button.**

REMEMBER

When you export a presentation, your original Keynote presentation remains untouched in its original location.

Sharing your Keynote presentation

You have two ways to share your presentation: Upload the presentation to iCloud.com and then share the link, or share the actual presentation. When you share the link, anyone who opens it can make changes to it, and those changes will sync to your Mac and iOS devices that access the presentation.

Here's how you can share your presentation via iCloud:

1. **Make sure that you've saved your presentation on iCloud.**

    If you aren't sure how to save your presentation on iCloud, see the "Choosing a theme and saving your presentation" section.

    Your presentation must be saved on iCloud for this option to work.

2. **Click Share in the toolbar, and then choose Share Link via iCloud.**

    Choose one of the options:

    - *Email:* Opens a new message with a link to your presentation. Address the message and click Send.

    - *Messages:* Opens a new message with a link to your presentation. Address the message and click Send.

    - *Twitter:* Opens a dialog so you can tweet a link to the presentation. If you aren't logged in or don't have a Twitter account, you're prompted to log in or create an account.

    - *Facebook:* Share the link to your presentation in a status update.

    - *LinkedIn:* Share your presentation with your connections.

    - *Copy Link:* Places the link in the Clipboard so you can paste it somewhere else, such as on your website or in another presentation.

Here's how you can send a copy of your presentation to the person who wants to see it:

Click Share in the toolbar, and then choose Send a Copy, which sends a copy of your entire Keynote presentation to the destination you choose. Depending on your choices, the results are slightly different:

The Email, Messages, and AirDrop choices open a dialog that lets you send the presentation as a Keynote file or as a PDF, QuickTime, or PowerPoint file. Click the file type and then click Next. The file is converted if you chose an option other than Keynote. Depending on your choice, the following happens:

- Email or Messages: A new E-mail or Message opens. Type in the address(es) to which you want to send the presentation, and then click Send.

- AirDrop: A file is created that other people with Macs using AirDrop can see and access.

Choose YouTube, Facebook, or Vimeo, and Keynote converts your presentation to a self-playing movie and a dialog lets you choose the delay time for slides and builds. Click Next.

The movie is created. A dialog prompts you to either sign in to your YouTube, Facebook, or Vimeo account or to post directly, giving the access level that each social network allows.

Click View Share Settings to see the link as well as who else is editing it, click the Stop Sharing button to remove the link from any place that you've shared it, or click the Send Link button to share it via Mail, Message, Twitter, Facebook, or LinkedIn.

For more tips on using iWork and Keynote, go to Book V, Chapter 6.

Chapter 5: Crunching with Numbers

In This Chapter

✔ Getting to know the Numbers spreadsheet

✔ Creating a spreadsheet

✔ Using sheets

✔ Working with tables and charts

✔ Polishing a spreadsheet

✔ Printing and sharing your spreadsheet

*N*umbers is a spreadsheet application designed to help you manipulate and calculate numbers for a wide variety of tasks, such as balancing a budget, calculating a loan, and creating an invoice. The Numbers application also lets you create line, bar, and pie charts that help you analyze your data graphically. What's more, Numbers offers organizational and layout capabilities that you won't find in other spreadsheet apps.

In this chapter, we explain the parts of a spreadsheet; then we explain how to create a new spreadsheet on your Mac or iCloud, or open an existing spreadsheet created in a different application. We show you how to work with your data on a spreadsheet, including setting up tables, entering data, and using formulas. We give you some tips for personalizing a spreadsheet to make it aesthetically pleasing. At the end of the chapter, we go over printing and sharing your spreadsheet, even if the person you want to share with doesn't use Numbers.

Numbers is part of the iWork suite. If you bought a new Mac after November, 2013, iWork apps are included. If you have an older Mac, you can purchase and download Numbers from the App Store for $19.99. If you have an iPhone, iPad, or iPod touch, the iOS version of Numbers lets you create and work on documents on those devices when you don't have your Mac handy. And, by saving your Numbers documents to iCloud, you can open them on the iCloud website on computers running Windows or Linux.

Understanding the Parts of a Numbers Spreadsheet

The Numbers window is divided into two main sections: the sheet and the Format/Filter pane. You place charts, tables, data, functions, and even graphics and media on the sheet. The Format pane is where you apply styles and color to the fonts and data you select in the worksheet, and the Filter pane is where you establish criteria to sort data on tables. Other things you can see on the Numbers window are

✦ **Toolbar:** Across the top is the toolbar, which has buttons for frequently performed tasks.

✦ **Sheet tabs:** As you add new sheets to the file, tabs appear across the top, which you click to move from one sheet to another.

✦ **Rulers:** If you choose View⇨Show Rulers, you see rulers above and to the left of the active sheet, which help you determine the final size of your spreadsheet, especially if you want to print it.

A sheet may have zero or more *tables,* which are distinct gridworks comprising *rows* (identified by incremental numbers down the left margin) and *columns* (in alphabetical order by a letter at the top). The intersection of a row and column is a *cell,* and that's where you type and store numbers, text, and formulas, as shown in Figure 5-1. A cell has the coordinates of the row and column; E4, for example, is the intersection of the fifth column (E) and the fourth row (4).

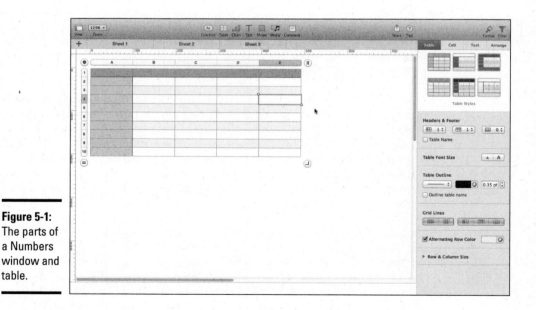

Figure 5-1:
The parts of a Numbers window and table.

Besides the mundane-but-fundamental cells that form the backbone of any spreadsheet, you can also place the following eye-catching (and useful) items in your sheets by clicking the buttons on the toolbar, as shown in Figure 5-2:

✦ **Table:** A *table* consists of rows and columns that can contain words, numbers, calculated results, or a combination of these types of contents.

✦ **Chart:** A *chart* displays data stored in a table. Common types of charts are line, bar, pie, and column. With Numbers, you can build two-axis and mixed charts as well as 2D, 3D, and interactive charts.

✦ **Text:** Text serves both decorative and informative functions. In a text box, you type and store text independent of the rows and columns in a table.

✦ **Shape:** Choose from three line styles and a dozen shapes to add pizazz to your sheet.

✦ **Media:** Add photos, music, or movies to your sheet.

✦ **Comment:** Comments are particularly useful when you share your sheets because others can give you feedback without changing the sheet itself.

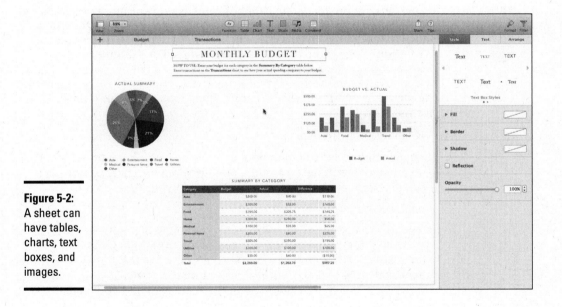

Figure 5-2:
A sheet can have tables, charts, text boxes, and images.

Putting together a spreadsheet is a simple process. The following list points out the basic steps:

1. Start with a sheet.

   When you create a new Numbers document, either from scratch or by using a template, Numbers automatically creates one sheet with one table on it. Your job is to fill that table with data — although you could delete it if you want to use that sheet as a cover page. Add more tables — yes, a sheet can hold multiple tables — or start spicing up your data presentation with charts or pictures. (More on that later.)

2. Fill a table with numbers and text.

   After setting up at least one table on a sheet, you can move the table around on the sheet and/or resize it. When you're happy with the table's position on the sheet and the table's size, you can start entering numbers into the table's rows and columns. Add titles to the rows and columns to identify what those numbers mean, such as *August Sales* or *Car Payments.*

3. Create formulas and use functions.

   After you enter numbers in a table, you'll want to manipulate one or more numbers in certain ways, such as totaling a column of numbers. Numbers offers 250 predefined functions to take your numbers or text and calculate a result, such as how much your company made in sales last month or how a salesperson's sales results have changed.

Functions are pre-loaded in Numbers and use one or more variables to calculate a result. You write formulas. Both are mathematical expressions that not only calculate useful results, but they also let you enter hypothetical numbers to see possible results. For example, if every salesperson improved her sales results by 5 percent every month, how much profit increase would that bring to the company? By typing in different values, you can ask, "What if?" questions with your data and formulas.

4. Visualize data with charts.

   Just glancing at a dozen numbers in a row or column might not show you much of anything. By turning numeric data into line, bar, or pie charts, Numbers can help you spot trends in your data.

5. Polish your sheets.

   Most spreadsheets consist of rows and columns of numbers with a bit of descriptive text thrown in for good measure. Although functional, such spreadsheets are boring to look at. That's why Numbers gives you the chance to place text and images on your sheets to make your information (tables and charts) compelling. You can even add audio effects!

Creating a Numbers Spreadsheet

To help you create a spreadsheet, Numbers provides 31 templates that you can use as-is or modify. Templates contain preset tables with formulas, which calculate the task at hand. For example, in the Savings Tracker template, you enter your goal, the length of time for your investment, and the interest rate, and then the template calculates how much you have to save each month to reach your goal. Changing those values changes the results.

Templates also have predefined font styles and color schemes. You can alter anything you want in a template — tables, charts, colors — but finding a template that is close to what you want to do gives you a head start. That way, you don't have to spend time designing, so you can concentrate on your figures.

If you prefer, use the Blank template to create a spreadsheet (one sheet with one table) from scratch. If you design a particularly useful spreadsheet, you can save it as a custom template (by choosing File⇨Save as Template).

Creating a new spreadsheet with a template

To create a spreadsheet based on a template, follow these steps:

1. **Double-click the Numbers icon in Launchpad or click the Numbers icon on the Dock (or choose File⇨New on the menu bar if Numbers is already running).**

   The icon looks like a 3D bar chart. When you click it, one of the following happens:

   • If you didn't turn on Numbers in iCloud, the Themes chooser opens.

   • If you turned on Numbers in the Documents & Data section of iCloud (see Book I, Chapter 3), you have to first choose where you want to work: iCloud or Mac. When you open Numbers to create a new document or work on an existing one, you have to click iCloud or On My Mac to choose where you want to save your new document (or to find an existing document) and then click New Document to open the Choose a Theme dialog, as shown in Figure 5-3.

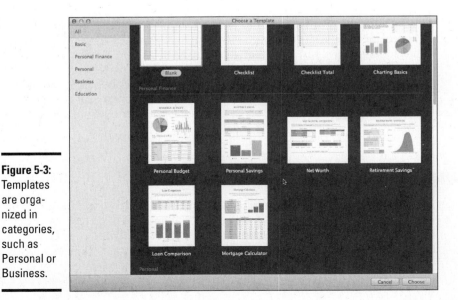

Figure 5-3: Templates are organized in categories, such as Personal or Business.

2. **Click a template category in the list on the left (or click All if you want to see all 31 templates).**

   Choose a template that is closest to what you want to do: for example, a household budget or a workout tracker.

3. **Double-click the template that you want to use, or click the template you like in the main pane. Then click the Choose button.**

   Numbers opens your chosen template.

   If you want to start with a blank spreadsheet, click Blank which is the first template under Basic.

4. **Choose File⇨Save.**

   The Save As dialog opens.

5. **Type a name for your spreadsheet and choose the folder where you want to store it on your Mac or save it to iCloud.**

Opening an existing file

If you're working on a Numbers document on one source (such as your Mac) and you want to open a document from another source (such as iCloud or an external drive), choose File⇨Open, and do one of the following:

✦ Click iCloud, click one of the documents in the list, and then click Open.

   You need an Internet connection to work on iCloud documents.

✦ Click On My Mac, scroll through the directories and folders to find an existing document you want to work on, click it, and then click Open. Choose On My Mac to access external drives and servers, too.

You might have spreadsheets that were created in a different application (such as Microsoft Excel, Quicken Open Financial Exchange [OFX], or AppleWorks 6), or you may have raw data that you want to bring into Numbers (such as comma-separated value [CSV] or tab-delimited text). You can open the file in Numbers, and Numbers will create sheets and tables with the data supplied. To open a non-Numbers file, drag the file you want to open over the Numbers icon on the Dock or follow the steps outlined earlier for opening a file via On My Mac.

Working with Sheets

Every Numbers spreadsheet needs at least one sheet, although you can have many (refer to Figure 5-1) . A sheet acts like a limitless page that can hold any number of tables, charts, and other objects. You want to use sheets to organize the information in your document, such as using one sheet to hold January sales results, a second sheet to hold February sales results, and a third sheet to hold a line chart that shows each salesperson's results for the first two months.

To help organize your sheets, Numbers stores the names of all your sheets in the tabs at the top of the sheet. Clicking the disclosure triangle on the right end of a sheet tab opens a list of all tables and charts stored on that particular sheet, along with options for copying, deleting, or renaming the sheet, as shown in Figure 5-4.

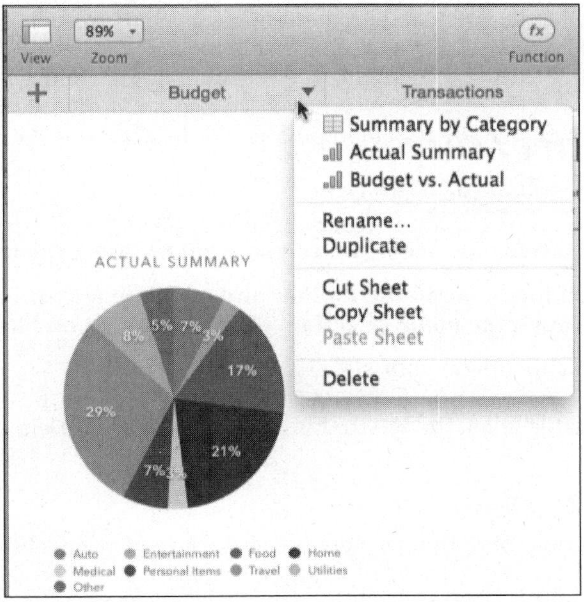

Figure 5-4:
View a sheet's elements.

To view the contents of a specific sheet, click that sheet name at the top of the sheet. To view a particular table or chart, find the sheet that contains that table or chart. Then click that specific table or chart.

Adding a sheet

You can always add another sheet. When you add a sheet, Numbers creates one table on that sheet automatically. To add a sheet, choose one of the following:

+ Choose Insert⇨Sheet from the menu bar.

+ Click the Add Sheet icon (a + sign) that appears at the far left of the row of sheet tabs.

Deleting a sheet

If you need a sheet to go away, clear out, disappear, whatever, you can delete it.

When you delete a sheet, you also delete any tables or charts stored on that sheet.

To delete a sheet, hover the cursor over the right end of the tab for the sheet you want to delete. Click the disclosure triangle when you see it, and then choose Delete from the pop-up menu (refer to Figure 5-4).

Adding or removing a table

As we mention earlier, a sheet can hold one or more tables, and the data you put in a table can be used as data references for charts you add to sheets. When you add a table, it uses the color scheme you choose and the type-faces associated with the template you're using, but it's empty — you have to input the data. Here, we show you how to add and format tables and then delve into how to use them to manipulate and display your data.

To add a table, follow these steps:

1. **Click the tab for the sheet where you want to insert the table.**

2. **Click the Table icon on the toolbar and click the left and right arrows to flip through the color selection. Click the table you like.**

   The table appears on your slide.

To remove a table, click the Resize button and then press Delete.

Resizing a table

You have a variety of options for changing the size of your table:

✦ **Resize handles:** Click the table and then click the Select Table button in the upper-left corner. Drag the handles around the edges to resize the table. This doesn't add rows and columns, just proportionately changes the table size.

✦ **Resize corner:** Click inside the table, and then click and drag the button in the bottom-right corner to add or remove columns and rows, and define the overall size and shape of your table.

✦ **Adding row/column button:** Click the Add button (two parallel lines in a circle) at the bottom-left corner to add rows or at the upper-right corner to add columns. Rows and columns are added to the table automatically.

✦ **Inserting or delete a row or column:** Hover the cursor by the row or column identifier (letters for columns, numbers for rows) before or after where you want to insert a row or column until you see a disclosure arrow. Click the arrow to open a menu that gives you choices to insert a row or column before or after the one you selected. You can also delete or hide the row or column you selected.

Delete multiple columns or rows by highlighting those column or row headings, clicking the Table menu, and then choosing Delete Columns or Delete Rows.

If you click the disclosure arrow of column A or B or row 1 or 2, you also have choices to insert header rows or columns or to convert the selected row or column into a header row or column. (See the "Inserting headers and resizing rows and columns" section for more information.)

✦ **Adjusting row height or column width:** Follow the steps for inserting but choose Fit Height/Width to Content adjust the height or width of the row or column to accommodate the contents of the cells in that row or column. Or, click the column or row and then hover the cursor over one of the edges of the row or column header until the cursor becomes a double-sided arrow. Click and drag the cursor/arrow to adjust the height or width of the row or column.

Changing the appearance of a table

Click the Format button on the toolbar to see the tools you can use to edit the appearance of your table. Select the cells, rows, or columns you want to edit, and click the tab of the Format pane for the things you want to change:

✦ **Table:** Use this tab's menus and buttons to adjust the color, font size, grid lines, and number of header and footer cells. These changes affect the entire table.

✦ **Cell:** Make changes to the cells, rows, or columns you select either singly or in multiples. Define how the data is formatted, such as currency or percentage, and assign fill and border colors and styles.

✦ **Text:** Define the text color, style, and alignment of text in selected cells, rows, or columns.

✦ **Arrange:** Reposition the table in relation to other objects on the sheet or align it on the sheet itself.

Inserting headers and resizing rows and columns

Headers are the first rows and columns of your table, where you usually type the names of the rows and columns. Footers are the final rows of the table, where you can repeat header names in particularly large tables. You can have header rows and columns that span up to five rows or columns, which is a handy way to use titles and subtitles for each row or column. Another way to insert header rows and columns is the following:

1. **Click the table, click the Format button on the toolbar, and then click the Table tab of the Format pane.**

2. **In the Headers & Footer section, use the pop-up menus to choose the number of row and column headers and column footers you want, up to five for each.**

3. **To make your header rows and columns stay put while you scroll through the rest of your table, click Freeze Header Row/Column in the pop-up menu.**

To insert header rows or columns after you already have data in your table, follow these steps:

1. Click a cell in one of the header rows or columns, either before or after where you want to insert another header row or column.

2. Click the Table menu and choose from the following:

- *Add Header Row Above:* Inserts an additional header row directly above the selected cell

- *Add Header Row Below:* Inserts an additional header row directly below the selected cell

- *Add Header Column Before:* Inserts an additional header column to the left of the selected cell

- *Add Header Column After:* Inserts a new column to the right of the selected cell

3. (Optional) Click a cell and use the menus in the Row & Column Size section to give a specific size to the row height or column width, or click the Fit button to have Numbers make automatic adjustments based on the amount of data in the cells in that row or column.

To emphasize the header rows and columns and footers and make them stand out from the contents of the table, you can outline single cells — or the entire row or column — with a border and/or fill the cells with a background color. Select the cells you want to emphasize and then do the following:

1. Click the Cell tab in the Format pane (click the Format icon on the toolbar if you don't see the Format pane).

2. Click the disclosure triangle next to Border to open the border options.

a. *Click the border style button (it looks like a paintbrush on a line) and choose a border style and the parts of the cells you want to apply it to.*

If you select one cell in the table and then choose the four-sided border, the four sides of that one cell will have the border.

If you select several cells, and then choose the four-sided border, the border surrounds the group but the lines between the cells remain unchanged.

If you want to add a border around all the selected cells, choose the border style that has both the outline and the inner lines emphasized.

b. *Click the pop-up menu beneath the word Border to change the border style from line to dash or dot.*

    c. *Use the up and down arrows beneath that pop-up menu to change the thickness of the border.*

    d. *Click the color swatch to choose a standard color or click the button next to the swatch to open the color pickers and choose a color from there.*

3. **Click the disclosure triangle next to Fill to add a background color to the headers or footers.**

    a. *Click the color swatch to choose a standard color or click the button next to the swatch to open the color pickers and choose a color from there.*

    b. *Click the Color Fill pop-up menu to choose the type of fill, such as Gradient.*

Typing Data into Tables

Now we get into the numbers part of Numbers. You need to know about the three types of data you can store inside a table: numbers, text, and formulas. You can also store images in a cell, which doesn't work as data per se but is useful to create documents such as an inventory or real estate listing.

We give you details about working with each type of data in the next three sections. However, in summary, to type anything into a table, follow these steps:

1. **Select a cell by clicking it or by pressing the arrow keys.**

2. **Type a number, text, or formula.**

   If you want to use a predefined function or create a formula of your own, type an equal sign (=) in the cell. The Function panel opens on the right side of the window.

3. **Press Return to select the cell below, press Tab to select the cell to the right, or click any cell into which you want to type new data.**

4. **Repeat Steps 2 and 3 for each additional formula or item of data you want to type into the table.**

Formatting numbers and text

When you type a number in a cell, the number will look plain — 45 or 60.3. To make your numbers more meaningful, you should format them. For example, the number 39 might mean nothing, but if you format it to appear as $39.00, your number now clearly represents a dollar amount.

To format numbers, follow these steps:

1. **Click to select one cell or click and drag to select multiple cells.**

   Numbers draws a border around your selected cell(s).

If you select empty cells, Numbers remembers the assigned format and automatically formats any numbers you type into those cells in the future.

2. **Click the Format button on the toolbar, and then click the Cell tab of the Format pane.**

3. **Choose how you want the data to appear in the Data Format pop-up menu, as shown in Figure 5-5.**

   Each choice has options that appear in the Format pane:

   • The numeric choices have submenus with further choices, such as how many decimals or the currency symbol.

   • When cells are formatted as Text, numbers have no numeric values. This is useful for typing in zip codes and phone numbers.

   • The Date & Time and Duration choices offer formatting options such as spelling out the month or using a number. Here, too, numbers are considered text.

   • The last set of choices are neither numeric nor text but instead let you create data entry cells that require an action, such as clicking to place a check mark in the box or limit your choices, such as a pop-up menu. (See "Formatting data entry cells," later in this chapter).

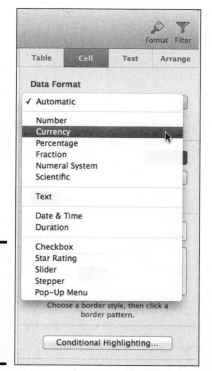

Figure 5-5:
Data looks, and works, differently depending on how it's formatted.

To add color to your cells and/or definition to them, click the disclosure triangles next to the Fill and Border options. Choose the options you want from the pop-up menus, as shown in Figure 5-6.

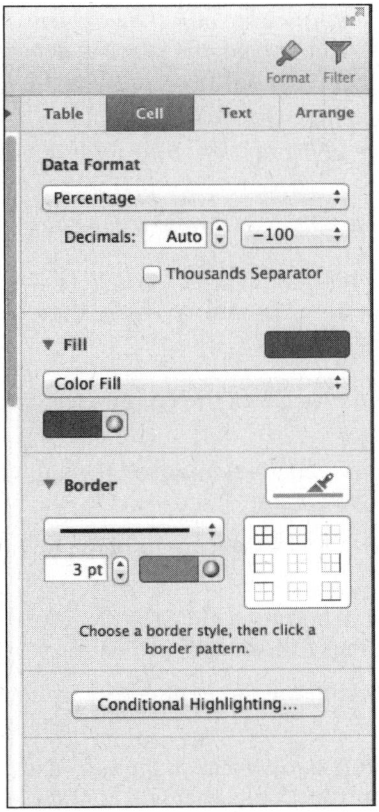

Figure 5-6:
Add background colors and borders to cells.

The cells automatically change as you try different effects.

✦ *Fill* puts a color, a gradient, or an image behind characters typed in the cell. Depending on the choice, you're presented with tools for choosing the color, the spectrum and direction (gradient), and scaling (image).

✦ *Border* surrounds your cell(s) with a line; define the width and color, and choose whether you want a border around each cell or around the group of cells or only on one side or in between.

✦ Click the *Colors icon* in either section to change the color of the fill or border. The color block opens a chooser that displays colors used in the theme; the color wheel opens the Colors window.

   a. *Click the color picker you prefer: Wheel, (which is the default), Slider, Palette, Spectrum, or Crayons.*

b. *Click the desired color in the color picker that appears in the Colors window.*

c. *(Optional) In the color picker, make the color lighter or darker by dragging the slider on the right up and down.*

d. *(Optional) In any of the color pickers, adjust the opacity by dragging the opacity slider left and right or type in a precise percentage in the text box to the right.*

e. *When you have a color you like, drag the color from the color box at the top to the color palette at the bottom. Your color is saved in the palette for future use.*

f. *Click the red Close window button or choose View⇨Close Colors.*

To format the style of the characters in the selected cell(s) — whether they're formatted as numbers, text, or data entry — click the Text tab and then the Style button in the Format pane.

✦ *To use a different font in the theme:* Click the Paragraph Styles menu and choose a different font.

✦ *To change the font style:* In the Font section, scroll through the Family menus to select the options you want.

The Family menu shows the fonts as they are to help you imagine your presentation using that font.

Click the font when you find it, and then click the Typeface, Size, and Style menus and buttons to make those changes to your type.

Change the font color by clicking the color wheel and following the steps mentioned previously.

✦ *To choose how you want your text to appear in the cell:* Click the horizontal and vertical Alignment buttons. Cells that will contain numbers usually have right alignment, and text in header cells is often centered.

If you're working with text, in a text box, you can select it and format the line and paragraph spacing, such as 1.5 line spacing and double-spacing between paragraphs. You can also create a bulleted or numbered list with the options in the Bullets & Lists section.

Typing formulas

The main purpose of a table is to use the data (numbers, textual data, dates, and times) you store in cells to calculate a new result, such as adding a row or column of numbers. To calculate and display a result, you need to store a formula in the cell where you want the result to appear.

Numbers provides three ways to create formulas in a cell:

+ Quick Formula
+ Typed formulas
+ Advanced functions

Using Quick Formula

To help you calculate numbers in a hurry, Numbers Quick Formula feature offers a variety of formulas that can calculate common results, such as

+ **Sum:** Adds numbers
+ **Average:** Calculates the arithmetic mean
+ **Minimum:** Displays the smallest number
+ **Maximum:** Displays the largest number
+ **Count:** Displays how many cells you select
+ **Product:** Multiplies numbers

To use a Quick Formula, follow these steps:

1. **Click the empty cell at the bottom or to the right of cells that contain the numbers you want to operate the function on.**

2. **Click the Function icon on the toolbar or choose Insert⇨Function on the menu bar.**

3. **From the pop-up menu (or sub-menu) choose Sum, Average, Minimum, Maximum, Count, or Product.**

   Numbers displays your calculated results.

Typing a formula

Quick Formula is handy when it offers the formula you need, such as when you add up rows or columns of numbers with the Sum formula. Often, however, you need to create your own formula.

Every formula consists of two parts:

+ **Operators:** Perform calculations, such as addition (+), subtraction (−), multiplication (*), and division (/)
+ **Cell references:** Define where to find the data to use for calculations

A typical formula looks like this:

```
= A3 + A4
```

This formula tells Numbers to take the number stored in column A, row 3 and add it to the number stored in column A, row 4.

To type a formula, follow these steps:

1. **Click (or use the arrow keys to highlight) the cell where you want the formula results to appear.**

2. **Type =.**

   The Formula Editor appears.

3. **Click a cell that contains the data you want to include in your calculation.**

4. **Type an operator, such as * for multiplication or / for division.**

5. **Click another cell that contains the data you want to include in your calculation.**

6. **Repeat Steps 4 and 5 as needed.**

7. **Click the Accept (or Cancel) button in the Formula Editor when you're done.**

   Numbers displays the results of your formula. If you change the numbers in the cells you define in Steps 3 and 5, Numbers calculates a new result instantly.

TIP

For a fast way to calculate values without having to type a formula in a cell, use Instant Calculations. Just select two or more cells that contain numbers, and you can see the results in the Instant Calculations results tabs along the bottom of the Numbers window, as shown in Figure 5-7. You can change the types of results you see in the Instant Calculations Results tabs by clicking the Action button (it looks like a gear) and selecting the functions you want to see from the pop-up menu.

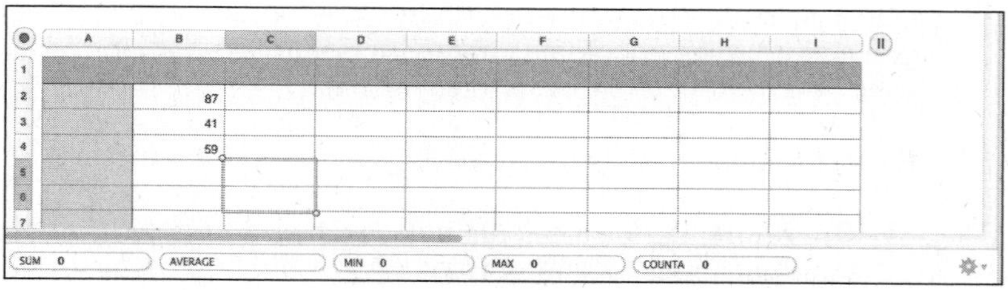

Figure 5-7:
Instant Calculations can show results without typing a formula first.

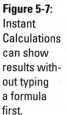

Using functions

Typing simple formulas that add or multiply is easy. However, many calculations can get more complicated, such as trying to calculate the amount of interest paid on a loan with a specific interest rate over a defined period.

To help you calculate commonly used formulas, Numbers provides a library of 250 *functions,* which are prebuilt formulas that you can plug into your table and define what data to use without having to create the formula yourself.

To use a function, follow these steps:

1. Click (or use the arrow keys to highlight) the cell where you want the function results to appear.

Some functions operate on data typed into the cell where the function is inserted. For example, if you insert the sine function, the sine of numbers you type into that cell will be calculated. Other functions use data in several cells to calculate a result, such as depreciation, which uses original cost, time in service, and some other business-y information. That type of information must be typed into the cells that the function refers to in order for it to work.

2. Press the equal (=) key.

The Formula Editor appears, and the Functions pane opens, as shown in Figure 5-8.

You can move the Formula Editor if you move the pointer to the left end of the Formula Editor. When the pointer turns into a hand, click and drag the Formula Editor to a new location so it doesn't hide the cells you're working on.

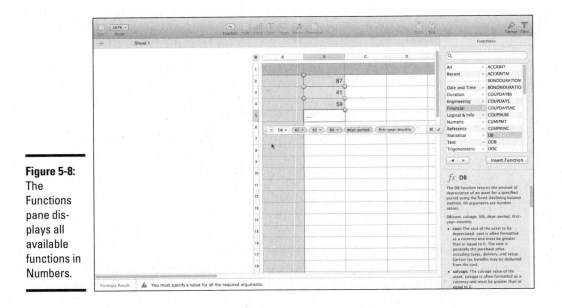

Figure 5-8:
The Functions pane displays all available functions in Numbers.

3. **Choose the type of function you want from the left column (or click All), and then scroll through the functions on the right and click the one you want to insert.**

   A definition for the selected function is shown at the bottom of the pane, along with an explanation of the types of data needed to complete the operation and an example of how it works.

4. **Click the Insert Function button.**

   The Formula Editor now contains your chosen function.

5. **Edit the formula by typing the cell names (such as C4) or clicking the cells that contain the data the function needs to calculate.**

6. **Click the Accept (check mark) or Cancel (x) button on the Formula Editor.**

   Numbers shows your result.

Choose View➪Show Formula List to see a list of all the formulas used in a spreadsheet. You can also see the formulas used in templates in this way.

Formatting data entry cells

After you create formulas or functions in cells, you can type new data in the cells defined by a formula or function and watch Numbers calculate a new result instantly. Typing a new number in a cell is easy to do, but sometimes a formula or function requires a specific range of values. For example, if you have a formula that calculates sales tax, you may not want someone to enter a sales tax more than 10 percent or less than 5 percent.

To limit the types of values someone can enter in a cell, you can use one of the following methods, as shown in Figure 5-9:

✦ **Sliders:** Users can drag a slider to choose a value within a fixed range.

✦ **Steppers:** Users can click up and down arrows to choose a value that increases or decreases in fixed increments.

✦ **Pop-up menus:** Users can choose from a limited range of choices.

You can also format the cell with a check box or star rating, as shown in Figure 5-9.

Formatting a cell with a slider or a stepper

Using a slider or stepper is useful when you want to restrict a cell to a range of values, such as 1–45. The main difference is that a slider appears *next to* a cell, whereas a stepper appears *inside* a cell.

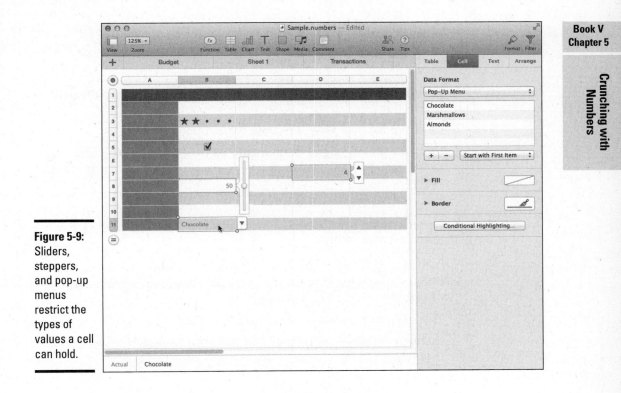

Figure 5-9:
Sliders, steppers, and pop-up menus restrict the types of values a cell can hold.

To format a cell with a slider or stepper, follow these steps:

1. **Click a cell that you want to restrict to a range of values.**

2. **Click the Format button on the toolbar, and then click the Cell tab of the Format pane.**

3. **Choose Slider or Stepper from the Data Format pop-up menu.**

4. **Enter the minimum acceptable value.**

5. **Enter the maximum acceptable value.**

6. **Enter a value in the Increment text box to increase or decrease by when the user drags the slider or clicks the up- and down-arrows of the stepper.**

7. **Use the Format and Decimals menus to edit the displayed number.**

   Numbers displays a slider next to the cell. Users have a choice of typing a value or using the slider to define a value. If you choose a value outside the minimum and maximum range defined in Steps 3 and 4, the cell won't accept the invalid data.

Formatting a cell with a pop-up menu

A pop-up menu restricts a cell to a limited number of choices. To format a cell with a pop-up menu, follow these steps:

1. **Repeat Steps 1 and 2 for inserting a slider or stepper (see the preceding section).**

2. **Click the list box under the Data Format pop-up menu.**

3. **Click the plus (+) sign button to add an item to the pop-up menu associated with the cell, and then type in the number or text you want added.**

    Repeat to add other items.

4. **To remove an item from the list, click the item and then click the minus (–) sign button.**

    Repeat to delete other items.

5. **Choose Start with First Item or Start with Blank from the pop-up menu next to the add/delete items buttons.**

    This determines what will be shown in the cell.

    Numbers displays a pop-up menu that lists choices when users click that cell.

You can also set a *conditional highlight* so that if your data meets a certain criterion or condition, Numbers will highlight the number or text in a color you want. Say you create a spreadsheet to track office supply inventory, and you want to know when you have fewer than five black pens. Set the conditional formatting of the cell to "less than or equal to 5." Then, when there are five pens or fewer, the cell changes color. Now, at a glance, you see pertinent information. To use conditional formatting, follow these steps:

1. **Select the cell(s) where you want to use conditional formatting.**

2. **Click the Format button on the toolbar, and then click the Cell tab of the Format pane.**

3. **Click the Conditional Highlighting button at the bottom of the pane.**

    You may have to scroll to find it.

4. **Click the Add a Rule button.**

    The Conditional Formatting window opens.

5. **Peruse the tabs and select the rule you want to use, as shown in Figure 5-10.**

    A field appears where you can type in a value.

- *If you want to refer to another cell:* Click the blue circle on the right end of the field and type in a cell reference. Or, click the cell in your sheet, and its reference appears in the field.

- *To change the value:* Click in the field and press the Delete key, and then type another value or enter a different cell reference.

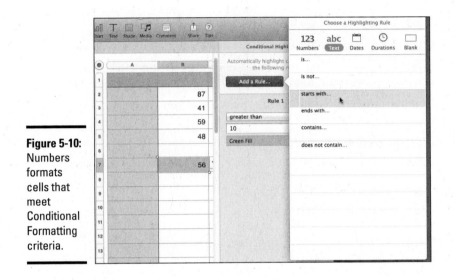

Figure 5-10:
Numbers formats cells that meet Conditional Formatting criteria.

6. **Click the pop-up menu to format how you want the data highlighted.**

   The sample box shows how the cell will appear if the data in it meet the conditional rule you set.

7. **(Optional) To add another rule, repeat Steps 4–6.**

8. **(Optional) To delete a rule, click the trash can icon that appears when you hover the cursor to the right of the rule name.**

9. **(Optional) To rearrange the order of the rules, hover the cursor to the left of the rule name and click and drag the Rearrange button (it looks like three horizontal lines).**

10. **Click Done.**

Sorting data

When you enter your data, you don't always do so in the order you want to see it. For example, to track invoices, you create a column for each piece of data, such as invoice number, date of purchase, customer name, and total, and then you enter the data from a stack of invoices so each row holds the data for one invoice. You may enter the data by invoice number first but then want to sort by customer name to see which customers have more than one outstanding invoice or by total to see who spent the most. You can sort the data by one of those columns. Here's how you do it:

1. **Click the table you want to sort or select a group of cells you want to sort.**

2. **Hover the cursor over the column indicator (the letters) that you want to use to define the sort.**

3. **Click the disclosure triangle that appears to open the pop-up menu.**

4. **Select Sort Ascending or Sort Descending to establish the order in which you want the data.**

   Numbers will sort your data by the column you chose.

Deleting data in cells

If you ever want to delete data in a cell, Numbers provides two ways:

✦ Delete data but retain any formatting.

✦ Delete data and formatting.

To delete data but retain any formatting, follow these steps:

1. **Select one or more cells that contain data you want to delete.**

2. **Press Delete or choose Edit⇨Delete from the menu bar.**

To delete both data and formatting in cells, follow these steps:

1. **Select one or more cells that contain data and formatting you want to delete.**

2. **Choose Edit⇨Clear All from the menu bar.**

Adding a chart

Charts are a graphical representation of data. Before you add a chart to your sheet, create a table and enter the data you want the chart to represent. Then, do the following:

1. **On the table where you input the data for your chart, click and drag to select the data, including row and column headers.**

2. **Click the Chart icon on the toolbar and then click the left and right arrows to flip through the color selection. First, click a tab for the type of chart you want — 2D, 3D, or Interactive — and, then choose the chart you want.**

   The chart with your data appears on your sheet.

If the data is on one sheet but you want to place the table on another sheet, do the following (you can also use these steps to create charts on the same sheet, if you want):

1. **Click that sheet where you want to place the chart.**

2. **Click the Chart icon on the toolbar and then click the left and right arrows to flip through the color selection. First, click a tab for the type of chart you want — 2D, 3D, or Interactive — and, then choose the chart you want.**

3. **Click the Add Chart Data button.**

4. **Click the sheet that holds the data.**

5. **Click and drag to select the cells, including headers, that contain the data you want in the chart.**

6. **Click the Done button.**

   The data selected from the table flows into the chart on the other sheet.

   Interactive charts are created the same way as 2D or 3D charts. Here's the difference. Rather than see, for example, eight columns that represent two types of data for four months, you see two columns at a time, and clicking the playback arrows animates the data.

7. **Click Format on the toolbar and then go through the tabs of the Format pane to edit the appearance and position of the chart and data:**

   - *Chart* gives you tools for changing the colors and fonts of the chart, as well as adding special effects such as shadow or opacity and a title and/or legend. At the bottom of the panel is the Chart Type menu. Click to change to a different type of chart, and any data you entered will appear on the new type.

   - *Axis* (all but pie charts) lets you name the axes and change the scale. Here you also find the menus for defining the value labels with percentage, currency, or others.

   - *Series* (all but pie charts) offers menus for naming the value labels.

   - *Wedges* (only pie charts) shows check boxes and menus for adding labels and defining the value data format. You can move the labels off the chart itself and separate the pieces of the pie by setting a greater distance from center with the respective slider bars.

   - *Arrange* lets you reposition the chart in relation to other objects on the slide or align it on the sheet itself. This doesn't change parts of the chart.

   - *Axis/Wedge Labels* lets you can define the label (number, percentage, and so on) and also change the font family, size, style, and color. Double-click any of the text on the chart, and the Axis or Wedge Labels tab appears in the Format pane.

8. **(Optional) To remove a chart, click it and then press Delete.**

You can also use the Numbers menu to add objects to your slides; choose Insert⇨Table/Chart/Shape/Line and then choose the specific type from the submenu that opens.

Naming sheets, tables, and charts

Numbers gives each sheet, table, and chart a generic name, such as Sheet 2, Table 1, or Chart 3. To help you better understand the type of information stored on each sheet, table, and chart, use more descriptive names, especially when you add multiple tables and charts. The sheet name appears on the sheet tab, and table and chart names appear when you click the disclosure triangle on the sheet tab.

To name a sheet, double-click the name on the sheet tab to select it and type a new name, or choose Rename from the sheet tab pop-up menu and then rename it.

Although you don't have to have a name for your charts and tables, it does help if you have more than one chart or table on a sheet. To name a table or chart, double-click the placeholder text to type a name for the table or chart. If you don't see the placeholder text, click the table or chart, and then click the Format button on the toolbar. Click the Table or Chart tab in the Format pane, and then select the check box next to Table Name or Title (for charts). Click the Table tab and Outline Table Name to put a box around the table name.

To move a table or chart from one sheet to another, click the table or chart and choose Edit⇨Cut. Click the sheet you want to move the table or chart to, and then choose Edit⇨Paste. Data and calculations remain unchanged. Click and drag the table or chart to the position you want on the sheet.

Making Your Spreadsheets Pretty

Tables and charts are the two most crucial objects you can place and arrange on a sheet. However, Numbers also lets you place text boxes, shapes, and pictures on a sheet. Text boxes can contain titles or short descriptions of the information displayed on the sheet. Shapes can add color or indicate navigational cues, such as arrows. Photos can make your entire sheet look more interesting, or they may be the focus of your sheet if you're creating an inventory.

Click the Table tab in the Format pane, and choose alternating Row Color to have that effect in your table. The colors will reflect those of the theme you chose, but you can change them with the color tool, which we explain in detail in the "Formatting numbers and text" section.

Adding a text box

To add a text box to a sheet, follow these steps:

1. Click the sheet tab to which you want to add the text box.

Numbers displays your chosen sheet and any additional objects that may already be on that sheet, such as tables or charts.

2. Click the Text icon (T) on the toolbar.

A text box appears on the sheet.

3. Double-click in the text box and type any text that you want to appear in the text box. Press Return to type text on a new line.

While you type, your text box lengthens to accommodate your text. You can widen the text box by clicking and dragging the handles on its sides.

4. (Optional) Select any text and choose any formatting options from the Format pane, as we explain earlier for formatting text in tables and cells.

Adding media

To add a photo, a movie, or audio file such as a TIFF, JPEG, or AIFF, to a sheet, follow these steps:

1. Click the sheet tab to which you want to add media.

2. Click the Media icon on the toolbar.

The Media Browser appears.

3. Do one of the following:

- *Photo:* Click the Photos tab, scroll through the thumbnails, and click one you want to insert.

- *Music:* Click the Music tab, and then click the song or spoken audio you want to add.

- *Movies:* Click the Movies tab, and then click the movie you want to insert.

Numbers displays your chosen image or movie on the sheet. If you added audio, a play icon indicates that. You can move the media around the sheet, resize photos and movies with the resizing handles, and use the editing tools of the Format pane to add borders or fills.

4. (Optional) To delete inserted media, click it and press Delete.

If you want to use an image as a background for a cell or group of cells, select the cells and then use the Fill tool of the Format pane.

Sharing Your Spreadsheet

You put a lot of effort into making your spreadsheet presentable. When you're ready to actually present it, you can share your spreadsheet with others by printing it or saving it as a file for electronic distribution.

Printing a spreadsheet

In other spreadsheet applications, it's not uncommon to print your spreadsheet and chart only to find that part of your chart or spreadsheet is cut off by the edge of the paper. To avoid this problem, Numbers displays a Content Scale, which lets you magnify or shrink an entire sheet so it fits and prints perfectly on a page.

To shrink or magnify a sheet to print, follow these steps:

1. **Click the sheet tab you want to print.**

2. **Choose File⇨Print.**

   Numbers displays a page and shows how the charts and tables on your sheet will print. If you can't see the whole page, change the view to 75% or 50% with the pop-up magnifying menu to see the borders of the page and where your tables and objects lie, as shown in Figure 5-11.

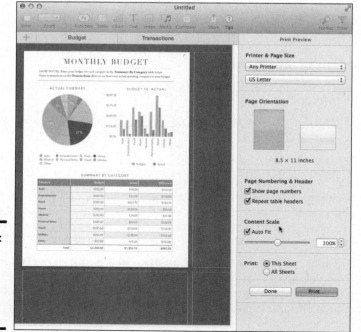

Figure 5-11: Use Print Preview to see how your sheet will print.

3. **Drag the Content Scale slider to magnify or shrink your data until it
   fits exactly the way you want on the page, or select the Auto Fit check
   box if you want Numbers to do the work for you.**

   The Content Scale slider is located at the bottom center of the Print
   Preview pane.

4. **Choose any other print options you want and click the Print button.**

Exporting a spreadsheet

When you choose File⇨Save, Numbers saves your spreadsheet in its own
proprietary file format. If you want to share your spreadsheets with others
who don't have Numbers, export your spreadsheet into another file format
by following these steps:

1. **Choose File⇨Export to⇨PDF/Excel/CSV/Numbers '09 on the menu bar.**

   The Export Your Spreadsheet dialog appears, as shown in Figure 5-12.

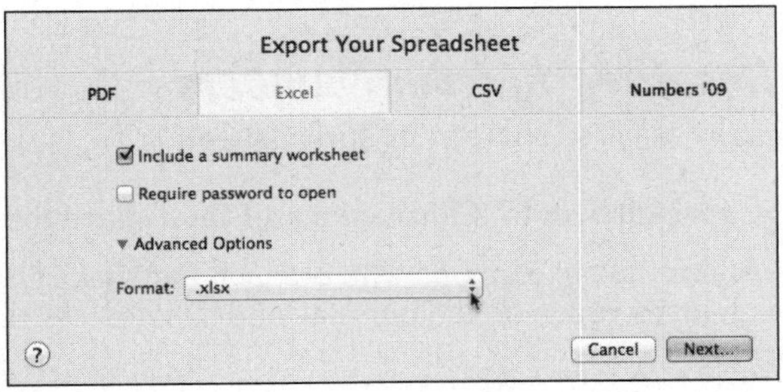

Figure 5-12:
Choose a
format to
save your
spread-
sheets.

	Export Your Spreadsheet		
PDF	Excel	CSV	Numbers '09

☑ Include a summary worksheet
☐ Require password to open

▼ Advanced Options

Format: .xlsx

Cancel   Next...

2. **Choose one of the following formats:**

   - *PDF:* Saves your spreadsheet as a series of static pages stored in the
     Adobe Acrobat Portable Document Format (PDF) that can be viewed
     by any computer with a PDF viewing application.

   - *Excel:* Saves your spreadsheet as a Microsoft Excel file, which can
     be opened and edited by any spreadsheet that can read and edit
     Microsoft Excel files.

   - *CSV:* Saves your spreadsheet in comma-separated value (CSV)
     format, which is a universal format that preserves only data, not any
     charts or pictures you have stored on your spreadsheet.

   - *Numbers '09:* Saves your spreadsheet as a file that's compatible with
     the previous version of Numbers.

The PDF file format preserves formatting 100 percent, but you need
extra software to edit it. Generally, if someone needs to edit your spreadsheet and doesn't use Numbers, choose File⇨Export to⇨Excel. The CSV
option is useful only for transferring your data to another application
that can't read Excel files.

The format you choose is highlighted, but you can switch to another one by clicking a different tab.

3. **(Optional) If you want to add a password to open the document, select the Require Password to Open check box (all except CSV).**

4. **Click Next.**

A dialog appears, where you choose a name and location to save your exported spreadsheet.

5. **Enter a name for your exported spreadsheet in the Save As text box.**

6. **Click the folder where you want to store your spreadsheet.**

You may need to switch drives or folders until you find where you want to save your file. You can also select an external drive or flash drive from the Devices section.

7. **Click Export.**

When you export a spreadsheet, your original Numbers spreadsheet remains untouched in its original location.

Sharing files directly from Numbers

You have two more ways to share your spreadsheet:

✦ **Upload the spreadsheet to iCloud.com and then share the link.**

When you share the link, anyone who opens it can make changes to it, and those changes will sync to your Mac and iOS devices that access the spreadsheet.

✦ **Share the spreadsheet itself.**

Either way, when you share the link or spreadsheet, all the sheets contained in the spreadsheet are included.

Here's how you can share your presentation via iCloud:

1. **Make sure that you saved your presentation on iCloud.**

If you aren't sure how to save your presentation on iCloud, see the "Creating a new spreadsheet with a template" section.

Your presentation must be saved on iCloud for this option to work.

2. **Click Share on the toolbar, and then choose Share Link via iCloud.**

Choose one of the options:

- *Email:* Opens a new message with a link to your spreadsheet. Address the message and click Send.

- *Messages:* Opens a new message with a link to your spreadsheet. Address the message and click Send.

- *Twitter:* Opens a dialog so you can tweet a link to the spreadsheet. If you aren't logged in or don't have a Twitter account, you're prompted to log in or create an account.
- *Facebook:* Share the link to your spreadsheet in a status update.
- *LinkedIn:* Share your spreadsheet with your connections.
- *Copy Link:* Places the link on the Clipboard so you can paste it somewhere else, such as on your website or in a Keynote presentation.

Here's how you can send a copy of your spreadsheet to the person who wants to see it:

1. **Click Share on the toolbar, and then choose Send a Copy.**

   This sends a copy of your entire spreadsheet to the destination you choose:

   - *Email*
   - *Messages*
   - *AirDrop*

   All these choices open a dialog that lets you send the spreadsheet as a Numbers file or as a PDF, an Excel file, or a CSV file.

2. **Click the file type and then click Next.**

   The file is converted if you chose an option other than Numbers.

   A new message opens.

3. **Type in the address(es) to which you want to send the spreadsheet and then click Send.**

   For AirDrop, a file is created that other people on your local network with Macs using AirDrop can see and access. See Book III, Chapter 4 to learn more about AirDrop.

   After you share a spreadsheet, the Share button on the toolbar changes from an arrow to two bodies.

4. **Click the Share button and then View Share Settings to see the link as well as who else is editing it.**

   Click the Send Link button to share it via Mail, Message, Twitter, Facebook, or LinkedIn.

To remove the link from any place that you've shared it, click the Stop Sharing button.

For more tips on using iWork and Numbers, go to Book V, Chapter 6.

Chapter 6: Getting the Most Out of iWork

In This Chapter

✔ Inserting photos, movies, and music in your iWork documents

✔ Copying and pasting in iWork

✔ Finding text and replacing it

✔ Editing photos

✔ Making comments in iWork documents

✔ Tracking down third-party iWork templates

If you read the last few chapters about using iWork applications — Pages, Keynote, and Numbers — you may have noticed that the window layout, the commands, and the tools are similar for them all. Some actions are exactly the same, and that's where this chapter comes in. We take you through some of the lesser-known (and some more advanced) functions of iWork that work the same whether you're writing a newsletter in Pages, preparing a presentation in Keynote, or building a budget in Numbers.

Inserting Media from Other Sources

Because documents are often shared electronically and viewed on a computer, media can be a fun — and informative — addition to any kind of document. A song might seem an odd addition to a spreadsheet, but a sound effect that screams "Wow!" when sales totals are over the top can be a way to compliment your sales team. Respectively, we show you how to insert photos, movies, and music from iTunes and iPhoto into your newsletters, presentations, and spreadsheets in Book V, Chapters 3, 4, and 5, but you can also add media from other sources by following these steps:

1. **In any of the iWork apps — Pages, Keynote, or Numbers — choose Insert⟹Choose.**

   A browser dialog opens, as shown in Figure 6-1.

Figure 6-1:
Insert
media from
sources
other than
iPhoto and
iTunes.

2. **Browse the directories and folders until you find the file you want to insert.**

   If the file is on a flash drive or another external drive, click that drive in the Devices section to see files stored there.

3. **Click the file, and then click the Insert button.**

   The media file is inserted in your document.

Audio and video can only be truly appreciated in electronically distributed documents — they don't do much for printed matter.

Copying and Pasting

Two of the most helpful functions when working with documents on computers are Copy and Paste. In Pages, Keynote, and Numbers, you can copy just about any text, image, object, table, or chart and then paste it somewhere else in the same document, in a new document in the same app, or in a different app. Here are the few simple steps it takes:

1. **Click the item you want to copy.**

2. **Choose Edit⇨Copy or press ⌘+C.**

3. **Go to the place you want to insert the item you copied.**

4. **Choose Edit⇨Paste or press ⌘+V.**

   • If the item you copied is formatted, choose Edit⇨Paste and Match Style.

   • If you copied cells from Numbers that contain formulas, choose Edit⇨Paste Formula Results to paste the data instead of the formulas.

Finding and Replacing

Product names change, a name has an unusual spelling, and version numbers are updated. When information throughout your document changes or needs to be corrected, use Find and Replace to find all occurrences of the data — text or numbers — and replace it with the new information. Follow these steps:

1. **Open the document that has the information you want to change.**

2. **Choose Edit⇨Find⇨Find.**

   The Find & Replace window opens, as shown in Figure 6-2.

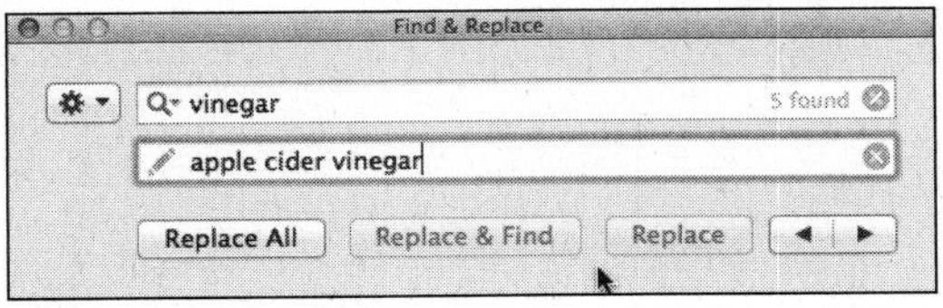

Figure 6-2:
Use Find &
Replace to
correct
certain info.

3. **Click the Action pop-up menu (looks like a cog) and choose Find and Replace.**

4. **(Optional) Refine your search.**

   - *Whole Words:* Select Whole Words to find the complete word — not just instances when the letters are part of a word.

     For example, if you search for "vine" and Whole Word is not selected, your results could include the word *vinegar* or *vineyard* or *grapevine*. When Whole Word is selected, the Find tool looks for a space after the last letter so the results show only the exact word you seek.

   - *Match Case:* Select Match Case if you want to use capitalization (or noncapitalization) as a search criterion.

5. **In the top field, type the word, phrase, or numbers you want to change.**

   The number on the right end of the top field indicates the number of occurrences of the found word or phrase within the document. In Figure 6-2, our search nets five matches.

6. **Type the replacement information in the second field.**

7. **Click one of these buttons:**

   - *Replace All* replaces all occurrences of the old information with the new information.

   - *Replace & Find* replaces the first occurrence and then shows you the next occurrence.

   - *Replace* replaces only the first occurrence. Then click the right arrow to move to the next occurrence found.

Modifying Photos

iWork applications — and Preview — provide some quick and easy ways to modify the appearance of a photo:

✦ **Masking:** Masking lets you display just a portion of an image, such as an oval or star-shaped area. Masking hides the other parts of the image; if you unmask an image, you see the whole thing again. This is different from cropping, which actually cuts off the portion of the image you don't want.

✦ **Instant Alpha:** Instant Alpha lets you make part of an image transparent, making the image seem cut out against the background of your document.

✦ **Adjust Image:** You can adjust contrast, exposure, and sharpness.

Masking a photo

A mask acts like a cookie cutter that you plop over a photo to save anything *inside* the cookie-cutter shape but hide anything *outside* the shape. iWork applications provide a variety of shaped masks, such as ovals, stars, arrows, and triangles. For example, in your school newspaper you could put the face of a sports winner in a star shape.

To apply a mask to a photo, follow these steps:

1. **Click the photo you want to mask.**

Handles appear around your chosen photo.

2. **Choose Format⇨Image⇨Mask with Shape, and then choose a shape, such as Polygon or Diamond.**

Your chosen mask appears over your photo, as shown in Figure 6-3. The to-be-masked portion appears dim. An editing tool appears at the bottom of the image.

3. **(Optional) Resize the photo or the mask or both.**

• *Photo:* Click the photo button on the editing tool and then resize the photo with the slider.

• *Mask:* Click the mask button on the editing tool to resize the mask with the slider.

You can also use the handles to resize the image or mask. Holding down the Shift key while dragging a mask handle retains the height and width aspect ratio.

Figure 6-3:
Use a mask
to save a
portion of a
photo.

4. **To choose which part of the picture appears within the mask, move the pointer to the dimmed portion of the photo outside the mask and then drag the dimmed portion.**

5. **Click the Done button or click outside the image.**

    Keynote applies the mask to your photo.

You can apply only one mask at a time to a photo. If you want to apply a different mask over a photo, you must remove the first mask by choosing Format⇨Image⇨Reset Mask.

Making a picture transparent with Instant Alpha

The Instant Alpha feature lets you remove an irregular portion of a photo. This can create unusual visual effects by stripping unwanted portions of a photo and keeping the parts you like. This differs from cropping, which is when you cut the edges off but the image remains rectangular. Look at these steps and the figure, and you'll see what we mean.

To use the Instant Alpha feature, follow these steps:

1. **Click the photo you want to modify.**

    Handles appear around your chosen photo.

2. **Choose Format⇨Image⇨Instant Alpha from the menu bar.**

    A dialog appears over your photo, telling you how to use the Instant Alpha feature.

3. **Place the pointer over the portion of your photo that you want to make transparent and then drag the mouse or on the trackpad.**

A common use of Instant Alpha is to eliminate a background and make the main subject stand out, maybe even then paste it over a different background. Instant Alpha uses color to identify the part you want to eliminate, so you may have to do Step 3 more than once to eliminate more parts. It highlights all parts of your photo that are similar in color to the area that you originally pointed to, as shown in Figure 6-4.

Figure 6-4: Highlight similar colors to eliminate.

26%

Click a color to make it transparent.
Drag to make similar colors transparent.   Reset   Done

4. **Release the mouse button or trackpad when you're happy with the portion of the photo that the Instant Alpha feature has highlighted and made transparent.**

5. **Click Done to save the changes or Reset to try again.**

You can use the Instant Alpha feature multiple times to remove different colors from the same photo. If you make a mistake, choose Edit⇨Undo Instant Alpha on the menu bar or press ⌘+Z.

Using Adjust Image

Another way to tweak your photos is to choose View⇨Show Adjust Image, which opens the window shown in Figure 6-5. Use the sliders to adjust contrast, exposure, sharpness, and other aspects of your photo. Click the Enhance button if you want the Adjust Image tool to auto-correct the image. You see the effects immediately on your image and need only click the close button to accept them. Click the Reset Image button if you don't like the changes you made; doing so returns your image to its original state.

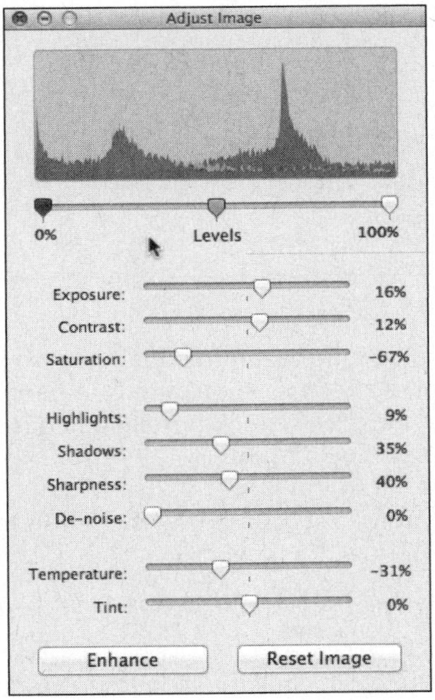

Figure 6-5:
Use Adjust
Image
to tweak
photos.

Adding Comments

Comments are like sticky notes in your document. You can leave notes for yourself or someone else reading your document, and other people can leave comments for you, too. To add comments, do the following:

1. **In an open document, click the Comment icon on the toolbar.**

   A virtual sticky note appears on your document.

2. **Type the comment you want to make, as shown in Figure 6-6.**

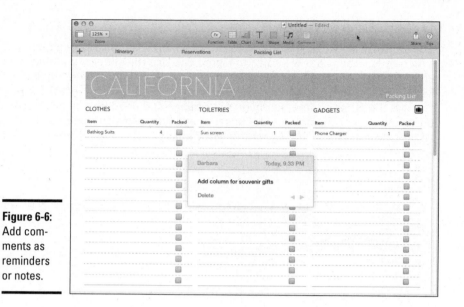

Figure 6-6:
Add com-
ments as
reminders
or notes.

That's it. In Pages, a yellow square appears in the document to indicate where you inserted a comment, while in Keynote and Numbers, your comment remains on the window, unless you hide it as explained next. To manage your comments, try these techniques:

✦ **Resize (Numbers and Keynote):** Click and drag the note's lower-right corner.

✦ **Move (Numbers and Keynote):** Relocate your comment by clicking and dragging the comment.

✦ **Edit:** Click the comment (in Pages, click the icon in the document to open it) and edit or add more to it.

✦ **Hide or display:** Choose View➪Comments (Comments and Changes in Pages)➪Hide Comment to hide the comment. (This won't delete it.) Choose View➪Comments/Comments and Changes➪Show Comment to see it again.

✦ **Delete:** Click Delete in the lower left corner to eliminate the note.

So you can track whose comments belong to whom, you — and other people with whom you share documents and who make comments on your documents — can add an author name to the comments. For each commenter, choose *App Name*➪Preferences➪General and type a name in the Author field. As extra ID-help, choose View➪Comments➪Author Color to assign a color to each comment author.

Finding More Templates

If the iWork templates and typefaces don't satisfy your creative needs, several third-party software developers offer free or sell templates that work with Pages, Keynote, and Numbers. We list a few here, but make sure to check out the App Store and search the Internet for others.

✦ **Facilisi:** (www.facilisi.com) Offers more than 1,600 templates for Pages.

✦ **Graphic Node:** (http://graphicnode.com/products/for-iwork) Offers still and motion themes and animations.

✦ **iWorkCommunity:** (www.iworkcommunity.com) iWork users post templates they've designed to share with other iWork users.

✦ **Jumsoft:** (www.jumsoft.com) Sells clip art for all three apps and templates for Pages and Keynote.

✦ **KeynotePro:** (http://keynotepro.com) Sells stylized templates for traditional presentations and kiosks.

✦ **Keynote Themes Plus:** (www.keynotethemesplus.com/home.html) Produces high-definition themes and presentations.

✦ **Numbers Templates:** (www.numberstemplates.com) The name says it all.

✦ **StockLayouts:** (www.stocklayouts.com) Free and paid Pages templates are available in various formats and specific to different industries such as health care, sports, and education.

Index

Special Characters and Numerics

D

N

O

T

About the Authors

Joe Hutsko is the author of *Green Gadgets For Dummies*, *Flip Video For Dummies* (with Drew Davidson), and *iPhone All-in-One For Dummies* (with Barbara Boyd). For more than two decades, he has written about computers, gadgets, video games, trends, and high-tech movers and shakers for numerous publications and websites, including *The New York Times*, *Macworld*, *PC World*, *Fortune*, *Newsweek*, *Popular Science*, *TV Guide*, the *Washington Post*, *Wired*, Gamespot, MSNBC, Engadget, TechCrunch, and Salon. You can find links to Joe's stories on his blog, joehutsko.com.

As a kid, Joe built a shortwave radio, played with electronic project kits, and learned the basics of the BASIC programming language on his first computer, the Commodore Vic 20. In his teens, he picked strawberries to buy his first Apple II computer. Four years after that purchase (in 1984), he wound up working for Apple, where he became the personal technology guru for the company's chairman and CEO. Joe left Apple in 1988 to become a writer and worked on and off for other high-tech companies, including Steve Jobs' one-time NeXT. He authored a number of video game strategy guides, including the bestsellers *Donkey Kong Country Game Secrets: The Unauthorized Edition* and *Rebel Assault: The Official Insiders Guide*.

Joe's first novel, *The Deal*, was published in 1999, and he recently rereleased a trade paperback edition of it with a new foreword by the author (tinyurl.com/hutskodeal).

Barbara Boyd writes mostly about technology and occasionally about food, gardens, and travel. She's the co-author, with Joe Hutsko, of the first, second, and third editions of *iPhone All-in-One For Dummies*, and the author of *AARP iPad: Tech to Connect* and *iCloud and iTunes Match In A Day For Dummies*. She also co-authored (with Christina Martinez) *The Complete Idiot's Guide to Pinterest Marketing*. At present, she's working on *Innovative Presentations For Dummies* with Ray Anthony.

Barbara worked at Apple from 1985 to 1990, beginning as Joe's assistant and the first network administrator for the executive staff. She then took a position as an administrator in the Technical Product Support group. Barbara recalls working with people who went on to become top names in technology. It was an exciting time to be in Silicon Valley and at Apple in particular. That experience instilled a lifelong fascination with technology and Apple products. Her interest and experience led to subsequent jobs in marketing and publishing at IDG (International Data Group) and later for a small San Francisco design firm. In 1998, she left the corporate world to study Italian, write, and teach.

Presently, Barbara stays busy writing, keeping up with technology, and tending her garden and olive trees. Barbara divides her time between city life in Rome and country life on an olive farm in Calabria, the toe of Italy's boot.

Dedication

Joe dedicates this book to: My fabulously thoughtful, kind, caring, smart, creative, beautiful, and amazing co-author — and lifelong friend (and karmic life preserver) — Barbara Boyd.

Barbara dedicates this book to: My sweet, patient husband, Ugo de Paula. Thank you for our "vita fatata." And to my talented, inspiring, since-childhood friend Joe Hutsko, without whom I wouldn't be doing any of this techie stuff.

Author's Acknowledgments

You see the author's names on the cover, but these books (like any books) are really a collaboration, an effort of a many-membered team. Thanks go to Bob Woerner at Wiley for commissioning the fourth edition of this book — we're going to miss you, Bob — and to Aaron Black for coming in mid-project and offering insight and support when we wanted to change this book for the better. Writers are only as good as their editors, and we were lucky to have not one but two amazing project editors, Heidi Unger and Elizabeth Kuball plus a super-duper copy editor, Teresa Artman. As always, technical editor Dennis R. Cohen is a joy to work with and an invaluable part of our revision team. Thanks, too, to the anonymous people at Wiley who contributed to this book — not just editorial, but tech support, legal, accounting, even the person who delivers the mail. We don't know you, but we appreciate the job you do; it takes a lot of worker bees to keep the hive healthy, and each task is important to the whole.

We continue to thank our literary agent, Carole Jelen, for her astute representation and moral support. Carole plays a key role in our success, promoting us and keeping an eye out for new opportunities.

Thanks to the folks at Apple who developed such cool products, and specifically to Keri Walker for her ongoing editorial product support.

Joe adds: Major thanks to my dear, long-time friend Barbara Boyd, who stepped up to the plate as co-author on both this book and *iPhone All-in-One For Dummies* when my life and work focuses shifted to other time-sensitive projects and matters; writing and making deadlines on both books would have been impossible without Barbara's contribution. I mean it quite literally when I say both books are more Barbara's than mine, from perspectives of total word count, attention to detail, and commitment. *Barbara adds:* I'm forever grateful to my co-author, Joe, for his collaboration but more than anything, for his solid, steadfast, ever-present friendship.

Publisher's Acknowledgments

Acquisitions Editor: Aaron Black

Project Editors: Heidi Unger and Elizabeth Kuball

Senior Copy Editor: Teresa Artman

Technical Editor: Dennis Cohen

Editorial Assistant: Anne Sullivan

Sr. Editorial Assistant: Cherie Case

Project Coordinator: Rebekah Brownson

Cover Image: ©iStockphoto.com/ LuckyBusiness; screenshot by Wiley

ple & Mac

ad For Dummies,
h Edition
8-1-118-49823-1

hone 5 For Dummies,
h Edition
8-1-118-35201-4

acBook For Dummies,
h Edition
8-1-118-20920-2

X Mountain Lion
r Dummies
8-1-118-39418-2

logging & Social Media

acebook For Dummies,
h Edition
8-1-118-09562-1

om Blogging
r Dummies
8-1-118-03843-7

interest For Dummies
8-1-118-32800-2

ordPress For Dummies,
h Edition
8-1-118-38318-6

usiness

ommodities For Dummies,
nd Edition
8-1-118-01687-9

nvesting For Dummies,
h Edition
8-0-470-90545-6

Personal Finance
For Dummies,
7th Edition
978-1-118-11785-9

QuickBooks 2013
For Dummies
978-1-118-35641-8

Small Business Marketing Kit
For Dummies,
3rd Edition
978-1-118-31183-7

Careers

Job Interviews
For Dummies,
4th Edition
978-1-118-11290-8

Job Searching with
Social Media
For Dummies
978-0-470-93072-4

Personal Branding
For Dummies
978-1-118-11792-7

Resumes For Dummies,
6th Edition
978-0-470-87361-8

Success as a Mediator
For Dummies
978-1-118-07862-4

Diet & Nutrition

Belly Fat Diet For Dummies
978-1-118-34585-6

Eating Clean For Dummies
978-1-118-00013-7

Nutrition For Dummies,
5th Edition
978-0-470-93231-5

Digital Photography

Digital Photography
For Dummies,
7th Edition
978-1-118-09203-3

Digital SLR Cameras &
Photography For Dummies,
4th Edition
978-1-118-14489-3

Photoshop Elements 11
For Dummies
978-1-118-40821-6

Gardening

Herb Gardening
For Dummies,
2nd Edition
978-0-470-61778-6

Vegetable Gardening
For Dummies,
2nd Edition
978-0-470-49870-5

Health

Anti-Inflammation Diet
For Dummies
978-1-118-02381-5

Diabetes For Dummies,
3rd Edition
978-0-470-27086-8

Living Paleo For Dummies
978-1-118-29405-5

Hobbies

Beekeeping
For Dummies
978-0-470-43065-1

eBay For Dummies,
7th Edition
978-1-118-09806-6

Raising Chickens
For Dummies
978-0-470-46544-8

Wine For Dummies,
5th Edition
978-1-118-28872-6

Writing Young Adult Fiction
For Dummies
978-0-470-94954-2

Language &
Foreign Language

500 Spanish Verbs
For Dummies
978-1-118-02382-2

English Grammar
For Dummies,
2nd Edition
978-0-470-54664-2

French All-in One
For Dummies
978-1-118-22815-9

German Essentials
For Dummies
978-1-118-18422-6

Italian For Dummies
2nd Edition
978-1-118-00465-4

e Available in print and e-book formats.

Math & Science

Algebra I For Dummies,
2nd Edition
978-0-470-55964-2

Anatomy and Physiology
For Dummies,
2nd Edition
978-0-470-92326-9

Astronomy For Dummies,
3rd Edition
978-1-118-37697-3

Biology For Dummies,
2nd Edition
978-0-470-59875-7

Chemistry For Dummies,
2nd Edition
978-1-1180-0730-3

Pre-Algebra Essentials
For Dummies
978-0-470-61838-7

Microsoft Office

Excel 2013 For Dummies
978-1-118-51012-4

Office 2013 All-in-One
For Dummies
978-1-118-51636-2

PowerPoint 2013
For Dummies
978-1-118-50253-2

Word 2013 For Dummies
978-1-118-49123-2

Music

Blues Harmonica
For Dummies
978-1-118-25269-7

Guitar For Dummies,
3rd Edition
978-1-118-11554-1

iPod & iTunes
For Dummies,
10th Edition
978-1-118-50864-0

Programming

Android Application
Development For
Dummies, 2nd Edition
978-1-118-38710-8

iOS 6 Application
Development For Dummies
978-1-118-50880-0

Java For Dummies,
5th Edition
978-0-470-37173-2

Religion & Inspiration

The Bible For Dummies
978-0-7645-5296-0

Buddhism For Dummies,
2nd Edition
978-1-118-02379-2

Catholicism For Dummies,
2nd Edition
978-1-118-07778-8

Self-Help & Relationships

Bipolar Disorder
For Dummies,
2nd Edition
978-1-118-33882-7

Meditation For Dummies,
3rd Edition
978-1-118-29144-3

Seniors

Computers For Seniors
For Dummies,
3rd Edition
978-1-118-11553-4

iPad For Seniors
For Dummies,
5th Edition
978-1-118-49708-1

Social Security
For Dummies
978-1-118-20573-0

Smartphones & Tablets

Android Phones
For Dummies
978-1-118-16952-0

Kindle Fire HD
For Dummies
978-1-118-42223-6

NOOK HD For Dummies,
Portable Edition
978-1-118-39498-4

Surface For Dummies
978-1-118-49634-3

Test Prep

ACT For Dummies,
5th Edition
978-1-118-01259-8

ASVAB For Dummies,
3rd Edition
978-0-470-63760-9

GRE For Dummies,
7th Edition
978-0-470-88921-3

Officer Candidate Tests,
For Dummies
978-0-470-59876-4

Physician's Assistant Exa
For Dummies
978-1-118-11556-5

Series 7 Exam
For Dummies
978-0-470-09932-2

Windows 8

Windows 8 For Dummies
978-1-118-13461-0

Windows 8 For Dummies
Book + DVD Bundle
978-1-118-27167-4

Windows 8 All-in-One
For Dummies
978-1-118-11920-4

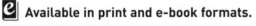 **Available in print and e-book formats.**